GROUPWARE:

Software for Computer-Supported Cooperative Work

GROUPWARE:
Software for Computer-Supported Cooperative Work
David Marca and Geoffrey Bock
The New Software Group
Digital Equipment Corporation
110 Spit Brook Road
Nashua, NH 03062

(The material in this book expresses only the views of the authors,
and is in no way a statement of Digital Equipment Corporation.)

GROUPWARE:

Software for Computer-Supported Cooperative Work

David Marca
Geoffrey Bock

Foreword by
Gerald Weinberg

IEEE Computer Society Press
Los Alamitos, California

Washington • Brussels • Tokyo

IEEE Computer Society Press Tutorial

Library of Congress Cataloging-in-Publication Data

Marca, David
    Groupware : software for computer-supported cooperative work /
David Marca, Geoffrey Bock.
        p.   cm.
    Includes bibliographical references and index.
    ISBN 0-8186-2637-2 (case). — ISBN 0-8186-2636-4 (fiche
    1. Work groups — Data processing. I. Bock, Geoffrey, 1946 -
II. Title.
    HD66.M365   1992
    658.4'036'028546—dc20   91-37373
                                                             CIP

Published by the
IEEE Computer Society Press
10662 Los Vaqueros Circle
PO Box 3014
Los Alamitos, CA 90720-1264

IEEE Computer Society Press Order Number 2637
Library of Congress Number 91-37373
IEEE Catalog Number EH0350-9
ISBN 0-8186-2636-4 (microfiche)
ISBN 0-8186-2637-2 (case)

Additional copies can be ordered from

IEEE Computer Society Press
Customer Service Center
10662 Los Vaqueros Circle
PO Box 3014
Los Alamitos, CA 90720-1264

IEEE Service Center
445 Hoes Lane
PO Box 1331
Piscataway, NJ 08855-1331

IEEE Computer Society
13, avenue de l'Aquilon
B-1200 Brussels
BELGIUM

IEEE Computer Society
Ooshima Building
2-19-1 Minami-Aoyama
Minato-ku, Tokyo 107
JAPAN

Second printing, 1992

Production Editors: Edna Straub and Anne Copeland
Copy Editor: Edna Straub
Cover: Alex Torres
Printed in the United States of America by Braun-Brumfield, Inc.

 THE INSTITUTE OF ELECTRICAL AND ELECTRONICS ENGINEERS, INC.

Foreword

We have already mentioned what may, perhaps, appear paradoxical to some of our readers — that the division of labor can be applied with equal success to mental as well as mechanical operations, and that it ensures in both the same economy of time. A short account of its practical applications, in the most extensive series of calculations ever executed, will offer an interesting illustration of this fact, whilst at the same time it will afford an occasion for shewing that the arrangements which ought to regulate the interior economy of a manufactory, are founded on principles of deeper root than may have been supposed, and are capable of being usefully employed in preparing the road to some of the sublimest investigations of the human mind.

So wrote Charles Babbage in his chapter, "On the Division of Mental Labor," in *Economy of Manufactures and Machinery*, published in 1832. In that chapter, Babbage described in some detail the group-working methods used by a joint French/English effort some years earlier to compute mathematical tables. This work aroused Babbage's interest in the possibility of "mills" for processing numbers, and thus he is credited with the invention of mechanical information processing.

Though we recognize him as the inventor of computers, Babbage was much better known in his own time as an organizer of work. Few people today know of his interest in the coordination of work. Failing to study the lessons of history, as Santayana remarked, we are destined to repeat them.

This, then, is the first reason for reading this collection of papers on groupware, *so that you won't simply repeat what others have done*. The collection is evidence that this discipline is maturing enough to allow us to learn the lessons of our history. The idea of groupware — if not the name — has been around for a long time. I'm old enough to be something of an historical figure myself (though contrary to rumor, I didn't know Babbage personally), and over twenty years ago I wrote in *The Psychology of Computer Programming*:

> ...the idea of the individual as the proper unit of study is never questioned at all, which is hardly unexpected since that assumption is built into the very hardware and software of all time-sharing systems! We do not, for example, have terminals that are suitable for two or more people working together at them and, lacking the terminals, we completely lack the software and even software ideas to support them.

I'm sure that the idea was not originally mine, but I quote it to illustrate how, in our business, software always seems to trail hardware. Like a number of other professional authors I've encountered, I had been consciously waiting for the day I could afford a large screen, a simple but effective form of groupware to facilitate collaboration. As soon as I got a large screen on my Macintosh, it became a "groupware" system. This brings us to the second reason for reading this collection, *so you'll have some perspective on how things really progress in our industry*.

Perhaps the single most distinguishing characteristic of human beings is their ability to work together. Other animals work together; wolves in hunting, beavers in building dams, penguins in raising their young. Other animals use tools; chimps use sticks to probe anthills, sea otters use stones to crack abalone shells, elephants use trees to whack down other trees. I believe, however, that humans are the only animals that we know who invent tools for working together — and they have done that as long as we have considered them human.

The construction of tools to foster group intellectual work should be no surprise. We've had such tools for a long time, and yet have tended to take them for granted. Isn't a slate or blackboard a piece of groupware? How about an overhead or slide projector? a megaphone or loudspeaker? the ordinary mail system? Babbage contributed a number of crucial ideas to our mail system, such as the postage stamps. What about a telegraph or telephone? Bell's work on the telephone started from his interest in developing a tool to help deaf students work with others. That he failed in his original goal does not diminish the magnitude of the telephone system as a groupware tool.

Because tool use and group work are so human, we tend to take them for granted. This, then, is the third reason for reading this collection: *to question your assumptions before you get too far into your career as a "groupware engineer."*

But there are other uses for this collection. It will also serve as a marker of the assumptions that we're making today, which in another generation will seem quite obvious. It also serves, even in its omissions, as a program guide for future research directions. For instance, none of the papers seriously addresses the emotional aspects of group work. To a large extent, most of the groupware pioneers seem to see the elimination of emotion as a major benefit of groupware. I believe they are wrong on two counts.

First, groupware won't eliminate emotion any more than computers did. Second, if it did eliminate emotion, the results would not be something to be desired, for the major driving force for group work is the desire to belong, to be loved. Why do you think AT&T's slogan, "Reach out and touch someone," has been so effective at selling *their* groupware system? And speaking of touch, that's another missing element for which effective remote groupware will have to find some substitute.

The emotional force driving people to work together will eventually make groupware succeed, overcoming all technical difficulties. But I wonder if we wouldn't get some of the benefit of groupware if similar attention were paid to the way people work successfully together without the aid of complex information systems? Keep that question in mind as you read these pioneering papers, and as you pick up your research where they left off.

Gerald M. Weinberg
June 12, 1992

Preface

Groupware: Software for Computer Supported Cooperative Work is a collection of readings about computing for groups. It takes a step into the field now called "Computer-Supported Cooperative Work" (CSCW). An emerging discipline, CSCW is concerned with bringing computing face-to-face with groups of people as they work. From this challenge comes software that enhances cooperation, augments human capability, and supports distributed teams. This kind of software is currently called "groupware." Unlike traditional computing, groupware computing has strong social and organizational dimensions, and exploits the capabilities of base-system technologies. It is this interdisciplinary framework that distinguishes groupware from the computing we have experienced in the past.

This tutorial was designed and written for the teachers, students, software engineers, and generalists in information systems and computer science who have recently become interested in group computing. Our goal is to provide an entry guide to the CSCW field. We approach CSCW from this perspective: *We see work as cooperative and social in nature; we see work being done by groups, not just by individuals.* Our perspective matches a growing trend, recognizing that the everyday problems we solve require an ever-growing dependence on others. Computer support for cooperative work must therefore concentrate on the problem of designing software to fit the way groups interact in the context of specific work situations.

This perspective has allowed us to write a tutorial that begins to bridge the social and technical aspects of developing groupware. As an introductory text, this volume presents the breadth of understanding needed to design group-related computer and information systems. To accomplish this, key papers have been selected to cover the conceptual underpinnings upon which groupware has been, and can be developed.

Overall, our presentation emphasizes the technical aspects of developing software *within the context of strong social and organizational factors:*

- Chapter 1, "Groups and Groupware," gives an overview of groups and their typical organizations, and summarizes the current status of CSCW.
- Chapter 2, "Conceptual Frameworks," makes the point that successful groupware systems are designed from the perspective most suited to the particular group and work being supported.
- Chapter 3, "Design Methods," presents ways to design software that augment, rather than replace human capabilities. It emphasizes designing software from intuitions derived by directly experiencing the users' work. It also stresses that designs are iteratively and collaboratively developed with users.
- Chapter 4, "Enabling Technologies — System-Related," presents a platform upon which groupware applications are typically built. It includes robust message transfer, directory structures to locate people, transparent distributed database services, and efficient hypertext mechanisms.
- Chapter 5, "Enabling Technologies — UI-Related," presents some important user interface technologies upon which groupware applications operate. It also discusses how the need for highly tailorable and extremely usable graphic user interfaces poses new challenges for groupware designers.
- Chapter 6, "Computer Supported Meetings," gives several case studies in which computers were brought into meeting rooms. These studies show how groupware spans a continuum of work tasks, emphasizes coauthoring and cooperative problem solving, and requires adapting to ever-changing meeting situations.
- Chapter 7, "Bridging Time and Space," includes applications that foster work across dramatically different time and distance barriers: (1) people working at the same time or at different times, (2) people working on exactly the same problem or on different parts of the problem at the same time, and (3) people working physically together or in separate locations.
- Chapter 8, "Coordinators," presents the latest methods and applications to help coordinate human activity. These methods and systems are intended to augment human capability by providing mechanisms for managing both the commitments and the overall dialogs pervasive in the workplace.

- Chapter 9, "What Makes Systems Effective?" includes several studies that evaluated the effectiveness of groupware, and found that successful systems (1) match the user's work, (2) never exploit any part of the intended user population, (3) are accompanied by training, and (4) are installed correctly.

Many papers and books of varying scope and quality have been published about groupware in the past eight years. Our goal here is to highlight key trends and ideas, and to be inclusive rather than critical or exhaustive. To provide proper coverage, each chapter includes a summary, followed by three or four important articles. We provide a set of additional references in the selected bibliography, and encourage those seeking more in-depth study to read these publications.

This tutorial has been designed to create a mood in which we can inquire into the often unquestioned assumptions that we personally bring to our computing practices and to our work in general.

We wrote this with the vision that CSCW will dramatically affect the way future computer systems are created and used. We see this shift keeping pace with that occurring in the field of management sciences. Achieving this change will provide enormous gain, and exploring it requires a commitment from both you, the reader, and us, the authors. So, we ask you now to approach this tutorial with a mind open to the chance that your software engineering practices will become quite different, yet much better. In return, we promise to make available to you a collection of distinctions, approaches, methods, and examples that have altered positively the practice of developing computer systems for groups.

David Marca
Geoffrey Bock
June 12, 1992
Nashua, New Hampshire

Acknowledgments

We first want to acknowledge our peers in the computing profession, whose work we reference herein. If not for their insight, hard work, and writings, we could not have created this tutorial.

We would like to thank John Whiteside, Howard Webber, Terry Winograd, Thomas Malone, and John Bennett for their personal support of our work in the groupware field. Thanks also to our management for their belief and support of our work here at Digital Equipment Corporation.

Acknowledgments go to Mark Ackerman, Scott Davis, Pamela Johnson, Michael Hammer, Paul Resnick, and anonymous technical reviewers from the IEEE for their helpful and constructive comments on early drafts. The Center for Coordination Science at the Massachusetts Institute of Technology helped provide the intellectual environment where we could begin to understand the breadth of groupware.

Our Digital colleagues in the Software Usability Group and the Advancement Development Section of the Office Systems Application Group provided ongoing conversations and helpful critiques so that we could validate our ideas.

Finally, we would like to acknowledge Gary Campen, who created the possibility for this tutorial.

Table of Contents

Introduction

Groupware: The Next Generation for Information Processing?*

Geoffrey Bock

With the advent of networked desktop devices, we must squarely face the issues and opportunities to capitalize on the enormous information resources at our fingertips. The notion of groupware provides a framework, the boundaries of a vision, for utilizing distributed information systems.

Some views of groupware

What do we mean by groupware? Some describe it as computer-based tools that can be used by work groups to facilitate the exchange and sharing of information (Bullen and Bennett, 1990). Others define it as computer-based systems that support two or more users engaged in a common task, providing an interface to a shared environment (Ellis and Rein, 1991). While it is important to consider both the enabling technologies and their interpersonal effects, these formal definitions are insufficient. We must also consider the organizational implications. Business managers, decision makers, and analysts, who routinely coordinate activities with many people, want to know what is excluded from the umbrella of groupware.

In my opinion, two likely types of systems are excluded. First are stand-alone personal computers. In this situation a person has an individual problem, and all the resources to solve it reside in a single box. This is an idealized environment, since few people actually work alone. Users seek systems through which they can communicate appropriately with one another, work together, and share information to achieve common goals.

The second type of system excluded from the groupware umbrella is the mainframe — the data warehouse — owned by the organization. A series of gatekeepers monitor access to its contents (the corporate data). But information is a corporate resource, the lifeblood of an organization. Beyond tracking ongoing operations, data should be useful for management and planning. It needs to be stored, protected, and shared, enabling the right people to access centrally organized information *just when they need it*.

In other words, personal computing is not groupware. It must evolve into various forms of interpersonal computing, enabling users to communicate and coordinate their activities with one another. Mainframe computing is not groupware. Corporate databases and secure storage systems often contain critical business information useful to decision makers, managers, and analysts. The real issues for business productivity are retrieval and sharing: first finding the information in the corporate store at the point when it is going to make a difference, then quickly sharing it with relevant individuals and groups in the organization. Between personal computing and the corporate data warehouse are many kinds of group-oriented systems.

Enabling technologies

From a software and hardware perspective, enormous advances in two underlying technologies, high-speed networking and distributed information systems, are propelling groupware applications to center stage.

With PC LANS, users are looking for ways to enhance their personal productivity by moving beyond a personal computing environment to one where two or more users can engage in a common task and support a shared environment. Users of networked personal computers can access a shared store of documents,

---

*   I would very much like to acknowledge the helpful comments of Mark Ackerman, Scott Davis, David Marca, and Howard Webber on earlier versions of this article.

send and receive electronic mail, exchange data, or even coordinate their calendars on line. These are rudimentary examples of groupware.

The impact of distributed-systems technologies is also far reaching. No longer do users think about storing all information in a single, centralized place. Rather, they want to distribute it around the network with rapid and efficient access. The corporate data warehouse becomes a single virtual entity located in many different physical places. Because users seek to maintain enterprise-wide stores of information, easily accessible to anybody on the network, they also need simple-to-use facilities for maintenance and updates.

No longer do we assume that all information processing will occur in a single, bounded, time-shared environment. With the advent of client-server architectures, we foresee a time when groups of cooperating processors communicate seamlessly with one another, each performing specialized, appropriately designed activities. Graphical user interfaces will enable users to express computationally complex tasks in simple, natural, intuitively obvious ways. Object-oriented technologies will enable users to make explicit the conceptual links between the real world of their work environments and the abstract entities, relationships, and actions of their information systems.

It is important to emphasize that these are enabling technologies. Groupware depends on applying these tools and techniques to solve users' emerging needs.

Computing needs of modern work groups

There are a number of social factors driving this sense about the possibilities for groupware. People are often overwhelmed by the volume and velocity of information in their daily work environments: the amount of information they might access and the speed with which it changes. Once on line, they have access to potentially important facts and figures, if they can focus their attention long enough to find the relevant information and derive its meaning. Simply collecting, disseminating, and delivering information from one desktop to another is a small part of the larger task. Interpersonal communication needs are more critical than ever before: getting in touch, staying in touch, and knowing when to move on.

Work in contemporary organizations is increasingly knowledge based. Organizational structures are changing: *ad hoc* teams that span formal organizational boundaries convene to investigate and resolve particular issues, and then disband.

Major tasks require sending and receiving information, frequently in nonpredictable ways. The modern work group is often networked and distributed across time and space. Somehow, information system technologies ought to help improve work group management and organizational productivity.

Users seek systems that will enable them to do their current jobs better, and that will permit them to accomplish new kinds of tasks with less effort. For example, groupware promises to fix the group scheduling problem by handling all the logistics of finding a common meeting time, getting the announcements on participants' calendars, disseminating the minutes, and then tracking the follow-up actions. A groupware application could help a task team sort and manage team information so that individuals could get the information they need, as they need it, and then track the requests, action items, and documents generated as part of the group activities.

Current groupware systems

Groupware applications simplify office work by removing the drudgery from seemingly routine tasks. To a limited extent many commercially available office systems already represent a first generation. Time-shared integrated office systems provide word processing, electronic mail, electronic calendars, and a consistent user interface to customized applications.[1] These are simple groupware systems that automate and expedite basic office procedures.

---

[1] Commercially successful office systems include ALL-IN-1* from Digital and PROFS from IBM.

Feature-rich electronic mail systems and faxes enable people in large organizations to communicate relatively effortlessly. Telephone tag is seemingly a bygone phenomenon with quick electronic messaging. Time delays are minimized by e-mailing or faxing documents for reviews, comments, and distribution. International standards now seek to make electronic messaging as robust and hassle free as mailing a hard-copy document or placing a phone call in real time. Electronic mail is an elementary groupware application to speed the dissemination of information.

Computer conferences and electronic bulletin boards are other first-generation applications. Popular in academic and technical circles for more than ten years, they are now being tried in a variety of different ways in commercial organizations. Potentially, groups of people can participate in conversations and meetings that bridge time and space. But all comments are treated equally, so that informal chatter is stored (and retrieved) with the same dexterity as substantive discussion.

In their current form, networked personal computers and workstations are part of the first generation as well. Ostensibly, the impetus is to share expensive physical resources via file or print servers while continuing to exercise direct, personal control over desktop devices. Once the desktops are connected, users begin to imagine the possibilities: sharing information, coordinating the myriad activities of small work-group teams, and collaborating on joint tasks (coauthoring a report, planning a customer visit, or rolling up the financials for a quarterly statement).

Nevertheless, today's realities are primarily personal-productivity tools. Integrated office systems, full-feature electronic mail, computer conferences, and networked desktop devices are designed largely to enhance an individual's effectiveness by providing immediate access to all kinds of electronic information. That they fulfill a vision for group-oriented applications is secondary.

The paradox of unrestricted connectivity

Without careful planning and design, simply connecting PCs into networked, shared environments creates an unfortunate paradox. Making it easy for people to talk to one another and share information does not necessarily improve the quality of their discussions, analyses, or decision making. Unrestricted connectivity is likely to lead to chaos and confusion.

Even if it is very easy to send and receive mail, the "right people" are not guaranteed to get the right information when they need it. Mailing a request does not assure the sender of a timely response or a satisfactory answer. Simply accessing shared information does not automatically teach the user what to do with it.

Networked information systems deliberately remove many of the social cues, clues, and controls that people in organizations traditionally take for granted when judging the quality, accuracy, and authenticity of the information they receive. Both anonymity and appearance can be deceiving. Sometimes we even risk losing the interpersonal touch so necessary for effective organizational life. Successful groupware should provide some answers to this paradox about the limitless dissemination of information.

We must be aware of another factor as well. When we think about ways to improve organizational effectiveness, we begin to address the underlying issues about how groups of people seek to run their business. We need to develop information systems that explicitly promote a sense of teamwork and coordination.

Potential groupware applications

Currently, few real groupware systems are commercially available. We can point to a few PC-LAN-based applications right now.[2] However, with a number of promising prototype and pilot efforts under way, we can begin to envision the outlines of powerful groupware applications. The market for groupware applications is changing very dramatically.

---

[2] For an assessment of some current applications, see Bullen and Bennet (1990).

3

Active information agents. The first kinds of applications help us deal with problems of information overload. Electronic mail is an immediate concern, particularly when there is too much of it. Somehow we want to use the structure of messages — the addressing information in the header fields — to sort mail into meaningful categories.

Information filters are intuitive and obvious: they mirror what happens in offices when we confront an unsorted stack of mail. It seems perfectly natural to read the important mail first, based on the sender, subject, or summary of the contents, then get to the "junk mail" later. For an electronic mail filter, we simply write an "IF-THEN" rule: IF the message meets certain criteria, THEN the system should perform a designated set of actions. For instance, a person could request that the system automatically sort the mail from his/her boss into a specific folder, the mail about a specific project into another, and automatically print all documents over a specific size. In this way the system functions like a personal administrative assistant.

The key is recognizing that many forms of information in the office have a specific structure. The address on an envelope has certain predefined fields. A purchase order or a travel request as an electronic form has a set of semistructured fields that can be completed before forwarding it to designated people for approval and action. Once we understand how business communications contain many different kinds of semistructured information, we can begin to anticipate how autonomous agents might filter or route messages, triggered by predefined criteria.

For example, a user who is out of the office on a trip could leave an autonomous agent running to routinely sort electronic mail, automatically forwarding certain designated topics to a colleague and everything else to his or her secretary. In another case, the user could encode all of the required steps to process a travel request into a series of rules. Then, after completion of the fields in an appropriate electronic form, designated agents could sort and route it, and take predefined actions based on prespecified criteria. Work-flow applications can encode organizational policies and procedures. With automatic form routing we can use the power of the system to handle many routine tasks, improving the coordination within a work group.

To do this, however, we need highly flexible design procedures and very easily modifiable software tools, enabling us to capture the implicit knowledge of organizational tasks. Office procedures frequently change, and we need to take many subtle personal relationships into account. Users will expect a groupware application to "do the right thing" without their being able to explicitly define what this "right thing" might be.

Links and activity coordination. Beyond semistructured messages, work-flow applications, and easily modifiable rule-based agents, another class of groupware systems involves hypertext links. This is hardly a new idea. In the waning days of World War II, Vannevar Bush observed that "the human mind . . . operates by association. With one item in its grasp, it snaps instantly to the next that is suggested by the association of thoughts."[3] Rather than using artificial indexing schemes, finding information should be as natural as first thinking about one idea then drawing an association to another. With the increased power of desktop devices and client-server architectures, we can now anticipate systems that will use *ad hoc* associations (or links) among seemingly random nodes of information.

Coordinators should help with the explicit problems of managing interrelated activities, such as designing a new software system for a financial institution. The immediate task might be to prepare a functional description, or perhaps a request for quotation, to send to a group of potential bidders. If the project is at all complex, the work will involve a host of organizational problems: identifying the participants, scheduling meetings, discussing issues, perhaps doing some market research or technical analysis, assigning action items, and so forth. Finally, we will prepare some kind of document (a report, a proposal, etc.) and formally declare the task "done."

---

[3] Vannevar Bush, "As We May Think," *Atlantic Monthly*, May 1945.

In the midst of these activities, we will be managing a series of requests, actions, and assignments. Each of these is a specific node of information which we can identify informally as the work progresses. We can make various associations, in a seemingly *ad hoc* manner, to identify linkages among tasks and coordinate group-related activities. To continue the example, when it comes time for a follow-up meeting for the new software system, we should be able to pull together an agenda from the list of outstanding action items. Then we can ensure that all of the required supporting documents are complete, review the comments received, and send the necessary information to the meeting attendees.

What is new about hypertext is that users need not determine links according to any predefined schema. They can define them as they go, as they make connections between various thoughts and observations, in a nonserial and nonprocedural way. Potentially, this *ad hoc* flexibility will enable task teams to work together with increased effectiveness.

Meeting support. A third kind of potential groupware system involves electronic meetings, which may have participants in the same room, or may have some individuals remotely located. Certainly, users have had communication devices in conference rooms for many years: telephones, speaker phones, and projection screens. However, desktop devices and distributed systems provide something new: the possibility of supporting meetings in a more focused, task-oriented, and interactive manner.

For instance, meeting participants might share visual displays. When users are working together on a problem, all could be viewing the same information on individual workstations, much like everybody looking at a common whiteboard. Participants may not be together in the same room; they could be scattered around the country, yet viewing a single display. In a multiple-windowing environment, we might set up situations where each member in the meeting has a shared group window plus a series of personal windows for individual work (like taking a personal notebook into a meeting).

Meeting support systems could be used to integrate many activities associated with task teams. Some systems enable participants to track actions and commitments so that all understand their assignments and responsibilities in real time. Others allow for anonymous commenting or issue-related voting as techniques for assisting group decision making. Meeting support systems may be linked to the underlying network so the minutes and action items can be quickly disseminated at the end of the meeting.

Components of effective systems. In the foreseeable future, effective groupware applications will include information filters, work-flow systems, hypertext linkages, and real-time meeting support. Users will interact intuitively with their environments. These systems are being designed in pursuit of a simple vision: that information systems should embody a sense of teamwork and collaboration. In pursuit of this vision, these systems promise to have a far-reaching effect on the design of organizational tasks, on how people actually organize their work to take maximum benefit from information technology.

Implications for groupware designers

A couple of years ago, a designer working on an executive support system candidly observed that "If you automate a mess, you are going to get an automated mess." No longer are we simply applying technology to expedite standard operating procedures. Rather, we are concerned with altering operations and policies so that business teams can "work smarter." This is a tall order. Information systems professionals are thrust, without preparation, into a central role, helping to improve organizational effectiveness, becoming change agents. Groupware promises to have substantial implications in the practice of systems analysis and design.

First, roles for information systems professionals are no longer confined to implementing technical solutions to other people's problems (delivering the functional specifications to build a system whose requirements are defined by another group). Quite the contrary, systems analysts now need to be part of the entire systems development life cycle, including working with end users and "client" organizations to help identify their information problems and define their requirements.

Accomplishing this requires new analysis methods of top-down systems design. It means getting involved at the very early stages of the design process, when people are exploring their problems and groping for some kinds of solutions. This means finding techniques that allow for rapid prototyping of potential solutions, and iterative design and testing of possible alternatives.

Second, the design of groupware systems must be tied to the strategic business objectives of the organization. Groupware systems offer the possibility of improving coordination and collaboration, capturing the logic of readily routinized tasks. The notion of "just-in-time" information is becoming a technical reality. Organizational structures in the future are going to be flatter, with managers having extensive responsibilities for a wide range of activities. Theorists talk about the advent of "ad-hocracies," where task teams from diverse groups in a firm will convene to solve a specific business problem and then disband.

Potentially, task teams will need fewer people to accomplish the same sets of activities. Possibly the same number of people will do more, enabling organizations to "work smarter" and become more productive. Smart organizations are going to deploy information technology as part of their core business strategy. They will be concerned with more than simply linking desktops and improving the flow of information. They will be concerned with improving the coordination of work tasks and business activities, changing how task teams actually use specific facts and figures. Information systems professionals need to play a role in the development of business strategy.

Finally, it is absolutely essential to keep a sense of perspective as we envision groupware systems. We are in the midst of a major evolution in hardware and software architectures with the deployment of local area networks, the advent of distributed software systems, and the revolution of graphical user interface designs. Many of the technical debates about the basic system components are winding down. We now need to thoroughly understand how to use the desktop resources for organizational benefits: how to harness the potentials of network-wide cooperative processing.

References

1. Christine Bullen and John Bennet, "Learning from User Experiences with Groupware," *Proc. CSCW*, October, 1990.
2. Clarence Ellis and Gail Rein, "Groupware: The Research and Development Issues," *Comm. ACM*, 1991.

Chapter 1:
Groups and Groupware

Chapter 1: Groups and Groupware

This section presents an overview of groups and group behavior. It focuses on how our definitions and conceptions of group life can be of direct use to groupware designers. This section also describes the field of computer supported cooperative work as it exists today. It sees groupware as software designed with a sensitivity to the ever-changing needs of a work group or task team. It introduces some basic social issues for groupware while balancing social and technical factors.

Background: The complexity of groups

There are many different kinds of groups: formal or informal, centralized or decentralized, structured or unstructured, work oriented or social — just to name a few. Individuals are members of a group, and yet the essence of the group transcends the experiences and activities of its members. The whole takes on a life of its own, greater than the sum of its component parts. Groups rarely remain static, nor do they exist at just one point in time. They are ongoing, living organisms that proceed through various stages of growth and development. As group members, individuals experience groups in a multitude of different ways.

Both the work of the group, and the process by which that work is done evolve on an ongoing basis. Groups have many tasks to fulfill simultaneously. They are concerned not only with doing the work and being productive, but also with maintaining their existence, preserving their identity, and fulfilling their mission. Within a group, individual members assume, transfer, and abandon a variety of roles. Group norms evolve. Some are explicit and readily identified, while others are implicit and often concealed. The volatility of these norms depends on the stage of the group. Groups form, establish a structure for working together, create major norms, settle into high performance, finish their work, and ultimately disband.

Themes: Understanding context from a group perspective

We view groupware as software designed from a group perspective, explicitly seeking to enhance various aspects of group life. Through this perspective we anticipate a spectrum of groupware applications including messaging systems, shared information sources, multiuser editors, electronic meeting rooms, computer conferencing, and group decision support tools.

Moreover, groupware can significantly influence the ways people are able to process, manage, and manipulate a wide range of knowledge and information. Groupware raises the possibilities for new forms of organizational design and business practices. Groupware is a new potential for how work groups or task teams might enhance the coordination of their activities in performing their assigned tasks. To understand the effects of groupware, we must examine it within the context of users' work environments.

Learning from user experience. Bullen and Bennett report on the experiences of users of various kinds of group-oriented software systems. They interviewed more than two hundred people in twenty-five enterprises, to see how software tools facilitated group work. Not surprisingly, they found that some tools are more successful than others, and that some groups have more successful experiences within their working environments than others.

Bullen and Bennett describe general themes that account for the relative success of certain kinds of group tools, considering the situation first from a software design perspective and then from an organizational perspective. They discuss how the users' views depend on the underlying functionality, the management environment, and the subtle interactions between technology and users' experiences.

From the design perspective, Bullen and Bennett identify electronic messaging as the primary tool to support group work. Users seek the ability to link messages into ongoing conversations (similar to face-to-face meetings). The functionality provided should correspond to the users' work environment: the tools need to be seen as logical, consistent extensions to ongoing business tasks, rather than as isolated and inconsistent applications.

From an organizational perspective, Bullen and Bennett find that groupware presents both a technical and a social intervention in the ongoing activities of a group. Users need to feel that the benefits of group support tools will outweigh their costs, and that the tools will directly help them in their everyday tasks. Moreover, group support tools may lead to business process redesign, in ways that mutually benefit users in work groups and the organization as a whole.

Some research and development issues. Ellis, Gibbs and Rein summarize key research and development issues for groupware. They present two taxonomies to define a comprehensive system. The first describes groupware in terms of a time/space continuum, considering group activities that are likely to take place simultaneously in one location (a meeting), and those that will be done at different times (document preparation) and/or at different places (working from home). The second describes groupware in terms of core technical components: message systems, multiuser editors, group decision support systems, computer conferencing, intelligent agents, and coordination systems.

Ellis et al. discuss some of the emerging enabling technologies for groupware, assessing their likely effects on group behavior. Much depends on how particular technologies are able to support (and facilitate) group processes. For instance, shared editing might enable people to work together to coauthor a document or discuss a common set of ideas. To be effective, the software technology must wrap social protocols around both information sharing and concurrency controls. To continue the example, the system must indicate to all participants when one person is modifying a document. One user cannot automatically overwrite another person's contributions. The system needs to make all participants aware when somebody modifies something.

In other words, successful groupware environments must promote key elements of group behavior, interpersonal conversations, and other kinds of social interactions. To do this, it is essential to understand how groups work, and how people function effectively in a group environment.

A primer on group dynamics. Cole and Nast-Cole provide a primer on group dynamics for groupware developers, outlining the basic processes of group life within the context of typical business situations. All too often people will try to use software solutions, expecting to solve particular work-group problems, only to discover that the proposed system does not meet their *real* needs. Cole and Nast-Cole identify a number of ways that group-work "solutions" fail to meet users' objectives by failing to correspond to basic aspects of group life. Similarly, they describe how successful groupware might enhance group functions when it is able to meet group needs.

Cole and Nast-Cole explain how groups can exist along many different psychological dimensions. Two or more people can be a group; they can share a common purpose and work to create a set of shared experiences. Communications, the processes by which people exchange information and develop mutual understanding, form a key component. Exchanging information will advance task-oriented activities as well as maintenance (group function) activities. Individual group members will assume various roles, and the group itself will develop specific behavioral norms.

Finally, Cole and Nast-Cole describe why effective groupware must support and enhance basic factors of group life: improving communications to create a sense of shared experiences. They suggest that groups will proceed through various developmental stages, sometimes characterized as "forming," "storming," "norming," "performing," and "adjourning." It is important to understand how groups function and exchange information during each of these stages. It is also important to identify the kinds of situations where groupware technologies will improve communication, and to recognize situations where these technologies will hinder communications and impede group development.

The future: Meeting organizational needs

The implementation of effective groupware will require both knowledge of how groups behave and corresponding innovations in systems analysis and design methodologies. Designers will need business analysis techniques that address group-level interactions, focusing on actual business practices and the interplay between group-oriented software and group behaviors. Finally, groupware will require very flexible systems environments, so that it can rapidly adapt to changes in group life.

Organizations of the 1990s are under enormous pressure to handle information effectively and efficiently. Managers need to find better ways to achieve group objectives. This is not simply a matter of exchanging more information, but also of understanding how the evolution of enabling technologies might affect management practices. Groupware holds the promise of providing innovative tools and techniques to improve communications, coordination, and collaboration among work groups or task teams. Groupware technologies themselves are only part of the overall situation, and they must be understood within the context of the group experience.

LEARNING FROM USER EXPERIENCE WITH GROUPWARE

Christine V. Bullen

Center for Information Systems Research
MIT Sloan School
77 Massachusetts Avenue
Cambridge, MA 02139

John L. Bennett

IBM Research Division
IBM Almaden Research Center
650 Harry Road
San Jose, CA 95120-6099

INTRODUCTION

Observers have identified a potential for major improvements in organizational productivity made possible through the use of personal computers serving as a means to link people into task-oriented teams. Our study offers an examination of how people are using personal computers for such electronic exchanges via networking. We interviewed 223 people who were using several "groupware" systems in a sample of 25 enterprises to see how they employ these software tools to support their group work. An explanation of our research design and a more complete discussion of the results can be found in Bullen and Bennett [Bull90].

We summarize here our findings to suggest relationships among function provided, user patterns of access to that function, individual perspectives on the role of groupware, and organizational factors that influence degree of use. Table 1 shows the 25 companies (pseudonyms are used to protect the confidentiality of participating companies), number of people interviewed at each company, and some of the groupware systems available. Table 2 lists the systems used in the organizations we visited, indicating the general categories of system functionality.

In making our observations and drawing conclusions we were struck by the importance of understanding the complex interplay of factors which influenced the specific organizations we studied. However, in order to simplify the presentation, we have sorted our conclusions into two categories:

I. From a Design Perspective - findings which designers ought to consider when conceptualizing functionality for groupware systems; suggestions for ways to improve systems.

II. From an Organizational Perspective - findings which management ought to consider when planning for and implementing groupware systems; cautions regarding the importance and complexity of organizational considerations in the context of group-oriented systems.

As with any categorization, this dichotomy of conclusions is an oversimplification that we make for analysis purposes. The groupings clearly overlap, and we believe designers will find useful information in the second grouping, and managers will benefit from the conclusions in the first category.

COMPANY	REVENUES IN BILLIONS*	NUMBER OF PEOPLE INTERVIEWED	GROUPWARE SYSTEMS
BigChem	$30.00	8	PROFS, Higgins, The Coordinator (V.I)
SoapCo	17.00	30	Other, Metaphor, ForComment
InsurCo	12.00	5	PROFS, Higgins
OilCo	11.00	5	PROFS
ExploreCo	10.00	3	Other
ConstrucCo	10.00	3	PROFS, Other
FoodCo	9.50	3	PROFS, The Coordinator (V.I), Higgins
TerminalCo	9.40	10	All-In-1
RBOC	8.40	10	PROFS, Higgins
HealthCo	8.00	20	All-In-1
BankCo	6.50	5	All-In-1
MedCons	6.00	3	PROFS, ForComment
LawCo	5.00	3	Higgins
ServBuro	4.40	13	The Coordinator (V.I)
SnackCo	2.00	35	The Coordinator (V.I), Other
BeerCo	1.40	6	Metaphor
SmallCons	1.40	10	Other
CableCo	1.00	15	The Coordinator (V.I)
SmallChem	1.00	8	The Coordinator (V.I)
PubServBuro	0.90	3	PROFS, Other
TransDist	0.18	10	The Coordinator (V.I)
SmallRes	**	3	Other
IndCons	**	2	The Coordinator (V.I)
StateBuro	n/a	3	PROFS, ForComment
BigU	n/a	10	PROFS, ForComment, Other

*Revenues approximate, 1988
**Revenues less than $1 million
Note: PROFS available in many places; studied in 2

Table 1 - Companies Studied

	CONSTRUCTION/ EDITING FACILITIES	ELECTRONIC EXCHANGE OF TEXT	DIRECTORY	TIME MARKING/ TIME KEEPING	GENERAL TOOLS
All-in-1	Yes	Yes	Yes	Yes	Some
ForComment	Yes	Specialized	Specialized	No	No
Higgins	Yes	Yes	Yes	Yes	Yes
In-House System 1	Yes	Yes	Specialized	No	Some
In-House System 2	Yes	Yes	No	No	No
Metaphor	Yes	Yes	Specialized	Some	Specialized
PROFS	Yes	Yes	Yes	Yes	Some
The Coordinator Version I	Yes	Yes	Specialized	Yes	Some

Table 2 - Tools Studied

KEY ISSUES AND CONCLUSIONS

I. From a Design Perspective

● Electronic Message Communication is the Primary Tool.

The functionality for sending and receiving electronic messages, available in all the products we studied, was by far the function most heavily used and universally stated as valuable. The desire to have support for communication within a work group was usually the primary motivation for acquiring the tool. People quickly learned the electronic messaging functions, and this contrasted with their failure to use many of the other functions available in these systems. Messaging was used extensively regardless of its user interface design, ease of access, or sophistication of function.

For example, the interface provided by The Coordinator (Version I) contains language related to the underlying theory of speech acts [Sear69]. This terminology is intended to lead the user to think about what s/he is doing and then to characterize a particular communication as one of several choices, e.g. a request or promise, etc. While the software provides a category for simple e-mail (called "free form"), we found people consistently sending each other "requests" regardless of the content of the message. Not surprisingly, "request" is the first menu choice and where the cursor falls by default. Many of those we interviewed reported that they ignored the choices and just "hit enter" to send a message.

In conclusion, our field observations show that the tool people use the most is electronic messaging. The message-flow needs of work groups appear to be so great that messaging overshadows other system-based functions. If we can assume that these busy people use just those system portions essential for their work, we may conclude that electronic messaging support is what is most needed.

● Message linking: a key improvement provided by electronic communications.

One aspect of the electronic message communication that stood out was the ability to link messages concerned with one subject area or associated with a distribution list. This functionality is provided in two of the tools (Higgins and The Coordinator) and it is also inherent in the concept of computer conferencing, which is available in All-In-1 (VAX Notes) and in In-House System I.

People reported in our interviews that they gained much value by being able to "look in one place for all discussion pertaining to project XYZ." In contrast, users of e-mail systems like PROFS and All-In-1 (without Vax Notes), complained about the difficulties of tracking down related messages and managing their mail folders (i.e. files for grouping messages by categories).

In The Coordinator (Version I) this functionality is embodied in a concept basic to the underlying theory: the "conversation" is the primary unit of interaction. Because of this, each time someone replies to a message, the reply is automatically linked to all previous messages in the stream and becomes part of the "conversation." Users found this feature one of the most valuable aspects of the tool.

Historically, knowledge workers have always sought ways to organize the volume of information to be managed. As an early innovation (1892), the vertical file system, facilitated the grouping of correspondence by subject:

"[Vertical files] had several advantages over [other forms of filing]. Most importantly, the folders allowed related papers to be grouped together and easily removed from the files for use." [Yate89]

In effect nothing has changed: groupware message linking or conferencing allows people to carry out this task for electronic correspondence!

The need represented in our interviews, (i.e., comments on the value of message linking), is one which should be carefully investigated by both designers and installers of groupware. People use message linking to:

- manage communications and documents
- keep records
- develop "group memory."

This conclusion may be telling us a great deal more than what is at first obvious: rather than looking at "fancy," innovative functions for groupware systems, designers should be focusing on how to better solve the basic need of office workers, i.e. managing large volumes of information. There may well be ways other than those we see today for designers to address these needs.

● What functionality is included and how it is offered are important factors.

What functionality is included.

One of the best examples of function requested by "the marketplace" but not used effectively by the people we interviewed is the calendaring function. The explanations we were given in our interviews focused on one fact: electronic calendars in their current form can not replace traditional paper ones. Here we can mention two of the key problems.

■ Traditional calendars are not simply places where you record times for events to take place on dates, though electronic calendars are usually limited to such a simple function. Traditional calendars have notes on them, contain telephone numbers, are often color coded, and have other papers attached (such as yellow sticky notes or paper-clipped memos, letters, etc.). The non-homogeneity of traditional calendars is actually an asset for finding important information (there are parallels here with Malone's [Malo83] findings on desk organization).

■ Electronic calendars are not portable, and paper copies of the information contained in the computer are inadequate substitutes. Notes on the paper copies often do not get keyed back into the computer-based version.

The calendar function has potential for supporting important group activities (keeping track of time commitments), but the current combination of software and hardware is seen by users as "not up to their needs."

How the functionality is offered.

The second aspect of functionality relates to the way it is offered to users. Aside from the functional limitations mentioned above, calendaring was not used in several

14

of the systems because people found the process of use awkward (e.g., no easy way to indicate recurring events). In other examples people reported that they could not use a tool effectively because they could not remember how to access a particular function and could find no effective help on-line or in the written manuals.

It has long been recognized that user interface design is a critical element in the successful use of a software product [Mart73]. Therefore it is not surprising that it continues to be an important element in the case of groupware tools. However, it may be that because people in a work group use these tools, additional factors must be considered. For example, in a single-user product, like the spreadsheet, designers must be concerned about how each user interprets menus and takes action. In a groupware tool the designer must be concerned about the individual user, and in addition, must address the issue of how what that user does is interpreted by many others, individually and as a group. The individual is acting as a representative of the group which may influence how the tool is used and interpreted:

> "... an intergroup transaction is not the same as an interpersonal one, although both take place between individuals. A group member involved in intergroup transactions [is] a representative of the group in accordance with the group's expectations. The member is not acting solely on an individual agenda." [Anco87]

In conclusion, it is clear from our interviews that the quality of design, both in terms of functionality provided and access to that functionality, is an important factor in how and whether people use groupware tools. People we interviewed frequently stated that they chose groupware systems because of the range of functions offered, but we noted system features that were often either ignored or adapted by the people to accomplish a simplified process of communicating electronically. Given that developers commit resources to provide function, it is important to understand what acts as a barrier between "offered" (by the system) and "used" (by the people).

- Isolated tools hinder productive use of groupware systems.

Tools may be considered isolated with respect to two aspects of integration: flow of control and flow of data [Bull90]. In some cases the process of accessing the function of a second tool when using one tool (i.e. flow of control) requires an awkward sequence of user actions. Other cases require the transfer of data from one tool to another (i.e. flow of data). (See also Nielsen et al., [Niel86])

Transfer of User Control - In several of the organizations we studied, it was necessary for the people to go through a series of steps in order to move from the groupware tool they were using for their business group/team work to other tools they had to use for tasks relating to the firm as a whole. For example some groups used a personal computer e-mail system like those available on Higgins or The Coordinator within their departments, but they changed to a mainframe-based tool like PROFS or All-In-1 for e-mail access to other parts of their companies. This was universally considered to be an aggravation and a waste of time, regardless of the ease or difficulty associated with the switch.

Transfer of Data - Tools that were not completely integrated required that the result from one task be consciously moved into the environment of another tool in order to perform additional tasks. Most users were annoyed by this step, irrespective of its ease or difficulty. The ForComment system, highly praised in most respects, was singled out here. In order to use ForComment, the person must import text created elsewhere. Although this is a straightforward step, users consistently commented that they would prefer that the functionality provided by ForComment be available as part of the word processor they used to create the text.

With respect to both flow of control and flow of data our interviews showed very clearly that a lack of integration from either integration perspective was a barrier to use of some groupware tools. In addition Ancona's [Anco87] research on boundary management (i.e. the management of the group's relations with environments and individuals external to the group) raises an interesting point with respect to flow of control. She found that, teams equally matched on group process characteristics, could be differentiated based on their boundary management capability. This implies that boundary management is a key aspect of team performance and, therefore, productivity. If teams are using groupware systems that interfere with their ability to perform boundary management (e.g., the team e-mail system is not easily connected to the company e-mail system), productivity may be adversely affected by isolated tools.

II. From An Organizational Perspective

● People report most value from tools paralleling non-electronic activities.

Those we interviewed reported that use of e-mail, for example, was "easy" because it was analogous to, but better than, what they did without groupware tools. People saw computer messaging as an improvement over "the old way" because it was faster, traceable, geography- and time-independent, and accessible from almost any location (e.g. at home, while traveling). Therefore it was easy for people to see the benefits to them in learning how to communicate electronically.

Other functions provided by the systems either differed significantly (e.g. electronic calendars) or presented capabilities that they were not currently using. In the latter category, functions such as project tracking, reminders, directories, and expense tracking all represent tasks that the people interviewed were not doing. Therefore, to use the electronic version of these tools would require them to expend resources for activities they did not normally carry out or carried out only infrequently.

We therefore conclude that designers, developers, and installers of groupware tools are presented with an interesting challenge: how are people going to make a transition to new practices which some of the functionality enables? Part of the answer lies in designing functionality that is easy to learn and to remember after long periods of non-use. However another part of the answer is found in the organizational considerations related to examining current work processes.

● Benefits gained need to balance or outweigh the invested resource.

The benefits from some of the functionality (other than that provided for messaging) were not clear, nor balanced in the minds of those we interviewed. In fact users often perceived extra effort on their part for no corresponding gain.

For example, people currently do not have an incentive to maintain an electronic calendar to support group use. They see the work involved as redundant (since most also want to have a portable calendar on paper in any case). Though they agreed that their managers and groups would benefit, the value to them personally was too far removed to motivate their behavior. They likened maintaining calendars and project information to "keypunching" activities. Yet the group value of electronic calendaring is realized only when everyone cooperates.

In addition, people object to the notion that others (not their secretaries) may schedule their time. Further, the process of setting up meetings is not always a mechanical one. Negotiation may be required to secure the presence of all desired parties. Therefore, people see an economic imbalance of input effort to output value. (See also Grudin, [Grud88].)

Messaging functions, however, offered a direct benefit. People experienced the satisfaction of "getting the message out," "putting the ball in the other guy's court," assigning tasks to group members, etc. On the receiving side, they had a record of what they were expected to do, and through being on copy lists, had a sense of being in touch with what was going on in the group. They had no need to conceptualize a higher order benefit.

Other functions, as mentioned previously (e.g. project tracking, reminders, etc.) actually required additional effort on the part of the users to learn to work in a different way. While the people we interviewed often said things like "I should do expense tracking", "I know it would be more efficient if I kept an electronic directory", "I could really benefit from the reminder function", invariably they were unwilling to adapt their behavior and invest the personal resources necessary to use this functionality. They had not identified benefits to using the technology which equalled or exceeded their resource investment.

Therefore, we can conclude that unless there is a balance between the perceived effort required on the part of the user and the benefit delivered to that user, a person is not likely to employ the functionality present in a tool. Other forms of motivation (e.g. management directives, group agreement, education) can be important in influencing the perception of balance.

● Groupware implementation is simultaneously a social and technical intervention.

Our research observations support Kling and Iacono [Klin89]: "computerization is simultaneously a social and technical intervention." One of the most important aspects of this complex intervention is that it is a "strategic intervention" [Klin89]. Whether the strategy of technology introduction is made explicit or kept implicit, it exists and can have a significant impact on the organization.

In our research we saw the effects of strategies on the individuals we interviewed. For example, when a groupware system was introduced as a way to streamline procedures by merely training new users in the mechanics of the tools, we saw people using a minimum of the functionality present in the systems. When instruction went beyond mechanical steps to include, for example, a presentation on the concepts of groupware, or material on how to relate the groupware functionality to accomplishing their work tasks, then people made use of, and applied creative thinking to using, the functionality present in the tool.

Organizational factors in the following four general categories showed up as consistently important as we interviewed people in the twenty-five firms.

Champions - Management support for the introduction of groupware tools varied significantly in our sample, ranging from the top executive levels to middle management supporters who felt they could engineer successful pilots and demonstrate the value of the tools to upper management. While these instances of managerial support represent very different levels of power within each organization, they demonstrate the importance in general of a committed leader in the introduction of a new technology.

Expectations - We observed two different work groups in one organization where the same software had been introduced. In one of these groups the tool was originally described as a new technology that people should familiarize themselves with and see what they could use it for. In the second group the tool was described as an important new technology for improving communication throughout the organization. Five years later, when we conducted our interviews, the original attitudes were still present and were influencing the software use.

It is clear from our studies and those of others (e.g., Carroll and Perin, [Carr88]) that the way in which new groupware tools are introduced into the work group will influence the ways in which they are used.

Training - Those interviewed generally described the training that they had received in the use of their software as directed toward building procedural or mechanical skills -- basic instruction in what keys to push to accomplish specific tasks. This was true for all the tools we studied. However, in the case of The Coordinator, we did interview some users who had received training that included an introduction to the theory underlying this product. While a subset of this group reported that the ideas were too sophisticated for them and their colleagues to assimilate, a few reported that knowledge of the theory helped them to use the tool and to implement the communication practices which the tool supports.

Given our previous observations that people are not using the functionality provided by these tools, the fact that they have also received only basic, mechanical training, would tend to indicate that the training is not adequate.

Evolution - After an initial introduction into the use of a groupware tool, the users we interviewed tended to "practice" only those procedures that they needed to accomplish their most urgent business tasks. As a result, much of what they were initially trained to do but did not continue to do regularly was forgotten.

In the use of any system, people will encounter special case needs for functions from time to time in their work. Those interviewed seldom looked up procedures in a manual when these situations arose. When online help was available, most who used it were unable to find what they needed. Instead, the typical form of help sought was to ask a colleague or subordinate.

Some of the organizations provided a person or group to serve as the designated support source to which the users would turn for help. These organizations appeared to understand the evolutionary nature of a person's use of software, and they supported that evolution through a formal organizational entity. Other sites we studied assumed that once the initial training had taken place, no formal corporate role of an on-going nature was needed. In these cases, *de facto* support grew up in the form of individuals in work groups who became "local gurus."

We observed what might be called a "plateau of competence" in using a tool. Without a timely and user-appropriate incentive to move beyond self-standardized use, people tend to settle into routine operations [Ross85]. This suggests that such stimuli must be in the form of easily tried procedures with immediately visible value so that they fit into the practices carried out during a busy day.

In each of the categories - champions, expectations, training, evolution - we saw a need for sensitivity to organizational issues. In addition the degree and timing of organizational intervention must be planned. The risk of failure increases when the multiple organizational factors are not considered. In the case of groupware technology, there is very little experience in understanding these factors, which may be particularly complex because of the "group" aspects of the application.

● Process redesign may be required to realize productivity improvement.

We have just suggested that organizations should consider the perspectives of people at all levels when introducing technology. It is also interesting to consider the extent to which organizations need to alter their basic processes in order to achieve higher levels of coordination and productivity.

For example, the process for coordinating work in a department or for conducting meetings may be areas in which productivity gains could be achieved through rethinking and redesigning the traditional forms (e.g., Whiteside and Wixon, [Whit88]). In our field work we observed instances where management expected substantial productivity improvement to result from the simple act of putting a groupware system into place. In these instances our interviews did not uncover any significant change in how people approached their jobs. Some felt that the new technology created more work for them and therefore made them less productive.

In some cases when groupware systems are implemented, we conclude that not enough attention is being placed on examining the basic processes of work and how technology may enhance these processes. Therefore, process redesign may be required to achieve productive benefits in using groupware technology.

Managers in some of the organizations we studied had explicit goals of changing the way work was carried out, moving their groups to new planes of performance, and creating "paradigm shifts." Management must take specific actions to bring forth these productive team characteristics. It is clear that accomplishment of many of these goals is not dependent on adding new technology. However, in the fast-paced, geographically-dispersed environment of today's corporation, groupware technology could enhance the individual's ability to carry out the appropriate tasks.

SUMMARY

Is groupware too new to study conclusively? We have learned from innovation research [Roge83] that it takes time for new ideas to be assimilated by people. Although the technology for electronic mail and conferencing has been available for fifteen years ([Enge64], [Joha88]), the concept of technology to support work groups has only been discussed for about four years. (Engelbart in the early '60's developed pioneering technology especially designed to support high-performing teams, but this work was not well known outside the computer science community.) We may therefore be observing the use of these new tools when they are in their infancy and before people have learned to think of them as essential tools for effective office work.

Experiences gained from studying people as they learn to use new tools can benefit the designers of the next tool generation, thereby helping to accelerate the process of acceptance and use of these tools. We also believe that managers can learn to be sensitive to the complex balance that exists between the organization and the technology. The observations and conclusions that we have discussed can inform us about what is taking place in organizations today, and they present an interpretation of the factors underlying the observed behavior. This research, as well as the reports of others on social and psychological factors (e.g., [Bair88], [Ehrl87], [Grud88], etc.), helps to shed light on the complexities of designing and implementing information technology that is used by work groups to help coordinate their communication and actions.

We see an important interplay of factors in our major conclusions. For example, people seem to need training beyond the simple mechanical instruction that usually accompanies groupware tools. Because groupware is a relatively new technology, this may change in the future as the tools are more widely known and used. Their inherent value may become more obvious to people and they will adapt to their use more easily.

However, the organizational inhibitors that we observed cannot be dismissed. Recognizing the long-lasting constraints of history and the power of politics in the organization at the same time as considering the new possibilities for technological support may result in new insights. These contrast with insights suggested when using traditional requirements analysis, often focused on individual users to the exclusion of organizational factors.

We have stated earlier that managing the volume of information has been traditionally, and still is, the major task facing knowledge workers. As we have interviewed, observed teams, and better understood the tasks they are undertaking, we have come to the conclusion that a groupware system like The Coordinator, for example, could have an effect on knowledge work by compressing it. That is, The Coordinator, if used as its designers intended, could reduce the volume and complexity of information so that managing the content and meaning of interaction would dominate managing volume.

Revolutionizing work may be an effective role for groupware systems in organizations. Most of today's groupware systems are not designed to do this. Instead they attempt to provide electronic support for the tasks people are believed to carry out in performing knowledge work in groups. If indeed the concept of work groups and business teams is the organizational concept of the future, it becomes critical to understand the interaction of individuals in these groups, and how information technology can support or even enhance the work of groups.

REFERENCES

[Anco87]   Ancona, Deborah Gladstein, "Groups in Organizations," **Group Processes and Intergroup Relations**, Editor Clyde Hendrick, Sage Publications, Newbury Park, CA, 1987, pp 207-230.

[Bair88]   Bair, James H., and Stephen Gale, "An Investigation of the Coordinator as an Example of Computer Supported Cooperative Work," Extended Abstract, submitted to the Second Conference on Computer-Supported Cooperative Work, Portland, Oregon, September 1988.

[Bull90]   Bullen, Christine V., and John L. Bennett, "Groupware In Practice: An Interpretation of Work Experiences," CISR Working Paper No. 205, MIT Center for Information Systems Research, Cambridge, MA 02139, March 1990.

[Carr88]   Carroll, John S., and Perin, Constance, "How Expectations About Microcomputers Influence Their Organizational Consequences," Management in the 1990's Working Paper 88-044, Sloan School of Management, MIT, Cambridge, MA, 02139, April 1988.

[Ehrl87]   Ehrlich, Susan F., "Social and Psychological Factors Influencing The Design of Office Communication Systems," in **Proceedings of Human Factors in Computing Systems and Graphics Interfaces** (Toronto, April 5-9, 1987), ACM, New York, pp 323-329.

[Enge63]   Engelbart, Douglas C., "A Conceptual Framework for the Augmentation of Man's Intellect," in **Vistas in Information Handling**, Vol. 1 (P. Howerton, Ed.), Spartan Books, Washington, D.C., 1963, pp 1-29.

[Grud88]   Grudin, Jonathan, "Why CSCW Applications Fail: Problems in the Design and Evaluation of Organizational Interfaces," **Proceedings of the Conference on Computer-Supported Cooperative Work**, September 26-28, 1988, Portland, Oregon, pp 85-93.

[Joha88]   Johansen, Robert, **Groupware: Computer Support for Business Teams**, The Free Press, New York, 1988.

[Klin89]   Kling, Rob and Suzanne Iacono, "Desktop Computerization & the Organization of Work," **Computers in the Human Context**, by Tom Forester, MIT Press, Cambridge, MA., 1989.

Malo83]   Malone, Thomas W., "How Do People Organize Their Desks? Implications for the Design of Office Information Systems," **ACM Transactions on Office Information Systems**, Vol.1, No. 1, January 1983, pp 99-112.

[Mart73]   Martin, James, **Design of Man-Computer Dialogues**, Prentice-Hall, Englewood Cliffs, New Jersey, 1973.

[Niel86]   Nielsen, J., R. Mack, K. Bergendorff, and N. Grischkowsky, "Integrated Software Usage in the Professional Work Environment: Evidence from Questionnaires and Interviews," in **Proceedings of CHI'86 Human Factors in Computing Systems** (Boston, April 13-17, 1986), ACM, New York, pp 162-167.

[Roge83]   Rogers, Everett, **The Diffusion of Innovation**, Free Press, New York, NY, 1983.

[Ross85]   Rosson, Mary Beth, "The Role of Experience in Editing," **Proceedings of INTERACT'84**, Elsevier North-Holland, Amsterdam, 1985, pp 45-50.

[Sear69]   Searle, John R., **Speech Acts**, Cambridge University Press, Cambridge, England, 1969.

[Whit88]   Whiteside, John, and Wixon, Dennis, "Contextualism as a World View for the Reformation of Meetings," in **Proceedings of the Conference on Computer-Supported Cooperative Work**, Association for Computing Machinery, New York, 1988.

[Yate89]   Yates, JoAnne, **Control Through Communication: The Rise of System in American Management**, Johns Hopkins University Press, Baltimore, MD, 1989.

GROUPWARE

Groupware reflects a change in emphasis from using the computer to solve problems to using the computer to facilitate human interaction. This article describes categories and examples of groupware and discusses some underlying research and development issues. GROVE, a novel group editor, is explained in some detail as a salient groupware example.

"Groupware: Some Issues and Experiences" by C.A. Ellis, S.J. Gibbs, and G.L. Rein, from *Communications of the ACM*, Vol. 34, No. 1, January 1991, pages 38-58. Copyright © 1991, Association for Computing Machinery, Inc., reprinted with permission.

SOME ISSUES AND EXPERIENCES

**C.A. Ellis,
S.J. Gibbs, and
G.L. Rein**

Society acquires much of its character from the ways in which people interact. Although the computer in the home or office is now commonplace, our interaction with one another is more or less the same now as it was a decade ago. As the technologies of computers and other forms of electronic communication continue to converge, however, people will continue to interact in new and different ways.

One probable outcome of this technological marriage is the electronic workplace—an organization-wide system that integrates information processing and communication activities. The study of such systems is part of a new multidisciplinary field: *Computer-Supported Cooperative Work* (CSCW) [29]. Drawing on the expertise and col-

laboration of many specialists, including social scientists and computer scientists, CSCW looks at how groups work and seeks to discover how technology (especially computers) can help them work.

Commercial CSCW products, such as *The Coordinator*™ [24] and other PC-based software [67], are often referred to as examples of *groupware*. This term is frequently used almost synonymously with CSCW technology (see [8] or [44] for general descriptions of, and strong motivation for groupware). Others define groupware as software for small or narrowly focused groups, not organization-wide support [30]. We propose a somewhat broader view, suggesting that groupware be viewed as the class of applications, for small groups and for organizations, arising from the merging of computers and large information bases and communications technology. These applications may or may not specifically support cooperation.

This article explores groupware

in this larger sense and delineates classes of design issues facing groupware developers. It is divided into five main sections. First, the **Overview** defines groupware in terms of a group's common task and its need for a shared environment. Since our definition of groupware covers a range of systems, the second section provides a **Taxonomy of Groupware Systems.** The third describes the widely ranging **Perspectives** of those who build these systems. The fourth section, **Concepts and Example,** introduces some common groupware concepts, and applies these to GROVE, one example of a groupware system. The fifth section contains a discussion of some Design Issues facing groupware designers and developers. Our emphasis in this section is upon system-level issues within real-time groupware. In our conclusion to this article we both issue a note of caution concerning the difficulty of developing successful groupware due to social and organizational effects, and indicate that there is much interesting work remaining to be done in this field.

Overview

Most software systems only support the interaction between a user and the system. Whether preparing a document, querying a database, or even playing a video game, the user interacts solely with the computer. Even systems designed for multiuser applications, such as office information systems, provide minimal support for user-to-user interaction. This type of support is clearly needed, since a significant portion of a person's activities occur in a group, rather than an individual, context. As we begin to focus on how to support this group interaction, we must attend to three key areas: communication, collaboration, and coordination.

The Importance of Communication, Collaboration, and Coordination

Computer-based or computer-mediated communication, such as electronic mail, is not fully integrated with other forms of communication. The primarily asynchronous, text-based world of electronic mail and bulletin boards exists separately from the synchronous world of telephone and face-to-face conversations. While applications such as voice mail or talk programs blur this distinction somewhat, there are still gaps between the asynchronous and the synchronous worlds. One cannot transfer a document between two arbitrary phone numbers, for example, and it is uncommon to originate a telephone conversation from a workstation. Integrating telecommunications and computer processing technologies will help bridge these gaps.

Similar to communication, collaboration is a cornerstone of group activity. Effective collaboration demands that people share information. Unfortunately, current information systems—database systems in particular—go to great lengths to insulate users from each

other. As an example, consider two designers working with a CAD database. Seldom are they able to simultaneously modify different parts of the same object and be aware of each other's changes; rather, they must check the object in and out and tell each other what they have done. Many tasks require an even finer granularity of sharing. What is needed are shared environments that unobtrusively offer up-to-date group context and explicit notification of each user's actions when appropriate.

The effectiveness of communication and collaboration can be enhanced if a group's activities are coordinated. Without coordination, for example, a team of programmers or writers will often engage in conflicting or repetitive actions. Coordination can be viewed as an activity in itself, as a necessary overhead when several parties are performing a task [62]. While current database applications contribute somewhat to the coordination of groups—by providing multiple access to shared objects—most software tools offer only a single-user perspective and thus do little to assist this important function.

A Definition of Groupware

The goal of groupware is to assist groups in communicating, in collaborating, and in coordinating their activities. Specifically, we define groupware as:

computer-based systems that support groups of people engaged in a common task (or goal) and that provide an interface to a shared environment.

The notions of a *common task* and a *shared environment* are crucial to this definition. This excludes multiuser systems, such as time-sharing systems, whose users may not share a common task. Note also that the definition does not specify that the users be active simultaneously. Groupware that specifically supports simultaneous activity is called *real-time groupware;* otherwise, it is *non-real-time groupware.* The emphasis of this article is real-time

groupware and system-level issues.

The term groupware was first defined by Johnson-Lenz [46] to refer to a computer-based system plus the social group processes. In his book on groupware [44], Johansen restricts his definition to the computer-based system. Our definition follows the line of reasoning of Johansen since this article is primarily concerned with system-level issues. All of the authors mentioned agree with us that the system and the group are intimately interacting entities. Successful technological augmentation of a task or process depends upon a delicate balance between good social processes and procedures with appropriately structured technology.

The Groupware Spectrum

There is no rigid dividing line between systems that are considered groupware and those that are not. Since systems support common tasks and shared environments to varying degrees, it is appropriate to think of a groupware spectrum with different systems at different points on the spectrum. Of course, this spectrum is multidimensional; two dimensions are illustrated in Figure 1. Following are two examples of systems described according to our definition's common task dimension:

1. A conventional timesharing system supports many users concurrently performing their separate and independent tasks. Since they are not working in a tightly coupled mode on a common task, this system is usually low on the groupware spectrum.
2. In contrast, consider a software review system that electronically allows a group of designers to evaluate a software module during a real-time interaction. This system assists people who are focusing on the same specific task at the same time, and who are closely interacting. It is high on the groupware spectrum.

Other systems, such as those described in the following examples, can be placed on the groupware spectrum according to how they fit the shared environment part of our definition. In other words, to what extent do they provide information about the participants, the current state of the project, and the social atmosphere?

1. The typical electronic mail system transmits messages, but it provides few environmental cues. Therefore it is rather low on the groupware spectrum.

2. In contrast, the "electronic classroom" system [74] uses multiple windows to post information about the subject being taught, and about the environment. Emulating a traditional classroom, this system allows an instructor to present an on-line lecture to students at remote personal workstations. In addition to the blackboard controlled by the teacher, windows display the attendance list, students' questions and comments, and the classroom status. Many commands facilitate lecture delivery and class interaction. This system is high on the groupware spectrum.

Over time, systems can migrate to higher points on the groupware spectrum. For example, Engelbart's pioneering work on augmenting the intellect in the 1960s demonstrated multiuser systems with groupware capabilities similar to some of today's research prototypes. Engelbart's On-Line System [NLS] [21], an early hypertext system, contained advanced features such as filters for selectively viewing information, and support for on-line conferencing. Today's improved technology and enhanced user interfaces have boosted this type of system higher on the groupware spectrum. Additionally, the technological infrastructure required for groupware's wide use—an infrastructure missing in the 1960s—is now emerging.

Taxonomy of Groupware Systems

This section presents two taxonomies useful for viewing the variety of groupware. The first taxonomy is based upon notions of time and space; the second on application-level functionality.

Time Space Taxonomy

Groupware can be conceived to help a face-to-face group, or a group that is distributed over many locations. Furthermore a groupware system can be conceived to enhance communication and collaboration within a real-time interaction, or an asynchronous, non-real-time interaction. These time and space considerations suggest the four categories of groupware represented by the 2x2 matrix shown in Figure 2. Meeting room technology would be within the upper left cell; a real-time document editor within the lower left cell; a physical bulletin board within the upper right cell; and an electronic mail system within the lower right cell.

A comprehensive groupware system might best serve the needs of all of the quadrants. For example, it would be quite helpful to have the same base functionality, and user interface look and feel (a) while I am using a computer to edit a document in real-time with a group (same time/same place or same time/different place) and (b) while I am alone editing in my office or home (different time). Of course, there are other dimensions, such as group size, that can be added to this simple 2x2 matrix. Further details of this taxonomy are presented by Johansen [45].

Application-Level Taxonomy

The second taxonomy presented in

FIGURE 1. Two Dimensions of the Groupware Spectrum.

FIGURE 2. Groupware Time Space Matrix.

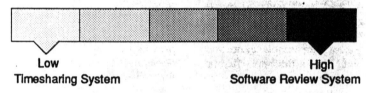

Common Task Dimension

Low
Timesharing System

High
Software Review System

Shared Environment Dimension

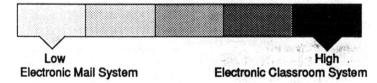

Low
Electronic Mail System

High
Electronic Classroom System

	Same Time	Different Times
Same Place	face-to-face interaction	asynchronous interaction
Different Places	synchronous distributed interaction	asynchronous distributed interaction

this section is based on application-level functionality and is not meant to be comprehensive; furthermore, many of the defined categories overlap. This taxonomy is intended primarily to give a general idea of the breadth of the groupware domain.

Message Systems

The most familiar example of groupware is the computer-based message system, which supports the asynchronous exchange of textual messages between groups of users. Examples include electronic mail and computer conferencing or bulletin board systems. The proliferation of such systems has led to the "information overload" phenomenon [37]. Some recent message systems help manage information overload by easing the user's processing burden. "Intelligence" is sometimes added to the message delivery system; for example, the Information Lens [63] lets users specify rules that automatically file or reroute incoming messages based on their content. Other systems add intelligence to the messages themselves; the Imail system [38], for example, has a language for attaching scripts to messages. Scripts are sender-specified programs that execute in the receiver's environment and that can, for example, query the receiver, report back to the sender, or cause the message to be rerouted.

Multiuser Editors

Members of a group can use multiuser editors to jointly compose and edit a document. Some of these editors, such as ForComment™ [67], are for asynchronous use, and conveniently separate the text supplied by the author from the comments of various reviewers. Real-time group editors allow a group of people to edit the same object at the same time. The object being edited is usually divided into logical segments; for example, a document could be split into sections or a program into procedures or modules. Typically, a multiuser editor allows concurrent read access to any segment, but only to one writer per segment. The editor transparently manages locking and synchronization, and users edit the shared object as they would a private object. Examples include the Collaborative Editing System (CES) [28], Shared Book [58], and Quilt [22, 57].

Some multiuser editors provide explicit notification of other users' actions. For example, Mercury [47], an editor intended for programming teams, informs users when their code needs to be changed because of program modifications made by others. The DistEdit system [49] tries to provide a toolkit for building and supporting multiple group editors.

Group Decision Support Systems and Electronic Meeting Rooms

Group Decision Support Systems (GDSSs) provide computer-based facilities for the exploration of unstructured problems in a group setting (see [51] or [16] for recent surveys). The goal is to improve the productivity of decision-making meetings, either by speeding up the decision-making process or by improving the quality of the resulting decisions [51]. There are GDSS aids for decision structuring, such as alternative ranking and voting tools, and for idea generation [2] or issue analysis [11].

Many GDSSs are implemented as electronic meeting rooms that contain several networked workstations, large computer-controlled public displays, and audio/video equipment (examples are discussed in [2, 12, 16, 64, 77 and 78]). Some of these facilities require a specially trained operator; others assume operational competence among the group members.

A well-known example is the PlexCenter Planning and Decision Support Laboratory at the University of Arizona [2]. The facility provides a large U-shaped conference table with eight personal workstations; a workstation in each of four break-out rooms; a video disk; and a large-screen projection system that can display screens of individual workstations or a compilation of screens. The conference table workstations are recessed to enhance the participants' line of sight and to encourage interaction. They communicate over a local area network and run software tools for electronic brainstorming, stakeholder identification and analysis, and issue analysis.

Recent work at the University of Arizona has concentrated on the support of larger groups. The current large group facility has 24 workstations designed to support up to 48 people. The support of large groups presents unique challenges and opportunities.

Computer Conferencing

The computer serves as a communications medium in a variety of ways. In particular, it has provided three new approaches in the way people carry out conferences: real-time computer conferencing, computer teleconferencing, and desktop conferencing.

Real-Time Computer Conferencing

Real-time computer conferencing allows a group of users, who are either gathered in an electronic meeting room or physically dispersed, to interact synchronously through their workstations or terminals. When a group is physically dispersed, an audio link, such as a conference call, is often established.

There are two basic approaches to implementing real-time computer conferencing software [73]. The first embeds an unmodified single-user application in a *conferencing environment* that multiplexes the application's output to each participant's display [42]. Input comes from one user at a time, and a *floor passing* protocol (determining who has the floor) exchanges input control among users [56]. Examples include *terminal linking* (a service found in some time-sharing systems) and *replicated windows* (typically implemented by a window server that drives a set of displays in tandem). The second approach is to design the application specifically to account for the presence of multiple users. Some examples are Real Time Calendar [RTCAL] [73], a meeting scheduling system, and Cognoter [78], a real-time group note-taking system.

Each approach has its advantages and disadvantages. While the first allows existing applications to be used, each user has an identical view of the application—there is no per-user context. The second approach offers the possibility of a richer interface, but the application must be built from the ground up or with considerable additional effort.

Computer Teleconferencing
Telecommunication support for group interaction is referred to as teleconferencing [43]. The most familiar examples of teleconferencing are conference calls and video conferencing. Teleconferencing tends to be awkward, requiring special rooms and sometimes trained operators. Newer systems provide workstation-based interfaces to a conference and make the process more accessible. Xerox, for example, established an audio/video link for use by a project team split between Portland and Palo Alto [26]. Most video interactions occurred between large Commons areas at each site, but project members could also access video channels through their office workstations. A similar system, CRUISER [72], lets users electronically roam the hallways by browsing video channels.

Desktop Conferencing
Teleconferencing is not only relatively inaccessible, but it also has the disadvantage of not letting participants share text and graphics (see [18] for a discussion of the failure of video conferencing). Real-time computer conferencing does not offer video capabilities. A third type of computer-supported conferencing combines the advantages of teleconferencing and real-time

conferencing while mitigating their drawbacks. Dubbed *desktop conferencing*, this method still uses the workstation as the conference interface, but it also runs applications shared by the participants. Modern desktop conferencing systems support multiple video windows per workstation. This allows display of dynamic views of information, and dynamic video images of participants [80].

An example of desktop conferencing is the MMConf system [14]. MMConf provides a shared display of a multimedia document, as well as communications channels for voice and shared pointers. Another example is the Rapport multimedia conferencing system [1]. Rapport is designed for workstations connected by a multimedia network (a network capable of transmitting data, voice, and video). The system supports various forms of interaction, from simple telephone-like conversations to multiparty shared-display interaction.

Intelligent Agents
Not all the participants in an electronic meeting are people. Multiplayer computer games, for example, might automatically generate participants if the number of people is too low for a challenging game. Such nonhuman participants are a special case of intelligent agents (a similar concept is "surrogates" [44]). In general, intelligent agents are responsible for a specific set of tasks, and the user interface makes their actions resemble those of other users.

As a specific example, we have developed a groupware toolkit that includes an agent named Liza [25]. One of the tools in the toolkit displays the pictures and locations of all session participants. When Liza joins a session, a picture of an intelligent-looking android is also displayed, indicating to the group that Liza is *participating*. Liza's participation means that a set of rules owned by Liza become active; these rules monitor session activity and result

in Liza suggesting changes of content or form.

Coordination Systems
The coordination problem is the "integration and harmonious adjustment of individual work efforts toward the accomplishment of a larger goal" [76]. Coordination systems address this problem in a variety of ways. Typically these systems allow individuals to view their actions, as well as the relevant actions of others, within the context of the overall goal. Systems may also trigger users' actions by informing users of the states of their actions and their wait conditions, or by generating automatic reminders and alerts. Coordination systems can be categorized by one of the four types of models they embrace: form, procedure, conversation, or communication-structure oriented.

Form-oriented models typically focus on the routing of documents (forms) in organizational procedures. These systems address coordination by explicitly modeling organizational activity as fixed processes [59, 83]. In some of the more recent systems there is an effort to make process support more flexible. For example, in Electronic Circulation Folders [ECF] [48] exception handling is addressed through migration specifications that describe all the possible task migration routes in terms of the steps to be carried out in processing organizational documents.

Procedure-oriented models view organizational procedures as programmable processes; hence the phrase "process programming" [3, 68, 69]. This approach was first applied to coordination problems in the software process domain and takes the view that software process descriptions should be thought of and implemented as software. The development of process programs is itself a rigorous process consisting of specification, design, implementation, and testing/verification phases [69].

Conversation-oriented models are based on the observation that people coordinate their activities via their conversation [15, 24, 65, 81]. The underlying theoretical basis for many systems embracing the conversation model is speech act theory [75]. For example, The Coordinator [24] is based on a set of speech acts (i.e., requests, promises, etc.) and contains a model of legal conversational moves (e.g., a request has to be issued before a promise can be made). As users make conversational moves, typically through electronic mail, the system tracks their requests and commitments.

Communication structure-oriented models describe organizational activities in terms of role relationships [10, 39, 77]. For example, in the ITT approach [39, 40], a person's electronic work environment is composed of a set of centers, where each center represents a function for which the person is responsible. Within centers are roles that perform the work and objects that form the work materials for carrying out the function of that center. Centers and roles have connections to other centers and roles, and the behavior of the connections is governed by the role scripts of the interacting roles.

Summary

As mentioned, overlap exists in these categories. As the demand for integrated systems increases, we see more merging of these functionalities. Intelligent message systems can and have been used for coordination. Desktop conferencing systems can and have been used for group editing. Nevertheless, many systems can be categorized according to their primary emphasis and intent. This, in turn, may depend upon the perspectives of the system designers.

Perspectives

As the preceding section's taxonomy suggests, groupware relies on the approaches and contributions of many disciplines. In particular, there are at least five key disciplines or perspectives for successful groupware: distributed systems, communications, human-computer interaction, artificial intelligence (AI), and social theory. It is important to note that the relationship between groupware and these five domains of study is a mutually beneficial one. Not only does each discipline advance our understanding of the theory and practice of groupware, but groupware presents challenging topics of research for all five domains—topics that without groupware might never be explored.

Of equal importance is the notion that a given groupware system usually combines the perspectives of two or more of these disciplines. We can see the desktop conferencing paradigm, for example, as having been derived in either of two ways:

1. by starting with communications technology and enhancing this with further computing power and display devices at the phone receiver, or
2. by starting with the personal workstation (distributed systems perspective) and integrating communications capabilities.

Distributed Systems Perspective

Because their users are often distributed in time and/or space, many multiuser systems are naturally considered to be *distributed* systems. The distributed systems perspective explores and emphasizes this decentralization of data and control. Essentially, this type of system infers global system properties and maintains consistency of the global state by observing and manipulating local parameters.

The investigation of efficient algorithms for distributed operating systems and distributed databases is a major research area in distributed systems theory. Some of these research results are applicable to groupware systems. For example, implementing electronic mail systems evokes complex distributed-systems issues related to robustness: recipients should be able to receive messages even when the mail server is unavailable. One solution is to replicate message storage on multiple server machines [6]. Discovering and implementing the required algorithms—algorithms that will keep these servers consistent and maintain a distributed name lookup facility—is a challenging task.

Communications Perspective

This perspective emphasizes the exchange of information between remote agents. Primary concerns include increasing connectivity and bandwidth, and protocols for the exchange of many types of information—text, graphics, voice and video.

One of the commonly posed challenges of groupware to communications technology is how to make distributed interactions as effective as face-to-face interactions. Perhaps the correct view of this challenge is that a remote interaction, supported by appropriate technology, presents an alternative medium. While this will not replace face-to-face communication, it may actually be preferable in some situations for some groups because certain difficulties, inconveniences, and breakdowns can be eliminated or minimized. For example, distributed interactions allow participants to access other relevant information, either via the computer or in a book on the shelf, without interrupting the interaction flow. This is analogous to findings on the use of telephone, electronic mail, and other technologies. While none of these replace face-to-face interaction, each has a niche where it is a unique and useful mode of communication. The challenge, then, is to apply appropriate technological combinations to the classes of interactions that will benefit the most from the new medium.

Human-Computer Interaction Perspective

This perspective emphasizes the importance of the user interface in computer systems. Human-computer interaction is itself a multidisciplinary field, relying on the diverse skills of graphics and industrial designers, computer graphics experts (who study display technologies, input devices, and interaction techniques), and cognitive scientists (who study human cognitive, perceptual, and motor skills).

Until recently, most user interface research has focused on single-user systems. Groupware challenges researchers to broaden this perspective, to address the issues of human-computer interaction within the context of multiuser or *group* interfaces. Since these interfaces are sensitive to such factors as group dynamics and organizational structure—factors not normally considered relevant to user interface design—it is vital that social scientists and end users play a role in the development of group interfaces.

Artificial Intelligence Perspective

With an emphasis on theories of intelligent behavior, this perspective seeks to develop techniques and technologies for imbuing machines with human-like attributes. The artificial intelligence (AI) approach is usually heuristic or augmentative, allowing information to accrue through user-machine interaction rather than being initially complete and structured.

This approach blends well with groupware's requirements. For example, groupware designed for use by different groups must be flexible and accommodate a variety of team behaviors and tasks: research suggests that two different teams performing the same task use group technology in very different ways [71]. Similarly, the same team performing two separate tasks uses the technology differently for each task.

AI may, in the long run, provide one of the most significant contributions to groupware. This technology could transform machines from passive agents that process and present information to active agents that enhance interactions. The challenge is to ensure that the system's activity enhances interaction in a way that is procedurally and socially desirable to the participants.

Social Theory Perspective

This perspective emphasizes social theory, or sociology, in the design of groupware systems. Systems designed from this perspective embody the principles and explanations derived from sociological research. The developers of Quilt [22], for example, conducted systematic research on the social aspects of writing, and from this research they derived the requirements for their collaborative editing environment. As a result, Quilt assigns document access rights according to interactions between users' social roles, the nature of the information, and the stage of the writing project.

Systems such as this ask people to develop a new or different awareness, one that can be difficult to maintain until it is internalized. For example, Quilt users must be aware when their working styles—which are often based on informal agreements—change, so that the system can be reconfigured to provide appropriate access controls. With The Coordinator [24], users need to learn about the language implications of requests and promises, because the system makes these speech acts explicit by automatically recording them in a group calendar. Both examples suggest the need for coaching. Perhaps the systems themselves could coach users, both by encouraging and teaching users the theories on which the systems are based.

Real-Time Groupware Concepts and Example

The vocabulary and ideas embodied in groupware are still evolving. In this section, we list some important terms useful for explanation and comparison of groupware systems, followed by an illustrative real-time groupware system. Our emphasis throughout the remainder of this paper is on real-time groupware. Functionality, design issues, and usage experience of GROVE, a real-time group text editor allowing simultaneous editing of private, shared, and public views of a document will also be explained.

- *shared context*. A shared context is a set of objects where the objects and the actions performed on the objects are visible to a set of users. Examples include document objects within coauthoring systems and class notes within electronic classrooms. This notion of shared context is a subset of the larger, more elusive concept of a *shared environment* discussed earlier.
- *group window*. A group window is a collection of windows whose instances appear on different dis-

The artificial intelligence (AI) approach is usually heuristic or augmentative, allowing information to accrue through user-machine interaction rather than being initially complete and structured.

play surfaces. The instances are connected. For example, drawing a circle in one instance makes a circle appear in the other instances, or scrolling one instance makes the others scroll.

- *telepointer*. A telepointer is a cursor that appears on more than one display and that can be moved by different users. When it is moved on one display, it moves on all displays.
- *view*. A view is a visual, or multimedia representation of some portion of a shared context. Different views may contain the same information but differ in their presentation (for instance, an array of numbers can be presented as a table or as a graph), or they can use the same presentation but refer to different portions of the shared context.
- *synchronous and asynchronous interaction*. In synchronous interactions, such as spoken conversations, people interact in real time. Asynchronous interactions are those in which people interact over an extended period of time such as in postal correspondence. Most groupware systems support only one of these interaction modes.
- *session*. A session is a period of synchronous interaction supported by a groupware system. Examples include formal meetings and informal work group discussions.
- *role*. A role is a set of privileges and responsibilities attributed to a person, or sometimes to a system module. Roles can be formally or informally attributed. For example, the person who happens to like to talk and visit with many people may informally take on the role of information gatekeeper. The head of a group may officially have the role of manager [37].

GROVE: A Groupware Example
The *GR*oup *O*utline *V*iewing *E*ditor (GROVE), [20], is an example of real-time groupware that illustrates some of the concepts just intro-

duced. GROVE, implemented at MCC, is a simple text editor designed for use by a group of people simultaneously editing an outline during a work session.

Within a GROVE *session*, each user has his or her own workstation and bitmap display. Thus each user can see and manipulate one or more *views* of the text being worked on in multiple overlapping windows on his or her screen. GROVE separates the concept of a view from the concept of a viewer. A *view* is a subset of the items in an outline determined by read access privileges. A *viewer* is a group window for seeing a contiguous subset of a view. GROVE views and viewers are categorized as private, shared, and public. A *private view* contains items which only a particular user can read, a *shared view* contains items readable by an enumerated set of users, and a *public view* contains items readable by all users.

Figure 3 shows a GROVE group window—group windows provide the shared viewers for synchronous interactions among users.

In addition to displaying views, group windows indicate who is able to use the window and who is actually participating in the session at any given time. This information is provided by displaying images of the people who are members of the view (or simply printing their names if their images are not available) along the bottom border of the window. Thus as users enter or leave the session, their pictures appear and disappear in all appropriate group windows. The window in Figure 3 appears on the workstations of the three users shown along the bottom border, and each user knows that the others have joined the session. Users can modify the underlying outline by performing standard editing operations (insert, delete, cut, paste, and so on) in a group window. When this is done, all three of the users immediately see the modification. Outline items which are grey (like the last item, in Figure 3) rather than black on a particular user's screen cannot be

modified by that user. Users can also open and close parts of the outline (by mousing on the small buttons on the left-hand side) or change the read and write permissions of outline items.

Participants can enter and leave a GROVE session at any time. When users enter (or reenter) a session, they receive an up-to-date document unless they choose to retrieve a previously stored version. The current context, is maintained even though changes may have occurred during their absence from the session. A session terminates when there are no remaining participants.

Design Issues and Rationale
GROVE was built as an experimental prototype to explore systems implementation issues, and to gain usage experience. We chose to build this system from scratch rather than beginning with the code of an existing editor because we wanted to understand, control, and modularize the code in particular ways. We were especially concerned with the user interface, and wanted to carefully architect the system's features and its look and feel. In keeping with the experimental nature of this tool, we chose to minimize the functionality and coding time spent on the standard editing features, and to concentrate on its groupware features. These features include the private, shared, and public group window support; the shared context present in the user interface; and the replicated architecture to allow fine-grained (keystroke level) concurrent editing and notification.

The architecture uses a local editor and replicated document at each user's workstation, and a centralized coordinator that serializes the operations of the various editors. This forced us to immediately face problems of response times, concurrent actions, and data inconsistencies. These are problems that plague real-time groupware systems in general. We have investigated this further, and using some concepts from the distributed systems literature, have devised an algorithm for distributed concurrency control. This eliminates the need for centralized coordination as will be shown in the later section on concurrency control.

GROVE proposes an alternative style of interaction. It is designed to encourage and assist in tightly coupled interaction as opposed to the majority of systems for editing documents or doing multiuser computing. The default in GROVE is a mode where everyone can see and edit everything, and there is absolutely *no locking* while editing. New users ask "Isn't it chaotic to all edit in the same document, even the same paragraph, at the same time?" and "Why would a group ever want to edit in the same line of text at the same time?" Indeed, this editor is at the opposite extreme from most CASE systems which force a group of software engineers to lock modules and work in a very isolated and serial manner. The answer to the above questions are related to groups learning to work in new and original ways. Part of the answer is that after a learning period, it is not chaotic, but rather surprisingly useful, because social protocol mediates. The above questions imply that we can learn a lot by observing teams using this editor for *real work*. In the next subsection, we report on our observation and reflection on some of this usage.

Usage Experience

Groupware developers need to be conscious of the potential effects of technology on people, their work and interactions. A sensitivity to this dimension can make the difference between a groupware system which is accepted and used regularly within an organization, and one that is rejected [32]. Issues of user friendliness, flexibility, and technological control must be considered during design and implementation. Much can be learned from ongoing observation and empirical study of groupware systems.

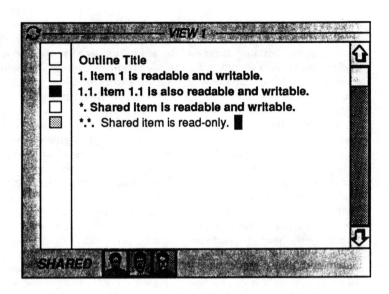

FIGURE 3. A GROVE Group Window.

GROVE has been used by several groups for a variety of design activities, from planning joint papers and presentations to brainstorming. In general, sessions can be divided into three types:

1. **face-to-face sessions** in the electronic meeting room at our lab where there are three Sun workstations and an electronic blackboard,
2. **distributed sessions** where the participants work from machines in their offices and use a conference call on speaker phones for voice communication, and

3. **mixed-mode sessions** where some of the participants are face-to-face and others are distributed.

Table 1 lists the session type, group size, and task for fifteen GROVE sessions. The early sessions were mostly face-to-face sessions where we (the GROVE creators) used the tool and fine-tuned it. More recent sessions have primarily been distributed or mixed-mode sessions

TABLE 1. *Summary of GROVE Sessions*		
Session Type	**Number of Users**	**Task**
distributed	3	Identify issues in a project description.
face-to-face	3	Refine list of issues in project description.
face-to-face	3	Outline a technical report.
distributed	3	Plan a managerial presentation.
face-to-face	3	Continue planning a managerial presentation
face-to-face	2	Plan a tutorial.
face-to-face	3	Discuss project plans.
face-to-face	3	Discuss software enhancements for a system.
face-to-face	3	Continue to discuss project plans.
face-to-face	3	Continue to discuss project plans.
mixed-mode	5	Identify similarities/differences of two projects
distributed	3	Remote session test.
distributed	5	Brainstorm on two related topics.
distributed	5	Outline a paper.
mixed-mode	6	Outline a paper.

Groupware developers need to be conscious of the potential effects of technology on people, their work and interactions.

across thousands of miles, and have included participants at remote locations at the MCC Human Interface Program, from the University of Michigan, and from the Arthur Andersen Consulting Company. Distributed and mixed-mode sessions frequently involve as many as five or six people.

From the user's perspective, distributed editing sessions are distinctly different experiences from face-to-face editing sessions. Here are some pro and con observations regarding distributed sessions:

Increases information access. Participants in distributed sessions who reside in their offices have access to their local books and files. This sometimes allows easy access to important information that would not otherwise be available during the session. People have commented positively on the convenience, comfort, and familiarity associated with remaining in their offices.

Encourages parallel work within the group. People often divide into subgroups to work on different parts of the task by using a social protocol and shared views. Then their work is merged with the rest of the group's work by changing the access rights on the shared items to public items. This is also done in face-to-face sessions, but not as frequently as in distributed sessions (perhaps because there are more participants in a typical distributed session).

It is easy for distributed members to drop out for a while, do something else (such as work on some code in another window or

get a drink), then return. This is not socially acceptable in most face-to-face situations, but is accepted in distributed sessions.

Makes discussion more difficult. Distributed sessions have a noticeably different communication pattern from face-to-face sessions. Because our phones are not full-duplex, only one person's voice is transmitted at a time. Consequently, people tend to take turns and are unusually polite—if they are impolite or uncooperative, remarks get cut off and the discussion is incomprehensible.

Makes group focus more difficult, requiring more concentration. People have commented that in general, face-to-face sessions feel shorter, seem to accomplish more in less time, and are frequently more exhilarating. In contrast, distributed and mixed-mode sessions seem to require more concentration and are more tiring. Since discussion is more difficult when some of the group members are distributed, people appear to work harder (i.e., they make a conscious effort) to get and give feedback.

Cuts down on social interaction. Distributed sessions tend to be more serious. Since there is less interchange about nontask-related topics, people tend to focus on the task immediately. The effect is a possible efficiency gain from time saved and a possible loss from social needs.

Most of the face-to-face sessions seem to have more intense, richer interactions, but we think the reasons are deeper than simply the

ability to look directly at other participants. Group members rarely look directly at each other during face-to-face sessions, but being in the same room seems to increase the awareness of other members' activities to the point where highly cooperative work can be done. Most of the GROVE cooperative usage techniques have emerged in the face-to-face sessions, then have been used again in the distributed sessions because they were successful in the face-to-face environment.

In addition to comparing distributed with face-to-face sessions, it is interesting to compare group editing (in the synchronous or real-time sense) with single-user editing. Our observations regarding group editing are:

Can be confusing, unfocused, and chaotic. Many things can be going on at once. Several people may be busy in different parts of the outline. At times someone starts wordsmithing a public item while another is still working on it. Since GROVE does not provide a telepointer or other explicit turn-taking mechanisms, actions on the public view (such as scrolling or opening and closing items) are generally disruptive unless accompanied by some verbal explanation. Without verbal explanations, such as "Let's scroll to the next page" or "I'm opening line 2," one wonders "Who is doing this?" and "Why is this being changed?"

Collisions are surprisingly infrequent. Awareness of others' activities is frequently at a subconscious level. As one user expressed it, "During the brainstorming phase, I remember feeling that I was totally occupied with entering my own thoughts as fast as I could. I didn't feel at the time that I was paying much attention to what others were doing—but I know I was . . . First of all, there was very little duplication (most of the items were fresh material), so I must have been reading others' contributions without being aware of it. Secondly, there were very few collisions with people working in the same item at the same time—I was aware of where others were working and steered clear of their space."

Can be efficient. Group editing provides many opportunities for parallel work. The most interesting cooperation patterns also involve an agreed-upon social protocol for using the tool. For example, GROVE does not have an easy way to move a subtree: one group's protocol was that one person should create new empty items where he or she wanted to move the existing lines, then each person took responsibility for cutting and pasting certain agreed-upon lines to new locations in the outline. The group accomplished the subtree move in less time than if one person had done it alone.

Can help prevent information loss, leading to a tangible group product. All the groups observed have produced significant outlines at the end of their GROVE sessions. These outlines are *group compositions that emerge out of the contributions of individuals.* The mechanism for generating the outline is a fascinating process which can consist of any of the following actions:

- **independent entry**—a user enters information while paying little attention to what is already there or what is being discussed,
- **reflective entry**—a user comments on, appends to, or modifies what has already been entered (perhaps by other users),
- **consensus entry**—as the result of discussion the group decides on an appropriate entry or modification,
- **partitioned entry**—the group assigns particular members to refine or reorganize particular parts of the outline, and
- **recorded entry**—a user paraphrases what is being discussed verbally.

This variety of contribution styles has two effects. First, there is little information loss (as compared with having a single person enter information), and consequently all groups have a significant, tangible product at the end of their sessions. The production of tangible output leads to interactions with high satisfaction/productivity ratings. Second, different groups tend to use the tool in different ways, perhaps adapting it to how they already work or experimenting with new formats.

Can make learning a natural aspect of tool use. Since people are using the same tool at the same time for a shared purpose, when one has a question, friendly help is right at hand. The shared context makes the exchange between requester and provider efficient and relevant.

An unexpected finding is that GROVE users say they now find using single-user tools frustrating. Once one has experienced the flexibility and support provided by a groupware tool, one wants groupware features in all tools. For example, one group had a distributed session in which they used a document-processing system to review slides for a joint talk. This system was basically a single-user tool, despite its shared desktop feature. People could not edit slides on the spot and effect a shared view of the slide. They were constantly saving and closing-and-reopening document files. There was no support for multiple writers—whoever saved last was what the system remembered. Although this system had powerful graphics and formatting capabilities, it was not adequate for the task at hand and users missed GROVE's collaborative editing features.

Design Issues

Groupware systems of the future will probably incorporate contributions from most, if not all, of the five disciplines of study previously outlined. Furthermore, the groupware designer will increasingly be called on to grapple with several important issues that bear directly on a system's success. Researchers are currently exploring methods and techniques for resolving these issues, but many key research problems remain to be solved. This section focuses on groupware research, describing the problems that continue to face groupware designers and developers. The emphasis of this section is on real-time groupware designed for use by small- to medium-sized groups. We focus on this form of groupware since we feel it is here that technical challenges faced by groupware designers are most apparent.

Group Interfaces

Group interfaces differ from single-user interfaces in that they depict group activity and are controlled by multiple users rather than a single user. One example of a group interface is the GROVE group window illustrated in Figure 3. Other examples include interfaces to real-time computer conferencing systems and to multiplayer games.

Group interfaces introduce design problems not presented by single-user interfaces. A basic problem is how to manage complexity: multiple users can produce a higher level of activity and a greater degree of concurrency than single users, and the interface must support this complex behavior.

Other important questions are: What single-user interface techniques and concepts are useful for constructing group interfaces? Where do they fail, pointing to the need for new concepts? For example, is something like a scrollbar useful when it can be manipulated by more than one person, or is it simply too distracting?

WYSIWIS Issues

One approach to constructing group interfaces is known as WYSIWIS [78]. This acronym stands for "What You See Is What I See" and denotes interfaces in which the shared context is guaranteed to appear the same to all participants. The advantages of WYSIWIS are a strong sense of shared context (e.g., people can refer to something by position) and simple implementation. Its major disadvantage is that it can be inflexible.

Experience has shown that users often want independent control over such details as window placement and size, and may require customized information within the window. The contents of the GROVE window in Figure 3, for example, vary among users in that color indicates user-specific write permissions (i.e., black text is read/write, gray text is read-only). This is an example of *relaxed* as opposed to *strict* WYSIWIS. Stefik et al. [78] have suggested that WYSIWIS can be relaxed along four key dimensions: display space (the display objects to which WYSIWIS is applied), time of display (when displays are synchronized), subgroup population (the set of participants involved or affected), and congruence of view (the visual congruence of displayed information).

Group Focus and Distraction Issues
A good group interface should depict overall group activity and at the same time not be overly distracting. For example, when one user creates or scrolls a group window, opens or closes a group window, or modifies an object another person is viewing/working on, other users can be distracted.

This points up a fundamental difference between single-user and multiuser interfaces. With single-user interfaces, users usually have the mental context to interpret any display changes that result from their actions. As a result, the sudden disappearance of text at the touch of a button is acceptable; in fact, much effort goes toward increasing the system's responsiveness. By contrast, with group interfaces, users are generally not as aware of others' contexts and can less easily interpret sudden display changes resulting from others' actions.

What is needed are ways to provide contextual clues to the group's activity. A simple solution is for participants to audibly announce their intentions prior to taking action—suitable in some situations but often burdensome. A promising alternative is to use real-time animation to depict smoothly changing group activity. For example, text could materialize gradually or change in color as it is entered. This approach, however, introduces a new set of problems. First, animation is computationally expensive and requires specialized workstation hardware. Second, it is difficult to find visual metaphors that are suitable for animating operations, although work on artificial realities and responsive environments [54, 55] seems promising. Finally, any solution to this problem must take into account the dual needs for speed and continuity: the system's real-time responsiveness to the user making changes must not be sacrificed for the smooth, continuous notification to other users.

Issues Related to Group Dynamics
Group interfaces must match a group's usage patterns. Single-user text editors often rely on simple interfaces; characters appear and disappear as they are inserted and deleted. Multiuser text editors, must contend with a diversity of usage patterns as we observed with GROVE. The text was generated as independent, reflective, consensus, partitioned, and recorded entries and, therefore required much richer interfaces.

An experimental *cloudburst*

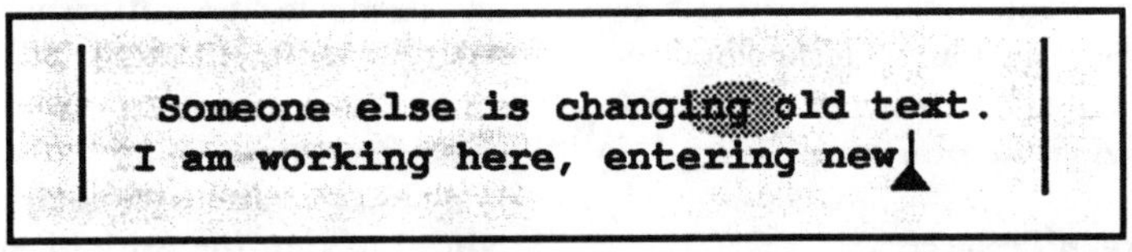

FIGURE 4. Portion of an Editing Window Using the Cloudburst Model.

model of multiuser text editing illustrates some needed group interface techniques. This model applies two techniques and is illustrated in Figure 4.

First, the text is aged so that recently entered text appears in bright blue and then gradually changes to black. Second, while textual modifications (insertions and deletions) are immediately visible to the person who initiates them, they are indicated on other users' displays by the appearance of clouds over the original text. The position and size of a cloud indicates the approximate location and extent of the modification. When a user has stopped typing for some time, the clouds on his or her display disappear and the new text is displayed, first in blue and gradually changing to black. The rationale for this interface is that an active user is only marginally interested in others' changes, which should therefore be indicated subtly and not disruptively. By the same token, when the changes are merged, everyone should be made aware of their contents.

Issues Related to Screen Space Management
Screen space is a limited resource in single-user applications, but it is even more of a problem with group interfaces in which each user can create windows that appear on other users' screens. Techniques for managing window proliferation are needed.

One approach is to aggregate windows into functional sets, or *rooms*, each of which corresponds to a particular task [9, 61]. Participants can move from room to room or be *teleported* by other users. When a room is entered, the windows associated with that room are opened.

Someone else is changing old text.
I am working here, entering new

A second approach is to let one of the users bear some of the burden of maintaining window order. The LIZA system [25] provides a monitor tool, for example, which allows one user to open and close windows used by participants. This approach is particularly useful with inexperienced users.

Issues Related to Group Interface Toolkits

Single-user interface technology has matured significantly during the past decade. The advances can be attributed in part to the work on user interface management systems (see [60] for a summary) and in part to the proliferation of window systems and their interface toolkits.

Many of these single-user interface concepts can be generalized to multiuser interfaces. Group windows are one example, telepointers another. Several questions remain open, because there is little experience with these generalized techniques. Should there be group windows for subgroups? Should there be multiple telepointers for the multiple subgroups? What are the intuitive ways to share telepointers? Experience with showing all users' cursors on every screen suggests that groupware developers must be careful not to clutter the screen or overload the participants [78]. The point is that group interface toolkits must not simply be extensions of existing toolkits; rather, they must introduce new constructs that better accommodate shared usage.

Group Processes

Some well-defined tasks, such as code walk-throughs, require the participation of a set of users and are called *group processes*. Group processes offer increased synergy and parallelism, but the required coordination overhead can burden the group and dampen its effectiveness. Groupware technology seeks to enhance the benefits while minimizing the overhead.

Group Protocols

Protocols are mutually agreed upon ways of interacting. These protocols may be built into the hardware and software, called *technological protocols*, or left to the control of the participants, called *social protocols*. Examples of technological protocols are the floor control mechanisms in several conferencing systems [1, 27, 56]. These systems can only process one user's input requests at a time, imposing on participants a group process of turn-taking.

Alternatively, control of the group process can be left to the group's social etiquettes which are mutually understood and agreed upon, but not enforced by the groupware system. Social protocols include formal rules or policies, such as *Robert's Rules of Order*, and less formal practices, such as polite turn-taking or hand-raising. In GROVE, social protocols control the use of public windows. For example, anyone can scroll a public window at will, but a group quickly learns that this is disruptive unless accompanied by a verbal explanation along the lines of "Let's scroll to the next page."

Each approach to group processes has advantages and disadvantages. Leaving the processes to social protocols encourages collaboration: the group must develop its own protocols, and consequently the groupware itself is more adaptive. Social protocols (in particular, ad hoc protocols), however, can be unfair, distracting, or inefficient. In contrast, embedding a group process in software as a technological protocol ensures that the process is followed, provides more structure to the group's activity, and assists less experienced users. Technological protocols can be overly restrictive: a group's idiosyncratic working style may not be supported, and the system can constrain a group that needs to use different processes for different activities.

Group Operations

At times, it is appropriate and insightful to view the work of multiple people as a single operation. We call the resultant operations *group operations*. There are many cases of groups accomplishing a task with more speed and accuracy than would be possible by a single individual. Examples include basketball teams, and fire-fighting teams. In other cases the complex procedures carried out by a group are easier to understand if they are not divided into specific tasks performed by specific individuals.

Group operations occur in both synchronous and asynchronous situations. Office procedures present an asynchronous situation and have been studied extensively in the context of the office information systems [5, 13, 83]. Problems associated with supporting these procedures include the following: organizational knowledge, exceptions, coordination and unstructured activity. Knowledge of an organization's structure, history and goals, is useful when following office procedures [5], yet this knowledge is volatile and difficult to specify. Exceptions are frequent since offices are *open systems* [33]; in particular, they contain incomplete and partial information about their day-to-day activities, making it impossible to identify all the situations encountered by an office procedure. Office procedures consist of many parallel asynchronous tasks related by temporal constraints. There is a need for coordination—a mechanism for informing users of required tasks and reminding them of commitments. Finally, since office procedures are not entirely routine, unstructured activities, such as planning and problem solving, can occur at various points within an office procedure [70].

Synchronous group operations are one of the characteristics distinguishing groupware from other systems. The problems described above for asynchronous group operations also apply in the synchronous realm. This can be illustrated by considering a hypothetical vote tool intended for small groups. Suppose the tool functions as follows:

When a user activates the tool, a window containing a type-in area and "Start Vote" and "Stop Vote" buttons appears on that person's display. After this user enters the issue to be voted on and selects "Start Vote," a group window appears on all session participants' displays. The group window contains four buttons for voting ("Yes," "No," "Undecided," and "Uncast"), and a bar chart showing the tallies of the participants' votes.

The following paragraphs refer to this tool in discussions of the issues involved in supporting synchronous group operations.

Organizational and Social Factors. It is easy to build a tool with the above functionality; the difficulty lies in designing it to be useful in a number of different situations. The tool allows participants to change their votes, displays partial results, lets anyone pose an issue for voting, and provides anonymity (unless the users can see each others' actions). How closely this functionality matches a given group's needs depends on both organizational factors (e.g., whether it is a group of peers or a stratified, and perhaps less democratic, group) and social factors (e.g., how open or trusting the group is). In general, specializing a tool to meet a group's particular needs requires *group* knowledge (e.g., user and group profiles) as well as *organizational knowledge.*

Exceptions and Coordination. The voting tool example also points out the need for exception handling and coordination in synchronous group operations. Typical exceptions occur when a noncooperative user fails to complete his or her role in the operation, or when the group composition changes (a person unexpectedly leaves or enters during a vote). Coordination is necessary since group operations impose obligations on the participants and response times vary. A simple solution is to let the group resolve such

difficulties using alternative communication channels, such as audio. The system should at least help detect problems, however, (e.g., by monitoring the progress of vote) and allow dynamic reconfiguration of the operation's parameters (e.g., changing role assignments or group size).

Integration of Activity Support. Asynchronous and synchronous operations are complementary subparts of larger tasks or activities. For example, system design projects include both high-level asynchronous tasks, such as requirements analysis, and synchronous activity, such as face-to-face meetings. A meeting proceeds in a largely unstructured way, but it can contain islands of structured synchronous operations—such as voting or brainstorming. This calls for integrating support for structured/unstructured activity on the one hand and for synchronous/asynchronous activity on the other. For instance, our voting tool should store vote results so that the group can use the results in the context of other tools and activities. In other words, the designer of group process support tools should look beyond the group and account for factors such as the group's goals and its place in the larger context of the organization or society.

Concurrency Control

Groupware systems need concurrency control to resolve conflicts between participants' simultaneous operations. With a group editor such as GROVE, for example, one person might delete a sentence while a second person inserts a word into the sentence. Groupware presents a unique set of concurrency problems, and many of the approaches to handling concurrency in database applications—such as explicit locking or transaction processing—are not only inappropriate for groupware but can actually hinder tightly coupled teamwork.

The following lists some of the

concurrency-related issues facing groupware designers.

- **Responsiveness**—Interactions like group brainstorming and decision making are sometimes best carried out synchronously. Real-time systems supporting these activities must not hinder the group's cadence. To ensure this, two properties are required: a short *response time*, or the time it takes for a user's own interface to reflect his or her actions; and a short *notification time*, which is the time required for these actions to be propagated to everyone's interfaces.

- **Group Interface**—Group interfaces are based on techniques such as WYSIWIS and group windows, which require identical or near identical displays. If the concurrency control scheme is such that one user's actions are not immediately seen by others, then the effect on the group's dynamics must be considered and the scheme allowed only if it is not disruptive. A session's cohesiveness is lost, for instance, when each participant is viewing a slightly different or out-of-date version.

- **Wide-Area Distribution**—A primary benefit of groupware is that it allows people to work together, in real time, even when separated by great physical distances. With current communications technology, transmission times and rates for wide-area networks tend to be slower than for local area networks; the possible impact on response time must therefore be considered. In addition, communications failures are more likely, pointing out the need for resilient concurrency control algorithms.

- **Data Replication**—Because a real-time groupware system requires short response time, its data state may be replicated at each user's site. Many potentially expensive operations can be performed locally. Consider, for instance, a joint editing session between a user in Los Angeles and one in New York. Typically, each user would be working in a shared context with group windows. If the object being edited is not replicated, then even scrolling or repairing window damage could require communication between the two sites—leading to a potentially catastrophic degradation in response time.

- **Robustness**—Robustness refers to the recovery from unusual circumstances, such as component failures or unpredictable user actions. Recovery from a site crash or a communications link breakdown—typical instances of component failure—is a familiar concern in distributed systems and a major one in groupware. Groupware must also be concerned with recovery from user actions. For example, adding a new user to a set of users issuing database transactions is not normally problematic—but adding a participant to a groupware session can result in a major system reconfiguration. The system's concurrency control algorithm must adapt to such a reconfiguration, recovering easily from such unexpected user actions as abrupt session entries or departures.

We will now describe several concurrency control methods. Of particular interest are techniques useful to real-time groupware, because real-time systems exaggerate the concurrency problems we have just outlined. The discussion begins with traditional distributed systems techniques and ends with the newer groupware approaches, which strive for greater freedom and sharing.

Simple Locking
One solution to concurrency is simply to lock data before it is written. Deadlock can be prevented by the usual techniques, such as two-phase locking, or by methods more suited to interactive environments. For example, the system might visually indicate locked resources [58], de-

creasing the likelihood of requests for these resources.

Locking presents three problems. First, the overhead of requesting and obtaining the lock, including wait time if the data is already locked, causes a degradation in response time. Second, there is the question of granularity: for example, with text editing it is not clear what should be locked when a user moves the cursor to the middle of a line and inserts a character. Should the enclosing paragraph or sentence be locked, or just the word or character? Participants are less constrained as the locking granularity increases, but fine-grained locking adds system overhead. The third problem involves the timing of lock requests and releases. Should the lock in a text editor be requested when the cursor is moved, or when the key is struck? The system should not burden users with these decisions, but it is difficult to embed automatic locking in editor commands. If locks are released when the cursor is moved, then a user might copy text in one location, only to be prevented from pasting it back into the previous location. The system, in short, hinders the free flow of group activity.

More flexible locking mechanisms have been investigated and reported in the literature. Tickle locks [28] allow the lock to be released to another requester after an idle period; soft locks [17] allow locks to be broken by explicit override commands. Numerous other schemes notify users when locks are obtained or conflicting requests submitted.

Transaction Mechanisms
Transaction mechanisms have allowed for successful concurrency control in non-real-time groupware systems, such as CES [28] and Quilt [22, 57]. For real-time groupware, these mechanisms present several problems. Distributed concurrency control algorithms, based on transaction processing, are difficult to implement, incurring a cost in user

response time. Transactions implemented by using locks lead to the problems described above. Other methods, such as timestamps, may cause the system to abort a user's actions. (Only user-requested aborts should be shown by the user interface.) Generally, long transactions are not well-suited to interactive use, because changes made during a transaction are not visible to other users until the transaction commits. Short (e.g., per-keystroke) transactions are too expensive.

These problems point to a basic philosophical difference between database and groupware systems. The former strive to give each user the illusion of being the system's only user, while groupware systems strive to make each user's actions visible to others. Shielding a user from seeing the intermediate states of others' transactions is in direct opposition to the goals of groupware. There has been some work on opening up transactions [4], but the emphasis of this work has been on coordinating nested transactions and not on allowing for interactive data sharing.

Turn-Taking Protocols
Turn-taking protocols, such as floor control, can be viewed as a concurrency control mechanism. The main problem with this approach is that it is limited to those situations in which a single active user fits the dynamics of the session. It is particularly ill-suited for sessions with high parallelism, inhibiting the free and natural flow of information. Additionally, leaving floor control to a social protocol can result in conflicting operations: users often err in following the protocol, or they simply refuse to follow it, and consequently, several people act as though they have the floor.

Centralized Controller
Another concurrency control solution is to introduce a centralized controller process. Assume that data is replicated over all user workstations. The controller re-

ceives user requests for operations and broadcasts these requests to all users. Since the same operations are performed in the same order for all users, all copies of the data remain the same.

This solution introduces the usual problems associated with centralized components (e.g., a single point of failure, a bottleneck). Several other problems also arise. Since operations are performed when they come back from the controller rather than at the time they are requested, responsiveness is lost. The interface of a user issuing a request should be locked until the request has been processed; otherwise, a subsequent request referring to a particular data state might be performed when the data is in a different state.

Dependency-Detection
The dependency-detection model [79] is another approach to concurrency control in multiuser systems. Dependency detection uses operation timestamps to detect conflicting operations, which are then resolved manually. The great advantage of this method is that no synchronization is necessary: nonconflicting operations are performed immediately upon receipt, and response is very good. Mechanisms involving the user are generally valuable in groupware applications, however, any method that requires user intervention to assure data integrity is vulnerable to user error.

Reversible Execution
Reversible execution [73] is yet another approach to concurrency control in groupware systems. Operations are executed immediately, but information is retained so that the operations can be undone later if necessary. Many promising concurrency control mechanisms fall within this category. Such mechanisms define a global time ordering for the operations. When two or more interfering operations have been executed concurrently, one (or more) of these operations is undone and reexecuted in the correct order.

Similar to dependency-detection, this method is very responsive. The need to globally order operations is a disadvantage, however, as is the unpleasant possibility that an operation will appear on the user's screen and then, needing to be undone, disappear.

Operation Transformations
A final approach to groupware concurrency control is operation transformation. Used in GROVE, this technique can be viewed as a dependency-detection solution with automatic, rather than manual, conflict resolution.

Operation transformation allows for high responsiveness. Each user has his or her own copy of the GROVE editor, and when an operation is requested (a key is typed, for example), this copy locally performs the operation immediately. It then broadcasts the operation, along with a *state vector* indicating how many operations it has recently processed from other workstations. Each editor-copy has its own state vector, with which it compares incoming state vectors. If the received and local state vectors are equal, the broadcast operation is executed as requested; otherwise it is *transformed* before execution. The specific transformation is dependent on operation type (for example, an insert or a delete) and on a log of operations already performed [19].

Other System Issues
As this article has shown, groupware encompasses a wide range of systems—from relatively straightforward electronic mail systems to state-of-the-art, real-time, multiuser tools. Regardless of a system's place on the groupware spectrum, groupware designers face a common set of implementation issues. Some of these issues are described in this section.

Communication Protocols
Effective communication is vital to successful groupware. Unfortu-nately, current communications technology is not as fully capable of supporting groupware as one might hope.

First, fully integrated data communications and digitized audio/video is not universally available. Groupware developers need protocols that account for the differing requirements of the various media. With audio or video, for example, the occasional loss of data is not disastrous, but a short transmission time is crucial. Additionally, the telephone and the workstation need to be integrated at the system level. Existing prototypes, such as the Etherphone™ [82], are promising, but there is no single network and addressing scheme with an inclusive protocol suite that is accepted as a standard.

A second problem is inadequate support for multiparty communication [73]. Real-time computer conferences often require that messages be sent to a specific set of addresses; such restricted broadcasts are called *multicasts*. Current protocols, whether virtual circuit or datagram based, are better suited for communication between two parties than for general multicasts.

Finally, standardization of data exchange formats is essential if groupware systems are to be useful across organizational boundaries. The office document architecture [41] and other information exchange protocols are steps in this direction.

Access Control
Access control determines who can access what and in what manner. Effective access control is important for groupware systems, which tend to focus activity and to increase the likelihood of user-to-user interference. Theoretical and applied research on protection structures, such as capability lists, has dealt only with non-real-time multiuser systems where users are not tightly coupled [23]. These results need to be thought about in the context of groupware's requirements.

Groupware's access control re-

Effective access control is important for groupware systems, which tend to focus activity and to increase the likelihood of user-to-user interference.

quirements have been described in other literature [27]. For example, if a group task is viewed in terms of its participants' roles, access constraints are usefully specified in terms of roles rather than individuals. Access permissions are not static, but can be granted and revoked. A system can simplify the process of obtaining appropriate access rights by supporting negotiation between parties.

Groupware's requirements can lead to complex access models, a complexity that must be managed. Since access information changes frequently, there must be *lightweight* access control mechanisms that allow end-users to easily specify changes. User interfaces should smoothly mesh the access model with the user's conceptual model of the system. Changing an object's access permissions should, for example, be as easy as dragging the object from one container to another.

Notification

In a single-user environment, it is important to notify the user when constraints are being violated, or when automatic operations provoke triggers or alerters. Notification is even more vital in a multi-user environment, because users must know when other users make changes that affect their work. This points out the need for a *notification mechanism*—a way of alerting and modifying one user's interface in response to actions performed by someone at another interface.

In synchronous interactions, *real-time notification* is critical; in fact, notification and response

times should be comparable. There are different granularities of notification; at the finest level, any user action—keystrokes, mouse motion—results in notification. For example, GROVE is based on keystroke-level notification: as one user types a character, this text becomes visible to the other users. Coarser levels of notification occur as user actions are chunked into larger aggregates. A text-editing system, for instance, could notify once a line or paragraph is completed. Factors such as performance, group size, and task are involved in choosing an appropriate level and style of notification. In general, however, we suggest that a fine-grained level of notification is useful for groups working in a tightly coupled manner, such as when reviewing a document or jointly operating a spreadsheet. As the focus shifts from group tasks to individual tasks—leading toward more asynchronous interaction—coarser notification becomes more appropriate.

Concluding Remarks

We have shown how the conceptual underpinning of groupware—the merging of computer and communications technology—applies to a broad range of systems. We have explored the technical problems associated with designing and building these systems, showing how groupware casts a new light on some traditional computer science issues. Information sharing in the groupware context leads, for example, to unexplored problems in distributed systems and user interface design that emphasize group inter-

action.

Although the prospects of groupware appear bright, we must take into account a history of expensive and repetitive failure [30]. Applications such as video conferencing and on-line calendars have largely been disappointments. These failures are not simply the result of poor technology, but can also be traced to designers' naive assumptions about the use of the technology [7].

Thus, an important area not covered in this article is the social and organizational aspects of groupware design—introduction, usage, and evolution. It should be noted that frequently a tool's effect on a group is not easily predicted or well understood [46]. As mentioned earlier, the system and the group are intimately interacting entities. A substantial literature explores the impact of computer technology on organizations and individuals [34,52,53,66]. Ultimately, groupware should be evaluated along many dimensions in terms of its utility to groups, organizations and societies.

Groupware research and development should proceed as an *inter*disciplinary endeavor. We use the word interdisciplinary as opposed to multidisciplinary to stress that the contributions and approaches of the many disciplines, and of end users, must be *integrated,* and not simply considered. It is our belief that in groupware design, it is very difficult to separate technical issues from social concerns—and that the methods and theories of the social sciences will prove critical to groupware's success.

Acknowledgments.
The authors would like to thank Les Belady, Pete Cook and Bill Curtis for encouraging and supporting groupware research at MCC. Michael Begeman, Kim Fairchild, John Fehr, Mike Graf, Bill Janssen and Tom Smith provided many contributions to MCC's early groupware projects. For their many thought-provoking conversations,

we thank Jeff Conklin, Ira Forman, Jonathan Grudin, Nancy Pennington, Steve Poltrock and Baldev Singh. We are indebted to Peter Marks, Glenn Bruns, Nancy Gore, as well as numerous colleagues at other institutions, and anonymous referees for their constructive reviews of early drafts of this article. Finally we would like to express our appreciation to those people who provided us with excellent technical support at MCC. ▣

References

1. Ahuja, S.R., Ensor, J.R., and Horn, D.N. The Rapport multimedia conferencing system. In *Proceedings of the Conference on Office Information Systems* (Palo Alto, Calif., Mar. 23–25). ACM, New York, 1988, pp. 1–8.

2. Applegate, L.M., Konsynski, B.R., and Nunamaker, J.F. A group decision support system for idea generation and issue analysis in organization planning. In *Proceedings of the First Conference on Computer-Supported Cooperative Work* (Austin, Tex., Dec. 3–5). ACM, New York, 1986, pp. 16–34.

3. Balzer, R., Process programming: passing into a new phase. In *Proceedings of the Fourth International Software Process Workshop* (Devon, UK, May 11–13). *Softw. Eng. Not.*, ACM SIGSOFT *14*, 4 (June 1989), 43–45.

4. Bancilhon, F., Kim, W., and Korth, H. A model of CAD transactions. In *Proceedings of the Eleventh International Conference on Very Large Data Bases* (Stockholm, Sweden, Aug. 21–23). Very Large Data Base Endowment, Saratoga, Calif., 1985, pp. 25–33.

5. Barber, G. Supporting organizational problem solving with a work station. *ACM Trans. Off. Inf. Syst. 1*, 1 (Jan 1983), 45–67.

6. Birrel, A.D., Levin, R., Needham, R.M., and Schroeder, M.D. Grapevine: An exercise in distributed computing. *Commun. ACM 25*, 4 (Apr. 1982), 260–274.

7. Bodker, S., Knudsen, J.L., Kyng, M., Ehn, P., and Madsen, K.H. Computer support for cooperative design. In *Proceedings of Conference on Computer-Supported Cooperative Work* (Portland, Oreg., Sept. 26–28). ACM, New York, 1988, pp.

377–394.

8. *Byte.* December, 1988.

9. Card, S., Henderson, D.A. The use of multiple virtual workspaces to reduce space contention in a graphical user interface. *ACM Trans. Graphics.* ACM, New York, 1987.

10. Cashman, P.M., Stroll, D. Developing the management systems of the 1990s: The role of collaborative work. In *Technological Support for Work Group Collaboration.* M.H. Olson, Ed., Lawrence Erlbaum Associates, Publishers, Hillsdale, N.J., 1989, 129–146.

11. Conklin, J., and Begeman, M. gIBIS: A hypertext tool for exploratory policy discussion. In *Proceedings of Second Conference on Computer-Supported Cooperative Work* (Portland, Oreg., Sept. 26–28). ACM, New York, 1988, pp. 140–152.

12. Cook, P., Ellis, C., Graf, M., Rein, G., and Smith, T. Project Nick: Meetings augmentation and analysis. *ACM Trans. Off. Inf. Syst. 5*, 2 (Apr. 1987), 132–146.

13. Croft, B.W., and Lefkowitz, L.S. Task support in an office system. *ACM Trans. Off. Inf. Syst. 2*, 3 (July 1984), 197–212.

14. Crowley, T. et.al. MMConf: An infrastructure for building shared multimedia applications. In *Proceedings of the Third Conference on Computer-Supported Cooperative Work* (Los Angeles, Calif., Oct. 8–10). ACM, New York, 1990.

15. DeCindio, F., DeMichelis, G., Simone, C., Vassallo, R., Zanaboni, A.M. CHAOS as coordination technology. In *Proceedings of the First Conference on Computer-Supported Cooperative Work* (Austin, Tex, Dec. 3–5), 1986, pp. 325–342.

16. Dennis, A.R., Joey, F.G., Jessup, L.M., Nunamaker, J.F., and Vogel, D.R. Information Technology to Support Electronic Meetings. *MIS Quarterly 12*, 4 (December 1988), pp. 591–619.

17. Ege, A., and Ellis, C.A. Design and implementation of GORDION, an object base management system. In *Proceedings of the International Conference on Data Engineering* (Los Angles, Calif., Feb. 3–5). IEEE, Washington, D.C., 1987, pp. 226–234.

18. Egido, C. Video conferencing as a technology to support group work: A review of its failures. In *Proceedings of the Second Conference on Computer-Supported Cooperative Work* (Portland, Oreg., Sept. 23–25). ACM, New York, 1988, pp. 13–24.

19. Ellis, C.A., and Gibbs, S.J. Concurrency control in groupware systems. In *Proceedings of the ACM SIGMOD '89 Conference on the Management of Data* (Seattle Wash., May 2–4 1989) ACM, New York.

20. Ellis, C.A., Gibbs, S.J., and Rein, G.L. Design and use of a group editor. In *Engineering for Human-Computer Interaction.* G. Cockton, Ed., North-Holland, Amsterdam, 1990, 13–25.

21. Engelbart, D.C., and English, W.K. A research center for augmenting human intellect. In *Proceedings of the Fall Joint Computer Conference* (San Francisco, Calif., Dec. 9–11). AFIPS, Reston, Va., 1968, pp. 395–410.

22. Fish, R., Kraut, R., Leland, M., and Cohen, M. Quilt: A collaborative tool for cooperative writing. In *Proceedings of the Conference on Office Information Systems* (Palo Alto, Calif. Mar. 23–25). ACM, New York, 1988, pp. 30–37.

23. Fites, P.E., Kratz, P.J., and Brebner, A.F. *Control and Security of Computer Information Systems,* Computer Science Press, Rockville, Md, 1989.

24. Flores, F., Graves, M., Hartfield, B., and Winograd, T. Computer systems and the design of organizational interaction. *ACM Trans. Off. Inf. Syst. 6*, 2 (Apr. 1988), 153–172.

25. Gibbs, S.J. LIZA: An extensible groupware toolkit. In *Proceedings of the ACM SIGCHI Conference on Human Factors in Computing Systems* (Austin, Tex., April 30–May 4). ACM, New York, 1989.

26. Goodman, G.O., and Abel, M.J. Collaboration research in SCL. In *Proceedings of the First Conference on Computer-Supported Cooperative Work* (Austin, Tex. Dec. 3–5). ACM, New York, 1986, pp. 246–251.

27. Greif, I., and Sarin, S. Data sharing in group work. In *Proceedings of the First Conference on Computer-Supported Cooperative Work* (Austin, Tex., Dec. 3–5). ACM, New York, 1986, pp. 175–183.

28. Greif, I., Seliger, R., and Weihl, W. Atomic data abstractions in a distributed collaborative editing system. In *Proceedings of the 13th Annual Symposium on Principles of Programming Languages.* (St. Petersburg, Fla., Jan. 13–15). ACM, New York, 1986, pp. 160–172.

29. Greif, I., Ed., *Computer-Supported Cooperative Work: A Book of Readings.* Morgan Kaufmann, San Mateo, Calif., 1988.

30. Grudin, J. Why CSCW applications fail: Problems in the design and evaluation of organizational interfaces. In *Proceedings of the Second Conference on Computer-Supported Cooperative Work* (Portland, Oreg., Sept. 26–28). ACM, New York, 1988, pp. 85–93.

31. Grudin, J., Poltrock, S. Computer-supported cooperative work and groupware. Tutorial presented at the *ACM SIGCHI Conference on Human Factors in Computing Systems.* (Seattle, Wash., Apr. 2). ACM, New York, 1990.

32. Harper, R.R., Hughes, J.A., Shapiro, D.Z. Working in harmony: An examination of computer technology in air traffic control. In *Proceedings of the First European Conference on Computer-Supported Cooperative Work.* (Gatwick, London, UK, Sept. 13–15). 1989.

33. Hewitt, C. Offices are open systems. *ACM Trans. Off. Inf. Syst. 4*, 3 (July 1986), 271–287.

34. Hiltz, S.R. *Online Communities: A Case Study of the Office of the Future.* Ablex Press, 1984.

35. Hiltz, S.R., Turoff, M. *The Network Nation: Human Communication via Computer.* Addison Wesley, 1978.

36. Hiltz, S.R., and Turoff, M. The evolution of user behavior in a computerized conferencing system. *Commun. ACM 24*, 11 (Nov. 1981), 739–751.

37. Hiltz, S.R., and Turoff, M. Structuring computer-mediated communication systems to avoid information overload. *Commun. ACM 28*, 7 (July 1985), 680–689.

38. Hogg, J. Intelligent message systems. In *Office Automation*, D. Tsichritzis, Ed. Springer-Verlag, New York, 1985, pp. 113–133.

39. Holt A.W. Diplans: A new language for the study and implementation of coordination. *ACM Trans. Off. Inf. Syst. 6*, 2 (April 1988), 109–125.

40. Holt, A.W., Ramsey, H.R., and Grimes, J.D. Coordination system technology as the basis for a programming environment. *Electrical Commun. 57*, 4 (1983), 307–314.

41. Horak, W. Office document architecture and interchange formats: Current status of international standardization. *IEEE Comput. 18*, 10 (Oct. 1985), 50–60.

42. Ishii, H. Design of Team WorkStation: A realtime shared workspace fusing desktops and computer screens. In *Proceedings of the IFIP WG 8.4 Conference on multi-User Interfaces and Applications* (Heraklion, Greece, Sept. 24–26). IFIP, 1990.

43. Johansen, R. *Teleconferencing and Beyond: Communications in the Office of the Future.* McGraw-Hill, N. Y., 1984.

44. Johansen, R. *Groupware: Computer Support for Business Teams.* The Free Press, N. Y., 1988.

45. Johansen, R. *Leading Business Teams.* Addison-Wesley, Reading, Mass. (to be published 1991).

46. Johnson-Lentz, P. and Johnson-Lentz, T. Groupware: The process and impacts of design choices. In *Computer-Mediated Communication Systems: Status and Evaluation*, E.B. Kerr, and S.R. Hiltz, Academic Press, New York, N. Y., 1982.

47. Kaiser, G.E., Kaplan, S.M., and Micallef, J. Multiuser, distributed language-based environments. *IEEE Softw. 4*, 6 (Nov. 1987), 58–67.

48. Karbe, B. Ramsperger, N. Weiss, P. Support of cooperative work by electronic circulation folders. In *Proceedings of the Conference on Office Information Systems* (Cambridge, Mass., April 25–27). ACM, New York, 1990, pp. 109–117.

49. Knister, M.J., Prakash, A. DistEdit: A distributed toolkit for supporting multiple group editors. In *Proceedings of the Third Conference on Computer-Supported Cooperative Work* (Los Angeles, Calif., Oct. 8–10). ACM, New York, 1990.

50. Koszarek, J.L. et.al. A multi-user document review tool. In *Proceedings of the IFIP WG 8.4 Conference on Multi-User Interfaces and Applications* (Heraklion, Greece, Sept. 24–26). IFIP, 1990.

51. Kraemer, K.L., and King, J.L. Computer-based systems for cooperative work and group decision making. *ACM Comput. Surv. 20*, 2 (June 1988), 115–146.

52. Kraut, R.E. Social issues and white-collar technology: an overview. *Technology and the Transformation of White-Collar Work*, Erlbaum Associates, Hillsdale, Calif., 1987, 1–21.

53. Kraut, R., Egido, C., and Galegher, J. Patterns of contact and communication in scientific research collaboration. In *Proceedings of the Second Conference on Computer-Supported Cooperative Work* (Portland, Oreg, Sept. 26–28). ACM, New York, 1988, pp. 1–12.

54. Krueger, M.W. *Artificial Reality.* Addison-Wesley, Reading, Mass., 1983.

55. Krueger, M.W., Gionfriddo, T., and Hinrichsen, K. VIDEOPLACE: An artificial reality. In *Proceedings of the CHI '85 Conference on Human Factors in Computing Systems* (San Francisco, Calif., April 14–18). ACM, New York, 1985, pp. 35–40.

56. Lantz, K. An experiment in integrated multimedia conferencing. In *Proceedings of the First Conference on Computer-Supported Cooperative Work* (Austin, Tex., Dec. 3–5) ACM, New York, 1986, pp. 267–275.

57. Leland, M.D.P., Fish, R.S., and Kraut, R.E. Collaborative document production using Quilt. In *Proceedings of the Conference on Computer-Supported Cooperative Work* (Portland, Oreg., Sept. 26–28). ACM, New York, 1988, pp. 206–215.

58. Lewis, B.T., and Hodges, J.D. Shared Books: Collaborative publication management for an office information system. In *Proceedings of the Conference on Office Information Systems* (Palo Alto, Calif., Mar. 23–25). ACM, New York, 1988, pp. 197–204.

59. Lochovsky, F.H., Hogg, J.S., Weiser, S.P., Mendelzon, A.O. OTM: Specifying office tasks. In *Proceedings of the Conference on Office Information Systems* (Palo Alto, Calif., March 23–25). ACM, New York, 1988, pp. 46–53.

60. Löwgren, J. History, state and future of user interface management systems. *SIGCHI Bulletin 20*, 1 (July 1988), 32–44.

61. Madsen, C.M. Approaching group communication by means of an office building metaphor. In *Proceedings of the First European Conference on Computer-Supported Cooperative Work* (Gatwick, London, UK, September 13–15). 1989.

62. Malone, T., and Crowston, K. What is coordination theory and how can it help design cooperative work systems? In *Proceedings of the Third Conference on Computer-Supported Cooperative Work* (Los Angeles, Calif., Oct. 8–10). ACM, New York, 1990, pp. 357–370.

63. Malone, T., Grant, K., Turbak, F., Brobst, S., and Cohen, M. Intelligent information-sharing systems

Commun. ACM 30, 5 (May 1987), 390–402.

64. Mantei, M. Capturing the capture lab concepts: A case study in the design of computer supported meeting environments. In *Proceedings of the Second Conference on Computer-Supported Cooperative Work* (Portland, Oreg., Sept. 26–28). ACM, New York, 1988, pp. 257–270.

65. von Martial, F. A conversation model for resolving conflicts among distributed office activities. In *Proceedings of the ACM Conference on Office Information Systems* (Cambridge, Mass., Apr. 25–27). ACM, New York, 1990, pp. 99–108

66. Olson, M.H., and Lucas, H.C. Jr., The impact of office automation on the organization: Some implications for research and practice. *Commun. ACM 25*, 11 (Nov. 1982), 838–847.

67. Opper, S. A groupware toolbox. *Byte* (December, 1988).

68. Osterweil, L. Software processes are software too. In *Proceedings of the 3d International Software Process Workshop* (Breckenridge, Colo., Nov. 17–19). Computer Society Press of the IEEE, Washington, D.C., 1986, pp. 79–80.

69. Osterweil, L. Automated support for the enactment of rigorously described software processes. In *Proceedings of the Fourth International Software Process Workshop* (Devon, UK, May 11–13, 1988). *Soft. Eng. Not*, ACM SIGSOFT *14*, 4 (June 1989), 122–125.

70. Panko, R.R. 38 offices: Analyzing needs in individual offices. *ACM Trans. Off. Inf. Syst. 2*, 3 (July 1984), 226–234.

71. Rein, G., and Ellis, C. The Nick experiment reinterpreted: implications for developers and evaluators of groupware. *Office: Tech. and People 5*, 1 (January 1990), 47–75.

72. Root, R.W. Design of a multi-media vehicle for social browsing. In *Proceedings of the Second Conference on Computer-Supported Cooperative Work* (Portland, Oreg., Sept. 26–28). ACM, New York, 1988, pp. 25–38.

73. Sarin, S., and Greif, I. Computer-based real-time conferencing systems. *IEEE Comput. 18*, 10 (Oct. 1985), 33–45.

74. Scigliano, J.A., Centini, B.A., and Joslyn, D.L. A Real-time Unix-based Electronic Classroom. In *Proceedings of the IEEE Southeastcon '87* (Tampa, Fla., April 5–8). IEEE, New York, 1987.

75. Searle, J.R. *Speech Acts: An Essay in the Philosophy of Language.* Cambridge University Press, 1969.

76. Singh, B. Invited talk on coordination systems at the *Organizational Computing Conference* (November 13–14, 1989, Austin, Texas).

77. Sluizer, S., and Cashman P.M. XCP: An experimental tool for managing cooperative activity. In *Proceedings of the 1985 ACM Computer Science Conference.* ACM, New York, 1985, pp. 251–258.

78. Stefik, M., Bobrow, D.G., Foster, G., Lanning, S., and Tartar, D. WYSIWIS revised: Early experiences with multiuser interfaces. *ACM Trans. Off. Inf. Syst. 5*, 2 (Apr. 1987), 147–186.

79. Stefik, M., Foster, G., Bobrow, D.G., Kahn, K., Lanning, S., and Suchman, L. Beyond the chalkboard: Computer support for collaboration and problem solving in meetings. *Commun. ACM 30*, 1 (Jan. 1987), 32–47.

80. Watabe, K., et.al. A distributed multiparty desktop conferencing system and its architecture. In *Proceedings of the IEEE Phoenix Conference on Computers and Communications* (Phoenix, Ariz., Mar.). IEEE, New York, 1990, pp. 386–393.

81. Woo, C.C. SACT: a tool for automating semi-structured organizational communication. In *Proceedings of the Conference on Office Information Systems* (Cambridge, Mass., Apr. 25–27). ACM, New York, 1990, pp. 89–98.

82. Zelleger, P.T., Terry, D.B., and Swinehart, D.C. An overview of the Etherphone system and its applications. In *Proceedings of the Second IEEE Conference on Computer Workstations* (Santa Clara, Calif., Mar. 7–10). IEEE, Washington, D.C., 1988, pp. 160–168.

83. Zisman, M.D. Representation, specification, and automation of office procedures. Ph.D. dissertation, Wharton School, Univ. of Pennsylvania, Philadelphia, Pa., 1977.

Categories and Subject Descriptors: D.2.2 **[Software Engineering]:** Tools and Techniques—*user interfaces;* H.1.2 **[Models and Principles]:** User/Machine Systems—*human information processing;* H.4.3 **[Information Systems Applications]:** Communications Applications; K.4.0 **[Computers and Society]:** General

General Terms: Design, Human Factors

Additional Key Words and Phrases: Computer-Supported Cooperative Work, coordination, multiuser interfaces, organizational interfaces

About the Authors:
CLARENCE ELLIS is a senior member of the technical staff in the Software Technology Program at the Microelectronics and Computer Technology Corporation (MCC) and adjunct professor at the University of Texas. His research efforts have recently been in the areas of collaboration and coordination systems, office information systems, and distributed systems.

SIMON GIBBS is an assistant professor at the Centre Universitaire d'Informatique, University of Geneva, Switzerland. He is currently working on software information systems and multimedia programming. Author's Present Address: Centre Universitaire d'Informatique, University of Geneva, 12 Rue du Lac, Geneva 1207, Switzerland. simon@cuisun.unige.ch

GAIL REIN is a member of technical staff in the Software Technology Program at Microelectronics and Computer Technology Corporation (MCC). Her research interests are in multiuser interfaces, visual languages, distributed systems, group work dynamics, and technology transfer.

Authors' Present Address: Clarence Ellis and Gail Rein are with MCC, 3500 Balcones Center Drive, Austin, TX, 78759-6509. ellis@mcc.com, rein@mcc.com

A Primer on Group Dynamics for Groupware Developers

Paul Cole and Judith Nast-Cole
14 Adelaide Avenue
Wayland, MA 01778

Abstract

Group dynamics can be an essential set of concepts for developers who are designing products for groups and teams. This paper identifies common issues for business groups trying to integrate information technology into their daily operations. Group dynamics concepts are presented and then a management team's use of group-oriented, information technology is analyzed using these concepts. From this perspective, usability becomes as much a factor of group dynamics as an evaluation of functionality. Group development guidelines are then presented suggesting an evolving use of information technology by groups and a requirement for increasingly flexible and customizable products.

The importance of group dynamics

Computer support has evolved from individual to group work. Groupware technology has focused on communication and coordination, that is, the linking of individuals. These individuals use a variety of existing information technologies. We have begun to see extraordinary benefits of increased group productivity through these efforts. These initial gains constitute only the first wave of computer-supported increases in group productivity. In actuality, they represent collections of computer-supported individuals rather than computer support for the "group as a whole." In order to create the next level of "group as a whole" productivity gains, it is necessary to understand group behavior from a perspective of group dynamics. It will be important that developers and users, or individuals introducing and customizing groupware technology, have a conceptual grounding in group dynamics.

This paper reviews theories of group dynamics, and illustrates the concepts with one team's experience using several group-oriented information technologies. In addition this primer describes some guidelines about when and how groups might utilize group-oriented information technologies. This paper does not identify a specific set of capabilities a groupware system should have or what aspects of group work could be enhanced by information technology. Instead, its purpose is to illustrate fundamental group dynamics concepts as a foundation to help software developers better understand group behavior. The concepts and case study analysis are most immediately applicable to the individual who is actually working with a group to integrate information technology. The concepts and case study represent a customer view and a framework for developers to better understand the feedback they may be receiving on their groupware applications to help them develop increasingly effective products.

Introduction to the case study

It is best to understand group dynamics in terms of the practical experiences of a group. Consequently, we will first describe the evolution of a management team and then use it to illustrate the fundamentals of group behavior and groupware. This case study is a composite of several groups with which we have consulted on issues of information technology.

Description of the group. In a Fortune-500 firm, a new engineering group was created from previously separate ones as part of a corporate-wide effort to align organizational groups so that expertise was better utilized and costs reduced. This new group was responsible for the development of workstations, personal computers, terminals, keyboards, and printers. The previously separate organizational groups had 50 to 100 engineers each, and were located at a number of different facilities.

This new organizational group created an opportunity to capitalize on the different strengths and experiences of engineering managers. However, these managers' different views of the business, customers, and technology, as well as different ways of doing business, made this task difficult. For example, one group of engineering managers on the new management team had previously worked together. They considered themselves to be from established, proven organizations that embodied the "right" way of operating. A second subgroup consisted of several other engineering managers who were relatively new to the company and were in new, high-growth organizations. They thought that the first subgroup of "established" managers was not willing to take risks and practiced "state of the shelf" engineering. The third subgroup was engineering managers from other, smaller groups that had always been peripheral to the large engineering groups in the company.

The executive manager of the new organizational group quickly moved to establish a common direction for the new organizational group. He pushed to get the goals of the individual departments better aligned with those of the whole. The executive manager hoped to improve compatibility between the products and to create a consistent architecture for the products. This executive was generally liked and accepted as an idealist and visionary by his staff. On many occasions, however, the management team was unsure about his expectations and specific objectives. For example, he wanted to create a significant shift in the work of the management team from technology focused to business and market focused. He was very concerned about the industry slowdown and wanted increased emphasis on profitability, feasibility, and consistency, rather than solely technical elegance. His management style was considerably more formal than most of the management team had been accustomed to. He was interested in establishing formal goals and metrics for all aspects of the business, and felt that formal processes were essential to the health of the organization. He was also quite concerned about the productivity of both the organization and his management team, with one of his priorities being to better utilize information technology as a key strategy in improving productivity.

Use of groupware technology. The executive manager's intention was to use information technology to maximize productivity. He believed that groupware technology was the critical vehicle for discussion and planning the activities of his geographically dispersed staff. In order to maximize the productivity of staff meetings, he wanted work to be done outside of meetings, leaving the meetings themselves for discussion on key areas that truly needed whole staff, face-to-face exchange. The tools he utilized were an electronic mail product, a computer conferencing product and an electronic meeting room used during the staff meetings. All the sites were linked by a common network which facilitated electronic communication. The meeting product included a prototype workstation with an attached device that would allow the workstation monitor to be projected onto a screen. The software included an editor for taking and displaying minutes of the meeting and an adapted spreadsheet used to record and track action items. The workstation was hooked up to the network, and consequently, individuals could access their own accounts to obtain and display individual information. The staff meeting room was also equipped with a fax machine, a printer, and several terminals located in the back of the room, so individuals could access information no matter where it existed on the network and could access their own accounts.

The executive manager had successfully used meeting software and computer conferencing in a previous organization and was anxious for his new management team to adopt the technology. When the system was first made available, he spoke of his own experience: it was useful for the immediate capturing of action items and it facilitated clear agreement on the specifics of an action item so a staff member was less likely to return to the next meeting with questions about the intent of the action item. A number of the staff members also had used meeting software, so they were amenable to using a system in the meeting. The only concern expressed was that it not interfere with or constrain the real work of the meetings.

The meeting system was used by the staff most frequently for displaying and modifying the agenda and taking minutes. The minutes were generally not displayed during the meeting. However, occasionally a staff member would suggest that the notes of a discussion be displayed to ensure that the group had a common understanding of a certain item. From time to time one of the participants mentioned a document in a discussion and the meeting secretary, who ran the meeting system, would retrieve the document from the staff notes file and display it. At the end of the meeting the system was used to review action items. The list of action items would be displayed on the screen and as the group reviewed each item, the status of the action was recorded.

The executive manager established a computer conference for use by his direct management team outside of staff meetings. The computer conference contained agendas of upcoming staff meetings, staff minutes from prior meetings, the list of open action items, new proposals or information of common interest, and other regular reports from the various groups. The executive manager expected budget proposals or plans for new efforts to be entered in the computer conference and reviewed by others prior to the assigned staff meeting. A different computer conference, for broader distribution than the direct management team, was also created and information that could be more widely distributed was posted there. The management team also communicated via an electronic mail product that was commonly available and had been actively used throughout the organization for many years.

Organizational impact of technology. The groupware technology available to this management team included electronic mail, computer conferencing and an electronic meeting system. The benefit of the technology to the group was significant, but the full capacity of the groupware system was not used and the manager's hopes for improved group productivity were not fully realized. The electronic mail system was used regularly by managers for distribution of information and for ongoing communication. The use of electronic mail for communication and decision making tended to occur between two individuals rather than the whole group. Individuals on the staff much more readily used electronic mail than the computer conferencing system to communicate with others. Electronic mail allows private communication, which is far more frequent in most work groups than public communication.

In the arena of public communication, the management team used the electronic meeting system far more effectively than the computer conference. The information technology enhanced communication within the group meetings rather than outside of the meetings.

The electronic meeting system minimized the administrative support necessary for the management team by having minutes recorded and immediately available. It improved the effectiveness of the group, particularly in the process of assigning actions to individuals. Recording and displaying action items increased the likelihood of follow-through. Misunderstandings were immediately clarified and recorded, minimizing one major cause of failure to complete action items.

The electronic meeting system was extremely useful when unplanned issues needed to be addressed. The electronic access that resulted from the linkage of the meeting system, the conferencing system, and the electronic mail meant that minimum time was wasted searching and retrieving information. Most importantly, current and accurate information could be accessed and acted upon. The electronic meeting system was not used frequently for presentations. Managers preferred to use overhead projectors, most likely because the quality and flexibility of the overhead projector was far better and more reliable than the meeting system. The executive manager chose not to require staff to use the electronic meeting system for presentations, and since staff managers were accustomed to using the overhead projector, they continued its use.

The use of the computer conference outside of the staff meeting produced less satisfactory results. Despite the extensive use of the computer conferences by the engineers in their organizations, the engineering managers were reluctant to use the product for transacting their daily business. Engineers regularly used computer conferences to exchange ideas on technical issues, get feedback on drafts of technical position papers and designs, or get help in problem areas. Managers, on the other hand, in private, spoke of their lack of comfort putting information in the management computer conference. They were uncertain about how much detail to provide, or how to describe certain things, such as business objectives, so that they would be commonly understood. They were also hesitant to comment in the computer conference on other managers' proposals or budget requests for fear of having comments misinterpreted or taken out of context. Consequently, much of the information posted in the computer conference was not adequately reviewed. Individuals who received little feedback on their work tended to take it less seriously as a viable mechanism for communication. Many of the engineering managers regularly had their secretaries print the computer conference rather than learn how to use the product themselves.

Groupware technology changed how this team did its work, although it did not create the anticipated increases in productivity the executive manager expected. In order to understand the reasons, one must look at group process, in addition to the technical processes. Certainly the use of technology had top management support, the failure of which is often identified as a key cause for lack of productivity gains and optimum utilization of technology. The group was generally knowledgeable about the technology and certainly comfortable with these and other software products. Were the products failing in a specific piece of functionality or was the style of work and pattern of interaction that the products created too discrepant from the managers' previous experience? Was it the wrong information to automate? One would anticipate that this management team's experience with computers and information technology would make them adept at utilizing group-oriented products. However, familiarity with the technical aspects of products is not the only variable to consider when seeking to understand the ways in which a group uses software. The use of information technology by this management team is better understood by examining how the group functions and works together.

Understanding group behavior

Behavior in groups is the result of a number of complex, simultaneous, and mutually reinforcing variables that are essentially "human," that is, not totally predictable. Groups cannot be adequately described by linear cause-and-effect formulas, so instead we will use several explanatory concepts in different combinations to understand group behavior. These concepts, referred to as group dynamics, will be reviewed and illustrated in the following section.

As we begin to analyze behavior and interaction among its members, we see that human behavior in the group can be understood on three levels: individual, interpersonal, and group. All three levels exist simultaneously, but we can identify different levels as primary when explaining a certain set of behaviors. For example, consider a project team member who frequently and loudly complains about the current work of the team. If we are using individual level of group analysis, we can characterize this behavior as a function of that member's style, personality, personal preferences, or experience. From an individual level, an explanation for his behavior is, "He's acting that way because he's just an angry kind of guy," or "He has a bad attitude." Most people use individual levels of analysis to describe and understand behavior. If we are using an interpersonal level of group analysis, that behavior is a function of that team member's interpersonal communication skills. An explanation for his behavior is, "He's acting that way because he's not very good at giving feedback and expressing his feelings," or "He's just upset with the project leader and has been acting that way since they had a blow-up several weeks ago." If we were using a group level of analysis we can perceive this same behavior as a function of group dynamics, which often transcend the individual and interpersonal, and as involving interplay within the social context called the group. Possibly the project team members and the manager had significant differences of opinion about critical schedule versus functionality tradeoffs and the unresolved differences created uncertainty for the whole group. In this situation it may be that many team members are dissatisfied, engaging in hallway and office discussions. Yet, at a team meeting this one person is vocal while everyone else sits in silence. The person's behavior can be understood as not only one person's opinion, but the preference and feelings of the whole team.

All three levels of analysis are valid ways to understand behavior, yet our tendency as individuals is to view behavior from an individual perspective. The group dynamics concepts covered in this paper will provide a framework to understand behavior at the group level of analysis. Moving the level of analysis from an individual or interpersonal to a group level is a natural transition, and simply requires us to describe events that are familiar but perhaps not clearly named.

Purpose and communication. Common purpose and communication are two key variables that can be used to define a group. A group is two or more people who interact and share a common purpose. For example, a number of people waiting at a bus stop does not constitute a group. When it begins to rain and one person opens his or her umbrella offering shelter to several others (a common purpose), then a group has been formed. Communication in the context of a group is the exchange of information between two or more individuals where a common meaning is assigned to the information exchanged. Communication occurs between a sender and receiver. Both parties must have a common understanding of the information to create effective communication.

New groups often spend time discussing and clearly establishing the common purpose of the group. On an individual level, group members go through a process of assessing the degree of compatibility between their own goals and the group's goals as they decide whether to commit themselves to the group goals. They also determine the fit between their own style of communicating and the group's style to ensure that they will be an effective operating group. Effective groups frequently have clearly stated, common goals that the team members feel committed to because they are consistent with their own goals.

For example, the management team described earlier had the common purpose to develop desktop products. In the early staff meetings the executive manager spent a considerable amount of time reviewing the company's goals and discussing how he felt the goals of this group fit the company goals and reviewed how each of the engineering manager's goals fit into the company goals. We do not know the degree to which the individual managers felt that the goals of the whole group were consistent with the goals of their subgroup. In strong, effective groups, the group goals are equally valued as individual or subgroup goals but the commitment to group goals generally becomes established over time.

At the point of this analysis, this management team was five months old and, therefore, the behavior of team members would be primarily derived from their individual goals. The executive manager also talked about his own management style and way of operating in the early meetings. He had hoped to establish open communication and he recognized that he could help set a tone of openness, if he were willing to set an example. The staff responded enthusiastically to discussion of his management style and his openness to feedback, but since he was the new manager they were reluctant to disclose very much.

Content and process. Perhaps you might be familiar with an illustration that plays upon our perceptual processes. Two profiles face one another. The viewer may either see the two faces in relief or see the shape of a candlestick, that is, the space between the two faces. Both perceptions are correct. One is not subordinate to the other. The notions of group content and process are similar. Content refers to the work of the group: the information it is sharing, the analysis it is performing, the decisions it is pondering, the project it is planning. Process refers to the way in which the group does its work: how decisions are made, the level of members' participation, the patterns of how information is communicated.

An example of content and process is embodied in the role of a sports announcer. The announcer is a process expert. If the content of a basketball game were announced, there would be long silences punctuated with "Two point, field goal," or "Free throw, one point." Instead, the announcer paints a vivid picture by describing who passes, who takes it down court, who goes up for the shot, who blocks, and so forth.

Returning to a hypothetical staff meeting of the management team discussed above, we can begin to identify its process, that is, how the staff meeting works. We might observe that the executive manager begins the discussion of agenda items; there is spirited debate by some members on technical topics; some members participate more that others; discussion often gets off the topic; and spirited discussion is often cut off and a decision is made by the executive manager.

Being able to see group process allows us to evaluate the efficiency with which a group approaches its work. Like the sports team that the announcer watches, we can see if the team is optimizing its time and human resources to accomplish its task. Content and process happen simultaneously.

Task and maintenance activities. Spend time observing a group working together at a staff meeting and you will observe two distinct types of activities: task and maintenance. Task activities are often what is thought of as "work" in organizational settings, and are directly related to the job at hand or the purpose for the group's existence. Maintenance activities, on the other hand, are often "invisible" in work settings and are those activities that focus on the well-being and solidarity of the group. These are activities that are often either taken for granted or not seen as important. However, maintenance activities are essential to insuring that a group is successfully completing its tasks. Examples of task activities include setting goals, prioritizing goals, getting information, coordinating individual effort, developing procedures, making decisions, and evaluating group effort.

Maintenance activities include seemingly simple things such as providing for group members' physical and social needs. A physical need could involve the place for a meeting (often rooms are too small or too stuffy), or the need to include breaks for rest or refreshment. Even committed group members may find themselves yawning after sitting for three hours in a room that is too warm or too small. Social needs are the needs people have to connect with others in some personal way. We have often seen well-intentioned managers fail to respond to the social needs of a group. For example, they may not have attendees introduce themselves in a meeting, so that others find themselves wondering who people are and why they are present. Or managers may discourage informal chatting with which meetings can often begin. They may fail to take into account that groups are composed of individuals as well as tasks and goals. This oversight often results in decreased motivation and effectiveness. Other group maintenance activities include settling conflict and differences, keeping communication open, and providing support and encouragement to group members. Groups that build relevant maintenance activities into their daily operations are able to resolve differences (rather than letting them fester), promote an open flow of information, and generally have a high level of morale.

The relationship between task and maintenance activities might be likened to a high-performance race car at the Indianapolis 500 or some other competition. The goal of the driver, crew, and car is to move the car around the track to win the race. Task activities are focused on going as fast as you can around the track and implementing a winning strategy. Cars are not on the track to take pit stops, yet what would happen if they failed to do so? Obviously the car would run out of fuel, the tires would go bald, and the driver could faint from dehydration. You can't win if you don't take pit stops, and, in fact, winners have learned to take quick and effective stops. So, too, for groups. High-performing groups understand the value of activities that maintain people's energy and involvement. Effective groups have learned to integrate maintenance activities into the very fabric of the group's work, and to view maintenance activities as the route to excellence.

Returning to the management team, we can now look for task and maintenance activities. Under "task," we notice that the group has clear goals established by the executive manager with added input from the group, and that these goals seem to be generally understood. Under "maintenance," there is a disagreement about how to achieve those goals, and differences of opinion are neither clearly delineated by members, nor fully discussed by the group as a whole. The executive manager directs those group members with conflicting views to work the issues off line, causing the group to move forward with no resolution and no mechanism to guarantee that resolution will follow.

The concepts of task and maintenance activities serve as ways to assess the group dynamics that contribute to an esprit de corps and high levels of productivity.

Roles. As you stay a little longer and observe the group in which you've just noticed task and maintenance activities, you will see that group members are not only talking about the work at hand, but they are also taking up different roles in relation to one another. Roles are simply positions or stances from which people operate for a period of time, and are not related to formal job titles. Roles are changeable and related to the social context, unlike personality and personal style, which are more permanent. One researcher (Kantor, 1975) suggests that there are four roles that group members can assume: mover, opposer, follower and bystander. When a group member is being a mover, that person is initiating the action in the group. For example he or she is setting the direction, establishing the focus, or making a suggestion on the way to proceed. An opposer role is one in which the person challenges the action. Person A says, "Let's go left." Person B is an opposer when he says, "No, let's go right, we went left last time and got lost." When a group member plays a follower, she or he is supporting the action of the mover or the opposer by saying, "Yes, that sounds like a good idea, I'm for that," or "Here's another good reason to do that." A bystander is a group member who is witnessing the action, simply observing and not actively participating at that time.

In American culture, the mover role is highly valued, many people like to think of themselves as being leaders, initiators, and self-starters. Yet, what would a group be with only movers? It might resemble the fourth of July with one good idea going off that way and another suggestion going off this way and a thorough lack of coordination and follow through. Similarly, the opposer role is often seen as the stick-in-the-mud, the difficult group member who slows the momentum of the group, yet it is also one with a critical eye, which is often essential to coming up with a well reasoned idea.

If you were to watch a group interaction, you could track the roles of group members: A moves, B follows, C opposes, and D stands by. In a group, balance and flexibility are the keys. That is, people can play all four roles depending on the immediate topic and their interest or expertise in it, as well as other factors. Some groups become stuck in habitual patterns of interaction. That is, A and B always oppose one another. Groups lose a large part of their potential creativity and problem solving abilities when members are constrained to limited roles. Leaders who can only move and are not able to follow or stand by do not allow others to be leaders. Group members who only follow or stand by are not able to initiate their own ideas, which might be of tremendous value.

Norms. Norms are another aspect of group functioning that powerfully influence how groups proceed with their work. Norms are defined as commonly shared beliefs, understandings, attitudes, and viewpoints that group members hold. Norms differentiate acceptable behavior from unacceptable behavior and operate as a set of standards for a group. Norms are developed over time and are influenced by how critical events involving the leader and members are handled. Take, for example, one manager who sought to change chronic lateness to staff meetings. He began the meeting on time and, as each latecomer entered the room, he stopped the discussion, pointed his finger at the person and demanded "Why are you late?" The group sat silently while he waited for the person's response before resuming the meeting. This manager wanted to begin on time and it did not take too many meetings with his behavior before people were there promptly. Was he successful? Perhaps he can now run timely meetings but he inadvertently created a group with the norm: cross the boss and be publicly ridiculed. Not surprisingly, group members were either intimidated or angry or both. People became more cautious in the meeting. Often vital discussion was truncated because people chose to avoid the potential of a "public trial." The manager's behavior strongly influenced norms of communication, participation, and trust.

Norms develop naturally and usually people are not aware or cannot articulate just what the group's norms are. Often the experience of entering a new group or organization with different norms can be quite startling. For example, in one group, status and titles confer a great deal of authority, while in another group titles and degrees are ignored and the successful completion of high quality projects is highly respected. A person moving from the first group to the second may be waiting to be addressed as Dr. A, and is greatly surprised when his opinion seems no more highly valued than that of someone else with an associate degree. Norms develop about all aspects of a group: timeliness, participation, the degree of cooperation among members, the level of personal sharing and familiarity, the use of humor, and how decisions tend to be made.

If we turn to the management staff meeting in the case study, we can observe a number of norms: differences of opinion are encouraged; debate is direct and becomes heated; projects are set up to compete with one another; there is almost no joking or lighthearted comments; the manager lectures the group at the beginning and end of the meeting; and the group listens politely and does not challenge the manager's perspective.

Leadership. Leadership is often identified as the key variable of successful groups, yet it is difficult to define what good leadership is. In part this is because leadership is dependent on the group contract, and effective leadership is defined by the needs of the group, the task, the needs of the individuals in the group, and the demands of the larger environment. A leader of a work group is responsible for establishing the direction and goals, monitoring progress toward goals, and obtaining the necessary resources to accomplish the task of the group. From a group perspective, leaders must be able to address the task and maintenance issues of a group.

In the case study management team, the manager's style was considerably more formal than the team was accustomed to. The manager insisted on formal processes and agreements between groups rather than undocumented, *ad hoc* discussions. Will this be a problem for the effectiveness of the team? If the manager is able to establish a common goal for the different groups, and effectively address their task and maintenance needs, then the issue of differences in style will be resolved. If the leader is unable to provide leadership in these domains, then the differences in style will become a point of increasing friction.

Stages of group development

Groups, whether a project team or a softball team, go through predictable stages of development much as individuals do. Although each group is obviously unique and made up of unique individuals, there are developmental milestones, dilemmas, and challenges that all groups experience in their development — just as there are predictable patterns of human development despite the fact that we're all different. When we talk about stages of individual or group development, we specify models of development that are unidirectional and have an invariant sequence of stages, that is, one stage is completed before we proceed to the next. The degree of group maturity is not determined by the degree of individual maturity, but rather by the length of time the group has met and how, as a group, the developmental challenges have been met. According to Tuckman, there are five stages of group development (Tuckman, 1965,1977): forming, storming, norming, performing, and adjourning. Each stage will be described in terms of the group's focus, members' feelings, and challenges for the leadership.

Forming. When a group first begins to meet it is in the forming stage of group development. The members' concerns typically focus on inclusion and orientation. Basically people are asking themselves, "Who else is in this group?" "Will I find a place for myself? " "Is the work at hand going to be of value?" "What is the task and how are we going to proceed?" People are generally going to wait to collect more data on the work and other group members before fully committing to be part of a group. It's the equivalent of sticking a toe in the water to check the temperature before jumping in. Although there are certainly people who belly flop in with little regard to the temperature or the depth of the water into which they're entering, most people proceed with more caution. In a very new group you would typically see group members being rather polite toward each other, staying on safe topics, "Did you have any trouble finding this conference room?" "Oh, you work with that group, do you know so and so?" People begin to identify other group members who are similar to them in terms of style, technical experience, or work preferences.

In the forming stage, group members may typically feel some level of confusion about what the work really will entail in terms of time, process, and scope. People may feel nervous because they may not know just what to expect. The leader's task in a new group is to orient the membership to the task and to one another. A new group, unsure of it's task or membership, is dependent on the leader (more so than in later stages) to provide ways for them to familiarize themselves with the goals, the work, and one another.

Storming. After some time working together the group develops a better sense of its work and the individuals in the group. The group moves from its "childhood" to its "teenage years," and enters the storming stage. Just as teenagers often test limits and challenge parental and institutional authority on their road toward maturity, so the group must grapple with similar issues of power, control, and authority. In storming, the group's primary focus is grappling with who is leading — who has authority to make decisions, establish priorities, and give direction. In a forming group, the group members are typically comfortable giving the designated leader that authority. However, during storming, members begin to forge a group identity by working through core issues of power, control, and authority. When a group is in storming you might see the rise of competitive subgroups who snipe or openly attack one another's positions or attack the leadership, the task, or the methods. "Who decided on the order of the agenda? That group does not understand the complexity of the problems. Why are we using these procedures? They're sure to fail." Other behaviors commonly exhibited are harsh evaluations of the work or the members, nonsupport of members, and rebellion against the leader. Members' emotions often run high and there are common feelings of anger, jealousy, intimidation, disapproval, and frustration. It is at this stage that members often question their involvement with such a "crazy" group, and group leaders feel as though they must have done something terribly wrong for the group that was once so reasonable and polite to suddenly explode with dissension and conflict.

This may be a point in the group's life where there's a turnover in membership, particularly if the leader fails to support the group as it grapples with these issues, and people end up feeling hopeless and stuck. The leader's task at this point is to help the group resolve differences by diffusing the high levels of emotionality in discussion, and helping subgroups and individuals to listen to one another and work toward resolution. Leaders can mismanage the storming either by squashing all conflict so that it goes underground instead of being worked out, or by abandoning the group, telling them to work it out without the leader's help. Conflict and anger can spiral out of control and the discussion can move from differences about substance to personal attacks. When this occurs, members may leave, morale can plummet, and the group may try to retreat to the forming stage as a way to avoid or deny the tension in the group.

Returning to that staff meeting we watched earlier, we observe that this management team is just entering the storming stage of group development: those three subgroups described earlier are more actively disagreeing with one another's positions and seem to be competing for their executive manager's attention and approval, each vying to install its priorities as most important; and while there have been no direct challenges to the leadership, there have been a number of comments about the viability of this new organization structure.

Norming. Eventually groups move through the storming stage to norming. The group has resolved issues of power and control and has been formed into a team. Often strong bonds and alliances come from successfully resolving conflict and differences of opinion. Adversaries may find that they share developed relationships from really working tough issues. The core issue for a group in norming is to develop group coordination and integration. How will the members work together to achieve the group's goal? The high level of emotionality in the group subsides and people typically find themselves drawn to the group, having friendships with other members and developing close ties. There are more negotiating roles and procedures and interjections of personal thoughts, feelings, and perspectives into the work. Common member feelings are a new sense of comfort and team spirit, a "we-ness." Often this is the time in a group's life when the group names itself, or finds some way to signify that this group of people is a team. The leader's task is to help the group define and plan the coordination and integration among functional relationships. At this point the leader is beginning to shift the responsibility for leading and facilitating onto the group itself.

Performing. A group in the performing stage is a mature, high-performing group. The basic issue is the work at hand. People have worked together long enough to know the work and each other very well. The whole group's energy can be directed toward the task. A performing group is productive, energetic, and effective. Members are able to collaborate and configure in ways that are most beneficial for reaching the team's goal. People typically feel a sense of satisfaction and competence. Being a member of a group in the performing stage is an exhilarating experience. The leader's task is simply to get out of the way and let the group do what it knows how to do. The leader at this point becomes much more of a consultant or coach, providing resources and advice or managing intergroup relations at the request of the group itself.

Adjourning. Groups end because they have completed their work, they are reorganized, or the organization's mission changes. When a group "begins to end" it is in the adjourning phase, regardless of what stage of development it has reached. The focus of adjourning is finishing, wrapping-up, and saying goodbye. Often in this stage groups regress, that is, they return to earlier behaviors and issues. A group that is working smoothly may suddenly develop conflict or old problems may re-emerge. A group that is adjourning needs to find ways to mark the end of the group's life. Parties, pictures, and opportunities to reflect on the group's accomplishments and failures, its learnings and blind spots, are all ways to end. People may have many different feelings in this stage of group development: sadness, anger, relief. The leader's task is to help people end the group, debrief the experience, hold a postmortem, and set up a final ending for the group.

Groups in organizations

Organizations can be thought of as one large group containing various smaller groups. An organization is made up of both formal and informal groups. Formal groups can comprise individuals who work for a common manager, on a specific project, or in a specific function, e.g. finance. Informal groups may include individuals in like functions but working for different managers, or individuals who are linked by common interests, similarities, or proximity.

The dynamics that occur in a group, i.e. norms, communication, task or maintenance, leadership, and development, also occur in the whole organization. The groups become the players in a large organization and the norms based on the environment, the task, and the leadership, determine to a great degree the relationships between the groups. Organizations develop through the same stages as groups, and are faced with the same dilemmas. The groups within an organization share certain elements of culture and leadership and also develop specific sub-cultures, ways of doing business, and leadership styles related to their work and position in the larger organization. The issues that groups face in organizations and the ways they approach and solve problems often mirror the larger organization. Organizations function as systems, in that any change in one part of the organization impacts the whole organization. The degree to which groups are interdependent increases this phenomenon.

Group dynamics and groupware technology

Group theory suggests that the use of computer technology in a group or organization needs to be understood in the context of overall group functioning. Assessing the functionality of the software is only part of the equation in understanding a group's acceptance and effective use of information technology. The following analysis will utilize the previously discussed group dynamics concepts to understand the group's use of information technology.

The electronic meeting system was used to record meeting minutes and the conferencing system was used as a common library of information that could be easily accessed. However, these technologies were not fully utilized or well integrated into the operation of the group. The management team was able to effectively use the information technology in the meeting, but it had difficulty using it, as a group, outside of the meeting. The following discussion will focus primarily on the management team's difficulty in fully using the computer conferencing system outside of the face-to-face meetings. Understanding this difficulty is critical because it represents a significant area of opportunity for groupware technology.

Leadership. Leadership is a key variable in understanding the behavior of any group, and likewise in a group's use of groupware technology. In many cases the lack of use of information technology is related to the leader's lack of commitment to or inexperience with the technology. In the case of this management team, the new executive manager had prior success with the technology and was actually providing the impetus for its use. Particularly in new groups the leader sets the initial parameters for acceptable behavior by his or her own actions and by the direction given to others. The executive manager believed that the availability of information technology and increased access to information would automatically result in increased productivity of his staff. This belief was the basis for introducing and requiring the use of group-oriented information technology by his staff. The executive manager in this case was very comfortable with groupware, but he underestimated the degree of change required by his staff to fully use the groupware applications. Unfortunately he had unrealistic expectations of how the technology would be used by his group. This difference in expectations between the executive manager and the staff members led, in part, to inconsistent use and acceptance of the groupware technology. Knowledge and appreciation of its impact on the group would have helped the manager more fully integrate and exploit the technology.

Communication and group norms. One of the primary advantages of groupware technology is the efficient and timely distribution of information in a form that can be utilized by a group or organization. Despite the significant efficiencies that groupware technology has created, too often the exchange of information does not result in effective communication or in the intended goal. In the management team, the new manager hoped to make efficient use of his staff's time by having documents reviewed in the management team's computer conference prior to a meeting — yet the behavior that resulted was inadvertently a decrease in the actual communication of the group. The manager, assuming documents had been reviewed, limited general presentations and discussions in the staff meeting and quickly pushed toward resolution of issues. The staff complied with the manager's request to use the computer conference, but used it primarily as a mechanism to document and centrally file information rather than as a vehicle for communication and dialogue. The management computer conference provided a channel for increased communication that was not fully used.

In order to evaluate the improvements in productivity and quality that groupware technology can bring, it is critical to distinguish between the exchange of information and communication. The exchange of information is a prerequisite for communication, yet communication requires that the parties involved have a common understanding of the information exchanged. Availability of information increases the effectiveness and productivity of an individual, but it is communication (common understanding of information) that results in increased group effectiveness and productivity. Communication is necessary for a group to transform information into decisions and actions. In the case of the management team, establishing norms about communication and interaction interfered with full acceptance of the information technology.

The engineering managers had never used a computer-conferencing product for regular communication. The norms of the organization were such that engineers worked regularly with detailed written material, whereas managers were less often required to work in this mode. The changes in behavior necessary to make the effective use of the computer conference were significant for the managers individually and as a group. Individually, the managers had to build into their day time to carefully review proposals. Managers who were accustomed to being quick on their feet in staff discussions had to learn to articulate their thoughts in writing. Managers who were accustomed to being persuasive in presentations found themselves at a loss trying to capture their thoughts in writing. The immediate, non-verbal cues of the group demonstrating interest or boredom were not available, and managers felt isolated and awkward, especially when submitting important proposals.

The executive manager's requirement to use the computer conference as a major vehicle for communication introduced an unknown into the group and represented a loss of face-to-face opportunity to develop norms of working. The management team was a new group, and therefore in the early stages of establishing sufficient trust to work effectively together. The management team had not reached a level of trust that allowed staff members to feel comfortable giving each other public feedback through the computer-conferencing system. The norms of a group also develop over time, and the norms about how to manage disagreement and conflict had not been firmly established. Being put in a position to comment on others' work in the computer conference, put individuals in the position of negotiating those norms without face-to-face feedback. Groups establish patterns of interaction through trial and error and using the computer conference may have created sufficient uncertainty and ambiguity to cause the staff to avoid it.

Maintenance activities. The lack of attention to the maintenance issues of the group also interfered with the management team's ability to more fully utilize the groupware technology. In the case of this management team, the operations manager was responsible for the setting up and running of the system. He set up the computer conference and entered the staff minutes and actions into the computer conference, but was not responsible for monitoring its use. The operations manager did not work with the managers to ensure that they were comfortable with the new communication process and had the sufficient skills to use it effectively.

The computer conference created a dilemma for the management team members that they resolved by avoiding its intended use. The use or lack of use of the computer conference was never discussed in staff once the system was in place. Individuals needed simple guidance on issues such as whether to post things in finished form or rough draft. Staff members did not want to waste time refining documents that were not going to be carefully reviewed, yet at the same time they did not want to submit rough drafts that would be rejected because of their lack of completeness or form. An explicit discussion in staff may have helped individuals feel more comfortable in using the computer conference. A demonstration of the conferencing system and a practice session with the staff using the system as intended, e.g. commenting on a document, would have helped establish new norms that included the active use of the information technology.

Group development guidelines. In the management team scenario the lack of established norms for communication, especially around conflict, and the lack of history in working together made the computer-conferencing application difficult for the group to use. The newness of the group amplified its experience with the new technology as an increase in the level of uncertainty — resulting in increased anxiety rather than increased productivity. From this perspective, usability becomes more a factor of group dynamics than an evaluation of functionality. Ironically, the groupware technology may have been used effectively by the group given its stage of development. A group's use of the technology will evolve as the group matures and negotiates the various developmental tasks in the group life cycle. The central question becomes how to introduce groupware technology that matches the developmental stage of the group, and how to design groupware applications that have the capacity to unfold as the group changes its relationship to the technology.

The developmental level of the group will most likely influence how a group will use a specific groupware application rather than what application the group will use, although it is possible that certain applications will be more appropriate at certain stages of the group's life. The focus of the following discussion will be how the use of groupware applications may change over the life span of a group and guidelines for their usage.

The primary issues of inclusion and membership characteristic of the forming stage result in relatively safe, congenial interactions that allow individuals to assess their fit with the group. The groupware technology available in the forming stage is also likely to be used in a relatively superficial, passive manner. Groups need to establish patterns of interaction and communication prior to using an electronic mail or computer-conferencing system for complex, controversial, or emotional issues. As in the management team example, a computer-conferencing system will probably be used to post or store information rather than as a mechanism for dialogue and debate. Electronic mail, especially between individuals, will be used more frequently than the conference system.

As the group is beginning the process of establishing norms for how it will work, it is important to have explicit conversations about the use of groupware technology. It is difficult and time-consuming for a group using predominantly electronic means of communication to establish common norms because of the ambiguous feedback and the absence of common group learning. An explicit discussion on norms and guidelines for using electronic communication would have been very useful in the management team presented here. The need to explicitly articulate a process for communication is even more critical in the forming stage of groups running electronically distributed meetings. To ensure maximum usage the leader or manager in the forming stage must set the direction for the group regarding use of groupware technology. He or she needs to set clear and high expectations of the group, yet be willing to negotiate and guide group members through any change and learning process that may be required.

In the storming stage issues of power and influence come to the forefront of the group and there is a tendency for the group to show signs of dissatisfaction and frustration with the leader and the work. The groupware technology may falsely appear to become more central as a communication tool in the storming stage, but it is critical to ensure that the predicable conflicts and disagreements be managed primarily in face-to-face meetings. Conflicts may escalate inadvertently when handled through electronic means because of the lack of immediate feedback, the increased likelihood of misinterpretation, and the emotional distance the technology falsely creates, reducing awareness of the impact of one's communication. What may appear to be increased usage of groupware applications in the storming stage may be counterproductive sub-grouping and bids for influence rather than the negotiation of differences about the actual work. The use of groupware technology may be one of the dissatisfactions expressed by the group as it confronts the difficulties of the work and the limits of technology. It is important that the manager be able to clearly articulate the risks and benefits of the technology and be able to maintain consistent expectations of the group regarding it usage.

In the norming and performing stages, when the group has established effective working relationships and is able to more flexibly address the work, the groupware technology will likely be optimally used. The issues of integration and role negotiation are central especially in the norming stage. The group will increasingly trust and use the groupware technology for coordination of the group's work. The need of all the group members to fully participate in face-to-face meetings will diminish and they will be increasingly able to work effectively in smaller and different configurations. As the whole group continues to effectively subdivide its work the reliance on electronic communication and groupware technology will increase. The group's early reliance on electronic mail for individual exchanges will most likely reduce as the group is more comfortable with public communication through the computer-conferencing system.

In the adjourning stage the group wraps up its work, or significantly changes direction, essentially creating, from a group dynamics point of view, a new group around a new task. The initial issues around trust, inclusion, and influence re-emerge in this phase and it is likely that the group's usage of groupware technology will diminish. The group will most likely return to its initial superficial and relatively passive use of groupware.

Summary

This paper illustrates how group dynamics — leadership, roles, norms, development, and communication — directly impact how effectively a group will utilize information technology. Assessing the dynamics of a group, in addition to the functionality of the group-oriented information technology, will give developers a more accurate understanding of a group's use of technology. The acceptance of the technology will be greatly determined by the existing group norms about communication and interaction and the degree of change required by the technology. The management team case study demonstrates that, in addition to committed leadership, training and periodic discussions about the use and assimilation of the technology are essential.

The critical issue in thinking about group development and groupware technology is the phasing of technology that is consistent with the task and social needs of the group. It is important to set realistic expectations of the capacity of the group to use the technology. It is important to have the group experience continued success with the technology as they develop, rather than becoming overwhelmed and frustrated by the technology in the early life of the group. The risks of groupware technology include the potential for a group to use the technology as mechanisms for avoidance and distance rather than as the tools of work. This paper illustrates, from a group dynamics point of view, how information technology can assist in the work of a group.

Bibliography

Argis, C., *Integrating the Individual and the Organization*, Wiley and Sons, New York, 1964.

Bader, L.,"Guidelines for Facilitating Groups," unpublished paper, 1982.

Bales, R., *Interaction Process Analysis: A Method for Study of Small Groups MA*, Addison-Wesley Press, 1951.

Bass, B.M., *Stogdill's Handbook of Leadership*, (Revised), New York Free Press, 1981.

Beck, A.P., "Developmental Characteristics of the System Forming Process," in *Living Groups: Group Psychotherapy and General Systems Theory*, J.E. Burlin, ed., Brunner/Mazel, New York, 1981.

Beckhard, R., *Organization Development: Strategies and Models*, Addison-Wesley, Reading, Mass., 1969.

Beckhard, R., and R.T. Harris, *Organizational Transitions: Managing Complex Change*, Addison-Wesley, Reading Mass., 1977.

Benne, K.D., et al., *The Laboratory Method of Changing and Learning*, Science and Behavior Books, Calif., 1975.

Bennis, W.G., *Organization Development: Its Nature, Origins, and Prospects*, Addison-Wesley, Reading, Mass., 1969.

Bennis, W.G., and H.A. Shepard, "A Theory of Group Development," *Human Relations*, Vol. 9, No. 4, 1956, pp. 415-437.

Bennis, W., et al., *Interpersonal Dynamics*, Dorsey Press, Homewood, Ill., 1968.

Berne, E., *The Structure and Dynamics of Organizations and Groups*, Grove Press, New York, 1963.

Berne, E., *Games People Play*, Grove Press, New York, 1964.

Bion, W., *Experiences in Groups*, Basic Books, New York, 1959, and Tavistock, London, 1959.

Bowditch, J., and A. Buono, *A Primer on Organizational Behavior*, John Wiley and Sons, New York, 1985.

Bradford, L.P., J.R. Gibb, and K.D. Benne, *T-Group Theory and Laboratory Method: Innovation and Reeducation*, Wiley, New York, 1964.

Cohen, A., and R. Smith, *The Critical Incident in Growth Groups*, University Associates, La Jolla, Calif., 1976.

Cole, P., and J. Nast-Cole,, "Small Group Processes: Two Contemporary Applications," in *Groups, Theory and Experiences*, R. Napier, and M. Gershenfeld, eds., Houghton Mifflin, Boston, 1985.

Cooper, G. ed., *Theories of Group Process*, Wiley, New York, 1975.

Deal, T.E., and A.A. Kennedy, *Corporate Cultures*, Addison-Wesley, Reading Mass., 1982.

Durkin, H.E., *The Group in Depth*, International University Press, New York, 1964.

Durkin, J.E., ed., *Living Groups: Group Psychotherapy and General Systems Theory*, Brunner/Mazel, New York, 1981.

Dyer, W.G., *Team Building*, Addison-Wesley, Reading, Mass., 1977.

Gibbard, G.S., J.J. Hartman, and R.D. Mann, eds, *Analysis of Groups: Contributions to Theory, Research, and Practice*, Jossey-Bass, San Francisco, 1973.

Hackman, J.R., ed., *Groups That Work (and Those That Don't)*, Jossey-Bass, San Francisco, Calif, 1989.

Haley, J., *Uncommon Therapy*, Norton, New York, 1973.

Kanter, R., *Men and Women of the Corporation*, Basic Books, New York, 1977.

Kantor, D., *Inside the Family: A Systems Approach*, Jossey-Bass, San Francisco, Calif., 1975.

Katz, D., and R.L. Kahn, *The Social Psychology of Organizations*, John Wiley, New York, 1966.

Lawrence, P., and J. Lorsch, *Developing Organizations: Diagnosis and Action*, Addison-Wesley, Reading, Mass., 1969.

Lewin, K., *Field Theory in Social Sciences*, Harper, New York, 1951.

Liken, R., *New Patterns of Management*, McGraw-Hill, New York, 1961.

Liken, R., *The Human Organization*, McGraw-Hill, New York, 1967.

Liken, R., *The Nature of Highly Effective Groups*, McGraw-Hill, New York, 1961.

McGregor, D.M., *The Human Side of Enterprise*, McGraw-Hill, New York, 1960.

Miller, E.J., and A.K. Rice, *Systems of Organization*, Tavistock, London, 1967.

Mills, T.M., *The Sociology of Small Groups*, Prentice Hall, New Jersey, 1967.

Newton, P., and P. Levinson, "The Work Group within the Organization: A Sociopsychological Approach," *Psychiatry*, Vol. 36, 1973, pp. 115-142.

Rioch, M.J. "The Work of Wilfred Bion on Groups," in *Group Relations Reader*, A.D. Colman and W.H. Bexton eds., GREX, Sausalito, Calif., 1975.

Rosenfeld, L.B., *Human Interaction in the Small Group Setting*, Merrill, Columbus, Ohio, 1973.

Schein, E., *Process Consultation*, Addison-Wesley, 1988.

Schein, E., *Organizational Culture and Leadership*, Jossey-Bass Publishers, San Francisco, Calif., 1987.

Schein, E.H., *Organizational Psychology*, Third ed., Prentice-Hall, Englewood Cliffs, New Jersey, 1980, (First published 1965, Second ed., 1970).

Schein, E.H., "The Role of the Founder in Creating Organizational Culture," *Organizational Dynamics*, Summer 1983, pp. 13-28.

Schein, E.H., and W.G. Bennis, *Personal and Organizational Change through Group Methods*, Wiley, New York, 1965.

Singer, D., et al., "Boundary Management in Psychological Work with Groups," *The Journal of Applied Behavioral Science*, Vol. 11, 1975, pp. 137-176.

Smith, P., *Groups in Organization*, Harper and Row, London/New York, 1973.

Snivastva, S., S. Obert, and E. Nielsen, "Organizational Analysis through Group Process: A Theoretical Perspective for Organization Development," in *Organizational Development in the United Kingdom and USA*, G.L. Cooper, ed., PBI Books, New York, 1977.

Thelen, H., *Dynamics of Groups at Work*, Chicago Univ. Press, Chicago, 1964.

Thibaut, J.W., *The Social Psychology of Groups*, John Wiley, New York, 1959.

Tichy, N.M., *Managing Strategic Change*, Wiley, New York, 1983.

Tuckman, B., and M.A. Jensen, "Stages of Small Group Development Revisited," *Group and Organizational Studies*, Vol 2, 1977, pp. 419-427.

Tuckman, B., and M. Jensen, "Developmental Sequence in Small Groups," *Psychological Bulletin*, Vol 63, 1965, pp. 384-399.

Chapter 2:
Conceptual Frameworks

Chapter 2: Conceptual Frameworks

In one sense, groupware is a conceptual shift: a shift in our understanding. The traditional computing paradigm sees the computer as a tool for manipulating and exchanging data. The groupware paradigm, on the other hand, views the computer as a shared space in which people collaborate; a clear shift in the relationship between people and information. Groupware designers are concerned with the human relationships computers can support as well as with traditional information processing matters. What shifts in conceptual foundation are necessary for designing effective groupware systems?

This section discusses the conceptual foundations that allow us to see the varied ways people organize their work, and to describe the complex social situations in which groupware must operate. The selected papers for this section create a vision of work based on human interaction, and on the critical role of language in the workplace.

Background: The evolution of groupware concepts

To understand how groupware concepts evolved, let us employ the concept called "world view". A world view is *the* fundamental metaphor from which we interpret our work. Using this concept, we could say each of us practices computing from a particular world view. For example, the traditional world view of software designers is "mechanism," which sees information as rules and data that are stored and manipulated. An emerging world view being adopted by the groupware community is "contextualism," which sees information in relation to who created it, why it was created, and how it is used in specific situations. Let us now explore these two world views in more detail.

Traditionally, the mechanistic world view has influenced computer science and computer technology by suggesting a variety of assumptions that underlie current design practices: people process information and make decisions; people carry out functional roles, using materials, according to rules; people create and maintain a structure of authority; and people negotiate and promote competing interests.

Some groupware developers see the mechanistic aspects of current computing practices as suitable for designing software for individuals but inadequate for designing software to support social interaction.

Groupware, with its natural focus on group interaction, shapes the evolution of computing practices and technology by opening the door for the contextualistic world view: people interpret information in the context of their work; people learn together as a team; people enter into personal relationships; and people support each other's interests.

Several advanced development groupware efforts have successfully adopted contextualism, creating new computing practices for understanding group work and the complex social interactions that underlie that work.

Themes: Augmentation, language, coordination

The most effective groupware systems to date come from designs that have been consciously created from particular conceptual frameworks, each focusing on a particular aspect of group work. The papers in this section suggest three conceptual frameworks within which groupware can be developed: *augmentation*, *language*, and *coordination*. Our experience suggests that once a framework is chosen, designers are better able to uncover the richness of a group's work. As a result, the system makes a better fit with the people and their work.

Augmentation. Engelbart asserts that computers and people must evolve together, and that computers should be designed to augment (in contrast to *replace*) human capabilities. In fact, augmentation is really a simultaneous growth for people and computers. The computer side comprises tools, methods, skills, knowledge, language, training, and organization. The human side adds high-performance work, specific roles in the workplace, and the ability to be engaged in work while not physically being present at the scene of the work.

Engelbart sees the computer as a tool supporting wide-scale augmentation, which requires software designed for interoperability and openness. Interoperability allows a person to access the materials of any other person, with software tools that operate correctly in work contexts that vary over time and distance. Openness comes from an underlying hypertext system, and provides a common facility for creating, transporting, storing, and manipulating work materials. Interoperability and openness are key concerns for the computing industry today. As a result, appropriate features, architecture, and user interfaces are coming to the fore in groupware design activities. For example, groupware designs must address both the transparency of information access, regardless of its locale, and the evolution of the system to suit users' needs. These requirements call for thoughtful deliberation during design, and an architecture that separates user interface and user profiles from application and network functionality.

Language. Bodker et al. suggest designing computer applications for cooperative work by first seeing that design is itself a cooperative process. From this viewpoint, design is a process that *creates computer artifacts in participatory ways*. Participation is a collective approach stressing industrial democracy, quality of work and product, and human-centered design. Bodker et al. emphasize participation, because many aspects of group work can only be made explicit through cooperative practice, that is, by practicing, we learn the nuances of the work.

Because cost-effective systems have time frames associated with their implementation, some kind of structure is required for practicing group work as a context for system design. Bodker et al. suggest structuring practice through language games. In a language game, users teach designers the "game of work" and designers teach users the "game of design." This method of joint learning equalizes the contributions people make and creates an atmosphere of openness to new ideas.

Employing language games to develop group work encourages everyone to participate in the totality of the work. Providing a total experience of the work helps in the development of a design that addresses the whole work situation. Language games also help users and designers bring out their different backgrounds and understandings of terms. Through this practice, the individuals on the design team make known their skills, and achieve a more interdisciplinary design effort.

The experience of Bodker et al. with language games suggests that computers are used in multilingual environments, evidenced by the variations in terminology used by different organizations within the same company. The "language of the work" comprises all these differences. Groupware designers are tasked with ensuring that their computer solutions address the human language differences. Designers also need to understand that users cannot anticipate all future situations; users tend to be traditional in their view of both the work and the computer's potential.

Sensitivity to these cultural truths will enable designers to understand the users' work and will lead to more widespread practice of collaborative design.

Coordination. The concept of the workplace centering around the interactions of actors (people) and agents (computerized procedures) is a central theme for coordination theory. Malone and Crowston define coordination as the act of working harmoniously, and thus they define coordination theory as a body of principles about how actors can work together in harmony. Their framework for coordination theory is developed from the components of coordination and associated processes. They suggest first, identifying work *goals*; second, mapping goals to *activities*; third, assigning activities to *actors*; and fourth, managing the *interdependencies* among actors.

The actors involved in a specific work situation may or may not distinguish all these components. For example, an entire manufacturing group may be viewed as a single actor at one time, while at other times each manufacturing station may be viewed as a distinct actor. Therefore, Malone and Crowston focus specifically on those aspects of a situation that are unique to coordination, defining coordination as "the act of managing interdependencies between activities performed to achieve a goal."

Managing interdependencies is a key to good coordination. Malone and Crowston classify the interdependencies among agents as *generic* (for example, sequenced actions, a shared resource, or simultaneous actions), or *domain-specific* (for example, a part designed by an engineering team must be able to be manufactured in quantity). They also see domain-specific coordination as an extremely common requirement of today's systems, asserting that the effectiveness of a general theory of coordination is measured by its transferability to a variety of work domains.

Futures: Shifting the framework underlying computing practices

There is a rapidly growing need for cooperation among many large organizations. This cooperation depends heavily on groups to plan and build artifacts of increasing complexity. These groups will need to use an infrastructure that supports wide-scale cooperative work. *The mechanistic approach that underlies current computing practices is proving to be inadequate for building this infrastructure.*

A major trend is underway to shift the framework from mechanistic to contextual, replacing "standard practice" with practices that emphasize augmentation, language, coordination, and other conceptual foundations yet to be discovered. We expect this shift to continue through this decade.

AUTHORSHIP PROVISIONS IN AUGMENT

Douglas C. Engelbart
Tymshare, Inc., Cupertino, CA
Journal (OAD,2250,)
December 9, 1983

1

Note: Published in "COMPCON '84 Digest, " Proceedings of the 1984 COMPCON Conference, San Francisco, CA, February 27 - March 1, pp. 465-472.

ABSTRACT

2

AUGMENT is a text processing system marketed by Tymshare for a multi-user, network environment. In AUGMENT's frontend is a User Interface System that facilitates flexible evolution of command languages and provides optional command recognition features. Exceptionally fast and flexible control of interactive operations is enabled by concurrent action of mouse and optional one-handed chord keyset. Files are hierarchically structured, and textual address expressions can flexibly specify any text entity in any file. The screen may be divided into arbitrary, rectangular windows, allowing cross-file editing between windows. Many options exist for controlling the "view" of a file's text in a window, e.g.: level clipping, paragraph truncation, and content filtering. Structural study and modification of on-line documents are especially facilitated. A Journal system and "Shared Screen Teleconferencing" support collaboration among authors and their colleagues. Graphic illustrations may be embedded in the same file with text.

2a

INTRODUCTION

3

AUGMENT was designed for augmenting human intellectual capabilities. It was targeted particularly toward the core work of professionals engaged in "tough knowledge work" -- e.g., planning, analyzing, and designing in complex problem domains. And special attention was paid to augmenting group collaboration among workers pursuing common goals.

3a

Authorship has received a great deal of attention in AUGMENT's evolution, as one of the central human activities to be augmented. An important set of provisions within AUGMENT -- in its architecture, design principles, and specific features -- is directly aimed toward bringing high performance to the authorship activities of knowledge workers. For the purposes of this paper, we thus speak interchangeably of "knowledge worker" and "author."

3b

We recognize explicitly that highly skilled workers in any field, and knowledge work is no exception, are those with good command of their tools. Our basic design goal was to provide a set of tools that would not themselves limit the capabilities of the people using them. A system designed to encourage more skilled workers will always enable higher human performance than one designed to support less skilled workers.

3c

In this regard, our design goal was to provide as much capability as possible for each level of system usage skill, and a continuous evolution path between skill levels. We believe firmly that knowledge workers are motivated to grow in knowledge and skill and that provisions in system design should support this. As the rest of the paper reveals, this approach translates into a rich set of AUGMENT provisions, aimed at providing speed and flexibility for skilled workers in organizing and pursuing their core knowledge work -- in which "authorship" is a primary activity.

3d

An explicit sub-goal in AUGMENT's development was to "augment" the development, production and control of complex technical documentation -- through the whole cycle of gathering information, planning, creating, collaborating, reviewing, editing, controlling versions, designing layout, and producing the final documents.

3e

This paper concentrates upon the development phase of this cycle. AUGMENT has well-developed tools to support the later, production phase, but their discussion is not included here.

3f

Studying another's work provides a well-recognized challenge, but one of the toughest jobs is to study one's own work during its development: to see what it really says about Issue X; to see if it does provide for Concept Y; to see if it is reasonably organized and structured -- and to do these over a body of material before it is "polished", i.e., before it is well structured, coherently worded, non-redundant and consistently termed.

3g

SOME BACKGROUND

4

HISTORY

4a

AUGMENT is an integrated system of knowledge-worker tools that is marketed by Tymshare's Office Automation Division. The system was developed at SRI International over an extended period under the sponsorship of NASA, DARPA, and RADC. Commercial rights were transferred to Tymshare in 1978 (where the system has since been renamed from NLS to AUGMENT) and its evolution continued. A short history of AUGMENT's development may be found in <Ref-1>, along with a summary of system characteristics and features. The general R&D philosophy and the design principles behind AUGMENT'S development are laid out in <Ref-2>.

4a1

The system evolved on time-shared, mainframe computers, and in a packet-switched network environment. In 1970 our computer was the second to be attached to the ARPANET, and since 1978 we have also operated extensively in the TYMNET environment. We have benefited directly from both the time-sharing and the network environments in matters that are important to the authorship process -- especially in dealing with large documents and multi-party documentation activities. In 1976-77 we conducted some applied studies for the Air Force, as reported in <Ref-3> and <Ref-4>, which concentrated upon this latter application.

4a2

RELEVANT ARCHITECTURAL FEATURES

4b

Perhaps AUGMENT's most unique architectural feature is its User Interface System (UIS), a special software module, which handles the human/computer interfaces to all interactive programs. It takes care of all command-language dialog and connection protocols, and provides a framework for building a coherent and integrated user environment while supporting flexible evolution on both sides: on the user's side, with evolution of command function and terminology; and on the technology side, with evolving hardware and software. (Design details are outlined in <Ref-5>; rationale and utilization in <Ref-6>.)

4b1

The UIS provides a reach-through service to non-AUGMENT systems, and can optionally translate back and forth to a foreign program's command language. It also supports the shared-screen, remote collaboration capability discussed below.

4b2

AUGMENT's architecture provides for open-ended expansion and flexible evolution of system functionality and worker command languages.

4b3

It is assumed that for any class of knowledge workers, specialized application systems developed by other parties, perhaps running on other computers, will provide services worth integrating. The "author class" of worker should be no exception. Continuing evolution toward the "author workshop of the future" will certainly depend upon some such features in workshop architecture.

4b4

It provides adaptation for different terminal characteristics, enabling application programers to work as though with a virtual terminal.

4b5

FILE CHARACTERISTICS

4c

AUGMENT employs explicitly structured files, with hierarchically organized nodes; each node can contain either or all of: up to 2,000 characters of text, a graphic structure, or other forms of useful data (e.g., digitized speech). The worker has a definite model in mind for the structuring of any file that he works with; in composing and modifying it he can organize and modify structure using the same verbs as for working with text strings (e.g. Insert, Replace, Move, Copy, Delete), with appropriate structural-entity nouns (e.g., Statement, Branch, Group, Plex). For any existing hierarchical structure, he has many flexible alternatives for addressing its entities, modifying its organization, jumping around within it, and viewing it in a most beneficial manner.

4c1

(Note: AUGMENT workers generally use the term "statement" to refer to a file node, which is natural enough since the terminology became established before we added the graphic capability. Now an AUGMENT "statement" can contain either or both a text statement and a graphic diagram.)

4c2

CONTROLLING THE TOOLS

5

Many of AUGMENT's unique author-support provisions address basic operations common to almost every task, things done over and over again. These operations, executed with speed and flexibility, provide for composing and modifying one's working material, and for studying what is there over a wide range of substantive levels -- from a single text passage to a collection of end-product draft documents and their associated set of working notes, reference material, and recorded-message dialog (assuming all to be on line).

5a

In the early stages of our program at SRI, we did a great deal of detailed work on what we called the "control interface" -- how users control the functional application of their tools. These details can be very important to "low-level" interactions which are done hundreds of times during a working day. Some of these details are quite relevant to bringing high performance to the authorship process.

5b

AUGMENT commands are expressed with verbs, nouns, and appropriate qualifier words; every command word is designated by entering one or more characters. The UIS recognizes the command word from these characters according to the command-recognition options designated in each individual's "profile file." Users seem to migrate fairly rapidly to "expert" recognition modes, where a minimum number of characters will elicit recognition of command words. The fully spelled-out command words are presented in the Command Feedback Window as soon as they are recognized. The Backspace Key will cause backup, one command word at a time.

5c

Of the system requirements behind our choice of this noun-verb command form, two are particularly relevant here: (1) The "vocabulary" of the functions of the tools, and of the entities they operate upon, must be as extensible as is a natural language; (2) Textual lists of commands must conveniently lend themselves to writing, documenting, and executing as "macro" commands.

5d

Screen selection is done with a mouse. If the command's noun is a single, defined text or structure entity, e.g., a "word", then there is only one selection needed (e.g., to pick any character in the designated word).

5e

Besides using a standard keyboard for character entry, an AUGMENT user may optionally use a five-key, one-hand, chord keyset. Remarkably little practice is required in order to enter alphabetic characters, one hand-stroke per character. With less than five hours practice, a person can begin profitably working in a two-handed, concurrent mode -- operating the mouse with one hand and simultaneously entering command characters and short literal strings with the other hand.   5f

Here is an example of a low-level action which reveals some basic characteristics of high-performance execution. It is a very simple situation, but representative of what is met over and over and over again in doing hard knowledge work. The worker is composing or modifying something in one area of the screen, when his eye catches a one-character typo in another area. For a skilled AUGMENT worker, the typo could be corrected in less time than it would take someone to point it out to him -- with three quick strokes of the keyset hand during a casual flick of the mouse hand, and an absolute minimum of visual and mental attention taken from the other ongoing task.   5g

Fast, flexible, graceful, low effort -- these are important to all high-frequency, low-level, knowledge-work actions. This same kind of speed and flexibility are achieved by skilled AUGMENT workers in executing all of the other functional features described below. Description of mouse and keyset, and their concurrent employment, may be found in <Ref-7>.   5h

ADDRESSING THE WORKING MATERIALS   6

There is a consistent set of addressing features that a worker may use in any command to designate a particular structural node or some element of text or graphics attached to that node. It adds appreciably to the power and flexibility of the system commands to have a rich, universally applicable vocabulary for directly addressing particular entities within the working files. Below are some examples.   6a

EXPLICIT STATEMENT ADDRESSES   6b

There are four "handles" by which a given statement may be directly addressed: 6b1

Structural Statement Number. This designates the current "structural location" of the statement. It is assigned by the system, depending upon where the worker installs or moves a statement within an existing structure, or how that structure might have been re-organized subsequently. It is usually expressed as an alternating sequence of number-letter fields -- e.g. "1", "1a", "1a1", "1a2", and "1b". At a worker's option, these same statement numbers could be shown as "1", "1.1", "1.1.1", "1.1.2", or "1.2", but this bulkier alternative is seldom chosen.   6b2

Statement Identifier, or SID. This is a unique integer, assigned in sequential order by the system as each statement is first inserted, and which stays with a statement no matter how much its content may be altered or where it may be moved in its file structure. To make it uniquely recognizable for what it is, a SID is always displayed, printed, or designated with a prefixed "0" -- e.g., "012", "0417", etc. SIDs are particularly useful for referencing passages in a document while it is evolving.   6b3

A Worker-Assigned Statement Name (or label). For any statement or part of the file structure, an author can designate as "name delimiters" a pair of characters that indicate to the system when the first word of a statement is to be treated as a name for that statement. For instance, if "(" and ")" are set by the author as name delimiters for a specified part of the file, any parenthesized first word in a statement would be recognized by the system as that statement's name.   6b4

(Note: It is optional whether to have any of the above three identifiers displayed or printed with the statements' text.)   6b5

A Direct Screen Selection. When a statement to be designated is displayed in a window, usually the best way to "address" it is to use the mouse to position the cursor anywhere on the statement and depress the mouse's "Select" key (indicated below by "<Select>"). This mode is generally used for text manipulation -- selecting characters, words, numbers, visibles, invisibles, etc. (any of the text entities which have been made system recognizable).   6b6

MARKERS   6c

As one "holds a place" in a book by leaving a temporary place marker in it, an author can place "markers" at arbitrary locations within an AUGMENT file. When placing a marker, he attaches it to a specific character in the text and gives it a name or label. Marker names are local to each file. Simple commands provide for displaying where one's markers are located and what their names are, for deleting or moving a marker, or for installing a new one.   6c1

A marker name may be included in an address expression, to provide another way of designating an address. A marker name can designate not only a particular statement, but a specific character within that statement. For example, "Copy Word #x (to follow word) <Select>" would designate that a word located somewhere in the file and marked with an "x" is to be copied to follow the cursor-selected word. There are many unique ways in which markers may be employed by an author who has integrated their artful use into her working methodology.   6c2

As a comparative example of some of the foregoing addressing forms, consider a statement whose SID is "069", whose statement number is "3b5", that has

statement-name delimiters designated for it as "NULL" and ":", that starts
with the text "Capacity: For every ...", and that has a marker named "x"
positioned on one of its characters. A command to move this statement could
optionally be expressed as: 6c3

    "Move Statement <Select> ...",   6c3a

    "Move Statement 3b5 ...",   6c3b

    "Move Statement 069 ...",   6c3c

    "Move Statement Capacity ...", or   6c3d

    "Move Statement #x ...".   6c3e

RELATIVE-ADDRESS EXTENSIONS   6d

A sequence of characters may be appended to the address of a given statement
to specify an address of a position "relative" to that statement. A major class of
these designations deals with relative structural location, such as: Up a level,
Down a level, Successor at same level, Predecessor at same level, Head at this
level, Tail at this level, and End statement at last and lowest position in this
branch. A period (".") in the address string indicates that relative addressing
is beginning, and each of these relative-location designators is indicated with a
directly mnemonic, one-letter designation.   6d1

For example, "Move Statement 0609 (to follow statement) 4b.dt" would move
Statement 0609 to follow the tail statement of the substructure one level down
from Statement 4b -- or, to conceptualize the associated address-location
pathway, "go to 4b, then Down a level and to the Tail".   6d2

EMBEDDED CITATION LINKS   6e

A special use of address expressions is within an explicit text entity that we
call a "Citation Link" (or "Link" for short). Links are used as textual citations
to some specific file item within the workshop domain. A link is delimited by
parentheses or angle brackets and contains a valid address string whose path
leads to the cited file entity. For example, "(0306)" or "(4b.dt)" are valid links.
Also, the reference items at the end of this paper are statements named "Ref-
1", "Ref-2", etc., and as such can be cited with links "<Ref-1>", "<Ref-2>", etc.
An AUGMENT reader may travel via such a link directly to the referenced
bibliographic citation.   6e1

A special feature in AUGMENT's link provisions is the use of "indirect link
referencing". In path-following terms, including ".l" in an address string
stipulates, "scan forward from this point to the next link, and follow that link

to its target." For example, to follow the path prescribed by link "(4b.l)", one would "go to 4b, then find the first link in that statement and follow the path that it specifies." This latter path in turn could prescribe use of another link, etc. There is no intrinsic limit to the number of these indirect links that may be employed in a given path -- only a natural caution against such a path looping back upon itself.   6e2

As an example, note that "<Ref-1>" is a link to the statement named "Ref-1", a bibliographic citation at the end of this paper. In that citation, there is a link to the original source document of the referenced publication, permanently stored in the AUGMENT Journal as Item 71279 (the Journal is described below). The point to be made here is that with the link "<Ref-1.l>", I can reference the original source document -- and a Jump Link command would "take me there."   6e3

TEXT AND CONTENT ADDRESSING   6f

Other addressing options include scanning for a content match, and/or stepping backward and forward a given number of characters or words (or other text entities). For instance, the foregoing link could have involved a bit more smarts in designating which link to follow: e.g., the path for '(4b "*D" .l)' would be "to 4b, scan for first occurrence of "*D", then follow the next link found in that statement."   6f1

OTHER-FILE ADDRESSING   6g

By preceding an in-file address string with a file address, and separating the two strings with a comma, one obtains a composite address designating a given entity within a given file. Extending this principle lets one prefix the file name with a directory name in which the file is to be found; and further, one can prefix this with a host-computer name.   6g1

For example, '(Office-5, Program-Documentation, Sequence-Doc, Specifications "Journal")' specifies the path: to the Office-5 host computer, to its Program-Documentation file directory, to its Sequence-Doc file, to its statement named "Specifications", and then scan to the location of the text "Journal".   6g2

If a person were working on the Office-5 host, he would only have to specify '(Program-Documentation, Sequence-Doc, Specifications "Journal")'. If he were already working within a file with its "link default" set to the Program-Documentation directory, he would only have to specify '(Sequence-Doc, Specifications "Journal")'. And if he were already working within the Sequence-Doc file, he would only have to specify '(Specifications "Journal")'. And if he were planning to reference items relative to the Statement named

"Specifications" very often, he could affix a marker (e.g., named "s") to its front and would then only have to specify '(#s "Journal")'. 6g3

Or, suppose he were working in another file in a different directory on Office-5 and wanted to reference items relative to that ame "far off" statement with special ease: in some temporary place in that file he could install a statement named "Ref" (for example) containing the textual link, "(Program-Documentation, Sequence-Doc, Specifications)". He could then cite the above reference with the link, '(Ref.l "Journal")'. This path description is: go to the statement in this file named "Ref", take the first link that you find there (traveling across intervening directories and files and statements), and beginning in the statement on the other end of that link, scan forward to the string "Journal". 6g4

This is only a cursory treatment, but should illustrate well enough what is meant by "a rich and flexible addressing vocabulary." As with other high-performance features in AUGMENT, a beginner is not forced to become involved in the larger vocabulary in order to do useful work (with productivity on at least a par with some other, restricted-vocabulary system). But an AUGMENT worker interested in higher performance can steadily pick up more of the optional vocabulary and skills in a smooth, upward-compatible progression. 6h

CONTROLLING THE VIEWS 7

A user of a book, or of most on-line text systems, is constrained to viewing the text as though he had a window through which he sees a fixed, formatted document. But as described below, our worker can view a section of text in many ways, depending upon his need of the moment. 7a

MULTIPLE WINDOWS 7b

For whatever total screen area is available to the worker, his general performance will be improved significantly if he can flexibly allocate that area into arbitrary-sized windows whose contents can be independently controlled. AUGMENT has long provided this basic capability, along with the provision that material from any accessible file may be shown in any window, and also that screen-select copying or moving can be done across the different windows.

7b1

(Note: Cross-file editing can be done at any time, between any two legally accessible files. If one or the other file's material or destination is not being displayed in any of the windows, one may always opt to employ a textual address expression instead of a <Select> within any editing command.) 7b2

User-adjustable parameters are used to control the view presented on the display. Adjusting one's view parameters is a constantly used AUGMENT feature that has solidly proved its value. To facilitate their quick and flexible use, the view-specification actions evolved into cryptic, single-character codes, called "viewspecs." The syntax of all Jump commands (used for traveling) includes the option of designating new viewspecs, and a special combination of mouse buttons enables quick, concurrent, keyset action to change the viewspecs for a given window. Here are a few of the frequently used view controls:

7b3

WINDOW VIEWS

7c

Structure Cutoff. Show only the statements that lie "below" this statement in the structure (i.e., this "branch"); or show only those following statements that are at this level or deeper; or show all of the following statements that will fit in this window.

7c1

Level Clipping. For the designated structure cutoff, show only the statements down to a specified level. Lower-level statements are "clipped" from the view; the worker can thus view just a selected number of the upper levels of his document/file.

7c2

Statement Truncation. For those statements brought into view (as selected by other view specifications), show only their first n lines. Truncation to one line is often used, along with level clipping, in order to get an effective overview.

7c3

Inter-Statement Separation. For viewing ease -- blank lines can be optionally installed between statements.

7c4

(Note: The foregoing view controls are extremely helpful when studying and modifying a document's structural organization.)

7c5

Statement Numbers and Names. Optionally, for a given window, show the Statement Number (or the SID) of each statement -- with an option for showing them at either the right or at the left margin. Independently, the showing of statement names may be turned on or off.

7c6

Frozen Statements. A worker may select a number of statements, in random order, and designate them as "frozen." One of the view-specification options is to have the frozen statements appear at the top of the frame, with the rest of that window left for normal viewing and editing. The frozen statements may be edited, or even cross-edited between any other displayed (or addressable) statements.

7c7

User-Specified Content Filters. A simple content-analysis language may be used in a "Set Content Pattern" command, which compiles a little content-checking program. One of the view-specification options will cause the system to display only those statements which satisfy both the structure and level conditions imposed by other viewspecs, and which also pass the content-analysis test applied by this program. Where desired, very sophisticated content-analysis programs may be written, using a full-blown programming language, and placed on call for any user.

7c8

USER-SPECIFIED SEQUENCE GENERATORS

7d

In the foregoing, a "view" is created by beginning at a designated location in a document (file) and selecting certain of the the "following" statements for display, according to the viewing parameters -- possibly suppressing statements that don't pass the test of a content-analysis program. This is essentially a "parameterized sequence generator," and provides very useful options for selectively viewing statements within a document; however, it works only by selectively discarding statements from a sequence provided in standard order.

7d1

Application programmers can provide alternate sequence-generator programs, which any user can invoke in a straightforward manner. In such a case, the apparent structure being presented to the user could be generated from a sequence of candidate statements according to any rules one may invent -- and the actual views could be further controlled by the above-described viewspecs for level clipping, truncation, content filtering, etc.

7d2

Perhaps the most commonly used, special sequence generator is one that provides an "Include" feature, where specially tagged links embedded in the text will cause their cited passages to be "included" in place of the Include-Link statements, as though they were part of this file. This provision enables arbitrary assemblage of text and formatting directives, from a wide collection of files, to represent a virtual, one-document, super file. For instance, the whole assemblage could be passed to the formatter, by means of a single user action, to generate a composite, photo-typeset document.

7d3

TRAVELING THROUGH THE WORKING FILES

8

An important provision in AUGMENT enables an author to freely "travel around" in his on-line file space to reach a particular "view point" of his choice -- i.e., the position within a file from which the system develops the desired form of "view" according to the currently invoked view specifications.

8a

Traveling from one view point to another is accomplished by Jump commands, of which the simplest perhaps is a direct Jump to a statement designated by a screen selection. Then, for a worker grown used to employing address strings, a next form would be a Jump on an embedded link, or to a statement designated by a typed-in address string -- using any combination of the addressing elements and viewspecs described above. For example, the link

"<4b:mI>" points to the Statement 4b, while invoking viewspecs "m" and "I" which cause the statements' SIDs to be displayed. The link "<Ref-1.l:i;LL>" points to the document referenced by the link in the statement named "Ref-1", invoking viewspec "i" for user content filtering, and sets the filter to "LL" to show only those statements beginning with a lower-case letter. The applications are effectively endless.

8b

MODIFYING THE DOCUMENT STRUCTURES

9

Given the array of capabilities described above, it is very simple also to provide for very flexible manipulation of the file structure. For operating on a small, basic set of structure-entity nouns, essentially the same basic verbs may be used as for text manipulation -- i.e. Insert, Delete, Move, Copy, Replace, and Transpose are quite sufficient for most cases. For instance, "Move Branch 2b (to follow) 3c" immediately moves Statement 2b and all of its substatements to follow Statement 3c -- and their statement numbers are automatically changed from 2b, 2b1, etc., to 3d, 3d1, etc.

9a

A few extra verbs are useful for structure manipulation. For instance, a "Break" command will break a given statement off at a designated point in its text string, and establish the rest of the text as a new, separate statement. And an "Append" command does the reverse -- i.e., it appends the text of one or more existing statements to the end of a designated statement.

9b

A major source of structure-modification capability derives from the associated "studying" capabilities. For example, if an author can view a file (document) with specifications that show him only one line each of just those statements in the top two levels, he gets an overview of the high-level organization that helps immensely to study his current structure or outline.

9c

Concurrent use of mouse and keyset also provide considerable gains in speed and flexibility for studying and modifying document structure. For example, if when studying the overview described in the previous paragraph, the author perceives that Statement 2b really belongs in Section 3, following Statement 3c, he can execute the necessary move command in a very quick, deft manner:

9d

Keyset hand strikes "m" and "b" (for Move Branch), while the mouse hand is positioning the cursor anywhere in the text line of Statement 2b. [Two chord strokes.]

9d1

The mouse hand depresses the <Select> button on the mouse while the cursor is on Statement 2b, then moves to Statement 3c and depresses it again, and then depresses it again to say, "OK, do it." [Three button pushes, synchronized with the mouse movement as it made two selections on easy, window-wide, whole-line targets.]

9d2

(Note: I just had myself timed for this above operation -- an unhurried 2.5 seconds.)

9e

In our view, interactive computer support offers an author a priceless opportunity to get away from the geometric bondage inflicted by pages, margins, and lines -- things which have very little if any bearing upon the content and organization of one's text. In terms of value to the authoring process, we differ sharply from those who advocate a "What you see is what you get" working mode during the development of a document's content and organization. For this kind of work, experienced users of the foregoing kind of flexible facility for addressing, viewing, and manipulating structured documents, would consider a "What you see ..." mode as a relative handicap.

9f

SUPPORTING MULTI-PARTY COLLABORATION

10

The support that advanced technology can provide for close collaboration among knowledge workers is a very important and much under-rated possibility. For multiple-author activities, collaborative support is an important aspect of system capability. Some years ago, we introduced the following provisions into AUGMENT. (A more complete, overview treatment of these is given in <Ref-8>.)

10a

Electronic Mail. Its primary attributes of speed, automatic distribution, and computer-to-computer directness are well recognized -- and are generally accepted now as important to the effectiveness of knowledge workers. AUGMENT Mail has features that are beyond what most electronic mail systems offer, and which provide unique benefit to the authorship process.

10b

AUGMENT's mail system allows one to "send" complete, structured documents as well as small messages. In an authorship environment, an important role for "electronic mail" is for the control and distribution of documents -- where small, throw-away messages are considered to be but a special class of document. An author should be able to bundle up any combination of text and graphics, in the forms that he has been using for studying and manipulating them -- and send the bundle to other workers. In AUGMENT, such a bundle is just like any other file structure, and can be studied and manipulated, incorporated into other files (documents), saved or deleted.

10b1

Recorded Mail -- AUGMENT'S Journal System. When mailing a document, an AUGMENT worker may optionally specify that it be installed as a "recorded" item. In this case, before distributing the item, the system will make a permanent record if it, as a file in a specified Journal collection. And, just as though it had been published, this recorded Journal item cannot later be changed. The system assigns a straightforward accession identifier (a simple number), and any authorized worker is henceforth guaranteed access to that Journal item by specifying the name of the Journal-collection and the Journal-item number -- e.g., as specified in the link "<OAD,2237,>".   10c

A given journal may be set up to serve multiple hosts and is much like a special library. It has its collection of documents, and AUGMENT provides associated support processes for entry, cataloging, retrieval, and access.   10c1

Together with the linking capability described above, a Journal system provides an extremely effective form of "recorded dialog." Cross-reference links between a succession of Journal items produces an inter-linked network of collaborative contributions -- plans, outlines, document drafts, schedules, short comments, detailed critiques, reference material, etc. The on-line worker can follow these links very easily and, using multiple windows and flexible viewing options, can make very effective use of such records.   10c2

For instance, consider a detailed commentary directed toward a "preliminary design" document recorded in a given Journal collection. The author writing the commentary could view the design document in one window and his developing commentary document in another. He can easily establish links in his commentary to cite any passage in the design document -- e.g., a statement, a term in the statement, or a diagram. Then this author would submit his commentary into the Journal, perhaps specifying a list of colleagues for "distribution." Each listed user would automatically receive a mail item announcing this new Journal entry, giving subject, author, date, etc., and the all-important link to the new Journal file containing the commentary. Any such recipient can subsequently study both the commentary and its cited planning document in a similar, multi-window, link-assisted manner.   10c3

Furthermore, this second reader could develop and submit his own recorded commentary, which because of the citation power of AUGMENT links could be as short and to the point as: "Frankly, John, I think your comment in (DDD,xxx,aa) is a mistake! Didn't you notice the earlier assumption in (DDD,xxx,bb)? Maybe you should go back to Tom's earlier requirements document -- especially at (EEE,yy,cc)." (Here, "DDD" and "EEE" represent Journal names, "xxx", "yyy", and "zzz" represent Journal item numbers, and "aa", "bb", and "cc" represent addresses pointing to specific passages in those Journal files.)   10c4

In official parlance, "retrieval" is the finding out about the existence of a relevant piece of information, whereas "access" is the subsequent process of gaining possession of the information. For users of AUGMENT's Journal system, retrieval is immensely facilitated by the widespread use of citation links. When one can follow them as easily as can a practiced AUGMENT worker, these links provide extremely effective retrieval support. We have supplemented this with some simple, automatically generated catalog files, which made a rather nice balance. Access is provided by direct Jump on a reference link if the file is on line; if it isn't, AUGMENT asks the worker if she wants it retrieved, and a simple affirmative response automatically launches a request for the system operator to retrieve the file from its archive tape, after which the worker is notified of its availability via electronic mail.

10c5

A private document can be submitted into a Journal. In this case, only those workers listed at Journal-entry time can get access to the central copy. Such a private item would not be listed or indexed in the "public" catalogs.

10c6

We have used the Journal system very heavily since 1970 to support AUGMENT's development activity; many customers have employed it heavily since 1975. There are about 100,000 entries recorded in the original Journal now (I don't know about other, newer AUGMENT Journal collections). We found that as workers became at home in this environment, they were increasingly free about submitting their items to the "public." It became evident that the scientific tradition of active and open interchange has some solid relevance to the collaborative processes in our smaller, "colleague communities." Time and again a worker would come across others' dialog and be able to contribute some valuable information (sometimes a one-sentence comment with a critical citation link). Often the payoff went the other way: the new party found immediate value in an old piece of recorded dialog.

10c7

Shared-Screen Teleconferencing. Consider a case where two people sit down to work together at a terminal, where they can both see the screen(s), and where either one can take over the controls. This is being done countless times every day throughout the country, in different combinations of expert-expert, expert-novice, novice-coach, etc. When talking together on their telephones, two or more distantly separated AUGMENT users can collaborate in a manner very similar to this.

10d

Suppose that two workers, Smith and Jones, want to set up and operate in a Shared-Screen Conferencing mode. Smith is in Princeton, working on host Office-4, and Jones is in San Francisco, working on host Office-12 -- and both of these host computers are connected to the same network. Assumedly they are in telephone contact when they decide to work in this shared-screen mode to collaborate on Smith's current job.

10d1

Jones will enter the command "Share (display with user) SMITH! On host OF12! Viewing (other display)!!"

10d2

Smith will enter the command "Share (display with user) JONES! On host OF4! Showing (this display)!!"

10d3

To give these commands, each person only entered the characters shown in upper case (entry case actually irrelevant), plus the digits, plus an "OK Key" action where each exclamation point is shown.

10d4

Whatever tool that Jones is currently using will continue responding to his controlling actions, as evidenced by various feedback and portrayal actions in the windows on his screen. Smith's screen image will clear, and be replaced with a replica of Jones' screen image -- multiple windows and all. For the duration of the shared-screen session, Smith's screen image will continue to replicate what is shown on Jones' screen.

10d5

There are provisions for passing control back and forth between workers. For instance, Jones can pass control to Smith so that Smith can show him some material or method of work. There are also provisions for the subsequent entry and departure of other conference participants.

10d6

EMBEDDING THE GRAPHIC ILLUSTRATIONS

11

For complete support of document development, it is important to provide integrated means for developing, viewing, and manipulating graphical portrayals. These portrayals should be part of the working files from the very start, to be studied, passed about in mail, shared in Conferencing mode, edited, captioned, labelled, and moved about within the document structure. Furthermore, active, relevant citation links pointing to these graphical constructs would be installed in and followed from textual passages throughout the associated set of documents (including Mail and Journal documents).

11a

AUGMENT's architecture and file structure were designed for this end, and a good bit of the associated implementation is in place.

11b

A graphical data structure can be attached to any given file node, and there are basic capabilities for composing, studying, and modifying graphical diagrams. When formatting for a suitably equipped photo-typesetting device, there are formatting directives to designate the position and scale for placing these diagrams on a page. An AUGMENT file with integrated text and graphics can thus be mapped automatically onto a high-quality document whose pages contain both text and line drawings.

11c

Our goal here was for what we call an "illustrative graphics" capability -- basic to which is a command that, when directed toward any conventional "plotter" file, will translate it into a diagram attached to a designated node. In this way we can make use of graphic constructs developed within almost any applications system, most of which have provision for outputting "conventional" plotter files.

11d

The most important next step is to adapt a bit-mapped display as an AUGMENT workstation, so the integrated text and graphics can be viewed and manipulated on the same screen. Heretofore, to do graphic work, an author has had to attach a Tektronix 4014 storage-tube display to the special printer/graphic port of her AUGMENT workstation. This has made use of AUGMENT graphics slow and expensive enough to limit the number of user groups who have developed the integrated use of mixed text and graphics.

11e

CONCLUSION

AUGMENT's unique provisions stemmed for the most part from the conceptual framework within which AUGMENT was developed. For instance, consider the pervasive and significant changes in the environment in which humans will be doing their knowledge work. Note that the habits, methods, conventions, intuitions, etc., that comprise the "ways" in which we think, work and collaborate, are for the most part products of many centuries of cultural evolution -- in a radically different environment. With a radically different environment, this constant process of cultural evolution can be expected to take some radical turns.

12a

The AUGMENT developmental framework assumed that many of these "ways" are candidates now for change in directions that heretofore would not have been beneficial. The AUGMENT system emerged as a first step in considering a few such changes, which perhaps can improve human capability for doing knowledge work because their new "ways" will enable us more effectively to harness the new tools toward more effective basic capability. (This is very different from trying to "automate" our old "ways" of doing things.)

12b

As an example, consider the "What You See Is What You Get" (WYSIWYG) syndrome. It is a highly touted feature for many vendors. It provides a definite advantage for the final process of converting a computer-held document to a nicely formatted hard copy. But what does it do for authorship? Well, in our framework, it has a negative impact. We were happy to abandon those constraints of lines and pages and other formatting geometry which did not contribute to matters of content and structure. We have chosen instead to provide the authorship process with structured files, flexible addressing, flexible window-size viewing, level and truncation viewspecs, etc. -- things that would be awkward or impossible to provide in a WYSIWYG environment. This provides the authorship phase with flexibility and power for studying and manipulating content and structure that we wouldn't consider trading off for WYSIWYG. Save it for the production phase.

12c

Here is another bit of culture that deserves re-examination. Consider the dictum, "Easy to learn, and natural to use." Or, "User friendly." The question is, for whom are you judging that things will be easy, or natural, or friendly? For designers of craft-work tool systems, very different perceptions of this issue are warranted between a system for the occasional, weekend do-it-yourself person and a system to be heavily used day after day by professionals. The AUGMENT User Interface System enables us easily to configure either kind of a tool collection.

12d

This paper describes part of what is provided to professional knowledge workers who do a significant amount of authorship work. We observe no more difficulty in their learning how to employ this relatively large collection of tools than one would expect for professional woodworkers in their learning about the relatively large collection of chisels and other tools of their trade. 12e

It is a basic part of our framework that, to augment human knowledge workers, attention must be given not only to tools, but to methods and skills as well. Because of space limitations, the scope of this paper was restricted to a summary of those tool provisions within AUGMENT that especially facilitate the authorship process. A full description of "How to use AUGMENT to ..." would definitely need to include methods of work that effectively harness these tool provisions, and the special kinds of skills that yield unique payoff in executing these methods. This is true for every tool system, of course, but it seems especially true in this case because many AUGMENT provisions do not fit into the general cultural background of our authorship process. 12f

Perhaps the best way for very brief summarization of what AUGMENT's users feel about its unique features is simply to say that those who leave its working environment really miss them. 12g

REFERENCES

Ref-1: **"Toward Integrated, Evolutionary Office Automation Systems,"** Douglas C. Engelbart, *Proceedings of the Joint Engineering Management Conference*, Denver, CO, October 16-18 1978, pp. 63-68. (AUGMENT,71279,).

13a

Ref-2: **"The Augmented Knowledge Workshop,"** Douglas C. Engelbart, Richard W. Watson, and James C. Norton, *AFIPS Conference Proceedings,* Vol. 42, National Computer Conference, June 4-8, 1973, pp. 9-21. (AUGMENT,14724,).

13b

Ref-3: **"Document Production and Control Systems,"** Elizabeth K. Michael, Dirk H. van Nouhuys, Beverly R. Boli, Raphael Rom, and Ann C. Weinberg, *Phase One report of Document Production and Control Systems Design Study*, by the Augmentation Research Center, SRI International, for AF Rome Air Development Center, Contract F30602-76-C-003, March 1, 1977. (AUGMENT,37730,).

13c

Ref-4: **"A Model Document Production System,"** Beverly R. Boli, Harvey G. Lehtman, Elizabeth K. Michael, Raphael Rom, Dirk H. van Nouhuys, and Nina Zolotow, *Phase Two report of Document Production and Control Systems Design Study*, by the Augmentation Research Center, SRI International, for AF Rome Air Development Center, Contract F30602-76-C-003, July 30, 1977. (AUGMENT,29000,).

13d

Ref-5: **"Toward High-Performance Knowledge Workers,"** Douglas C. Engelbart, *OAC '82 Digest*, Proceedings of the AFIPS Office Automation Conference, San Francisco, CA, April 5-7 1982, pp. 279-290. (AUGMENT,81010,).

13e

Ref-6: **"User Interface Design Issues for a Large Interactive System,"** Richard W. Watson, *AFIPS Conference Proceedings*, Vol. 45, AFIPS Press, Montvale, NJ, 1976, pp. 357-364. (AUGMENT,27171,).

13f

Ref-7: **"Design Considerations for Knowledge Workshop Terminals,"** Douglas C. Engelbart, *AFIPS Conference Proceedings*, Vol. 42, National Computer Conference, June 4-8, 1973, pp. 221-227. (AUGMENT,14851,).

13g

Ref-8: **"Collaboration Support Provisions in AUGMENT,"** Douglas C. Engelbart, *OAC '84 Digest*, Proceedings of the 1984 AFIPS Office Automation Conference, Los Angeles, CA, February 20-22, pp. 51-58. (OAD,2221,).

13h

COMPUTER SUPPORT FOR COOPERATIVE DESIGN

Susanne Bødker
Jørgen Lindskov Knudsen
Morten Kyng
Computer Science Department,
Aarhus University, Ny Munkegade 116,
DK-8000 Aarhus C, Denmark.
Phone: +45 6 12 71 88.
E-mail: bodker@daimi.dk, jlk@daimi.dk,
mkyng@daimi.dk.

Pelle Ehn
Kim Halskov Madsen

Department of Information and Media Science,
Aarhus University, Niels Juelsgade 84,
DK-8200 Aarhus N, Denmark.
Phone: +45 6 13 67 11.
E-mail: ehn@daimi.dk, halskov@daimi.dk.

ABSTRACT

Computer support for design as cooperative work is the subject of our discussion in the context of our research program on Computer Support in Cooperative Design and Communication. We outline our theoretical perspective on design as cooperative work, and we exemplify our approach with reflections from a project on computer support for envisionment in design – the APLEX and its use. We see envisionment facilities as support for both experiments with and communication about the future use situation. As a background we sketch the historical roots of our program – the Scandinavian collective resource approach to design and use of computer artifacts, and make some critical reflections on the rationality of computer support for cooperative work.

INTRODUCTION

Design of computer applications and cooperative work will be discussed in two different ways. First we look at design as a process which may create the conditions for cooperation in use. Secondly, we look at the design process itself as one kind of cooperative work. To do so we identify and discuss the ideal that has become dominant in understanding cooperative work in and around the CSCW conferences: The small research group of the 1980s. Rooted in the Scandinavian tradition of designing in projects together with trade unions, we discuss some alternatives to the ruling ideal. We emphasize that it is important that designers of computer support for cooperative work do not just impose their own understanding or ideal of cooperative work onto other groups in other domains. Instead of heading for some ideal which may be more suited for the cooperation of researchers than for that of the users, we suggest that design is understood as a process which can help identifying and emphasizing future cooperation among the users.

Moreover, designers and users need tools and techniques to facilitate design as a cooperative process. We present our research program [4], in particular a part of it concerning computer support for cooperation among users and professional designers. Since design of computer support is design of the conditions for the future work situations of the users, these conditions need to be designed with concern for the practice and cooperation of the involved groups. We argue that an active participation of users in design is necessary to deal with this.

To be able to utilize the practical knowledge of the users and to be able to consider not only describable aspects of the computer support and future work situations, we advocate design by doing: A process of envisionment where the users can experience the future: Working with the (simulated) application. We present a computer-based object-oriented environment,

APLEX, which is intended to support such cooperative design among users and professional designers. Finally we discuss some of the technical challenges deriving from the design of APLEX.

Hence, the paper start out with a broad introduction to our social and anthropological perspective on cooperative work, then focus on the design process as cooperative work, and finally zooms in on our more technical efforts to design computer support for this situation. In a concluding example we discuss the relations between these different levels of understanding computer support for cooperative work.

To set the stage, we will start out by making some critical reflections of the rationality of computer support for cooperative work.

RATIONALITY OF COOPERATIVE WORK

Briefly outlining the ruling ideal, we see a tendency to define the ideal for cooperative work as a small group of equally qualified people working together with very little managerial guidance or intervention. In other words, the ideal for a small research group in the 1980s.

One of the problems with the small research group ideal is that it is an ahistorical ideal. Conditions for scientific work have changed dramatically in this century. Researchers have been forced into large project teams where the outcome is partly determined on beforehand, and is to be achieved under great time pressure. The cooperative ideal seems to have developed in the same period of time as a way of preserving some of the freedom of the "real" scientist, who was before a creative loner in his study. The ideal of cooperative research work is something new, and it may change again, depending on the development of the conditions for research.

Few researchers have explicitly defined cooperative work, and those who do often base their definition on sharing of tools, materials and the like [14, 25, 26]. Is shared instruments a precondition for cooperative work, and does it make a difference if we talk about real-time sharing or sharing of a tool-box? Can office workers only work cooperatively if they also share typewriter, paper and pens? It is claimed that cooperation means no specialization or division of labor. As an example of the opposite, consider a woman giving birth to her child aided by a midwife, a nurse, and possibly a doctor. Specialization and division of labour is obvious, and at the same time it is definitely an example of cooperative work.

The definitions typically focus on cooperative work in general as an ideal, decontextualized from history, society and situation. The emphasis is on use of artifacts and materials, on communication and coordination of activities in general. We share this ideal with great sympathy. We think, however, that it is important to go beyond this abstract level, trying to understand computer support for cooperative work in a historical and social context – *to understand cooperative work in practice.*

By *practice* we refer to human everyday practical activity. In practice we produce the world. Both the world of objects and our knowledge about this world. Practice is both action and reflection. But practice is also a social and historical activity. As such it is being produced cooperatively with others, being-in-the-world. To share practice is also to share understanding of the world with others. However, this production of the world and our understanding of it takes place in an already existing world. It is the product of former practice. Hence, practice has to be understood socially: as our producing and reproducing social processes and structures as well as our being the product of them.

Rationality
The practical "reality" for cooperative work is often far from as rational and democratic as seems to be presumed in the "research group ideal". To get to a somewhat different conception, we will give two examples of totally different ways of looking at cooperation: *care ra-*

tionality – the "motherly" way of cooperation; and the *rationality of solidarity* – cooperation in the workers' collective. We do not introduce these examples to say that THEY are better ways of looking at cooperation than the research group ideal, but they definitely deal with communities where cooperation means something different.

Care rationality

In her book, *Caring. A Feminine Approach To Ethics & Moral Education* [20], Nel Noddings discusses caring as a philosophical alternative to the ruling ideal – "the father's voice" – the rational model, which is based on hierarchical thinking and abstract categories such as fairness and justice.

A person cares about somebody by taking on this person's situation, based on her former experiences with caring. Basically, we can only care about somebody because we, ourselves, have been exposed to the full-fledged experience of being cared for at some point of time in our lives. The caring relation is, in other words, not a relation between equals, and we cannot just decide to care about each other as an explicit or implicit commitment.

The caring relation is a rather complicated one. The "one-caring" starts to care and determines how to act, not from an abstract categorization of different types of needs, but from making specific to herself the situation of the cared-for-to-be, and trying out that situation. In other words the rationality of caring relates to situations, whereas traditional, scientific, "male" rationality relates to abstract categories.

The main points which challenge our understanding of cooperative work are, first of all, that we deal with relations between people, which are mutual but not on equal terms. The degree of freedom to act, etc., is very different on the two sides. Secondly, commitment to participate in a caring relation from the one-caring's side is not sufficient. To be able to take on the role as the one-caring, the person must herself have been cared-for. Thirdly, the ara-

tionality and situation dependence of the caring relation, and the resolution of unresolved situations by prototypical investigations: the one-caring investigates prototypical situations based on the situation of the cared-for and tries out these prototypical situations – "how would I like it to be if my girl was in this situation...?"

Rationality of the workers' collective

The sociologist Sverre Lysgaard has analyzed how factory workers together form a *workers' collective*; a support and protection mechanism against the ever ongoing exploitation by the managerial technical/economical system [18]. To Lysgaard, the workers' collective is a result of the tension between the individual on the one hand and the technical and economical exploitation on the other hand.

In a factory we would normally not call work cooperative. What Lysgaard describes is, however, a strong informal system which enable the workers to act together, instead of as outstanding and vulnerable individuals. The norms and values of the workers' collective become a buffer between the individual worker on the one hand, and the technical/economical system on the other. The conditions for this collective are not what the small research group ideal says: a multi-person tasks aided by technology, work done in an informal, normally flat organization, relatively autonomous. Rather it is determined by a complicated, dialectic relation with an inexorable, formal, hierarchical organization.

Different rationalities and cooperative work

Where the discussions about cooperation based on the small research group ideal have adapted "the father's voice" means-end rationality, the workers' collective represents a case of a different kind of rationality – the rationality of solidarity. This is still bound to contracts or commitments whereas the care rationality is an example of a kind of rationality which is not as directly bound to commitment – the commitments can only be seen over time, as one person carries on the caring-for to another person.

Our point is that we do not need to see research work as an ideal for cooperative work to conduct a discussion of computer support for cooperative work. Rather we need to realize that there are many other ways of conducting cooperative work, and that these ways exists under a wide range of conditions; political, economical, gender-based, etc.

Cooperative work is many-folded and domain dependent. But still we believe in cooperative work, and we want to support situations of cooperative work. To build or introduce computer support for cooperative work is a process of change; not only of technology but also of the work place as such. Much in line with the Scandinavian collective resource approach we suggest that in trying to understand computer support for cooperative work we should supplement the focus on the "product" with a concern for the *design process*, including also the specific work practice and setting.

THE COLLECTIVE RESOURCE APPROACH

The *collective resource approach* in Scandinavia constitutes a major part of our background. It is based on two design ideals: The first is *industrial democracy*, the attempt to extend political democracy by also democratizing the work place – the social life of production inside the factory gates and office walls. The second is *quality of work and product*, the attempt to design skill-enhancing tools and environments for the production of highly useful quality products and services.

Both design ideals are of importance in the context of cooperative design. To have workers and designers cooperatively design skill-enhancing environments for users is a very direct way of having the workers influence their own work situation. Hereby, cooperative design contribute to industrial democracy.

Cooperation with the Trade Unions: The Scandinavian Projects

Practice along the lines of the collective resource approach has developed in Scandinavia during more than 15 years [9, 10]. In research as well as in design, the approach includes the workers who ultimately will be exposed to its results. The process was initiated in 1970 by the Norwegian Iron and Metal Workers Union (NJMF), which in cooperation with researchers from the Norwegian Computing Center embarked on a research project on planning, control and computerization from a trade union perspective. It was decided, as part of the project, to try out the work practices that the people in the project believed would become commonplace in the future: that the local unions themselves investigate their important problems at the work place and in the relation between the work place and the local community, and that in this work they use external consultants as well as internal consultants and other resources provided by the company.

The NJMF project inspired several new research projects throughout Scandinavia. In Sweden the DEMOS project on trade unions, industrial democracy and computers started in 1975 [8]. A parallel project in Denmark was the DUE project on democracy, education and computer-based systems [17].

Although growing, the extent and impact of these activities did not meet the initial expectations. It seemed that one could only influence the introduction of the technology, the training, and the organization of work to a certain degree. From a union perspective, important aspects like the opportunity to further develop skill and increase influence on work organization were limited. Social constraints, especially concerning power and resources, had been underestimated, and in addition the existing technology constituted significant limits to the feasibility of finding alternative local solutions which were desirable from a trade union perspective.

As an attempt to broaden the scope of the available technology, we decided to try to supplement the existing elements of the collective resource approach with union based efforts to *design* new technology. The main idea of the first projects, to support democratization of the design process, was complemented by the idea of *designing tools and environments for skilled work as well as for quality products and services.* To try out the ideas in practice, the UTOPIA project was started in 1981 in co-operation between the Nordic Graphic Workers' Union and researchers in Sweden and Denmark with experiences from the 'first generation' of collective resource projects [2].

The position we took in NJMF, DEMOS, DUE, UTOPIA and other collective resource projects was that decentralization of decision-making and a participative approach to the design process are not sufficient. Instead our position goes back to the different interests of management and workers concerning industrial democracy.

Conflicts and emancipation
Hence, we rejected the *harmony view* of organizations, according to which conflicts in an organization are regarded as pseudo-conflicts to be dissolved by good analysis and increased communication. Consequently we also rejected an understanding of design as fundamentally a rational decision-making process based on common goals. Instead our research was based on a *conflict view* of industrial organizations in our society. Within a conflict view it does make a difference whether you design cooperatively with management or with workers. In the interest of emancipation, we deliberately made the choice of working together with workers and their organizations, supporting the development of their resources for a change towards democracy at work. We found it necessary to identify ourselves with the "we-feeling" of the workers' collective, rather than with the overall "we-feeling" of modern management which focuses on gaining more productivity out of the work force. In short: Trade unions were seen as organizations with a structure that was problematic when functioning as vehicles for

designing for democracy at work, at the same time they were seen as the only social force that in practice could be a carrier of this ideal.

Human Centered Design
The political reason for involving end-users in the design process, and for emphasizing their qualifications and participation as resources for democratic control and change is only one side of the coin. The other is the role of skill and participation in design as a creative and communicative process.

This complementary concern has grown out of our dissatisfaction with traditional theories and methods for systems design – not only with how systems design has been politically applied to deskill workers, but more fundamentally with the theoretical reduction of skills to what can be formally described. Hence, one can say that the *critique of the political rationality* of the design process points to a *critique of the scientific rationality* of methods for systems description.

Our approach to cooperative design include users in a double sense. We claim the importance of rethinking the design process to include structures through which ordinary people at their work place more democratically can promote their own interests. We also claim the importance of rethinking the use of descriptions in design, and of developing new design methods that enable users of new or changed computer artifacts to anticipate their future use situation, and to express all their practical competence in designing their future.

This approach is a challenge to rethink traditional understanding of the process of design and its relation to the use of computers in working life. However, it is not only a strategy to include users and their trade union activities in the design process, but more fundamentally to include a cultural and anthropological understanding of human design and use of artifacts, to rethink the dominating objectivistic and rationalistic conception of design. At least in this sense, the collective resource approach reaches beyond the borders of Scandinavia.

THE OBJECT-ORIENTED PERSPECTIVE

The collective resource approach is one part of our background. The other major part - *the object-oriented perspective on programming* - can be traced back to the Norwegian Computing Center as well. Simula67 was initially developed as a simulation language, but its object-oriented approach was found useful as a general programming perspective. Since then there have been major research efforts in Scandinavia within various aspects of object-oriented programming, including also the idea of languages rooted in the professions of the (non-computer professional) users. It is outside the scope of this paper to discuss our view on object-oriented programming further, but we will point out that our way of thinking about programs and programming is strongly influenced by this tradition. Further discussion can be found in [15].

UNDERSTANDING DESIGN AND USE OF COMPUTERS ARTIFACTS

Given this background we will now turn to our philosophical understanding of design. We focus on understanding of the role of computer applications in use, on the phenomenology of design, and on design as language-games, rather than on design as consciously planned and executed processes.

An understanding of the role of a computer application in use is important for design. Our inspiration for a new approach to design, based on an understanding of the use of *artifacts* in human work activity, comes from many fields of research. They include the human activity theory of A. N. Leontjew [3], the language-game approach by L. Wittgenstein [10], and recent contributions to the theory of design and computer artifacts by H. and S. Dreyfus [7] and T. Winograd and F. Flores [29].

With these approaches, we take as our point of departure what people *do* with computers in their daily work, how they cooperate with each other by means of computers, and how this co-

operation can be enhanced. The basis for design is involved, practical use and understanding, rather than detached reflection. "Hands-on" experiences come into focus. We comprehend design of computer artifacts as concerned social and historical activity in which these artifacts and their use are anticipated. An activity and form of knowledge that is both planned and creative, and that deals with the contradiction between tradition and change.

Design and practical experience

The future use situation is the origin of design, and we design with this situation in mind. To design with the future use activity in mind also means to start out from the present practice of the future users. It is through their experiences that the need for design has arisen, and it is their practice that is to be applied and changed in the future use activity.

Some aspects of practice can be made *explicit*. In design, they can be formally represented in systems descriptions and requirement specifications. But there are other aspects of practice which we can learn only through practical experience. We call these aspects *practical*. The practical aspects are important in design exactly because they are what characterize professional and skillful use of an artifact, as opposed to the use by a novice who basically follows explicit rules.

Design and phenomenology

As mentioned above, our approach is inspired by the one taken by Winograd [29] and Dreyfus [7]. With their phenomenological framework, the point of departure in design is that the different participants understand the situation they come from. They are used to act in situations of "normal resolution". This goes for users as well as designers. The normal resolution or understanding includes the blindness created by the tradition they come from. The design process is characterized by a breakdown of this understanding, by which a situation of irresolution is created. Design is resolving these situations of irresolution, based on commitments between the participants. This is neither objective problem solving nor rationalistic decision making. It is *concerned* human activity, where different traditions and backgrounds meet.

The concept of breakdown is fundamental to design. Breakdown is both desirable and undesirable. On the one hand it is necessary to break down the everyday understanding and use within a specific tradition to create new knowledge and new designs. Breakdown of our understanding of a well known situation is the opening to new knowledge and eventually an understanding of something new. On the other hand, design which is not based on the understanding and use within a tradition – the users' practical skills – are likely to fail, because knowledge "embedded" in the tradition is lost. To be able to deal with this contradiction between involved understanding of the artifact in use and detached reflection on the artifact and the use situation is fundamental to design.

Design as a language-game

Our way of understanding prototyping, mock-ups, and experimental methods in design is also heavily influenced by the ordinary language philosophy of Wittgenstein. Following Wittgenstein, we think of design and use activities as *language-games* that people play: we learn to participate, interact and communicate in games. We use our *ordinary language*, and we acquire competence by learning *in practice*. This means that we view *language as action* rather than *language as description* as fundamental.

Designers are involved in changing computer artifacts and the way people use them. Hence, the language-game of design is one that changes the rules for another language-game – that of use of the artifacts.

Playing the game of design

If designers and users share the same *form of life* it will be possible to overcome the gap between the different language-games. It will at least in principle be possible to develop the practice of design so that there is enough *family resemblance* between a specific language-game of design and the language-games in which the design of the computer artifact is intervening.

The language-games played in design can be viewed both from the point-of-view of the users and of the designers. We can focus on design as a language-game in which the users learn about possibilities and constraints of including new computer artifacts in their ordinary language-games. The designers' practical knowledge will primarily be expressed as the ability to construct specific language-games of design in such a way that the users can develop their reflective and practical knowledge of future use by participating in design processes. However, in order to set up these kinds of language-games the designers have to learn from the users. To possess the competence involved in using a professional language requires a lot of learning within that practice.

The users can, in an involved and influential way, participate in the language-game of design, when the methods applied give their design activities a family resemblance to the language-games they play in ordinary use situations. In order to stress this important involvement of the users in the design process, we often refer to the users participating in a design process as *lay designers*. They have expertise within the work domain, but no particular expertise as designers.

According to Wittgenstein [30], language-games are also characterized by how we play and make up the rules as we go along. And there are even games where we alter them as we go along. This is in our view a good characterization of the language-games of design.

Descriptions and models in design

In understanding design as language-games, systems descriptions are seen as speech acts we have learned within a specific language-game. If they are good, it is because they are good "moves" within that game. As such they can create breakdowns of understanding as well as help avoid them, depending on what kind of moves they are within the game.

To use descriptions in design is to participate in the playing of a language-game. This is the language-game of anticipating new or changed computer artifacts and use situations. What is created are artifacts that we can *reflect upon*, and some times get "hands-on" involved *practical experience* from (e.g. by using a prototype). Especially artifacts for involved experience as a basis for later reflections are fundamental to our approach.

New design methods?

In summary, it is our position that
- a new design approach must take the specific use activity as its point of departure;
- focus on language as *action* rather than as *description*; and that
- users must be allowed to examine the artifact being designed through hands-on experiences.

What is needed most urgently at the moment is not better linguistic notations for more or less formal descriptions of the functionality of a system, but descriptions that are *reminders of use of the intended computer artifact*. This points in the direction of description methods as support for *concerned involvement*, rather than *correct* description. Such support may be achieved by the use of scenarios, prototypes, mock-ups etc. This is design as a language-game of *doing, learning and playing*.

However, few traditional computer-based design tools are flexible enough to support this kind of design. Traditional prototyping methods exhibit a potential conflict between accessibility (not too much computing competence and programming effort should be needed to use them), and flexibility, both in terms of how the tools can be applied, and in terms of which products can be designed.

With this background and theoretical perspective we now turn to our current research program on computer support in cooperative design and communication.

THE RESEARCH PROGRAM: COMPUTER SUPPORT IN COOPERATIVE DESIGN AND COMMUNICATION

The research program started in May 1987. It is a long term effort planned jointly by the Computer Science Department and the Department of Information and Media Science at Aarhus University [4]. One aspect of the program focus on computer support for experimental design and for communication. The other aspect of the program focuses on the language usage of design and use of computer systems, and the way it relates to the work processes of which it is a part. The purposes are:
- to develop exploratory and object-oriented programming methods into something which, in combination with other design methods, can be applied in practical design;
- to do research into the possibilities of making better user interface design, by means of different theoretical frameworks, and better computer support (such as pluggable software);
- to investigate the possibilities of creating better computer support for cooperative work in small groups.
- to provide empirical knowledge of the interplay between the computer medium and the professional communication that takes place through it, or is motivated by it, and
- to investigate the possibilities for exploiting this knowledge as a basis for design.

As a summary we characterize the theoretical perspective of the program with the following stipulations and reflections:
- *In designing a computer application, conditions for the whole use situation are implicitly or explicitly designed as well.*
  In design of computer support for cooperative work we have to be able to understand the cooperative work the application is to be

used for. This can only be done in cooperation with experienced users acting as lay designers.

- *Users and designers often have different backgrounds, different professional languages, and are used to different language-games.*

The construction of language-games unique to the specific design situation, but with family resemblance with the lay designers normal professional language-games, is an important aspect of cooperative design. In this way, cooperative design becomes a process of mutual learning.

- *Normally, a computer application is used in a multi-lingual environment, comprising the technical support staff and (possibly several) user professions.*

All parties can make legitimate, but sometimes contradictory, demands to the computer application. To design the computer application in such a way that it takes the multi-linguistic environment into account is a challenge in cooperative design.

- *The needs and demands of the prospective users are essential to good design, but are hard to express before the future situation has been experienced.*

In design of computer support for cooperative work this obstacle can be surmounted by using prototypes, mock-ups, scenarios, etc. which make it possible to get experiences, not only by reflection, but also by involvement in possible future use situations and through use of possible future computer applications.

- *Professional users tend to be rather traditional in their views on how to organize their work and on the potential computer applications for it.*

Methods in design have to relate to both *tradition and change*, and especially to the interplay between the two positions. Computer applications are often understood metaphorically, and metaphors can be used in design to support the interplay between tradition and change.

We now turn to our own considerations in a project on a computer-based artifact for early envisionment in cooperation between professional designers and lay designers. First we discuss some dimensions of the design situation, we then turn to APLEX, a computer-based environment for cooperative design.

DIMENSIONS OF THE DESIGN SITUATION

As outlined above, we consider the role of the lay designers as a key issue. End-user involvement is needed but to be fruitful, the design situation must have family-resemblance with their work situation and allow them to get "hands on" experiences in situations resembling the (future) work. We call what is demonstrated or examined in the design situation a *prototype*. In doing this we are hopefully not to much in conflict with emerging terminology in the area.

In understanding the design situation we must consider *the people involved*. Are the designers professionals, lay designers, or a combination? Today, the only active designers are professionals. End-users are at best only competent evaluators. Many 4th generation tools advocate that lay designers can design their future computer applications themselves, but this is rarely seen in real projects. Most often we have seen the professional designers as the ones suggesting changes. The users accept or reject, but do not take the initiative to make changes. Furthermore, situations where only lay designers with one type of use background participate differ from situations where more user groups are active. The computer professionals in those situations often take on the responsibility of transferring opinions and choices from one group to the other.

We must also consider different *aspects of the design process*.

One aspect is that of demonstration versus use. In *demonstration* the lay designer watches the professional operating the prototype. By *use* we mean that the lay designer try out the prototype in the (simulated) work activity. In case of *modification* the prototype is changed during a session, whereas in the case of *exploration* the prototype is examined without change. Most practical situations deal only with exploring. This relates to demonstration: a demonstration, which is driven by the professional designers, often resembles a film or video with no possibility of stopping or going behind the screen.

There is also a difference between *laboratory* and *field* (or on location) evaluation: the difference between evaluation of prototypes in an artificial setting and their actual use in the work activity. When we talk about the early stages of the process where envisionment is the main purpose, this is mostly done as laboratory evaluation, or in fact often without considerations for an explicit use setting. Prototyping by versioning can be seen as field evaluation, but at a very late stage of the design process. *Controlled experiment* where the aspects to be tried out are settled in advance differs from *exploratory experiment*. Outside the human factors research, there seems to be little practical or theoretical understanding of the needs or methods for setting up controlled experiments. At the same time, many of the human factors methods are too limited when it comes to the rather complex situations of human work. Furthermore, many approaches remain analytical and do not support design based on the evaluation.

Envisionment may have the character of *brain storm, outline of alternatives or test of a single solution followed by minor changes*. Presently, computer support for brain storming is seldom applied in practice. Often only one basic architecture is prototyped, and then a few different screen layouts, report formats etc. are tested.

Each of these dimensions related to the process are of relevance when creating a cooperative design situation which stimulate active lay designers involvement. For instance, compare a situation where the professional designer in a laboratory demonstrates a prototype with a situation where the lay designer on location tries out various alternatives as part of a brain storming process.

We now turn to some more technical aspects of computer support for design in general.

Depending on the *degree of integration* with the computer resources in the organization, an evaluation in real work situations is made easier or harder. Furthermore, if there is a large degree of integration, all the designers, including lay designers, have a possibility of knowing the computers on beforehand.

Access to other design tools and ways of *combining* various design tools determines the extent to which envisionment have to be done with only one tool or whether it is possible to apply several supplementary tools simultaneously.

Is it possible to reuse and modify modules from existing applications or prototypes? Access to a *component library* helps the designers to rapidly and easily get from one prototype to another. For instance, is it possible to reuse an existing database and build or experiment with different interfaces? To what extent is it possible to experiment with new types of hardware?

The degree of *incrementability* says something about how easily prototypes can be changed: How is it possible to intervene into a prototype in the design session and make the next version running?

Finally, but not of least importance, we draw to the attention the conditions under which the design takes place. The resources available in terms of time for the designers, equipment available and qualifications of the designers are essential. Moreover, the authority of the designers to make decisions about the design process and product is important too.

Based on our theoretical perspective we can conclude that:

- These users should be able to explore and to modify in the field.
- The construction of prototypes should be so effective, and the prototypes so flexible, that different prototypes in fact will be constructed and thus different alternatives tried out.
- The prototypes developed should be based on a suitable spectrum of different computer support. They should be integrated with other systems in the work situation in such a way that the future work situation may be experienced.
- The organizational setting and the resource situation of the designers should allow them to spend the time needed to develop design skills directed towards the specific area of use, and to make decisions based thereon.

This is the design setting for which we need computer support. Unfortunately existing computer support gives rise to systems that are rather closed, with very little support for multiuser applications, for multiple activities, for reuse of existing applications, or for integration with existing applications or newly created applications. Hence, the challenge to design the APLEX.

COMPUTER SUPPORT FOR ENVISIONMENT – APLEX

The design environment APLEX is a means for cooperative design. It is intended to support involved communication among professional and lay designers about future use situations. This communication is based on practical hands-on and organizational experience using APLEX. We see the future design situation using APLEX as being a cooperative design situation between one or more professional designers and one or more lay designers. The different designers are directly involved in the design process and APLEX must be able to respond to the needs of the whole group. This implies that it should be possible for both the professional and for the lay designers to conduct their own experiments using APLEX. Furthermore, it should be possible to engage the designers in intensive design work where the different designers are conducting a mutual experiment using APLEX.

This implies that APLEX must be able to support envisionment ranging from mock-ups over prototyping to application construction/integration, using various techniques such as "intelligent" slide shows, guided tours, and exploratory programming.

On the design of APLEX

APLEX will not primarily aim at *implementing* the computer application which is being constructed. Instead we will experiment with development systems where the prototypes do not need to be running versions of the future computer program, as well as with systems for actual application development. It is one of the aims of this project to develop a designer's workbench, where both possibilities exist as supplementary tools for the designers. The flexibility of APLEX should allow for evaluation of various types of user interfaces, various interaction styles, different functionalities as well as various target applications. APLEX should include generalizations of the facilities that 4th generation tools provide. Furthermore, we will examine the use of various kinds of simulation and visualization techniques. APLEX should also include possibilities of simulating different, specific computer workstations and other types of technology.

Technically, APLEX presents several research challenges. First, it must offer a comprehensive and device independent interface framework. Secondly, it tries to expand the capabilities of prototype systems outside the limits of traditional implementability (parts of the functionality and the interface might be simulated by means of video-disks, "dummy" screen images, or human beings). Thirdly, it explores the capabilities of strongly interdependent interfaces on different workstations connected through high-capacity networks. Fourthly, it explores the relationship between the application and the underlying interface framework through investigation of the technical implications of this concept. To achieve these goal we find that full support of the I^3 concept (*Incremental, Integrated, Interactive*) is necessary. Furthermore, the design of APLEX will be based on many aspects of traditional workstation environments.

Cooperative

From the point-of-view of cooperation, the issue of robustness versus flexibility is important. Often it is the professional designers who need the flexibility whereas it is the lay designers that need the robustness in order to have any realism in their examinations.

In case of demonstration or use in restricted situations where the designers actually sit together and examine the prototype, the "side-tracking" may be avoided by the interference of the professional designer, but in situations where the lay designers are "on their own" this is not the case. Such errors may create breakdowns which cannot be interpreted in the use situation. Hence, they cannot contribute to the development of the lay designer's understanding of, or unreflected action in this use situation.

Furthermore, cooperation entails that creation of multi-user applications is an important aspect of APLEX, and that even in the design situation multi-person use of APLEX is needed. The multi-user situations create a need to let APLEX include network facilities as well as facilities for sharing of objects.

Multi-person use results furthermore in requirements to documentation and communication support in the design situations. A shared hypermedia is one exiting idea which is, as yet, unexplored. Hypertext technology [6] seems to be an obvious idea for a way of structuring this documentation, because it allows reference pointers among different parts of the text, and even of the prototype. This possibility is primarily intended for reflection in breakdown situations where the "illusion" of being in the future world breaks down for the users.

Incremental

We have described the need for rapid modification of the substrate being created. One important means for achieving the capability for rapid modification is obtained by a high degree of incrementability. Several systems contain such high degree of incrementability, most notable the various Lisp-systems [24] and the Smalltalk-80 system [11]. However, these systems have shown that we face an overall dilemma - the contradiction between flexibility and robustness. Incrementability is obtained by having very flexible programming languages that allow for dynamic binding. At the same time, such dynamic substrates pose serious problems in terms of security. This implies that errors occurring during use are usually indicated at a very low level in the system, which make it very difficult for a lay designer to interpret the actual cause of the error. It should be possible to construct substrates that are consistent, and where errors messages etc. can be interpreted within the substrate.

We also need a powerful debugger (in the line of the Smalltalk-80 debugger) making it possible to cancel erroneous computations, ignore errors, make minor local modifications in order to make progress possible, or follow a chain of activities leading to the erroneous state. The debugger must be able to grant specific capabilities temporarily to an object in order to allow for further examination. We find, however, that this ability must be very explicit in order to ensure that the designer is aware of the change of capabilities of the object. Thus, APLEX should support the manipulation of capabilities of the individual objects.

The above discussion of robustness leads to our view of incrementability. APLEX should be incremental in the sense that it should be possible to modify objects in a substrate without restructuring the whole substrate.

Integrated

By integrated is meant that APLEX is well-integrated with the various other applications in the organization, and that substrates created with APLEX themselves can be integrated with other substrates. The guiding metaphors of integration in APLEX will be: "access to anything anytime" and "living within the full environment". The metaphor of total access is of course relative to the present capabilities in the system as discussed above. Furthermore, APLEX must keep track of the relations between the objects, and their corresponding source, documentation, help facilities, tutorials, as well as their relations with other objects in the environment.

Having a design tool isolated from the other computer facilities in the organization will give rise to numerous problems. It is therefore important that facilities for connecting APLEX to the existing computer resources are designed to overcome those problems.

The substrates in APLEX will be organized in easy-to-access libraries (or databases) and structured with re-usability and pluggability as some of the most important design strategies. We will extend this view to hardware, such that hardware components in APLEX will be considered similar to software components (pluggable hardware components). Thus allowing for experimentation with alternative hardware devices in the design process and for experiments with advanced hardware, e.g. video.

Besides being well-integrated with itself, APLEX must be well-integrated with other design tools. It should e.g. be possible to use a sequence of screen images made in Hyper-Card™ [13] or VideoWorks™ [28].

Interactive

Without the need for any arguments, APLEX must contain extensive graphical capabilities for creating highly interactive interfaces both to existing computer facilities, and to APLEX applications. Since we are envisioning APLEX being used for experimenting with the development of applications to be realized on specific com-

puters, we intend, within APLEX, to create simulations of various existing interactive systems, such as the Macintosh desktop [12], the Smalltalk-80 and the Microsoft window systems. This will make it possible, in the design situation, to experiment with the impact of imposing computer-specific constraints on the future application.

Further Design Issues

The above design space gives rise to further important issues, that will be addressed during the design of APLEX. These include:

Domain dependence: APLEX must support application domain specific substrates. This makes it possible to make APLEX "grow" into application domains slowly, and thereby make it possible to create more and more advanced substrates within a specific application domain by creating more and more domain specific substrates.

Enforcement versus conventions: Our main points of reference in the above discussions were Smalltalk-80 on the one hand, and HyperCard on the other. Very alike in some aspects, very different in others. A comparison of the two easily leads to a discussion of what support for programming the prototype designers need – do they need a specific number of different types of objects, or is a flexible possibility for using and modifying examples of objects better? In general this is a discussion of to what extent a certain style of use of APLEX should be enforced by strict typing and syntax, and to what extent a more flexible guiding of the user by examples, convention patterns, etc., works better. At the moment we do not know, experiences from programming languages are ambiguous in this respect, and we hope to be able to try out different ways of doing this.

Architectural Overview of APLEX

Throughout the development of APLEX we will experiment with object-oriented design. One of the motivations for this is that object-oriented design principles facilitate creation of what can be called pluggable software. That is, software that is open–ended in the sense that a given substrate, created by means of object-oriented design principles, is a substrate that in a future application can be expanded and modified. We will hopefully benefit from this open-ended nature in two ways: First, it will be a well-suited structure for the implementation of the above mentioned components of APLEX, since they both internally and externally are substrates that will be subject to expansion/modification during the design process. Secondly, the strategy for combining substrates will benefit from the use of object-oriented design principles [31]. As such, this part of the project will also be an experiment in realistic application of object-oriented design principles. This leads to the need for a programming language supporting object-oriented design principles. The language chosen is the Beta programming language [16].

The architecture of the graphical interaction system of APLEX contains the following three components:

Graphical library which is primarily concerned with supporting the construction of graphical items. The graphical library is a toolbox with capabilities like drawing (and manipulating) of such items. Presently, APLEX will be designed using the page composition language PostScript as its graphical library [22].

Windowing environment which is primarily concerned with supporting the sharing of the display by various applications running on a workstation, as well as sharing of windows between workstations via a local area network. Within each window, graphical capabilities may be supported, or each application is responsible for utilizing the inside of each window. Presently, APLEX will be designed utilizing the NeWS™ [19] window system.

User interface framework. The design of APLEX is a research effort in the direction of creating a framework by which the interaction between the user and the computer application can be envisioned. The capabilities of such a framework are extensions of the capabilities of

the windowing environment. In addition to the capabilities of the windowing environment, the framework contain capabilities for defining more fine-grained structures on the display by defining graphical structures that are not windows, but more tightly connected with the application. Examples of such structures are icons, buttons, menus, and scroll bars. Furthermore, the framework is concerned with the definition, distribution and handling of events, both hardware events (e.g. mouse movement, keyboard events, etc.) and software events (e.g. window exposed, icon selected, spreadsheet – cell selected). Our view on user interface framework is inspired by the MVC concept in Smalltalk-80 [11]. The semantics of interactive graphical communication are discussed further in [5].

It is important to stress that our view on user interface frameworks is not part of a discussion in favor of separating the design of the interface from the design of the functionality of the application. In fact, we find that such separation is neither possible nor feasible in general [27]. However, it is our aim to create a set-up of pluggable components, some of which deal with the interaction and some with the *underlying components*, e.g. databases.

Some applications may be constructed with more than one interface associated with it. There are several architectural reasons for this: Each interface may, for instance, focus on specific aspects of the application, and the structure of each interface is designed in order to ease the manipulation of these specific aspects. These interfaces might all be active at the same time, and manipulations of the application through one of the interfaces might influence the other interfaces. Each interface defines a protocol that the application must support, and the interfaces must be dynamically connected to the underlying components. Furthermore, interfaces may utilize various predefined interface components, such as buttons, scroll bars, or menus. Such a framework will allow for rapid modifications of a prototype, as well as for design of different alternative prototypes, some of which show different styles of interaction based on the same underlying components.

The above structure is what we, with respect to user interfaces, mean by pluggable components. The protocols define the *slots* by which interfaces and underlying components can be *plugged* together. In the design of APLEX, we will examine the usage of object-oriented design principles in this area.

The underlying extensibility in object-oriented systems seems to be well suited to pluggability. The design of APLEX will utilize this pluggability as the fundamental architecture of the system. This implies that all components of APLEX will be constructed as objects, including hardware components. In this way, we will be able to simulate not yet constructed specialized hardware by constructing a software simulation (software object) of that component and conduct experiments. Furthermore, we will be able to experiment with different hardware solutions to specific interaction problems by defining common properties of types of hardware (e.g. pointing devices or picking devices) and then select different actual devices (e.g. soft screen vs. mouse vs. tracker ball). In the same way, it is possible to encapsulate the functional behavior of external (to APLEX) software systems as objects in APLEX with a protocol, modeling the functionality. Furthermore, we will be able to treat external resources on equal terms with APLEX resources and experiment with using different external resources as alternatives in a design process.

Using APLEX

We would like to conclude our treatment of APLEX with a "Please try it!". At the moment, however, APLEX exists only as envisionment. We are now conducting experiments, based on HyperCard, Smalltalk-80, NeWS and other systems in order to try out and look further into the ideas outlined above. We have also initiated the construction of the first prototype of APLEX,

while still continuing to develop the conceptual framework underlying APLEX.

As a weak substitute for "hands-on" experience we make use of a fictious example. The example is, however, firmly rooted in our empirical research [3].

Imagine a project where a group of professional designers work together with a group of office workers in a government institution to help these office workers achieve new kinds of computer support for their work. The project is managed by a steering committee with representation from management and the employees. It is a basic idea of the project that the employees should, in project groups, take part in designing the computer applications that they are to use themselves. The specific case deals with the filing and retrieval system for incoming and outgoing mail etc., the so-called Journal. The purpose of this project is to find out how the Journal can be reorganized to be more efficient, eventually by means of a computer application.

From the beginning, the group work with three different alternatives:

- a restructuring of the existing paper based Journal without the use of computers.
- a restructuring of the paper files with computer support for retrieval of documents and computer-based mail lists to inform the workers who draw on the services of the journal in their daily work (case workers) about incoming mail.
- a computer based Journal where all documents are scanned in upon arrival in the Journal office, and with computer based retrieval and mail lists.

In the early meetings it is a major task to delimit the type of computer application wanted from the three general solutions. Some of the important issues are the organization of work – who should use the application and how?, what are the hardware choices?, and how are they connected to the physical organization of work? Depending on whether the documents are to be filed in a traditional paper file or scanned into the computer, the women in the Journal office have to conduct their work differently - the role of e.g. a photo copier would differ. Much of the internal mail circulation would not be needed with the scanner solution, i.e. the traditional communication patterns would be changed fundamentally.

In this situation, the professional designer initiate the discussions by building two small *demonstration* prototypes by means of APLEX: scanner or no scanner. Together with simple mock-up's supplementing the physical layout of the future work-place, the prototypes are used to demonstrate to the group what the possibilities and constraints of the *alternatives* would be. Maybe APLEX doesn't really contain a pluggable scanner, in which case the designer uses images on a videodisk made with a drawing program, just simualting the scanning procedure. The main idea is to get a discussion about technical and organizational implications of the two different proposals.

In this situation, APLEX is a flexible environment for the professional designers: it allows them to reuse parts from one prototype in constructing the other; to make use of other design tools in building the prototypes, and to use pluggable hardware devices.

Next we consider a situation where a professional designer and a group of lay designers, women from the Journal office, sit down to find out exactly what information should be filed, how it should be entered, what the screen images should look like, and what interaction they want. Based on earlier talks with the users and on the previous meetings, the professional designer has made a first prototype. This prototype is merely a sequence of screen images, which are based on the appearance of the mail lists presently used at the institution. When necessary, information is added to the prototype. The discussion focuses on the information needed - on the screen and in the files, and how much of this should be entered by the office workers - and on the possible changes in ways of cooperating. This is a situation where the designers are *modifying* the prototype, si-

muitaneously with the *use* of it. The component library is used to look at different types of screen layouts and interaction styles: a direct manipulation version, a form-filling one, etc.

At a later state, the prototype, which have been elaborated on by the involved group, can be used in its *real organizational setting*. The prototype is still running by means of APLEX, but now APLEX needs also to be hooked up to, or running some of the other computer programs that are normally used in the Journal office, e.g. a word processing program. For a period of time, the Journal office tries out their design in their daily work. Some changes are made in the way the system is used. Problems still come up about the information needed to file and retrieve the documents, but also about the speed of the application. The situation is one where the *robustness* of the prototype is important since the professional designers, although present, cannot help each user all the time.

SUMMING UP

We have seen examples of the use of APLEX in different *situations* in a design process. This process is one in which the participants could make use of their different backgrounds as office workers or as designers in playing the language-game of design. The APLEX prototypes have made it possible, under different conditions, for the office workers to experience their future work situation. The APLEX is an environment that facilitates such language-games. We do not see APLEX as the only way of doing this. Rather, APLEX ought to be one of many more or less integrated tools and techniques belonging to the practice of the professional designer.

The design process is very important for the future work situation of the users. The kind of computer support needed for cooperative work in different settings may differ a lot, and as we have argued, it is important to investigate and develop new possibilities of cooperation in a design process where prospective users are actively involved. In other words, we do not primarily see cooperative work, or computer support for it, as a static entity. We view design as a cooperative process out of which new possibilities of cooperation is created.

In the presentation of our example we have made a number of gross simplifications, especially with respect to the degree of harmony in the project: first of all, management doesn't interfere with the process. Secondly, there is only one user group. From the real life case we have reduced complexity by not considering the group of case workers. Thirdly, we assume that the professional designers have no interests of their own, which contradicts those of the workers. Real design processes are surrounded by many conflicting interests: the conflicts between management and labor, workers collectives which question why they should do a job that they are not hired to do: help management design computer applications, and conflicts among groups of workers who belong to different trades. Another simplification, closely related to our neglect of conflicts, concerns the rationality of the cooperation in the design process described: it does not differ significantly from the small research group ideal discussed in the beginning of our paper.

To get beyond the small research group ideal and reach a fuller understanding of what cooperation means in real life situations is a major challenge for our research program. Not least because design is a process of change in which the tools and materials of a group are often replaced by something new. If we restrict ourselves to the shared material, shared tools, etc. definition, we cannot understand how groups cope with situations of change, such as design, when their traditional "sharedness" - the tools and materials - are taken away from them. Such a group needs not only cooperative work as an ideal, but as a (design) process leading in a democratic direction.

REFERENCES

1. Bjerknes, G. et al. (eds.): *Computers and Democracy – a Scandinavian Challenge*, Avebury 1987.
2. Bødker, S. et al.: A Utopian Experience, in [1].
3. Bødker, S.: *Through the Interface – a Human Activity Approach to User Interface Design*, DAIMI PB-224, Computer Science Department, University of Aarhus, 1987.
4. Bøgh Andersen, P. et al.: *Research Programme on Computer Support in Cooperative Design and Communication*, DAIMI IR-70, Computer Science Department, University of Aarhus, 1987.
5. Bøgh Andersen, P., Knudsen, J.L.: *Semantics for Interactive Graphical Systems*, Preliminary version, Computer Science Department, Aarhus University, 1988.
6. Conklin, J.: *Hypertext: An Introduction and Survey*, IEEE Computer, 20(9), September 1987.
7. Dreyfus, H. L., Dreyfus, S. D.: *Mind over Machine – the power of human intuition and expertise in the era of the computer*, Basil Blackwell, 1986.
8. Ehn, P., Sandberg, Å.: Local Union Influence on Technology and Work Organization, some results from the Demos Project, in Briefs, U. et al. (eds.): *System Design, for, with, and by the user*, North-Holland, 1983.
9. Ehn, P., Kyng, M.: The Collective Resource Approach to Systems Design in [1].
10. Ehn, P.: *Work-Oriented Design of Computer Artifacts*, Almqvist & Wiksell International, Falköping, 1988.
11. Goldberg, A., Robson, D.: *Smalltalk-80: The Language and its Implementation*, Addison-Wesley Publishing Company, 1985.
12. *Human Interface Guidelines: The Apple Desktop Interface*, Addison-Wesley Publishing Company, 1987.
13. *HyperCard User's Guide*, Apple Computer, 1987.

14. Johnson, B., Weaver G.: Using a Computer-Based Tool to Support Collaboration: A Field Experiment, in [23].
15. Knudsen, J.L., Madsen, O.L.: Teaching Object-Oriented Programming is more that Teaching Object-Oriented Programming Languages, in *Proceedings of Second European Conference on Object-Oriented Programming (ECOOP'88)*, Oslo, Norway, August 1988.
16. Kristensen, B.B. et al.: The BETA Programming Language, in Shriver, B., Wegner, P. (eds.): *Research Directions in Object-Oriented Programming*, MIT Press, 1987.
17. Kyng, M., Mathiassen, L.: Systems Development and Trade Union Activities, in Bjørn-Andersen, N. (ed.): *Information Society, for Richer, for Poorer*, North-Holland, 1982.
18. Lysgaard, S.: *Arbeiderkollektivet*, Universitetsforlaget, Oslo 1976 (In Norwegian).
19. *NeWS Technical Overview*, Sun Technical Report, 800-1498-05, 1987.
20. Noddings, N.: *Caring. A Feminine Approach To Ethics & Moral Education*, University of California Press, 1984.
21. Polanyi, M.: *Personal Knowledge*, Rutledge & Kegan Paul, 1967.
22. *PostScript Language Reference Manual*, Addison-Wesley Publishing Company, 1985.
23. *Proceedings of the Conference on Computer-Supported Cooperative Work*, 1986.
24. Shiel, B.: *Power Tools for Programmers*, Datamation, 29(2), February 1983.
25. Stasz, C., Bikson, T.: Computer-Supported Cooperative Work: Examples and Issues in One Federal Agency, in [23].
26. Sørgaard, P.: A cooperative work perspective on use and development of computer artifacts, Järvinen, P. (ed.): *Proceedings of the 10th Information Systems Research Seminar in Scandinavia*, Tampere, 1987.
27. Tanner, P., Buxton, W.: Some Issues in Future User Interface Management System (UIMS) Development in Pfaff, G.(ed.): *User Interface Management Systems*, Springer Verlag 1985..
28. *VideoWorks II Manual*, MacroMind, Inc., 1987.
29. Winograd, T., Flores, C. F.: *Understanding Computers and Cognition: A New Foundation for Design*, Ablex Publishing Compagny, 1986.
30. Wittgenstein, L.: *Philosophical Investigations*, Oxford University Press, 1953.
31. Yankelovich, N. et al.: *Intermedia: The Concept and the Construction of a Seamless Information Environment*, IEEE Computer, 21(1), January 1988.

What is Coordination Theory and How Can It Help Design Cooperative Work Systems?

"What is Coordination Theory and How Can It Help Design Cooperative Work Systems?" by T.W. Malone and K. Crowston from *Conference on Computer-Supported Cooperative Work*, October 1990, pages 357-370. Copyright © 1990, Association for Computing Machinery, Inc., reprinted with permission.

Thomas W. Malone and Kevin Crowston

Center for Coordination Science (E53-333)
Massachusetts Institute of Technology
Cambridge, MA 02139

It is possible to design cooperative work tools based only on "common sense" and good intuitions. But the history of technology is replete with examples of good theories greatly aiding the development of useful technology. Where, then, might we look for theories to help us design computer-supported cooperative work tools? In this paper, we will describe one possible perspective—the interdisciplinary study of coordination—that focuses, in part, on how people work together now and how they might do so differently with new information technologies.

In one sense, there is little that is new about the study of coordination. Many different disciplines—including computer science, sociology, political science, management science, systems theory, economics, linguistics, and psychology—have all dealt, in one way or another, with fundamental questions about coordination. Furthermore, several previous writers have suggested that theories about coordination are likely to be important for designing cooperative work tools (e.g., [Holt88], [Wino86]).

We hope to suggest here, however, that the potential for fruitful interdisciplinary connections concerning coordination is much greater than has as yet been widely appreciated. For instance, we believe that fundamentally similar coordination phenomena arise—unrecognized as such—in many of the fields listed above. Though a single coherent body of theory about coordination does not yet exist, many different disciplines could both contribute to and benefit from more general theories of coordination. Of particular interest to researchers in the field of computer-supported cooperative work is the prospect of drawing on a much richer body of existing and future work in these fields than has previously been suggested.

In this paper, we will first describe what we mean by "coordination theory" and give examples of how previous research on computer-supported cooperative work can be interpreted from this perspective. We will then suggest one way of developing this perspective further by proposing tentative definitions of coordination and analyzing its components in more detail.

What is coordination?

We all have an intuitive sense of what the word "coordination" means. When we attend a well-run conference, when we watch a winning basketball team, or when we see a smoothly functioning assembly line we may notice how well coordinated the actions of a group of people seem to be. Often, however, good coordination is nearly invisible, and we sometimes notice coordination most clearly when it is lacking. When we spend hours waiting on an airport runway because the airline can't find a gate for our plane, when the hotel room we thought had been reserved for us is sold out, or when a company fails repeatedly to capitalize on innovative ideas its researchers develop we may become very aware of the effects of poor coordination.

In order to proceed it is helpful to have a more precise idea of what we mean by "coordination." Appendix A lists a number of definitions that have been suggested for this term. The diversity of these definitions illustrates the difficulty of defining coordination, and also the variety of possible starting points for studying the concept. For our purposes here, however, we believe it is most useful to start with the following "common sense" definition of coordination taken from a dictionary [Amer81]:

the act of working together harmoniously.

We will refer to this as the "broad" definition of coordination, and will suggest a more restrictive "narrow" definition below. It is important to note here, however, that we intend for working together "harmoniously" to include conflict as well as cooperation. Even when a group of actors has strong conflicts of interest or belief, they may still produce results that observers would judge to be "good" or "harmonious." For example, different groups in a company often compete for budget resources and people, and this competition sometimes contributes to the company's ability to produce useful products.

What is coordination theory?

We define *coordination theory* as a body of principles about how activities can be coordinated, that is, about how actors can work together harmoniously. It is important to realize that there is not yet a coherent body of theory in this domain. However, there are theories, concepts, and results from many different fields that could both contribute to and benefit from the development of such general theories.

For instance, it is clear that questions about how people coordinate their activities are central to parts of organization theory, sociology, social psychology, anthropology, linguistics, law, and political science. Important parts of economics and management science also analyze how people can coordinate their work with a special focus on rational ways of allocating resources. Computer science does not deal primarily with people, but different computational processes must certainly "work together harmoniously," and as numerous observers have pointed out, certain kinds of interactions among computational processes resemble interactions among people (e.g., [Fox81], [Hewi86], [Hube88], [Mill88], [Smit81]).

These potential overlaps suggest that coordination theory will be like other interdisciplinary fields that arise from the recognition of commonalities in problems that have previously been considered separately in different fields. For instance, the field of cognitive science grew out of the recognition by researchers in several different fields (e.g., psychology, computer science, and linguistics) that they were dealing separately with similar problems: how can information processing systems (people or computers) do things like use language, learn, plan, remember, and solve problems (e.g., see [Gard85], [Norm80])? Most observers would agree that progress in the new field has benefitted significantly from emergent cross disciplinary connections, and the paradigms used have in turn been quite influential in the older fields [Gard85].

In coordination theory, the common problems have to do with coordination: How can overall goals be subdivided into actions? How can actions be assigned to groups or to individual actors? How can resources be allocated among different actors? How can information be shared among different actors to help achieve the overall goals?

In its attempts to find generalizations that apply across disciplines and across levels of analysis, coordination theory resembles earlier work on systems theory and cybernetics (e.g., [Beer67], [Boul56], [Emer69], [Forr80], [vonB50], [Wien61]). We are significantly better equipped for the task of identifying and analyzing coordination processes now,

101

however, than systems theorists were several decades ago. For instance, new qualitative languages from computer and cognitive sciences (such as object inheritance networks and Petri nets) seem especially promising as tools for formalizing "mid-level theories" like Winograd and Flores' [Wino86] "conversations for action." These qualitative mid-level theories are more specific than the quantitative abstractions of systems theory, but more general than specific case studies.

What isn't coordination theory?

If coordination theory can draw upon so many different fields, is it any more than just the union of these fields? How can we look at a theory and decide whether it is or is not an example of coordination theory? While it is certainly not helpful to include everything in coordination theory, neither do we think it is essential to draw sharp boundaries between what is and is not coordination theory. Instead, as in cognitive science and many other fields, we think certain characteristic questions and approaches will come to typify central examples of coordination theory. For example, theories that apply to only one kind of actor will probably be less important to coordination theory than theories that can be applied to several kinds of actors.

Previous examples of coordination theory and CSCW

With the definition of coordination theory we have just presented, it is clear that some of the work already done in the field of computer-supported cooperative work can be viewed as examples of the use of coordination theory. Even though these authors did not use the term "coordination theory," each of the following examples involves using ideas about coordination from other disciplines to help develop cooperative work tools:

(1) Holt [Holt88] describes a theoretical language used for designing coordination tools that is based, in part, on ideas about Petri nets, a formalism widely used in computer science to represent process flows in distributed or parallel systems. This language is part of a larger theoretical framework called "coordination mechanics."

(2) Winograd and Flores ([Flor88], [Wino87], [Wino86]) have developed a theoretical perspective for analyzing group action based heavily on ideas from linguistics (e.g., [Sear75]) about different kinds of "speech acts," such as "requests" and "commitments." This perspective was a primary basis for designing the Coordinator, a computer tool that helps people make and keep track of requests and commitments to each other.

(3) Malone [(Malo90] describes how ideas from organization theory about flexible organizational structures called "adhocracies" [Mint79] and ideas from artificial intelligence about "blackboard architectures" for sharing information among program modules ([Erma80], [Nii86]) contributed to the design of the Information Lens, a system for helping people share information in organizations [Malo87].

(4) Conklin & Begeman [Conk88] and Lee [Lee90a] describe systems to help groups of people record the structure of arguments (e.g., positions, arguments, and counterarguments) that are based in part on ideas from philosophy and rhetoric about the logical structure of decision-making.

(5) Turoff [Turo83] used ideas about prices and markets to suggest a computer-based system to help people to exchange services within organizations.

Clearly, drawing a line around these examples and calling them "coordination theory" does not, in itself, provide any benefit. Nor does using ideas about coordination from other disciplines provide any guarantee of developing useful cooperative work tools. Nevertheless, we feel that considering these examples within the common framework of coordination theory provides two benefits: (1) it suggests that no one of these perspectives is the complete story, and (2) it suggests something about how we might look for more insights of the sort that many people feel have resulted from these previous examples.

In particular, the perspective of coordination theory suggests (1) that we should look to previous work in various disciplines for more insights about coordination, (2) that we should attempt to develop frameworks or concepts that will facilitate such interdisciplinary transfers, and (3) that we should attempt to develop new concepts and theories focused specifically on the questions of coordination that seem central to building cooperative work tools. In the next section, we will take a step in this direction.

TOWARD A FRAMEWORK FOR COORDINATION THEORY

So far, we have claimed that many different disciplines can contribute to our understanding of coordination and that better understanding of coordination will help build useful cooperative work tools. But is it really sensible to use the term "coordination" in describing all the different kinds of phenomena to which we have alluded? For that matter, is there anything in common among these different phenomena, other than some occasional similarities in terminology? As a first step toward answering these questions, we will present in this section our preliminary efforts toward developing a framework for analyzing coordination. This framework is not a "theory of everything;" it is only one approach which we have found helpful in seeing the relationships between different views of coordination.

Components of coordination

According to our broad definition of coordination above, coordination means "the act of working together harmoniously." What does this broad definition of coordination imply? First of all, what does the word "work" imply? The same dictionary defines "work" as "physical or mental effort or activity directed toward the production or accomplishment of something" [Amer81]. Thus there must be one or more *actors*, performing some *activities* which are directed toward some ends. In what follows, we will sometimes refer to the ends toward which the activities are directed as *goals*. By using the word "harmoniously," the definition implies that the activities are not independent. Instead, they must be performed in a way that helps create "pleasing" and avoids "displeasing" outcomes, that is, that achieves the goals. We will refer to these goal-relevant relationships between the activities as *interdependencies*. These components and the coordination processes associated with them are summarized in Table 1. (See [Bali86], [Bali81], [Barn64;], [Malo87b], [Malo88], [McGr84], [Mint79] for related decompositions of coordination.)

Components of coordination	*Associated coordination processes*
Goals	Identifying goals
Activities	Mapping goals to activities (e.g., goal decomposition)
Actors	Selecting actors Assigning activities to actors
Interdependencies	"Managing" interdependencies

Table 1. Components of coordination.

For example, an automobile manufacturing company might be thought of as having a set of goals (e.g., producing several different lines of automobiles) and a set of actors (e.g., people) who perform activities that achieve these goals. These activities may have various kinds of interdependencies such as using the same resources (e.g., an assembly line) or needing to be done in a certain order (e.g., a car must usually be designed before it is built).

One use of this set of components of coordination is to help facilitate conceptual transfers between disciplines. For instance, elsewhere [Malo88], we have shown how research in selected areas of economics and artificial intelligence can be compared in terms of these dimensions. This comparison suggested a novel insight for economic theorists about the importance of product descriptions, as well as prices, in coordinating resource allocation in markets.

Coordination is attributed to a situation by observers

It is important to realize that the actors involved in a situation may or may not all agree on the identification of all these components. Instead, one or more of these components may be attributed by an observer in order to analyze the situation in terms of coordination. For instance, we may sometimes analyze everything that happens in a manufacturing division as one "activity", while at other times, we may want to analyze each station on an assembly line as a separate "activity."

One very important case of this occurs when the actors have *conflicting goals*, but we choose to analyze the results of their behavior in terms of how well it achieves some goals in which we are interested. For instance, even though two designers on a project team may have strongly opposing views about how a product should be designed, we can evaluate their collective behavior in terms of the quality of the final design. Another important example of conflicting goals occurs in market transactions: All the participants in a market might have the goal of maximizing their own benefits, but we, as observers, can evaluate the market as a coordination mechanism in terms of how well it achieves some global goal such as allocating economic resources to maximize consumer utilities (e.g., [Debr59]).

In practice, situations in which actors have at least partly conflicting goals are nearly universal, and mixtures of cooperation and conflict are quite common (e.g., [Cibo87], [Will85], [Sche69]). When we analyze the coordination in these situations, we must (at least implicitly) evaluate the actors' collective behavior in terms of how well it achieves some overall goals (which may or may not be held by the actors themselves).

A narrow definition of coordination

The broad definition of coordination we have been using includes almost everything that happens when actors work together: setting goals, selecting actors, and performing all the other activities that need to be done. For some purposes, it is useful to be able to focus explicitly on the elements that are unique to coordination, that is, on the aspects of "working together harmoniously" that are not simply part of "working." In our analysis of the broad definition above, the element of coordination that was implied by the word "harmoniously" was interdependencies. Therefore, when we want to focus specifically on the aspects of a situation that are unique to coordination, we will use the following narrow definition of coordination:

> *the act of managing interdependencies between*
> *activities performed to achieve a goal.*

Clearly, many important coordination situations involve multiple actors, and in our previous work (e.g., [Malo88]), we defined coordination as something that occurs only when multiple actors are involved. Since then, however, we have become convinced that the essential elements of coordination listed above arise whenever multiple, interdependent activities are performed to achieve goals—even if only one actor performs all of them.

Kinds of Interdependence

Both our definitions of coordination give a prominent role to interdependence: If there is no interdependence, there is nothing to coordinate. There is also a long history in organization theory of emphasizing the importance of interdependence in determining how organizations are structured (e.g., [Thom67], [Galb73], [Lawr67], [Pfef78], [Rock89], [Har90]). This suggests that one useful way to extend the theory of coordination is to ask what kinds of interdependence between activities are possible and how different kinds of interdependence can be managed.

Our preliminary investigations of this question have led us to believe that interdependence between activities can be analyzed in terms of *common objects* that are involved in some way in both actions. For example, the activities of designing and manufacturing a part both involve the detailed design of the part: the design activity creates the design and the manufacturing activity uses it.

These common objects constrain how each activity is performed. Different patterns of use of the common objects by the activities will result in different kinds of interdependences. For example, the parts can be manufactured only after the design is complete and the actor doing the manufacturing has received a copy. We call this pattern of usage (one task creating an object that is used by others) a *prerequisite* constraint. In general, the common object may constrain any or all of the activities that use it. In this case, for example, it might make sense for a designer to consider the constraints that the manufacturing process places on the design and to create a design that will be easier to manufacture.

Table 2 presents a preliminary list of types of interdependencies and coordination processes that can be used to manage them. The table includes both generic kinds of interdependence and specific examples of interdependence that arise in particular situations. We labeled this list "preliminary" because we suspect that there is more structure in the space of kinds of interdependence and processes than is currently reflected in the table.

One use of this table (especially the generic parts of it) may be to help show the relationships between previous work in different disciplines. For instance, much of economics is focused on analyzing market mechanisms for resource allocation, and parts of computer science have focused on questions of synchronizing activities to meet simultaneity constraints.

An even more important use of the approach suggested by this table may be to help generate possible alternative ways of coordinating in a particular situation. For instance, it may be possible to characterize a situation in terms of the kinds of interdependence it involves, and then use a "catalog" of interdependencies and their associated processes to generate a set of alternative processes that could be used to manage the interdependencies. This ability to characterize a space of possible coordination processes for a given set of activities would be useful in understanding how new kinds of coordination tools could lead to new ways of organizing cooperative work.

Kinds of Interdependence	Common object	Example of interdependence in manufacturing	Examples of coordination processes for managing interdependence
Generic:			
Prerequisite	Output of one activity which is required by the next activity	Parts must be delivered in time to be used	Ordering activities, moving information from one activity to the next
Shared resource	Resource required by multiple activities	Two parts installed with a common tool	Allocating resources
Simultaneity	Time at which more than one activity must occur	Installing two matched parts at the same time	Synchronizing activities
Domain-specific:			
Manufacturability	Part	Part designed by engineering must be made by manufacturing	Decision-making (e.g., negotiation, appeal to authority)
Customer relations	Customer	Both field service and sales personnel deal with same customer	Information sharing (e.g., sharing problem reports)

Table 2. Preliminary examples of kinds of interdependence.

Example: Coordinating interdependencies between design and manufacturing

This example illustrates how knowing the interdependencies in a situation may suggest alternative ways to manage them. The example is based, in part, on extended field studies of engineering change processes in several manufacturing organizations [Crow90]. In the case of design and manufacturing, an important kind of interdependence results from the common object that is the design of the product to be manufactured.

One simple way technology can help manage these interdependencies is simply by helping to detect them in the first place. For instance, one of the applications we have investigated for the Information Lens and Object Lens systems ([Lai88], [Malo87]) is routing engineering change notices to engineers to whose work is likely be be affected by a given change, even when the person making the change does not know who else it will affect.

Whether all the interdependencies are recognized or not, there seem to be at least four basic ways to manage them:

(1) At a minimum, the designer must create a design and give it to the manufacturer to build. One simple effect of CAD systems, for example, is to make this transfer process easier.

(2) The designer and the manufacturer can negotiate what the design should be, for example, by iterating the design process or in joint meetings. A variety of electronic meeting support and communication tools could help this process and could make it more desirable relative to alternative ways of managing the same interdependencies.

(3) Sometimes the need for explicit negotiation can be eliminated by moving some of the knowledge about the constraints of either task from one engineer to another. For instance:

    (a) Some of the manufacturer's knowledge (the knowledge about the manufacturing constraints, not about how to do the manufacturing) can be made available to the designer, for example, by training the designer in methodologies such as design for manufacturing or by embodying the knowledge in an intelligent CAD system.

    (b) Some of the designer's knowledge can be transferred to the manufacturer. For example, if a system like gIBIS [Conk88] is used to capture more of the designer's intent as well as the details of the part, the manufacturing engineer might be able to change some details of the design to make the parts easier to build while preserving the intent.

(4) A third party, such as a common superior, may be able to resolve problems as they arise or to give enough initial direction that problems do not arise.

This analysis seems to be easily transferred to other domains. For example, a bank and a potential borrower have to agree on a common object, a loan. The typical approach seems to be case (1) above: the bank offers a loan with its standard terms and a person who wants the loan takes it or leaves it. In some cases, the bank and the borrower negotiate the details of the loan, case (2) above. Finally, one can imagine transferring some of the bank's knowledge about making loans, for example, to a computer program that a potential borrower could run to explore possible loan conditions (case (3a)), or to a third party who would suggest which bank would be best for a given applicant (case (4)).

Processes underlying coordination

In attempting to characterize more precisely different coordination processes, we have found it useful to describe them in terms of successively deeper levels of underlying processes, each of which depends on the levels below it. Table 3 shows a preliminary diagram of the levels we have used. For instance, most of the coordination processes listed in the last column of Table 2 require that some decision be made and accepted by a group (e.g., what goal will be selected or which actors will perform which activities). Group decisions, in turn, require members of the group to communicate in some form about the goals to be achieved, the alternatives being considered, the evaluations of these alternatives, and the choices that are made. This communication requires that some form of "messages" be transported from senders to receivers in a language that is understandable to both. Finally, the establishment of this common language and the transportation of messages depends, ultimately, on the ability of actors to perceive common objects such as physical objects in a shared situation or information in a shared database (e.g., see [Such87]). These layers are analogous to abstraction levels in other systems, such as protocol layers for network communications.

Even though the strongest dependencies appear to be downward through these layers, there are also times when one layer will use processes from the layers above it. For instance, a group may sometimes use decision-making processes to extend the common language it uses to communicate (e.g, see [Lee90b]), or a group may use coordination processes to assign decision-making activities to actors.

Process Level	Components	Examples of Generic Processes
Coordination	goals, activities, actors, resources, interdependencies	identifying goals, ordering activities, assigning activities to actors, allocating resources, synchronizing activities
Group decision-making	goals, actors, alternatives, evaluations, choices	proposing alternatives, evaluating alternatives, making choices (e.g., by authority, consensus, or voting)
Communication	senders, receivers, messages, languages	establishing common languages, selecting receiver (routing), transporting message (delivering)
Perception of common objects	actors, objects	seeing same physical objects, accessing shared databases

Table 3. Processes underlying coordination.

Example : Selecting actors to perform activities

To see how this framework can be used to analyze coordination processes, let us consider the part of the activity assignment process that involves selecting which actors will perform which activities. For this example, we will analyze one particular method that can be used for this process: a competitive bidding scheme like that used in many kinds of markets. Our analysis will draw upon the version of this process formalized by Smith and Davis [Smit81] and extended by Malone ([Malo87b], [Malo88]).

In this scheme, a client first broadcasts an announcement message to all potential contractors. This message includes a description of the activity to be performed and the qualifications required of potential contractors. The potential contractors then use this information to decide whether to submit a bid on the action. If they decide to bid, their bid message includes a description of their qualifications and their availability for performing the action. The client uses these bid messages to decide which contractor should perform the activity and then sends an award message to notify the contractor that has been selected.

In this case, the decision to be made is which contractor will perform a specific action. The choice results from a multi-stage process in which contractors decide whether to propose themselves as alternatives (by submitting bids) and clients decide which contractor to select based on their evaluations of the contractors' bids. The actors communicate by exchanging messages, and we can regard these messages as including representations of common objects (such as activities and bids) which both senders and receivers can perceive.

Viewing the activity assignment process in this way, immediately suggests other possibilities for how it can be performed. For instance, an authority-based decision-making process might be used in which a manager simply assigns activities to people who have implicitly already agreed to accept such assignments. This view also suggests how computer tools could be used to support a bidding process for task assignments in human organizations (e.g., see [Malo87a], [Turo83]).

CONCLUSIONS

In this paper, we have argued that many different disciplines can contribute to our understanding of coordination and that a better understanding of coordination can help us build useful cooperative work tools. In order to support these claims, we have shown examples of interdisciplinary transfers of ideas about coordination that have already provided useful insights for cooperative work tools, and we have sketched out the beginnings of a framework that can facilitate such interdisciplinary transfers and lead to the development of new general theories about coordination.

Clearly there is much left to be done. We hope, however, that the perspective we have suggested here will help build tools that enable people to work together more effectively and more enjoyably.

ACKNOWLEDGEMENTS

This work was supported, in part, by Digital Equipment Corporation, the National Science Foundation (Grant Nos. IRI-8805798 and IRI-8903034), the MIT International Financial Services Research Center, and General Motors/Electronic Data Systems.

Parts of this paper were included in a previous working paper [Malo88] and in proposals submitted to the National Science Foundation. We are especially grateful to Deborah Ancona, John Carroll, Michael Cohen, Randall Davis, John Little, and Wanda Orlikowski for comments on earlier versions of the paper, and to participants in numerous seminars and workshops at which these ideas have been presented.

APPENDIX:
PREVIOUSLY SUGGESTED DEFINITIONS OF COORDINATION

"The operation of complex systems made up of components." [NSF89]

"The emergent behavior of collections of individuals whose actions are based on complex decision processes." [NSF89]

"Information processing within a system of communicating entities with distinct information states." [NSF89]

"The joint efforts of independent communicating actors towards mutually defined goals." [NSF89]

"Networks of human action and commitments that are enabled by computer and communications technologies." [NSF89]

"Composing purposeful actions into larger purposeful wholes." [Holt89]

"Activities required to maintain consistency within a work product or to manage dependencies within the workflow." [Curt89]

"The additional information processing performed when multiple, connected actors pursue goals that a single actor pursuing the same goals would not perform." [Malo88]

REFERENCES

[Amer81]   American Heritage Dictionary. Boston: Houghton Mifflin, 1981.

[Bali86]   Baligh, H. H. Decision rules and transactions, organizations and markets. *Management Science, 32*, 1480–1491, 1986.

[Bali81]   Baligh, H. H., Burton, R. M. Describing and designing organizational structures and processes. *International Journal of Policy Analysis and Information Systems, 5*, 251–266, 1981.

[Barn64]   Barnard, C. I. *The Functions of the Executive.* Cambridge, MA: Harvard University, 1964.

[Beer67]   Beer, S. *Cybernetics and Management* (2nd ed.). London: English Universities Press, 1967.

[Boul56]   Boulding, K. E. *The Image.* Ann Arbor, MI: University of Michigan, 1956.

[Cibo87]   Ciborra, C. U. Reframing the role of computers in organizations: The transaction costs approach. *Office Technology and People, 3*, 17-38, 1987.

[Conk88]   Conklin, J., Begeman, M. L. gIBIS: A hypertext tooling for exploratory policy discussion. In Tatar, D. (Ed.), *Proceedings of the 2nd Conference on Computer-supported Cooperative Work* (pp. 140–152). New York: ACM, 1988.

[Crow90]   Crowston, K. *Modeling Coordination in Organizations.* Ph.D. Dissertation, Sloan School of Management, Massachusetts Institute of Technology, Forthcoming (1990).

[Curt89]   Curtis, B. Modeling coordination from field experiments. In *Organizational Computing, Coordination and Collaboration: Theories and Technologies for Computer-Supported Work.* Austin, TX, 1989.

[Debr59]   Debreu, G. *Theory of value: An axiomatic analysis of economic equilibrium.* New York: Wiley, 1959.

[Emer69]   Emery, J. C. *Organizational Planning and Control Systems: Theory and Technology.* New York: MacMillan, 1969.

[Erma80]   Erman, L. D., Hayes-Roth, F., Lesser, V. R., Reddy, D. R. The HEARSAY-II speech understanding system: Integrating knowledge to resolve uncertainty. *Computing Surveys, 12*(2), 213–253, 1980.

[Flor88]   Flores, F., Graves, M., Hartfield, B., Winograd, T. Computer systems and the design of organizational interaction. *ACM Transactions on Office Information Systems, 6*(2), 153–172, 1988.

[Forr80]   Forrester, J. W. *Systems dynamics.* New York: North-Holland, 1980.

[Fox81]   Fox, M. S. An organizational view of distributed systems. *IEEE Transactions on Systems, Man and Cybernetics, 11*(1), 70–79, 1981.

[Galb73]   Galbraith, J. R. *Designing Complex Organizations.* Reading, MA: Addison-Wesley, 1973.

[Gard85]   Gardner, D. *The Mind's New Science: A History of the Cognitive Revolution.* New York: Basic, 1985.

[Hart90]   Hart, P. & Estrin, D. Inter-organization computer networks: Indications of shifts in interdependence. *Proceedings of the ACM Conference on Office Information Systems,* Cambridge, MA, April 25-27, 1990.

[Hewi86]   Hewitt, C. Offices are open systems. *ACM Transactions on Office Systems,* 4(3), 271–287, 1986.

[Holt89]   Holt, A. *Personal communication.,* 1989.

[Holt88]   Holt, A. W. Diplans: A new language for the study and implementation of coordination. *ACM Transactions on Office Information Systems,* 6(2), 109–125, 1988.

[Hube88]   Huberman, B. A. (Eds.). *The Ecology of Computation* . Amsterdam: North-Holland, 1988.

[Korn81]   Kornfeld, W. A., Hewitt, C. The scientific community metaphor. *IEEE Transactions on Systems, Man, and Cybernetics, SMC-11,* 24–33, 1981.

[Lai88]   Lai, K. Y., Malone, T., Yu, K.-C. Object Lens: A spreadsheet for cooperative work. *ACM Transactions on Office Information Systems,* (Oct), 1988.

[Lawr67]   Lawrence, P. R. & Lorsch, J. W. *Organization and Environment.* Boston: Graduate School of Business Adminsitration, Harvard University, 1967.

[Lee90a]   Lee, J. Sibyl: A qualitative decision management system. In Winston, P. (Ed.), *Artificial Intelligence at MIT: Expanding Frontiers* Cambridge, MA: MIT Press, 1990.

[Lee90b]   Lee, J., Malone, T. W. Partially Shared Views: A scheme for communicating among groups that use different type hierarchies. *ACM Transactions on Information Systems, 8,* 1-26, 1990.

[Malo87a]   Malone, T. W. Computer support for organizations: Towards an organizational science. In Carroll, J. (Ed.), *Interfacing Thought: Cognitive Aspects of Human Computer Interactions* Cambridge, MA: MIT Press, 1987.

[Malo87b]   Malone, T. W. Modeling coordination in organizations and markets. *Management Science, 33,* 1317–1332, 1987.

[Malo88a]   Malone, T. W. *What is coordination theory?* (Working paper #2051-88). Cambridge, MA: MIT Sloan School of Management, 1988.

[Malo90]   Malone, T. W. Organizing information processing systems: Parallels between organizations and computer systems. In Zachary, W., Robertson, S., Black, J. (Ed.), *Cognition, Computation, and Cooperation* (pp. 56–83). Norwood, NJ: Ablex, 1990.

[Malo87c]   Malone, T. W., Grant, K. R., Turbak, F. A., Brobst, S. A., Cohen, M. D. Intelligent information-sharing systems. *Communications of the ACM, 30,* 390–402, 1987.

[Malo88b]   Malone, T. W., Smith, S. A. Modeling the performance of organizational structures. *Operations Research, 36*(3), 421–436, 1988.

[McGr84]   McGrath, J. E. *Groups: Interaction and Performance.* Englewood Cliffs, NJ: Prentice-Hall, 1984.

[Mill88]   Miller, M. S., Drexler, K. E. Markets and computation: Agoric open systems. In Huberman, B. A. (Ed.), *The Ecology of Computation* (pp. 133–176). Amsterdam: North-Holland, 1988.

[Mins87]   Minsky, M. *The Society of the Mind.* New York: Simon and Schuster, 1987.

[Mint79]   Mintzberg, H. *The Structuring of Organizations.* Englewood Cliffs, NJ: Prentice-Hall, 1979.

[Nii86]   Nii, P. The blackboard model of problem solving. *The AI Magazine,* (Spring), 38–53, 1986.

[Norm80]   Norman, D. A. Twelve issues for cognitive science. *Cognitive Science, 4,* 1–32, 1980.

[NSF89]   NSF-IRIS. *A report by the NSF-IRIS Review Panel for Research on Coordination Theory and Technology.* Available from NSF Forms & Publications Unit, 1989.

[Pfef78]   Pfeffer, J. & Salancik, G. R. *The External Control of Organizations: A Resource Dependency Perspective.* New York: Harper & Row, 1978.

[Sche60]   Schelling, T. C. *Strategy of Conflict.* Cambridge: Harvard University Press, 1960.

[Sear75]   Searle, J. R. A taxonomy of illocutionary acts. In Gunderson, K. (Ed.), *Language, Mind and Knowledge* (pp. 344–369). Minneapolis, MN: University of Minnesota, 1975.

[Rock89]   Rockart, J. F. & Short, J. E. IT and the networked organization: Toward more effective management of interdependence. In M. S. Scott Morton (Ed.), *Management in the 1990s Research Program Final Report.* Cambridge, MA: Massachusetts Institute of Technology, 1989.

[Smit81]   Smith, R. G., Davis, R. Frameworks for cooperation in distributed problem solving. *IEEE Transactions on Systems, Man and Cybernetics, 11*(1), 61–70, 1981.

[Such87]   Suchman, L. A. *Plans and Situated Actions: The Problem of Human Machine Communication.* Cambridge: Cambridge University Press, 1987.

[Thom67]   Thompson, J. D. *Organizations in Action.* New York: McGraw-Hill, 1967.

[Turo83]   Turoff, M. *Information, value, and the internal marketplace* (Unpublished manuscript). New Jersey Institute of Technology, 1983.

[vonB50]   von Bertalanffy, L. The theory of open systems in physics and biology. *Science, 111,* 1950.

[Wien61]   Wiener, N. *Cybernetics: Or Control and Communication in the Animal and the Machine* (2nd ed.). Cambridge, MA: MIT Press, 1961.

[Will85]   Williamson, O. *The Economic Institutions of Capitalism.* New York: Free Press, 1985.

[Wino87]   Winograd, T. A language/action perspective on the design of cooperative work. *Human Computer Interaction, 3*, 3–30, 1987.

[Wino86]   Winograd, T., Flores, F. *Understanding computers and cognition: A new foundation for design.* Norwood, NJ: Ablex, 1986.

Chapter 3:
Design Methods

Chapter 3: Design Methods

The design of a new technology like groupware is an intervention into an ongoing world of activity. It alters people's practices and concerns. The design of groupware technology also leads to new work practices, which in turn create new design possibilities. Thus, it could be said that the methods used to design groupware enable interventions in the workplace. Which design methods enable effective interventions into people's day-to-day work?

This section presents methods for designing groupware systems. The papers cover design from three points of view: understanding the cognitive aspects of design activities, studying the interruptions in the ongoing activity of the workplace as a basis for design, and enhancing traditional design methods to address contextual and linguistic aspects of group work.

Each paper explores, in some way, the nature of participatory design (designing *with* users), a key groupware principle.

Background: A growing need for balanced designs

In early years, engineers designed general-purpose computing systems to address a wide variety of programming tasks. The systems were, in turn, used to design applications that usually satisfied the needs of individual users.

Typically, computer professionals developed applications based on the requests of end users. This traditional separation of responsibilities for designing and using computing solutions is becoming increasingly untenable, as evidenced by the increasing concern for understanding the needs of user groups as part of the software development process.

Early systems analysis and design practices developed software that automated routine and operational-level business transactions. Early designs structured software according to the form of the data; the activities, their triggers and data flows; and the functions of active elements. Supporting group work was never a consideration for those who practiced these early methods.

These methods were founded on two basic beliefs: that computers manipulate data, and that computer systems embody the process of decision making.

In contrast, groupware designs address the social as well as the technical aspects of people's work. In other words, a groupware designer considers both how people intend to work and how people will use technology in their work. The resulting designs address the social and technical dimensions of the users' work, how technology can be used in the work situations, the anticipated work problems, and how technology can be used to handle those problems.

Themes: Cognition, intervention, enhancement

Software designs are generated from the *assumptions* made about the users' work: what they expect the software to do, and how they intend to operate that software during their collaborative endeavors. Recent evidence has indicated, time and again, that correct assumptions can only come from first-hand experience of people's work. The user-centered design approach is seen today as the best method for acquiring this first-hand experience. Following are some themes within the general paradigm of user-centered design.

Design as cognition. Olson and Olson categorize traditional methods into technology-driven design, design by prescription, intuitive design, analogical design, and evolutionary design. They note that all these traditions lack a focus on users' needs and capabilities.

An alternative design process that centers on users suggests that we observe and analyze users at work, understand relevant theory about users to assist design activities, and iteratively validate the design through prototypes and mock-ups.

Olson and Olson use these techniques not only to build effective systems, but also to study their own design activities. In effect, they continually update their user-centered design approach as they practice it. This gives other groupware designers an insightful model for continually improving their own methods.

For example, we can look at design as a distributive cognition problem. From this viewpoint, design meetings are group phenomena that require artifacts and memory. Design-team activities can be categorized into coordinating activities, issue development and resolution, and role participation. Using this framework, Olson and Olson develop plots of design activities. These plots have potential for groupware designers as economical summaries of design events, baselines of current practice, and descriptions of the design process. The plots also point out where the issue identification and resolution process deserves conscious design and maintenance, and where particular artifacts are useful as design aids. As summaries of the users' work, plots embody groupware requirements.

Design as intervention. Flores et al. suggest that technology is the design of practices realized through artifacts. This view of technology sees computers encompassing the design of work practices, implying that the design process intervenes in the ongoing activity of the world. This implies that the design of information systems intimately affects everyone's life. Called "language/action," their theory treats language as something that creates. In other words, people use language to act together to create the world they live in. This use of language, embodied in the distinctions of requests, promises, declarations, and assertions, is extremely interesting for groupware designers, because of its contrast with the prevailing view that language is something for representing designs.

Using the language/action theory, Flores et al. demonstrate how computer tools are designed by always focusing on how people create action through their spoken words. The authors suggest first identifying "breakdowns" (circumstances that interrupt the normal course of events), then preparing "interventions" (activities that create new action in light of the current circumstances). For example, consider a group of people following a project plan. A breakdown could be a major schedule slip in that plan. An intervention could be a "what if" analysis of the slip and the actions required to get back on schedule. Application of this theory can be aided by using the computer to record, distribute, and restructure people's requests and promises, thereby using the computer as a coordination device. (Chapter 8 covers these software systems in more depth.)

Enhancing design methods. Marca asserts that traditional design methods embody an underlying assumption that effective software can be created by studying users from afar. These methods overlook the unique context of people's work: its history, its continual tendency to change, and the situations within which specific work happens. As an alternative, designing software by understanding the nuances and cooperative aspects of people's work is advocated. He suggests that this understanding can only be acquired by actually working with users. He then shows how to enhance traditional design methods so this direct understanding can be acquired and specified collaboratively *with* users.

Marca's paper describes how to combine several theories that include focusing on the users' work, participating in the redesign of the users' work, adopting a consistent viewpoint for the design, and generating questions whose answers help shape the design. This combination leads to an overall method where: *systems analysis* means doing the work, *interviews* happen when group members share their norms and work practices, *information* is left open to continuing reinterpretation, *design* is a collaboration between users and developers, and *verification and validation* involve rapid prototyping at the actual work site.

Futures: Participatory design becomes standard practice

User-centered design will continue to mature. We foresee a simplification of the process as well as a resolution of currently undefined issues, leading to parallel development of machine and human skills. In support of human skill growth, computer artifacts will include a variety of capabilities, each matching a particular skill level. New groupware methods will emerge in concert with the evolution of groupware tools and human skills.

Future design methods will recognize the value of subjectivity in the design process. Most importantly, they will emphasize relevance, suitability, and adequacy, three qualities that expand the current notion of usability. Groupware designers will gain deeper understandings of the phenomenon of designing computer artifacts. Working from a knowledge of how design methodologies have developed in mature fields such as architecture, they may develop theories that cover operational and substantive aspects of groupware design. Finally, since the design of groupware is collaborative in nature, expect the teaching of design to be done in a master-apprentice relationship.

User-Centered Design of Collaboration Technology

Gary M. Olson and Judith S. Olson
University of Michigan

Groupware, like other forms of information technology, should be designed with the users' needs and capabilities as the focus. User-centered system design consists of observation and analysis of users at work, assistance in design from relevant aspects of theory, and iterative testing with users. We illustrate the various stages of this approach with our development of groupware for software designers. We have extensive studies of designers at work, have developed the beginnings of a theory of distributed cognition, and are at the first stages of iterative testing and redesign of a prototype of a shared editor to support their work.

---

design,   collaboration,   software engineering,   cognition

INTRODUCTION

New information technologies, called *collaboration technologies,* are being developed to facilitate the work of groups. Since collaboration is both frequent and difficult, there is growing pressure to deploy these technologies in business, education, research, and government. Will these systems benefit collaboration? This is, of course, a familiar question for design in general: How can we build things that are useful and usable? There is an answer, at least an *approach to*

Our work on collaboration technology is supported by the National Science Foundation (Grant IRI-8902930), by Andersen Consulting, by Steelcase, Inc., and by Apple Computer. The work described in this article is from a highly collaborative project involving many participants, including Lola McGuffin, Elliot Soloway, Marty Sonntag, Brian Holtz, Dan O'Leary, Mark Carter, and Marianne Storrosten at Michigan; Libby Mack and Beth Lange at Andersen; Skip Ellis, Gail Rein, and Bill Curtis at MCC; and Allan MacLean, Victoria Bellotti, and Richard Young at Rank Xerox EuroPARC. This article was written during sabbatical leaves in Cambridge, England, and we are grateful to our hosts, Rank Xerox EuroPARC and the Applied Psychology Unit, for providing supportive environments. We also thank Allan MacLean, Libby Mack, Richard Young, and Gail Rein for critical readings of an early draft.

Correspondence and requests for reprints should be sent to Gary M. Olson, Cognitive Science and Machine Intelligence Laboratory, University of Michigan, 701 Tappan, Ann Arbor, MI 48109-1234.

design, that seems so right that it is startling when we find that it is so often ignored: Focus the design process from the outset on the users, what they need to do and what they can do.

As Norman [25] has shown for many design areas, however, this principle is honored more often in word than deed. Collaboration technologies seem to be no exception to this. In this article, we argue for design being driven by paramount consideration of what the users need to do and what the users can do, called *user-centered design*. We illustrate what we mean with material drawn from our research.

User-centered design is very difficult, which is part of the reason why it is often ignored. It is particularly difficult in the building of large, complex systems, where the designers and implementers are parts of organizationally complex teams. In these situations, it is often not clear when in the development process these user-centered activities should take place, how to conduct them, and whose responsibility it is.

In addition, using theory to aid our design of collaborative systems is also difficult. In the case of single-user systems, we have a knowledge base from cognitive psychology on which to draw for critiques of design possibilities. However, in designing collaboration technology, we have a much weaker knowledge base. We know much less about how collaborative activities work than we do about individual problem solving and cognition. But this also provides an opportunity. We believe that user-centered design of collaborative systems will generate not only good systems but also will advance our fundamental knowledge about how collaboration works.

APPROACHES TO THE DESIGN OF COLLABORATION TECHNOLOGY

As with the design of any technological system to support human needs, there are a variety of ways in which systems actually are designed. Some of the most common are listed below.

Technology-driven Design. Systems are built because the technology exists. Classical video conferencing is an instance of this. A technology was proposed before anyone understood fully what the problem was or what was the best way to solve it [9].

Rational Design. This is design by prescription. A system is built to change the way people behave, to a way that does not exist presently but is felt to be of value. The Coordinator [42], which requires senders of messages to declare the purpose of their message in formal terms, or the Activity Manager System [41], which provides a formal framework for routine office activities, are examples of this.

Intuitive Design. This is the most common kind of design. Here, a designer builds something because it seems intuitive that the new functionality provided by the system would be good. Electronic mail systems are examples of this approach. Clearly, intuition is right in that shipping material electronically from one location to the other is very functional. But, unfortunately, intuition does not serve well by itself in guiding the design of exactly what action should follow what in a dialog and what to call the actions (e.g., post, mail, or send). The intuitions of designers often do not match those of users [25].

Analogical Design. Systems are built to be very much like nonelectronic things that people presently use. Electronically editable whiteboards are examples of this [35]. They are designed to allow the same kinds of actions that people make on ordinary whiteboards, but then add new functionality related to storing, editing, and printing the material.

Evolutionary Design. These are systems that extend the capabilities of systems that people already use. An example would be Timbuktu on the Macintosh [13] or various shared window systems [19], which allow a group of users to share access to regular single-user applications. There is no guarantee that migrating from something that works will yield something new that also works. In particular, in the example mentioned, the shift from solo to group use of an application is a fundamental change, raising many issues, such as communication and coordination among users' work.

Any of the strategies just described can lead to excellent, useful systems. In particular, analogy-based designs and evolutionary designs start from something that makes sense to users, something familiar. However, even these strategies need to be carried out in a framework that stresses several additional points.

User-Centered Design

According to this strategy (described most completely in sources such as Refs. 16 and 26), design begins with detailed considerations of users' tasks and capabilities. Who are the potential users of a system? How varied are they? What is their current work like? Which aspects of their work are difficult? What are their needs? Answers to these questions are arrayed against technology opportunities; prototypes of systems are designed and evaluated with users before final designs are set. There are three key aspects to this design strategy: involving users, iterative design, and the role of theory about users.

Involving Users. There are many ways to carry out a user-centered design strategy. One method is to have users as active, coequal partners on the development team. This is a hallmark of the Scandinavian approach to user design [10, 14]. Probably a more common strategy is to have early and frequent user contact during the course of system design. Users are queried and interviewed. Initial designs are critiqued by them. Users' work practices are observed (e.g., with videotape records), both prior to the introduction of technology and during the iterative, prototyping stages of system development. This provides an objective record of what users do under these various circumstances, as well as information about the detail and timing of activities to supplement the reports from the users themselves. However, whatever the details of the strategy, the key feature is to have the needs of the ultimate users of the system as the focus of design. It is only too easy for the designers to believe, usually falsely, that their needs and preferences are representative of actual end users. Although designers are sometimes themselves the intended users, this case is rare.

Grudin [17] points out that the organizational complexities of collaborative systems makes the involvement of users trickier. Many collaborative systems have been designed according to the specifications and inputs from the managers of the ultimate users, not the users themselves. Managers rarely understand the details of the task and the interpersonal practices that affect the successful adoption of a collaborative system. It is not surprising that such applications often fail.

Electronic calendaring systems provide a cogent example. It is usually managers that advocate their design and use, and we do not argue with the value these systems may have for them. Electronic calendars for an entire group can be of great value for managers in calling meetings or in tracking individuals' progress. However, they may also have severe impacts on the way individuals work. Calendar systems require constant updating from the individuals and may instill feelings of invasion of privacy and loss of control. In short, there may be a complex pattern of costs and benefits across the users, who vary in their roles, organizational status, and work habits.

The role of theory. We also believe in theory-assisted design. By theory we mean primarily theory about users, either individually or collectively. We chose the term "assisted" very carefully. Even in the traditional engineering disciplines, design is rarely based on theory. Design is a generative process, and the starting point for design is seldom "first principles." Rather, design is evolutionary, analogical; it builds on other designs. Theory, however, provides a check, a filter against which designs can be evaluated.

In the design of computer systems, the design is assessed for how well it fits the user's theoretical perceptual, motor, and cognitive abilities. Designs are then altered when the theory indicates that the design makes excessive demands on the user's capabilities. In single-user systems, this strategy is quite sophisticated [31]. In collaborative systems, we know less about group processes, communication, and group problem solving, but still can use what we know about the cognitive capacities of the individuals who make up the group.

Iterative design. Iteration is another key aspect of user-centered design. As soon as possible, users are shown mock-ups or prototypes of systems. This means it must be possible to do rapid prototypes. For some systems, this can be done with paper-and-pencil or cardboard mock-ups on a first cut of the functionality. A running mock-up usually is produced, even with many functions incomplete or handled in a Wizard of Oz manner. The key is to get users using something like the intended system long before commitments are made to the functions and form of the final system.

User-Centered Design as an Approach to Research

Our work focuses on the design of technology to support group work. While we want to build good systems, we also want to use our system building activities as a way of contributing to the general knowledge base about how collaboration works. We feel these two goals fit together quite well. The interplay of systems with group behavior can make aspects of the group processes more explicit, offering the possibility of understanding better the nature of these processes.

There are several aspects to our research strategy. First, our *observational studies* of potential users allow us to:

> Analyze their current practice so we can identify opportunities for technology intervention, and

> Establish a baseline of current practice in order to assess the effects of introducing our new technologies.

In parallel with this, we ourselves use as many different current technologies as we can acquire to learn about both functionality and usability through firsthand experience. We do not feel we have to invent something entirely new, but rather can build on, refine, and integrate the good ideas of others.

Second, throughout the observation and generation of ideas regarding technological support, we are using *theory*, what we know about human capacities, to guide our thinking. We look for cases, for example, where known limits of human retention and perception are exceeded, for cases where communication fails because of limits in the speed with which people can process information, or for cases of misunderstanding because of limits in one's ability to generate a clear idea in someone else's framework. Put differently, we use theory to help us interpret failures and breakdowns that we observe, so that we generate possible technology solutions that are principled rather than ad hoc.

Third, as we build prototypes of technology for collaborative tasks, observing them in use provides an opportunity for *quasi-experimental assessment*. For example, we can build different versions of systems that vary on some critical feature, and watch different groups use them. Since we are studying real work groups in real workplaces, we cannot carry out traditional experiments in order to pin down exact causes and effects. However, with a large number of such groups available for possible observation, we ought to be able to acquire some systematic and general knowledge.

OUR CONCEPTUAL PERSPECTIVE

We come to our work with a particular perspective about how to look at the collaborative activities of our groups.

Focus on Cognition. We focus on the problem-solving activities involved in work. We realize that lots of other things happen during collaborations, pertaining to the interpersonal, social, and organizational aspects of our collaborators' lives. However, we feel that, at the present time, the kinds of collaboration technologies we can build are easiest to apply to the cognitive aspects of work. This does not mean that we ignore these other elements. As we build tools to aid the cognitive, problem-solving activities of their work, we may well affect these other aspects of their work. Thus, although we focus on cognition, we will monitor and assess these other elements.

Our work focuses on groups who are doing difficult cognitive tasks, such as designing computer systems. In such tasks, groups engage in the full spectrum of problem-solving activities, including stating the goal, ideating, structuring, evaluating, selecting, and implementing. In design tasks, the implementation phase is replaced by a specification phase: the essence of doing design is specifying what ought to be built, not actually building it. People carrying out difficult cognitive tasks, whether working as individuals or in groups, do not proceed through these various activities in an orderly fashion. But they generally do all of these activities at some point during their problem solving.

Cognition is Distributed. Cognitive activities, such as collaborative problem solving, are prime examples of the distribution of cognition across individual minds and their social, physical, and cultural environments [27]. The core idea of *distributed cognition* is that the processes and representations of the internal cognitive system are continuous with representations and processes in the external world. Or, put differently, cognition does not occur exclusively or principally in the mind. Cognition involves external artifacts, such as regularities in the natural world, information from other people in the social world, and tools in the designed world. Our cognition is essentially, not accidentally, distributed among elements of the social and physical world. It is no accident that we, the most cognitive of organisms, are also the most artifacted and most social.

Our core cognitive capabilities can be fully understood only if viewed as a blend of internal and external activities. Take the example of working memory. This is the immediately available store of information used during cognitive processing; its limited capacity is a classic example of a bottleneck. However, in most natural tasks, our functional working memory is a blend of internal and external storage. We do most arithmetic with paper and pencil, using algorithms that are a smooth blend of internal and external processing. Similarly, in reading, our functional working memory includes whatever can be apprehended within our momentary eye fixations.

Similarly, functional long-term memory is not internal traces of facts or procedures but indices to where this information is in the world. For example, I cannot remember my colleagues' phone numbers, so I write them down and tape them up next to the phone. These serve as part of my functional long-term store just as much as those few phone numbers I have committed to memory. At a more social level, rather than learn specific bodies of knowledge, I learn who knows various things and ask them when I need to know something from those domains.

We make extensive use of external *cognitive representations* in conceptualizing and understanding things. My interactions with the sketches, drawings, and models that I construct to help me understand something embody my understanding as much as anything that is in my mind. The symbol systems we construct to help us understand abstract domains such as mathematics and logic are effective because they are concrete, external representations that we can manipulate on paper and whiteboards. This externalization is essential to their power.

This view of cognition is critical to understanding the processes and structures of collaborative work. Collaboration proceeds through interaction with others, mediated by a variety of very interesting cognitive artifacts. In collaborative work, the components of a task are distributed among individuals, who use a range of social procedures to coordinate their work. The language and paralanguage of collaborative work are extremely interesting, as a number of investigators have pointed out already [36–38]. In addition, collaborators make extensive use of artifacts such as paper, whiteboards, and projected images [38]. These designed artifacts are critical for coordination, communication, information representation, storage, and retrieval—indeed, the whole range of core cognitive capabilities. Understanding their role is a key to carrying out user-centered design of collaboration technology.

OUR RESEARCH PROJECT

The relatively short-term, goal-driven collaborations that characterize task forces or ad hoc work groups [23, 32] are the principal focus of our research. There are several reasons for this. First, such groups constitute both a natural form of group activity and their study is methodologically tractable [23], making *in situ* research feasible. A representative work group has fewer than 10 members, and works on their task for a period of weeks or months. Many work groups last only as long as their task takes to complete. Second, their members are often organizationally and geographically dispersed, and represent several disciplines, meaning that problems of coordination, representation, and communication are central—problems that new collaboration technology might help solve. Third, they are organizationally interesting as well as important. Their effective use has been pointed to as a characteristic of organizations that work exceptionally well [32]. They constitute a key aspect of what have been referred to as "adhocracies" [1, 40], a more flexible form of organization that is contrasted with bureaucracies.

Another major aspect of our research is that we have chosen to focus on the group work involved in the early stages of system design and specification. Much software is designed collaboratively, and at least since Brooks [3], it has been widely recognized that there are large coordination costs in software design by teams. This seems like a rich domain for the investigation of collaboration technology. In addition, currently there are very few tools for this software development stage, even though it is widely recognized as both a difficult and

125

an extremely important stage in the software life cycle. Finally, our collaborative research team has extensive experience in either the study of software engineering as a human activity or its actual implementation.

Our project contains a number of major components. First, for all the above-mentioned reasons, we are carrying out observational studies of collaborative design. We will turn to this in greater detail in a moment, since it is this work that is the focus of the present article. Second, we are building experimental software tools, or groupware, that might support this work. In part, this work is based on our evaluations of existing experimental and commercial software systems, including groupware, and in part it is based on our observational work. We will briefly allude to some of this work later. Third, as these tools emerge, we will be carrying out systematic evaluations of their use by collaborators, including the very same ones whom we are studying in our initial observational work. Fourth, we are also exploring innovative physical environments, including rooms and furniture, for the support of collaboration. This latter work is described in more detail in Refs. 7, 8, 20, 28 and 29.

EMPIRICAL STUDIES OF DESIGN

The understanding of the work situations of our target population is critical to our user-centered design strategy. Thus, empirical studies of design constitute a major focus of our research at present. This work is being carried out in several settings. First, we are studying real-life design groups at Andersen Consulting. Initially, we have collected a number of tapes of design meetings that are part of ongoing projects. These thus constitute cross-sectional samples of design activity. In most of these cases, we have rich background information about the organizational status of the participants, the prior history and subsequent progress of the project, and the significance of the issues addressed in the meeting we taped. We focused on meetings because they are a particularly accessible component of collaboration, but we know that work important to the project goes on elsewhere. We also intend to collect longitudinal data in which we track a design project over time, with repeated video samples of interactions among the participants, periodic interviews with the participants, and a collection of copies of work materials.

A second source of empirical studies is a range of materials collected by the Software Technology Program at Microelectronic and Computer Technology Corporation (MCC). A number of these materials have been described in technical papers [6, 18, 33]. Some of these materials are tapes of design meetings very similar to the ones we are collecting at Andersen Consulting. Others come from various special-purpose studies carried out by investigators at MCC, such as an experimental study of the Nick Laboratory [6, 33].

Third, investigators at Rank Xerox EuroPARC have been collecting material of designers working on a specific design task given to them "in the zoo"[1],

[1] This phrase is attributed to Victoria Bellotti at EuroPARC.

meaning that they work under realistic but controlled circumstances in the laboratory (as contrasted with artificial circumstances of purely laboratory tasks or uncontrolled free behavior in the field). These materials are being collected as part of a project on the analysis and explication of Design Rationale [21]. We have examined in detail a videotape of two designers, who have a history of working together on system designs in a company, as they redesign a bank automatic teller machine (ATM).

There are three areas we could look at in characterizing the behavior of our design groups:

1. Coordination Activities. These have to do with the organization and coordination of group activity both during the course of a meeting and over the course of a project, including such activities as goal stating, agenda setting, history keeping, floor control, activity tracking, and project management.

2. Issue Development. The content of design discussions centers on issues, potential solutions, arguments for and against each solution, and resolutions, as well as how they relate to each other. These describe the details of the design as well as its evolution and justification. The process of design discussion follows fairly traditional stages of problem solving: stating the goal, ideating, structuring, evaluating, selecting, and implementing.

3. Roles and Participation. There are numerous organizational, social, and personality factors that affect group behavior. These are the traditional focus of much of social psychology. We feel it is important to track these factors as we study the impact of technology aids on group behavior, but they are not the focus of our design efforts.

In all of our work with these materials, we have two complementary goals. One is to characterize the nature of present practice, both so we understand the work of these teams and so we have a baseline against which we can characterize the effects of later interventions with collaboration technology. To achieve this goal, we need to monitor all three areas described earlier. The second goal—the one we focus on here—is to analyze present practice for opportunities for technology intervention. Since we are focusing on developing aids to support the problem-solving activities of our designers, we have focused our efforts on developing analysis schemes for the first two areas.

Given our views about distributed cognition, we feel it is essential to understand the *use of artifacts* in these activities. Most face-to-face interactions take advantage of such artifacts as words and graphics on paper, blackboards and whiteboards, viewgraphs and slides, and, increasingly, computer-based displays. These artifacts serve a variety of purposes, including the coordination of activities (e.g., a printed agenda or minutes) or the development of issues (e.g., a picture of a system design or a list of features of a design). Analysis schemes that illuminate how such artifacts are used are critical to our development of new software-based artifacts. We need to understand both how existing artifacts are used and how our new artifacts will be used. Of course, many current artifacts are quite limited, and thus we do not want to be misled into thinking that a narrow evolutionary approach based on current artifacts is the only design strategy. This is why it is necessary to analyze current practice within some type of explicit framework, where design features for totally novel artifacts might emerge.

In the following sections, we describe briefly our progress in assessing these activities in early design tasks.

STREAMS OF ACTIVITY DURING DESIGN MEETINGS

One important goal of our observational work is to characterize the general overall flow of activities in representative design meetings. We have developed a graphical description of this, which we call a *meeting plot*. Figures 1–3 show a series of examples from an array of different kinds of meetings. In these plots, the x axis is time, and the y axis is various classes of activities. For example, in all of the plots, we classify the activities associated with forming or understanding the *goal*, with tracking progress from meeting to meeting and making assignments (called *project management* in these plots), and setting and keeping to the *agenda*. In the center—the grayed band—we enumerate the major topics of the meeting, using a different set for each of the plots. In addition, we code time spent in *digressions* such as joke-telling or side conversations, and the use of specific visual aids such as flip charts or whiteboards. The running solid line in these plots shows what kind of activity was occurring during each moment. These graphs provide an economical description of the stream of activity in these sessions.

Figure 1 shows a meeting plot for one of the design meetings at Andersen Consulting. In this meeting, seven designers are discussing how to redesign a particular large system that had recently become overloaded. They discuss how to move pieces of the software from a mainframe to PCs that are networked to it. Each participant brings his or her home group's perspective on this particular task, noting both what problems might be encountered in the process of off loading functions to the PCs, and who has the skill and time to take on this extra work. The first half of the meeting involves generating the aspects of the problem, and the second half reviews how to staff the exploration of these issues and the actual work. At the very end, they discuss a second overall solution to the problem of overload, but quickly dismiss it to proceed with assignment of people to the current plan. They use a whiteboard heavily to keep track of the various issues and to note who agrees to take on the work.

Figure 2 shows three one-hour design meetings of a group of seven designers at MCC who were asked to develop a conceptual framework for a large software development project that integrated four important research areas. The conceptual framework had to describe the concepts of each research area and the interdependencies between them. One interesting thing about this set of plots is that the first meeting involved a great deal of time understanding the goal (e.g., understanding what was to go into this conceptual framework), the first and

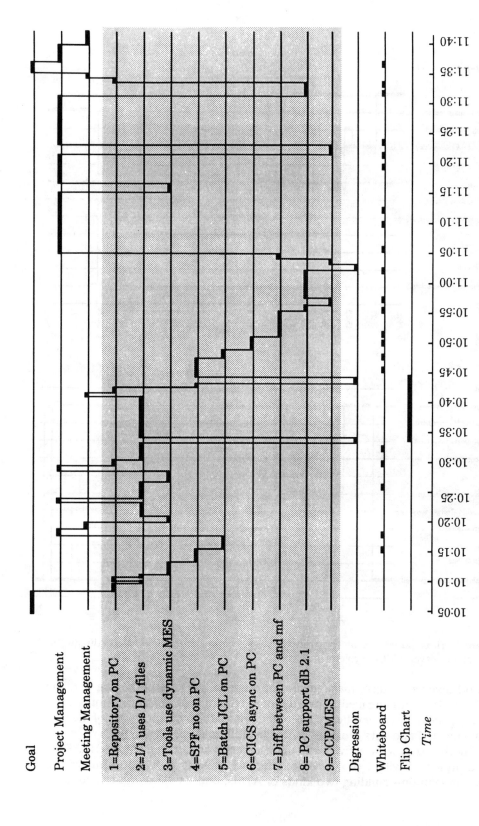

Figure 1. Meeting at Andersen in which they consider the problems involved in moving functions from the mainframe to the PC environment.

129

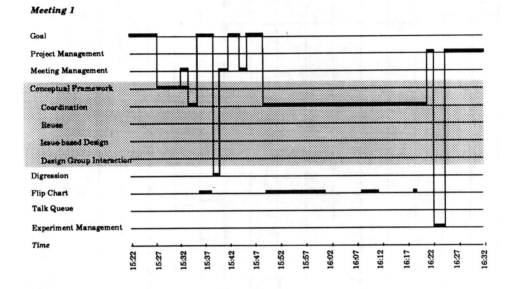

Meeting 1

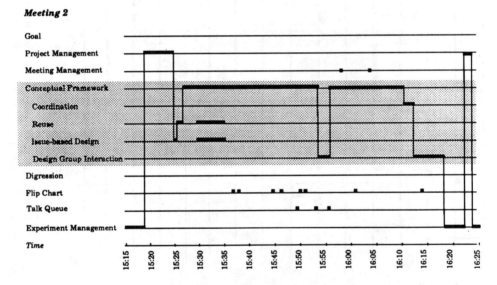

Meeting 2

Figure 2. Three successive meetings in which a group explores how to coordinate the missions of several MCC projects.

second involved project management appropriately at the beginning and the end, and the third engaged in project management only at the beginning (also appropriately). There was heavy use of the flip charts in keeping track of ideas as they emerged and lists of issues yet to be addressed.

Figure 3 shows the activity of two designers working on a bank ATM. They were presented with a problem—long queues at existing ATMs'—and with a possible solution—building two kinds of ATMs, one standard and one for cash

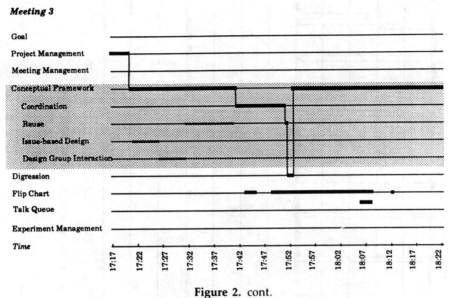

Figure 2. cont.

withdrawals only (a fast ATM). They were asked to review this design, and were encouraged to come up with an alternative one if they wished. They did, in fact, develop a design that combined the idea of a regular and a fast ATM into one machine that would have different modes. In this meeting, the designers immediately begin to critique the two designs without discussing among themselves how to go about this whole task (there was no goal understanding and agenda setting until 4–5 minutes into the meeting). Most of the time was spent designing new features, some of which were foreshadowed in the discussion of advantages and disadvantages of the previous designs. Only at the end of the meeting did they discuss the constraints that were implied in the problem statement, pushing the design space that they had worked in for the majority of their time. Similar to the meeting in Figure 1, they returned to the solution they had spent most of their time on and concluded with a summary of that design. They used a printing whiteboard extensively, both taking notes as they went and referring back to previously noted ideas.

These three examples illustrate the use of meeting plots. We find them useful for at least three reasons. First, they provide an economical summary of what are very complex events. In one compact drawing, one gets a good impression of what happened in a design session. If these were implemented so that they could be produced on line, these plots could even serve as an excellent graphical index to either the original video record of the meeting or to a transcript. Second, they constitute a potentially useful datum in constructing a baseline account of current practice. We plan to do studies in which we explore the sensitivity of various features of these plots to interventions in the activities of our designers. Third, in conjunction with the issue representations described in the next section, they provide a clear framework for the description and

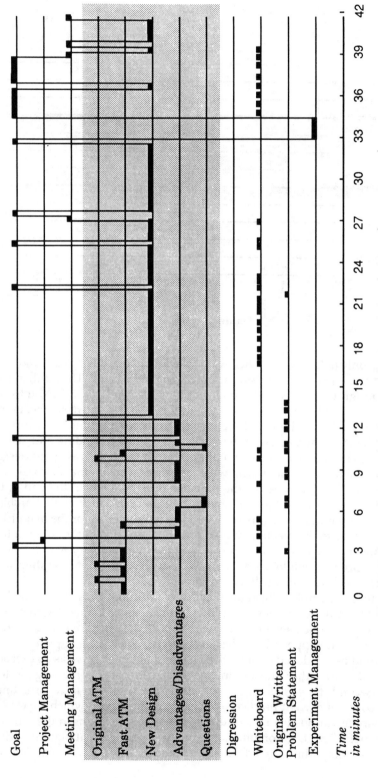

Figure 3. Meeting of a pair of designers evaluating existing designs of an automated transaction machine (ATM) and designing a new one.

analysis of the process of design, the aspect of design activity that we are most interested in supporting with collaboration technology.

ISSUE DEVELOPMENT

The task of collaborative designers during the early stages of their work is to achieve some consensus on the general characteristics of a new target system. This usually involves generating a number of design options, and discussing many specific issues raised by these possibilities. A major problem in group design as it is done now is keeping track of the fragments of design alternatives raised, and tracking the progress of the discussion on the various issues opened. These are complex information management tasks, and current procedures and artifacts do not work well.

We are exploring several ways of representing how design issues develop in current practice. One is closely related to our meeting plots in that it tracks various activities over time. In these plots, however, we trace the development of a specific design issue over the course of a design session (or over multiple sessions in a longitudinal study). We illustrate this for the design session shown in Figure 3. In the course of that design session, a number of general and specific design issues are discussed. Figure 4 shows the temporal evolution of three issues, one very general and two very specific.

Figure 4a shows the history of one of the most general design issues, namely, whether to develop a fast ATM capability by using one machine with different modes or to develop two separate machines. The design they are given to critique involves two separate machines, whereas their final design is based on one machine. As in the meeting plots, the x axis is time. The y axis lists standard problem-solving stages adapted to fit the major activities encountered in design. The highest level is a *statement* of the design issue itself. Under this are specific *positions* on this issue, and *evaluations* of these positions. There are potentially many positions, and in more complex designs a large number might be considered. In the examples shown here, usually only two are considered. The next line is the act of *selecting* a position on this issue. Below it is a line to cover the *detailed design* activities that follow the selection of a design alternative. For a general decision such as one versus two machines, much specific activity follows the selection of an alternative. This consists of generating details of the top-level design and raising many new specific design issues for various details of the design. Finally, the last line is *evaluation* of the detailed design.

The three issues shown in Figure 4 reveal an interesting array of patterns. Not surprisingly, the top-level issue is discussed throughout much of the session. More interesting are the specific issues shown in panels 4b and 4c. These represent detailed aspects of the final design about which there was some discussion of alternatives. In panel 4b, the issue is how to present the receipt to the user of the ATM machine. In the initial design that they are given to critique, one machine, the regular ATM, presents the receipt in a slot and the money in a

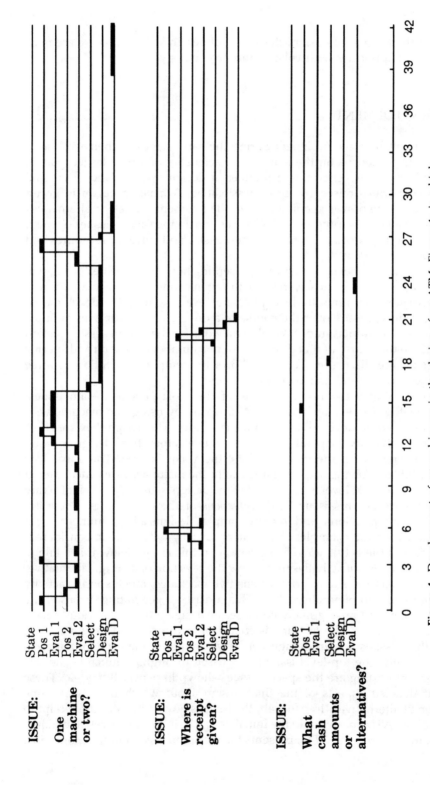

Figure 4. Development of several issues in the design of an ATM. Figure 4a is a high-level view of the major design issue, that of whether there should be one machine or two. Figures 4b and 4c show the development of two subissues, both of them more detailed issues in the overall design of an ATM.

drawer; in the other machine, a fast ATM, it presents both in the drawer. One of them notices this, and the other writes it down:

Pause

00:05:44

Denis: Ah, I'll tell you what I do like though is this "cash and receipt from drawer." Taking both from the same place is quite a good idea. You know, in the top one it says "take cash from drawer and receipt from slot." This is indeed something that you have to do.

John writes down "cash and receipt from same place" in the Advantages column.

Later, when they are working on the design of their own ATM, they appear to retrieve this earlier design decision directly. They briefly reconsider the possible reasons for the alternative of having it in a slot.

Pause

00:19:05

Denis: Right, so select . . . cash amount.

John labels his diagram with "select cash amount →" with the arrow pointing at it.

Denis: Remove card; you've got to remove the card before you take the cash, because otherwise people forget taking their card.

John: Whereas they might not forget the cash.

John writes "Remove card" on the board.

Denis: (laughing) They probably won't, yes. That's why the card always comes out, I think. It doesn't on all of them, but on most of them it does.

John writes "Remove cash" on the board.

Denis: ". . . and receipt from drawer . . ."

John adds "and receipt from drawer."

Denis: We've got to be absolutely clear about having the receipt in the drawer. Again that might be difficult . . . if possible I suppose, because if their ATMs already bung it out through a slot, it might be difficult to do it another way. . .and if you bung it in the drawer for other things, like when you're doing a transfer, then no one's going to remember to take it out of the drawer.

In panel 4c, the issue is what specific cash amounts to offer as alternatives to users of their newly designed ATM machine when it is in its fast cash mode. Again, they consider a specific design alternative in the course of discussing the initial design. One of them sketches a design idea on the back of a sheet of paper, using the cash alternatives 10, 20, 30, 40 and 50 pounds. Later, in the course of doing their own design, they take something very close to this and just assert it as part of their design. Only much later, after finishing their design, do they evaluate their idea in more depth:

Pause

00:22:50

John: Is there any way we can improve on preset amounts?

Denis: No, well . . . I don't think so, I mean that's the easiest way . . . I mean as to deciding which was the best piece out of that . . . I'm not sure whether you need that many. It would depend, you could just do a survey though. Couldn't you just sort of attach something from the inside which just looked at what most people mostly chose. In fact that's probably what they've already done.

John: Yes.

Denis: Trying to decide which were the most common ones. They probably are twenty and fifty are the most common ones. In fact that would probably do, almost. Just a big red button and a big blue button.

John writes "4. Survey most common cash withdrawals."

Denis: Especially since people tend to fit in.

John: That's right, I mean if you've got ten, twenty, fifty, and a hundred this covers the spectrum doesn't it?

Denis: That's it.

John: A fiver maybe, for people like me (laughs).

Denis: Yes . . . Well no they wouldn't like that because . . . I suppose yes actually it's best to let people draw very small amounts, because you keep it in the bank. Unless they're overdrawn, in which case, let them take out as much as they want (laughs).

These examples are illustrative of the treatment of issues during a design session. Issues are raised, discussed, decided upon, and evaluated in bits and pieces throughout a session. An overriding issue such as one machine versus two comes up again and again, as one might expect. But even little issues— details of a design—are treated in a temporally fragmented way. In this case, the entire session lasts only a little more than 40 minutes, and the two designers keep notes on the whiteboard and on paper. However, in the more complex designs materials that we have from Andersen Consulting and MCC, where designs are worked on over many multiple-hour sessions, many issues and ideas are raised and lost.

How can one keep track of design ideas? One proposal is the IBIS representation scheme developed by Rittal and Kunz [34] and used in the graphical hypertext system gIBIS [5]. Figure 5 shows the general IBIS scheme, with the notation including *issues* (connected to other issues), their alternative proposed *positions*, and the *arguments* for or against each position. A network of relationships grows because other issues arise as generalizations or specializations of earlier issues. Another form of representation is the Design Rationale framework [21]. Adapting one of these schemes to capture the swift activity and to accommodate the peculiarities of real-time interactions among designers may be one way technology could support the content of group design.

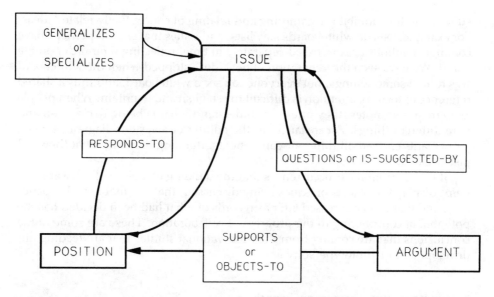

Figure 5. Schematic of the elements in an Issue-Based Information System (IBIS) which makes explicit the various issues, arguments, and decisions as a design develops.

THE USE OF ARTIFACTS

Designers working both alone and in groups make extensive and varied use of artifacts [2, 24, 37, 38]. This is the essence of distributed cognition: people have developed ways of extending their limited personal capabilities through judicious use of paper, books, whiteboards, flip charts, other people, etc. Also, we have seen in our tapes that people often use gestures to convey ideas about a design, to refer to past ideas in a brief way, to indicate aspects of agreement, and to seize or relinquish the floor. Thus, understanding how designers currently use artifacts and gestures, and how this relates to their shared knowledge assumptions, is a key aspect of user-centered design.

Our high-level meeting plots record when various physical artifacts are used, but do not indicate which topic is being addressed at the time (e.g., the agenda item being ticked off or the assignment of a person to do some work) nor the way in which it is being used (to clarify a point or to refer to a point made earlier). Our analysis of the use of artifacts will take the form suggested by both Tang and Bly: each use of an artifact will be coded by whether it is expressing a new idea, emphasizing or clarifying an existing idea, storing information for later use (such as a visual reminder of some action to be taken later), or referring to an idea presented earlier. Once again, we will take the idea of a meeting plot and extend it to note the uses and limits of artifacts as they relate to other aspects of the meeting and how they are used over time.

In our informal observations of our taped meetings, we have already seen serious limits in the use of artifacts, some limits we believe can be overcome by the judicious use of technology. We have seen that current artifacts are not easily edited, and thus inhibit the gathering and relating of conceptually related ideas. For example, lists on whiteboards stay lists, and issues that should perhaps have common solutions are discussed separately in time, reflecting their order on the board. We have seen the generation of new ideas stopped when the whiteboard was full. In some settings, not everyone can see a whiteboard, and thus a shared reference or focus of attention is difficult to establish and maintain. When people keep their own notes, they often misunderstand what is being decided on and note different things. For instance, in the editing of a system diagram, several participants crossed off different components, thinking that was what they had just decided.

It is clear from these occurrences that the building of a piece of software that helps display the objects or issues being discussed, that is editable and expandable, and that can be accessed later as records of what had been decided has the potential of contributing to the progress of collaboration. These are some of the conclusions that are coming from the observational studies that are feeding our development of prototype software.

TOWARD USER-CENTERED DESIGN OF COLLABORATION TECHNOLOGY

The extensive observational work we are conducting is helping us implement user-centered design of collaboration technology. We have been analyzing the cognitive processing that occurs in these design meetings for insights as to where technology might play a useful role. One promising line has been to use categories such as those that appear on the y axes of the meeting plots and the issue plots (Figures 1–4), and analyze them according to the following scheme:

The goal: What is the purpose of this activity?

How should the activity be done, ideally?

What potential problems are there with doing it the way it is typically done?

How do current technologies or processes support this activity?

What are the limits to these?

What are the requirements for new aids?

How can information technology meet these requirements?

What costs might be incurred by new technology aids?

What special characteristics of our specific domain, early software design, must be taken into account?

What are the potential differences from groups with various natures and size?

The complete analysis is far too complicated to explicate here. But this framework is a principled way of sorting out what currently works well in collaborations and what does not. The kinds of difficulties in the use of artifacts previously described suggest some possible technology aids. From observations such as these, we concluded that one candidate technology to assist these kinds of groups would be a shared workspace, where all collaborators could have easy access to a single information object for purposes of viewing it or changing it. The information object itself might be anything, such as text, structured drawings, a spreadsheet, a multimedia document, a hypertext structure—whatever the collaborators need. However, the kinds of new functionalities our collaborators might find useful would include such things as:

A single information object in the workspace

No constraint on size or complexity

Easy editing

An ability to construct a variety of useful views of the object

Both shared and private views

It is of course more complex than this. Once you open the design space for a system with a shared workspace, lots of details need to be filled in about what kinds of functions and what kinds of interface features would produce a useful tool. Furthermore, these design questions might have somewhat different answers, depending on the kinds of objects in the shared workspace. This is where iterative design is critical.

A number of other designers have felt that a shared, electronically editable workspace would be useful for collaborators. A few examples are Cognoter [15], GROVE [12], the Capture Lab [22], Diamond/Slate's mmconf [39], and shared windowing systems [17]. Similarly, commercial products such as Timbuktu on the Macintosh allow a group to share an application. In all of these cases, a number of functions have been implemented, but each design offers a slightly different constellation. In most of these cases, the features of these systems are based on the designer's intuitions rather than on a user-centered observational base. This has helped to surface many issues about what functions might be useful and how to present them to users, but iterative design with users will be needed to sort out what is useful.

Members of our project have used most of the existing shared workspace systems, some of them at great length. This type of informal "user" testing is a useful step in understanding the issues in building such systems. However, in most cases, these systems are unavailable or are no longer under development. Thus, another aspect of our research is to build an experimental platform on which we can begin the process of iteratively designing a shared workspace that might help our collaborators. We call this project ShrEdit, for shared editor [4]. Currently, we are settling some computer science infrastructure issues, so we have a platform on which we can build prototypes of tools that may help our collaborators. Consistent with our user-centered design strategy, what prototypes to build and how they are modified subsequently will be guided by our analyses of the work of our designers and their experiences with our emerging prototypes.

CONCLUSIONS

We have stressed the need to pursue a user-centered design strategy in building collaboration technology, and have illustrated our approach through work in progress. It is clearly much easier, and often much more satisfying in the short run, to plunge into new, exciting technologies and build systems that seem like they ought to be useful to someone. The path we advocate, namely, understanding the needs of users and using iterative design strategies to evolve the technology tools, is much more tedious. The range of unknown issues in this area is far too great, all the way from how to craft interfaces for collaborative systems [11, 27] to the social and organizational issues involved in the acceptance of such systems [17]. But it strikes us as the best way to develop technologies and to develop the kind of fundamental understanding of group work that will contribute to design of many technologies and processes in the future.

REFERENCES

1. Bennis, W.G. The temporary society. In *The Temporary Society*, W.G. Bennis and P.E. Slater (Eds). Harper & Row, New York, 1968
2. Bly, S.A. A use of drawing surfaces in different collaborative settings. In *Proceedings of the Conference on Computer-Supported Cooperative Work*. Portland, Or., 1988, 250–256.
3. Brooks, F.P., Jr., *The Mythical Man Month: Essays on Software Engineering*. Addison-Wesley, Reading, Mass., 1975.
4. *Cognitive Science and Machine Intelligence Laboratory, ShrEdit, A Multi-user Shared Text Editor: Users Manual*. University of Michigan, 1989.
5. Conklin, J., and Begeman, M.L. gIBIS: A hypertext tool for exploratory policy discussion. In *Proceedings of the Conference on Computer-Supported Cooperative Work*. Portland, Ore., 1988, 140–152.
6. Cook, P., Ellis, C., Graf, M., Rein, G., and Smith, T. Project Nick: Meetings augmentation and analysis. *ACM Trans. on Office Info. Syst. 5*, 2 (1987), 132–146.
7. Cornell, P., and Luchetti, R. Ergonomic and environmental aspects of computer supported cooperative work. In *Proceedings of the 1989 Annual Meeting of the Human Factors Society*. Denver, Colo., 1989.
8. Cornell, P., Mack, L.A., Luchetti, R., and Olson, G.M. CSCW anecdotes and directions. In *Proceedings of the 1989 Annual Meeting of the Human Factors Society*. Denver, Colo., 1989.
9. Egido, C. Video conferencing as a technology to support group work: A review of its failures. In *Proceedings of the Conference on Computer-Supported Cooperative Work*. Portland, Ore., 1988, 13–24.
10. Ehn, P. *Work-oriented Design of Computer Artifacts*. Arbetslivscentrum, Stockholm, 1988.
11. Ellis, C.A., Gibbs, S.J., and Rein, G.L. Groupware: The research and development issues. Tech. Report STP 414-88. Microelectronics and Computer Technology Corp. Austin, Tex., 1988.
12. Ellis, C., Gibbs, S.J., and Rein, G.L. Design and use of a group editor. MCC Technical Report STP-263-88, 1988.
13. Farallon Computing, Timbuktu: The next best thing to being there. 1987.
14. Floyd, C. Alternative software design and development in Scandinavia. *Human-Computer Interaction* (in press).
15. Foster, G., and Stefik, M. Cognoter: Theory and practice of a Collaborative tool. In *Proceedings of the Conference on Computer-Supported Cooperative Work*. Austin, Tex., 1986, 7–15.
16. Gould, J.D., Boies, S.J., Levy, S., Richards, J.T., and Schoonard, J. The 1984 Olympic message System—A test of behavioral principles of system design. *Commun. ACM 30*, 9 (1987), 758–769.
17. Grudin, J. Why CSCW applications fail: Problems in the design and evaluation of organizational

interfaces. In *Proceedings of the Conference on Computer-Supported Cooperative Work.* Portland, Ore., 1988, 85–93.

18. Jarvenpaa, S.L., Rao, V.S., and Huber, G.P. Computer support for meetings of groups working on unstructured problems: A field experiment. *MIS Q.* (1988), 645–666.

19. Lantz, K.A. An experiment in integrated multimedia conferencing. In *Proceedings of the Conference on Computer-Supported Cooperative Work.* Austin, Tex., 1986, 267–275.

20. Mack, L.A. Technology for computer-supported meetings. In *Proceedings of the 1989 Annual Meeting of the Human Factors Society.* Denver, Colo., 1989.

21. MacLean, A., Young, R.M., and Moran, T.P. Design rationale: The argument behind the artifact. In *Proceedings of CHI'89, Human Factors in Computing Systems.* 1989, 247–252.

22. Mantei, M. Capturing the Capture Lab concepts: A case study in the design of computer-supported meeting environments. In *Proceedings of the Conference on Computer-Supported Cooperative Work.* Portland, Ore., 1988, 257–270.

23. McGrath, J.E. *Groups: Interaction and Performance.* Prentice-Hall, Englewood Cliffs, N.J., 1984.

24. Minneman, S.L., and Bly, S.A. Experiences in the development of a multi-user drawing tool. Xerox PARC Technical Report, SSL 89-00089, 1989.

25. Norman, D.A. *The Psychology of Everyday Things.* Basic Books, New York, 1988.

26. Norman, D.A., and Draper, S.W. *User Centered System Design.* Lawrence Erlbaum Assoc., Hillsdale, N.J., 1986.

27. Olson, G.M. Distributed Cognition (in preparation).

28. Olson, G.M., Olson, J.S., McGuffin, L., Mack, L.A., Cornell, P., and Luchetti, R. Designing flexible facilities for the support of collaboration. In *Computer Augmented Teamwork: A Guided Tour,* G.R. Wagner (Ed.)., Van Nostrand Reinhold (in press).

29. Olson, G.M. The Nature of Group Work. In *Proceedings of the 1989 Annual Meeting of the Human Factors Society.* Denver, Colo., 1989.

30. Olson, J.S., and Olson, G.M. The growth of cognitive modeling since GOMS. *Human Computer Interaction 5,* 1990, 221–265.

31. Olson, J.S., Olson, G.M., Mack, L.A., and Wellner, P. Concurrent editing: The group's interface. In *Proceedings of INTERACT '90.* Cambridge, England, 1990.

32. Peters, T.J., and Waterman, R.H., Jr. *In Search of Excellence: Lessons from America's Best-Run Companies.* Harper & Row, New York, 1982.

33. Rein, G.L., and Ellis, C. The Nick experiments reinterpreted: Implications for developers and evaluators of groupware. *Office: Technology and People,* 1989.

34. Rittal, H., and Kunz, W. Issues as elements of information systems. Working paper #131. Institut fur Grundlagen der planug I.A., University of Stuttgart, 1970.

35. Stefik, M., Foster, G., Bobrow, D., Kahn, K., Lanning, S., and Suchman, L. Beyond the chalkboard: Computer support for collaboration and problem solving in meetings. *Commun. Assoc. Comput. Machin., 30,* 1 (1987), 32–47.

36. Suchman, L.A., *Plans and Situated Actions: The Problem of Human Machine Communication.* Cambridge University Press, Cambridge, England, 1987.

37. Tang, J.C., and Leifer, L.J. A framework for understanding the workspace activity for design teams. In *Proceedings of the Conference on Computer-Supported Cooperative Work.* Portland, Ore., 1988, 244–249.

38. Tang, J.C. Listing, drawing, and gesturing in design: A study of the use of shared workspaces by design teams. Xerox PARC Technical Report SSL-89-3, 1989.

39. Thomas, R.H., Forsdick, H.C., Crowley, T.R., Schaaf, R.W., Tomlinson, R.S., Travers, V.M., and Robertson, G.G. Diamond: A multimedia message system build on a distributed architecture. *IEEE Computer 18,* 2 (1985), 65–78.

40. Toffler, A. *The Third Wave.* Morrow, New York, 1980.

41. Tueni, J. Knowledge based office automation and CSCW. In *Proceedings of the First European Conference on Computer Supported Cooperative Work.* London, UK, 1989, 317–330.

42. Winograd, T. A language/action perspective on the design of cooperative work. *Human Computer Interaction 3,* 1 (1988), 3–30.

Computer Systems and the Design of Organizational Interaction

FERNANDO FLORES

Action Technologies

MICHAEL GRAVES

Logonet, Inc.

BRAD HARTFIELD and TERRY WINOGRAD

Stanford University

"Computer Systems and the Design of Organizational Interaction" by F. Flores, M. Graves, B. Hartfield, and T. Winograd, from *ACM Transactions on Office Information Systems*, April 1988, pages 153-172. Copyright © 1988, Association for Computing Machinery, Inc., reprinted with permission.

The goal of this paper is to relate theory to invention and application in the design of systems for organizational communication and management. We propose and illustrate a theory of design, technology, and action that we believe has been missing in the mainstream of work on office systems. At the center of our thinking is a theory of language as social action, which differs from the generally taken-for-granted understandings of what goes on in an organization. This approach has been presented elsewhere, and our aim here is to examine its practical implications and assess its effectiveness in the design of The Coordinator, a workgroup productivity system that is in widespread commercial use on personal computers.

Categories and Subject Descriptors: H.4.1 [**Information Systems Applications**]: Office Automation; H.4.3 [**Information Systems Application**]: Communications Applications—*electronic mail*

General Terms: Design, Human Factors, Management

Additional Key Words and Phrases: Conversation, coordination, language/action, ontology, speech act, The Coordinator

1. INTRODUCTION

In using the word "technology" people are generally concerned with artifacts—with things they design, build, and use. But in our interpretation, technology is not the design of physical things. It is the design of practices and possibilities to be realized through artifacts. Computer technology involves machines, but that is not what is ultimately significant. It encompasses the design of new practices (including those of word processing, electronic communication, printing, accounting, and the like), and beyond that it opens the possibility for new realms of practice.

Authors' addresses: F. Flores, Action Technologies, 2200 Powell St., Emeryville, CA 94608; M. Graves, Logonet, Inc., 2200 Powell St., Emeryville, CA 94608; B. Hartfield, 2096 Yale St., Palo Alto, CA 94304; T. Winograd, Department of Computer Science, Stanford University, Stanford, CA 94305.

Computer technology can change what it means to manage and to act in an organization. In fact, such a change is happening and is going to happen regardless of what the designers think they are doing. When we accept the fact that computer technology will radically change management and the nature of office work, we can move toward designing that change as an improvement in organizational life.

At one level this is a paper about a particular system designed to provide computer support for communication in organizations. At another level, it is about the design of computer systems in general, and beyond that about the nature of the design process and its relation to theory. We argue that careful, conscious theorizing at a foundational level should precede design and can increase the likelihood of its effectiveness. We begin by expanding on what we mean by "theory."

2. THEORY AND DESIGN

The design of new technology is always an intervention into an ongoing world of activity. It alters what is already going on—the everyday practices and concerns of a community of people—and leads to a resettling into new practices, which in turn create new future design possibilities.

The designer is someone who steps back from what is already going on to create an intervention. In doing this he or she applies, implicitly or explicitly, a background orientation toward the activity in which the technology is to be employed. This orientation may rest on taken-for-granted conventional wisdom or may emerge from an explicit theoretical articulation of what it is that is going to be facilitated. For example, the design of a tool for communication and management in an organization will embody an orientation toward action and the management of action. As one possibility, the designer may assume that the relevant activity can be characterized as the generation and movement of objects (papers, reports, products, etc.) through some space (the office or a network of offices and receiving and dispatching points).

One can increase the coherence of a design by developing a theoretical "ontology," which lays out basic dimensions and distinctions. In saying that this explication is theoretical we are not attributing to it a predictive structure like that of mathematical theories of physics. What we mean is that it clarifies the preunderstanding of what kinds of things exist, what kinds of properties they can have, and what kinds of events and relationships they can enter into. The "objects," "forces," "velocities," and the like of Newtonian physics provide this kind of basis for the more quantitative aspects of the theory.

A theory, as an ontology, is a set of key distinctions for observing, participating, and designing. It is (to use a metaphor) the eyes with which we see what is going on. For example, one distinction in our common sense ontology of organizations is that of "messages" that people send to one another. As observers in this ontology we see messages going back and forth; as participants, we send and receive messages; and as designers we may design systems for facilitating message composition and transmission. But "messages" is only one possibility for constituting ourselves as observers, participants, and designers. We might, as theorizers, offer other interpretations of what is happening on the basis of other key distinctions, such as those of shared tasks and goals or of speech acts.

Every theory or every ontology of distinctions will allow us to make some observations, actions, and designs and prevent us from making others. Designers who work with "messages" can devise systems for making the preparation and passing of messages more efficient. But the possibilities are also limited by this ontology—they cannot escape designing something to do with messages. The question is what ontology of distinctions—what theory of management and organizational action—will prove effective in designing systems for organizations.

The effectiveness of a work of design, and of a theory as a basis for design, must be assessed in the context of the consequences of the intervention. Some theories will prove better as a basis for design than others. That is to say, some will be more effective for orienting us toward new possibilities that can be developed into useful artifacts. For some purposes, the understanding we already experience will be a satisfactory basis. In others, reorientation can open new and better possibilities.

Two prominent orientations underlie most of the computer systems in common use today. Each of them offers distinctions from which users and designers observe and participate in the activities of concern. The most prevalent, which underlies traditional electronic data processing, has been based on an ontology of "data" and "information." Its distinctions are those of data, formatting, and algorithms for data storage and manipulation. A computer system contains and manipulates information and is related to the "real world" through operations of "data entry" and "reporting" or "data access."

This orientation is embodied in the design of "management information systems" (MISs), which focus their intervention on the task of providing quantities of accurate, up-to-the-minute data to managers. They carry the assumption that the greater the quantity and accuracy of the information available, the more able are people to consider alternatives and make decisions. These systems have largely failed in their attempt to improve management because the problem is not one of insufficient or stale data. Management is not management of information. Information is only important to managers because they need to take actions, for which they sometimes require grounding that can take the form of statements, summaries, and reports. By focusing on an ontology defined in terms of data, MISs operate in a secondary domain and more often than not swamp the manager in distracting information.

A second orientation takes "decision making" as the central task of managers and is expressed in the design of "decision support systems" and more recently of "expert systems." Here the focus moves away from the data itself to the process of problem solving and decision making. This process can be roughly characterized as a series of steps, which include defining the problem space, listing alternatives within that space, assessing the consequences of each alternative, and finally selecting from among them. Decision, evaluation, search, and cognition are taken as the key distinctions.

Hidden within this ontology is a focus on evaluation and search for solutions that rest on a relatively well-established and formalizable problem space. We believe that much of the work in this area is foundering because this assumption is rarely appropriate in practice. Coming to terms with the ill-defined background within which we feel there is a problem or state of irresolution is one of the fundamentally unsolved central issues in this line of research.

Both traditional data-processing and problem-solving orientations convey an attitude that there is an "objective" external world that can be neutrally observed and fully characterized in symbolic representations. This kind of approach (which we have labeled "rationalistic" in [6]) has a long and useful history, but it is not the one best suited to design in the office. The more urgent need is to understand the role of background and language in setting the dimensions of the space in which people interpret and generate their possibilities for action.

In line with this, a third theoretical orientation underlies our own work, with "action through language" as the key domain of distinctions. The design of conversational systems focuses on interventions into the recurrent patterns of communication in which language provides the coordination between actions.

3. A LANGUAGE/ACTION PERSPECTIVE

Our principal theoretical claim is that human beings are fundamentally linguistic beings: Action happens in language in a world constituted through language. What is special about human beings is that they produce, in language, common distinctions for taking action together. Language then is not a system for representing the world or for conveying thoughts and information. Language is ontology: a set of distinctions that allows us to live and act together in a common world.

The orientation within which we go about design is one that allows human beings to observe their producing and acting in a world linguistically, to design their actions together, and to recognize and respond to breakdowns. The designer's job is to identify recurring breakdowns, or interruptions in ongoing activities, and prepare interventions to resettle the activities in ways that cope with or avoid those breakdowns.

In using the term "breakdown" here, we do not intend it to have a tone of "upset" or "catastrophe." A breakdown is any interruption in the smooth unexamined flow of action. It includes events that participants might assess as negative (as when the pen you are writing with runs out of ink) or as a positive new opportunity (e.g., a stray useful thought that interrupts your flow of writing or a friend knocking at the door).

In turning our attention to this ontology, we are not designing something new for human beings to do. People already produce a world together in language and they already coordinate their actions in that world. A fundamental condition of human action is the ability to affect and anticipate the behavior of others through language. Design can improve the capacity of people to act by producing a reorganization of practices in coherence with the essential, ineliminable nature of human interaction and cooperation. The crucial distinctions—the ontology— of our design are the fundamental linguistic actions: requests, promises, assertions, and declarations. A brief summary of the dimensions of linguistic action is given by Aurämaki et al. (pp. 126–152, this issue) and is based on a taxonomy developed by Searle [3]. We do not lay out all of the distinctions here but indicate the direction of our theory with the cases of requests and promises.

When you request that someone perform an action in the future, you anticipate the fulfillment of certain conditions. The conditions explicitly stated in the request are interpreted within an implicit background of standard practices—what is "normally" done in your community in similar situations—and within the shared understanding of speaker and hearer. Not all conditions will be or need be explicitly stated when the background itself is sufficient. For example, in requesting "Meet me tomorrow at two o'clock," you specify an action and a description of those conditions of fulfillment that are not taken for granted. In this case, the time is explicit, whereas the place and any other conditions are implicit in the preunderstanding of the speaker and listener. We speak of the "conditions of fulfillment" of a request as including not just the explicit statement, but the larger interpretation (which may differ between speaker and hearer) of the conditions under which the requester will declare that the request has been satisfactorily fulfilled.

People promise actions to one another. That is, they offer to perform some action in the future, or they agree to perform some future action that has been requested of them. This act need not involve any mention of "promise." A promise might be "Okay," or "You're the boss," a nod, or even in some contexts just a mutually recognized silence.

A request and promise (or a declining) make up an initial segment of a "conversation for action," which initiates a simple structure of possibilities for continuing to some kind of completion. The promiser may later report performance of the action, and the requester may declare the conversation and the action completed. Alternatively, the request or promise may be canceled, or a further request made (by either party) to clarify or modify the conditions of fulfillment.

Organizations are structures for the social coordination of action, generated in conversations based on requests and promises. These distinctions of linguistic action are crucial to building technology for organization and management. They are also universal with respect to time and culture. So long as people live and work together, they will coordinate their actions in requests and promises and the expectations that derive from them.

It is important to separate out these basic constitutive phenomena of social action from the particular cultural and linguistic forms in which they appear. As mentioned above, many different kinds of utterances (or nonutterances) can be interpreted as promises in a particular cultural background. The same words may lead to very different interpretations in different contexts.

In some cases the forms depend on the details of the situation. "It's cold in here" may be a request for action in some situations and not in others. In other cases there are cultural norms. In adapting The Coordinator to Italian, the programmers were told to avoid the term corresponding to "request" because "Only the government requests. Other people 'invite.'" Similarly, a popular observation about Japanese culture concerns a reluctance to appear to offend the listener. It is said that the Japanese will "never decline a request." In the immediate visible sense, this may be true: A direct expression of a request is never (in polite discourse) answered with "No." But in the deeper interpretation there must be recognizable means for conveying all of the basic possibilities of promising, declining, and negotiating. If I enter into a conversation with you about meeting at two o'clock tomorrow, I need to go away from that conversation knowing whether it is worth my effort to show up at the appointed time on the expectation that you will be there. Without the fundamental distinctions of social coordination, we cannot carry out activity that involves other people in anything but the immediate present or in predictable recurrent patterns.

These distinctions will be implemented with different tools and regularized practices, depending on context and culture and on what technology is available. Much of our own work has concerned computer-based tools for conversation. We have also implemented our theory of language as action in other areas, such as the design and presentation of courses in management and effective communication, and for generally allowing people to learn and embody new distinctions for observing, assessing, and designing social actions.

By teaching people an ontology of linguistic action, grounded in simple, universal distinctions such as those of requesting and promising, we find that they become more aware of these distinctions in their everyday work and life situations. They can simplify their dealings with others, reduce time and effort spent in conversations that do not result in action, and generally manage actions in a less panicked, confused atmosphere.

4. COMPUTER TOOLS FOR ACTING IN LANGUAGE

As computer networks become more widely available and easier to use, they are generating new phenomena relevant to management. They introduce more than just the connectivity of being able to send, store, and receive information. Via networking, one can extend the effective reach of actions, record them, and structure them. Although this new potential rests on the technology of computer networks, that is not where the relevant understanding lies. The potential for designing new and more effective tools and practices lies in the domain of networks of people engaged in conversation and in the networks of actions that connect them. This is where the fundamental distinctions are made and where the salient breakdowns occur.

As we described above, the rationalistic tradition leads people to think that as they become more electronically connected, the ensuing availability of information will greatly improve the effectiveness of organizations and the execution of management. It is tacitly assumed that information quantity can somehow be correlated with enhancement of alternatives and hence more effective decision making. But productivity in the office is not quantity of information—it concerns the effectiveness of people getting things done. As more and more databases, electronic bulletin boards, online query systems, and the like become routinely available, people often become less rather than more certain of what actions are appropriate. The breakdown that arises is one of overload. It becomes more difficult to assess the available information in a meaningful way: to determine what is relevant to actual and potential concerns, what legitimacy to grant to the information and its speaker, and what structure to impute or assign to it.

Electronic mail, for example, has led to new possibilities for communication that cuts across many of the older structures in organizations [4]. At the same time, it has created a new source of breakdown for many people, who find themselves swamped by messages that demand their attention. As Kiesler observes, "If you just add technology to the office, you may wind up having more communications to monitor, more things to type, and more projects initiated

147

that don't get completed; you may not improve performance" [2, p. 48]. In the authors' personal experiences working within a community of researchers dedicated to the design and use of computer systems, we are continually jolted back to reality by statements like "Oh, sorry I didn't get to that—I'm two weeks behind in getting through my e-mail."

For older media, specialized roles and institutions have evolved to deal with this breakdown. Libraries, universities, publishers, editors, commentators, and the media marketplace help to digest information for us. Receptionists, secretaries, and assistants manage the flow in a variety of organizational situations. The range and quantity of information readily accessible via the computer appears to have temporarily outpaced the growth of new roles and institutions for handling information. And so, to view networks as simply a mechanism for information connectivity leads to a fundamental breakdown. The management of information becomes an additional task—a burden, not a support.

Tools continually emerge to handle this flow as people attempt to cope with the breakdowns they experience. A survey of the software available for use in offices reveals a great potential for innovative practices. Calendar programs, project management tools, spreadsheets, and the like can be used effectively to associate information with the human environment that makes the information meaningful. Users adapt generic technologies such as spreadsheets to the immediate tasks at hand in a pragmatically effective way (often in ways other than those anticipated by their designers) without a theoretical foundation.

If design is based on a theoretical framework, a unified and coherent approach can be developed. The vast number of specialized and idiosyncratic tools and practices can be incorporated into a coherent theory that leads to an effective redesign of already existing tools and to fruitful new possibilities. Database systems offer an example of this process in a different domain. The jumble of practices for storing structured data in computer-accessible files has gradually evolved into a relatively small and coherent theory on which powerful generic tools such as relational databases and query languages can be built and standardized, thereby not only providing a way to clean up existing systems, but, as these database tools become standard in operating systems, offering new possibilities for their use.

We propose that the language/action theory offers such a unified foundation for designing the support of interactive work in organizations. We illustrate the relevance of this analysis to computer systems by describing The Coordinator,[1] a workgroup productivity system currently used on IBM PC-compatible machines for everyday operations in sales, finance, general management, and planning in organizations of a variety of sizes and types. The Coordinator provides facilities for generating, transmitting, storing, retrieving, and displaying records of moves in conversations. However, unlike electronic mail systems that take messages and information as their starting points, it is based on the language/action theory outlined above. The description here focuses on the "conversation manager," which is one part of an integrated system that also includes word processing, formatting, calendar maintenance, and connectivity over phone lines and local-area and wide-area networks.

---

[1] "The Coordinator" is a registered trademark of Action Technologies.

4. THE COORDINATOR

The Coordinator is a system for managing action in time, grounded in a theory of linguistic commitment and completion of conversations. Conversations are essentially temporal, both as a sequence of acts and in the wider context of conversations and actions in a community or organization.

In making a request or promise, the speaker brings into a shared domain of interpretation a set of conditions to be fulfilled through action in the future. A conversation that develops from this opening can be viewed as a kind of "dance" in which particular linguistic steps move toward completion: If an action has been requested of you, you promise or decline; if you have promised to complete the action, you report completion or revoke your promise; if you have requested an action, you cancel your request, ask for a progress report, or declare that your conditions have been fulfilled and the action completed. What drives the design here is our theoretical claim that social action happens through language. The conversational dance is a social dance of bringing forth conditions of fulfillment, commitment to fulfill them, and completion.

The user interface of The Coordinator is based on menus that reflect the underlying theory. The primary menu for conversing is shown in Figure 1. Some of the menu items initiate new conversations. Others bring up records of existing conversations.

Instead of providing a uniform command to initiate a new message, The Coordinator provides options that identify different linguistic actions. When "Request" is selected, the user is prompted to specify an addressee, recipients of copies, a domain (a keyword that groups related conversations under a common concern), and a brief action heading (corresponding to the subject header in traditional mail systems). The body of the message is prompted with the phrase "What is your request?" to which the user enters any text whatsoever. The system makes no attempt to interpret this text but relies on the user's understanding and cooperation that the message is properly identified as a request. This is a key design issue: Let people interpret the natural language, and let the program deal with explicit declarations of structure (such as the user's declaration that this is a request). The conditions of fulfillment rest in the interpretations of speaker and hearer, not in the structure of the text. A perfectly understandable request (one with mutually understood conditions of fulfillment) might contain the single word "Noon?" if the participants have a shared understanding (e.g., they often go to lunch together).

When the user signals that the text is complete, the system prompts for three dates associated with the completion of the action: a "respond-by" date, a "complete-by" date, and an "alert" date. Date entries are optional, but experienced users almost always include one or more of them. Not only do they provide the primary structure for retrieval and for monitoring completion, but the identification of completions with specific dates plays a surprisingly large role in producing effective conversations. A requester will specify a completion time for the action based on assessing when this action is crucial in dealing with wider concerns, preparations for other actions, and so on. The response time will reflect an assessment of how soon other actions need to be taken if the request is declined. For example, suppose that someone requests preparation of a financial

```
                    C O N V E R S E


OPEN CONVERSATION FOR ACTION        REVIEW / HANDLE
    Request                             Read new mail
    Offer                               Missing my response
                                        Missing other's response

OPEN CONVERSATION FOR POSSIBILITIES
    Declare an opening                  My promises/offers
                                        My requests
ANSWER                                  Commitments due: 24-May-88


NOTES                                   Conversation records
```

Fig. 1. Converse menu from The Coordinator. (Reprinted by permission from F. Flores, C. Bell, M. Graves, and J. Ludlow. *The Coordinator Workgroup Productivity System I. Version 1.5 P.* Action Technologies, Emeryville, Calif., 1987.)

```
SPEAKING IN A CONVERSATION FOR ACTION

   Acknowledge       Promise
   Free-Form         Counter-offer
   Commit-to-commit  Decline
   Interim-report    Report-completion
```

Fig. 2. Menu for responding to a request. (Reprinted by permission from F. Flores, C. Bell, M. Graves, and J. Ludlow. *The Coordinator Workshop Productivity System I. Version 1.5 P.* Action Technologies, Emeryville, Calif., 1987.)

report that is crucial to a meeting on Thursday. The request includes, as a condition of its fulfillment, that it be satisfied by the meeting time, and the response must be soon enough to find another way to get the report or alternative information for the meeting.

When a request is received, the recipient responds by selecting "Answer" from a menu of mail-reading operations, which calls forth a subsidiary menu as shown in Figure 2. This menu is automatically generated by a conversational state interpreter that keeps track of the current state of the conversation (as determined by the preceding acts). For a detailed description of conversation structure and its embodiment in The Coordinator see [5] and [6].

The first three items in the right-hand column (Promise, Counter-offer, and Decline) represent the standard actions available in response to an initial request. The fourth choice (Report-completion) is also possible, since in some cases, it will turn out that the recipient of a request has already done what was requested.

The left-hand column introduces conversation acts concerned with the conduct of the conversation itself, which do not advance its state. "Acknowledge" sends a standard reply informing the requester that the request was received. "Free-form" allows any kind of communication relevant to the conversation—most frequently, notes, comments, and questions—that does not fit into the formal structure. "Commit-to-commit" would be conveyed in natural language with sentences like "I'll let you know by Thursday if I can do it." That is, the speaker is committing to take the next conversational step (promising or declining) by a specific time.

When any answering action is selected, a new message is automatically generated with markers corresponding to the choice of act and with a generic text. For example, if the response is "Promise," the initial message is "I promise to do as you request," whereas for "Counter-offer" it is "No; I counteroffer: ..." The user can augment or replace this text using embedded word processing facilities. Experience has shown that a surprising number of messages need only the initial pro forma composition. The message initiating a request or offer needs to contain text that sets forth the action such as "This is a reminder to send me that report we were talking about at lunch." But often the subsequent steps are made by simply selecting the appropriate menu item and hitting the button that sends a message.

Whenever "Answer" is selected, the menu displays only those actions that could sensibly be taken next by the current speaker, given the direction of the conversation toward completion of action. For example, after making a commitment, the next time the promiser answers in that conversation (assuming no intervening action by the requester), the menu offered will be as shown in Figure 3. At this point, there is no longer an option to decline, but the promiser can "Report-completion" or "Cancel" with or without initiating a new promise.

The Coordinator has no magic for coercing people to come through with their promises, but it provides a straightforward structure in which they can review the status of their commitments, alter commitments they are no longer in condition to fulfill, anticipate coming breakdowns, make new commitments to take care of breakdowns and opportunities appearing in their conversations, and generally be clear (with themselves and others) about the state of their work. The structure and status of conversations is the primary basis for organizing retrieval and review in the system. To put it simply, the structure is organized to provide straightforward and relevant answers to the implicit question "What do I have to do now?"

Several things are of note:

—The basic unit of work in the system is a conversation, not a message. In conventional electronic mail systems, messages are often linked by conventions such as the use of "Re: ..." in headers. For The Coordinator, each message (including a Free form) belongs to a particular conversation. The retrieval structure is a two-level one with the user first identifying a conversation, then selecting particular messages within it to be displayed.

—The explicit use of conversation theory in the generation of messages makes it possible for retrieval to be based on status. There is a way to display answers to questions such as "In which conversations is someone waiting for me to do something?" or "In which conversations have I promised to do things?" Note

```
┌────────────────────────────────────────────────┐
│  SPEAKING IN A CONVERSATION FOR ACTION           │
│                                                  │
│  Free-Form         Cancel/New-Promise            │
│  Interim-report    Cancel                        │
│                    Report-completion             │
└────────────────────────────────────────────────┘
```

Fig. 3. Answer menu generated in continuing a promise. (Reprinted by permission from F. Flores, C. Bell, M. Graves, and J. Ludlow. *The Coordinator Workshop Productivity System I. Version 1.5 P.* Action Technologies, Emeryville, Calif., 1987.)

that these two queries are different. For example, if you make an offer to me, then our conversation is in a state in which the next move characteristically belongs to me, but I have made no promise to you.

—The distinction of "completion" is central to monitoring the progress of conversations. An "open" conversation is one in which additional steps are required to reach a state of closure. Note that completion is not the same as satisfaction. If I withdraw a request, the conversation is complete even though the request was never satisfied. The distinction between open and closed conversations is one of the primary ones used to filter out those to be retrieved. Unless the user designates otherwise, The Coordinator will display only those conversations that are still open to further action.

—Explicit response, completion, and alert dates identify potential breakdowns in the progress toward completion and are used for time-oriented retrieval. The calendar subsystem is integrated, so that all of these items can optionally appear at the appropriate places in a personal calendar, along with more conventional entries such as meetings and appointments.

—The Coordinator applies theories of language without attempting to automate language understanding. All of the interpretations (e.g., that a particular message is a request, or that it should be done by a certain time) are made by the people who use the system, guided by appropriate menus and prompts. This is not experienced by users as an extra job of annotating but in fact replaces typing parts of the contents.

—It is a generic tool in the same sense as a word processor or a spreadsheet, but in a different domain of elements, that is, a different ontology. A word processor is not equally well suited to generating all kinds of character sequences but is specially designed for the words, sentences, and paragraphs of ordinary written text. Similarly, The Coordinator is not built for arbitrary sequences of messages, but for the requests, promises, and completions that are at the heart of coordinated work.

We want to reiterate our point that, although The Coordinator exemplifies a new design and a new theory of action and management as a basis for design, the distinctions of linguistic acts and completion of action are not those of new entities or new proposals for doing something. What we are doing in our theory is reconstructing constitutive distinctions of human social action. These are distinctions for generating any socially coordinated actions: bringing, in a request, a future action and its conditions of fulfillment into a publicly shared world and producing, in a promise, a commitment to complete the action. These distinctions are simple, universal, and generative of the complex organizational and management phenomena with which we need to deal.

Managers are often faced with apparently overwhelmingly complex projects and sets of actions to manage, recurrent miscoordinations of action (misunderstandings of requests, conditions of fulfillment, and promises), and information overload. By interpreting the situation as a network of requests and promises with certain regular logical and temporal structures, we can help bring order. Information is information that appears within a conversation with relevance to action: It is not piled up as contextless facts. The activity of management is the creation and development of conversations for completing action. These constitutive distinctions give managers an improved awareness of what they are managing and an increased capacity to observe, monitor, and intervene in the flow of activity.

Everyone makes requests and promises, but we are not typically aware of them in a fashion that helps to identify breakdowns or intervene in the constitutive dimension of our actions. The Coordinator expands the individual's capacity to observe and assess a situation and intervene into what is already going on. When you make a request with The Coordinator, you are presented with the fact that you are making a request—you choose "request" from its menu for conversations. When you make a promise, it is the same. And, more important than the names on the screen, the request or promise you make in the conversation sets in motion a conversational structure and a structure for observing your conversation that is defined by the linguistic move you have made. You have tools, in other words, for anticipating and identifying breakdowns on the way to the completion of action, for intervening consistently with breakdowns that have occurred, and generally for making the next appropriate moves in the conversation.

What is crucial, we are saying, to the effectiveness of The Coordinator is that it produces in its user a capacity to observe action in its constitutive dimension. The system will "coach" its user to operate in a system of distinctions that constitute and promote effective coordination of action. The effectiveness of the tool is not limited to its actual occasions of use. The Coordinator also has an educational dimension. By operating consistently within the distinctions embodied in it, people begin to acquire a "new common sense" about social action. Even away from The Coordinator itself, they will begin to observe and act in ways that are consistent with the theory. Their taken-for-granted understanding or way of observing will embody those distinctions on which The Coordinator is designed, and they learn to observe, assess, identify, and intervene in accordance with them.

5. THE SOCIAL ENVIRONMENT

Since The Coordinator embodies an orientation toward language as social action, its effects must be examined beyond the context of a single user—in the social interaction of an organization as a whole. The key observation about a tool like

The Coordinator is that it intervenes and creates change by making explicit a structure of conversation that was already there.

The most visible impact is to facilitate the shared clarity of communication. Participants who share a grounding in observing, assessing, and intervening in conversations for action will have the basis for a more effective mutual understanding of actions to be taken. A request is a request, with a well-understood structure of consequences, in the understanding of all participants. They share a language of distinctions for attacking ambiguity and ensuring that they share an understanding of what they are doing together.

In a sense, this clarity is something that needs to be recovered as we move from older social forms to the complex computer-mediated modern organization. In a simple closely knit society, there is a tremendous degree of overlap in people's backgrounds. They share a common set of social mores and understandings and can anticipate close similarity in their interpretations. In a small group, furthermore, each individual is familiar and everyone's behavior can be frequently anticipated on the basis of prior personal experience. In such a context, there is a relative clarity of knowing what people really mean by what they say.

In today's modern society, there is much less cultural commonality, and organizations tend toward being collections of nameless and faceless "functional roles." Communication structures are mechanized and regularized in order to regain some degree of predictability. Kiesler describes how "computer-mediated communication can break down hierarchical and departmental barriers, standard operating procedures, and organizational norms" [2, p. 48]. She documents a number of ways in which the use of electronic messages can lead to breakdowns in the face of the relative absence of what she terms "static and dynamic personal information" and argues that "the real challenge is to build electronic communication facilities so that it is easy for people to negotiate and to implement procedures and norms—in other words, to design systems that somehow give back the social context that computer mediation wipes out" [2, p. 54].

In a way, the drive toward "computerization" is an overreaction in this direction. A rigidly specified set of procedures can help ensure context-independent predictability at the cost of a mindless lock-step pattern in which the individual cannot vary from the prescribed routines. In contrast, by making the network of requests and promises explicit in its structure and temporality, systems such as The Coordinator can provide a means of improving the degree to which people have adequately shared interpretations of their commitments and actions, while leaving them the individual choice and responsibility for dealing with them.

The success of systems based on the language/action ontology depends on the development of a new shared culture or "tradition" in which the commitment dimension of language is taken seriously within a shared interpretation of explicitly marked language acts. Although the dance of request and promise is universal, doing it and being explicit about it are two very different things. In all areas of social interaction, the experienced phenomenon of acting is very different from what happens when we make an interpretation of our acts explicit by describing or characterizing them. If I discreetly behave in a way that I hope will make you want to leave (e.g., looking at my watch and stacking up things on my desk while we talk), my act is socially different from directly saying "I request that you leave." These kinds of subtleties are extremely important in maintaining the network of relationships and assessments of other people.

In some contexts, standard practices lead us to associate indirectness with politeness. A request to have the window closed can be "Close the window!" or "My, but it's chilly in here." The explicit prefacing of a request with a marker ("I request that you close the window") is an additional act, which in the background of everyday interaction has a stiff and rather formal sound. The same explicitness as signaled by the message type in a Coordinator request can be heard (especially by new users) as having a less-than-friendly tone. But as practices evolve in a group, the listening evolves to suit the medium.

By explicitly marking the action structure, The Coordinator changes the space of possibilities for communication—the form of the dance. It is not possible, for example, to be ambiguous as to whether or not a message is intended to convey a request. It is hard to "suggest" an action to test whether it is taken as something you want the hearer to do. Each message carries a label that distinguishes it as a request or as not-a-request (e.g., a conversation for possibilities). The labeling itself constitutes part of the meaning. Even the need for the sender to consider "Am I making a request here?" changes the situation.

New users who interpret The Coordinator as a "message system" are sometimes frustrated by what they perceive as undue restrictiveness or regimentation; they see it as restricting the range of possibilities for communication by imposing categories such as "offer" and "request." At a superficial level, it is easy to refute this by noting that these categories are not forced on all messages: It is always possible to send a "free-form" which has no status in the conversation structure, and there are "conversations for possibilities" in which no pattern of request and promise is expected or made possible. But it should be clear that this is not the whole story. The fact that there is a conversation initiated with "request" means that when a sender chooses to label something as "free-form" or "possibilities" it can be interpreted as *not* making a request. The overall space of possible choices conditions the interpretation of everything made within it.

Relative to a seemingly unstructured language such as that associated with standard electronic mail systems, conversation systems such as The Coordinator present constraints. This is not surprising; all language always does that by creating a space of distinctions in which to interpret the world and our actions. The questions are then, "Relative to what is it constraining?" and "What is gained by these constraints?"

There is a spectrum having at one end unstructured message systems and at the other traditional information systems, that are limited to a particular conversation that they help to administer effectively (e.g., customer service requests). Information systems impose significant constraints and provide efficient tools for dealing with the specified conversations. There is little confusion about which set of conversations can best be mediated by the particular system and which are best dealt with in some other way.

Electronic messaging systems seem quite unstructured, but in fact they do impose some structure, such as forcing explicit declaration of recipients and, sometimes, of the subject. They do not provide, for example, the potential found in ordinary conversation for making a remark without making it clear whether a particular person was supposed to hear it. Even though this could be seen as a limitation in the design of mail systems, it is a limitation that people are accustomed to and which for the purpose of most conversations is not serious. The Coordinator comes in the middle. It offers more structure than conventional mail systems in order to better organize and more rapidly assess the conversations one is engaged in, that is, to deal with the barrage of messages that can be quickly produced and transmitted with computer networks. On the other hand, it is less confining than the customer-order system.

The underlying claim of The Coordinator is that such explicitness is beneficial, overall, for the kinds of conversations that go on among managers and other workers in settings like offices. This claim can be refined in several dimensions as outlined in the following sections.

5.1 Conversation Types

With The Coordinator, we are only dealing with some of the conversations in an office setting. It is misleading to see the future "electronic office" as one in which all communication is mediated by computers. There is a vital place for everything from highly structured messages to the open-ended discourse that thrives around the coffeepot or in chance encounters in the corridor. In fact, an important question is what aspects of language in the office should be incorporated into computer systems at all. The medium is well suited to some types of conversation (especially those in which structured records and recall are important) and ill suited to many types that have traditionally been carried on face-to-face or by voice.

As we move from face-to-face encounter, to telephone, to written text, to online data, we progressively narrow the basis for interpretations. A shrug and a smile may be a perfectly adequate response to a request in face-to-face conversation because the listener (who listens with eyes as well as ears) has a wealth of observations on which to ground assessments of what to expect. On the other hand, not everything can be done face-to-face. The airplane, postal system, telephone and telegraph coexist. We select the medium on the basis of its suitability, cost, and convenience.

The Coordinator is a machine for conducting conversations for action and also provides facilities (equivalent to conventional electronic mail) for other types of conversation. For a broad range of work-related interactions we believe much can be gained from the introduction of commitment management in conversations for action. There are also interesting new possibilities for different kinds of machines that would provide support for conversations with different structures. But computer-based communication cannot take over the wide range of spoken communications, including those in which vagueness serves an important social purpose and in which the (often unconscious) interpretation of "tone of voice" and "body language" are essential to understanding. It may well be that as office communication systems evolve, there will be a mix in which computer-based text is used for the more explicit forms, while recorded and transmitted voice and video images become the preferred mode for less structured types of conversation that must occur at a distance.

5.2 Stability of Role Structure

We are primarily designing for settings in which the basic parameters of authority, obligation, and cooperation are stable. The typical office presents a structure of recurrent patterns of conversation in mutually understood domains of possibilities associated with formally declared roles such as "group manager," "assistant," and "programmer." The issue here is not whether the role structure is hierarchical, democratic, or whatever, but whether it is basically agreed upon and is not itself a matter of ongoing active negotiation. In an unstable organization, for example, it might be very useful to be able to "suggest" an action without explicitly requesting that anyone do it in order to gauge people's responsiveness.

This is not to imply the absence of such negotiations within the structure of The Coordinator, since they always occur in every social setting. For example, authority roles are negotiated as people judge whether it is acceptable for them to decline (or even counter) a request of a given kind from a particular party, upon considering the consequences of doing so. But successful functioning depends on this not being the primary concern in the bulk of interactions.

An observation that goes along with this is that The Coordinator has been most successful in organizations in which the users are relatively confident about their own position and the power they have within it. This does not mean that the organization is democratic or that power relations are equal. It means that there is clarity about what is expected of people and what authority they have (e.g., what requests can be clearly declined without fear of negative impact). In such an environment, people can be comfortable with making (and then possibly changing) commitments and accepting commitments from others in the same spirit.

5.3 Cooperation and Competition

We are primarily concerned with work settings in which the cooperative aspects of achieving mutually declared results dominate over the competitive aspects of interpersonal or intergroup conflict. Of course, no setting, no matter how visibly "cooperative," can be understood without recognizing the internal conflicts of interest and the ways in which they generate the space of actions. The Coordinator's successful use does not depend on an idealized cooperative spirit in which everyone is working for the good of all. But it does depend on basic assumptions that the overall interests are shared and that the parties recognize that honest dealings with one another will be the best for their shared benefit. This is true, for example, in successful market structures in which each party competes with the others, but recognizes the joint advantage in maintaining (through legal systems and the like) a communication mechanism based on mutual trust.

Our philosophy of communication rests on an interpretation of individual responsibility and autonomy in which people take responsibility for their language acts and behave in accordance with shared standards. This does not mean a utopia in which people always tell the truth or always come through with what they promise. We can design to facilitate the positive aspects of social interaction but we cannot magically change human nature. People can use any communication device whatsoever to lie, deceive, and manipulate. They will always promise things they cannot or will not do and will generate further conversations to deal with the consequences.

With The Coordinator, we are not proposing a change in the nature of action and cooperation in the office. What we are doing is laying bare the constitution of action and cooperation in order to open the way to diagnosing breakdowns, increasing effectiveness, and in general designing the workplace as an effective, healthy environment. To do so requires building and implementing practical tools on the basis of a theory of organizational life. We believe it is imperative that constitutive theories of organization and cooperation be embodied in tools and practices. Only in that way can our understandings shape the reality of work. Work, and the organization of work, can be designed only when practices are designed and implemented on the basis of sound theory.

6. TECHNOLOGY, CHANGE, AND LEARNING

Our view of design is consciously oriented toward improving the quality and effectiveness of organizational life, not just providing computer support for current practices. As we emphasized in the first section, all innovative technology leads to new practices, which cause social and organizational changes whether anticipated or not. Some of these will be effective and others may be counterproductive. Our firm belief is that this process can be done with awareness. Although we can never fully anticipate the changes a technology will trigger, we can make conscious choices in the directions of change we facilitate.

This attempt to do conscious design in this domain is both worthwhile and difficult. A system that is intended to have certain positive impacts (as assessed by the designer and/or the users) may turn out to do quite the opposite when it is put into practice. Although all aspects of design gain from being done in collaboration with the users (see [1]), it is especially essential that the explicit interpretation and implementation of social changes be generated jointly with the people who participate in them.

There needs to be a shared understanding within the organization that there is an ongoing breakdown in the domain of conversation and commitment that is relevant to productivity. There is wisdom in the aphorism "If it ain't broke, don't fix it"; people only seek change when they experience breakdown. The problem is that it is relatively easy for people to identify small-scale breakdowns ("I can't get invoices to the branch offices fast enough") and difficult to recognize the large-scale breakdowns of organization and communication that pervade their work. Most people (including most managers) do not experience "lack of coordination" as a breakdown even though they face the consequences of it every day under a variety of names.

In addition to recognizing the problem, people must understand the intervention well enough to identify and anticipate the new breakdowns it will create when integrating with preexisting structures, practices, and tools. The use of an explicit conversation manager will lead to changes in the social practices with potentially complex ramifications. In every organization a background of practices has evolved in conjunction with the mixture of previous technologies and circumstances. Any change to this background, planned or not, will affect power relations, stability of roles, and individual satisfaction. With the introduction of any new technology (hardware, software, or practices), some people will see themselves as gaining and others will anticipate (often appropriately) being put at a relative disadvantage. Education cannot eliminate the underlying power struggles but can be the basis for dealing with them explicitly in the context of potential changes.

It must be understood that a system can be used as the basis for an ongoing process of mutual education in which the people who use the system envision possibilities for new ways of working, interpret those possibilities in light of their own experience, and choose what will be implemented. The technology in turn can play a role in "coaching" the users. We are all aware of cases in which our verbal understanding of what we should do is not effective in generating the acts we want. For example, understanding the advantages of getting things done on time is rarely sufficient to prevent procrastination. An effective reminder system cannot prevent it either, but it can help by offering opportunities for self-examination, that is, by getting us to ask the question "When am I really going to work on this?"

In the domain of commitment and conversation, this kind of coaching is offered by the structure of The Coordinator. The simple need to characterize a message as an "offer," "request," or "opening for possibilities" leads the user to ask "What am I trying to do here?" At a later stage in a conversation, the need to explicitly declare it "complete" or to choose a speech act that leaves it "open" leads the user to ask questions about what is still missing and who is responsible for resolving it. Our experience in introducing The Coordinator has convinced us that this kind of coaching can be valuable and that it leads to a kind of continuing education that goes well beyond training for technical facility in using software. As people use the system they develop their understanding of the acts that go with it.

Programs like The Coordinator, which are based on an explicit theory of organizations and of directions for change, have at times been referred to pejoratively as "missionary software." The implication is that organizational or social change is being imposed on an unwilling populace by outsiders with a dogmatic theology. Although this kind of manipulation is possible in principle, the technology is likely to be rejected, ignored, or subverted in practice. But from a different perspective, The Coordinator is a new kind of "educational software" in which the everyday use of its communication tools serves to educate users in the principles of conversation and action. Learning is integrated into the practice of working so that the skills for understanding the organization as a network of negotiated commitments for operating within it can be developed.

7. CONCLUSION

In this paper, we have been talking primarily about The Coordinator. Here we want to reemphasize that The Coordinator design, with its particular screens, buttons, and so forth, is an initial example of a large family of potential tools, based on some fundamental theoretical claims about design and organizational action:

—Design is for transparency of action and expansion of possibilities. It is always an intervention into the practices, breakdowns, and possibilities already present in a community: an intervention that will shift and resettle practices, breakdowns, and possibilities. All design embodies an ontology, a set of constitutive distinctions, of the domain in which the design is an intervention. Good design is an ontologically grounded intervention that allows work to flow smoothly with a minimum of breakdowns in completing an action and that expands positive possibilities for participants and production in the domain.

—The ontology in which we are designing is one of action happening through language. The constitutive dimension of social and organizational interaction can be laid out as a structure of linguistic actions in a temporal dance. The key distinctions in this structure, as we have interpreted it, are requests, promises, assertions, and declarations as moves in conversations for the completion of action.

The Coordinator is a generic tool for conversations for action. Many customizations and extensions of the design are possible. For example, in The Coordinator people make requests and promises by typing in English text. But this is not the only possibility; the interpretation of linguistic acts can be based on embodiments that include figures, drawings, oral content, symbols, and formalized data relations. In another direction, tools can be developed to fit particular organizational situations, standard practices, and domains of work. The actions can be tailored to particular recurrent conversations that include the ones handled in traditional data processing such as order entry, inventory, and accounting.

By taking language/action theory as a basis, we are asking people to go about their business with a different awareness. We design in a fundamental domain of social interaction, which calls for the explicit recognition of the autonomy and responsibility of communicating individuals within a social network that is defined and maintained through the action of language. The evolving nature of computers and of work in organizations will inevitably lead to the widespread development and use of computer tools grounded in this domain of design.

REFERENCES

1. BJERKNES, G., EHN, P., AND KYNG, M. *Computers and Democracy*. Avebury, Aldershot, England 1987.
2. KIESLER, S. Thinking ahead: The hidden messages in computer networks. *Harvard Bus. Rev.* (Jan.–Feb. 1986), 46–60.
3. SEARLE, J. R. A taxonomy of illocutionary acts. In *Language, Mind and Knowledge*, Minnesota Studies in the Philosophy of Science, vol. 11, K. Gunderson, Ed. University of Minnesota Press, Minneapolis, 1975.
4. STASZ, C. AND BIKSON, T. K. Computer supported cooperative work: Examples and issues in one federal agency. In *Proceedings of the Conference on Computer Supported Cooperative Work* (Austin, Tex., Dec. 3–5).
5. WINOGRAD, T. A language/action perspective on the design of cooperative work. *Human-Computer Interaction 3*, 1 (1987–88), 3–30.
6. WINOGRAD, T., AND FLORES, F. *Understanding Computers and Cognition: A New Foundation for Design*. Ablex, Norwood, N.J., 1986 and Addison-Wesley, Reading, Mass., 1987.

BIBLIOGRAPHY

FLORES, F. C.   Management and communication in the office of the future. Unpublished Ph.d. dissertation, Univ. of California at Berkeley, 1981.

FLORES, F. C., AND LUDLOW, J. J.   Doing and speaking in the office. In *DSS: Issues and Challenges*, G. Fick and R. Sprague, Eds. Pergamon Press, London, 1981.

Received February 1988; revised March 1988; accepted May 1988

Augmenting SADT[TM] To Develop
Computer Support for Cooperative Work

David A. Marca

Digital Equipment Corporation[1]
Software Development Technology Group
110 Spit Brook Road Nashua, NH 03062

Abstract

Traditionally, systems analysis methodologies have been used to describe office work from an information flow perspective. The language-action perspective of Winograd and Flores suggests that work results come from the conversations people have at the office. Using the language-action perspective, this paper creates a general framework for both systems analysis and its practice. Structured Analysis And Design Technique (SADT), a systems analysis methodology, is augmented using this framework. This work took place on the CONTRACT (COmmitment Negotiation and TRACking Tool) project. This paper includes the experiences of both users and systems analysts during the project, and emphasizes how to develop SADT descriptions *with* users to represent the richness and complexity of social interactions at work. The resulting software specification is also presented, including how it aided the work of the people who actually helped developed it.

1. An Introduction To The SADT Methodology

Structured Analysis And Design Technique (SADT) is both a language and a process for systems analysis. Originally, it was created for describing systems and their operations (Ross 1977). The box-and-arrow language of SADT allows a systems analyst to draw diagrams of the activities, information, and physical components of a system. For example, a box could represent an assembly activity and the arrows could identify parts, tools, and assembly instructions (Figure 1). The SADT process helps a systems analyst elicit requirements from users through interviews (Ross & Schoman 1977). The process also advocates iterative review of documented requirements by users (Figure 2). Together, the SADT language and iterative modeling process form a comprehensive methodology for describing systems and specifying requirements.

The SADT language and process are artifacts of a methodology rooted in general systems theory. This fact distinguishes SADT from all other widely-used systems analysis techniques, which have their origins in software design. Thus, the SADT graphic language has representations for describing system qualities such as coordination, real-time interactions, and feedback. And so SADT practitioners are able to describe: computer-aided manufacturing (Ramirez 1989, Bailey & Thornhill 1990), real-time systems (Stockenberg 1989), banking (McDermott & Cot-trell 1989), decision support (Ellis 1989), process improvement (Preston 1989), technology planning (Thornhill 1989), software engineering (Snodgrass 1989), and enterprise integration (Pyryemybida 1989, Joyce & Nolan 1989).

Coordination, interactions, and feedback are characteristics of both automated systems like those mentioned above, and systems dominated by human interaction. For example, a variety of human interactions can be observed in the way people cooperate at work (e.g. negotiation, feedback). Focusing on cooperation in the workplace is an emerging discipline, currently called Computer-Supported Cooperative Work, or CSCW (Greif 1988). CSCW blends computer and social sciences. CSCW researchers have noted that human interaction plays a dominate role in the design of software (Bullen & Bennett 1990). *This is in contrast to the view of technology being the sole design center for automated systems.*

These facts and trends led us to using SADT to describe a cooperative workplace. For example, imagine SADT being used to describe people co-authoring documents, coordinating tasks, providing feedback to each other, or any other collaborative situation in a typical workplace. Using SADT to model aspects of cooperative work seemed plausible, because SADT had suitable descriptive mechanisms in its graphic language. There was also precedent for aug-

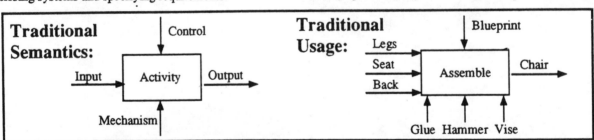

Figure 1: SADT Graphics For Systems Analysis

0-8186-2637-2/92 $03.00 © 1991 IEEE

menting SADT to handle specific application domains (Brackett & Mc-Gowan 1977, Schoman 1979, Stockenberg 1989). This paper presents experiences in using SADT to describe a cooperative work-place and for eliciting requirements of cooperative group work situations. As it turned out, the entire practice of systems analysis had to be re-examined and augmented before an SADT description of a cooperative workplace could be created. The next section of this paper explains why this occurred.

2. A Language-Action Framework For Systems Analysis

Systems analysts have traditionally sought to model the information flow of a workplace. This tradition has been profoundly shaped by software engineering practice, which fundamentally considers "information" as a "thing" that needs to be managed by computers. As systems analysts, we have all experienced workplaces and have, by tradition, modeled their processes as tasks and information flow. This kind of systems analysis works well, for example, when an anticipated computer system is being designed to merely replace all or part of the paper flow in an organization.

But we have also experienced the workplace as something more than just paper flow. The workplace appears to be very dynamic, where even the most "well-defined" processes have a "plastic" quality to them (found in Ehn 1988). For example, in a manufacturing process for assembling computers, a process which people consider to be quite "fixed", people are continually adjusting their tasks to suit their ever-changing work context (Marca, May 1989). Take, for instance, the situation where a person assembling a computer changes the order of the steps based on his or her knowledge of part availability on the floor for that day. In this case, that person is not strictly follow "the process".

So if people are not following a pre-specified process, what *is* going on at work? In the case of computer manufacturing, people spend a considerable amount of time talking to each other. On closer study, it was discovered that people converse to align their organizations and teams in order to accomplish the coordination needed to build a computer. For example, a "new product group" exists to expedite and manage the handover of hardware prototypes from engineering groups to manufacturing groups. The role of this group is primarily an *orchestrator of conversations* between engineers and manufacturing personnel.

Systems analysts practicing traditional methods can experience extreme difficulty creating specifications of this kind of work from the perspective that the information is *the* thing to be studied. The reason is that a vital part of group members' work is their conversations: who they spoke with, what they said, and the business reasons for those discussions. Systems analysis can be simplified by first considering an alternate framework for understanding how people work cooperatively. The paradigm put forth by Winograd and Flores (see Win-ograd and Flores 1986) suggests studying the conversations people have at work. This paradigm provides a design center for developing a suitable framework for systems analysis.

Using the Winograd and Flores paradigm, one can approach system analysis with the following question: "How should I practice systems analysis if I fundamentally shift my focus away from 'people just sharing information' and consider instead 'people having conversations'?" By continually asking this question during systems analysis, one can see the results of group work as artifacts that stem from what people said they would do. For example, here are some building blocks of conversations that one can imagine happening in a large computer company for creating and improving products:

*1) A **declaration** made by the president of a company (e.g., "We build workstations.") creates a context for engineers to create new products (e.g., engineers then begin designing a workstation-class computer).*

*2) A **commissive** made by an engineer (e.g., "I will finish estimating the cost of the workstation redesign by next week.") can impact the work done by other team members.*

*3) An **assertion** made by a marketing expert determines the business value of the engineering project (e.g., "We estimate people will buy 1000 workstations/week over the next year. If, in four months, we can implement a redesign which saves $100 per computer, we can spend up to $100,000 to make that change and recover the cost over the product's life.").*

Notice how these statements interrelate, build upon each other, and create a context in which cooperative work can take place. ("Context" is a business situation and a corresponding rationale within which work takes place.) One could therefore say that speaking these statements in some sense *creates* the work. Looking at the workplace from a

Systems Analysis Practices	Methods Advocated In SADT
Understand Work Tasks	Observe current operations, work flow, work tasks; Investigate databases, reports, etc.
Interview Users	One-on-one discussions regarding a person's work tasks and the information needed to do those tasks.
Validate Requirements	Requirements are iteratively reviewed and approved by users ("the SADT Author/Reader Cycle").

Figure 2: SADT Methods For Systems Analysis

language-action perspective suggests that work is fundamentally social in nature (verified in Ehn 1988). This suggests that "conversation", and not just "information", is fundamental to people's work, and that all work is fundamentally social (Whiteside & Wixon 1988). Therefore, *a language-action perspective focuses on the social interactions in the workplace, and considers information within the context of these interactions.*

With this insight, formerly missing from the general practice of systems analysis, the SADT methodology can be augmented for describing workplaces where people carry on a variety of complicated and interconnected conversations. Shifting perspective is a serious step. It requires augmenting the foundation upon which old analysis practices are based, in order to develop computer systems that correctly support cooperative work. The next section of this paper explains what impact such a perspective shift can have on the practice of systems analysis.

3. A New Interpretation For Systems Analysis Practices

We observe an increasing interest in understanding how to develop software that supports the work of groups, in contrast to supporting just the work of individuals. Such software is currently being termed "Groupware" (Johansen 1988). Currently, the computing industry as a whole is not aware that traditional systems analysis practices may not be adequate for developing effective software for cooperative work. To explain why this may be so, let us look at the current practice of software design.

Software designs are created in part from the assumptions made about how users intend to use a future software system to accomplish their work. By practicing systems analysis, software engineers acquire an understanding about users. This understanding leads to assumptions about the way people intend to use software systems. Traditionally, systems analysts study people working at their individual desks, offices, or workplaces. The assumptions that come from these observations have been effective for designing software for the desktop, that is, for the individual (e.g. spreadsheets). Unfortunately, these assumptions do not transfer to groups -- Group work is about human *interaction,* and assumptions about the work of individuals fail to map to the complex social situations that arise when groups of people work cooperatively (Grudin 1988).

To see why this happens, let us investigate scheduling meetings using group calendars: In one organization, managers kept their work schedules in on-line calendars because they had secretarial support. However, other potential meeting participants (e.g. engineers) rarely kept their work schedules in on-line calendars because their secretarial support was minimal. Automatic meeting scheduling, seen as beneficial by the managers, was seen as a burden by potential meeting participants because those people had to do extra work to maintain their calendars while receiving no perceived benefit from that work. One can imagine that a very good software requirements specification for automatic meeting support has little value for this organization. These findings, initially reported by Grudin, confirm what was discovered on the CONTRACT Project: present-day systems analysis practices might be inadequate for gaining an appropriate understanding of group interaction. For SADT in particular, three aspects of inadequacy in the methodology were discovered (see Figure 3):

Understanding The User's Work By Doing It

First, traditional systems analysis emphasizes "studying" users. The closest one usually gets to the actual work being done is to observe the current system in operation by walking through the work site. Traditionally, interviewing sessions encourage people to *talk about* their work, as opposed to *actually doing* the work in front of (or with!) the systems analyst. In order to understand the nuances of group interaction, systems analysts need to understand users by actually doing the work with them (advocated in Ehn 1988). For example, CONTRACT Project members worked as part of the user team. This team expedited cost-effective efforts that redesign computer parts. That experience gave the systems analysts a first-hand understanding of the people and the conversations required to make redesign efforts successful.

Uncovering Group Norms And Shared Work Practices

Second, traditional interviewing techniques emphasize questioning individuals on how they do their particular job. The nature of this questioning style makes it difficult to discover how the work of one person actually affects the work of others, and vice versa. That person being interviewed has an *individual interpretation* of his or her work. More informative and detailed is the *group interpretation* of work. Eliciting this interpretation requires interviewing

Systems Analysis Practice	Practices From An Interpretive Framework Of:	
	Work As Individuals Doing Tasks	**Work As Group Interaction**
Understand Work Tasks	Studying people doing their individual work.	Systems analysts do actual work with users.
Interview Users	One-on-one questioning about a person's individual work tasks.	Users demonstrate their group norms and shared work practices.
Validate Requirements	Requirements are iteratively written, reviewed, and revised.	Requirements come from seeing the system actually being used.

Figure 3: Systems Analysis Practices Differ Based On Perspective

the entire team at the same time *while they work* in order to uncover their norms and their shared work practices (Mumford 1983, Ehn 1988). A group interviewing session provides both the systems analysts and the users with an opportunity to better understand the work being done as it progresses. For example, systems analysts noticed that users often met as a team to do group problem solving of difficult cases. So, group interviewing sessions were held with the entire user team in their meeting room, modified slightly to resemble the one in Figure 4. The room allowed users to share with each other how they work during a problem solving session. They described their work from both individual and team perspectives. SADT diagrams were periodically sketched in front of the group as the meeting proceeded. Sometimes, documents were referred to, or phone calls were made to other people, to clarify or verify facts. During these sessions users discussed the criteria for successful redesign projects. These discussions heightened each person's work, because everyone learned both the business issues surrounding a redesign project and the successful techniques for expediting such projects. These issues and techniques were not commonly known nor understood among team members (see also Ehn 1988).

Rapid Prototyping For Validating Requirements

Third, traditional systems analysis emphasizes defining software requirements and designs in documents, which are iteratively written, reviewed, and revised (e.g. using the SADT Author/Reader Cycle). Such specifications and their traditional iterative review process are useful in the very early part of system development, because they create a baseline from which to build an initial version of the envisioned system. Unfortunately, these specifications are usually seen as the *only* requirements for the system. Traditionally little, if any, software requirements elicitation and validation happens *at the actual work site* -- the place where nuances and "special" cases are observed.

On the CONTRACT effort, an initial specification led to a prototype that was used to manage a few, very simple redesign projects. From this experience, many of the initial software requirements for supporting the user team were verified by seeing the people use the system on a day-by-day basis (Marca et. al., April 1989). This approach helped validate the requirements of how the group worked *as a team* within the context of particular redesign projects. We also discovered a few additional information objects and their interrelationships. So by taking the approach of supporting redesign projects of ever-increasing complexity, the system value grew incrementally as each new project

was supported. This led to adding only small of new functions to support each new re-design project. This step-wise approach to system development also made simple the discovery and correction of invalid system requirements.

4. A New Interpretation For SADT Graphics And Models

Initially, traditional SADT graphics (see Figure 1 and Figure 5) and models (Figure 6) were used in conjunction with the new systems analysis practices given in the previous section of this paper. From this first modeling task, it became evident that the traditional interpretation of both SADT graphics and models was not corresponding exactly to the language-action framework. From the perspective that sees work as group interaction, an SADT model describes current work practice as interrelated conversations. Contrast this to the traditional interpretation, where an SADT model describes workflow or information flow. Models that specify workflow reveal a perspective where being precise about the information flow has value. Unfortunately, this kind of precision has limited utility for understanding the dynamics of group interaction.

To see why this may be so, consider the situation where a person is trying to follow a set of work rules, but is unable to do so because the context for that work is inappropriate. Imagine we are following a plan to redesign a part for a particular computer, and half-way through the redesign we discover the computer is not selling as we expected. This drop in sales causes our planned return on investment to fall below acceptable business limits. The original plan can no longer be followed and must be revised. The drop in sales is a context which negatively impacts the plan. A software specification or design for support of this work that failed to accommodate this changing context would lead to a system that could not handle the full range of co-operation in redesign projects.

Now consider a description of the conversations people have with the contexts in which those conversations take place. This description allows a system analyst to identify a particular work situation and to then see what conversations, actions, and people are required to produce the most effective results. In the example just given, a description of this kind would first identify falling sales as a context. The specification would then tie this context to the conversations for replanning a redesign project. This approach represents (and ties together!) both the business situations and the work tasks in a way that creates a description of cooperative work from the language-action perspective.

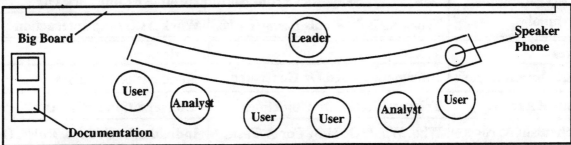

Figure 4: The Group Problem-Solving and Interviewing Room

The graphics of the SADT Activity Modeling Language (Marca & McGowan 1988) are sufficient for creating descriptions that can describe cooperative work situations like the one just given if their "semantics" are correctly altered (Figure 5). The SADT box, input arrow, output arrow, control arrow, and mechanism arrow take on new meanings from the perspective of "work as conversation": 1) boxes represent actions, 2) input and output arrows represent requests and promises, 3) control arrows represent the context within which requests and promises are made, and 4) mechanism arrows represent persons, groups, etc.

With these augmented SADT graphics, a new model was attempted. As soon as this model was started, however, the "semantics" of SADT models themselves also had to change to reflect the shift away from representing work as tasks and information and towards representing work as conversations. Since SADT models are rich in distinctions about systems in general, the semantics werechanged so as to create an alternate modeling framework for cooperative work situations. Figure 6 summarizes the framework for SADT models developed during the CONTRACT Project, contrasted with its traditional interpretation.

A systems analyst would use this framework in roughly the following way. A **Model** describes one or more people working collaboratively, describing what they say (conversations) and do (actions). The **Purpose** is a set of questions about these conversations and actions. A question has the general form: "Given a particular business context, what now will people say and do?" Answers to these questions provide the understanding needed to design a software system for the group. The **Viewpoint** states the vantage point (i.e. appropriate person or group) from which conversations are interpreted. Describing the workplace from a *single* viewpoint keeps the interpretation consistent, and thus consistent answers to the question set are obtained. The **Precision** determines the level of detail to which the model must be taken in order to answer all questions related to the Purpose. Precision, therefore, determines the level of granularity of conversations, below which no additional value is gained by asking more questions. The **Boundary** defines the range over which the conversations and the actions take place. Since conversations take place with other groups of people, the Boundary marks the "organizational interface" (Malone 1985) between groups. Boundary is thus useful for specifying how the resulting software system will ultimately fit into the workplace. Redefining SADT model semantics completes the augmentation of the traditional SADT methodology.

5. Using Augmented SADT To Specify A Coordination Program

The framework for systems analysis given in Section 2, the new practices for systems analysis given in Section 3, and the alternate semantics for SADT graphics and models given in Section 4 together constitute an augmented SADT methodology. We now claim augmented SADT is sufficient for specifying the requirements of a computer-based system that supports cooperative work. A "coordination program" is the generic name currently given to one kind of software tool for cooperative work (Winograd 1988). As background, a brief history of some past research and advanced development projects on coordination programs is given in order to show why the augmented SADT methodology was needed to specify a coordination program for the team responsible for expediting redesign projects.

From a software engineering perspective, coordination programs are distinguished from traditional software applications in that they contain embedded protocols which describe how a group cooperates (Holt & Cashman 1981). Early coordination programs like Monster (Holt & Cashman 1981) and XCP (Sluzier & Cashman 1984) took the approach of specifying group work as a set of rules. These rules defined *sequential* work tasks and the information that interrelates those tasks. Such rule-based specifications were found to be somewhat limited in the kinds of group work situations they can describe. To explain, people using this approach found it difficult to specify rules without also considering their execution sequence. These specifications were thus difficult to quickly and reliably modify when the work process changed (Marca & Cashman 1985). Given these experiences, the CONTRACT Project started with the following question: "How could specifications be written so the resulting software could support cooperative work situations exhibiting rapid change and complex human interaction?"

Other researchers have attempted to answer this question by writing specifications that defined rules for those work tasks which are independent of time. Task sequencing is left up to the group as they work. Coordination programs like COSMOS (Bowers 1988) adopted this approach, and used a declarative specification language to define "timeless" work tasks. Another approach is to consider conversation being common to all work (Winograd & Flores 1986). Specifications written from this perspective concentrate on defining how to manage the commitments people make to each other. Two examples are: CHAOS (De-

SADT Graphic Symbol	Semantics From An Interpretive Framework Of:	
	Work As Individuals Doing Tasks	**Work As Group Interaction**
Boxes	Tasks	Actions
Input/Output Arrows	**Information Used Or Generated**	**Requests & Promises**
Control Arrows	**Triggers, Rules, Or Guidelines**	**Conversation Contexts**
Mechanism Arrows	**Who, What, Or How For A Task**	**Individuals, Groups, Roles, Orgs**

Figure 5: Two Interpretations Of SADT Graphics

Cindio et. al. 1988), which emphasizes elaborate negotiation protocols, and The Coordinator (Winograd 1988), which supports mail message manipulation according to a fixed negotiation protocol.

Two shortcomings exist in all the above theories and systems. The first shortcoming is the lack of a well known requirements specification methodology centered around the language-action perspective. None of the aforementioned efforts successfully employed a *widely-used* systems analysis methodology consistent with the perspective of "work as conversation". Using SADT addresses this first shortcoming.

The second shortcoming is the lack of an *architecture* that identifies and separates the major elements of a coordination program. These elements are: 1) contexts and conversations, 2) the information embodied in conversations, and 3) how conversational information is maintained. This second shortcoming is addressed with a specification architecture created from a paradigm of multiple, interconnected models (Marca & McGowan 1982). This paradigm suggests a set of small models, each focuses on one element and each connects in some meaningful way to the other models. Applying this paradigm results in the specification architecture summarized in Figure 7.

This architecture *encapsulates* the major elements of cooperative work into three models: 1) the **Cooperation Model** describes conversations and the context (i.e. the situation) in which they occur; 2) the **Conversation Model** defines the informational content of the conversations; 3) the **Negotiation Model** describes the process by which some conversations are maintained through the process of negotiation. In addition, this specification architecture associates each model to a particular level. Each level is created so that a model lower in the architecture must rely on the model higher in the architecture.

For example, the Conversation Model describes the informational content for particular commitments without needing to know the details of how the negotiation process is actually defined in the Negotiation Model. The Coopera-

tion Model, in turn, contains the situational context for any particular conversation in the Conversation Model (i.e. the context strongly influences what information people must share during a conversation). Here are some details:

The **Cooperation Model**, the SADT model of Level 1, describes the contexts (i.e. business situations) for the group and the conversations the group has when a particular business situation arises. To create this model, an analyst works along side users in order to understand and define the work contexts and their resulting conversations. Each context and conversation is worked into the model, thereby evolving it into a generalized description of cooperation for the group. For example, in the Cooperation Model of Figure 8, notice how "Problems", one result of implementing a Part Change, is a feedback that becomes a *second* context within which future "Part Change" proposals are made.

The **Conversation Model**, the Entity-Relation-Attribute model (Batra, et. al. 1990) of Level 2, defines the informational content of each relevant conversation have at work. The model is created by using the SADT arrows found in the Cooperation Model to create conversation *types* (i.e. objects), one type for each relevant conversation. For example, Figure 9 depicts how "Product" and "Part" became two separate conversation types because the Cooperation Model of Figure 8 described Product Volumes being the context within which a Part Change is proposed.

The **Negotiation Model**, the state-transition model (Winograd & Flores 1986) of Level 3, defines a protocol (i.e. a method) for maintaining the information for each conversation that is negotiated. Such conversations, called "conversations for action" (Searle 1969), are the speaking that occurs between a specific "Asker" and a specific "Doer". For example, a portion of the CONTRACT negotiation protocol is given in Figure 10. Notice how the specification architecture allows the negotiation protocol to be associated with only those conversation types requiring negotiation (i.e. promises), as in the case of Part. The lack of an attached protocol indicates that a conversation type is an assertion (i.e. fact), as in the case of Product.

SADT Model Characteristics	Semantics From An Interpretive Framework Of:	
	Work As Individuals Doing Tasks	**Work As Group Interaction**
Content	Tasks and information.	People's work context, conversations and actions.
Purpose	Find out how the system generates outputs given certain inputs.	Find out what people say and do in a particular work context.
Precision	How detailed tasks and information have to be.	How detailed conversations have to be.
Boundary	System Interface.	Organizational Interface.

Figure 6: Two Interpretations Of SADT Models

6. How Systems Analysts Experienced Augmented SADT

While using the augmented SADT methodology, the systems analysts on the CONTRACT Project experienced their systems analysis work in new ways. These experiences led to insights about coordination programs and to better ways to specify those kinds of software systems. Some details follow.

Experiencing Users' Work: Eliciting the requirements for a group cooperating at work became easy when the work of users was *directly* experienced. This practice brought the systems analysts close to their users. This closeness had a significant, positive impact on the specification and the process by which it was developed. In particular, their experiences of doing work with the user were superior to their previous intuitions about designing coordination programs. For example, system analysts gained an understanding of the complexities of redesigning parts and managing projects. They used this understanding to discuss with users how difficult redesign scenarios could be correctly supported with the negotiation protocol. These discussions led to a simple specification of negotiation that correctly handled complex redesign projects.

Compressed Review Cycles: The collaborative authoring sessions held in the special meeting room substantially compressed the SADT Author/Reader Cycle. For example, when systems analysts created a model of the redesign process right in front of the users (who were engaged in that process), they gave immediate confirmation of the model's validity and pointed out where the model was inaccurate and deficient. No time was wasted distributing documents that might not have been reviewed in a timely manner (a serious problem for systems analysis projects). Similarly, the typical problem of users forgetting how they actually reviewed documents was avoided.

Integrated Specifications: The interpretive framework of "work as conversation" is a valid perspective from which the traditional SADT methodology can be augmented. The augmentation outlined in this paper was carefully crafted so that SADT descriptions of a cooperative workplace could directly feed the software design. For example, the specification architecture given in Figure 7 ties the SADT Cooperation Model directly to the other models (Stockenberg 1989). The complete set of models provides substantial requirements traceabil-ity and enables software to be written in a direct manner with little additional translation.

Maintainable Specifications: Linking the Negotiation Model to a conversation type creates a model network that can be easily maintained and extended. For example, a change to the Negotiation Model in Figure 10 simultaneously affects all conversation types to which it is linked. This scheme maps directly to the same principles found in object-oriented programming, where the conversation type is the object and the negotiation protocol is the method for that object (Lai & Malone 1988). Thus, the augmented SADT methodology can be used with object-oriented software development methods.

Viewpoint Is Critical: Skillful use of "viewpoint" is essential for producing a useful specification. In particular, the Conversation Model is useful when its conversation types are defined from a single viewpoint. Clarity is obtained when *the single viewpoint consistently interprets any particular act of speech as a commissive or an assertion.* In other words, we need a single viewpoint to see one person's promise as being another person's assertion. For example, Product Volumes are promises when seen from the viewpoint of the Sales Organization. These same statements, however, are seen by the expediting team as assertions, which are the context for Part Changes (i.e. sales are the rationale which justifies funding a redesign project). So, the expediting team sees some conversations as negotiable and others as facts. Thus, a Part Change is a promise (i.e. commissive) made by the expediting team to redesign a part so it costs less to manufacture, and Product Volumes are their facts (i.e. assertions) about the future sales of a particular computer which uses that part.

7. How Users Experienced Augmented SADT

Throughout the CONTRACT project, users gave systems analysts feedback on the utility of the augmented SADT methodology. For example, users said that, during collaborative authoring sessions, the sharing of their work practices made them more effective on their redesign projects. They also said that the specification resulted in an invaluable system for creating accurate reports that allowed them to be the first group ever to successfully pass all internal audits for product redesign. Some details follow.

Computing Business Value: From a business pespective, it does little good to make requests and promises that have little, no, or negative value to the company. The value of a particular promise is determined by the assertions that surround it. Users said the augmented SADT methodology enabled them to distinguish assertions from promises. For

Level	Model	Content	Architectural Intent
1	Cooperation	Contexts And Resulting Conversations	Isolate the conversations and explain why they take place.
2	Conversation	Informational Content Of Conversations	Isolate the informational content of conversations.
3	Negotiation	Negotiation Process	Isolate how conversational information is maintained.

Figure 7: An Architecture Of Interconnected Models

example, Product Volumes are facts used to compute the expected savings of a Part Change, thus enabling a comparison of savings against cost. Users said that augmented SADT let them specify Product Volume assertions so that business value could be computed at any step in a Part Change negotiation. They said this allowed them to evaluate alternate proposals in minutes, and that this system capability was *the most important* to their daily work.

Integrity Of Commitments: Coupled to the aspect of computing business value is ensuring the integrity of a commitment. Users said that for them, any change made to a particular commitment (i.e. a renegotiation) had to "work". They defined "work" as follows: "The savings promised for a particular Part Change must always pay back its redesign costs." This requirement was satisfied by specifying in the Part Change conversation type both "originally promised" and "newly proposed" values for each information element. This additional information ensured that business value could be computed for these commitments, regardless of their negotiation status. For example, users who wanted to renegotiate a commitment could propose a new date and then quickly determine the cost of that renegotiation across all affected products. Users said this capability was critical for doing impact analysis when they renegotiated changes to existing work plans.

Closing And Renegotiating Commitments: Users said that the two-party negotiation protocol accurately specified closing and renegotiating conversations. The specification was a hybrid of those found in Winograd 1986 and DeCindio et. al. 1986. For closing, the "Doer" first asserts the work is done, and then the "Asker" accepts or rejects the work. Users said these distinctions helped them focus their discussions around task acceptance criteria, a trouble spot on previous redesign projects. For renegotiating, the "Doer" has the choice of "reneging" or "revoking" a promise. Users said this distinction helped them clarify whether an existing commitment was being revised from whether it was being terminated, a major source of miscommunication on previous redesign projects.

Granularity Of Commitments: There is a point of diminishing returns with regard to the granularity of commitments on record. Users explained this concept in the following way: "It is not necessary to record that two people will meet to discuss the funding status of a re-design project. It is critical, however, to record the funding decisions they make in that meeting." To satisfy this requirement, the Conversation Model contains only those conversations held during a redesign project that were deemed critical to its success (e.g. funding, product volumes, part changes). Users identified these conversations as being sufficient business information for managing their redesign projects.

8. Closing Remark

The positive experiences voiced by both users and systems analysts indicate augmented SADT has merit for developing cooperative work systems. These experiences were positive because systems analysts took into account social aspects of the user's work. *As system analysts, we choose or not choose to be responsible for the social aspects of people's work.* Research indicates that computer professionals do not realize that they always make this choice when they build a system, whether they do it consciously or not (Zuboff 1984). When systems are developed without this awareness, the quality of people's work can degrade dramatically. For example, some have experienced a decrease in the social interactions that make their work enjoyable and fulfilling *after* automation occured (Zuboff 1984). So, what might be at stake for us as systems analysts is finding ways to combine a responsibility for the social quality of the workplace with our technical expertise.

Acknowledgments

The CONTRACT coordination program was developed within Digital Equipment Corporation by the Intelligent Systems Technology Group, and was usability engineered by the Software Usability Engineering Group. The project was sponsored in part by the Engineering & Technology Group of Computer Systems Manufacturing. The author would like to thank John Bennett, Terry Winograd, and John Whiteside for their extremely valuable review, coaching, and support during the writing of this paper.

Notes

[TM]SADT is a trademark of SofTech, Inc. [1]The views expressed in this paper are those of the author, and do not represent the views of Digital Equipment Corporation.

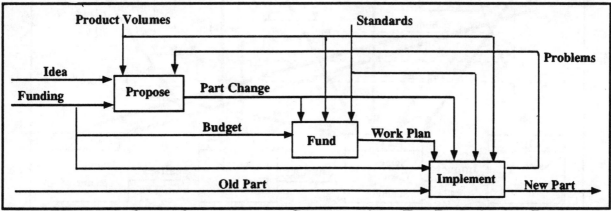

Figure 8: Some Contexts And Conversations For Redesigning Parts

References

Bailey, J., Thornhill, D. "Product Change Process: Meeting Digital's Future Needs" Proc. IDEF Users Group; April 1990

Batra, D., Hoffer, J., Bostrom, R. "Comparing Representations with Relational and EER Models" CACM Vol 33 No 2; February 1990

Bowers, J. "Local And Global Structuring Of Computer-Mediated Communication: Developing Linguistic Perspectives On CSCW in COSMOS" Proc. 2nd Conference On Computer-Supported Cooperative Work; September 1988

Brackett, J., McGowan, C. "Applying SADT to Large Systems Problems" SofTech Tech Paper TP059; Jan 1977

Bullen, C., Bennett, J. "Groupware in Practice: An Interpretation of Work Experiences" MIT, Center for Information Systems Research; 1990

DeCindio, F., DeMichelis, G., Simone, C. "CHAOS As A Coordination Technology" Proceedings Of The 1st Conference On Computer-Supported Cooperative Work; 1986

Ehn, P. "Work-Oriented Design Of Computer Artifacts" Almqvist & Wiksell International; 1988

Ellis, R. "IDEF as a Decision Support System in a CIM Enterprise" Proc. of the IDEF Users Group; May 1989

Flores, C.F., Ludlow, J. "Doing and Speaking in the Office" G. Fick and R. Sprague (eds.) DSS. Issues and Challenges, Pergamon Press, London; 1981

Greif, I. "Computer-Supported Cooperative Work: A Book Of Readings" Morgan Kaufmann Publishers; 1988

Grudin, J. "Why CSCW Applications Fail" Proc. 2nd Conf. On Computer-Supported Cooperative Work; September 1988

Holt, A., Cashman, P. "Designing Systems To Support Cooperative Work" 5th International Conference on Computer Software and Applications Proc; November 1981

Johansen, R. "Groupware: Computer Support For Business Teams" The Free Press; 1988

Joyce, R., Nolan, M. "Interactive Knowledge Acquisition for Tomorrow's Enterprise" Proc. IDEF Users Group; May 1989

Lai, K., Malone, T. "Object Lens: A Spreadsheet For Cooperative Work" ACM Trans. on Info. Systems; Oct 1988

Malone, T. "Designing Organizational Interfaces" Proc. of the Conference on Computers and Human Interaction; April 1985

Marca, D. "Experiences In Building Usable Meeting Support Software" Proc. 1st Groupware Tech. Workshop; Aug. 1989

Marca, D. "Specifying Group Work Applications" Proc. 5th Inter. Workshop On Soft. Spec. & Design; May 1989

Marca, D., McGowan, C. "SADT: Structured Analysis And Design Technique" McGraw-Hill; 1988

Marca, D., McKenna, N., White, S. "Computer-Aided Support For Coordination Technology" CASE'87 Proc.; May 1987

Marca, D., Schwartz, S., Casaday, G. "A Specification Method For Coordinated Work" Proc. Of The 4th Inter. Workshop On Software Spec. And Design; April 1987

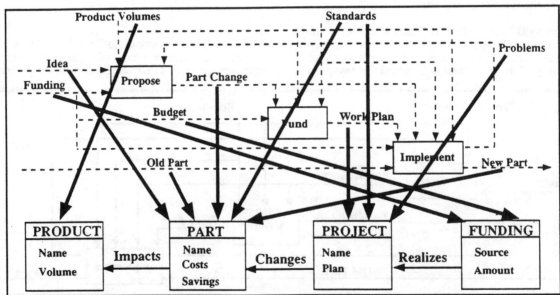

Figure 9: Creating Conversation Types From The Work Description

Marca, D., Cashman, P. "Towards Specifying Procedural Aspects of Cooperative Work" Proc. of 3rd Inter. Workshop On Software Spec. And Design; August 1985

Marca, D. McGowan, C. "Static And Dynamic Data Modeling For Information Design" Proc of the 6th International Conference On Software Engineering; Sept 1982

McDermott, J., Cottrell, R. "Application of IDEF to Banking" Proc of the IDEF Users Group; Oct 1989

Mudge, A. "Value Engineering: A Systematic Approach" Library of Congress number 70-145618; 1971

Mumford, E. "Designing Human Systems" Manchester Business School; 1983

Preston, R. "Process Improvement Through IDEF Methodology" Proc of the IDEF Users Group; May 1989

Pyryemybida, S. "An Enterprise Description -- A Case Study" Proceedings of the IDEF Users Group; Oct 1989

Ramirez, M. "IDEF Applications To Production Systems Definition Proc of the IDEF Users Group; May 1989

Ross, D. "Structured Analysis: A Language for Communicating Ideas" IEEE Trans. Soft. Eng. Vol 3 No 1; Jan 1977

Ross, D., Schoman, K. "Structured Analysis for Requirements Definition" IEEE Trans. on Soft. Eng. Vol 3 No 1; Jan 1977

Schoman, K. "SADT and Simulation" SofTech Technical Paper Number TP072; May 1979

Searle, J.R. "Speech Acts" Cambridge University Press, Cambridge; 1969

Sluzier, S., Cashman, P. "XCP: An Experimental Tool For Managing Cooperative Activity" Conf. on Office Automation; August 1984

Snodgrass, B., "Information Asset Management using IDEF" Proceedings of the IDEF Users Group; May 1989

Stockenberg, J. "Extending IDEF for Modeling and Specifying Real-Time Systems" Proc. IDEF Users Group; May 1989

Thornhill, D. "IDEF: A Management Perspective" Proceedings of the IDEF Users Group; May 1989

Whiteside, J., Bennett, J., Holtzblatt, K. "Usability Engineering: Our Experience And Evolution" Handbook Of Human-Computer Interaction (ed) Martin Helander, North-Holland; 1988

Whiteside, J., Wixon, D. "Contextualism As A World View For The Reformation Of Meetings" Proc Of The 2nd Conf On Computer-Supported Coop Work; Sept 1988

Winograd, T. "A Language/Action Perspective On The Design Of Cooperative Work" Proc Of The 1st Conference On Computer-Supported Cooperative Work; 1986

Winograd, T. "A language/action perspective on the design of cooperative work" Journal Of Human-Computer Interaction, Vol 3; 1987

Winograd, T. "Where The Action Is" BYTE; Dec. 1988

Winograd, T., Flores, F. "Understanding Computers and Cognition" Ablex Publishing Co; Norwood, NJ; 1986

Zuboff, S. "In The Age Of The Smart Machine" Basic Books; 1984

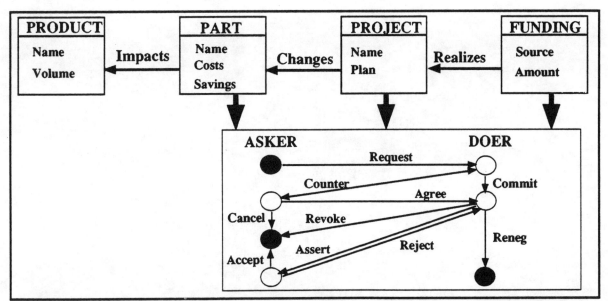

Figure 10: Linking The Protocol To Only Negotiated Conversation Types

Chapter 4:
Enabling Technologies —
System-Related

Chapter 4: Enabling Technologies — System-Related

As more work is kept on line, the need increases for additional communication support including telephone and computer workstations, desk-to-desk conferencing, and data sharing. The growing pervasiveness of these systems requires architectures for the effective integration of their capabilities. What architectures can enable groupware?

This chapter presents major software technologies upon which groupware applications are typically built. The papers in this section create a software platform for groupware (for example, personal name spaces, hypermedia, and replicated databases). Our intention is to give a broad view of the underlying software technologies necessary to design effective groupware applications.

Background: Early architectural work

Engelbart's seminal work, NLS, was the first system designed with a concern for architectural issues in the context of using computers to support groups. The NLS system was built using an architecture comprising a user-interface system separate from specific application processes, a protocol to provide effective communication between application processes, a central collection of tools and services for all users, and special tools for particular work tasks.

These components required messaging, objects, distributed information bases, and hypertext. Though not widely embraced for years, Engelbart's early work ultimately became a cornerstone for CSCW.

Themes: Multimedia, naming, connectivity, hypertext

Today, groupware systems typically run on a platform of general capabilities such as (1) replicated, interlinked, multimedia information; (2) a reliable and responsive communication network; (3) group work session management over time and distance; and (4) a common and consistent user interface. Groupware applications also have to account for performance, scalability, security, and usability. Experience with developing and using these systems indicates the need for a groupware platform that includes a hypermedia network of information; objects for group communication; a customizable user interface; a distributed file system that is secure and scalable; and a reliable, high-performance wide area network.

For groupware application designs, specific system capabilities have to be fully identified during the requirements definition phase. They also have to be fully tested under real usage conditions as early as possible during the development phase. Some field-tested capabilities for today's groupware applications follow.

Multimedia electronic mail. For the users of a distributed system to collaborate effectively, easy sharing of data is vital. Borenstein & Thyberg set a goal to improve their existing base of tools, particularly the underlying file system. Their theory for supporting cooperative work has three main parts: (1) a networked file system that provides the illusion of a uniform central file system; (2) a programming library independent of any particular windowing system; and (3) a very large scale, multimedia mail and bulletin board system. From this theory, Borenstein and Thyberg contributed to the design of the Andrew File System, by applying six principles:

(1) Network computers are commonplace and generally underutilized; let them share the task of maintaining a distributed database.
(2) Given current network throughput rates, use cache to reduce contention on centralized resources and to make data available, as well as transparent, in its origination.
(3) Group work patterns cannot be anticipated; use real-time data access and modification patterns to optimize the database.

(4) Distributed databases can be enormous; minimize system-wide knowledge-and-change information, avoiding continuous updating and replicating of data structures.

(5) Any given computer cannot be guaranteed reliable; depend only on the minimal number of system entities to maximize security.

(6) Database operations are background tasks; use batch operations whenever possible (yet be aware of the latency this may cause).

Bornstein and Thyberg also discuss the need for the distributed file system to address scalability and security issues. A *scalable* file system easily copes with the addition of users and sites, grows with minimal expense, demonstrates little performance degradation when its size increases, and has little administrative complexity built into it. A *secure* file system protects information from undesired access while ensuring that security mechanisms do not inhibit legitimate use of the system. Security issues include authentication, file protection, and resource usage.

Personal naming. Prinz and Pennelli cite two practical problems in supporting group communication: the growing number of message-handling systems and the need for a distributed message directory system. They note how current systems focus strictly on asynchronous communication, creating the need for (1) storage and management of objects, (2) information structuring to match organizational structure, (3) explicit relationships between message entities and their descriptions, (4) a distributed database of messages, and (5) a repository of information about the organization.

Prinz and Pennelli assert the clear need for a directory that supplies information about the users of a message-handling system. They suggest a mail directory structured according to the organization. They recommend the design be established within the context of both the overall work and all the relationships that make that work happen. They recommend an implementation that extends the X.400 Mail Standard to incorporate the concept of group communication. For example, to support organized events taking place between two or more people to achieve a specific goal, they propose: roles, message objects, functions, and rules as building blocks for organizing group communication.

Connectivity for conferencing. Kawell et al. provide a design and an implementation for a replicated database that can support computer conferencing over wide area networks. Specifically, their target is groups of people working with shared sets of documents on a computer network that is *rarely connected*. They exploit the following properties of electronic conferencing: adding documents to a database, limited modifications to documents within the database, no updating of sets of documents, and background operation of database changes. Their design is guided by six principles:

(1) Database replication will be a background activity.
(2) Computers will seldom be connected to one another.
(3) Database replicas must converge over time.
(4) There will be no master copy of the database.
(5) No database replica directory will be provided.
(6) Replication will be extremely fast.

Here is the resulting replication algorithm:

(1) Create a list of databases needing replication;
(2) Create indices to the remote databases;
(3) Copy over newer remote documents;
(4) Delete documents if remote database entries are flagged for deletion; and
(5) Copy necessary remote documents that are missing from the local database.

Experience with this algorithm has demonstrated several benefits. First, replication can occur even though computers are rarely connected to each other. Second, replication becomes a mechanism for automatic, unattended backup. Third, permanent connections to the network need not be maintained by users. Fourth, information can be shared with unsecured sites without losing database integrity. And finally, additional users are supported by simply adding database servers. These benefits make this database system an extremely inexpensive and secure means of supporting computer conferencing.

Hypertext. Conklin provides an extensive survey of 20 hypertext systems, featuring machine-supported links between and within documents. These systems demonstrate new possibilities for using computers as communicating and thinking tools. He categorizes the 20 systems into macro-library systems, problem exploration tools, browsing systems, and general hypertext technology.

Conklin describes the essence of hypertext and its potential. Hypertext is a hybrid technology that blends a database method for creating and accessing interlinked information, a representation scheme that mixes text within a semantic network of links, and an interface modality featuring arbitrarily embedded control buttons. Hypertext linking, the computer support for tracing references, can support idea structuring, categorizing, and referencing. The semantic network created from links enables quick navigation to closely related ideas. The control button interface allows navigation jumps with the single click of a mouse button.

Conklin concludes by describing two problems with current hypertext technology: disorientation and cognitive overhead. *Disorientation* is failing to understand or recognize your present location in the hypertext network. This happens when an unnatural break in your thought occurs because of the need to create "idea units" that do not match your conceptual thinking right at that moment. *Cognitive overhead* is the additional effort required to maintain (simultaneously) several navigation tasks or trails. It is the extra mental energy required to create, name, and keep track of links during your work. Creating "good" names, building "sufficient" links, choosing which link path to follow, and remembering how to backtrack on paths are potentials for cognitive overloading.

Futures: Mail standards, improved hypertext, better networks

The future will most likely see the maturing and standardizing of mail systems. For example, a mail directory standard will probably include three artifacts: (1) a directory information model comprising objects, attributes, object classes, and schemas; (2) a directory information tree, which implements a hierarchy of directory entries down to the object level; and (3) directory system agents (servers that can fragment the directory information tree). This standard will enable organizations to link with one another.

Future hypertext systems will have to expand their capabilities before they can be fully utilized by groupware applications. In navigational capabilities, hypertext must provide contextual versus structured search strategies, search and query of heterogeneously structured networks, versioning for simultaneous exploration of alternatives, and query-based access.

Required computational improvements include computation across the network, choice of built-in or user-defined functions, inference functions that derive and enter new information, reconfiguration of the network in response to new information, and maintenance and manipulation of change history.

For group work support, hypertext must expand to allow applications to create groups of nodes and links, and to manipulate these groups as unique entities. It must keep up with alterations in users' conceptual structures and must provide multiple organizations, message transfers, and notifications. Other characteristics of group work support in hypertext will be annotating, multiple viewing, message transferring, and mutual intelligibility, as well as extensibility (providing an open system), and tailorability (allowing users to reprogram their applications).

The future will also bring significant improvements in today's standard packet-switched networks. The reliability and latency of current networks interfere with synchronous group work situations. Networks exhibiting high bandwidth, high throughput, low error rates, and high reliability are critical for future groupware applications. Groupware developers may be required to trade off these network capabilities, depending on the specific groupware application being built. For example, a computer conferencing system can be effective on a wide area network that guarantees to be only partially operational at any given time. In contrast, a real-time distributed meeting system would be wholly ineffective if it ran on such a network.

Power, ease of use and cooperative work in a practical multimedia message system

NATHANIEL S. BORENSTEIN†

Bellcore, Room MRE, 2A274, 445 South Street, Morristown, NJ 07960, USA

CHRIS A. THYBERG

Room 3017, Hamburg Hall, Carnegie Mellon University, Pittsburgh, PA 15213, USA

(Received April 1990 and accepted in revised form August 1990)

The "Messages" program, the high-end interface to the Andrew Message System (AMS), is a multimedia mail and bulletin board reading program that novices generally learn to use in less than an hour. Despite the initial simplicity, however, Messages is extremely powerful and manages to satisfy the needs of both experts and novices through a carefully evolved system of novice-oriented defaults, expert-oriented options, and a help system and option-setting facility designed to ease the transition from new user to sophisticated expert. The advanced features of the system facilitate types of cooperative work that are not possible with other mail or bulletin board systems, but which would also be impossible in large heterogeneous communities if the system were not so easily used by both novices and experts. A major example of such cooperative work is the Andrew Advisor system, a highly-evolved and sophisticated system that uses the AMS to solve the problems of distributed support for a very diverse user community in a heterogeneous computing environment. The evolution of the Advisor system and its uses of the AMS mechanisms are considered as a detailed example of the power and limitations of the AMS.

Introduction

This paper describes one notably successful user interface program for reading and sending mail and bulletin board messages, the "Messages" interface to the Andrew Message System. This system is currently in use at hundreds of sites, and at some sites its use has become virtually ubiquitous. In such environments, where its advanced features can be universally relied on at both ends of the communication, it has facilitated new kinds of computer-based cooperative activities. In this paper, we will describe the Messages program in order to understand the factors underlying its success, both its popularity with users and its effectiveness as a tool for cooperative work. In particular, we will focus on the question of how it manages to accommodate the diverse needs of novices and experts alike. Finally, we will look at an example of how the system has been successfully used by an independent group to support a rather complex form of cooperative work, the Andrew Advisor system.

† This paper describes work carried out while the author worked at the Information Technology Center, Carnegie Mellon University, Pittsburgh, Pennsylvania.

A good user interface is, of course, always good news to the people who have to use it. All too often however, it has proven difficult or impossible to determine after the fact, what has made a user interface successful or popular. The lessons of popular user interfaces are often idiosyncratic and difficult to generalize, or just plain obscure, as noted in Borenstein and Gosling (1988). In the case of the Messages program, as with all others, a great deal of debate could be made over the reasons for its strengths and weaknesses, or indeed over the precise nature of those strengths and weaknesses. In this case, however, the program was initially built and subsequently remodeled on a clear foundation of assumptions and beliefs about user interface technology, so that the end product may justifiably be viewed as the result of an experiment, an empirical application of one set of user interface design principles. We will make these principles explicit before describing the program itself.

The principles put forward here were not explicitly stated or committed to print prior to the Andrew project, but they were certainly strongly held beliefs that were often expressed in conversation. One of the authors has recently produced an expanded attempt to enunciate these as general principles for user interface design (Borenstein, in press *a*). In that book, arguments are made to justify the principles. Here however, we will treat the principles as axioms, and will consider the resulting artifact, the Messages program, as empirical result of the application of these axioms. Or, to put it more simply, we describe the principles and the result in the hope that the connection between the two will tend to support the validity of the basic design principles involved.

Assumption 1: The actual utility of applications that promise to support Computer-Supported Cooperative Work (CSCW) cannot be judged in the absence of a real user community. Any system, therefore, that claims to make a contribution to CSCW, but has no significant base of regular users, is making an empty or unverifiable claim.

Assumption 2: Usability is an essential prerequisite for any software system with a significant user interface component, which includes all systems to support cooperative work. Even in "research" systems, if the focus of the research is on doing something for end users, as it necessarily must be in all CSCW research, then a highly polished and usable interface is essential. The absence of such an interface will make it nearly impossible to obtain a realistic user community, and will thus necessarily skew any research results in such a way as to make it nearly impossible to evaluate the underlying ideas.

Assumption 3: In user interfaces, there is *no* fundamental trade-off between power, complexity and usability. The most complex and powerful systems can also be the easiest to use, if designed properly, subject to ongoing, consciously evolutionary development.

Assumption 4: In a complex user interface, all defaults should be carefully tuned for the most common novice user responses and expectations.

Assumption 5: Powerful but potentially confusing user interface features should be turned off by default, so as to not conflict with novice learning.

Assumption 6: Mechanisms must be provided to ease the transition from novice to expert, especially in systems where powerful expert-oriented features are not made available without explicit user action to request them.

Assumption 7: Good user interfaces grow and evolve. The most essential part of the design process is the evaluation of, and improvement upon, previous versions of the interface, based on feedback from, and observation of real users of the system.

This paper views the Messages program as an uncontrolled field test of the above assumptions. The successes and failures of the system cannot be absolutely demonstrated to have resulted directly from these assumptions, but it is the authors' belief that a substantial connection does exist. At the very least, the principles provide the philosophical background against which the system should be understood.

Andrew and its message system

Besides the philosophical background, there is also a technical background that must be understood in order to have a clear understanding of the Messages program. Messages was produced as a part of the Andrew project, about which a brief explanation is in order.

The Andrew Project (Morris, Satyanarayanan, Conner, Howard, Rosenthal & Smith, 1986; Morris, 1988; Borenstein, in press *b*) was a colloborative effort of IBM and the Information Technology Center at Carnegie Mellon University. The goal of the Andrew project was to build a realistic prototype of a university-wide distributed computing environment. That is, particular emphasis was paid to the needs of the academic and research communities. The success of that effort can be measured in part by the fact that the prototype has been taken up and is now fully supported by the University's central computing organizations.

As the project evolved, it concentrated on three main parts. The Andrew File System (Howard, 1988; Howard, Kazar, Menees, Nichols, Satyanarayanan, Sidebotham, & West, 1988; Kazar, 1988; Kazar & Spector, 1989) is a distributed network file system designed to provide the illusion of a uniform central UNIX file system for a very large network (10 000 workstations was the design goal).†
The Andrew Toolkit (Palay, Hansen, Kazar, Sherman, Wadlow, Neuendorffer, Stern, Bader, & Peters, 1988; Borenstein, 1990) is a window-system-independent programming library to support the development of user interface software. It currently supports a number of applications, including a multi-media editor that allows seamless editing of text, various kinds of graphics, and animations.

The third main piece of Andrew is the Andrew Message System, or AMS. The AMS, which makes heavy use of the file system and the toolkit, provides a large-scale mail and bulletin board system. It transparently supports messages which include text, pictures, animations, spreadsheets, equations, and hierarchical drawings, while also supporting "old-fashioned" text-only communication with low-end machines such as IBM PCs and with the rest of the electronic mail world. The Andrew Message System has in recent years become widely available. While the Carnegie Mellon installation is still the largest by some measures, there are other

† The Andrew File System technology, AFS 3.0, is a product of Transarc Corporation.

large Andrew sites, one of which has a bulletin board system at least twice as large as Carnegie Mellon's. This paper primarily reflects experience with the system at Carnegie Mellon however, as that is where the system was developed, has been used for the longest time, and has been most readily observed by the authors.

There are many parts to the Andrew Message System, including several non-multimedia user interfaces for reading mail and bulletin board messages from low-end terminals and PCs. There are also several AMS subsystems that have relatively small user interface components, such as the distributed message delivery system. A detailed description of the Andrew Message System is beyond the scope of this paper and can be found elsewhere (Rosenberg, Everhart & Borenstein, 1987; Borenstein, Everhart, Rosenberg & Stoller, 1988; Borenstein & Thyberg, 1988; Borenstein, Everhart, Rosenberg & Stoller, 1989). This paper will concentrate on the high-end user interface, the "Messages" program, and on the manner in which it has proven to be particularly conducive to cooperative work.

Messages: the system functionality

Although the AMS is a complex system made of many parts, to most users the term "AMS" is virtually synonymous with the Messages user interface program, which is all they actually see of the AMS. Messages presents a basic user interface that is quite similar to many other mail and bulletin board readers, easing the learning process for many users. Hidden behind the superficial similarity, however, is a wealth of powerful features that await the interested user.

THE MESSAGES WINDOWS

Messages runs under any of several window management systems, the most common of which is the X11 window system from MIT (Scheifler & Gettys, 1987). The program can open multiple windows on the screen, but typically the novice user is confronted with the single window shown in Figure 1, in which the screen is divided into several subwindows for message bodies, message "captions" (one-line summaries), and the names of message "folders" (collections or directories of messages, analogous to mail classes in some other systems).

Within this main window, the novice user can do everything one might need to do in the course of *reading* mail and bulletin board messages. The most common actions—selecting a new message or folder—are accomplished by pointing and clicking. Other actions, such as deleting messages, are available via the standard Andrew pop-up menu mechanism. For the novice user, there is never any reason to touch the keyboard in the course of reading messages.

To send a message, a user may either choose the Send Message menu item or one of the *Reply* menus. This will cause a new "messages-send" window to appear on the user's screen, as pictured in Figure 2.

MULTIMEDIA FEATURES

A major area in which Messages offers more functionality than most mail and bulletin board systems is in the integrated manner in which it includes formatted text and multimedia objects. In Figure 3, for example, the user is reading a message that

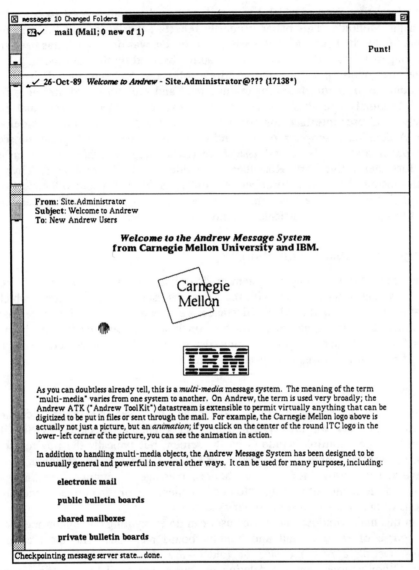

FIGURE 1. The main window of the Messages user interface as it might look to a new user receiving his first piece of multimedia mail.

contains a picture within formatted text. It is important to note that users can read, print, and otherwise manipulate such messages with absolutely no knowledge about the multimedia system. Multimedia messages are fundamentally no different from the user's perspective, to any other messages in the system, and the user need learn nothing new in order to read most of them, and only a few new things in order to compose them.

The multimedia capability of Messages has, perhaps not surprisingly, proven to be one of its most admired and successful features. Crucial to its success has been the

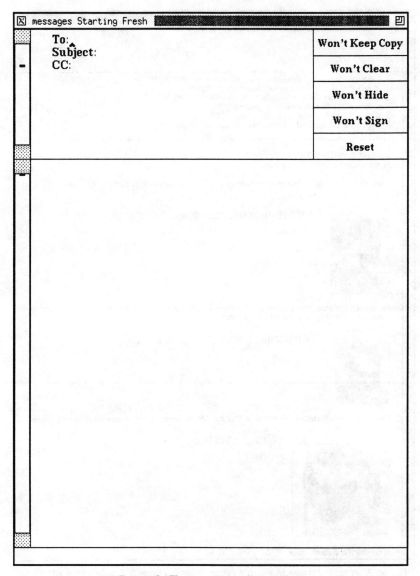

FIGURE 2. The message-sending window.

fact that novices can receive and appreciate multimedia features with essentially no extra effort or learning. Also critical has been the ease with which new and casual users can master a subset of the multimedia authoring capabilities and still get substantial benefit from that subset. Nearly all Messages users quickly learn, for example, the ease and value of using multiple fonts within mail messages.

ACTIVE MESSAGE FEATURES

Another aspect of Messages that has proven extremely useful and popular is a set of features known collectively as "active messages". These are a set of specialized

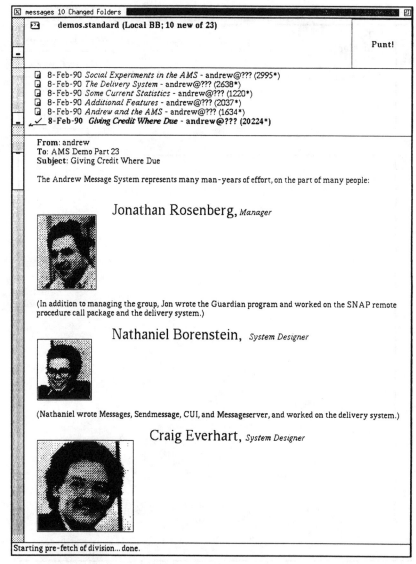

FIGURE 3. A mail message in which a raster image is embedded within formatted text.

message types that carry with them, in addition to a normal (and possibly multimedia) message body, information that directs a particular interaction with the user. For example, one type of active message is the "vote" message. Here special headers direct the user interface to ask the user a multiple choice question, the answer to which will be mailed to a designated address for collection and tabulation. Figure 4 shows a user reading a vote message. In addition to votes, the Andrew Message System supports four other types of active messages: return receipt requests, enclosures, folder subscription invitations, and redistribution notices. (See Borenstein *et al.*, 1989, for details on active messages).

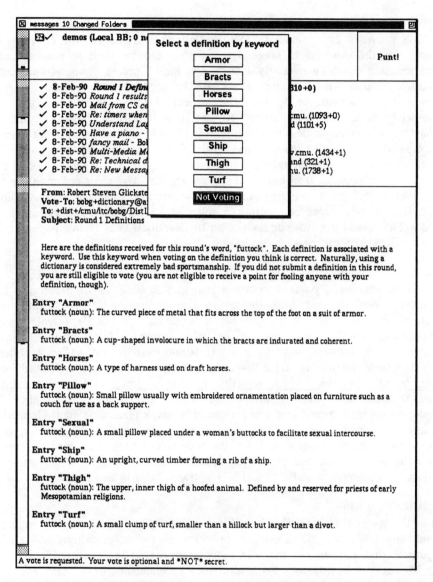

FIGURE 4. A "vote" message, inviting the reader to answer a question and have that answer automatically sent back to a specified destination.

As with multimedia messages, active messages require no special training to be of value to the receiver. For the receiver, they appear simply as messages that magically bring up dialog boxes and ask questions using mechanisms that are easily understood. The amount of expertise required to create an active message is also surprisingly small and is easily mastered by new users of the system.

It seems likely that the notion of "active messages" can be generalized substantially. This is the subject of recent research by Borenstein, unpublished data.

THE FLAMES MESSAGE FILTERING LANGUAGE

The AMS provides an embedded LISP-like language called FLAMES (Filtering Language for the Andrew Message System) that can be used to automatically classify new mail when it arrives. By default, new mail is placed in an automatically-created folder called "mail". However, a FLAMES program can sort incoming mail by keywords, by sender, or by any other aspect of the mail message, and can automatically place mail in the correct folder. (It is important, however, that the user "subscribe" to any folders in which mail is placed automatically, or the system will not automatically show the user the new messages in those folders.) Indeed, a FLAMES program can even reject mail by returning it to its sender, or it can automatically process the mail and send out an answer. The most common use for personal FLAMES programs is to automatically sort new incoming messages into folders. Beyond this, however, several complex FLAMES-based applications have been developed, and the Advisor system, to be described later in this paper, relies heavily on FLAMES for message processing.

PRIVATE BULLETIN BOARDS AND NEW BULLETIN BOARD CREATION

The Andrew Message System supports a rich and flexible set of protection and configuration options that facilitate group communication. In particular, the protection mechanisms permit the creation of public bulletin boards, private boards (readable and postable only by members of a group), official bulletin boards (readable by all, postable only by a few), administrative and advisory bulletin boards (postable by all, readable by only a few), administrative and advisory bulletin boards (postable by all, readable by only a few), and various hybrids thereof. In addition, the protection mechanisms can be (and are) used to allow, for example, a secretary to read and process someone else's electronic mail. (Indeed, a secretary could create something like a magazine for an employer, containing only those pieces of the employer's mail that the secretary thought the employer would really want to see.) The rich protection options make it possible to use message "databases" in innovative ways, as will be illustrated later in this paper.

CUSTOMIZATION OPTIONS

Most of the optional features that have been described are relatively easy to learn. Beyond this however, the Messages program is radically customizable using mechanisms that require substantially more expertise. The Andrew Toolkit, on which Messages is based, provides several such mechanisms, on several levels. In particular, it includes an "init file" mechanism, which offers a simple macro facility for creating compound commands. For situations where such a simple facility is inadequate, the toolkit includes Ness, an extension language described in Hansen (1990), which allows fully programmable customizations and extensions to the behavior of AMS, as well as the creation of powerful interactive objects that can be sent and received with Messages.

Though these mechanisms are complex enough to require substantial time and expertise to master, they are sufficiently useful and accessible to have been used on many occasions to create customized or extended versions of the AMS for specialized purposes, one of which will be discussed at some length later in this paper.

OTHER ADVANCED FEATURES

The AMS supports many other advanced features, too many to describe in detail here. These include:

- Electronic "magazines" which allow one user to act as an "information filter" for many other users and thus reduce the problem of "information flood".
- An unusually rich set of mechanisms for replying to messages.
- Support for easily including excerpts from one message in another in an aesthetically pleasing way.
- Heuristic validation of destination addresses.
- A rich set of variants on the basic notion of "subscribing" to a message folder.
- A large amount of functional support for manipulating message folders.
- Mechanisms for marking groups of messages and manipulating them as a group.

LEARNING ABOUT AND USING THE OPTIONAL FEATURES

As the Messages interface evolved, in every case where a choice had to be made between the needs of novices and the needs of experts, the default behavior of the program was targeted at novice users. The resulting program is undeniably easy for novices to use. For experts, the desire for extended functionality is accommodated through the use of options.

This in general, is a tricky and risky enterprise, because there is really no difference between a non-existent feature and a feature that the expert doesn't know about or can't figure out how to use. In order to successfully meet the needs of experts, it was important to ensure that no major expertise would be required in order to use the expert-oriented features.

The most important mechanism by which this is accomplished in the Messages program is the "Set Options" interface. In any message-reading window, the user can choose the Set Options menu option. When this menu action is initiated, the display is altered, as shown in Figure 5. Here the contents of the "captions" area have been replaced with a scrollable list of user-settable options, and the "bodies" area now displays a scrollable set of option-related information, including interaction objects that can be used to actually change the options.

Using the "Set Options" interface, users can easily learn about and use a large number of sophisticated options. By the time they have exhausted the potential of this interface, they are already expert Messages users by any reasonable definition. Beyond this point, further customization is still possible using more complex mechanisms, as previously mentioned. Although the Andrew help system provides significant assistance to users who want to master these mechanisms, they remain significantly harder than the "Set Options" mechanism. Most users never even attempt to learn to use the other mechanisms, so it is important that the needs of the majority of sophisticated and expert users be satisfied by the use of "Set Options".

The myth of the power/usability trade-off

There is a popular and widespread belief among programmers and end users alike that a fundamental trade-off exists between easy-to-use, novice-oriented programs on the one hand and very powerful and customizable expert-oriented programs on the

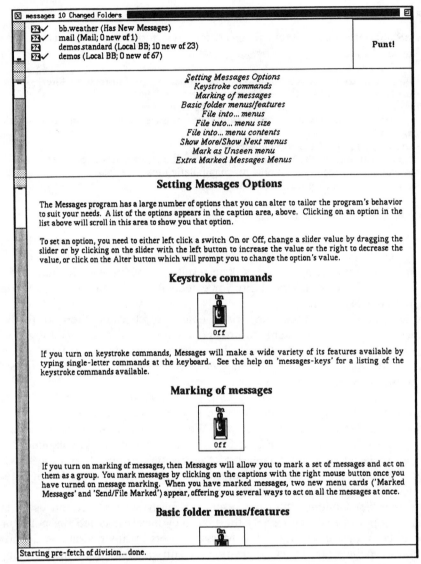

FIGURE 5. The "Set Options" interface, by which users gradually learn about and enable some of the more advanced capabilities of the system.

other. This belief persists in the absence of any really compelling evidence, and in spite of the existence of at least a few examples of programs that successfully "have it both ways".

Along with a handful of other programs, the Messages interface can be viewed as a proof-by-example of the fact that this is not a fundamental trade-off. There is no reason *in principle* why an interface cannot meet the needs of both experts and novice users. Indeed, doing so is startlingly simple in theory, though exceedingly difficult in practice. Basically, only three things are required:

(1) An easy-to-use, novice-oriented default interface.
(2) A large set of powerful features and options that are not visible or enabled for new users.
(3) A smooth, obvious and easy-to-use mechanism by which users can gradually learn about the more advanced features.

Of course, all three requirements are much more easily stated than done. In the case of Messages, these three requirements were successfully obtained only after a great deal of evolution, user testing, and independent evaluation. But it is important to understand that the popularity and success of the Messages interface was not attributable to any particular intuitive genius on the part of the builders, but rather to the process and environment in which the interface was developed.

The initial public releases of the Messages program in particular, satisfied almost none of the users. Novices found the screen layout of the initial version, which mixed folder names and the new messages within each folder in a single scrollable text region, to be confusing and unintuitive. Experts, meanwhile, were frustrated by the many features that had been omitted in the name of usability (and also expediency). In fact, the initial version was met with such hostility that it would have been reasonable to consider simply abandoning the whole project. The fact that the program was able to evolve into the popular interface described in this paper, is indicative of the fact that something did go right in the process by which the system evolved.

The first salient feature of that evolutionary process was the fact it was long and painful. It took about four years of full-time programming work by one person, with additional work by many others at many points. Most of this time was spent trying to get a great number of details right. It is not at all obvious how the process could have been significantly streamlined. There may simply be no substitute for sweat and hard work.

Another aspect of the evolution worth noting is that, from the second version on, the Messages program always had a large community of experienced users as a well as a continuous influx of novice users (in the form of incoming freshman students at CMU). The expert users helped guarantee the continuing accretion of expert oriented features, while the steady stream of new users ensured that the default settings would continue to be refined towards ease of use for novices.

Also crucial during this period, was the fact that Messages captured the attention of a number of non-technical specialists who helped to guide its evolution. The Andrew project was able to hire as consultants, a graphic designer to study the visual aspects of the program, technical writers to improve the documentation and interaction messages, and a human factors expert to study how novices and experts actually used the system and where they got stuck.

Most important, the Messages interface was able to evolve successfully because of the tenacity or stubbornness of many of the parties involved. The author bullheadedly proceeded from the assumption that nothing could possibly be wrong with the interface that couldn't be fixed with enough work—an attitude which, while it produced a good interface in the end, may well have produced a much bigger system than was strictly necessary. The managers supported the project unflaggingly, possibly fearing that the failure of the flagship application would produce domino-like conclusions of failure for the Andrew File System and the Andrew Toolkit, on which the message system was based. The funding had been secured for several years by the initial CMU/IBM contract, so there was essentially no one inclined to put the brakes on the project. Thus, a project that might have appeared to be headed for failure in the early years succeeded in some measure because it was given enough time to evolve naturally. Many other promising projects have surely died due to the absence of such patience and stability.

One useful practice that helped ensure that changes to Messages would be viewed as *positive* was that the author kept a permanent log of all functional changes made to the system. As the system matured through over one hundred releases of the software, this list became increasingly important. When changes were contemplated, the list could be used to determine why the current functionality worked the way it did. Without this list, it is easy to imagine an endless cycle of changes that undid each other to please diverse audiences. The list made it easier to relate new user feedback to the earlier feedback that had shaped the prior evolution of the system.

It is interesting to note that while the Messages interface grew into a form pleasing to experts and novices alike, it did not do this smoothly or continuously. After the disastrously unpopular first release in the spring of 1986, the next few versions were targeted explicitly at increasing the satisfaction of those who were currently using the system, and thus displayed an increasing bent towards expert users. Later, with the influx of new students in the fall, concern shifted abruptly to the difficulties experienced by new users of the system. This pattern continued for several years—expert-oriented refinements occurred in the spring and summer, and novice-oriented work was concentrated in the fall and winter. Good user interface projects are often driven by the needs of their users; in this case, the structure of the academic year was a fortunate coincidence that helped keep the Messages interface balanced between novice and expert concerns.

As the system developed, one of the last major pieces to be put in place was the "Set Options" interface. The evolutionary process just described had created a somewhat schizophrenic user base, with an artificially strong division between the novices and experts. Experts would request a new feature, it would be added, and an announcement would tell them explicitly what magic operation they had to perform in order to enable the new feature. But while established experts were able to assimilate one new bit of magic at a time, the growing body of such magic gradually became a major hurdle that prevented new users from growing into experts. That problem was substantially solved with the introduction of "Set Options".

Probably the hardest part of the evolutionary process was determining, whenever an expert-oriented change was made or contemplated, how that change would affect novices who were rarely part of the discussion about the functional change. It is very difficult for experts to predict how novices will react. Thus it is often hard to determine whether or not a new feature should be available by default. Indeed, the wrong decision was made on more than one occasion, though this was only found out via feedback from later novices. The only useful principle in this regard is to at least make an effort to view each new feature through novice eyes; this will catch many, though not all of the potential problems. The remainder simply have to be caught by experience with future novices.

To the authors, in hindsight at least, much of this appears to be little more than the application of common sense to practical user interface design. It is worth pausing, therefore, to consider why the myth of the power/usability trade-off is so widespread. Here too, the answer is mostly common sense: the above approach to interface evolution is quite costly, frustrating and time-consuming. It is so sufficiently hard and rare to build an interface that is exceptionally good for novices, or exceptionally good for experts, that most projects are more than satisfied with either achievement. For that reason, many users have rarely, if ever, been exposed to an interface that works well for both categories of user. The myth, then, is a simple case of unjustified extrapolation: "if I've never seen an elephant, then elephants must not exist".

Unfortunately, the analogy may apply equally to the future prospects for interfaces that work well for novices and experts. Like the elephants, which are being slaughtered wholesale for their ivory, such interfaces may be almost doomed to extinction by the laws of economics. It is far from clear that there is any substantial economic advantage to building programs that are tuned for both novices and experts, but it is all too clear that building them in such a way entails substantial extra costs. It seems sadly unlikely, therefore, that we will see a proliferation of such programs in the near future.

Putting it all together: cooperative work in the Andrew Message System

The Andrew Message System has proven to be exceptionally popular with its user community in general. Weekly statistics indicate that roughly 5300 people use it at Carnegie Mellon to read bulletin boards regularly. Even more users read their personal mail with the system. The AMS is also in use at over a hundred other universities and research sites. This would be indication enough that the system is a success; however, the greatest enthusiasm has in fact been found among those who are using the AMS for substantial cooperative activity. Most notable among these devoted users are the people who provide support services on Andrew at CMU. The Andrew Advisor is a singular example of real-life cooperative work, conducted with the Andrew Message System.†

THE ADVISOR SYSTEM

Centrally supported and distributed UNIX computing at CMU has a long and diverse history. The most recent milestone is the Andrew Project, as described above. Quite apart from the Andrew project is the much longer tradition of departmental UNIX computing, especially among such UNIX sophisticates as are to be found in the School of Computer Science. This tradition is a major influence on the development of centrally supported, distributed UNIX computing. Indeed, "collaboratively supported" is a better phrase than "centrally supported" since it indicates the (sometimes stormy) marriage of departmental and central facilities, systems administration, and user services.

† Substantially different versions of the following discussion of the Advisor electronic mail consulting service have appeared in Borenstein and Thyberg (1988) and Thyberg (1988).

The central computing organizations at Carnegie Mellon face unusual challenges in supporting their computing constituency. Four factors complicate the task. First, the distributed UNIX computing environment we provide has grown substantially beyond the Andrew project, and is now a complex assemblage of vendors' operating systems, the Andrew File System (now provided by Transarc Corporation), the X11 windowing environment from M, the Motif user interface offerings from the Open Software Foundation, third-party and campus-contributed software and, of course, the components of the Andrew project: ATK and AMS. Furthermore, this environment is provided for and supported by hardware from many manufacturers. Second, although the environment has been widely deployed and promoted, it is an ever developing, rapidly changing environment. As a result, it is not too inaccurate to characterize the computing environment as a 9000-user beta-test site. Third, campus computing expertise is widely, but unevenly, distributed. The users span the entire spectrum from technophobe to technophile. Fourth, the people involved in software development and maintenance, system administration, and user services belong to several organizations and work in different buildings.

To cope with these challenges, members of the Distributed Workstation Services group (DWS), with the help of the AMS group, developed an extensive electronic mail consulting service called "Advisor". Advisor presents the user with a single, private, and personal help resource for every conceivable problem a user might encounter in the complex system described above. The user simply mails a query to Advisor's account. In 24 to 48 hours, private mail comes back to the user from Advisor's account, prepared by a DWS staff member. In fact, however, Advisor is the front-end of a vast network of bulletin boards that enlist the cooperative efforts of all the professional staffs in the central computing organizations.

ADVISOR I

Advisor has been in use since January 1985. In the earliest days, it was simply another Andrew account. One person logged in as "advisor", read the incoming mail, handled it with what limited tools were available (online lists, hardcopy lists, hand written notes, and a good memory for the status of a given request), gathered information by talking with the programmers, and sent out replies to the user. This worked reasonably well during the deployment of Andrew when there were a small number of carefully selected users and the Andrew consultant had an office among the Andrew developers.

The first public Andrew workstation lab appeared in the spring of 1986. Shortly thereafter, Andrew accounts were made generally available. Advisor was immediately overwhelmed with mail. An additional consultant picked up Advisor duties, but there were always problems with how to divide the work between the two staff members and how to keep track of the status of any given message. A rudimentary method for classifying messages did exist, but the mechanism was clumsy, time-consuming and not that useful because all the messages were lumped together in one large, flat mail directory. The combination of the large volume of the easy questions and the genuine difficulty of the hard questions made it difficult to process Advisor mail in a timely fashion. We clearly required some way of getting almost immediate assistance from the right people in other organizations.

In the fall of 1986, the first version of what is now the Andrew Message System was released to campus. It marked a major advance in the integration of electronic communication. Personal mail and bulletin boards, though conceptually distinct, were now no longer different in kind. A public bulletin board and a user's private mailbox are both examples of message databases. The only real difference is the degree of accessibility to other users. As indicated above, the AMS supports a rich and flexible set of protection options that permit the creation of public bulletin boards, private bulletin boards, official bulletin boards, semi-private bulletin boards and shared mailboxes, and other variations on the theme. Furthermore, since message databases are built on top of the UNIX hierarchical directory structure, bulletin boards could now be nested within each other.

One of the authors hit on the idea of using bulletin boards as folders for classifying Advisor's mail. The authors created a suite of semi-private bulletin boards, postable by the whole community, but readable only by those in the central computing organizations, and wrote a program in a primitive stack-oriented language for automatically filing messages. (The stack-oriented language was the predecessor to the FLAMES language described earlier). The result was Advisor II.

ADVISOR II

Tom Malone, in his discussion of the Information Lens system (Malone, Grant, Turbak, Brobst & Cohen, 1987), has identified three fundamental approaches for handling large volumes of electronic information. The first approach, *cognitive filtering*, attempts to characterize the contents of a message and the information needs of the recipient. The system then matches messages about XYZ with readers who have expressed an interest in XYZ. The second approach, *social filtering*, focuses on the relationships between the sender and the recipient. In addition to the message's topic, the status of the sender plays a role in the reader's interest in the message. The final approach, *economic filtering*, looks at implicit cost-benefit analyses to determine what to do with a piece of electronic mail. Advisor II relied heavily on both cognitive and social filters as the criteria for automatic message classification.

Each message to Advisor that did not come from a member of a known set of Advisor "helpers" was assumed to be from a user requesting assistance. The message was then placed on a bulletin board called "*advisor.open*". The Advisor staff subscribed to this bulletin board and used it as an inbox for new questions. A copy of mail from the user was also placed in *advisor.trail,* to assist the staff in keeping track of requests, and to *advisor.qa,* to which answers would also eventually go, thus forming a repository of useful past work. Thus, the first criterion for sorting the mail was a social one—is the sender a helper or a user? The list of the helpers, that is, the staffs of the various computing organizations, had to be kept current as constants within the stack language program that did the automatic filing of messages.

An incoming question from a user was also copied to one of a series of subject-specific bulletin boards, according to keywords in the subject line. For example, if a subject line was "mail bug", the message was copied to *advisor.mail.* These bulletin boards, though not open to the public, were readable by the developers, system administrators, etc. who subscribed to the bulletin boards covering their areas of interest and responsibility. To continue the example, the AMS group members subscribed to *advisor.mail*, thereby increasing the likelihood of seeing only those messages generally relevant to them. Uninformative or nonexistent subject lines caused the message to be copied to *advisor.misc*. All good Advisor helpers were expected to subscribe to *advisor.misc*, in addition to their other subscriptions. Thus, the second criterion for sorting mail was a cognitive one—is the mail likely to be of interest to a particular group of people?

Cognitive and social filtering were combined at several critical junctures. For example, when the Advisor staff requested more information from the user, Advisor received a blind carbon copy of that request. Because the message was from Advisor, it did not go into *advisor.open* by virtue of the social filter which stipulated that Advisor was never to be taken as a user asking for help. Instead the message went to *advisor.trail* and to the relevant subject-specific bulletin board by virtue of cognitive filtering of the subject line. Another example was in the processing of contributions from Advisor helpers. A helper would see a question on some topical bulletin board. By choosing the Reply to Readers menu option (which prepends "Re:" to the same subject line as the user's initial post), the helper sent the answer, not to the user, but directly back to that subject-specific bulletin board. By virtue of social filtering, mail from helpers never went into *advisor.open*, but only to some topic-oriented bulletin board. And when a final answer was sent to the user, the blind carbon receipt once again bypassed *advisor.-open* because it was from Advisor and ended up on *advisor.trail* and the correct topical bulletin board. In addition, the Advisor would carbon copy the final answers to the *advisor.qa* bulletin board. Unfortunately, the questions and answers were not paired, but in chronological order, due to early limitations in the AMS.

To summarize: the Advisor staff answered questions from *advisor.-open* as they were able. They kept an eye on the relevant subject-specific bulletin boards for help with the difficult problems. Having collected the information from the helpers, the Advisors sent polished answers back to the users. As far as the users could see, they had sent mail to Advisor and received an answer from Advisor. The fact that there was additional internal consultation was kept behind the scenes.

EVALUATION OF ADVISOR II

The key feature of the first automated Advisor mechanism was the automatic filing of messages into subject-specific bulletin boards. The positive effect of this was two-fold. First, messages came to the immediate attention of the other technical groups. Often, the Advisor staff found that someone in another group had already answered the question before Advisor had even looked at it. This kind of pro-active assistance was greatly appreciated. Second, because requests for more information and final answers passed back to the subject-specific bulletin boards, the other groups could provide problem-solving advice and assure technical accuracy.

However, the negative effects outweighed the positive. First, poorly phrased questions from the users led to many "misclassifications". The message filing algorithm worked quite well, but so many subject lines were virtually contentless, e.g. "Help!", that far too many messages ended up on *advisor.misc*: close to 50%

of all mail to Advisor, according to the authors' estimate. Without better characterization of the message's content in the subject line, the Advisor staff were helpless to get the right mail to the right parties. The designers of Advisor considered the possibility of also searching the body of a message for sort keys, but the pre-FLAMES filtering language was not powerful enough to support free-text information retrieval techniques. Advisor settled for pattern matching on the subject line, rather than suffer too many false keyword hits.

Second, with every question going to a subject-specific bulletin board, the Advisor helpers had no easy way to distinguish between the questions the Advisor staff knew how to answer and those they didn't. Hence, they wasted time answering some questions unnecessarily and neglected other questions for which help really was required. In retrospect, it seems like a truism, but actual use of the mechanism vividly showed that cooperative work disintegrates if what is expected, and from whom, is not clearly articulated. Computer-supported methods can just as easily exacerbate the problem of undefined expectations as alleviate it.

Third, because every blind carbon from Advisor and every message from an Advisor helper also went to the subject-specific bulletin boards, these soon became too cluttered to be of much use. On the one hand, helpers got tired of wading through them. On the other, Advisor, at that time, had no way to show a message and all the replies to it in a single chain, so it was sometimes very hard to find the answers that were already available. There is nothing so deadly to cooperation as seeming to ignore another's efforts. Despite Advisor's best intentions, this problem appeared far too often.

Fourth, because every question and every answer went to *advisor.qa*, but the question and the answer were not adjacent messages, *advisor.qa* proved to be virtually worthless as a resource for the Advisor staff.

These four failings were compounded by the rapidly growing amount of mail being sent to Advisor. More staff were needed, contributing to difficulties working from a single inbox, and the helpers were becoming frustrated beyond their willingness to assist in the support of Andrew. It was clear that Advisor needed a significant overhaul.

ADVISOR III

The third version of the Advisor system was implemented in 1988, and, with the exception of the recent changes described below, Advisor III represents the current state of the system. In Advisor III, the only automatic sorting of incoming mail is by the day it arrived. This sorting is done by a FLAMES program. Mail goes into one of *advisor.inbox.monday, .tuesday,* etc. Student Advisors are each responsible for a particular day's worth of Advisor mail. They acknowledge every piece of user mail, handle most of the requests, and then cross-post the tough questions on topic-oriented bulletin boards with names like "*advisor.helpbox.mail*". Figure 6 gives a sampling of the current suite of helpboxes. They are very similar to the "magazines" mentioned previously—they are, in essence, journals compiled by the Advisor staff of just those questions that require the help of some other group to answer. The technical staffs subscribe to appropriate helpboxes and to the parent bulletin board, *advisor.helpbox.* Posts to the parent bulletin board notify Advisor helpers of the

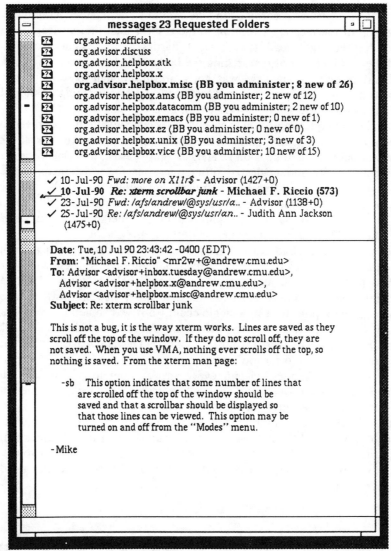

FIGURE 6. A partial listing of the Advisor suite of bulletin boards; a sampling of helpboxes.

creation of a new helpbox, give a synopsis of its purpose, and invite them to subscribe. All this is done automatically, via folder subscription invitations, one of the "active message" features mentioned above.

Some members of the technical staff prefer to receive as personal mail the postings to the helpbox they've agreed to monitor. FLAMES makes it trivial to combine any helpbox with a distribution list of interested individuals: these helpers get direct mailings while the bulletin board serves as a shared archive. The helpers' replies go back to Advisor' mailbox, where the FLAMES program processes them and, on the basis of a special reply-to header, places them on the correct helpbox and sends them to any associated distribution lists. The Advisor on whose day the question came in collects the information posted to the helpbox and sends a well-crafted reply to the user.

In addition to the helpboxes, there are *advisor.questions* and *advisor.trail* which provide rudimentary measurement and tracking. Copies of the incoming user mail get placed in *advisor.questions* and *advisor.trail* automatically, thanks to the FLAMES program. Monthly daemons take messages off these bulletin boards and archive them in date-stamped subsidiary bulletin boards, for example, *advisor.questions-Apr-1990*. There is even an Advisor bulletin board, *advisor.daemons,* where the daemons report their activities.

To assist Advisors in getting good answers to the users, a collection of interesting questions and their answers is generated on *advisor.outbox,* which replaces *advisor.qa* from Advisor II. The Advisor uses improved message-filing commands to move back-to-back question/answer pairs to the *advisor.outbox.* Also, there are two bulletin boards for internal dialog; *advisor.discuss,* for meta-Advisor debate and general Advisor information, and *advisor.official* where official pronouncements from other groups can be posted. *Advisor.official* is how Advisor receives such technical and policy "FYI" ("For Your Information") items, insuring that every Advisor sees the information, not just the Advisor on the day the FYI was sent.

It is important to note that Advisor III no longer applies any social filtering to separate the folks who are likely to be qualified to send us official FYIs from those who are not. Staff in other groups who wish to send us an official FYI are simply told to send it directly to the address *"advisor + official".*† We apply social pressure on our peers should we ever get information on this channel that is not accurate or useful. In fact, what usually happens is that the Advisors themselves and their supervisors see official pronouncements elsewhere and resend them to *advisor + official.* Another benefit of removing Advisor II's social filtering mechanism is that we no longer discriminate against staff; our peers are able to ask questions of Advisor just as our users do. And by no longer having to maintain lists of who are the helpers, we have been able to expand our assistance base significantly since it is trivial to create and maintain an access group for a particular helpbox using the protection mechanisms mentioned earlier.

EVALUATION OF ADVISOR III
By putting human intelligence to work at the heart of the system, the Advisor staff solved in one stroke several of the problems that troubled Advisor II. First, Advisor can support a far more fine-grained suite of helpboxes than it could with automatic filing. Poorly phrased subject lines are less of a concern because humans read the mail and digest its contents before passing it to a topical bulletin board. Second, when an Advisor staff member puts a question on a helpbox bulletin board, everyone knows this means help is genuinely needed. Third, because clutter does not automatically accumulate in the helpboxes, these have become "high-content" bulletin boards that the programmers and administrators feel are worth

† The Andrew Message System interprets any address of the form "userid + text" to be deliverable to the user named on the left of the " + " character. It is up to the FLAMES program processing that user's mail box to take whatever action the user would like, keying off the text to the right of the " + " character. If the user has no FLAMES program, or his FLAMES program doesn't recognize the text, the message is dropped off into the user's mail folder.

reading regularly. The pay-off for Advisor is a much more reliable information resource. And just in case there are a number of items pending on a given helpbox, the AMS now has a Mark Related Messages menu option which puts a marker beside all the messages in a given reply-chain. Advisor rarely misses a helper's contribution in the new scheme. Fourth, *advisor.outbox* is a useful repository of previously answered queries because the Advisors themselves decide to post only those question/answer pairs that are likely to be of future use. The questions are now adjacent to their answers with the addition of the message filing command, Append to Folder, which takes a set of marked messages and adds them to the end of a folder, rather than shuffling them into the folder in chronological order.

In summary, though Advisor III lacks the pro-active help and the quality assurance that was evident in Advisor II, the Advisor staff is better equipped to handle the load than before. Currently, Advisor receives, on average, 450 new messages per month; 714 messages received is the current single-month record. Note that these are new requests from users; the total number of messages that pass through the Advisor system, including help from Advisor helpers, requests for more information, and replies to users, averages 50 messages per day, or 1500 per month. The student Advisors do an admirable job of performing triage on incoming mail. Full-time DWS staff now function much more as Advisor supervisors, taking areas of technical responsibility, expediting helpbox requests, and insuring that the answers that go out from Advisor are timely and accurate. Messages in Advisor III filter up "manually" through different levels of expertise: the simplest questions are answered by the students, the harder ones are answered by the full-time consultants, and the hardest are tackled by the programmers and administrators themselves. At each level, humans work diligently and efficiently to minimize time-delays inherent in the system. But all parties involved feel that the Advisor scheme focuses and streamlines their efforts.

There were, however, some aspects of Advisor III that cried out for significant improvement. First, there was the problem of correctly routing follow-up mail to the inbox where the initial mail was placed. For example, if the first piece of mail about a particular problem came on Monday and thus was placed in *advisor.inbox.monday,* how would Monday's Advisor continue a dialog with the user on Tuesday, without having all that mail end up in the inbox of the Tuesday Advisor? If the follow-up mail is delivered to the Tuesday Advisor, parallel processing or deadlock can occur as both Tuesday's and Monday's Advisors try to figure out what's going on.

Second, we had no good way of tracking requests to Advisor. We would have liked to have been able to find out quickly, for any particular piece of mail from a user, when that mail arrived, who on the Advisor staff first handled it, who in some other organization was then working on it, what the current status of the item was, and so on. This was just one aspect of a larger need for good monitoring tools on Advisor. We needed ways to measure the flow of questions, their types, the steps taken to answer them, and the mean time to find an answer for a user.

Third, Advisor handles a huge load of routine items like requests for more disk quota. These are matters that rarely require attention from the Advisor staff, save to pass them along to a system administrator and send the users an acknowledgment of receipt. It would have been nice if it took little or no effort to handle such requests.

Fourth, routine filing operations were tedious and error-prone. For example, when closing an interesting exchange with a user, the Advisor had to move mail, one by one, into *advisor.outbox*. The messages that constituted the dialog were likely to be spread around in the inbox and were not necessarily connected by the same subject line. The Advisor would have to rummage around and find all the relevant messages, get them over to *advisor.outbox* in the correct order, and then delete the entire set from the inbox.

How the designers of Advisor have addressed these concerns, and what issues remain for future exploration, is discussed in the remainder of this paper.

ADVISOR TODAY

The Advisor III system was sufficiently successful to leave the basic scheme unaltered. Incoming messages are still classified primarily by the date of receipt, and then filtered upward as necessary through human action, allowing the simplest questions to be responded to by the least-expert Advisors. However, the authors believe that the powerful automatic classification features Messages provided encouraged over-automation. in Advisor II and that Advisor III was in large part a reaction against such over-automation. The further development of Advisor has been evolutionary, incremental, and in the direction of adding more automation back into the system. This time, automatic mail handling features have been added in a much more selective, principled, and informed way than was the case in the crude keyword-classification mechanisms of Advisor II. Automation has been added where it could solve specific problems in the Advisor mechanism, rather than attempting to automate the entire process at once.

Structuring routine advisor actions

While the Advisor designers were concerned to solve in a piecemeal fashion particular shortcomings with Advisor III, the authors believe that a pattern of development has been emerging which can be characterized as the application of the language-as-action paradigm (explicated in Winograd & Flores, 1986; Winograd 1988) to various aspects of the Advisors' actual work practices. This paradigm, along with the Information and Object Lens work of Malone, Grant, Lai, Rao and Rosenblitt, (1987) and Lai and Malone, (1988), has guided the Advisor staff toward the semi-formalizing of certain linguistic "steps" that Advisor frequently makes in the "language dance" from initial query to final answer.

We mentioned earlier that sorting Advisor mail by day creates the problem of how Monday's Advisor continues a dialog with a user on Tuesday, without getting in the way of the Tuesday advisor. This problem is solved with the Messages customization facilities mentioned earlier. The designers of Advisor have developed a suite of specialized message sending/replying commands on the *Advisor* menu card of the "messages-send" window as shown in Figure 7. These commands, which are also bound to keys, insert a special reply-to message header on the outgoing mail. That mail, and all mail in reply to it, get sorted into the correct day's inbox by virtue of that header. So even though the follow-up reply from the user comes in on Tuesday, it still goes to the Monday inbox, where Monday's Advisor is waiting for it. This mechanism is not foolproof. For example, a user may send in a piece of mail at 11:59 pm on Monday and follow it at 12:01 am on Tuesday with another piece of mail about the same matter, but with a completely different subject line. Since no reply from Advisor has come to the first message to provide the hook on which to hand subsequent dialog, the two messages are going to end up on different inboxes and the Monday and Tuesday Advisors are going to have to work it out. Still, the special reply-to header works in most cases to route extended mail exchanges correctly.

Notice in Figure 7 that these commands make no mention of any particular day of the week. The day-specific special message header is correctly inserted by virtue of an environment variable, *DAY,* which conditions the behavior of this single set of commands automatically and appropriately. This variable is set for each Advisor in a personal setup file he invokes whenever he logs into the Advisor account. Should this setup mechanism fail and the *DAY* variable be undefined, the sending/replying commands will prompt the Advisor for which day of the week it is that he is now answering. The Advisor can enter the day on the fly and can also set *DAY* for the rest of the session with the Change Advisor Day menu action. Staff members who work on more than one day's worth of incoming messages can, in a single Advisor session, trivially switch back and forth between, say, their identity as the "Tuesday advisor" and their identity as the "Wednesday advisor". With a single operation, they change all of the special header information that identifies and tracks their correspondence in these roles.

The second problem, tracking the actions that have been taken in response to a user's request for assistance, is one that Advisor continues to wrestle with. To provide the hooks for a solution, the Advisor staff introduced the notion of special message headers that indicate the "state" of each piece of Advisor mail in the progression from initial acknowledgment to closure. State is automatically set by use of the four sending/replying commands shown in Figure 7: Acknowledgment, Request for Information, For Your Information, and Final Answer, each of which marks the outgoing message with a distinct state message header: "ACK", "RFI", "FYI", and "ANS", respectively. A reply from the user to an Advisor message of a particular state can inherit the same state message header, which in turn can be processed by either Ness or FLAMES to generate rudimentary tracking and measurement. For example, one could go to advisor.trail, start with a user's initial request, and trace the entire exchange, noting Advisor's acknowledgment of the query, all requests for and provision of further information, and what Advisor believed to be the closing message. If the user replies to that "final answer" it indicates that the matter is still open. Unfortunately, there is currently no way to go back and change the state of Advisor's first "final answer" to something like "first try at an answer", "second try at an answer", and so on. As we have said, tracking a user's request is not yet fully developed in the current Advisor system.

The third area of concern in Advisor III is that of quickly handling the large volume of mail that requires nothing more than "message-shuffling" on Advisor's part. The most frequent request of this sort is the request for more disk quota. The Advisor neither dictates nor applies the quota policy and does not have the privileges required to actually change a user's quota. Thus, the Advisor does little more than acknowledge the user's request and pass it along to the Accounts group,

200

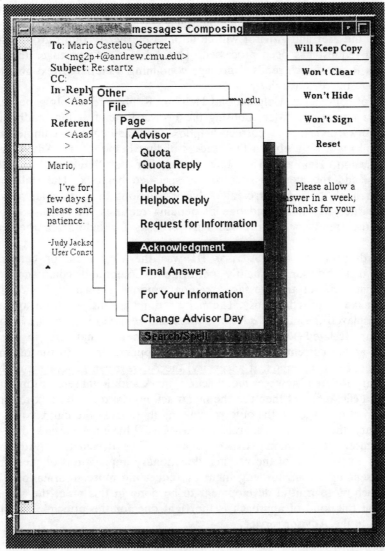

FIGURE 7. Custom Advisor commands for sending or replying to users' mail.

who makes the judgement whether additional quota should be granted and perform the necessary steps required to increase the user's quota. To streamline handling quota requests, the Advisor staff created the pair of menu actions Quota and Quota Reply, also shown in Figure 7. First the Advisor chooses the Forward menu action to create a message-sending window with the user's mail in it, giving the Advisor the opportunity to make annotations if warranted. Then the Advisor chooses Quota. The user's message is automatically addressed to *advisor.helpbox.quota,* and a command is run to generate some information about the requester's current disk usage. The results from this command, which are captured in a distinctive font, are prepended to the user's text and the resulting message is sent off with the state message header, "Quota", which gives us a hook for measuring the number of quota requests Advisor processes. The message also has a modified reply-to header so that both the user and Advisor will be notified by the Accounts group when the user's quota request has been processed. The Advisor acknowledges the user by using Quota Reply, which sends a message containing a prepared text about policy and current resource constraints.

The pair of commands, Helpbox and Helpbox Reply, are simply generalizations of the quota operation. After choosing the Forward menu action, addressing the mail-to-be-forwarded to the correct helpbox, and adding any commentary the Advisor thinks will be useful to the readers of that helpbox, the Advisor chooses the menu action, Helpbox. The state message header "Helpbox" is added to the message and the message goes to the specified helpbox. The state message header is a hook both for tracking Advisor's actions in getting an answer for the user, particularly to remind one of pending requests for assistance, and for measuring the frequency with which Advisor asks for help from the technical staff.

The fourth problem with Advisor III was the clumsiness of certain filing operations that Advisor frequently performed. Compound commands on the *Classify* menu card of the messages-reading window, shown in Figure 8, were created to make these actions easy. The menu action Current→ Outbox appends the currently displayed message to *advisor.outbox* and removes it from the inbox. The menu action Related→ Outbox gathers the messages that are in the same reply-chain as the currently displayed message, appends them to the outbox, and removes them from the inbox. If necessary, the Advisor can generate a reply-chain with the Mark Related Messages menu action, mark additional relevant messages by pointing and clicking, and then use the menu action Marked→ outbox to move the entire group of messages to the outbox, deleting them from the inbox.†

In summary, the four problem areas for Advisor III have been attacked by putting some structure into common Advisor behaviors. The designers of Advisor have made some investigation of the varying illocutionary implications of such linguistic actions as sending an acknowledgement or requesting more information. Though there is much more fruitful development to be done in this area, the authors are satisfied that this kind of approach is the right one for the principled addition of automation to the Advisor service.

Linking support groups

The Distributed Workstation Services group has for some time been exporting the Advisor concept and connecting the Advisor system to other help groups on campus. The most mature example to date is a bridge between the *advisor.helpbox.datacomm* bulletin board and a suite of bulletin boards attached to an account, dc0m, belonging to the Network and Communications group. Rather

† Another evolutionary change in the Advisor system has been the development of customized environments for each of the Advisor staff members. Staff members have developed their own auxiliary sub-systems, including additional bulletin boards for their own pending Advisor items, and have elaborately customized compound operations defined as well. The move-to-pending menu actions in Figure 7 are examples of a "personal" extension of the Advisor mechanism which has been adopted by all the Advisors.

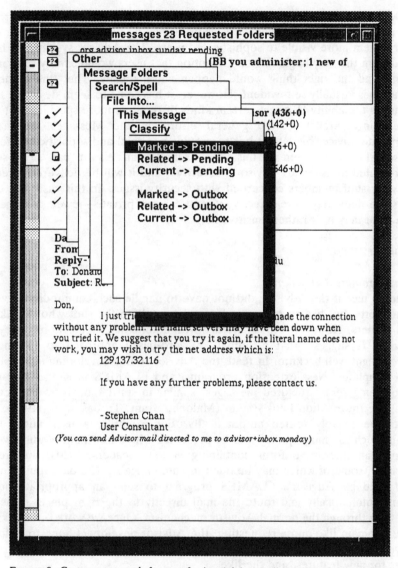

messages 23 Requested Folders

org advisor inbox sunday pending

Other   (BB you administer; 1 new of
  Message Folders
    Search/Spell
      File Into...
        This Message   sor (436+0)
          Classify   (142+0)
            Marked -> Pending   6+0)
            Related -> Pending
            Current -> Pending   646+0)

            Marked -> Outbox
            Related -> Outbox
            Current -> Outbox

Da
From
Reply-   u
To: Donald
Subject: R

Don,
        I just trie   nade the connection
without any problem. The name servers may have been down when
you tried it. We suggest that you try it again, if the literal name does not
work, you may wish to try the net address which is:
        129.137.32.116

        If you have any further problems, please contact us.

        - Stephen Chan
        User Consultant
        (You can send Advisor mail directed to me to advisor+inbox.monday)

FIGURE 8. Custom commands for transferring Advisor mail into the *advisor.outbox*.

than have these folks subscribe to the Advisor helpbox as a second source of input
to their group, the Advisor designers created a "hot link" between the two groups.
When Advisor puts mail into its datacomm helpbox, it is automatically resent to
dc0m with a special header. When someone in Data Communications replies to that
mail, by virtue of that header, it comes back directly to Advisor's helpbox, just
where the Advisor expects to find it. There are similar links to other groups who
employ Advisor-like systems that we have exported for both academic and
administrative use. In this way, DWS hopes to provide these groups with a common
front-end to the community—mail to Advisor—while allowing them to use whatever
internal consulting structures suit them best. It is our belief that a large part of
Distributed Workstation Services' role is to enable this kind of distributed support.

203

Revealing Advisor's inner workings to users

Another subtle but useful change has been in making the hidden structure of the Advisor system more visible to sophisticated users. The Advisor system was heavily oriented from the very beginning to the notion that users would simply send mail to "advisor" and the right thing would happen automatically. That this is ideal for novice users is virtually self-evident. However, it has come to seem desirable to give expert users the ability to direct certain kinds of requests more specifically. (This is an interesting parallel to the general effort, in the Messages interface, to accommodate novices by default but to provide powerful and sophisticated features to those who want them.) Thus, for example, an expert can now send a security-related message to "advisor + security", and it will be delivered directly to the Advisor staff members concerned with security issues. In this case, not only is the message delivered more directly, it is also more private—fewer staff members will see what may be a rather sensitive message.

ADVISOR'S FUTURE

Structuring routine user actions

It would be nice if the Advisors did not have to handle such commodity services as quota requests, but had them forwarded immediately to the staff who do take care of such matters. However, the experience with automatic classification by keywords in Advisor II suggests that a simple keyword-based approach to routing such messages might well backfire. Instead, the Advisor staff is developing a combination of mail templates, Ness extension programs, and FLAMES programs that permit users to create semi-structured messages, similar in spirit though not in detail, to those of the Information Lens system (Malone, Grant, Turbak *et al.*, 1987), which can then be reliably routed automatically. For example, a user might type a command such as "more-quota" and be presented with a new mail-sending window, containing an interactive form containing various headers, fields, and relevant information, some of which may be filled in automatically. The data thus generated is then used by Advisor's FLAMES program to send an appropriate acknowledgment automatically and route the mail directly to the right place, rather than have it filter through the normal Advisor mechanism. Once we work out the kinks in a limited domain like quota requesting, the Advisor developers hope to follow this prototype with interactive templates and FLAMES parsings for bug reports, requests for new features, and the like.

Automatic Advisor "claim checks" and social filtering

We indicated earlier that we have not completely solved the problem of routing all mail from a user about a given problem to a single Advisor's inbox. It has been proposed that the FLAMES file which processes incoming Advisor mail immediately sends back to the user a confirming message which will ask the user to send Advisor any further messages about the matter at hand by replying to this "claim check" message. While such a claim check could be implemented today, the Advisor staff feel it makes more sense to introduce this after we have supplied some Advisor-submission templates, because then the claim check that is returned can be made apropos of the type of query Advisor received. It is here Advisor may introduce social filtering again. For example, if the submission mechanism can automatically generate information about the status of the sender (e.g. faculty, staff, student, which department, etc.), then the handling of this mail, including the initial claim check, can be sensitive to the different needs of these constituencies and the (possibly) different computing policies that apply to various groups.

Structuring routine helper actions

Those who cooperate with Advisor by reading helpboxes and posting information there do so on a voluntary basis. It would be useful to develop tools for the helpers that semi-formalize their uptake of Advisor's requests for assistance. To design such tools will require careful thought about various illocutionary categories like directives—Advisor messages that attempt to get the helpbox reader to do something (e.g. answer the forwarded question), and commissives—helper messages that commit the helper to some action (e.g. fix some bug by a certain date). Furthermore, the helpers need some way to transfer ownership of a commitment, and both Advisor and the helpers need tools to facilitate the negotiation of help commitments, especially if they are subject to change as new information and technical and resource feasibilities warrant. Similarly, if the staffing model for Advisor changes significantly from that of an Advisor taking an entire day's worth of Advisor mail to a queue of requests that all the Advisors draw from, then there may be much greater need for internal mechanisms whereby different Advisor staff members can take up, transfer, and close responsibility for individual user requests. The work of Winograd and Flores, especially as it has begun to appear in software products like The Coordinator, is fundamental to our explorations in this area.

Tracking and measurement revisited

An experiment has been conducted with the Advisor system to use our FLAMES program to automatically generate an Informix database of tracking information about all the traffic through the Advisor system. This database, which was a course project for a group of students in the Social and Decision Science department, never went into full-scale use, largely due to a lack of programming resources. Nevertheless, the idea seems very promising, and also points strongly to the lack of database facilities as an underlying weakness in AMS. The Advisor staff is looking for additional resources to take up this project in earnest. The result will be a system parallel to Advisor's myriad bulletin boards that both the Advisors and their supervisors can use to get status on a particular user request, as well as to generate routine statistical measures and reports.

Question/answer service for users

The *advisor.outbox* is a fairly useful collection for Advisor's own use. But the notion of a database or a hyper-document of commonly asked questions and expert answers that grows in step with Advisor's question-answering is what we are aiming for. Such a tool would be enormously valuable to the Advisors themselves, their helpers, and other computing consultation services around campus. With careful user-interface design and expert system intelligence, it could also be most beneficial to the end user, provided that the information was timely, accurate, and easy to navigate. A recent example of the sort of system we would like to graft onto Advisor is the Answer Garden (Ackerman & Malone, 1990).

Other engines behind the AMS front-end

The infrastructure for the Advisor service was put together using AMS bulletin boards as much for the reason that was the tool we had available as for any intrinsic virtues of bulletin boards. Exploring other computer-based communication technologies would be a useful exercise. For example, computer conferences are a different breed of animal to bulletin boards. It would be very instructive to re-implement Advisor's helpboxes using an advanced conferencing system, one rich in mechanisms for assigning various roles and passing control of "the floor", in order to see how many of the tools for semi-formalizing Advisor and helper behaviors simply fall out as a consequence of the particular strengths of computer conferencing.

At a more fundamental level, it is clear to the authors that the Advisor service has nearly reached the limits of what current AMS bulletin boards can do as information repositories—AMS does not provide a general database mechanism, but Advisor often needs one. Then again, without AMS and its powerful kit of features and customization and extension mechanisms, the Advisor staff, who are neither academics nor researchers, but practising consultants and service providers, would likely never have pursued the vision of computer-supported cooperative consulting to the point where such limitations become apparent. When the son-of-AMS is available, whatever that might be, the designers of Advisors ars poised and ready to investigate the avenues of development outlined above.

Conclusions

The Messages interface has been highly successful as a user interface, easily learned and appreciated by novices, easily extended by experts, and powerful enough to support major cooperative work applications. Although one such program cannot be considered proof, it lends support to the notion that power and usability are not fundamentally incompatible. It demonstrates one approach to reconciling power and usability, which entails tailoring all default behavior to novices while providing a simple and graceful mechanism by which experts can extend its power.

The evolution of the Advisor system has taught its designers a great deal about computer-supported cooperative work. Our failed experiments have been the most instructive of all our experiences. But with each incarnation, Advisor feels more and more like an enduring technology for user support in times when central consulting services are lean and everyone looks to some form of distributed consulting to ease the load. We realize that we have only begun to scratch the surface, but we feel we are taking the right steps to exploit the ever-increasing power and sophistication of distributed computing in higher education. The Advisory staff, most of whom are not programmers, have proven able to use the expert-oriented features of the Andrew Message System to develop FLAMES programs, customized compound commands, hot links between support systems, Advisor-templates, and interfaces to alternative engines largely independent of the AMS developers. It is by virtue of putting these tools in the hands of cooperating workers that the Advisor system continues to be an interesting example of how the AMS supports a large, important, complex, "real-life" cooperative work application.

Messages is a part of the Andrew Message System, which was developed by Nathaniel Borenstein, Jonathan Rosenberg, Craig Everhart, Bob Glickstein, Adam Stoller, Mark Chance and Mike McInerny. Substantial parts of the Messages user interface reflect the suggestions and experiences of thousands of users, but most especially the suggestions of Dan Boyarski, Chris Haas, Chris Thyberg and Pierette Maniago, who devoted substantial time and effort to studying, deploying and extending the system. The Andrew Message System was built on top of the rich infrastructure provided by the Andrew File System and the Andrew Toolkit, which are themselves the product of a great deal of work by a great many top-notch software developers. The Andrew Message System and the Andrew Toolkit are part of the Andrew software as distributed on the X11R4 tape from MIT. They are freely available to all interested parties.

Advisor II was conceived by Chris Thyberg and implemented by Pierette Maniago, with help from Nathaniel Borenstein. Advisor III was designed and implemented by Chris Thyberg, Pierette Maniago, and Adam Stoller. Recent Advisor extensions are the work of Chris Thyberg, Wallace Colyer, Judith Jackson, Bob Glickstein and Michael Riccio.

Continued thanks also go to our frontline Advisors over the years. They are the real answer-givers and they have been an unfailing source of useful suggestions for the improvement of the Advisor mechanism and of distributed user support in general.

Finally, none of the work described here would have been possible without the encouragement and support of some very enlightened and visionary management at both CMU and IBM. This paper was written with the support of equally enlightened management at Bellcore.

Judith Jackson helped substantially with the description in this paper of the Advisor system. The paper also benefited greatly from the comments of several anonymous reviewers, as well as Terilyn Gillespie, Peter Clitherow, Bob Kraut and Steve Rohall.

References

ACKERMAN, M. & MALONE, T. (1990). Answer garden: A tool for growing organizational memory. In *Proceedings of the Conference on Office Information Systems,* Cambridge, Massachusetts. New York: ACM Press.

BORENSTEIN, N. S. & GOSLING, J. (1988). UNIX Emacs as a test-bed for user interface design. In *Proceedings of the ACM SIGGRAPH Symposium on User Interface Software,* Banff, Alberta.

BORENSTEIN, N. S., EVERHART, C. F., ROSENBERG, J. & STOLLER, A. (1988). A multi-media message system for Andrew. In *Proceedings of the USENIX 1988 Winter Technical Conference,* Dallas, Texas. Dallas, TX: USENIX Association.

BORENSTEIN, N. S. & THYBERG, C. (1988). Cooperative work in the Andrew Message System. In *Proceedings of the Conference on Computer-Supported Cooperative Work, CSCW 88,* Portland, Oregon.

BORENSTEIN, N. S., EVERHART, C. F., ROSENBERG, J. & STOLLER, A. (1989). Architectural issues in the Andrew Message System. In E. STEFFERUD, O.-J. JACOBSEN & P. SCHICKER, Eds., *Message Handling Systems and Distributed Applications.* Amsterdam: North-Holland.

BORENSTEIN, N. S. (In press *a*). *Software Engineering and Other Delusions.* Englewood Cliffs, NJ: Prentice Hall.

BORENSTEIN, N. S. (In press *b*). CMU's Andrew project: a report card. *Communications of the ACM.*

BORENSTEIN, N. S. (1990). *Multimedia Applications Development with the Andrew Toolkit.* Englewood Cliffs, NJ: Prentice Hall.

HANSEN, W. (1990). Enhancing documents with embedded programs: how Ness extends insets in the Andrew Toolkit. In *Proceedings of IEEE Computer Society 1990 International Conference on Computer Languages,* New Orleans.

HOWARD, J. (1988). An overview of the Andrew File System. In *Proceedings of the USENIX 1988 Winter Technical Conference,* Dallas, Texas.

HOWARD, J., KAZAR, M., MENEES, S., NICHOLS, D., SATYANARAYANAN, M., SIDEBOTHAM, R. & WEST, M. (1988). Scale and performance in a distributed file system, *ACM Transactions on Computer Systems*, **6**, (1).

KAZAR, M. (1988). Synchronization and caching issues in the Andrew File System. In *Proceedings of the USENIX 1988 Winter Technical Conference*, Dallas, Texas.

KAZAR, M. & SPECTOR, A. (1989). Uniting file systems, *UNIX Review*, March.

LAI, K.-Y. & MALONE, T. (1988). Object lens: a spreadsheet' for cooperative work. In *Proceedings of the conference on computer-supported cooperative work*, CSCW 88, Portland, Oregon.

MALONE, T., GRANT, K., TURBAK, F., BROBST, S. & COHEN, M. (1987). Intelligent information-sharing systems, *Communications of the ACM*, **30**, (3).

MALONE, T., GRANT, K., LAI, K.-Y. RAO, R. & ROSENBLITT, D. (1987). Semi-structured messages are surprisingly useful for computer-supported coordination. In I. GREIF, Ed., *Computer Supported Cooperative Work: A Book of Readings*. San Mateo, CA: Morgan Kaufman.

MORRIS, J., SATYANARAYANAN, M., CONNER, M., HOWARD, M., ROSENTHAL, D. & SMITH, F. (1986). Andrew: a distributed personal computing environment, *Communications of the ACM*, **29**, (3).

MORRIS, J. (1988). Make or take decisions in Andrew. In *Proceedings of the USENIX 1988 Winter Technical Conference*, Dallas, Texas.

PALAY, A., HANSEN, W., KAZAR, M., SHERMAN, M., WADLOW, M., NEUENDORFFER, T., STERN, Z., BADER, M. & PETERS, T. (1988). The Andrew Toolkit: an overview. In *Proceedings of the USENIX 1988 Winter Technical Conference*, Dallas, Texas.

ROSENBERG, J., EVERHART, C. & BORENSTEIN, N. (1987). An overview of the Andrew Message System. In *Proceedings of SIGCOMM '87 Workshop, Frontiers in Computer Communications Technology*, Stowe, Vermont.

SCHEIFLER, R. & GETTYS, J. (1987). The X window system, *ACM Transactions on Graphics*, **5**, (2).

THYBERG, C. (1988). Advisor—an electronic mail consulting service. In *Proceedings ACM SIGUCCS User Services Conference XVI*, Long Beach, California.

WINOGRAD, T. & FLORES, F. (1986). *Understanding Computers and Cognition*. Norwood, NJ: Ablex Publishing Corp.

WINOGRAD, T. (1988). A language perspective on the design of cooperative work. In I. Grief, Ed. *Computer Supported Cooperative Work: A Book of Readings*. San Mateo, CA: Morgan Kaufman. .

Relevance of the X.500 Directory to CSCW Applications

- Directory support for computer based group communication -

Wolfgang Prinz[a] and Paola Pennelli[b]

[a]German National Research Center for Computer Science (GMD), P.O. Box 1240, D-5205 St. Augustin, West-Germany, prinz@f3.gmd.dbp.de

[b]Tecnopolis - CSATA Novus Ortus, Str. Prov. Casamassima km 3, Valenzano (Bari), Italy, pennelli@ibacsata.bitnet

Abstract

In 1988 the standardization bodies ISO and CCITT released the first international standard of a distributed Directory Service [3]. The purpose of the Directory as it is described by the standard is to supply a global nameserver and an application independent management and information service. But these applications are not exhausting the possibilities of a Directory usage. It is the intention of this paper to present the possibilities and chances the Directory offers to applications in the CSCW area.

Our investigation focuses on CSCW models and applications that support and coordinate communications in groups [15]. First the paper identifies and analyses components which most of these applications have in common. For the analysis we introduce the classification of activity oriented models and conversation oriented models. Then, after a brief introduction into the X.500 Directory Service, it is shown in which way the identified components can be represented by the Directory Service. The paper concludes with a discussion of desirable improvements on the Directory Service.

1. Introduction

A consequence of the growing number of Message Handling System (MHS) users is the need for a directory that supplies information about MHS users. In 1984 this demand led to the constitution of a working group by the standardization bodies ISO and CCITT with the task to define a distributed directory system for OSI applications and users. The result is now available as the CCITT X.500 or ISO 9594 Directory Standard [3].

The standard describes two main purposes of the Directory. The first purpose is to supply an application independent management and information service for information about OSI-applications and their users. The second purpose is to serve as a global nameserver, i.e. for the management of globally unique 'user-friendly names' for objects of the real world which are represented by entries in the Directory.

Even if the idea of a globally unique Directory defined by the X.500 standard is very new and probably unknown to most people, it can be foreseen that the Directory will become a widespread and important support tool for communication systems similar to the success of e-mail systems. Therefore, it is worth to think about the possibilities of a Directory application in the CSCW area at this early stage. This paper presents the possibilities and chances the Directory offers to applications in the CSCW area. We will illustrate how developers and researchers in the area of CSCW can benefit from considering the possibilities of the X.500 Directory.

Our investigation focuses on CSCW models and applications that support and coordinate communication in groups [15]. Henceforth, we will call these models and applications Group Communication Support Systems (GCSS). Examples of such systems and models are CHAOS [5], Lens [11], DOMINO [10], COSMOS-SDL [2] and the AMIGO Activity model [6]. They also include models [6, 7] that consider an application of the Directory for a technical support. An additional application of the Directory Service for the administration of logical GCSS components avoids a distribution of that information among different information management systems or database applications and a unified management is achieved, instead.

2. Components of Group Communication Support Systems

It is the aim of this paper to describe the benefits of a Directory application for group communication support systems (GCSS). To this purpose we should first identify and analyze those components which are common to most CSCW applications and which are suitable for storage and administration by the Directory service.

2.1. The Basic Building Blocks of Group Communication Support Systems

The field of CSCW comprises a large number of different applications. That is why a comprehensive investigation of all kinds of applications within this paper is impossible. Instead, we will focus our considerations on applications which support *asynchronous* communication, i.e. group-communication based on e-mail systems. Henceforth, the term communication should be understood as asynchronous message based communication. Models and applications of that type have been available since several years, and research in that area is still going on. This offers us the opportunity of analyzing these applications in order to identify possibilities for a Directory support and to propose an appropriate Directory usage for future developments.

A useful basis for our analysis is a survey of group communication support systems presented in [13]. In this survey we compared models and systems developed in the context of office automation, group communication and conversation analysis (e.g. speech act theory). Since the different terminologies and terms used by the various models may lead to confusion, we used the basic components of the AMIGO Activity Model (AAM) [4] as a comparison schema. This was done by mapping components and elements of the considered models onto the AAM components which served as a platform for a uniform analysis of the different models.

An important result of this investigation is, that the elements of all considered models can be mapped onto the AAM components even if different representation methods are used. This enables us to abstract from concrete realizations and to concentrate on the AAM components illustrated below as the basic building blocks of GCSS:

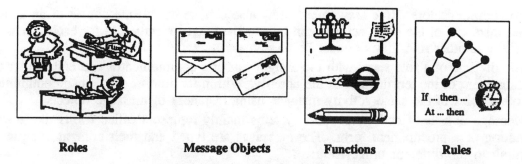

| Roles | Message Objects | Functions | Rules |

Figure 1: Basic building blocks of GCSS

The *message object* component describes the types and structures of messages that occur in a communication process. An abstract description of the characteristics of the communicators in communication is given in the *role* component. Operations that roles perform (e.g. on messages) are described by the *function* component. It is the purpose of a GCSS to support and coordinate the exchange of messages between roles and to describe the conditions under which roles have to perform which functions. These regulations are described in the *rule* component.

After this identification of the basic building blocks of GCSS we will now have a closer look on each component in order to see whether a representation in the Directory is possible and useful.

Representation methods for the function component range from the simple naming of functions to a procedural description. Within the rule component nets (DOMINO, Officetalk-D, CHAOS) or production rules (PAGES [8], Information Lens, COSMOS-SDL) are used for the description of the coordination. The Directory data model does not provide means for the representation of procedural descriptions, nets, or rules. Therefore, a representation of the rule and function component is only possible as a data stream without any semantics for the Directory. Consequently, a Directory representation of GCSS elements that realize these components is not of interest.

For the analysis of the role and message object component we distinguish between **activity oriented** systems and **conversation oriented** systems. We will see that the systems and models[1] of each group use different representations of roles and message objects.

2.1.1. Roles and Message Objects in Activity Oriented Models

Activity oriented systems are designed to support the cooperative execution of a goal oriented task. Characteristic of such tasks is that the regulations which structure the communication process can be described in advance. We will call the communication process described by the regulations an *activity*. Most of the systems developed as office procedure systems belong to this group. An example for activities, such systems are able to support, is a travel application procedure or a procurement procedure.

The models of this group use the role concept as a means for an abstract description of the function and behavior of a communicator within an activity. The description is independent of the individuals or automata that fulfill the roles. For example the roles of a date-planning activity [16] are *initiator* and *participant*, for a travel application activity the roles are *applicant*, *authorizer*, and *travel agent*. Each time an activity is instantiated, a communicator (e.g. a person or an automaton) is assigned to that role, i.e. a new role instance is created. One communicator may play several roles as well as one role can be fulfilled by

---

[1] The survey considers models as well as realized systems. Henceforth, we will use the terms system and model as synonyms when we mean both, realized systems and theoretical models.

several communicators. Role assignments may also change during the course of an activity. Several instances of the same activity can be executed concurrently and for each instance of an activity another role may or must be chosen.

The lifetime of a role starts with the assignment of a communicator and ends either with a reassignment or the termination of the activity. Within its lifetime a role can communicate with other roles of the same activity instance using instances of message objects.

Message objects of activity support systems mainly represent office forms like a travel application or a procurement form. The messages are typed and their content is structured according to the different office forms.

The definition of the roles and message objects of this group are activity specific. For each activity different roles and message types must be defined and their definition is meaningful only in the context of the activity in which it appears. Since the roles and message objects defined by models of this group are only referable in the activity-specific communication, we call them *communicational roles* or *communicational message objects* respectively. Addressing of a communicational role in a communication outside of the activity is not possible.

2.1.2. Roles and Message Objects in Conversation Oriented Systems

A user support for everyday conversations which are independent of a specific activity is provided by models and systems we want to classify as conversation oriented systems. For example, these systems automatically arrange the user mail according to its context or they propose appropriate message types for the next communication act within a conversation according to predefined rules. In most cases these rules are derived from the speech act theory, such as in CHAOS and Coordinator [18].

Other systems, e.g. Lens, make the attempt to support the user in filtering and sorting messages as a means to overcome the information overload and to eliminate junk mail.

Common to all of these systems is that they do not apply the role concept. The purpose of the systems is the support of users in individual communication. Therefore, it is not desirable to adopt the role concept as it is used by the activity oriented systems as a means to prescribe the behavior of a communicator in his/her communication. This technique is only required for activities where communicators must behave in a prescribed way in order to fulfill their task within the activity

Nevertheless, we want to propose an adaptation of the role concept that makes it also useful for conversation oriented models. The adaptation requires a specification of roles which is independent of a particular activity. Roles must be defined as components of the environment in which the conversations between the communicators take place. They should represent the status and function of the communicators within that environment. For the communication applications, we consider this environment to be determined by the organization. Consequently, we will call roles of that type *organizational roles* to differentiate them from activity specific communicational roles. Examples of such roles are *boss, project-leader, project-member, or secretary.*

In contrast to a communicational role, the assignment of a person to an organizational role is independent of a particular activity. The lifetime of the role and the role communicator assignment depends on the organization in which the organizational role is defined. This assignment will not change very often. Henceforth, there will be only one set of role instances, i.e. communicators assigned to a role, in contrast to the communicational roles where each activity instance results in an additional set of role instances. Therefore it is possible to specify the name(s) of the person(s) who fulfill the organizational role by the very role description. For communicational roles, instead of names of persons, predicates that express constraints and requirements may be given. The role player has to satisfy them in order to play the role as expected. These requirements can be used for the selection of a role player as well as a for a qualification test of a given person. Alternatively, names of organizational roles can be specified as role players. The role player selection is then restricted to those communicators that are allowed to play the organizational role. In that case a person is bound to a communicational role via the assignment to an organizational role.

Another advantage of the role concept is that persons can be addressed by their role name. In organizations this is useful because in most cases people do not know the names of the people that fulfill the different roles but they know the names of the departments and the roles within that department, e.g. finance dep. → cashier or project xyz → project leader and project members. In the last example, one role name denotes a group of people (project members), i.e. mailing a message to the role project member is like mailing it to a distribution list.

In almost every organization, formal or informal communication regulations exist by which people communicate which each other. These regulations determine who may communicate with whom for which purpose. Such regulations express, for example, that an employee has to consult his/her boss first before s/he negotiates with other departments, or that s/he has to ask the secretary first before s/he goes into the office of the director. Such regulations, which are expressed over the organizational roles people play, do not exist for electronic communication [12]. Therefore it happens, that users violate the communication regulations and etiquette either by intention or in the most cases unintentionally because they simply do not know the regulations. An inclusion of such regulations into communication support systems would increase the level of support and would help the user to behave more adequately, i.e. according to etiquette. A first attempt towards that direction was made by Tsichritzis and Gibbs in [19].

Conversation oriented systems offer the user a predefined, and in some cases extensible, set of structured message types. The different message types are composed according to the forms that exist within an organization. Consequently, we will call such messages *organizational message types*. Examples for organizational message types are *short-notice, inquiry, commitment*. Both techniques, the typing and structuring of messages, shall help the users to select an appropriate message type for communication and to fill out the message with the required information. Furthermore, these techniques allow a message type and content based filtering, arranging and sorting of incoming messages.

It should be noticed that the set of organizational and communicational message types is not disjoint. For example, a travel application might be either an organizational message type as well as a message type used within a travel apply activity. Messages, that initiate an activity always belong to both groups. When they are initially sent the activity has not yet been started. After the acceptance by an activity support system, the activity is initiated and from this time on its type can be regarded as a communicational message type.

2.2. Requirements

A comprehensive user support that includes support for cooperative activities as well as a support for individual communication requires a combination and integration of activity oriented and conversation oriented systems. An important integration aspect is that common and interrelated components of the different systems are managed and accessible by only one database management system (DBMS) in order to avoid multiple and inhomogeneous representations of the same information. So far, each system uses its own application specific database or knowledge base system. In the following we will list the most important requirements a general database should fulfill.

a. Roles and message types are objects with specific properties. Therefore, the database should provide means for the storage and management of objects.

b. For the description of organizational roles it is important to express its organizational context, i.e. the department to which the role belongs and its hierarchical level. A DBMS that provides means for a hierarchical ordering of entries would be suitable for that purpose.

c. Organizational and communicational roles are fulfilled by people or automated services (role players). The binding of a role to its role players is described by naming the role player or by describing possible role players using a predicate. Additionally, bindings from role to role are possible. Therefore, the DBMS should allow the description of relations between entries. Furthermore, it is important that the database stores all employees, services, roles and message types, etc. of an organization. Different and inhomogeneous DBMS each of them storing a different subset of the organizational information are not practicable for that purpose.

d. Communication systems are mostly distributed systems and organizations are very often locally distributed as well. Consequently, one should choose a distributed database that allows the storage of information at the places where it is produced and managed.

e. The information of large organizations will not be managed by a single authority but by all those authorities being responsible for the information. That entails the need for a distributed management of the database information.

f. Communication and cooperation is not bound to the borders of an organization. A database that additionally provides information about other organizations and their employees, roles, etc. would well support the cooperation of different organizations.

After a brief introduction into the X.500 Directory system in the following chapter, we will show in which way the Directory satisfies the previously listed requirements.

3. The X.500 Directory

A Directory System (DS) is a facility for storing and maintaining information about various objects in a distributed system. Such objects may be users, resources or services available, either within a single network or within several interconnected networks. The Directory is a distributed service offering a distributed administration of all information it contains. A DS hides changes in the network from the user because it enables him/her to refer to an object by name instead of by network address, for example. It also provides a more user-friendly view of the network so that users have an efficient method of referring to network information. In the following we will briefly describe the information model and the services of the Directory. A more comprehensive description of the Directory can be found in [1, 17].

3.1. The Directory Information Model

The information model describes the logical structure of the directory information. Each object of the 'real world' known to the Directory is represented by a so-called *(object) entry*. The collection of all object entries make up the *Directory Information Base* (DIB). An object entry contains a specific set of properties of a 'real world' object which are represented by several attributes of the entry. Each attribute consists of an attribute type, indicating the type of information represented, and one or more attribute values containing the information.

In order to avoid a multitude of different types of entries and to provide a guiding schema for the representation of 'real world' objects by Directory entries, object classes are defined. An object class is an identified family of 'real world' objects which share certain characteristics. The definition of object classes is managed by the *Directory Schema*. The schema consists of a set of rules that specify and control the structure of information. In particular, an object class describes and controls the contents of entries which belong to it in terms of mandatory and optional attributes.

In order to allow a distributed administration of the DIB, the object entries are arranged in a hierarchical structure called the Directory Information Tree (DIT), where the nodes of the tree are the Directory Entries. As the DS operates in a distributed environment, the DIT can be fragmented and allocated to different servers called Directory System Agents (DSAs). The DSAs, each of them only knowing and handling a part of the global directory information, cooperate to perform operations, assuring that a user can navigate through the global DIT and that s/he can access each entry in the DIT from each site.

Each entry in the DIB is labeled with a unique Relative Distinguished Name (RDN). A user can refer to an object entry through its "Distinguished Name". The Distinguished Name of an entry is the sequence of the Relative Distinguished Names of all superior entries and its own RDN. In this way, each object entry can be reached by a unique name, which is the pathname from the root of the tree to the object entry. An example of a DIT and of Distinguished Names determination is shown in the following diagram:

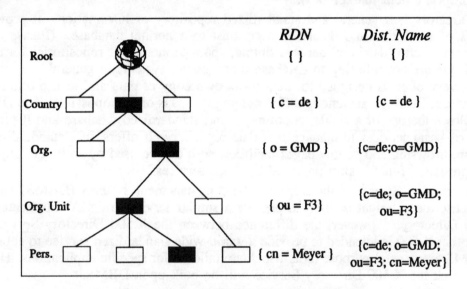

Figure 2: Determination of Distinguished Names

A single object may have several alternative names in the system. These alternative names are called "Alias Names". The alias is another entry in the DIB which points to the object entry and permits to reach a single node in the DIB via another path.

3.2. The Directory Services

According to their purpose the Directory operations are divided into three categories. Each category is described by one *port* that offers appropriate operations. It is distinguished between the Read Port, Search Port and Modify Port.

The Read Port supports the retrieval of information associated with a particular entry. That means that, by the Read Port, the Directory supplies a name to properties mapping service *(white pages facility)*. Additionally, a compare operation is provided that compares a supplied value with the values of a particular attribute type in a specified entry.

The Search Port enables a user to explore the DIB, looking for information associated with a particular object (browsing facility). Moreover, this port provides a yellow pages facility, that consists of looking for all the objects in the DIB, or in a subtree of the DIB, which match a particular set of attributes.

The Modify Port supports all modify operations. These are operations to add, to remove, or to modify an entry or to change the name of an entry.

As shown above, the Directory Service provides a variety of retrieval operations. These operations facilitate the access to and the usage of information contained in the DIB supplying "white pages", "browsing" and "yellow pages" facilities. Moreover, the Directory System offers the basic operations to modify the DIB in conformance with the Directory Schema.

4. Supporting GCSS by the Directory

Before we describe the Directory application for GCSS support in detail, it is shown that the X.500 Directory satisfies the requirements listed in section 2.2. Whenever one of the requirements is affected by the following considerations this will be indicated by referring to the appropriate item marker (a-f).

The Directory is a general and standardized repository of information. It provides all advantages of a standardized database in contrast to a normal database. (Please note: in this context, the term 'database' denotes simple, application specific repositories for data, i.e. data-bases; we are not referring to database management systems in general.) In particular, a database very often is designed to manage its own copy of data and to use different data access services. Sharing data among different applications is often impossible. The Directory, instead, allows the use of a single, coordinated and standardized database and it provides a single set of basic services to manage that data repository. It offers, in a standardized way, the look-up, browsing and yellow pages facilities, so it can be used by any other application which requires the functionality provided by these services.

It is obvious, that any of the large database management systems (DBMS) which are already in use today, might be used to provide a similar service to CSCW applications than the X.500 Directory. However, the difference between the X.500 Directory Service and a DBMS is, that X.500 is intended to provide a world-wide standardized service to applications while DBMS are general purpose tools which are tailored for specific applications. However, it is likely that the X.500 Directory Service will be built upon DBMS.

Real world objects are represented in the DIB according to the Directory data model as object-entries. Since these entries allow the representation of the characteristic properties of a real world object by attributes, requirement (a) is satisfied. Furthermore, the hierarchical naming schema (Fig. 2) enables a hierarchical ordering of entries (b).

The extensibility and flexibility of the Directory data model makes it possible to adapt the object classes in a way that the characteristic objects of an organization can be represented in the Directory. Since each entry is denoted by a unique name, relations between two entries are easily described by assigning the name of the referred entry as an attribute value to the referring entry (c). The type of the attribute determines the semantic of the link. Examples for this technique are given in Tables 1 and 2.

Another important aspect is the distributed management offered by the Directory. The Directory is distributed and provides distributed administration facilities for the information it contains (d,e). In particular, if the Directory is used for the storage of the logical components of the GCSS, such as Roles and MessageType, it will support the handling and distributed management of these components. Moreover, in conjunction with an X.400 MHS as the underlying communication media, the distributed administration of the network and the registering of users involved in a group communication application can be supported by the Directory. In this way, we can note that the use of the Directory System supports the implementation of group communication at two levels. The first level is given by management support for logical components of the GCSS and the second level is represented by the support the Directory offers to the communication service a GCSS is based on in order to store technical communication information (address, etc.).

The information stored in the Directory is organized according to the Directory Schema which is different from a normal database schema because it is open. Open means that each administrative authority establishes that part of the schema which applies to those portions of the DIB administered by the authority (e). So, it is possible to have different rules and object class at different sites. That is very suitable in the context of group communication applications, because the different organizations, represented in the Directory, can thus define their own internal structure in a quite independent way.

Finally, we want to point out the information service that the Directory offers to users and to other services. As the Directory is intended to serve as a world-wide distributed service, any user and service, stored in any site, can use the facilities that the Directory provides for retrieval purposes (f). In particular, a generic user inquiring the Directory can obtain information about his/her own or another organization, about the roles that s/he or another user may occupy and about available services and information required to access them.

These considerations show that the Directory satisfies the requirements listed in section 2.2. The following chapter will illustrate how to represent roles and message types as entries in the DIB.

5. Representation of GCSS Components by the Directory

The Directory provides a predefined set of object classes for the representation of 'real world' objects. The following considerations describe in which way these object classes can be used for our purposes and which extensions are necessary.

5.1. Representation of Roles

In chapter 2 we distinguished between organizational roles and communicational roles depending on the environment in which they are defined. Accordingly, two different object classes for the representation of roles as entries in the Directory are required.

Previously we defined organizational roles as an abstract means to describe status and function of employees within an organization. An organizational role can be described by the properties: name, description, collocation, telecommunication information, function, status, and responsibility of the role and the role player. For the communication context, the function, status, and responsibility of a role can be expressed by listing the message types the role may use and the activities the role may start or be involved in. A more detailed description of the rights and responsibilities of a role can be given using access control specification means. Since an explanation of that technique and its application would exceed the framework of this paper, the interested reader is referred to [14]

Further important pieces of information needed to characterize an organizational role are the names of the employees who can occupy the role. Although one role can be fulfilled by several employees, the DIB will contain only one entry per role. In each entry representing a role there will be an attribute that contains the names of those employees that can play the particular role.

The Directory standard already defines an object class for organizational roles. For the representation of the listed properties this object class must be extended. The following figure lists the attributes of the extended organizational role object class in ASN.1 notation. Additional attributes are typed in *italics*.[2]

```
OrganizationalRole OBJECT-CLASS
        SUBCLASS OF Top
                MUST CONTAIN{
                        commonName}
                MAY CONTAIN{
                        description,
                        localAttributeSet,
                        organizationalUnitName,
                        postalAttributeSet,
                        telecommunicationAttributeSet,
                        preferredDeliveryMethod,
                        roleOccupant,
                        seeAlso,
                        messageTypes,
                        activities,
                        startActivities}
```

The name of a role is stored in the attribute *commonName*. The *local*, *postal* and *telecommunication* attribute sets contain attributes for storing the description of the location of the role. The *organizationalUnitName* attribute stores the department to which the role belongs. The preferred delivery method for messages (e-mail, fax, paper mail) is stored in the corresponding attribute. The *seeAlso* attribute can be used to reference similar roles.

The attribute *roleOccupant* contains the Directory names of the people who are allowed to play that role. The attributes *messageTypes, activities*, and *startActivities* store the Directory name[3] of entries that represent either message types or activities. These attributes establish links between different Directory entries.

The following table shows an example of an entry of the OrganizationalRole object class that describes the role of a project leader.

commonName	*Project Leader*
description	Leader of the CSCW project
...	...
roleOccupant	{...; cn=Smith}
seeAlso	Project Member
messageTypes	shortNotice, travelApplication, procurementApplication
activities	travel, procurement
startActivities	travel, procurement

Table 1: Example of an entry of the *OrganizationalRole* object class

In the previous chapter, we spoke about the Communicational Roles as the roles existing only in the context of a particular activity. They are activity specific and they permit variable

---

[2] The correct technique for the extension of object classes is the definition of a *subclass*, but for simplicity we have chosen this technique.

[3] In following examples we use a descriptive name instead of a Directory name in order to make them easier to read and understand.

roles assignments. So, this kind of roles is characterized by its name, its description and by the activity it is located in. It is also necessary to describe, in a variable way, the people who can occupy the role and to define the kind of communicational message types it can handle and its responsibilities within the activity.

The Directory standard does not define any object class for the representation of communicational roles. So we should now define a new object class to be used to represent these roles. The definition of that object class is as follows:

```
CommunicationalRole OBJECT-CLASS
        SUBCLASS OF Top
            MUST CONTAIN{
                    commonName}
            MAY CONTAIN{
                    description,
                    activity,
                    owner,
                    commMessageTypeList,
                    responsibilities}
```

The *commonName* attribute specifies the name of a role. The *description* attribute allows a general description of the role. The *activity* attribute indicates the particular procedure which the role is defined in. The *owner* attribute contains a description of the person who occupies the role during the activity; that attribute does not contain an employee name because the owner of the communicational role is different for each activity instance. For example, values for that attribute can be organizational roles or descriptions like the following: 'The user who initiates the activity'. The *commMessageTypeList* attribute contains the message types which this role can handle during the procedure. Finally, the *responsibilities* attribute describes the responsibilities of that role within the activity.

The following table gives an example of an entry representing the *initiator* communicational role, defined within a date-planning activity.

commonName	*initiator*
description	Initiator of a date planning activity
activity	Date planning
owner	sender of the date-planning-init message
commMessageTypeList	date-planning-init date-request date-proposal date-decision date-cancelation
responsibilities	decide about a proposed date, authorized to send a date-cancelation

Table 2: Example of an entry of the *CommunicationalRole* object class

The proposed object classes should be regarded as an example. The application of the Directory by a specific GCSS might require modifications and extensions to these object classes.

In this way it is possible to represent roles as entries of the object classes organizationalRole and communicationalRole in the DIB. The DIB is organized as a tree structure (the

219

DIT) that represents geographical and/or organizational dependencies. Consequently, it is necessary to determine the place of entries of both object classes within that tree (see Fig. 3). Conforming to the Directory schema entries of the organizationalRole object class are immediate subordinates of entries of the Organization object class or OrganizationalUnit object class. The level at which an entry is added to the DIT represents the status of the role within the organizational hierarchy. An organizational diagram can be chosen as a guideline for the design of the part of the DIT that represents the organization. Communicational roles are defined in the context of an activity. Consequently, they are immediate subordinates of the entry representing the corresponding activity. (see [14] for a discussion about the representation of activities).

5.2. Representation of Message Types

In chapter 2 we also distinguished between organizational message types and communicational message types. Organizational message types were characterized as general message types existing in an organization which are used by users in daily work, independently of a specific activity.

The definition of organizational message types includes the assignment of a name, a description of its usage, and information about its organizational context (organizationName, organizationalUnitName for messages types which are used only in an specific department, e.g. the message type *software notice* of the software department). Moreover, the structure of the message type, that is the set of attributes composing the message itself, and the list of roles which can use this message type must be defined.

Based on these considerations the OrganizationalMessageType object class is defined as follows:

```
OrganizationalMessageType OBJECT-CLASS
        SUBCLASS OF Top
                MUST CONTAIN{
                        messageTypeName}
                MAY CONTAIN{
                        description,
                        organizationName,
                        organizationalUnitName,
                        structureDefinition,
                        roleList,
                        seeAlso}
```

This object class specifies the message type name and the purpose of that message (description). Apart from the information about the organization and organizationalUnit in which the message type is defined, there are two important attributes *structureDefinition* and *roleList*, which contain a description of the structure of this message type and the names of all roles that can handle it, respectively. The *seeAlso* attribute can be used for references to other message types which have a similar purpose. The following table shows an example of an entry representing an organizationalMessageType:

messageTypeName	short-notice
description	This message type should be used to exchange inofficial notices.
organizationName	Fantasia
structureDefinition	Message Attributes: - sender, recipient, date, subject - reference: your letter, telephone-call - with the request for: call-back, for your information, etc. - ...
roleList	all roles
seeAlso	notice, software-notice

Table 3: Example of an entry of the *organizationalMessageType* object class

Communicational message types, however, are message types defined and used within a particular activity. In order to represent these activity specific message types as entries in the DIB, we need to associate with them the message type name, a description concerning the content of the message, the activity in which it is defined and used, the structure of the message itself and, finally, a list of roles that will receive this message type during the course of the activity. The following object class is used to represent communicational message types:

```
CommunicationalMessageType OBJECT-CLASS
        SUBCLASS OF Top
              MUST CONTAIN{
                     messageTypeName}
              MAY CONTAIN{
                     description,
                     activity,
                     structureDefinition,
                     roleList,
                     seeAlso}
```

This object class contains a subset of attributes available in the OrganizationalMessageType object class. A new attribute is associated to the entries belonging to the CommunicationalMessageType object class. It is the *activity* attribute. This attribute is peculiar to this object class, since it specifies the particular activity the messageType is defined in. The following figure shows an example of a communicationalMessageType entry:

messageTypeName	date-planning-init
description	This message type is used to initiate a date-planning activity bu sending an instance of this message to the date-planning mediator.
activity	date-planning
structureDefinition	Message Attributes: - sender, recipient, date, meeting name - meeting description, date, time - participants
roleList	initiator, participants
seeAlso	date-request, date-proposal, date-decision, date-cancelation

Table 4: Example of a *communicationalMessageType* entry

In this way, all message types can be represented as entries in the DIB. The organizational message type entries will be immediate subordinates of entries representing the organization or organizational units, according to its definition context. Entries representing message types are leaf entries in the DIT. Since the communicational message types are only meaningful within a particular activity, the corresponding entries will be immediate subordinates of an entry representing the activity in which they are defined (see also communicational roles).

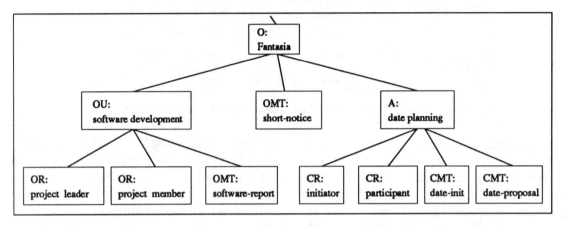

Figure 3: Subtree of the DIT showing entries representing the organization (O), organizational units (OU), activities (A), organizational roles (OR), communicational roles (CR), organizational message types (OMT), and communicational message types (CMT).

Figure 3 shows a subtree of the DIT that illustrates the placement of organizational and communicational roles and message types. The subtree shows an entry representing properties of the organization *Fantasia* and the organizational unit *software development*. Placing the entries for the organizational roles *project leader* and *project member* as subordinates of that entry indicates that these roles belong to that specific department. Only within this department the organizational message type *software report* is used. That is why the corresponding entry is placed in this subtree and not directly as a subordinate to the organization entry as done for the organizational message type *short notice*. The entry *date planning* represents the date-planning activity. Subordinates of this entry are the communicational roles *initiator* and *participants* and the communicational message types *date-init* and *date-proposal*.

5.3. Application of the Directory Information

Above, we explained how to represent the GCSS components by the Directory. In the following we will illustrate how this information can be applied. Three different types of applications can be distinguished: administration support for a single application, application overlapping info-service and user-infoservice.

The application of the Directory for the administration of the roles and message type description releases developers of GCSS from design and realization of their own databases. The distribution of the Directory is especially of advantage for distributed group communication applications, because Directory information is accessible in the same way from different sites. Besides the administrative support the Directory provides possibilities for the description of relations between entries by name-links or predicates. An example for that is the selection and assignment of role-players. A role to role-occupant relation can be described either in static way by naming the role-occupants with their Directory-names (organizational roles) or by the description of predicates (communicational roles). That is possible because the Directory allows the representation of heterogeneous objects in a unified and standardized way and because it provides a unique naming schema for all entries. Heterogeneous databases, each of them storing different pieces of information (e.g. about roles or employees) cannot provide this functionality.

The Directory is an application independent database offering its services to different kinds of (group communication) applications. Very often the information used and managed by different applications are the same. For example, O/R addresses, message type or role descriptions can be used by interpersonal mailing services and activity and conversation oriented GCSS as well. Consequently, this information should be stored and managed only by one service, instead of using different data management services. Therefore, the Directory application described in this paper avoids inconsistent data caused by the formation of different application-specific databases.

The Directory offers an infoservice to the users of group communication applications. Users can retrieve all information about the existing roles and message types within his/her organization or of other organizations. In particular, due to "browsing" and "yellow pages" facilities provided by the Directory, it is possible to get information about roles, such as to know who can occupy a particular role and, by "white pages" facilities, to map role names to O/R addresses of users that play a role. For example, in a travel apply activity, a user who wants to send a request, can use the Directory in order to find the employee that s/he has to inquire and the communication information, that s/he needs for sending the request. The Directory offers the same kind of services for message types. That is, when users need to exchange messages, they can retrieve information about available message types and their structure using the Directory facilities. For example, if an employee has to send a short-notice to another employee, s/he can find the form of the message type "notice" inquiring the Directory. Furthermore, we can think of user agents which are able to interpret the Directory information in order to supply the user with an appropriate form on the screen.

6. Open Aspects, Future Work

It is clear that the Directory standard does not meet all requirements of GCSS and that extensions to the Directory are required. We will work out these extensions in this chapter. As we have already seen, there are many relations between entries. For example, the organizational role entries contain the names of entries representing the users that can take on the corresponding role. The communicational role entries have a link to other entries in the DIB, too. This link is realized by the *owner* attribute pointing to possible entries for that role. The Directory standard does not provide support for the retrieval of relations between entries. Thus, a first extension that the Directory needs affects its capability to interpret and to maintain such sorts of relations.

Due to these links existing between entries, the removal of entries where other entries point to leads to an inconsistent DIB. Therefore, in order to maintain the integrity of the DIB, the Directory will have to be extended, including mechanisms for support and management of these kinds of updates. At GMD we are working on solutions for these aspects. Our future plan is to develop an organizational knowledge base which is based on Directory concepts. Currently, we are extending our Directory service, which is used as an information service for users of our message handling service, towards a general information service about our organization for services and users as well.

Another important issue is the security of data in the DIB. We said that the different organizations involved in Group Communication activities are represented in the DIB and that their own information (organizational structure, roles, message types etc.) are available to the Directory users. It can be necessary for an organization to protect and to hide parts of this information from other organizations. Moreover, also inside an organization it is not always desirable to allow every employee the access to every information. Therefore, the Directory has to provide an authorization policy and it must support the specification, enforcement and maintenance of access rights for the purpose of granting and refusing access to information. Current implementations of the Directory service [9] already offer means for access control.

7. Conclusion

This paper has outlined how group communication support systems (GCSS) can apply the emerging X.500 Directory service. For this purpose the basic building blocks of GCSS were identified. Two of these components, roles and message objects, were identified as suitable for a representation in the Directory. For a better analysis of these components we distinguished between activity and conversation oriented models. This distinction results in the definition of organizational and communicational roles and message types, respectively.

The demand arose that a comprehensive user support for co-operative group work can be supplied only when activity and conversation oriented systems are combined and integrated. Such an integration would benefit from a single database for the administration of role and message type description. We listed the requirements for such a database and it could be shown that the Directory satisfies them all. Finally, we illustrated how roles and message types can be represented and in what manner the Directory service and the contained information can be applied.

We hope that this paper will stimulate researchers and developers of group communication support systems an impulse to consider an application of the emerging X.500 Directory service for future developments.

Acknowledgments

We would like to thank our colleagues A. Jerusalem and H. Santo for their helpful comments on this paper and U. Bernhard for the English proofreading. Furthermore we want to express our thanks to Tecnopolis CSATA and FORMEZ that made the stay of P. Pennelli at GMD possible.

References

[1] S.D. Benford. *Research into the design of distributed directory services*. PhD thesis, University of Nottingham, Nottingham, GB, October 1988.

[2] John Bowers and John Churcher. Local and global structuring of computer medieated communication: Developing linguistic perspectives on cscw in cosmos. In *CSCW 88: Proceedings of the Conference on Computer Supported Cooperative Work*, Portland, Oregon, Sept. 1988. ACM SIGCHI & SIGOIS.

[3] CCITT. Data comunication networks directory, recommendations x.500-x.521, 1988. see also: ISO 9594- 1-8.

[4] T. Danielsen. Aam - the amigo activity model. In U. Pankoke-Babatz, editor, *Computer Based Group Communication, the AMIGO Activity Model*, pages 67–125. Ellis Horwood, 1989.

[5] F. de Cindio, G. de Michelis, C. Simone, R. Vasallo, and A. M. Zanaboni. Chaos as coordination technology. In *CSCW'86 Conference on Computer-Supported Cooperative Work*, Austin, Texas, Dec. 1986.

[6]   U. Pankoke-Babatz (Ed.), T. Danielsen, A. Patel, P.A. Pays, W. Prinz, and R. Speth. *Computer Based Group Communication, the AMIGO Activity Model.* Ellis Horwood, 1989.

[7]   R.E. Young et al. Interim report on the cosmos project, cosmos report. Technical Report 45.5 EXT, COSMOS Project, COSMOS Coordinator's Office, Queen Mary College, London., January 1988.

[8]   Heikki Heammaeinen, Reijo Sulonen, and Christian Berard. Pages: Intelligent forms, intelligent mail and distribution. In *IFIP WG 8.4 Working Conference Pisa*, Oct. 1986.

[9]   S. E. Kille. The quipu directory service. In E. Stefferud, O.J. Jacobsen, and P. Schicker, editors, *Message Handling Systems and Distributed Applications, IFIP 6.5, International Working Conference, Costa Mesa, Oct. 1988.* North-Holland, 1989.

[10] Thomas Kreifelts and Gerd Woetzel. Distribution and error handling in an office procedure system. In G. Bracchi and D. Tsichritzis, editors, *Office Systems: Methods and Tools, Proc. IFIP WG 8.4 Work. Conf. on Methods and Tools for Office Systems*, pages 197–208, 1987.

[11] T. W. Malone, K. R. Grant, K-Y Lai, R. Rao, and D. Rosenblitt. Semi-structured messages are surprisingly useful for computer-supported coordination. In *CSCW' 86 Conference on Computer-Supported Cooperative Work*, pages 102–114, Austin, Texas, Dec. 1986.

[12] U. Pankoke-Babatz. Requirements for group communication support in electronic communication. In R. Speth, editor, *Message Handling Systems, IFIP 6.5, International Working Conference, Munich*, pages 197–206. North-Holland, April 1987.

[13] W. Prinz. Survey of group communication models and systems. In U. Pankoke-Babatz, editor, *Computer Based Group Communication, the AMIGO Activity Model*, pages 127–180. Ellis Horwood, 1989.

[14] W. Prinz. *Application of the X.500 Directory by Office Services.* R. Oldenburg Verlag, 1990.

[15] W. Prinz and R. Speth. Group communication and related aspects in office automation. In R. Speth, editor, *Message Handling Systems, IFIP 6.5, International Working Conference, Munich.* North-Holland, April 1987.

[16] W. Prinz and M. Woitass. The date planning system - example of a cooperative group activity. In E. Stefferud, O.J. Jacobsen, and P. Schicker, editors, *Message Handling Systems and Distributed Applications, IFIP 6.5, International Working Conference, Costa Mesa, Oct. 1988.* North-Holland, 1989.

[17] D. Rotondi, A. Pepe, P. Penelli, and M. Waldow. The directory in heterogeneous computer networks: design and application aspects. In *Proceedings of the VIII - Seminar on Packet switching networks - Leningrad, USSR*, June 1989.

[18] Action Technology. *The Coordinator, Workbook & Tutorial Guide*, June 1987.

[19] D. Tsichritzis and S. F. Gibbs. Ettiquette specification in message systems. In D. Tsichritzis, editor, *Office Automation.* Springer, 1985.

Replicated Document Management in a Group Communication System

Leonard Kawell Jr., Steven Beckhardt, Timothy Halvorsen, Raymond Ozzie
Iris Associates, Inc.

Irene Greif
Lotus Development Corp.

Abstract

This paper is about the design and implementation of a replicated database that forms the basis for the Notes* group communication system. The system supports groups of people working on shared sets of documents and is intended for use in a personal computer network environment in which the database servers are "rarely connected". Most algorithms for guaranteeing consistency across replicas require more reliable network connections between servers for adequate performance. Analysis of many group communication applications, however, revealed relatively weak consistency requirements across copies of the database. These requirements can be met by a simple replication algorithm that works well in rarely connected environments. This kind of replication has been used previously for a limited set of applications such as name directory replication; we have applied this technique to a much larger class of applications. Our characterization of this class of applications suggests that this technique generalizes to support distributed database implementations of other group work systems, including computer conferencing and bulletin board systems.

"Replicated Document Management in a Group Communication System" by L. Kawell, Jr., S. Beckhardt, T. Halvorsen, R. Ozzie, and I. Greif, presented at the Second Conference on Computer-Supported Cooperative Work, September 1988. Printed with permission of the authors.

•*Notes is an internal project name*

Presented at the **Second Conference on Computer-Supported Cooperative Work**, Portland, Oregon, September 26-28, 1988

1. Introduction

Notes is a group communication system that is used by people to share textual, numeric, and graphical information. The system operates on personal computers in local-area and wide-area networks, and provides end-users the ability to design and create document databases for specific applications. This paper focuses on the Notes document manager, which supports replicated databases with a number of interesting characteristics, particularly when compared with replication technology typical in transaction-oriented databases.

In transaction-processing applications for record-oriented database management systems, replication algorithms must meet strict consistency criteria, usually defined in terms of serializability of transactions [Gray]. Most implementations of replication algorithms that provide strict consistency depend on high likelihood of continuous connection between database server machines. Notes has a strong requirement to support workgroups that cannot afford continuously available inter-network connections. We refer to such networks as *rarely-connected* networks. This level of connectivity is typical for PC users. Local area networks that connect small workgroups who share printers often are not interconnected to support cross-group collaboration. Dial-up line connections that cross organizational boundaries are expensive and have low bandwidth.

In rarely connected environments, replication that guarantees serializability would at best be possible only at enormous cost in performance. However, Notes applications do not require this level of consistency across replicas. As a result we are able to rely on a simple replication algorithm. It provides the replication that is crucial to the viability of the product in the PC environment, at a cost that is acceptable in that environment. The replication capability has had several additional benefits for the product, since it also provides a means of doing static load balancing on a single network, automatic backup of databases, and support of home or portable computers that operate in a standalone mode.

Similar approaches to replicated databases have been previously used for distributed directory services [Oppen] [Smith]. Our work extends this approach to a broader class of applications, including document sharing, electronic mail, and conferencing. The implementation is new as well, because it is optimized to work well over low bandwidth, dial up lines.

Section 2 briefly outlines the characteristics of typical applications. In section 3 we review the design goals for the document manager and replication process. Section 4 presents the algorithms and implementation. Section 5 provides some data on current usage of replication. The concluding section reviews our approach to bringing shared document databases to the PC user. This approach meets a wide-range of user needs, not least of which is the need to collaborate despite the reality of poor network connectivity for PC users in *ad hoc* workgroups.

2. Application Characteristics

Notes is based on a shared document database system that can be tailored to the needs of specific workgroups. A user might participate in a number of workgroup activities each supported by a different shared database. A database is a collection of related forms or semi-structured [Malone] documents, organized through views that sort or categorize information.

Users build specialized applications by tailoring the database to store, organize and present specific kinds of information. For example, a group managing a software development project would want a variety of different documents in the database: bug reports, bug fix notices, comments and suggestions, progress reports, etc. The documents would be organized to make it easy for a reader to find new items, and so that comments related to particular topics were grouped together.

The format of documents and appearance of information can vary from application to application: graphs, images, pictures and numerical information can be intermixed with textual information; layout and use of color can give individual

applications very distinctive looks. Databases have been designed to support group applications such as:

- ❑ Software Development Project Management
- ❑ Document Library Management
- ❑ Strategic Business Opportunities
- ❑ Market Research Consolidation
- ❑ Personnel Department Job Openings
- ❑ Group Status Reporting
- ❑ Customer Contact Tracking

The way that a group uses one of these databases is reminiscent of "computer conferencing" systems such as EIES [Hiltz] and electronic bulletin boards such as University of Illinois Plato Group Notes and VAX Notes [Gilbert]. As in these systems, the emphasis is on *many-to-many* communication, as opposed to the person-to-person communication of electronic mail. New documents are composed and entered in the database to be read by a group of individuals. Some group members act in special roles — e.g. moderator — and are therefore granted special privileges for accessing and modifying items in the database.

The primary differences between Notes and these kinds of systems have to do with the distribution and availability of information, the high quality screen presentation, multi-media documents and tailorability of applications. Most conferencing systems have been mainframe or mini-based with information viewed only through terminals and with user interfaces based on character displays. These conferences may have different purposes, but they always have the same message-like appearance. Tailorability is just beginning to be addressed in research prototypes of extensions to conventional conferencing sytems [e.g. the "Tailorable EIES" project].

Traditional conferencing systems make different guarantees about availability of data. A mainframe-based conferencing system is available only when the machine is accessible and operating. A networked system such as VAX Notes similarly depends on access to critical machines: although there may be a large number of geographically distributed servers in a network, each "conference" is on a single server in a system. This approach is viable for VAX Notes only because it is intended for use on a DECnet network, a network with continuous connections. In a rarely connected environment, dependence on a single machine as the sole repository for a group's database would be unacceptable. If the group is widely dispersed, some group members would have to reach the server over expensive phone lines. A local replica gives a low cost, highly available alternative.

Despite the differences in approach, both specifically designed Notes applications and general computer conference discussions share the following properties:

(1)   Group communication is accomplished primarily through adding documents to a database.

(2)   The applications do not rely heavily on modifying documents once placed in the database. (An exception is a situation in which one user can be identified from the outset as the sole editor of a document.)

(3)   The applications do not call for transaction processing that crosses document boundaries (that is, there are no updates to sets of documents that must be done to all or to none of the documents in the set).

(4)   Group members do not need to see "up-to-the-minute" data at all times.

Applications with these characteristics can be fully supported by replicated databases that meet weak consistency requirements. As we explain in Section 4, our replication algorithm assures "eventual consistency", a form of weak consistency.

A feature of this design is that a user need only communicate with a single server to modify a database. Propagation of database changes occurs between servers as a background activity. This ensures good response time as well as eventual convergence of the databases. Properties 2 and 3 are particularly important because exclusive locks to documents and two-phase commit protocols cannot be implemented under these conditions.

These application characteristics are shared by many asynchronous meeting support systems. Computer conferencing systems support generic electronic meetings that allow groups to accomplish many of the same goals of face-to-face meetings without co-locating, and without even attempting to all work at the same time. Tailored applications for specific kinds of group meetings and information sharing also fit these characteristics. The growing number of Notes applications forms a large class as well.

Sometimes special consideration has to be made for replication during application design. If, for example, the software development application were based on large documents intended to include bug report and repair information, many individuals might all need to update a single document (violating property 3 above). The bug reporter would write the initial report, but people working on fixing the bug would later have to update the document to indicate that they were working on it and the status of the fix. If instead a set of documents is used, each participant in the process can simply add comments in a new, briefer document that will be stored with the original document.

There are group work applications that do not fit within this class. If a group of co-authors requires immediate notification when more than one person is working on the same document (even if the co-authors are connected to separate servers) [Greif], they will have difficulties in a rarely connected environment. Either the database cannot be replicated, or it must be replicated by a more complex algorithm that will require more continuous connections between servers and stricter consistency across copies.

3. Document Manager

The document manager implements the basic operations for data storage and retrieval. These same operations are used in the replication process. This section outlines the design goals of the document manager, with particular attention paid to replication, concurrency and access control.

3.1 Document Manager Design Goals

The primary goal of the document manager is to provide permanent storage for free-form and semi-structured objects of arbitrary size. The document manager can handle many different types of data (e.g. floating point numbers, times and dates), and is exceptional in its ability to handle large blocks of text and graphics. The document manager is not a generalized database system; instead it is tuned for documents that are 2-3Kbytes in size and can handle documents of approximately 100-200Kbytes. (See [Smith] for comparison of relational databases and databases tuned for more general kinds of object storage.)

Conventional databases tend to work with small records or tables, so they can typically buffer large portions of the database in memory. Since we assumed that our "records" would be large, the Notes system maintains most of the database on-disk and only caches the most recently used parts of the database in memory. For this reason, the document manager does not provide a well-tuned way to store thousands of small records.

The document manager provides a relatively fast way to search for documents by any small field and very fast access to many, sorted views of the documents in the database. The searching capability is provided by storing the small fields in documents separated from the large fields. The view capability is provided by maintaining up-to-date indices containing sorted copies of fields in the selected documents. View indices can be hierarchical for use in tree-structured conferences and for multi-level "categorization" of documents (especially mail).

The document manager has programmatic interfaces for the following functions:

o Databases can be created, opened, closed, and deleted.

o Documents can be created, opened, updated, closed, and deleted.

o Documents can be retrieved based upon their modification time and/or the contents of fields within the documents.

o Search criteria are specified using a very comprehensive algebraic query language. Indexed views can be created, opened, closed, and deleted.

o Groups of index entries in a view can be read. The desired entries can be specified by either index position, using an infinite precision number (e.g. 2.1.3.4), or by key values.

The document manager protects the confidentiality of documents through access control lists. An access control list (ACL) is a system-managed object contained in the database. An ACL contains a list of the names of all the users and groups who are authorized to access the database. Associated with each name in the list is the access level that the user has been granted.

3.2 Replication Design Goals

Notes replication ensures eventual consistency of the documents in all replicas: changes made to one copy eventually migrate to all. If all update activity stops, after a period of time all replicas of the database will converge to be logically equivalent: each copy of the database will contain, in a predictable order, the same documents; replicas of each document will contain the same fields. In other words, a program cannot detect the difference between replicas through the document manager programmatic interface.

The goals of the replication design in Notes are as follows:

(1)   Background Replication. Automatic replication of additions (new documents), deletions, and modifications (edits) is a background activity that does not interfere with normal database access.

(2)   Rarely Connected Networks. Support replication of documents on servers that are only seldomly in communication with each other. Because Notes is designed to operate in an environment where servers are rarely in communication with each other, replication does not require any immediate server-to-server message exchanges when a document is added or updated. (See [Stonebraker] for a replication algorithm that does depend on immediate communication.) Instead, a goal of replication is that it be capable of being deferred until a user-defined time (e.g. once a day, once an hour).

(3)   Convergence. Over time, all replica databases must converge to contain the same versions of all documents.

(4)   No Master Copy of a Database. No database replica is known as the "master copy". Likewise, no instance of a document is viewed as the "master copy". Unless purposefully set up otherwise (via access control), all copies are viewed as peers. This means replicating with any copy of the database is sufficient to obtain a correct copy of all the documents.

(5)   No Database Replica Directory. There is no clearinghouse that enumerates the locations of the replicas of a particular database. There may be as many replicas as desired and each site is responsible for maintaining communication with at least one other replica of the same database. Creation of a new replica is a localized event. No centralized notification is required to alert other servers of the existence of a new replica.

(6)   Optimized Dial-up Connections. When replication occurs across slow and costly communication links (2400 baud is typical) it is essential that the replication process perform its work quickly. Communication line bandwidth is clearly the limiting factor in moving a large document from one server to another. However, communication costs can be minimized by ensuring that new or updated documents can be efficiently identified, so that only those documents are moved across the link.

229

Some additional considerations have to do with network administration dependencies and end-user visibility of replication. Unlike some replicated database systems (e.g. [Gifford]), the Notes system does not keep a separate transaction journal or log that causes the same transactions to be performed on each copy of the database. Instead, the Notes system uses time stamps indicating the time of the last update to determine how to produce a consistent copy of the data. With this approach, the only information that must be maintained in each database is the time of the last replication with any of the other replicas of the database. Although databases with rollback capability provide automatic recovery from failures, network administrator intervention of considerable sophistication is often enough required to rule this approach out for our environment.

We also wanted to shield end-users from the details of replication. We wanted it to appear as if each copy of the file magically became consistent with all other replicas. In reality, we've discovered that things like network propagation delays, access control (especially), propagated deletions, and ID-based database equivalency sometimes require at least the database administrators to understand replication. We are currently using our early customer sites to determine the extent to which they find they have to understand these issues. We are also investigating the extent to which we can educate the users using application-specific terminology as opposed to teaching them the details of the technology.

3.3 Concurrency

The goals of concurrency control in the document manager and Replicator process are to:

(1) Detect and signal occurrences of multiple updates to a single version of a document.

(2) Converge to a single version of an updated document.

We do not try to support multi-document update transactions or automatic merging of concurrent updates to a single document. This contrasts with the goals of other replicated database systems for continuously connected networks [Stonebraker] which provide transaction concurrency control by requiring agreement among the servers. These other systems tend to treat the inability to communicate with other servers as an exception condition. Notes treats this type of communication as the norm.

Interactive detection of multiple updates is handled by the document manager for a single database using optimistic concurrency control [Kung]. When a document is opened, its modification time and version number are recorded in memory. When the user chooses to store an updated version of the document, the in-memory modification time and version are compared with the copy in the database on disk. If they differ, then another user has modified the document since the original user opened his or her copy. When this occurs, the user is notified on the workstation and can choose to overwrite the other user's version.

4. Replication

The replication algorithm is given in the first part of this section and is followed by discussion of a number of interesting design and implementation issues.

4.1 Replication Algorithm

The replication algorithm is a one-way "pull model" [Demers] algorithm. It is so named because the algorithm is executed on the local computer and only pulls documents from a remote computer. However, the algorithm is executed simultaneously by the remote computer so the overall effect is that replication occurs in both directions at once. The replication algorithm is as follows:

(1) Create a list of databases requiring replication. Find the databases common to both local and remote computers, and for each database, verify that the remote database has been modified since the last replication with the local computer.

(2) Create document indexes.

a) Open the remote database and create a list of all the documents that have been modified since the last replication. For each document include its document IDs (see section 4.2) and its last modification time.

b) Open the local database and create a list of all the documents.

(3) Replicate. For each entry in the local list, find the corresponding entry in the remote list.

a) If the document in the remote database is a newer version than the version in the local database then copy the document to the local database.

b) If the document in the remote database is marked as "deleted" then delete the document in the local database.

c) If the document in the remote database is older than the version in local database or the document is not in the remote database then do nothing since the remote Replicator will copy the document from the local database.

d) For the remaining documents in the remote database list, copy them to local database since these are new documents.

4.2 Identifying Documents, Versions and Instances

At a given time, a document can exist in any number of replica databases. Each copy of the document is an *instance*. At most one instance of a document can appear in a single database at any time. An instance in one replica can be edited to produce a new *version* of the document. In that replica the new version replaces the old version. Two replicas of a database may have different versions of the same document if the databases have not gone through the replication process.

Thus at any given time across a set of replicas of a database, there can be many instances of a document, each of which can be a different version of that document. Immediately after replication, the pair of databases that have just replicated have exactly the same set of document instances and document versions.

Notes uses several identifiers to describe documents, document versions and instances. The *DocumentPositionID* denotes a particular version of a document in a particular database. It is specific to a database because it contains information about the relative storage position of the document in the database. As a result, it affords very fast access to the document (in a particular database), but it is not the same identifier for other instances of the document.

The *DocumentVersionID* is used to describe a particular version of a document. It changes as new versions are created. It consists of four components: a database identifier, the time of creation of the document, the time of last modification, and a sequence number. The use of the sequence number will be explained later.

The *DocumentID* is the unique identifier of a document across all replicas. In other words, it is invariant for all versions and all instances of the document. The DocumentID is actually the DocumentVersionID without the version information.

4.3 Identifying Replicas

The first step in replication involves determining what databases should be replicated. Since there is no master catalog or directory of databases that must be replicated, it is up to the server, at the moment of replication to determine what databases must be replicated. The server determines this by obtaining a complete directory listing of all databases on the remote system and comparing this with a directory of all local databases.

The server then determines which remote databases are replicas of local databases. The server must determine this either from file names or from internal identifiers. File names are not used for two reasons:

(1)   to allow for replication across heterogeneous operating systems with dissimilar file name syntaxes, and

(2)   to allow local control of file and directory names (a database may be given any name and placed in any directory and replication will still take place correctly).

Therefore replicas are determined by an identifier termed *ReplicaID*. The ReplicaID is assigned at creation of the first instance of the database, and is the same for all replicas of the database. The directory listing protocol includes for each database the ReplicaID and the name of the file in which it is stored. In addition, the time of last modification of each database is also provided. The modification time allows an important optimization because it allows the Replicator to ignore those databases that have not been modified since this server's last replication with the remote server. For servers that call each other frequently, this is the normal case for most databases. In our environment, servers typically call each other several times a day and find it necessary to replicate three or four files out of a possible two or three dozen.

4.4 Incremental Replication

In the above algorithm, the remote database must send a list of all documents added or modified since the last replication. This *incremental replica-*

tion is based on information stored in a small replication history table in each database. This table contains an entry for every other database that this database has ever replicated with. Each entry contains the remote database's name and the time of the last successful replication. This time is provided as an input to the procedure that builds the list of documents in the remote database. Only documents modified (added, edited, or deleted) since the last replication are added to the document list. Therefore, each replication only deals with documents modified since the last replication. This greatly reduces the time it takes to transfer the list and build an index from the list. In practice, each replication normally finds only a few new or modified documents, so it usually takes under a minute (of connect time) to determine which documents must be replicated. For new databases (and occasionally in problem situations) there is no useful time of last replication. In that case a full replication is done by sending a list of all documents in the remote database.

4.5 Concurrent Updating of Documents

Traditional locking cannot be used to prevent concurrent updates to a replicated document because copies of the document can be on servers that are not in communication with each other. Notes can detect concurrent updates only when they are updates to the same instance of a document (in the same database). For concurrent updates to instances in replica databases, Notes simply guarantees that after replication, both databases will have the same version of the document.

Notes uses two identifiers for each document to guarantee convergence to a single version. It might be expected that the time of last modification would be sufficient. Each server would simply choose the document with the latest modification time. However, we were concerned that in the haphazardly managed PC environment that a server, with its time incorrectly (or maliciously) set into the future, could store a document that simply could not be superseded (at least until time caught up with it). On the other hand, an increasing integer sequence number has the disadvantage that two concurrent updates could look like no update at all. As a result, Notes uses a sequence number and a modification time. The sequence number is the primary arbitrator between two documents, with the modification time used as a tie-breaker. This has the effect that a document edited and saved many times is chosen over a document updated only once.

This approach does not detect concurrent updates. Clearly, two documents with the same sequence number but different modification times are the result of a concurrent update. But if the sequence numbers are different, it is impossible to tell if one was a direct ancestor of the other or if they took divergent paths. This problem may be solved in a future version of Notes by storing the complete modification history of a document as a series of modification times. Thus, when presented with two versions of the same document, the document manager can determine if one was a direct ancestor of the other or whether a concurrent update resulted in a divergence.

4.6 Access Control as Concurrent Update Protection

Access control in Notes is based on an ordered set of *levels* and a set of user tailorable *privileges* that allow fine tuning of access to specific documents. The access levels correspond to conventional user roles such as Reader, Author, and Editor.

Access Control may be used to control concurrent editing of documents in a replicated database. The access control design provides for the following types of replicated databases:

(1) Single master copy and all others read-only (e.g. Corporate Policies and Procedures Handbook, Newsletter).

(2) Peer databases but only original authors may edit documents (e.g. Design Discussion, Status Reports).

(3) Peer databases and any user with the capability can edit any document (concurrency-control is just a matter of convention).

To set up a "master copy" database, all users are granted read/write access in the master copy and Reader access in all other copies. This ensures that changes only occur in the the master copy and prevents simultaneous updates from ever occurring.

The "master copy" style of access control can be relaxed by granting users Author access in the non-master copies of the database. This enables users to add and edit documents to any replica of the database but only the original author of a document can edit the document. This approach avoids simultaneous updates as long as each user works on a single instance of the database (typically on the user's "home" server).

4.7 Database Administration

Replication is initiated by a call schedule that instructs one server to call another for the purpose of replication (as opposed to calling to route mail, for example). Typical call schedules have one server call another once or several times a day. The frequency of calling depends on the desired group interaction and the type of database. For example, a conferencing database might replicate several times a day to promote a high degree of interaction while once a day is more than sufficient for a product catalog database.

5. Replication in Use

The main benefit of Notes replication is that it performs well in rarely connected environments. As long as a client workstation can communicate with a local server, the Notes user can complete database operations. Any changes made to a database on the local server can be propagated to other servers in the background. Communication between servers can be scheduled to optimize the use of the available communication lines, whether over dial-up, wide-area or local area network.

Replication also provides a number of other benefits. This section describes some of these additional benefits and the ways that replication is being used at one site.

5.1 Benefits of Replication

Originally conceived as a way to provide inter-network communication, the inexpensive form of replication provided by Notes has proved to be valuable for other reasons:

o Static load balancing on single networks - The servers are typically microcomputers of fairly limited capacity. Additional users can be supported by simply adding another server and creating replicas of the databases on the original server.

o Automatic backups - Replication can be used to provide unattended database backups. This is particularly important in the PC environment rife with low reliability PC file systems, disk system crashes, and inexperienced PC operators who make "user errors" managing files. If a server or database goes down, users can easily change their access to another server that has a replica of the affected databases.

o Off-line standalone use - One-person offices, portable computers, and home users have found that having a personal, but more or less up-to-date copy of shared documents is very handy. The isolated PC can periodically dial up and connect for replication, but a permanent connection is not necessary. Once the shared documents have been replicated to the standalone PC, quick access to documents is no longer limited by the slow speed of the dialup connection. In fact the dialup connection is no longer needed.

o Management domain isolation - The combination of Notes security and replication provides a way to ensure that information can be distributed to untrusted sites without danger of bad information flowing back from the sites. Also, workgroups can maintain control over the usage and administration of their own servers.

5.2 Observed Usage

At Lotus and Iris (the authors' companies), there are a large number of databases in use on a regular basis. We have collected information at Lotus, Iris, and our customer test sites (approximately 30 sites in all) to be compiled and analyzed at a later date.

Between Lotus and Iris there are a total of 275 different databases (with replicas counting as a single database) stored on 26 different servers. Of these 275 databases, 110 are either personal mail or inactive databases. Of the remaining 165 active databases, 82 databases have more than one instance and 15 databases have more than 5 instances. The databases with the most instances are:

Database	Number of Instances
Name & Address Book	14
Software Problem Reports	14
Notes User Notes	12

The Name & Address Book is a database used by the Notes distributed directory service. The Software Problems Reports database is a "tracking" application that contains bug reports and their resolution for the Notes project. The Notes User Notes database is a "discussion" database that is used to discuss features and suggestions (as well as complaints) for the Notes project. It is interesting to note that these three databases represent three completely different applications built using Notes. This shows that replication is indeed useful across a range of Notes applications. What these three applications have in common is their usefulness across the entire organization.

The Software Problems Reports database illustrates a number of the points made earlier in this paper. It is a medium sized database (approximately 950 documents) that combines very structured documents (e.g. Problem Reports) with relatively unstructured documents (e.g. Development's Responses). Users can enter a problem report on any of the 14 different servers containing a replica of the database. Generally, a new report appears in all replicas within 24 hours of its being entered. Although new problem reports and responses can be entered anywhere, by any user, certain edits made to existing reports (such as marking a problem as fixed) are made by a single individual (or a small group) with editor access.

We are also using replication as a way of moving problem reports and suggestions between the customer sites and our office. Since these sites are separate companies, the ability to isolate networks and servers into management domains and still replicate has proven to be an essential capability.

Conclusion

In this paper we have characterized the kinds of applications that are well-suited to implementation in a rarely connected environment and described an underlying database replication technology that can support these applications. Clearly, there are applications which cannot be supported with this kind of replication. These include applications that require exclusive locking or transaction serializability. Distributed database technology which supports these applications also requires more continuous connections between servers.

Just as groups have different working goals, they also have differing computer environments. The assumption that full connectivity and consistency is required can make systems very expensive and difficult to implement in some environments. A closer examination of workgroup needs reveals a large class of information sharing and collaborative applications which have much less stringent consistency requirements. These applications can be solved today with a relatively inexpensive rarely-connected network solution.

Additional applications can be accomodated through application design and through conventions about individuals' roles — author vs editor vs commentator — that make it possible for them to work in the rarely connected environment. One of the most interesting things about early tests of Notes has been the observation that workgroups are willing to analyze and adjust their working relationships in order to be in communication with each other today. The benefits of a rarely connected environment may indicate that future systems should allow workgroups to choose between a rarely connected solution and a continuously connected solution depending on their specific application needs.

Acknowledgments

We are grateful to Nancy Enright, David Reiner, Pito Salas, Eric Sall, Sunil Sarin, Steve Sneddon and Richard Wolf for their comments on early drafts of this paper.

References

[Demers] A. Demers, D. Greene, C. Hause, W. Irish, J. Larson, S. Shenker, H. Sturgis, D. Swinehart, D. Terry. Epidemic Algorithms for Replicated Database Maintenance. *ACM Operating Systems Review;* January, 1988

[Gifford] D. K. Gifford. Weighted Voting for Replicated Data. *Proceedings of the Seventh Symposium on Operating Systems Principles.* ACM SIGOPS 1979, Pages 150-159

[Gilbert] P. D. Gilbert. Development of the VAX NOTES System. *Digital Technical Journal* . No. 6 February 1988.

[Gray] Gray, J. N. et al. Granularity of Locks and Degrees of Consistency in a Shared Data Base, in Modeling in Data Base Management Systems, North Holland Publishing, 1976, pp. 365-394.

[Greif] I. Greif, R. Seliger and W Wiehl. Atomic Data Abstractions in a Distributed Collaborative Editing System. *Proceedings of the Thirteenth Annual ACM Symposium on Principles of Programming Languages,* St. Petersburg, Florida, January 1986.

[Hiltz] S. Hiltz and M. Turoff. The Network Nation: Human Communication via Computer. Addison-Wesley, 1978.

[Kung] H. T. Kung and J. T. Robinson. On Optimistic Methods for Concurrency Control. *ACM Transactions on Database Systems*, Vol. 6, No. 2, June 1981, Pages 213-226.

[Malone] T. W. Malone, K. R. Grant, Kum-Yew Lai, R. Rao, and D. Rosenblitt. Semistructured Messages Are Surprisingly Useful for Computer-Supported Coordination. *ACM Transactions on Office Information Systems*, Vol. 5, No. 2, April 1987, Pages 115-131.

[Oppen] D. C. Oppen and Y. K. Dalal. The Clearinghouse: A Decentralized Agent for Locating Named Objects in a Distributed Environment. Xerox Technical Report: OPD-T8103, 1981

[Smith] K. E. Smith and S. B. Zdonik. Intermedia: A Case Study of the Differences Between Relational and Object-Oriented Database Systems. OOPSLA '87 Proceedings

[Stonebraker] M. Stonebraker. Concurrency Control and Consistency of Multiple Copies of Data in Distributed INGRES. Proceedings of the Third Berkeley Workshop on Distributed Data Management and Computer Network. San Francisco, August 1978.

Hypertext: An Introduction and Survey

Reprinted from *Computer*, Vol. 20, No. 9, September 1987, pages 17-41. Copyright © 1987 by The Institute of Electrical and Electronics Engineers, Inc. All rights reserved.

Jeff Conklin

Microelectronics and Computer Technology Corp.

M ost modern computer systems share a foundation which is built of directories containing files. The files consist of text which is composed of characters. The text that is stored within this hierarchy is linear. For much of our current way of doing business, this linear organization is sufficient. However, for more and more applications, a linear organization is not adequate. For example, the documentation of a computer program* is usually either squeezed into the margins of the program, in which case it is generally too terse to be useful, or it is interleaved with the text of the program, a practice which breaks up the flow of both program and documentation.

As workstations grow cheaper, more powerful, and more available, new possibilities emerge for extending the traditional notion of "flat" text files by allowing more complex organizations of the material. Mechanisms are being devised which allow direct machine-supported references from one textual chunk to another; new interfaces provide the user with the ability to interact directly with these chunks and to establish new relationships between them. These extensions of the traditional text fall under the general category of *hypertext* (also known as *nonlinear text*). Ted Nelson, one of the

Documentation is the unexecutable English text which explains the logic of the program which it accompanies.

> **Hypertext systems feature machine-supported links—both within and between documents—that open exciting new possibilities for using the computer as a communication and thinking tool.**

pioneers of hypertext, once defined it as "a combination of natural language text with the computer's capacity for interactive branching, or dynamic display . . . of a nonlinear text . . . which cannot be printed conveniently on a conventional page."[1]

This article is a survey of existing hypertext systems, their applications, and their design. It is both an introduction to the world of hypertext and, at a deeper cut, a survey of some of the most important

design issues that go into fashioning a hypertext environment.

The concept of hypertext is quite simple: Windows on the screen are associated with objects in a database, and links are provided between these objects, both graphically (as labelled tokens) and in the database (as pointers). (See Figure 1.)

But this simple idea is creating much excitement. Several universities have created laboratories for research on hypertext, many articles have been written about the concept just within the last year, and the Smithsonian Institute has created a demonstration laboratory to develop and display hypertext technologies. What is all the fuss about? Why are some people willing to make extravagant claims for hypertext, calling it "idea processing" and "the basis for global scientific literature"?

In this article I will attempt to get at the essence of hypertext. I will discuss its advantages and disadvantages. I will show that this new technology opens some very exciting possibilities, particularly for new uses of the computer as a communication and thinking tool. However, the reader who has not used hypertext should expect that at best he will gain a perception of hypertext as a collection of interesting features. Just as a description of electronic spreadsheets will not get across the real elegance of that tool, this article can only hint at the potentials of hypertext. In fact, one must work in current hypertext environments for a while for the collection of fea-

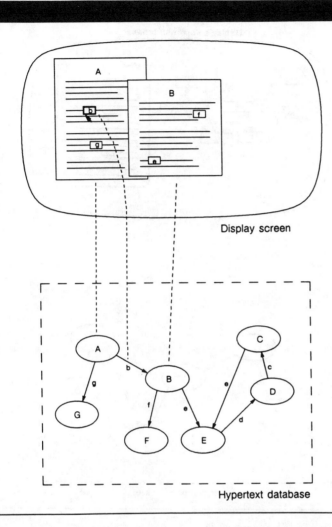

Figure 1. The correspondence between windows and links in the display, and nodes and links in the database. In this example, each node in the hypertext database is displayed in a separate window on the screen when requested. The link named "b" in window A has been activated by a pointing device, causing a new window named "B" to be created on the screen and filled with the text from node B in the database. (Generally, links can have names that are different from the name of the node they point to.)

that is common to many hypertext systems is the heavy use of windows that have a one-to-one correspondence with nodes in the database. I consider this feature to be of secondary importance.

One way to delimit hypertext is to point out what it is not. Briefly, several systems have some of the attributes of hypertext but do not qualify. Window systems fall into this category; while window systems do have some of the interface functionality, and therefore some of the "feel" of hypertext, window systems have no single underlying database, and therefore lack the database aspect of hypertext. File systems also do not qualify as hypertext; one could claim that a file system is a database, and that one moves among *nodes* (files) by simply invoking an editor with their names. However, to qualify as hypertext, a system must use a more sophisticated notion of links and must provide more machine support for its links than merely typing file names after a text editor prompt. Similarly, most outline processors (such as ThinkTank) do not qualify. They provide little or no support for references between outline entries, although their integrated hierarchical database and interface do approximate hypertext better than the other systems that I have mentioned. Text formatting systems (such as Troff and Scribe) do not qualify. They allow a tree of text fragments in separate files to be gathered into one large document; however, this structure is hierarchical and provides no interface for on-line navigation within the (essentially linear) document. Similarly, database management systems (DBMSs) have links of various kinds (for example, relational and object-oriented links), but lack the single coherent interface to the database which is the hallmark of hypertext.

As videodisc technology comes of age, there is growing interest in the extension of hypertext to the more general concept of *hypermedia*, in which the elements which are networked together can be text, graphics, digitized speech, audio recordings, pictures, animation, film clips, and presumably tastes, odors, and tactile sensations. At this point, little has been done to explore the design and engineering issues of these additional modalities, although many of the high-level design issues are likely to be shared with hypertext. Therefore, this survey will primarily address the more conservative text-based systems.

A glimpse of using hypertext. It is use-

tures to coalesce into a useful tool.

One problem with identifying the essential aspects of hypertext is that the term "hypertext" has been used quite loosely in the past 20 years for many different collections of features. Such tools as window systems, electronic mail, and teleconferencing share features with hypertext. This article focuses on machine-supported *links* (both within and between docu-

ments) as the essential feature of hypertext systems and treats other aspects as extensions of this basic concept. * It is this linking capability which allows a nonlinear organization of text. An additional feature

*While this article seeks to establish the criterion of machine-supported links as the primary criterion of hypertext, this is by no means an accepted definition. Therefore I will also review and discuss some systems which have a weaker notion of links.

ful to have a sense of the central aspects of using a hypertext system, particularly if you have never seen one. Below is a list of the features of a somewhat idealized hypertext system. Some existing systems have more features than these, and some have fewer or different ones.

• The database is a network of textual (and perhaps graphical) nodes which can be thought of as a kind of *hyperdocument*.

• Windows on the screen correspond to nodes in the database on a one-to-one basis, and each has a name or title which is always displayed in the window. However, only a small number of nodes are ever "open" (as windows) on the screen at the same time.

• Standard window system operations are supported: Windows can be repositioned, resized, closed, and put aside as small window icons. The position and size of a window or icon (and perhaps also its color and shape) are cues to remembering the contents of the window. Closing a window causes the window to disappear after any changes that have been made are saved to the database node. Clicking with the mouse on the icon of a closed window causes the window to open instantly.

• Windows can contain any number of *link icons** which represent pointers to other nodes in the database. The link icon contains a short textual field which suggests the contents of the node it points to. Clicking on a link icon with the mouse causes the system to find the referenced node and to immediately open a new window for it on the screen.

• The user can easily create new nodes and new links to new nodes (for annotation, comment, elaboration, etc.) or to existing nodes (for establishing new connections).

• The database can be browsed in three ways: (1) by following links and opening windows successively to examine their contents, (2) by searching the network (or part of it) for some string,** keyword, or attribute value, and (3) by navigating around the hyperdocument using a *browser* that displays the network graphically. The user can select whether the nodes and links display their labels or not.

The browser is an important component

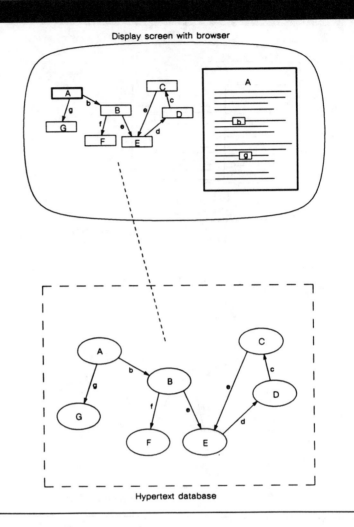

Figure 2. The screen at the top illustrates how a hypertext browser provides a direct two-dimensional graphic view of the underlying database. In this illustration, the node "A" has been selected for full display of its contents. Notice that in the browser view you can tell not only which nodes are linked to A but also how the subnetwork fits into the larger hyperdocument. (Of course, hyperdocuments of any size cannot be shown all at once in a browser—only portions can be displayed.)

of hypertext systems. As the hyperdocument grows more complex, it becomes distressingly easy for a user to become lost or disoriented. A browser displays some or all of the hyperdocument as a graph, providing an important measure of contextual and spatial cues to supplement the user's model of which nodes he is viewing and how they are related to each other and their neighbors in the graph. (See Figure 2.)

Using a browser can be likened to using visual and tactile cues when looking for a certain page in a book. Sometimes we remember the general way the page looked and about how far it was through the book, although we don't recall the page number or even which keyword terms would help us find it by using the index or table of contents. The browser display can be similarly scanned and scrolled when the

*Note that I am are describing two uses of icons: those that function as placeholders for windows that have been temporarily put aside, and those within windows that represent links to other nodes.

**A *string* is a series of alphabetic and numeric characters of any length, for example "listening" or "G00274."

user has forgotten all but the appearance or location of a node.

Hypertext implementations

The history of hypertext is rich and varied because hypertext is not so much a new idea as an evolving conception of the possible applications of the computer. Many people have contributed to the idea, and each of them seems to have had something different in mind. In this section, I will review these theorists and their ideas in an effort to present a historical perspective as well as to sketch some of the hypertext applications that have been devised to date. I do not describe the individual systems and ideas reviewed here in any detail. For more detailed information, the reader is invited to consult the literature directly.

One kind of manual hypertext is the traditional use of 3 × 5 index cards for note taking. Note cards are often referenced to each other, as well as arranged hierarchically (for example, in a shoebox or in rubber-banded bundles). A particular advantage of note cards is that their small size modularizes the notes into small chunks. The user can easily reorganize a set of cards when new information suggests a restructuring of the notes. Of course, a problem with note cards is that the user can have difficulty finding a specific card if he has many of them.

Another kind of manual hypertext is the reference book, exemplified by the dictionary and the encyclopedia. In the sense that each of these can be viewed as a graph of textual nodes joined by referential links, they are very old forms of hypertext. As one reads an article or definition, explicit references to related items indicate where to get more information about those items. The majority of people's transactions with a dictionary make use of the linear (alphabetic) ordering of its elements (definitions) for accessing a desired element. An encyclopedia, on the other hand, can best be used to explore the local nodes in the "network," once one has found the desired entry through the alphabetic index.

There are also many documents in which references to other parts of the document, or to other documents, constitute a major portion of the work. Both the Talmud, with its heavy use of annotations and nested commentary, and Aristotle's writings, with their reliance on references to other sources, are ancient prototypes of

hypertextual representation.

But if one insists, as most modern proponents of hypertext do, that navigation through hypertextual space must be computer-supported in order to qualify as true hypertext, then the field is narrowed considerably, and the history likewise shortened.

In some ways, the people who first described hypertext—Bush, Engelbart, Nelson—all had the same vision for hypertext as a path to ultimate human-computer interaction, a vision which is still alive today among hypertext researchers. Thus the historical review below stresses the early development of ideas about hypertext as much as the more contemporary implementation efforts.

Because of the difficulty of precisely classifying hypertext systems according to their features, my description will list systems according to application. There are four broad application areas for which hypertext systems have been developed:

- *macro literary systems*: the study of technologies to support large on-line libraries in which interdocument links are machine-supported (that is, all publishing, reading, collaboration, and criticism takes place within the network);
- *problem exploration tools*: tools to support early unstructured thinking on a problem when many disconnected ideas come to mind (for example, during early authoring and outlining, problem solving, and programming and design);
- *browsing systems*: systems similar to macro literary systems, but smaller in scale (for teaching, reference, and public information, where ease of use is crucial);
- *general hypertext technology*: general purpose systems designed to allow experimentation with a range of hypertext applications (for reading, writing, collaboration, etc.)

These categories are somewhat informal. Often the single application to which a system has been applied to date determines which category it is described in. Bear in mind that some of the systems mentioned below are full-scale environments, while others are still only conceptual sketches. Some systems have focused more on the development of the *front end*

(the user interface aspects), while others have focused on the database issues of the *back end* (the database server). Table 1 identifies various features of the different hypertext systems which have been implemented.

Macro literary systems. The earliest visions of hypertext focus on the integration of colossal volumes of information to make them readily accessible via a simple and consistent interface. The whole network publishing system constitutes a dynamic corpus to be enriched by readers without defacing the original documents; thus, the difference between authors and readers is diminished. The advent of the computer has brought this vision closer to reality, but it has also revealed the monumental problems inherent in this application area.

Bush's Memex. Vannevar Bush, President Roosevelt's Science Advisor, is credited with first describing hypertext in his 1945 article "As We May Think,"[2] in which he calls for a major postwar effort to mechanize the scientific literature system. In the article, he introduces a machine for browsing and making notes in an extensive on-line text and graphics system. This *memex* contained a very large library as well as personal notes, photographs, and sketches. It had several screens and a facility for establishing a labelled link between any two points in the entire library. Although the article is remarkably foresightful, Bush did not anticipate the power of the digital computer; thus his memex uses microfilm and photocells to do its magic. But Bush did anticipate the information explosion and was motivated in developing his ideas by the need to support more natural forms of indexing and retrieval:

> The human mind . . . operates by association. Man cannot hope fully to duplicate this mental process artificially, but he certainly ought to be able to learn from it. One cannot hope to equal the speed and flexibility with which the mind follows an associative trail, but it should be possible to beat the mind decisively in regard to the permanence and clarity of the items resurrected from storage.[2]

Bush described the essential feature of the memex as the ability to tie two items together. The mechanism is complex, but clever. The user has two documents that he wishes to join into a *trail* he is building, each document in its own viewer; he taps in the name of the link, and that name appears in a code space at the bottom of

Table 1. Hypertext systems and their features.

Hypertext Systems	Hierarchy	Graph-based	Link Types	Attri-butes	Paths	Ver-sions	Proced-ural Attach-ment	Keyword or String Search	Text Editor	Con-current or Multi-users	Pictures or Graphics	Graphical Browser
Boxer	Yes	Yes	Fixed¹	No¹	No	No	Yes	Yes	Emacs	No	Yes	Yes
CREF	Yes	Yes	Yes	No	No	By link	No	Yes	Zmacs	No	Yes	No
Emacs INFO	Yes	No	No	No	No	No	No	Yes	Emacs	No	No	No
IBIS	Yes	Yes	Yes	No	No	By link	No	No	A basic text editor	Yes	No	No
Intermedia	Yes	Yes	Yes	Yes	No²	No	No²	Yes	Custom	Yes	Yes	Yes
KMS	Multiple	Yes	Fixed	No	No¹	Yes	Yes	Yes	Text/graph. WYSIWYG	Yes	Yes	No
Neptune	Yes	Yes	Yes	Yes	No	Yes	Yes	Yes	Smalltalk-80 editor	Yes	Yes	Yes
NLS/Augment	Yes	Yes	Yes	Yes	Yes	Yes	Yes	Yes	Custom	Yes	Yes	No
NoteCards	Multiple	Yes	Yes	Nodes	No	No	Yes	Yes	Interlisp	Yes	Yes	Yes
Outline Processors	Yes	No	No	No	No	No	No	Yes	Various	No	No	No
PlaneText	Unix file sys.	Yes	No	No	No	No	No	Unix/grep	SunView text ed.	Yes	Yes	Yes
Symbolics Document Examiner	Yes	Yes	No	No	Yes	No	No	Yes	None	No	No	No
SYNVIEW	Yes	No	No	No	No	No	No	No	line ed./Unix	No	No	No
Textnet	Multiple	Yes	Yes	Yes	Yes	No	No	Keyword	Any	No	No	No
Hyperties	No	Yes	No	No	No	No	No	No²	A basic text editor	No	Yes	No
WE	Yes	Yes	No	Fixed	No²	No²	No²	No	Smalltalk-80 editor	No²	Yes	Yes
Xanadu	No	Yes	Yes	Yes	Yes	Yes	No	No	Any	No	Yes	No
ZOG	Yes	No	No	No	No	No	Yes	Full text	Spec. Pur.	Yes	No	No

¹ Can be user programmed.
² Planned for next version.

In this table, each column represents one possible feature or ability that a hypertext system can provide. The negative or affirmative entries in the table indicate whether the corresponding hypertext system meets the standard criteria for a specified feature. These criteria are listed below.

Hierarchy: Is there specific support for hierarchical structures?
Graph-based: Does the system support nonhierarchical (cross-reference) links?
Link types: Can links have types?
Attributes: Can user-designated attribute/value pairs be associated with nodes or links?
Paths: Can many links be strung together into a single persistent object?
Versions: Can nodes or links have more than a single version?
Procedural attachment: Can arbitrary executable procedures be attached to events (such as mousing) at nodes or links?
String search: Can the hyperdocument be searched for strings (including keywords)?
Text editor: What editor is used to create and modify the contents of nodes?
Concurrent multiusers: Can several users edit the hyperdocument at the same time?
Pictures or graphics: Is some form of pictorial or graphical information supported in addition to text?
Graphics browser: Is there a browser which graphically presents the nodes and links in the hyperdocument?

Figure 3. Engelbart at the NLS/Augment workstation. Note the chord key set under Engelbart's left hand. The chord key set is optional for Augment. It is a remarkable accelerator for character-driven commands and mouse-select screen operands.

each viewer; out of view, the code space is also filled with a photocell-readable dot code that names the other document and the current position in that document. Thereafter, when one of these items is in view, the other can be instantly recalled merely by tapping a button below the corresponding code space. Bush admitted that many technological breakthroughs would be needed to make his memex practical, but he felt that it was a technological achievement worthy of major expenditure.

Engelbart's NLS/Augment. Just less than two decades later Douglas Engelbart, at Stanford Research Institute, was influenced by Bush's ideas. In 1963, Engelbart wrote "A Conceptual Framework for the Augmentation of Man's Intellect."[3] Engelbart envisioned that computers would usher in a new stage of human evolution, characterized by "automated external symbol manipulation":

In this stage, the symbols with which the human represents the concepts he is manipulating can be arranged before his eyes, moved, stored, recalled, operated upon according to extremely complex rules—all in very rapid response to a minimum amount of information supplied by the human, by means of special cooperative technological devices. In the limit of what we might now imagine, this could be a computer, with which individuals could communicate rapidly and easily, coupled to a three-dimensional color display with which extremely sophisticated images could be constructed . . .[3]

His proposed system, H-LAM/T (Human using Language, Artifacts, and Methodology, in which he is Trained), included the human user as an essential element: The user and the computer were dynamically changing components in a symbiosis which had the effect of "amplifying" the native intelligence of the user. This is still a common vision among developers of hypertext systems.

Five years later, in 1968, Engelbart's

ideas about augmentation had become more specific, and had been implemented as NLS (oN Line System) by the Augmented Human Intellect Research Center at SRI. NLS was designed as an experimental tool on which the research group developed a system that would be adequate to all of their work needs, by

placing in computer store all of our specifications, plans, designs, programs, documentation, reports, memos, bibliography and reference notes, etc., and doing all of our scratch work, planning, designing, debugging, etc., and a good deal of our intercommunication, via the consoles.[4]

These consoles were very sophisticated by the standards of the day and included television images and a variety of input devices, including one of Engelbart's best known inventions, the mouse.*

Files in NLS were structured into a hierarchy of segments** called *statements*, each of which bore an identifier of its level within the file. For example, a document might have statements "1," "1a," "1a1," "1a2," "1b," etc., though these identifiers did not need to be displayed. Any number of reference links could be established between statements within files and between files. Note that this is a structure which is primarily hierarchical, but which allows nonhierarchical links as well. The importance of supporting both kinds of structures is a point to which I will return later. The system provided several ways to traverse the statements in files.

NLS, like other early hypertext systems, emphasized three aspects: a database of nonlinear text, *view filters* which selected information from this database, and *views* which structured the display of this information for the terminal. The availability of workstations with high resolution displays has shifted the emphasis to more graphical depictions of nodes, links, and networks, such as using one window for each node.

NLS provided viewing filters for the file structure: One could clip the level (depth) of hierarchy displayed, truncate the number of items displayed at any level, and write customized filters (in a "high-level content analysis language") that displayed only statements having the specified content. NLS also introduced the concept of

---

*Engelbart also introduced a five-key handset—a one-handed keyboard. The operator enters alphanumeric text by "chording" the five keys. Although this method is slower than two-handed typing, it has a considerable advantage for short commands when used with a mouse in the other hand.

**Segments were limited to 3000 characters in length.

multiperson distributed conferencing/editing.

NLS has evolved over the years. It is now called Augment (or NLS/Augment) and is marketed as a commercial network system by McDonnell Douglas. In developing NLS, the emphasis has been on creating a consistent environment for "knowledge workers" (that is, office automation for software engineers). The system now includes many forms of computer-supported communication, both asynchronous (email with links to all documents, journaling of ideas and exchanges, bulletin boards, etc.) and synchronous (several terminals sharing the same display, teleconferencing, etc.). It includes facilities for document production and control, organizational and project information management, and software engineering. (See Figures 3 and 4.)

Nelson's Xanadu Project. During Engelbart's development of Augment, another hypertext visionary, Ted Nelson, was developing his own ideas about augmentation, but with an emphasis on creating a unified literary environment on a global scale. Nelson coined the term "hypertext." His thinking and writing are the most extravagant of any of the early workers. He named his hypertext system Xanadu, after the "magic place of literary memory" in Samuel Taylor Coleridge's poem "Kubla Khan." In Xanadu, storage space is saved by the heavy use of links. Only the original document and the changes made to it are saved. The system easily reconstructs previous versions of documents. Nelson describes his objectives as follows:

> Under guiding ideas which are not technical but literary, we are implementing a system for storage and retrieval of linked and windowing text. The *document*, our fundamental unit, can have windows to any other documents. The evolving corpus is continually expandable without fundamental change. New links and windows can continually add new access pathways to old material. Fast proprietary algorithms render the extreme data fragmentation tolerable in the planned back-end service facility.[5]

The long range goal of the Xanadu project has been facilitating the revolutionary process of placing the entire world's literary corpus on line. In fact, Xanadu's design makes a strong separation between the user interface and the database server, with most of the emphasis placed on the latter. In particular, great care has been taken that copyright protection is main-

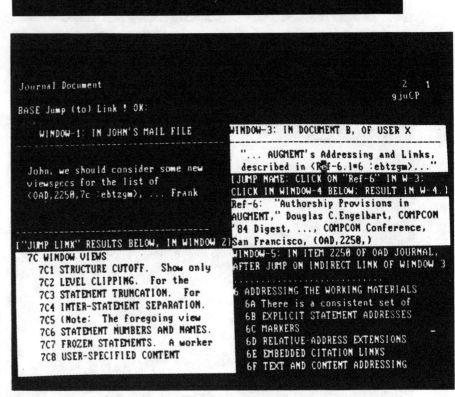

Figure 4. Augment display showing five windows. Window 1 (W-1) has a passage as if embedded in a message, showing a link to Branch 7c of Document 2250 in the OAD Journal. A ViewSpec ("ebtzgm") provides the following specifications: target level plus one, truncate to one line per statement, no blank lines between statements, show only that branch (e.g., not Branch 7d), and turn on Location Numbers. Window 2 (W-2) shows the view obtained with a jump link command. To perform a jump link command, the operator clicks on the link in W-1, then moves the cursor into W-2 for the final click. The very top-left system message announces that the desired Journal Item has been accessed, and the cluster at the top left of the screen verifies that the view is clipped to three levels and the statements truncated to one line each. Window 3 (W-3) shows an indirect link that specifies the linkage path. In effect, this link says "go to the statement in the file named 'Ref-6,' follow the link found there to its target file, and in that file find Location Number 6." Note that the same ViewSpec is specified here as for the link in W-1. Window 4 (W-4) identifies Ref-6 and provides its general reference source as the reference section at the end of the document; a user can jump from the link citation in W-3 to see this statement by using the jump name command. To perform this command, he clicks on "Ref-6" in W-3 then clicks on W-4. Window 5 (W-5) shows a view in the OAD-Journal Item 2250. The user can obtain this view by performing a jump link command on the indirect link of W-3. To perform this command, the user clicks on the indirect link of W-3 and then clicks in W-5.

tainable, and that a system for the electronic accounting and distribution of royalties is in place. Nelson predicts that the advent of on-line libraries will create a whole new market for the organization and indexing of this immense information store.

The back end of the Xanadu system has been implemented in Unix and is available in several forms, including as an on-line service (much like Engelbart's Augment). A crude front end for the Xanadu system is also available which runs on Sun workstations.

Trigg's Textnet. Randall Trigg wrote the first and to date the only PhD thesis on hypertext. In his thesis, he describes his Textnet system as supporting *nonlinear text*—text in which documents are organized as "primitive pieces of text connected with typed links to form a network similar in many ways to a semantic net." The thesis focuses on specific link types that support literary criticism.

In the tradition of the field, Trigg's system is just a first step in the direction of his vision:

> In our view, the logical and inevitable result [of the computer revolution] will be the transfer of all such [text handling] activities to the computer, transforming communication within the scientific community. All paper writing, critiquing, and refereeing will be performed on line. Rather than having to track down little-known proceedings, journals or unpublished technical reports from distant universities, users will find them stored in one large distributed computerized national paper network. New papers will be written using the network, often collaborated on by multiple authors, and submitted to on-line electronic journals.[6]

Textnet implements two basic types of nodes: those which have textual content (*chunks*) and those which hierarchically organize other nodes (*tocs*, for "table of contents"). Thus Textnet supports both hierarchical trees (via the toc nodes) and nonhierarchical graphs (via the typed links).

Trigg further proposes a specific taxonomy of link types for use by collaborators and critics in Textnet. He argues that there is generally a specific set of types of comments, and that there is a link type for each comment. For example, there are *refutation* and *support* links, and, more specifically, there are links to say that a point is irrelevant ("Pt-irrelevant"), that data cited is inadequate ("D-inadequate"), or that the style is rambling ("S-rambling"). Trigg describes over 80 such link types and argues that the disadvantage of having a limited set of link types is outweighed by the possibility of specialized processing on the hyperdocument afforded by a definite and fixed set of primitives.

In addition, Textnet supports the definition of *paths*—ordered lists of nodes used to browse linear concatenations of text and to dump such scans to hard copy. The path facility relieves the hypertext reader from having to make an *n-way* decision at each link; rather, the reader is provided a default pathway through the network (or part of the network), and can simply read the material in the suggested order as if he were reading a linear document.

Trigg joined Xerox PARC after completing his thesis and was one of the principal architects of the Xerox NoteCards system.

Problem exploration systems. These are highly interactive systems which provide rapid response to a small collection of specialized commands for the manipulation of information. They can be thought of as the early prototypes of electronic spreadsheets for text and symbolic processing. One important feature of most of these tools is a facility for suppressing detail at various levels specified by the user. For example, the outline processors all have single keystroke commands for turning on and off the display of subsections of a section. This is an unusual but natural facility. Hypertext and similar tools excel at the collection of large amounts of relatively unstructured information. But such collections are of little use unless adequate mechanisms exist for filtering, organizing, and browsing. These are the primary desiderata of these authoring/thinking/programming systems.

Issue-Based Information Systems. Horst Rittel and his students have introduced the notion of Issue-Based Information Systems (IBIS)[7] to handle systems analysis in the face of "wicked problems." Rittel describes wicked problems (as opposed to "tame" ones) as problems which cannot be solved by the traditional systems analysis approach (that is, (1) define the problem, (2) collect data, (3) analyze the data, (4) construct a solution). Wicked problems lack a definitive formulation; their problem space cannot be mapped out without understanding the solution elements; in short, the only way to really understand a wicked problem is to solve it. Wicked problems have no stopping rule. The design or planning activity stops for considerations that are external to the problem (for example, lack of time, money, or patience). Solutions to wicked problems are not "right" or "wrong"; they just have degrees of sufficiency. Rittel argues that solving wicked problems requires all those involved to exchange and argue their many viewpoints, ideas, values, and concerns. By coming to understand other viewpoints better, each participant is able to understand the whole problem better. This process enables a common understanding of the major issues and their implications to emerge. IBIS is designed to support this design/planning conversation.

IBIS systems are thus a marriage of (1) teleconferencing systems which enable many people to participate in one conversation, and (2) hypertext, which allows participants to move easily between different issues and the different threads of argument on the same issue. The current version of Rittel's IBIS runs on an Apple PC and is being ported to Sun workstations.* IBIS has three types of nodes (*issues*, *positions*, and *arguments*), and uses nine types of relations to link these nodes. In a typical application, someone posts an issue; then that person or others post positions about that issue; and then the positions are argued using argument nodes. Of course, any of the three types of nodes can be the seed of a new issue. (See Figure 5.) The current set of relationships between nodes is: *responds-to*, *questions*, *supports*, *objects-to*, *specializes*, *generalizes*, *refers-to*, and *replaces*. The research on IBIS concentrates on ways to summarize and present the issue network, both for participants and decision makers.

Lowe's SYNVIEW. David Lowe's SYNVIEW system is similar in concept to Rittel's IBIS but goes in a different direction. It proposes that the participants, in addition to posting their own issues and arguments, assess previous postings as to their validity and relevance. The assessment is done by a kind of quantitative voting. For example, if you think that Joe's response to Sam makes a good point but is not really a direct response to Sam's posting, you might grade it "5, 1" (where 5 is a high validity rating and 1 is a low relevance rating). These values are averaged into the existing values for that posting. The various displays of the argument structure show the values for each posting, allowing readers to focus, if they choose to, on those argument trails having the highest voted validity.

> Through debates on the accuracy of information and on aspects of the structures themselves, a large number of users can cooperatively rank all available items of information in terms of significance and relevance to each topic. Individual users can then choose the depth to which they wish to examine these structures for the purposes at

---

*A graphical Sun version, called gIBIS, is also being developed at the MCC/Software Technology Program.

hand. The function of this debate is not to arrive at specific conclusions, but rather to collect and order the best available evidence on each topic.[8]

UNC's WE. A group at the University of North Carolina at Chapel Hill has been developing a *writing environment* called WE.[9] Their research is based on a cognitive model of the communication process which explains reading as the process of taking the *linear* stream of text, comprehending it by structuring the concepts hierarchically, and absorbing it into long-term memory as a *network*. Writing is seen as the reverse process: A loosely structured network of internal ideas and external sources is first organized into an appropriate hierarchy (an outline) which is then "encoded" into a linear stream of words, sentences, etc.

WE is designed to support the upstream part of writing. It contains two major view windows, one graphical and one hierarchical, and many specialized commands for moving and structuring material (nodes and links with attached text) between these two views. Normally a writer will begin by creating nodes in the graph view, where he can place them anywhere within the window. At this stage, little or no structure is imposed on the conceptual material. The writer can place nodes in "piles" if they seem to be related, or he can place individual nodes between two piles if they are somewhat related to both. As some conceptual structure begins to emerge from this process, the writer can copy nodes into the hierarchy window, which has specialized commands for tree operations. The hierarchy window has four different display modes: (1) the tree can be laid out on its side, with the root node on the left; (2) the tree can be hung vertically with the root at the top; (3) child nodes can be displayed inside their parent node; and, (4) the hierarchy can be shown in the traditional outline view.

WE uses a relational database for the storage of the nodes and links in the network. The user points with a mouse to select a node. A third window is an editor for the material within the currently selected node. A fourth window on the screen is for queries to the database. A fifth window is used to control system modes and the current working set of nodes.

WE is designed to be an experimental platform to study what tools and facilities will be useful in a writer's environment. The real validation of these ideas, as with so many of the systems described here, will

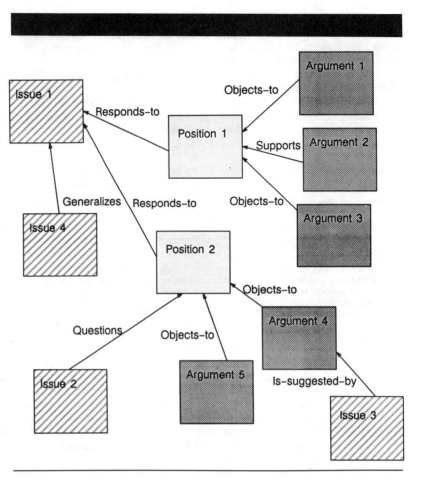

Figure 5. A segment of a possible IBIS-style discussion showing the topology of the IBIS network. Each node contains information on the type of the node, the time and date of creation, the author, a short phrase describing the content, a longer body of text with the text of the comment, a list of keywords, and a list of the incoming and outgoing links.

come with further experiments and analysis.

Outline processors. An *outline processor* is a word processing program which is specialized for processing outlines, in that its main commands deal with movement among, creation of, and modification of outline entries. In this respect, these programs commercialize many ideas from Engelbart's NLS/Augment. Outline processors also have at least simple text editors and do some text formatting, so that the user can use the same tool to go from outline to finished document. One of the most powerful features of outline processing is the ability to suppress lower levels of detail in the outline. As with Engelbart's NLS/Augment, the user can view just the top level of the outline, or the top *n* levels, or he can "walk the tree,"

opening up just those entries that are relevant or useful to the idea that he is working on. In addition, each outline entry can have a textual body of any length associated with it, and the user can make this body appear or disappear with a single keystroke. This feature is a real boon to the writing process, because it allows the user to have a view of both the immediate text that he is composing and the global context for it. It also facilitates rapid movement between sections, particularly in large documents, because in outline mode a remote section is never more than a few keystrokes away.

Most outline processors are personal computer programs, and they have done much to bring some of the concepts underlying hypertext into popularity. The first of these was called ThinkTank. It was released in 1984. It has since been joined

244

by a host of others, with names like Max-Think, Executive Writer/Executive Filer, Thor, Framework, Kamas, Fact Cruncher, Freestyle, Idea!, and PC-Outline.[10] There are two very recent additions to the field: Houdini is an extension of MaxThink that supports rich nonhierarchical internode references; and For-Comment is a word processor that allows up to 15 people to apply hypertext-like annotations to a document (and can operate over a Local Area Network (LAN) in real time).

Aside from Houdini, most outline processors do not support inter-entry references, except by "cloning" the whole entry and displaying it in the new location. Only a few others provide windows for nodes. None of them provide explicit "mousable" link icons. For these reasons, one could argue whether they qualify as hypertext as I have defined it here. However, ThinkTank was the first program to be billed—somewhat pretentiously—as an "idea processor," and all of these programs treat sections of text as first-class objects and support manipulations that coincide with the way one manages ideas. They share these features with hypertext, and in this sense, they anticipate the inevitable proliferation of hypertext features within the mainstream of computer applications.

Structured browsing systems. The systems reviewed in this section were designed primarily for applications involving large amounts of existing information or requiring easy access to information. These systems pose different problems for their designers. Ease of learning and ease of use are paramount, and great care goes into crafting the interface. On the other hand, writing (adding new information) is usually either not allowed to the casual user or is not particularly well supported.

CMU's ZOG and Knowledge Systems' KMS. ZOG is a menu-based display system developed in 1972 at Carnegie-Mellon University.[11] It consists of a potentially large database of small (screen-sized) segments which are viewed one at a time. ZOG was developed with the particular goal of serving a large simultaneous user community, and thus was designed to operate on standard terminals on a large timesharing system. In 1981 two of the principals on the ZOG Project, Donald McCracken and Robert Akscyn, started the company Knowledge Systems and developed a commercial successor to ZOG

called Knowledge Management System (KMS).

Each segment of the ZOG/KMS database is called a *frame*. A frame has, by convention, a one-line title at the top of the screen, a few lines of text below the title stating the issue or topic of the frame, a set of numbered (or lettered) menu items of text called *selections*, and a line of standard ZOG commands called *global pads* at the bottom of the screen. (Some of these commands are: *edit*, *help*, *back*, *next*, *mark*, *return*, and *comment*.) The selections interconnect the frames. When a user selects an item by typing its number or letter at the terminal keyboard, the selected frame appears on the screen, replacing the previous frame. The structure is generally hierarchical, though cross-referencing links can be included. In addition, an item in a frame can be used to activate a process.

In 1982 ZOG was installed and used as a computer-based information management system on the nuclear-powered aircraft carrier USS CARL VINSON. This system is probably the largest and most thoroughly tested hypertext system in service in the field. ZOG has also been used for more interactive process applications such as policy analysis, authoring, communications, and code management. Historically, however, ZOG made its name more as a bulletin board/textual database/CAI tool than as an interactive system. Hence it is included in this section on browsing. A drawback of the ZOG/KMS style of viewing a single frame at a time is that users may become disoriented, since no spatial event corresponds to the process of moving from frame to frame. In the KMS system, this tendency has been offset by minimizing system response time, so that frame-to-frame transition takes about half a second. The possibility of user disorientation is greatly reduced by the fact that the user can move very quickly among frames and thus become reoriented with very little effort. Creating text and graphics is also fast in KMS.

Emacs INFO Subsystem. The help system in the widely used text editor, Emacs, is called INFO, and is much like ZOG. It has a simpler set of standard commands, and its control input is done by single letters or

short commands typed at the keyboard. It is primarily hierarchical, but a user can jump to a different place in the hierarchy by typing in the name of the destination node. It is used as an on-line help system in Emacs. INFO has the same potential for user disorientation which is shared by all of the systems which display only a single frame at a time and have no browser.

Shneiderman's Hyperties. The University of Maryland Hyperties project* has been developed in two directions—as a practical and easy-to-learn tool for browsing in instructional databases and as an experimental platform for studies on the design of hypertext interfaces. As a practical tool, it has already seen some use in the field at a Washington, D.C. museum exhibit about Austria and the Holocaust. (See Figure 6.) Designers of the exhibit emphasized making the system easy and fun for users who have never used a computer before. As an experimental platform, it has been used in five experimental studies involving over 220 subjects.[12]

In Hyperties the basic units are short articles (50-1000 words typically), which are interconnected by any number of links. The links are highlighted words or phrases in the article text. The user activates the links by touching them with a finger (on a touch-sensitive screen) or using the arrow keys to jump to them.** Activating a link causes the article about that topic to appear in its own window on the screen. The system keeps track of the user's path through the network of articles, allowing easy return from exploratory side paths.

In addition to a title and a body of text, each article has a short (5- to 25-word) description which the program can display very quickly. This feature allows the user an intermediate position between bringing up the full article and trying to guess from the link name precisely what the article is about.

Hyperties runs on the IBM PC. Recently graphics capabilities have been added to the system. Current implementation efforts focus on support for videodisc images. Also, a browser is being developed

---

*The "ties" in "Hyperties" stands for "The Interactive Encyclopedia System."

**The Hyperties system uses a different convention than the mouse to select links. In the Hyperties system, some link is always selected. When the user pushes one of the arrow keys, the system responds by selecting the nearest link in the direction of the arrow. Studies showed this to be a faster and easier technique for selecting arbitrary highlighted fields on the screen.

which will provide string search, bookmarks, multiple windows, and user annotation.

Symbolics Document Examiner. The most advanced of the on-line help systems, this tool displays the pages from the entire twelve-volume manual set on the Symbolics Lisp machine screen.[13] Certain textual fields in the document (printed in bold) are mouse-sensitive. Touching one of these fields with the mouse causes the relevant section of the manual to be added to the current working set of manual pages. The system allows the reader to place *bookmarks* on any topic and to move swiftly between bookmarked topics. The protocol for link following is tailored to browsing in a reference manual or encyclopedia. Mousing a link only causes it to be placed on a list of current topics. Then, mousing an entry in this list causes that link to be followed, bringing up the referenced topic in the main viewing window.

The system also supports on-line string search of preidentified keywords, including the search for whole words, leading substrings, and embedded substrings. The system is thus well designed for the specific task of browsing through a technical manual and pursuing several aspects of a technical question or several levels of detail simultaneously. The user cannot make any changes or additions to the manual set (although it is possible to save personalized collections of bookmarks).

General hypertext technology. So far I have discussed hypertext systems that have particular practical applications. The following systems also have one or more applications, but their primary purpose is experimentation with hypertext itself as a technology. For example, while NoteCards has been used for authoring, programming, personal information management, project management, legal research, engineering design, and CAI, its developers view it primarily as a research vehicle for the study of hypertext.

Xerox PARC's NoteCards. Perhaps the best known version of full hypertext is the *NoteCards* system developed at Xerox PARC.[14] The original motivation in building NoteCards was to develop an information analyst's support tool, one that would help gather information about a topic and produce analytic reports. The designers of Notecards observed that an information analyst usually follows a general procedure that consists of a series

PLACES: AUSTRIA   PAGE 1 OF 3

Austria (see map) holds a special place in the history of the **Holocaust.**

Situated between Eastern and Western Europe, possessing a vibrant and

culturally creative **Jewish community** on the eve of World War II,

Austria had also provided the young **Adolf Hitler,** himself an Austrian

raised near Linz, with important lessons in the political uses of

antisemitism Leading **Nazis** came from Austria: the names of Adolf

Hitler, **Adolf Eichmann,** who organized the **deportations** of the Jews to

the **death camps,** and **Ernst Kaltenbrunner,** the head of the

Reich Main Office for Security, 1943-45, readily come to mind.   As

----

Linz - city in northern Austria; childhood home of Adolf Hitler and other

leading Nazis

NEXT PAGE   **RETURN TO GYPSIES**   **INDEX**

Figure 6. The Hyperties Browser enables users to traverse a database of articles and pictures by selecting from highlighted items embedded in the text of the articles. The photos show the IBM PC version of Hyperties. The upper node shows a map of Austria. The lower node shows double-spaced text with link terms highlighted. Either a touchscreen or jump-arrow keys are used for selection of brief definitions, full articles, or pictures. The Hyperties Author permits people with only word processing skills to create and maintain databases. Research versions of Hyperties run on the Enhanced Graphics Adapter to give more lines and multiple windows and on the Sun 3 workstation to show two full pages of text at a time. Current development efforts will enable readers to point at pictures and videodisc images to retrieve further information.

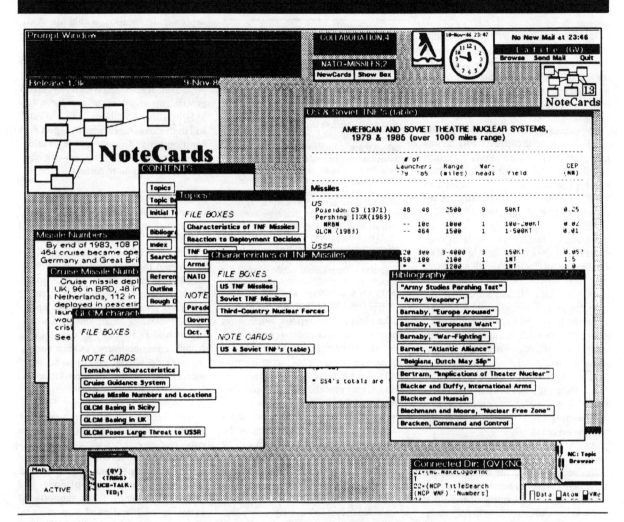

Figure 7. A typical NoteCards screen with five FileBox cards, two unformatted Text cards, and one Text card formatted as a table. Links between cards are represented by the boxed text inside the cards. The two menus at the top/middle of the screen control two different note files. The remainder of the icons on the screen belong to non-NoteCard applications running in the Xerox Lisp environment.

of steps: (1) reading sources (news reports, scholarly articles, etc.), (2) collecting clippings and filing them (in actual shoeboxes!), and (3) writing analytic reports. The designers also observed that throughout the process, the analyst forms analyses and conceptual models in his head. The research goal of the PARC team was to develop technology to aid the analyst in forming better conceptual models and analyses, and to find better expressions of these models and analyses.

A programmer's interface makes NoteCards an open architecture that allows users to build (in Lisp) new applications on top of NoteCards. Using this

interface, the user can easily customize the browser. NoteCards allows easy creation of new types of nodes. Forty or fifty such specialized node types have been created to date, including text, video, animation, graphics, and actions. * The new version also allows several users to work in the same Notefile at the same time.

Part of NoteCards' success is due to the fact that it was developed on Xerox D-series Lisp machines, which are powerful workstations that have high resolution

---

*An *action node* contains Lisp code which gets evaluated when a link to the node is activated.

screens allowing windows and link and node icons to be displayed in very high resolution. (See Figure 7.) Currently between 50 and 100 users use NoteCards, many of them outside of Xerox (even though it is not a supported product). Several of these users have constructed very large databases in the system (for example, 1600 nodes with 3500 links between them).

Brown University's Intermedia. One of the oldest and largest hypertext research groups exists at Brown University, at the Institute for Research in Information and Scholarship (IRIS).[15] The Intermedia project builds on two decades of work and three prior generations of hypertext systems.[16]

The first system was the Hypertext Editing System designed by Ted Nelson, Andy van Dam, and several Brown students for the IBM 2250 display in 1968. This system was used by the Houston Manned Spacecraft Center to produce Apollo documentation.

The second system was the File Retrieval and Editing System (FRESS). FRESS was a greatly enhanced multiterminal timesharing version designed by van Dam and his students. It became available in 1969 and was commercially reimplemented by Phillips in the early 1970's. FRESS was used in production by hundreds of faculty and students over more than a decade. Its users included an English poetry class that did all of its reading and writing on a communal hypertext document. Like NLS, FRESS featured both dynamic hierarchy and bidirectional reference links, and keyworded links and nodes. Unlike NLS, it imposed no limits on the sizes of nodes. On graphics terminals, multiple windows and vector graphics were supported.

The third project, the Electronic Document system, was a hypermedia system emphasizing color raster graphics and navigation aids.

As part of Brown's overall effort to bring graphics-based workstations into effective use within the classroom, the Intermedia system is being developed as a framework for a collection of tools that allow authors to create links to documents of various media such as text, timelines, diagrams and other computer-generated images, video documentaries, and music. Two courses, one on cell biology and one on English literature, have been taught using the system. Current applications include InterText, a text processor; InterDraw, a graphics editor; InterVal, a timeline editor that allows users interactively to organize information in time and date sequences; InterSpec, a viewer for sections of 3D objects; and InterPix, a scanned-image viewer. Under development are a video editor, a 2D animation editor, and more complex methods for filtering the corpus and creating and traversing trails.

Intermedia is being developed both as a tool for professors to organize and present their lesson material via computer and as an interactive medium for students to study the materials and add their own annotations and reports.

For example, in the English literature course the first time a student is searching for background information on Alexander Pope, he or she may be interested in Pope's life and the political events that prompted his satiric criticism. To pursue this line of thought the student might retrieve the biography of Pope and a timeline summarizing political events taking place in England during Pope's life. Subsequently, the student may want to compare Pope's use of satire with other later authors' satiric techniques. This time the student may look at the same information about Pope but juxtapose it with information about other satiricists instead of a time line. The instructor (and other students, if permitted) could read the student's paper, examine the reference material, and add personal annotation links such as comments, criticism, and suggestions for revision. While revising the document, the student could see all of the instructor's comments and examine the sources containing the counter-arguments.

Like most of the serious workers on hypertext, the Intermedia team is especially concerned with providing the user with ways of managing the increased complexity of the hypertext environment. For example, they contend that multiple links emanating from the same point in a document may confuse the reader. Their alternative is to have a single link icon in the material (text or graphics) which can be quickly queried via the mouse to show the specific outgoing links, their names, and their destination nodes.[15] They also propose a construct called a *web* to implement context-dependent link display. Every link belongs to one or more webs and is only visible when one of those webs is active. To view documents with the links that belong to a particular web, a user opens a web and then opens one or more of its documents. Although other webs may also reference the document, only the links which were made in the current web are displayed. As a result, the user does not have to sift through the connections made in many different contexts.

The Intermedia project is also studying ways of providing an effective browser for a network that can include hundreds or even thousands of nodes. The Intermedia browser has two kinds of displays: a *global map*, which shows the entire hyperdocument and allows navigation within it; and a *local map*, which presents a view centered on a single document and displaying its links and nearest neighbors in the web. In addition, a display can show nodes and links at several levels of detail. For example, it can show whole documents and the links between them, or each link and its approximate location within its documents. (See Figure 8.)

The Intermedia project has a long history, many participants, and a serious institutional commitment to long-term objectives. It conducts creative hypertext experiments and uses the classroom as a proving ground. Although this project is still in its early stages, we can expect it to contribute significantly to the development of effective cooperative work environments based on hypertext.

Tektronix Neptune. Tektronix Neptune is one hypertext system that has been particularly designed as an open, layered architecture.[17] Neptune strongly separates the front end, a Smalltalk-based user interface, from the back end, a transaction-based server called the Hypertext Abstract Machine (HAM). The HAM is a generic hypertext model which provides operations for creating, modifying, and accessing nodes and links. It maintains a complete version history of each node in the hyperdocument, and provides rapid access to any version of a hyperdocument. It provides distributed access over a computer network, synchronization for multiuser access, a complex network versioning scheme, and transaction-based crash recovery.

The interface layer provides several browsers: A *graph browser* provides a pictorial view of a subgraph of nodes and links; a *document browser* supports the browsing of hierarchical structures of nodes and links; and a *node browser* accesses an individual node in a hyperdocument. Other browsers include *attribute browsers*, *version browsers*, *node differences browsers*, and *demon browsers*. (See Figure 9.)

In Neptune, each end of a link has an offset within its node, whether that node is textual or graphical.* The link attachment may refer to a particular version of a node, or it may refer to the current version. The HAM provides two mechanisms that are useful for building application layers: Nodes and links may have an unlimited number of attribute/value pairs; and special high-speed predicates are included for querying the values of these pairs in the entire hyperdocument, allow-

---

*Unlike in most hypertext systems, the destination end of a Neptune link is an iconic point in the text of the destination node rather than the whole node.

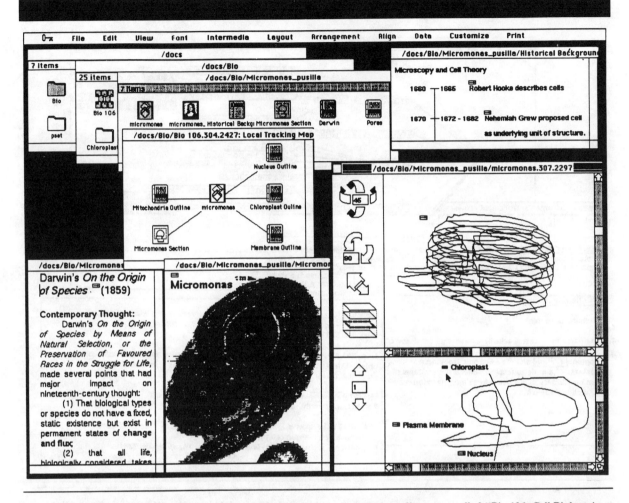

Figure 8. The Intermedia System. This figure illustrates materials from an Intermedia corpus called "Bio 106: Cell Biology in Context." Three folder windows containing hierarchically organized documents of different types are open in the upper left side of the display. An InterText document (lower left side) and an InterVal document (upper right side) are currently open, as well as an InterDraw document containing a scanned electronmicrograph (lower middle). This image has been linked to a corresponding three-dimensional image displayed in an InterSpect document (lower right). The "lower tracking map" (center) shows the links emanating from the current document. Authors or browsers can manipulate the three-dimensional image, edit text and graphics, follow links or create links at any time in this environment. (The electronmicrograph of *Micromonas* was published in the *Journal of Phycology* and is reprinted with the permission of the Editor.)

ing higher level applications to define their own accessing mechanisms on the graph. The HAM also provides a demon mechanism that invokes arbitrary code when a specific HAM event occurs.

diSessa's Boxer. Boxer[18] is a highly interactive programming language specifically tailored to be easy for noncomputer specialists to learn. Boxer uses a *box* to represent a unit of information in the system. In Boxer, one box can contain other boxes, or data such as text or graphics. For example, a program is a box that contains some boxes that provide input and output variables, and other boxes that specify behavior. The system also supports alternate views of some boxes: A box which specifies a graphics routine can also show that graphic display.

Since Boxer is a programming language, it treats cross-reference links in a special way. Rather than using mousable icons as links, Boxer uses a specialized box, called a "port," which gives a direct view into the destination. For example, a port from box

A to box B appears within A as a box which shows B. But a port is more than just a view of the destination box, because the destination box can be changed through any of the ports which lead to it, and the changes will be reflected in all of these ports.

Hierarchy is more naturally expressed in Boxer than in many of the other hypertext systems. Boxes are nested within each other two-dimensionally, and are filtered to reduce the level of clutter on the screen. This system of representation has the

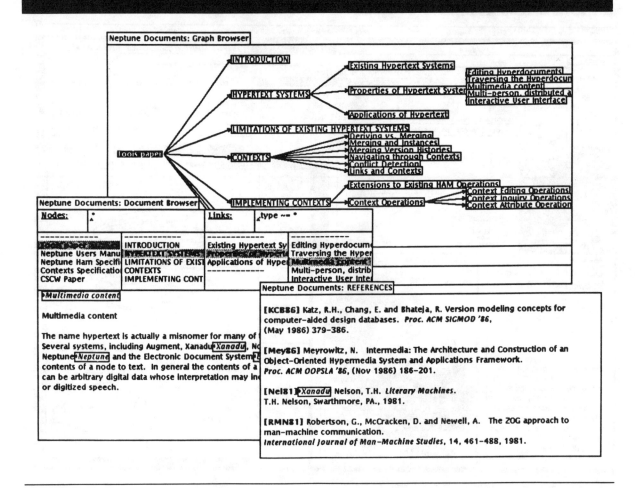

Figure 9. Neptune browsers. Three browsers from Neptune are illustrated. A pictorial view of a network of nodes and links is shown in the Graph Browser (the upper window). The lower right window and the lower pane of the Document Browser are viewers for text nodes. Icons representing link attachments are shown embedded within the text in each of the nodes.

advantage of showing a natural hierarchy of nodes: The windows of lower-level nodes are nested directly within their parents. In most hypertext systems, no attempt is made to display the parent-child relationship once the nodes are opened as windows.

Pitman's CREF. The Cross-Referenced Editing Facility (CREF) is a prototype of a specialized text and graphics editor which was developed originally as a tool for use in analyzing the transcripts from psychological experiments (known as *protocols*), but which was also used to inves-tigate more general hypertext design issues.[19] Much of the interactive feel of CREF reflects the style of use and pro-gramming of the Symbolics Lisp machine, on which it was built. Chunks of text, called *segments*, constitute the nodes in the system. Segments are arranged in linear series, and can have keywords and various kinds of links to other segments. The notion of a linear set of segments is natu-ral to the protocol analysis problem, since the first step with such protocols is to seg-ment them into the episodes of the exper-imental session.

CREF organizes segments into *collec-tions*, which can be defined implicitly by a predicate (called an *abstract collection*) or explicitly by a list (called a *static collec-tion*). At any time, the selected collection appears as a continuous length of text with the segment boundaries marked by named horizontal lines (such as "Segment 1," "Segment 2," etc.). This view can be edited as if it were a single document.

One way of forming an abstract collec-tion is by selecting segments using a boolean predicate over keywords. To extend the power of this keyword facility, CREF allows the user to define a type hier-archy on the keywords. For example, if "card 105" is defined as a type of (i.e., a *child* of) "card," then collections based on the keyword "card" will also contain segments which have only "card 105" as a keyword.

CREF supports four kinds of links: *references links* cross-reference among segments; *summarizes links* impose hierarchy (a *summary* is a segment which has one or more summarizes links to other segments); *supersedes links* implement versioning by copying the superseded segment and freezing it; and *precedes links* place a linear ordering on segments.

Finally, CREF allows multiple analysts to compose different *theories* about a protocol, using the same segmented data. Each theory imposes its own structure on the data, and has its own collections, diagrams, keywords, and annotations. This mode of selection is similar to the notion of contexts or webs used in other systems.

Hypertext on the Macintosh. At least two programs have been written for the Apple Macintosh that provide hypertext facilities: FileVision and Guide.

FileVision is primarily oriented to graphics nodes and to applications which can exploit visual indexing. The advertising for FileVision describes applications that encourage visual indexing. For example, in the database for a travel agency, the map of a region may contain icons for the main cities in that region. The user clicks on the icon for a city to obtain a display of a map of that city. The map of the city may have icons for the major landmarks in the city. The user clicks on one of these icons to obtain a display of data about the landmark, or perhaps even to obtain a picture of the landmark itself.

Guide is a more recent program which is based on an earlier Unix version developed in England.[20] It does not provide the graphics capabilities of FileVision (graphics are supported but cannot contain links), but it does support textual hypertext data very well. Guide uses three kinds of links: *replacement links*, which cause the text in the current window to be completely replaced by the text pointed to by the link; *note links*, which display the destination text in a pop-up window; and *reference links*, which bring up a new window with the destination text. Guide is now available for PCs as well.

As this article goes to press, there is news that Apple will soon have its own hypertext system, called HyperCards. HyperCards will be similar in some ways to Xerox PARC's NoteCards. It will provide special support for *executable links*, which will give it the flavor of a programming language. HyperCards will be bundled with the system software in new Macintoshes.

MCC's PlaneText. PlaneText, developed in the MCC Software Technology Program (STP), is a very recent addition to the family of general hypertext systems.* PlaneText is based on the Unix file system and the Sun SunView window manager. Each node is a Unix file. Links appear as names in curly brackets ({}) whose display can be turned on and off. Links are implemented as pointers saved in separate files, so that the linked files themselves are not changed by creating hypertext references between them. This design allows for the smooth integration of hypertext into the rest of the Unix-based computational environment, including such tools as Mail and News. It allows for the hypertext annotation of standard source code files. In addition, the Unix file directory system serves as a "free" mechanism for creating hierarchical structures among nodes.**

PlaneText supports color graphics nodes which can be freely linked into a hyperdocument.

Summary. The systems in this section were presented in terms of four broad categories: macro literary systems, problem exploration systems, structured browsing systems, and general hypertext technology. Table 1 summarizes this discussion and provides a breakdown of the various features which current hypertext systems can include.

One additional area of research currently is the development of systems which aid the entire process of design, particularly the informal upstream aspects. Such systems require the features of hypertext problem exploration and structured browsing systems as well as the advanced

---

*It is perhaps too early to say, however, how PlaneText will rank in the world of hypertext, since it will only be publicly available from the participant companies in the MCC/Software Technology Program. For more information call Bill Stotesbery at MCC, (512) 343-0978.

**The use of an existing tree-structuring mechanism limits any hypertext system to only being able to handle a single hierarchical structure. Single hierarchical organizations may be too limited for some advanced applications.

---

features of the experimental hypertext technologies. Indeed, this area of investigation may become an important fifth category for hypertext systems of the future.

The history of hypertext presented here suggests that the concept and the advantages of hypertext were clear several decades ago, but that widespread interest in hypertext was delayed until the supporting technology was cheap and readily available. This suggestion may be misleading. Many of the "elders" of the field feel that something else has changed as well. They feel that today computer users easily accept the role of the computer as a tool for processing ideas, words, and symbols (in addition to numbers and mere data), and as a vehicle of interhuman communication. Those theorists who gave presentations of their hypertext systems 20 years ago, using expensive state of the art hardware, report that the computer science community showed little interest. This lack of interest seemed to stem as much from a lack of understanding of the basic concepts of hypertext as from a lack of hardware resources.

If this is so, then the recent upsurge in interest in hypertext may signal that the computer community is now ready to consider its technology as much a tool for communication and augmenting the human intellect as for analysis and information processing. Hypertext is certainly a large step in that direction.

The Essence of Hypertext

It is tempting to describe the essence of hypertext as its ability to perform high-speed, branching transactions on textual chunks. But this is a little like describing the essence of a great meal by listing its ingredients. Perhaps a better description would focus on hypertext as a computer-based medium for thinking and communication.

The thinking process does not build new ideas one at a time, starting with nothing and turning out each idea as a finished pearl. Thinking seems rather to proceed on several fronts at one, developing and rejecting ideas at different levels and on different points in parallel, each idea depending on and contributing to the others.

The recording and communication of such entwined lines of thought is challenging because communication is in practice a serial process and is, in any case, limited by the bandwidth of human linguistic processing. Spoken communication of parallel themes must mark items with stresses, pauses, and intonations which the listener must remember as the speaker develops other lines of argument. Graphical forms can use lists, figures, and tables to present ideas in a less than strictly linear form. These visual props allow the reader/viewer to monitor the items which he must understand together. One of the challenges of good writing, especially good technical writing, is to present several parallel lines of a story or an argument in a way that weaves them together coherently.

Traditional flat text binds us to writing and reading paragraphs in a mostly linear succession. There are tricks for signalling branching in the flow of thought when necessary: Parenthetical comments, footnotes, intersectional references (such as "see Chapter 4"), bibliographic references, and sidebars all allow the author to say "here is a related thought, in case you are interested." There are also many rhetorical devices for indicating that ideas belong together as a set but are being presented in linear sequence. But these are rough tools at best, and often do not provide the degree of precision or the speed and convenience of access that we would like.

Hypertext allows and even encourages the writer to make such references, and allows the readers to make their own decisions about which links to follow and in what order. In this sense, hypertext eases the restrictions on the thinker and writer. It does not force a strict decision about whether any given idea is either within the flow of a paper's stream of thought or outside of it. Hypertext also allows annotations on a text to be saved separately from the reference document, yet still be tightly bound to the referent. In this sense, the "linked-ness" of hypertext provides much of its power: It is the machine processible links which extend the text beyond the single dimension of linear flow.

At the same time, some applications demonstrate that the "node-ness" of hypertext is also very powerful. Particularly when hypertext is used as a thinking, writing, or design tool, a natural correspondence can emerge between the objects in the world and the nodes in the hypertext database. By taking advantage of this object-oriented aspect, a hypertext user can build flexible networks which model his problem (or solution). In this application the links are less important

than the nodes. The links form the "glue" that holds the nodes together, but the emphasis is on the contents of the nodes.

From a computer science viewpoint, the essence of hypertext is precisely that it is a hybrid that cuts across traditional boundaries. Hypertext is a *database method*, providing a novel way of directly accessing data. This method is quite different from the traditional use of queries. At the same time, hypertext is a *representation scheme*, a kind of semantic network which mixes informal textual material with more formal and mechanized operations and processes. Finally, hypertext is an *interface modality* that features "control buttons" (link icons) which can be arbitrarily embedded within the content material by the user. These are not separate applications of hypertext: They are metaphors for a functionality that is an essential union of all three.

The power of linking. In the next two sections of this article, I will explore links and nodes in more detail as the basic building blocks of hypertext.

Link following. The most distinguishing characteristic of hypertext is its machine support for the tracing of references. But what qualifies a particular reference-tracing device as a link? How much effort is permissible on the part of a user who is attempting to trace a reference? The accepted lower limit of referencing support can be specified as follows: To qualify as hypertext, a system should require no more than a couple of keystrokes (or mouse movements) from the user to follow a single link. In other words, the interface must provide links which act like "magic buttons" to transport the user quickly and easily to a new place in the hyperdocument.

Another essential characteristic of hypertext is the speed with which the system responds to referencing requests. Only the briefest delay should occur (one or two seconds at most). Much design work goes into this feature in most systems. One reason for this concern is that the reader often does not know if he wants to pursue a link reference until he has had a cursory look at the referenced node. If making this judgement takes too long, the user may become frustrated and not bother with the hypertext links.

However, not all link traversals can be instantaneous. Perhaps as important as rapid response is providing cues to the user about the possible delay that a given query or traversal might entail. For example, some visual feature of the link icon could indicate whether the destination node is in memory, on the disk, somewhere else on the network, or archived off line.

Properties of links. Links can be used for several functions. These include the following:

• They can connect a document reference to the document itself.

• They can connect a comment or annotation to the text about which it is written.

• They can provide organizational information (for instance, establish the relationship between two pieces of text or between a table of contents entry and its section).

• They can connect two successive pieces of text, or a piece of text and all of its immediate successors.

• They can connect entries in a table or figure to longer descriptions, or to other tables or figures.

Links can have names and types. They can have a rich set of properties. Some systems allow the display of links to be turned on and off (that is, removed from the display so that the document appears as ordinary text).

The introduction of links into a text system means that an additional set of mechanisms must be added for creating new links, deleting links,* changing link names or attributes, listing links, etc.

Referential links. There are two methods for explicitly linking two points in hypertext—by reference and by organization. The reference method is a nonhierarchical method. It uses referential links that connect points or regions in the text.

Referential links are the kind of link that most clearly distinguishes hypertext. They generally have two ends, and are usually directed, although most systems support "backward" movement along the link. The origination of the link is called the "link source," and usually acts as the *reference*. The source can logically be either a single point or a region of text. At the other end, the "destination" of the link usually functions as the *referent*, and can

---

*Link deletion is problematical. For example, what should the policy be for nodes which are stranded when all their links have been deleted? Should they be placed in "node limbo" until the user decides what to do with them?

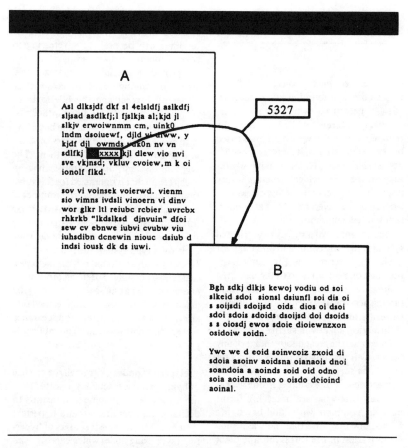

Figure 10. An example of a link with a point source and a region destination. The source of the link is a token in the text of document A which contains a textual identifier ("xxxx"). The identifier may be (1) the name of the destination node (in this case it would be "B"), (2) the name of the link, or (3) an arbitrary string which is neither the name of the link nor the destination node. The destination of this link is node B which is a region. The link has an internal name (5327) which is normally visible to the user.

also be either a point or a region. (See Figure 10.)

A *link point* is some icon indicating the presence of the link. It usually shows the link's name and perhaps also its type. Or it may show the name and/or type of the destination node. In systems such as Neptune which support links with both point source and point destination, the icon also indicates which type of link is indicated. In some systems, the display of links can be suppressed, so that the documents appear linear.

A *link region* is a set of contiguous characters which is displayed as a single unit. In Figure 10, the link destination is a link region, namely, an entire node. Fig-

ure 10 illustrates the most common form of hypertext link, in which the source is a point and the destination is a region. This example typifies many of the link applications listed above, because it shows how a chunk of text—a region—is written about or referenced by some smaller chunk of text, often a sentence. Since most readers are accustomed to single point references to sentences (i.e., footnotes), they have no problem accepting a link with a point source. There can be regions in graphics as well—either bordered regions or collections of graphic objects in a figure.

Link regions can pose difficult design problems. They are easiest to implement as whole nodes, since setting a region off

from its neighboring material within the same node raises a tough implementation issue—how to display the selected region to the user. It must be highlighted somehow, using reverse video, fonts, or color, but each of these options poses difficulties in keeping overlapping regions clearly highlighted. The Intermedia designers propose to draw a light box around regions and a darker box around region/region overlaps, thus showing a single level of overlapping[15]; however, this technique is not effective if there are more than two overlapping regions.

Another difficulty posed by link regions is how to show the name of the link. Unlike a link point, a link region has no obvious position for a title, unless it is placed arbitrarily at the beginning or end of the region.

Link regions can also be difficult to manipulate. Designers must devise a system for copying, moving, modifying, and deleting the region and the substrings within it. The movement of regions involves logistical dilemmas which are not easy to resolve: For example, when one moves a major portion of the text in a destination region to someplace else in the node, should the link destination move with it or stay with what remains? Also, designers must make special provisions for deleting, moving, or copying the defining end points of a region.

Organizational links. Like reference links, organizational links establish explicit links between points in hypertext. Organizational links differ from referential links in that they implement hierarchical information.

Organizational links connect a parent node with its children and thus form a strict tree subgraph within the hypertext network graph. They correspond to the *IS-A* (or *superconcept*) links of semantic net theory, and thus operate quite differently than referential links.* For example, rather than appearing as explicit highlighted tokens in each node, organizational links are often traversed by a separate mechanism at the node control level (i.e., special *goto-parent*, *goto-first-child*, and *goto-next-sibling* commands). In other cases, there are organizational nodes (such as toc nodes in Textnet and FileBoxes in NoteCards) which record the organizational structure.

---

*Note that organizational links are distinct from the class hierarchy links that would be used (in the object-oriented programming paradigm) to define types and subtypes of nodes in the hypertext system.

Keyword links. In addition to the explicit linking performed by referential and organizational links, there is a kind of implicit linking that occurs through the use of keywords. This type of linking is yet to be fully explored.

One of the chief advantages of text storage on a computer is the ability to search large and complex documents and sets of documents for substrings and keywords.* Naturally, this ability is also a valuable aspect of hypertext. Indeed, most users of large hyperdocuments insist on having some mechanism for scanning their content, either for selected keywords (which can apply to nodes, links, or regions) or for arbitrary embedded strings.

From a functional standpoint, link following and search are similar: Each is a way to access destination nodes that are of possible interest. Link following usually yields a single node, whereas search can yield many; hence, a keyword is a kind of implicit computed link. The value of this insight is that it may allow design of a hypertext interface which is consistent across all link-tracing activities.

To tree or not to tree. Some hypertext systems (for example, Emacs INFO) support only hierarchical structures, others (such as Xanadu and Hyperties) provide no specific support for hierarchical structures, and others (such as Textnet and NoteCards) support both kinds of structures.

One could question just how sufficient strictly hierarchical structures are, and for which applications they are sufficient and for which they are not. On the one hand, abstraction is a fundamental cognitive process, and hierarchical structures are the most natural structures for organizing levels of abstraction. On the other hand, cases obviously exist where cross-hierarchical links are required. Frank Halasz, one of the developers of NoteCards, has gathered statistics on the *hyperspace* of a single representative NoteCards user; this person had 1577 nodes (cards) in all, 502 of which were File-Boxes (hierarchical nodes). Connecting these nodes were a total of 3460 links, 2521

*There is some controversy over the relative merits of keyword retrieval as opposed to full text search. On the one hand, keyword retrieval is only as good as the skill and thoroughness of the person selecting the keywords. On the other hand, full text search does not find all the relevant documents, nor does it always find only the relevant documents. Its shortcomings are due in part to the commonness of synonyms in English. In addition, full text search can be computationally prohibitive in large networks.

(73 percent) of which connected FileBoxes to each other or to individual notecards, 261 (7.5 percent) of which were nonhierarchical referential links, and the remainder of which were mail links (used by the system to tie mail messages to other nodes). This example, for what it is worth, suggests that hierarchical structure is very important in organizing a hypertext network, and that referential links are important but less common.

One advantage of a strictly tree-oriented system is that the command language for navigation is very simple: From any node, the most one can do is go to the parent, a sibling, or a child. This simplicity also diminishes the disorientation problem, since a simpler cognitive model of the information space will suffice.

Of course, the great disadvantage of any hierarchy is that its structure is a function of the few specific criteria that were used in creating it. For example, if one wishes to investigate what sea-based life forms have in common with land-based life forms, one may find that the traditional classification of life forms into the plant and animal kingdoms breaks up the information in the wrong way. The creator of a hierarchical organization must anticipate the most important criteria for later access to the information. One solution to this dilemma is to allow the information elements to be structured into multiple hierarchies, thus allowing the world to be "sliced up" into several orthogonal decompositions. Any hypertext system which has hierarchy nodes, such as Textnet (toc nodes) and NoteCards (FileBox nodes), can perform this operation quite easily. These are the only systems which explicitly claim to support multiple hierarchies. Indeed, one early user of NoteCards used the system in doing the research and writing for a major project paper; he imposed one organization on the data and his writings while doing the research, and then quite a different (yet coexistent) organization on the same material to produce his paper. As a generalization, it seems that engineering-oriented hypertext users prefer hierarchical organizations, whereas arts- or humanities-oriented users prefer cross-referencing organizations.

Extensions to basic links. Certain features of the link enable it to be extended in

several ways. Links can connect more than two nodes to form *cluster links*. Such cluster links can be useful for referring to several annotations with a single link, and for providing specialized organizational structures among nodes. Indeed, the toc nodes of Textnet and the FileBoxes of NoteCards are both forms of cluster links.

One useful way to extend the basic link is to place attribute/value pairs on links and to query the network for them. The Neptune system, for example, has an architecture that is optimized for this function. Coupled with specialized routines in the database interpreter (the HAM), these attribute lists allow users to customize links in several ways, including devising their own type system for links and performing high-speed queries on the types.

It is also possible to perform procedural attachments on a link so that traversing the link also performs some user-specified side effect, such as customizing the appearance of the destination node. This ability is provided in Neptune and Boxer.

Hypertext nodes. Although the essence of hypertext is its machine-supported linking, the nodes contribute significantly to defining the operations that a hypertext system can perform. Most users of hypertext favor using nodes which express a single concept or idea, and are thus much smaller than traditional files. When nodes are used in this fashion, hypertext introduces an intermediate level of machine support between characters and files, a level which has the vaguely semantic aspect of being oriented to the expression of ideas. But this sizing is completely at the discretion of the hypertext writer, and the process of determining how to modularize a document into nodes is an art, because its impact on the reader is not well understood.[21]

The modularization of ideas. Hypertext invites the writer to modularize ideas into units in a way that allows (1) an individual idea to be referenced elsewhere, and (2) alternative successors of a unit to be offered to the reader (for instance, more detail, an example, bibliographic references, or the logical successor). But the writer must also reckon with the fact that a hypertext node, unlike a textual paragraph, tends to be a strict unit which does not blend seamlessly with its neighbors. Some hypertext systems (Notecards, CREF, Boxer, FRES, NLS) allow nodes to be viewed together as if they were one big node, and this option is essential for some applications (for example, writing and reading prose). But the boundaries around nodes are always discrete and require sometimes difficult judgements about how to cleave the subject matter into suitable chunks.

The process of identifying a semantically based unit, such as an idea or concept, with a syntactic unit, such as a paragraph or hypertext node, is not unique to hypertext. Manuals of style notwithstanding, traditional text has rather loose conventions for modularizing text into paragraphs. This looseness is acceptable because paragraph boundaries have a relatively minor effect on the flow of the reading. Paragraph boundaries are sometimes provided just to break up the text and give the eye a reference point. Thus, decisions about the distribution of sentences among paragraphs is not always critical.

Hypertext, on the other hand, can enforce a rather stern information hiding. In some systems, the only clue a user has as to the contents of a destination node is the name of the link (or the name of the node, if that is provided instead). The writer is no longer making all the decisions about the flow of the text. The reader can and must constantly decide which links to pursue. In this sense, hypertext imposes on both the writer and the reader the need for more process awareness, since either one has the option of *branching* in the flow of the text. Thus hypertext is best suited for applications which require these kinds of judgements anyway, and hypertext merely offers a way to act directly on these judgements and see the results quickly and graphically.

Ideas as objects. While difficult to document, there is something very compelling about reifying the expression of ideas into discrete objects to be linked, moved, and changed as independent entities. Alan Kay and Adele Goldberg[22] observed of Smalltalk that it is able to give objects a perceptual dimension by allocating to them a rectangular piece of screen real estate. This feature offers enhanced retrieval and recognition over computer-processed flat documents, because to a much greater degree abstract objects are directly associated with perceptual objects—the windows and icons on the screen.

Paragraphs, sections, and chapters in a book, viewed through a standard text editor or word processor, don't stand out as first-class entities. This is particularly apparent when one can view one's docu-

ment hierarchically (i.e., as an outline) at the same time that one adds new sections and embellishes existing ones. People don't think in terms of "screenfulls"; they think in terms of ideas, facts, and evidence. Hypertext, via the notion of nodes as individual expressions of ideas, provides a vehicle which respects this way of thinking and working.

Typed nodes. Some hypertext systems sort nodes into different types. These *typed nodes* can be extremely useful, particularly if one is considering giving them some internal structure, since the types can be used to differentiate the various structural forms.

For example, in our research in the MCC Software Technology Program, we have been implementing a hypertext interface for a design environment called the Design Journal. The Design Journal is intended to provide an active scratchpad in which the designer can deliberate about design decisions and rationale, both individually and in on-line design meetings, and in which he can integrate the design itself with this less formal kind of information. For this purpose we have provided a set of four typed nodes for the designer to use—*notes, goals/constraints, artifacts,* and *decisions.* Notes are used for everything from reminders, such as "Ask Bill for advice on Module X," to specific problems and ideas relating to the design. Goals/constraints are for the initial requirements as well as discovered constraints within the design. Artifacts are for the elements of the output: The Design. And decisions are for capturing the branch points in the design process, the alternatives considered by the designer, and some of the rationale for any commitment (however tentative) that has been made. The designer captures assumptions in the form of decisions with only one alternative. Our prototype of the Design Journal uses color to distinguish between note types in the browser, and we have found this to be a very effective interface.

Hypertext systems that use typed nodes generally provide a specialized color, size, or iconic form for each node type. The distinguishing features help the user differentiate at a glance the broad classes of typed nodes that he is working with. Systems such as NoteCards, Intermedia, and IBIS make extensive use of typed nodes.

Semistructured Nodes. So far I have spoken of the hypertext node as a structureless "blank slate" into which one might put a word or a whole document. For some applications, there is growing interest in *semistructured nodes*—typed nodes which contain labelled fields and spaces for field values. The purpose of providing a template for node contents is to assist the user in being complete and to assist the computer in processing the nodes. The less that the content of a node is undifferentiated natural language (for example, English) text, the more likely that the computer can do some kinds of limited processing and inference on the textual subchunks. This notion is closely related to Malone's notion of semistructured information systems.[23]

To continue with the example of the Design Journal, we have developed a model for the internal structure of decisions. The model is named ISAAC. It assumes that there are four major components to a design decision:

(1) an *issue*, including a short name for the issue and a short paragraph describing it in general terms;
(2) a set of *alternatives*, each of which resolves the issue in a different way, each having a name and short description, and each potentially linked to the design documents or elements that implement the alternative;
(3) an *analysis* of the competing alternatives, including the specific criteria being used to evaluate them, the trade-off analysis among these alternatives, and links to any data that the analysis draws upon; and
(4) a *commitment* to one of the alternatives (however tentatively) or to a vector of preferences over the alternatives, and a subjective rating about the correctness or confidence of this commitment.

Without getting into the details of the underlying theory, I merely wish to stress here that the internal structure of ISAAC suggests that the author of an ISAAC decision is engaged in a much more structured activity than just "writing down the decision," and the reader is likewise guided by the regularity of the ISAAC structure.

Of course, it may not be clear why we do not treat each of the elements listed above as its own typed hypertext node. The reason is that the parts of an ISAAC frame are much more tightly bound together than ISAAC frames are bound to each other. For example, we could not have an analysis part without an alternatives part; yet if we treat them as separate hypertext nodes, we have failed to build this constraint into the structure. The general issue here is that some information elements must always occur together, while others may occur together or not, depending on how related they are in a given context and how important it is to present them as a cluster distinct from "surrounding" information elements. This problem is recursive: An element that is atomic at one level may turn out on closer inspection to contain many components, some of which are clustered together.

In hypertext this tension presents itself as the twin notions of semistructured nodes and composite nodes.

Composite nodes. Another mechanism for aggregating related information in hypertext is the *composite node.* Several related hypertext nodes are "glued" together and the collection is treated as a single node, with its own name, types, versions, etc. Composite nodes are most useful for situations in which the separate items in a bulleted list or the entries in a table are distinct nodes but also cohere into a higher level structure (such as the list or table). This practice can, however, undermine the fundamental association of one interface object (window) per database object (node), and thus must be managed well to avoid complicating the hypertext idiom unduly.

A composite node facility allows a group of nodes to be treated as a single node. The composite node can be moved and resized, and closes up to a suitable icon reflecting its contents. The subnodes are separable and rearrangeable through a subedit mode. The most flexible means of displaying a composite node is to use a constraint language (such as that developed by Symbolics for Constraint Frames) which describes the subnodes as *panes* in the composite node window and specifies the interpane relationships as dynamic constraints on size and configuration.

Composite nodes can be an effective means of managing the problem of having a large number of named objects in one's environment. Pitman described the problem this way:

> In this sort of system, there is a never-ending tension between trying to name everything (in which case, the number of named things can grow quickly and the set can become quickly unmanageable) or to name as little as possible (in which case, things that took a lot of trouble to construct can be hard to retrieve if one accidentally drops the pointers to them).[19]

One problem with composite nodes is that as the member nodes grow and change the aggregation can become misleading or incorrect. A user who encounters this problem is in the same predicament as a writer who has rewritten a section of a paper so thoroughly that the section title is no longer accurate. This "semantic drift" can be difficult to catch.

Analogy to semantic networks. The idea of building a directed graph of informal textual elements is similar to the AI concept of *semantic networks.* A semantic network is a knowledge representation scheme consisting of a directed graph in which concepts are represented as nodes, and the relationships between concepts are represented as the links between them. What distinguishes a semantic network as an AI representation scheme is that concepts in the representation are indexed by their semantic content rather than by some arbitrary (for example, alphabetical) ordering. One benefit of semantic networks is that they are natural to use, since related concepts tend to cluster together in the network. Similarly, an incompletely or inconsistently defined concept is easy to spot since a meaningful context is provided by those neighboring concepts to which it is already linked.

The analogy to hypertext is straightforward: Hypertext nodes can be thought of as representing single concepts or ideas, internode links as representing the semantic interdependencies among these ideas, and the process of building a hypertext network as a kind of informal knowledge engineering. The difference is that AI knowledge engineers are usually striving to build representations which can be mechanically interpreted, whereas the goal of the hypertext writer is often to capture an interwoven collection of ideas without regard to their machine interpretability. The work on semantic networks also suggests some natural extensions to hypertext, such as typed nodes, semistructured nodes (frames), and inheritance hierarchies of node and link types.

The advantages and uses of hypertext

Intertextual references are not new. The importance of hypertext is simply that references are machine-supported. Like hypertext, traditional literature is richly interlinked and is hierarchically organized. In traditional literature, the medium of print for the most part restricts the flow of reading to follow the flow of linearly arranged passages. However, the process of following side links is fundamental even in the medium of print. In fact, library and information science consist principally of the investigation of side links. Anyone who has done research knows that a considerable portion of that effort lies in obtaining referenced works, looking up cross-references, looking up terms in a dictionary or glossary, checking tables and figures, and making notes on notecards. Even in simple reading one is constantly negotiating references to other chapters or sections (via the table of contents or references embedded in the text), index entries, footnotes, bibliographic references, sidebars, figures, and tables. Often a text invites the reader to skip a section if he is not interested in greater technical detail.

But there are problems with the traditional methods.

- Most references can't be traced backwards: A reader can not easily find where a specific book or article is referenced in a document, nor can the author of a paper find out who has referenced the paper.

- As the reader winds his way down various reference trails, he must keep track of which documents he has visited and which he is done with.

- The reader must squeeze annotations into the margins or place them in a separate document.

- Finally, following a referential trail among paper documents requires substantial physical effort and delays, even if the reader is working at a well-stocked library. If the documents are on line, the job is easier and faster, but no less tedious.

New possibilities for authoring and design. Hypertext may offer new ways for authors and designers to work. Authoring is usually viewed as a word- and sentence-level activity. Clearly the word processor *

---

*Actually, the term "word processor" is quite misleading. Most such tools accept input only at the character level, and manipulate characters, words, sentences, and paragraphs with equal facility. So these tools manipulate units of text, not words. But do they "process" these units? "Processing" implies that the computer performs some additional work, such as changing the verb form if the subject was changed from singular to plural, or performing real-time spelling and grammar correction. Since this is not the case, we really should return to the original term for these tools: "text editors".

is a good tool for authoring at this level. However, authoring obviously has much to do with structuring of ideas, order of presentation, and conceptual exploration. Few authors simply sit down and pour out a finished text, and not all editing is just "wordsmithing" and polishing. In a broad sense, authoring is the *design of a document*. The unit of this level of authoring is the idea or concept, and this level of work can be effectively supported by hypertext, since the idea can be expressed in a node. As the writer thinks of new ideas, he can develop them in their own nodes, and then link them to existing ideas, or leave them isolated if it is too early to make such associations. The specialized refinements of a hypertext environment assist the movement from an unstructured network to the final polished document.

New possibilities for reading and retrieval. Hypertext may also offer new possibilities for accessing large or complex information sources. A linear (nonhypertext) document can only be easily read in the order in which the text flows in the book. The essential advantage of nonlinear text is the ability to organize text in different ways depending on differing viewpoints. Shasha provides the following description of this advantage:

> Suppose you are a tourist interested in visiting museums in a foreign city. You may be interested in visual arts. You may want to see museums in your local area. You may only be interested in inexpensive museums. You certainly want to make sure the museums you consider are open when you want to visit them. Now your guidebook may be arranged by subject, by name of museum, by location, and so on. The trouble is: if you are interested in any arrangement other than the one it uses, you may have to do a lot of searching. You are not likely to find all the visual arts museums in one section of a guidebook that has been organized by district. You may carry several guidebooks, each organized by a criterion you may be interested in. The number of such guidebooks is a measure of the need for a nonlinear text system.[21]

Another advantage is that it is quite natural in a hypertext environment to suspend reading temporarily along one line of investigation while one looks into some detail, example, or related topic. Bush described an appealing scenario in his 1945 article:

> The owner of the memex, let us say, is interested in the origin and properties of the bow and arrow. Specifically he is studying why the short Turkish bow was apparently superior to the English long bow in the skirmishes of the Crusades. He has dozens of possibly pertinent books and articles in his

memex. First he runs through an encyclopedia, finds an interesting but sketchy article, leaves it projected. Next, in a history, he finds another pertinent item, and ties the two together. Thus he goes, building a trail of many items. Occasionally he inserts a comment of his own, either linking it into the main trail or joining it by a side trail to a particular item. When it becomes evident that the elastic properties of available materials had a great deal to do with the bow, he branches off on a side trail which takes him through textbooks on elasticity and tables of physical constants. He inserts a page of longhand analysis of his own. Thus he builds a [permanent] trail of his interest through the maze of materials available to him.[2]

As we have seen, Bush's notion of the "trail" was a feature of Trigg's Textnet,[6] allowing the hypertext author to establish a mostly linear path through the document(s). The main (default) trail is well marked, and the casual reader can read the text in that order without troubling with the side trails.

Summary. We can summarize the operational advantages of hypertext as:

- *ease of tracing references*: machine support for link tracing means that all references are equally easy to follow forward to their referent, or backward to their reference;
- *ease of creating new references*: users can grow their own networks, or simply annotate someone else's document with a comment (without changing the referenced document);
- *information structuring*: both hierarchical and nonhierarchical organizations can be imposed on unstructured information; even multiple hierarchies can organize the same material;
- *global views*: browsers provide table-of-contents style views, supporting easier restructuring of large or complex documents; global and local (node or page) views can be mixed effectively;
- *customized documents*: text segments can be threaded together in many ways, allowing the same document to serve multiple functions;
- *modularity of information*: since the same text segment can be referenced from several places, ideas can be expressed with less overlap and duplication;
- *consistency of information*: references are embedded in their text, and

if the text is moved, even to another document, the link information still provides direct access to the reference;
- *task stacking*: the user is supported in having several paths of inquiry active and displayed on the screen at the same time, such that any given path can be unwound to the original task;
- *collaboration*: several authors can collaborate, with the document and comments about the document being tightly interwoven (the exploration of this feature has just begun).

The disadvantages of hypertext

There are two classes of problems with hypertext: problems with the current implementations and problems that seem to be endemic to hypertext. The problems in the first class include delays in the display of referenced material, restrictions on names and other properties of links, lack of browsers or deficiencies in browsers, etc. The following section outlines two problems that are more challenging than these implementation shortcomings, and that may in fact ultimately limit the usefulness of hypertext: *disorientation* and *cognitive overhead*.

Getting "lost in space." Along with the power to organize information much more complexly comes the problem of having to know (1) where you are in the network and (2) how to get to some other place that you know (or think) exists in the network. I call this the "disorientation problem." Of course, one also has a disorientation problem in traditional linear text documents, but in a linear text, the reader has only two options: He can search for the desired text earlier in the text or later in the text. Hypertext offers more degrees of freedom, more dimensions in which one can move, and hence a greater potential for the user to become lost or disoriented. In a network of 1000 nodes, information can easily become hard to find or even forgotten altogether. (See Figure 11.)

There are two major technological solutions for coping with disorientation—graphical browsers and query/search mechanisms. Browsers rely on the extremely highly developed visuospatial processing of the human visual system. By placing nodes and links in a two- or three-dimensional space, providing them with

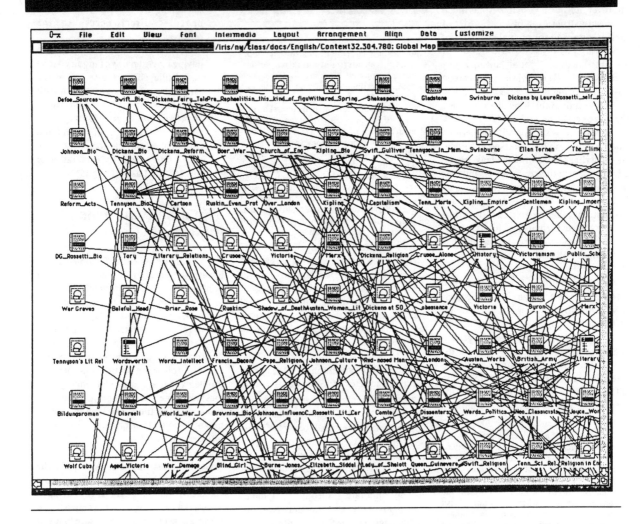

Figure 11. Tangled web of links. This experimental implementation of a global map in the Intermedia system shows the difficulty of providing users with spatial cues once a linked corpus contains more than a few dozen documents. This global map only represents about one tenth of the documents in a corpus designed for a survey of English literature course.

properties useful in visual differentiation (color, size, shape, texture), and maintaining certain similarities to our physical environment (for example, no two objects occupy the same space, things only move if moved, etc.), browser designers are able to create quite viable virtual spatial environments. Users orient themselves by visual cues, just as when they are walking or driving through a familiar city. However, there is no natural topology for an information space, except perhaps that higher level concepts go at the top or on the left side, so until one is familiar with a given

large hyperdocument, one is by definition disoriented. In addition, an adequate virtuality is very difficult to maintain for a large or complex hypertext network. Such parameters as (1) large numbers of nodes, (2) large numbers of links, (3) frequent changes in the network, (4) slow or awkward response to user control inputs, (5) insufficient visual differentiation among nodes and/or links, and (6) nonvisually oriented users combine to make it practically impossible to abolish the disorientation problem with a browser alone.

One solution to this dilemma is to apply

standard database search and query techniques to locating the node or nodes which the user is seeking. This is usually done by using boolean operations to apply some combination of keyword search, full string search, and logical predicates on other attributes (such as author, time of creation, type, etc.) of nodes or links. Similarly, one can filter (or *ellide*) information so that the user is presented with a manageable level of complexity and detail, and can shift the view or the detail suppression while navigating through the network. However, much research remains to be done on effective and standardized methods for ellision.

The cognitive task scheduling problem. The other fundamental problem with using hypertext is that it is difficult to become accustomed to the additional mental overhead required to create, name, and keep track of links. I call this "cognitive overhead." Suppose you are writing about X, and a related thought about Y comes to mind and seems important enough to capture. Ideally, hypertext allows you to simply "press a button" (using some mouse or keyboard action) and a new, empty hypertext window pops onto the screen. You record Y in this new window, then you press another button, the Y window disappears, and you are in the X window right where you were when Y occurred to you.

Unfortunately, the situation is a bit more complex than this scenario implies. If Y has just occurred to you, it may still be hazy and tentative; the smallest interruption could cause you to lose it. Coming up with a good word or short phrase to summarize Y may not be easy. You have to consider not just what is descriptive but also what will be suggestive for the reader when he encounters the link to Y within X. In addition, you must determine whether you should name the link to Y to suggest the contents of Y or to show Y's relationship to X. Some systems (for example, NoteCards) provide that links can have both a *type* (such as "idea") and a *label* (such as "subsume A in B"). Coming up with good names for both can impose even more load on an author struggling with an uncertain point. (One way to reduce this problem is for the authoring system to support immediate recording of the substance of the idea, deferring the creation and labeling of the link and/or the node until after the thought has been captured.)

Beyond that, you must also consider if you have provided sufficient links to Y before returning to work on X. Perhaps there are better ways to link Y to the network of thoughts than at the point in X where Y came to mind.

The problem of cognitive overhead also occurs in the process of reading hypertext, which tends to present the reader with a large number of choices about which links to follow and which to leave alone. These choices engender a certain overhead of metalevel decision making, an overhead that is absent when the author has already made many of these choices for you. At the moment that you encounter a link,

how do you decide if following the side path is worth the distraction? Does the label appearing in the link tell you enough to decide? This dilemma could be called "informational myopia." The problem is that, even if the system response time is instantaneous (which it rarely is), you experience a definite distraction, a "cognitive loading," when you pause to consider whether to pursue the side path. This problem can be eased by (1) having the cross-referenced node appear very rapidly (which is the approach of KMS), (2) providing an instantaneous one- to three-line explanation of the side reference in a pop-up window (which is the approach of Intermedia), and (3) having a graphical browser which shows the local subnetwork into which the link leads.

These problems are not new with hypertext, nor are they mere byproducts of computer-supported work. People who think for a living—writers, scientists, artists, designers, etc.—must contend with the fact that the brain can create ideas faster than the hand can write them or the mouth can speak them. There is always a balance between refining the current idea, returning to a previous idea to refine it, and attending to any of the vague "proto-ideas" which are hovering at the edge of consciousness. Hypertext simply offers a sufficiently sophisticated "pencil" to begin to engage the richness, variety, and interrelatedness of creative thought. This aspect of hypertext has advantages when this richness is needed and drawbacks when it is not.

To summarize, then, the problems with hypertext are

- *disorientation*: the tendency to lose one's sense of location and direction in a nonlinear document; and
- *cognitive overhead:* the additional effort and concentration necessary to maintain several tasks or trails at one time.

These problems may be at least partially resolvable through improvements in performance and interface design of hypertext systems, and through research on information filtering techniques.

I n this article, I have reviewed existing hypertext systems, the opportunities and problems of hypertext, and some of the top-level design issues of building hypertext systems. It has been my intention to give the reader a clear sense of what hypertext is, what its strengths and weaknesses are, and what it can be used

for. But I also intended something more: that the reader come away from this article excited, eager to try using hypertext for himself, and aware that he is at the beginning of something big, something like the invention of the wheel, but something that still has enough rough edges that no one is really sure that it will fulfill its promise.

To that end, I mention one more book that might be considered to belong to the literature on hypertext. *Neuromancer*[24] is a novel about a time in the distant future when the ultimate computer interface has been perfected: One simply plugs one's brain into the machine and experiences the computer data directly as perceptual entities. Other computers look like boxes floating in three-dimensional space, and passwords appear as various kinds of doors and locks. The user is completely immersed in a virtual world, the "operating system," and can move around and take different forms simply by willing it.

This is the ultimate hypertext system. The basic idea of hypertext, after all, is that ideas correspond to perceptual objects, and one manipulates ideas and their relationships by directly manipulating windows and icons. Current technology limits the representation of these objects to static boxes on a CRT screen, but one can easily predict that advances in animation, color, 3D displays, sound, etc.—in short, Nelson's *hypermedia*—will keep making the display more active and realistic, the data represented richer and more detailed, and the input more natural and direct. Thus, hypertext, far from being an end in itself, is just a crude first step toward the time when the computer is a direct and powerful extension of the human mind, just as Vannevar Bush envisioned when he introduced his Memex four decades ago. □

Acknowledgements

I wish to thank Les Belady, Bill Curtis, Susan Gerhart, Raymonde Guindon, Eric Gullichsen, Frank Halasz, Peter Marks, and Andy van Dam for their thoughtful reading of previous drafts.

References

1. T.H. Nelson, "Getting It Out of Our System," *Information Retrieval: A Critical Review*, G. Schechter, ed., Thompson Books, Wash., D.C., 1967.

2. V. Bush, "As We May Think," *Atlantic Monthly*, July 1945, pp.101-108.

3. D.C. Engelbart, "A Conceptual Framework for the Augmentation of Man's

Intellect,'' in *Vistas in Information Handling*, Vol. 1, Spartan Books, London, 1963.

4. D.C. Engelbart and W.K. English, ''A Research Center for Augmenting Human Intellect,'' *AFIPS Conf. Proc.*, Vol. 33, Part 1, The Thompson Book Company, Washington, D.C., 1968.

5. T.H. Nelson, ''Replacing the Printed Word: A Complete Literary System,'' *IFIP Proc.*, October 1980, pp. 1013-1023.

6. R.H. Trigg, *A Network-based Approach to Text Handling for the Online Scientific Community*, PhD. Thesis, University of Maryland, 1983.

7. H. Rittel and M. Webber, ''Dilemmas in a General Theory of Planning,'' *Policy Sciences*, Vol. 4, 1973.

8. D.G. Lowe, ''Cooperative Structuring of Information: The Representation of Reasoning and Debate,'' in *Int'l. J. of Man-Machine Studies*,'' Vol. 23, 1985, pp. 97-111.

9. J.B Smith et al, ''WE: A Writing Environment for Professionals,'' Technical Report 86-025, Department of Computer Science, University of North Carolina at Chapel Hill, August 1986.

10. W. Hershey, ''Idea Processors,'' *BYTE*, June 1985, p. 337.

11. D. McCracken and R.M. Akscyn, ''Experience with the ZOG Human-computer Interface System,'' *Int'l J. of Man-Machine Studies*, Vol. 21, 1984, pp. 293-310.

12. B. Shneiderman and J. Morariu, ''The Interactive Encyclopedia System (TIES),'' Department of Computer Science, University of Maryland, College Park, MD 20742, June 1986.

13. J.H. Walker, ''The Document Examiner,'' *SIGGRAPH Video Review*, Edited Compilation from *CHI'85: Human Factors in Computing System*, 1985.

14. F.G. Halasz, T.P. Moran, and T.H. Trigg, ''NoteCards in a Nutshell,'' *Proc. of the ACM Conf. on Human Factors in Computing Systems*, Toronto, Canada, April 1987.

15. N.L. Garrett, K.E. Smith, and N. Meyrowitz, ''Intermedia: Issues, Strategies, and Tactics in the Design of a Hypermedia Document System,'' in *Proc. Conf. on Computer-Supported Cooperative Work*, MCC Software Technology Program, Austin, Texas, 1986.

16. N. Yankelovich, N. Meyrowitz, and A. van Dam, ''Reading and Writing the Electronic Book,'' *Computer*, October 1985.

17. N. Delisle and M. Schwartz, ''Neptune: A Hypertext System for CAD Applications,'' *Proc. of ACM SIGMOD Int'l Conf. on Management of Data*, Washington, D.C., May 28-30, 1986, pp. 132-143. (Also available as SIGMOD Record Vol. 15, No. 2, June 1986).

18. A. diSessa, ''A Principled Design for an Integrated Computational Environment,'' *Human-Computer Interaction*, Vol. 1, Lawrence Erlbaum, 1985, pp. 1-47.

19. K.M.Pitman, ''CREF: An Editing Facility for Managing Structured Text,'' A.I. Memo No. 829, M.I.T. A.I. Laboratory, Cambridge, Mass., February 1985.

20. P.J. Brown, ''Interactive Documentation,'' in *Software: Practice and Experience*, March 1986, pp. 291-299.

21. D. Shasha, ''When Does Non-Linear Text Help? *Expert Database Systems, Proc. of the First Int'l Conf.*, April 1986, pp. 109-121.

22. A. Kay and A. Goldberg, ''Personal Dynamic Media,'' *Computer*, March 1977, pp. 31-41.

23. T.W. Malone et al, ''Intelligent Information-Sharing Systems,'' *Communications of the ACM*, May 1987, pp. 390-402.

24. W.Gibson, *Neuromancer*, Ace Science Fiction, 1984.

E. Jeffrey Conklin is a member of the research staff and GE's liaison to the Software Technology Program in the Microelectronics and Computer Technology Corporation (MCC). His research centers on constructing information systems for the capture and use of design rationale.

Conklin Received his BA from Antioch College and his MS and PhD from the University of Massachusetts at Amherst.

Readers may write to Conklin at MCC Software Technology Program, P.O. Box 200195, Austin, TX 78720; (512) 343-0978.

A more detailed version of this article, including an extended bibliography, is available from the author. To obtain a copy, circle number 181 on the Reader Service Card at the back of the magazine.

Chapter 5:
Enabling Technologies —
UI-Related

Chapter 5: Enabling Technologies — UI-Related

As far as end users are concerned, the user interface is the system. Anything and everything they want to do with computerized information must be available at the user interface. For designers and implementors, the user interface is a metaphor for the system. From an architectural perspective, the user interface provides the logical set of system services to collect inputs from end users and to display results, in a readily understandable fashion.

End users touch, feel, see (and sometimes hear) the hardware: keyboarding inputs, moving a mouse, viewing the results of their interactions, and interpreting the meanings behind the system responses. But what end users see, and how they respond, depends on the illusions that designers and implementors create in the user-system dialogue. How have user-interface metaphors evolved from an individual perspective, focused on sequential, individual tasks, to a group perspective, concerned with the interrelationships of tasks?

Background: Using illusions

From the mid-1970s through the mid-1980s, word processors and spreadsheets provided the primary user-interface metaphors for personal productivity applications — exploiting the capabilities of personal computers, and, to a lesser extent, those of time-shared computers. Word-processing applications sought to automate processes for creating and editing text, providing users with the illusion of a "computerized typewriter." Specific keyboard commands enabled users to insert, replace, format, or revise individual characters or various segments of text, ranging from words to lines, sentences, paragraphs, and pages. "Computerized typing" and "processing words" were the metaphors.

Similarly, spreadsheets sought to expedite procedures for computing numeric relationships, from a simple financial statement to a complex mathematical model. Rather than specifying a system of abstract equations, users could visualize relationships and calculate results in real time, computing values among various cells in a grid. Sets of rows, columns, and tables provided the metaphor of a "financial spreadsheet."

Effectively using character cell display devices and affordable personal computers, task-oriented applications revolutionized routine aspects of professional office work: writing documents, calculating budgets, maintaining lists, storing and finding everyday information. Yet word processors and spreadsheets primarily describe aspects of personal work. For example, users edit documents or calculate numeric relationships as a part of their individual activities, rather than as an aspect of a shared work environment. They work on individual tasks, one at a time, rather than on a set of related activities in context.

Themes: Metaphors for group activities

With a limited focus on personal productivity, a task-oriented metaphor is sufficient. But with the focus on group productivity, users now seek more powerful metaphors, more powerful ways to express interactions with relevant group information.

Emerging user-interface technologies promise to facilitate effective work group interactions by enabling users to initially define, and then effortlessly redefine their work contexts. Groupware capitalizes on varied system combinations: terminals or networked desktop devices (workstations or personal computers), some shared resources (such as file or mail servers), high bandwidth computer networks, and projection devices.

User interface metaphors are an important enabling component for groupware. Designers and implementors must choose an appropriate metaphor that both uses the capabilities of the hardware and system software, and represents clearly the underlying abstractions about the users' work environments.

The desktop metaphor. As Johnson et al. recall, the implementation of the Xerox 8010 (Star) was a landmark event. Introduced in 1981, the Star pioneered the desktop metaphor with familiar kinds of everyday things, such as folders, documents, an in-box, an out-box, and so forth. In effect, the Star gave people an electronic work environment.

The Star system was based on distributed personal workstations, connected by a local area network (LAN) to shared resources, and a highly visual, bitmapped display, together with a pointing device (mouse). These capabilities promised new styles of interpersonal office communication. The Star was also designed fundamentally from a group perspective, so that office workers could focus simply on doing their work, and not have to pay attention to the details of operating systems, software, applications or programs.

The resulting user-interface design for the Star emphasized a small set of generic commands, direct manipulation, good graphic designs, icons to represent things on the desktop, and objects that had observable properties. Users would communicate with one another and share information through a local area network. The system sought to provide the illusion of manipulable objects, with a revealed structure and a consistent, appropriate graphic vocabulary.

Compared to the user interface designs for character cell word processors and spreadsheets, the desktop metaphor was certainly a development ahead of its time. Though hardly a commercial success, the Star was a precursor of work-group oriented systems, offering an initial vision of how advanced information technology might improve interpersonal communications and provide useful tools to support group work.

The rooms metaphor. The desktop represents a single set of activities, where individuals might work with different people on various tasks, and seek to organize their work environments around specific groups of activities. Henderson and Card describe one approach for individual users to organize related activities into common task environments: the "rooms" metaphor.

Users might collaborate at different times on various kinds of activities: writing a report, working through the calculations for a new budget proposal, finding information from published sources, or debugging a program. Ideally, users should be able to organize their collaborative activities by work tasks, and to collect related task-specific tools into separate "rooms" or work areas.

Users simplify the management of multiple activities by creating different rooms for each task, and by providing indicators when one user has initiated or modified a shared object that others should view. Users work separately and asynchronously, relying on the system for communication and passing messages. Alternatively, users might project the contents of a shared room in a real-time meeting for group discussions, contending for group attention while exchanging information.

The office building metaphor. Rooms, too, seem limited to describing an individual user's view within the context of sets of group interactions. Madsen seeks to describe a group-oriented environment, based on group communications within an "office building." Through the office building metaphor, users would be able to tailor and modify their user-system environment at all levels, from global behaviors of window management and displays, to the detailed interactions with individual objects, allowing continual change.

Users may work alone one moment, switch to working in pairs for a while, then move to functioning within the context of a small group, or as part of a large organization. They might seek small group interactions in a "group working room," then move to a "conference room" for a formal meeting, go to a "library" to find publicly available information, or have an informal conversation in a "coffee room" or "hallway." A group communications environment calls up different kinds of metaphors (appropriate tools and principles for organizing and browsing information) depending on the nature of the tasks at hand.

Futures: Exploiting technologies

Looking to the future, user interface metaphors will support the activities of work groups and task teams in intuitive ways. For individual users, an effective groupware system will simply be a natural extension of their shared work experiences. New user interface designs will closely mirror the expanding bandwidth of user-system dialogues, capitalizing on hardware and software innovations.

Groupware designers and implementors will need to exploit the potentials of rapidly changing hardware and software technologies, improving existing metaphors, and pursuing group-oriented user interface designs. Color displays promise to have a profound effect on user interface designs, and on support for group work environments. Users will be able to indicate the state of an activity not only by its shape or screen message, but also by its color and texture.

Beyond color, three-dimensional representation of information promises to have a substantial impact. The 3D representation may describe an individual user's view of a personal hierarchy (for instance, a filing system) or a group's view of a shared work environment (for example, the formal and informal relationships of an organization). The information presented will generate a multimedia experience, going beyond words and icons to group information pictures, full motion video, and sound.

The experience to date with most computer usage is still primarily in the form of single-user/single-system situations. The emergence of groupware has significantly shifted the need to experience multiple-user/single-system and multiple-user/multiple-system situations. Furthermore, computer capabilities are emerging that will enable several people to collaborate simultaneously on a shared work surface, creating the metaphor of a shared notebook or logbook. User interface metaphors are changing to emphasize group-oriented modes of communication. In the future, they will embody team-oriented styles of problem solving, and capture explicitly interpersonal interaction.

The Xerox Star:
A Retrospective

Jeff Johnson and Teresa L. Roberts, US West Advanced Technologies

William Verplank, IDTwo

David C. Smith, Cognition, Inc.

Charles H. Irby and Marian Beard, Metaphor Computer Systems

Kevin Mackey, Xerox

Reprinted from *Computer*, Vol. 22, No. 9, September 1989, pages 11-26. Copyright © 1989 by The Institute of Electrical and Electronics Engineers, Inc. All rights reserved.

Xerox introduced the 8010 "Star" Information System in April of 1981. That introduction was an important event in the history of personal computing because it changed notions of how interactive systems should be designed. Several of Star's designers, some of us responsible for the original design and others for recent improvements, describe in this article where Star came from, what is distinctive about it, and how the original design has changed. In doing so, we hope to correct some misconceptions about Star that we have seen in the trade press and to relate some of what we have learned from designing it.

For brevity, we use the name "Star" here to refer to both Star and its successor, ViewPoint. "ViewPoint" refers exclusively to the current product.

What Star is

Star was designed as an office automation system. The idea was that professionals in a business or organization would have workstations on their desks and would use them to produce, retrieve, distribute, and organize documentation, presentations, memos, and reports. All of the workstations in an organization would

The Xerox Star has significantly affected the computer industry. In this retrospective, several of Star's designers describe its important features, antecedents, design and development, evolution, and some lessons learned.

be connected via Ethernet and would share access to file servers, printers, etc.

Star's designers assumed that the target users were interested in getting their work done and not at all interested in computers. Therefore, an important design goal was to make the "computer" as invisible to users as possible. The applications included in the system were those that office professionals would supposedly need: documents, business graphics, tables, personal databases, and electronic mail. The set was fixed, always loaded, and automatically associated with data files, eliminating the need to obtain, install, and start the right application for a given task or data file. Users could focus on their work, oblivious to concepts like software, operating systems, applications, and programs.

Another important assumption was that Star's users would be casual, occasional users rather than people who spent most of their time at the machine. This assumption led to the goal of having Star be easy to learn and remember.

When Star was introduced in 1981, its bitmapped screen, windows, mouse-driven interface, and icons were readily apparent features that clearly distinguished it from other computers. Soon, however, others adopted these features. Today, windows, mice, and icons are more common. However, Star's clean, consistent user interface has much more to do with its details than with its gross features. We list here the features that we think make Star what it is, categorized according to their level in the system architecture: machine and network, window and file manager, user interface, and document editor.

0-8186-2637-2/92 $03.00 © 1989 IEEE

Machine and network level. Important aspects of Star can be found in the lowest levels of its architecture: the machine and the network of which it is a part.

Distributed, personal computing. Though currently available in a stand-alone configuration, Star was designed primarily to operate in a distributed computing environment. This approach combines the advantages and avoids the disadvantages of the two other primary approaches to interactive computing: time-shared systems and stand-alone personal computers.

Time-shared systems, dominant through the sixties and seventies, allow sharing of expensive resources like printers and large data stores among many users and help assure the consistency of data that many must use. Timesharing has the disadvantages that all users depend upon the continued functioning of the central computer and that system response degrades as the number of users increases.

Personal computers, which have replaced timesharing as the primary mode of interactive computing, have the advantage, as one Xerox researcher put it, "of not being faster at night." Also, a collection of personal computers is more reliable than are terminals connected to a centralized computer: system problems are less apt to cause a total stoppage of work. The disadvantages of PCs, of course, are the converse of the advantages of timesharing. Companies that use stand-alone PCs usually see a proliferation of printers, inconsistent databases, and nonexchangeable data.

The solution, pioneered by researchers at Xerox (see "History of Star development" below) and embodied in Star, is to connect personal workstations with a local area network and to attach shared resources (file servers, database servers, printers) to that same network.

Mouse. An interactive computer system must provide a way for users to indicate which operations they want and what data they want those operations to be performed on. Users of early interactive systems specified operations and operands via commands and data descriptors (such as text line numbers). As video display terminals became common, it became clear that it was often better for users to specify operands — and sometimes operations — by pointing to them on the screen. It also became clear that graphic applications should not be controlled solely with a key-board. In the sixties and seventies, people invented many different pointing devices: the light pen, the trackball, the joystick, cursor keys, the digitizing tablet, the touch screen, and the mouse.

Like other pointing devices, the mouse allows easy selection of objects and triggering of sensitive areas on the screen. The mouse differs from touch screens, light pens, and digitizing pads in that it is a relative pointing device: the movement of the pointer on the screen depends upon mouse movement rather than position. Unlike light pens, joysticks, and digitizing pads, the mouse (and the corresponding pointer on the screen) stays put when the user lets go of it.

To achieve satisfactory mouse-tracking performance, Star handles the mouse at a very low level. In some workstations, the window system handles mouse tracking, with the result that the mouse pointer often jerks around the screen and may even freeze for seconds at a time, depending upon what else the system is doing. The mouse is a hand-eye coordination device, so if the pointer lags, users just keep moving the mouse. When the system catches up, the mouse moves beyond the user's target. We at Xerox considered this unacceptable.

Star uses a two-button mouse, in contrast with the one-button mouse used by Apple and the three-button mouse used by most other vendors. Though predecessors of Star developed at Xerox Palo Alto Research Center (see "History of Star development" below) used a three-button mouse, Star's designers wanted to reduce the number of buttons to alleviate confusion over which button did what. Why stop at two buttons instead of reducing the number to one, as Apple did? Because studies of users editing text and other material showed that a one-button mouse eliminated button-confusion errors only at the cost of increasing selection errors to unacceptable levels.

Bitmapped display. Until recently, most video display terminals were character-mapped. Such displays enable vast savings in display memory, which, when memory was expensive, made terminals more affordable.

In the seventies, researchers at Xerox PARC decided that memory would get cheaper eventually and that a bitmapped screen was worth the cost anyway. They thus developed the Alto, which had a screen 8.5 inches wide and 10.5 inches tall and an instruction set specially designed for manipulating display memory.

Like the Alto, Star's display has a resolution of 72 pixels per inch. The number 72 was chosen for two reasons. First, there are 72 printer's points per inch, so 72 pixels per inch allows for a smooth interface with the world of typesetting and typography. Second, 72 pixels per inch is a high enough resolution for on-screen legibility of a wide range of graphics and character sizes (down to about eight points — see Figure 1), but not so high as to cause an onerous memory burden, which a screen that matched the 300 dots-per-inch printer resolution would have. Unlike many PC graphic displays, the pixel size and density are the same horizontally and vertically, which simplifies the display software and improves image quality.

Window and file manager level. Just above Star's operating system (not discussed here) are facilities upon which its distinctive user interface rests.

Windows. Systems now commonly allow several programs to display information simultaneously in separate areas of the screen, rather than each taking up the entire display. Star was the first commercial system to provide this capability.

Some windowing systems allow windows to overlap each other. Other systems don't; the system adjusts the size and position of windows as they are opened and closed. Star's windowing system could overlap windows and often did (for example, property sheets appeared in windows overlapping application windows). However, early testing revealed that users spent a lot of time adjusting windows, usually so they did not overlap. Because of this, and because Star's 17-inch screen reduced the need for overlapping windows, the designers decided to constrain application windows to not overlap. However, some situations benefit from overlapping application windows. This, added to a subsequent reduction in the standard screen size to 15 inches (with a 19-inch screen optional), resulted in optional constraints for ViewPoint, Star's successor, with the default setting allowing application windows to overlap one another.

Integrated applications. "Integrated" has become a buzzword used to describe many things. Here, it means that text, graphics, tables, and mathematical formulas are all edited inside documents. In many other systems, different types of content are edited in separate application

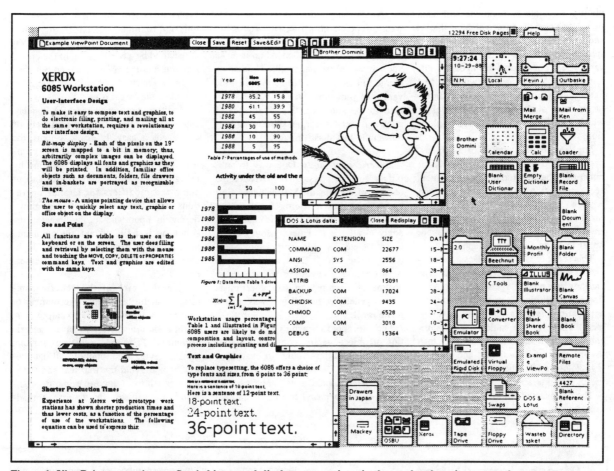

Figure 1. ViewPoint screen image. Star's bitmapped display, once unique in the marketplace, is now much more common. Such a display permits WYSIWYG editing, display of proportionally spaced fonts, integrated text and graphics, and graphical user interfaces.

windows and then cut and pasted together. For example, a MacDraw drawing put into a Microsoft Word or Aldus Pagemaker document can no longer be edited; rather, the original must be re-edited with MacDraw and then substituted for the old drawing in the document.

Not even Star is fully integrated in the sense used here. For example, though the original structured graphics editor, the new one (see "History of Star development" below), and the table and formula editors all operate inside text files, spreadsheets and freehand drawings are currently edited in separate application windows and transferred into documents, where they are no longer fully editable.

User-interface level. Star's user interface is its most outstanding feature. In this section we discuss important aspects of the interface in detail.

Desktop metaphor. Star, unlike all conventional systems and many window- and mouse-based ones, uses an analogy with real offices to make the system easy to learn. This analogy is called "the Desktop metaphor." To quote from an early article about Star:

Every user's initial view of Star is the Desktop, which resembles the top of an office desk, together with surrounding furniture and equipment. It represents a working environment, where current projects and accessible resources reside. On the screen are displayed pictures of familiar office objects, such as documents, folders, file drawers, in-baskets, and out-baskets. These objects are displayed as small pictures, or icons.

The Desktop is the principal Star technique for realizing the physical office metaphor. The icons on it are visible, concrete embodiments of the corresponding physical objects. Star users are encouraged to think of the objects on the Desktop in physical terms. You can move the icons around to arrange your

Desktop as you wish. (Messy Desktops are certainly possible, just as in real life.) You can leave documents on your Desktop indefinitely, just as on a real desk, or you can file them away.[1]

Having windows and a mouse does not make a system an embodiment of the Desktop metaphor. In a Desktop metaphor system, users deal mainly with data files, oblivious to the existence of programs. They do not "invoke a text editor," they "open a document." The system knows the type of each file and notifies the relevant application program when one is opened.

Most systems, including windowed ones, use a Tools metaphor, in which users deal mainly with applications as tools. Users start one or more application programs (such as a word processor or spreadsheet), then specify one or more data files to edit with each. Such systems do not explicitly associate applications with data files. Users bear the burden of doing that — and of remembering not to try to edit a spreadsheet file with the text editor or vice versa. User convention distinguishes different kinds of files, usually with filename extensions (such as memo.txt). Star relieves users of the need to keep track of which data file goes with which application.

SunView is an example of a window system based upon the Tools metaphor rather than the Desktop metaphor. Its users see a collection of application program windows, each used to edit certain files. Smalltalk-80, Cedar, and various Lisp environments also use the Tools metaphor rather than the Desktop metaphor.

This is not to say that the Desktop metaphor is superior to the Tools metaphor. The Desktop metaphor targets office automation and publishing. It might not suit other applications (such as software development). However, we could argue that orienting users toward their data rather than toward application programs and employing analogies with the physical world are useful techniques in any domain.

The disadvantage of assigning data files to applications is that users sometimes want to operate on a file with a program other than its ''assigned'' application. Such cases must be handled in Star in an ad hoc way, whereas systems like Unix allow you to run almost any file through a wide variety of programs. Star's designers feel that, for its audience, the advantages of allowing users to forget about programs outweighs this disadvantage.

Generic commands. One way to simplify a computer system is to reduce the number of commands. Star achieves simplicity without sacrificing functionality by having a small set of generic commands apply to all types of data: Move, Copy, Open, Delete, Show Properties, and Same (Copy Properties). Dedicated function keys on Star's keyboard invoke these commands. Each type of data object interprets a generic command in a way appropriate for it.

Such an approach avoids the proliferation of object-specific commands and/or command modifiers found in most systems, such as Delete Character, Delete Word, Delete Line, Delete Paragraph, and Delete File. Command modifiers are nec-

essary in systems in which selection is only approximate. Consider the many systems in which the object of a command is specified by a combination of the cursor location and the command modifier. For example, Delete Word means ''delete the word that the cursor is on.''

Modifiers are unnecessary in Star because exact selection of the objects of commands is easy. In many systems, the large number of object-specific commands is made even more confusing by using single-word synonyms instead of command modifiers for similar operations on different objects. For example, depending upon whether the object of the command is a file or text, the command used might be Remove or Delete, Duplicate or Copy, and Find or Search, respectively.

Careful choice of the generic commands can further reduce the number of commands required. For example, you might think it necessary to have a generic command Print for printing various things. Having Print apply to all data objects would avoid the trap that some systems fall into of having separate commands for printing documents, spread-

Direct manipulation

Jeff Johnson and Teresa L. Roberts

Star's Desktop metaphor is based upon the more general principle of "direct manipulation."[1,2] What, exactly, is direct manipulation? Consider the following passage from a description of Apple's Macintosh:

> Imagine driving a car that has no steering wheel, accelerator, brake pedal, turn signal lever, or gear selector. In place of all the familiar manual controls, you have only a typewriter keyboard.
> Anytime you want to turn a corner, change lanes, slow down, speed up, honk your horn, or back up, you have to type a command sequence on the keyboard. Unfortunately, the car can't understand English sentences. Instead, you must hold down a special key with one finger and type in some letters and numbers, such as "S20:TL:A35," which means, "Slow to 20, turn left, and accelerate to 35."
> No doubt you could learn to drive such a car if you had sufficient motivation and determination. But why bother, when so many cars use familiar controls? Most people wouldn't.[3]

Actually, it isn't familiarity that makes real cars easier to drive than the hypothetical "computer car" would be — cars are certainly not familiar to those who are just learning to drive them. What makes real cars easier to drive is the directness of their controls. Real cars have distinct interfaces to the speed control (the accelerator pedal), the direction control (the steering wheel), the gears (the gearshift handle), the radio (several knobs and buttons), etc. Each interface is specially designed for controlling its respective function. In contrast, the hypo-

thetical "computer-car" has only one control: a keyboard.

Direct manipulation requires that distinct functions be invoked and controlled in spatially distinct locations, in ways that are specific and appropriate for the particular function being controlled. Data objects should be selected and operated on by simulated physical contact rather than by abstract verbal reference: "*That* one" rather than "The one in row 6." Continuous functions (such as screen brightness and color saturation) should be controlled via continuous controls such as sliders, knobs, and dials. Discrete functions (such as character font family) should be controlled via discrete means such as commands, multiposition switches, or menus. In effect, a direct manipulation system has a different input channel for every function the user can have it perform.

Conventional interfaces are indirect in that there is a single, general interface to all functionality (such as a keyboard and command language or a menu). In other words, there is only one input channel for all kinds of input; different kinds of input are distinguished linguistically, rather than spatially.

Having a different interface to each function may seem to contradict the goal of having a consistent interface, but in fact does not. Similar functions should indeed have similar user interfaces across contexts. Direct manipulation requires, however, that different functions should have distinct interfaces, just as a car has distinct interfaces to its various functions.

Directness versus indirectness is not a simple dichotomy: we can speak of degrees of directness. Consider a graphics editor for creating illustrations. In the following sequence of interfaces, each contains all of the indirection of the previous one and adds a new level:

sheets, illustrations, directories, etc., but it is nonetheless unnecessary. In Star, users simply Copy to a printer icon whatever they want to print. Similarly, the Move command is used to invoke Send Mail by moving a document to the out-basket.

Of course, not everything can be done via generic commands. Some operations are object-specific. For example, a word might use italics, but italics are meaningless for a triangle. In Star, object-specific operations are provided via selection-dependent "soft" function keys and via menus attached to application windows.

Direct manipulation and graphical user interface. Traditional computer systems require users to remember and type a great deal just to control the system. This impedes learning and retention, especially by casual users. Star's designers favored an approach emphasizing recognition over recall, seeing and pointing over remembering and typing. This suggested using menus rather than commands. However, the designers wanted to go beyond a conventional menu-based approach. They wanted users to feel that they are manipulating data directly, rather than issuing commands to the system to do it. Star's designers also wanted to exploit the tremendous communication possibilities of the display. They wanted to move away from strictly verbal communication. Therefore, they based the system heavily upon principles that are now known as direct manipulation and graphical control.

Star users control the system by manipulating graphical elements on the screen, elements that represent the state of the system and data created by users. The system does not distinguish between input and output. Anything displayed (output) by the system can be pointed to and acted upon by the user (input). When Star displays a directory, it (unlike MS-DOS and Unix) is not displaying a list of the names of the files in the directory, it is displaying the files themselves so that the user can manipulate them. Users of this type of system have the feeling that they are operating upon the data directly, rather than through an agent — like fetching a book from a library shelf yourself rather than asking someone to do it for you.

A related principle is that the state of the system always shows in the display. Nothing happens "behind the user's back." You needn't fiddle with the system to understand what's going on; you can understand by inspection.

One of Star's designers wrote

> When everything in a computer system is visible on the screen, the display becomes reality. Objects and actions can be understood purely in terms of their effects upon the display. This vastly simplifies understanding and reduces learning time.[2]

An example of this philosophy is the fact that, unlike many window-based computer systems (even some developed at Xerox), Star has no hidden menus — all available menus are marked with menu buttons.

For a more detailed explanation of direct manipulation, see the sidebar.

Icons and iconic file management. Computer users often have difficulty managing their files. Before Star existed, a secretary at Xerox complained that she couldn't keep track of the files on her disk. An inspection of her system revealed files named memo, memo1, memo071479, letter, etc. Naming things to keep track of

---

(1) The most direct interface for moving a circle would have the user point directly at the screen and pull the circle to its new location.

(2) Introducing a mouse, bitpad, or joystick adds one level of indirection: moving the mouse, bitpad stylus, or joystick on the desk moves the pointer on the screen. Some users have difficulty with this indirection.

(3) Arrow keys introduce another level — and another kind — of indirection: the keystroke movements required to move the screen pointer, and hence the circle, do not resemble the desired movement of the circle.

(4) Typing a command to move the circle is still more indirect. Though typing a command involves movements (keystrokes), we are inclined to think of the movements as incidental; they could just as well be speech. Thus, it is no longer a matter of movement — similar or not — in one place corresponding to movement in another place; rather, it is the syntax and semantics of the command that determine what happens.

· Differences in directness can be very subtle. Contrast the following two methods of changing the size of a window on the display:

(1) Grabbing onto a corner of the window and stretching the window to the desired size.

(2) Clicking on the desired window, choosing Resize from a command pull-down menu, then pointing to where the window's new border is to be moved.

It is sometimes said that mouse-driven user interfaces are direct while keyboard user interfaces are indirect. Note, however, that both methods 1 and 2 above use a mouse, yet method 2 is less direct than method 1.

The above examples involve an illustration tool and a window manager. Such applications are actually in a special category with respect to direct manipulation, because the images on the screen are what the application is intended to manipulate. The purpose of many applications (such as databases, command and control, and file management) is to allow users to manipulate information that is only represented on the screen in some way (for example, pictorially or textually). Such applications therefore have one inherent level of indirection.

Systems having direct-manipulation user interfaces encourage users to think of them as tools rather than as assistants, agents, or coworkers. Natural-language user interfaces, which are inherently indirect, encourage the reverse. As direct-manipulation interfaces become more prevalent and as progress is made in natural-language understanding and generation, it will be interesting to see which way users prefer to think about their computers.

References

1. E. Hutchins, J. Hollan, and D.A. Norman, "Direct Manipulation Interfaces," in *User-Centered System Design*, D.A. Norman and S. Draper, eds., Erlbaum Associates, Hillsdale, New Jersey, 1986, pp. 87-124.

2. B. Shneiderman, "Direct Manipulation: A Step Beyond Programming Languages," *Computer*, Vol. 16, No. 8, Aug. 1983, pp. 57-68.

3. L. Poole, "A Tour of the Mac Desktop," *MacWorld*, Vol. 1, No. 1, 1984, pp. 16-21.

them is bothersome enough for programmers, but completely unnatural for most people.

Star alleviates this problem partly by representing data files with pictures of office objects called icons. Every application data file in the system has an icon representing it. Each type of file has a characteristic icon shape. If a user is looking for a spreadsheet, his or her eye can skip over mailboxes, printers, text documents, etc.

Furthermore, Star allows users to organize files spatially rather than by distinctive naming. Systems having hierarchical directories, such as Unix and MS-DOS, provide an abstract sort of "spatial" file organization, but Star's approach is concrete. Files can be kept together by putting them into a folder or simply by clumping them together on the Desktop, which models how people organize their physical worlds. Since data files are represented by icons, and files are distinguished by location and specified by selection rather than by name, users can use names like memo, memo1, letter, etc., without losing track of their files as easily as they would with most systems.

As bitmap-, window-, and mouse-based systems have become more common, the use of the term "icon" has widened to refer to any nontextual symbol on the display. In standard English, "icon" is a term for religious statues or pictures believed to contain some of the powers of the deities they represent. It would be more consistent with its normal meaning if "icon" were reserved for objects having behavioral and intrinsic properties. Most graphical symbols and labels on computer screens are therefore not icons. In Star, only representations of files on the Desktop and in folders, mailboxes, and file drawers are called icons.

Few modes. A system has modes if user actions differ in effects or availability in different situations. Tesler has argued that modes in interactive computer systems are undesirable because they restrict the functions available at any given point and force users to keep track of the system's state to know what effect their actions will have.[3] Though modes can be helpful in guiding users through unfamiliar procedures or for handling exceptional activities, they should be used sparingly and carefully.

Star avoids modes in several ways. One is the extensive use of generic commands (see above), which drastically reduces the number of commands needed. This, in turn, means that designers need not assign double-duty (that is, different meanings in different modes) to physical controls.

A second way is by allowing applications to operate simultaneously. When using one program (such as a document editor), users are not in a mode that prevents them from using the capabilities of other programs (such as the desktop manager).

A third way Star avoids modes is by using a noun-verb command syntax. Users select an operand (such as a file, a word, or a table), then invoke a command. In conventional systems, arguments follow commands, either on a command line or in response to prompts. Whether a system uses noun-verb or verb-noun syntax has a lot to do with how moded it is. In a noun-verb system such as Star, selecting an object prior to choosing a command does not put the system into a mode. Users can decide not to invoke the command without having to "escape out" of anything or can select a different object to operate on.

Though Star avoids modes, it is not completely modeless. For example, the Move and Copy commands require two arguments: the object to be moved and the final destination. Though less moded ways to design Move and Copy exist, these functions currently require the user to select the object, press the Move or Copy key, then indicate the destination using the mouse. While Star waits for the user to point to a destination, it is in Move or Copy mode, precluding other uses of the mouse. These modes are relatively harmless, however, because (1) the shape of the cursor clearly indicates the state of the system and (2) the user enters and exits them in the course of carrying out a single mental plan, making it unlikely that the system will be in the "wrong" mode when the user begins his or her next action.

Objects have properties. Properties allow objects of the same type to vary in appearance, layout, and behavior. For example, files have a Name property, characters have a Font family property, and paragraphs have a Justified property. Properties may have different types of values: the Name property of a file is a text string; the Size property of a character might be a number or a choice from a menu; the Justified property of a paragraph is either "on" or "off." In Star, properties are displayed and changed in graphical forms called property sheets.

Property-based systems are rare. Most computer systems, even today, allow users to set parameters for the duration of an interactive session or for the duration of a command, but not for particular data objects. For example, headings in Wordstar documents do not "remember" whether they are centered or not; whether a line is centered is determined by how the program was set when the line was typed. Similarly, directories in Unix do not "remember" whether files are to be listed in alphabetical or temporal order; users must respecify which display order they want every time they invoke the ls command.

Progressive disclosure. It has been said that "computers promise the fountains of utopia, but only deliver a flood of information."[4] Indeed, many computer systems overwhelm their users with choices, commands to remember, and poorly organized output, much of it irrelevant to what the user is trying to do. They make no presumptions about what the user wants. Thus, they are designed as if all possible user actions were equally likely and as if all information generated by the system were of equal interest to the user. Some systems diminish the problem somewhat by providing default settings of parameters to simplify tasks expected to be common.

Star goes further towards alleviating this problem by applying a principle called "progressive disclosure." Progressive disclosure dictates that detail be hidden from users until they ask or need to see it. Thus, Star not only provides default settings, it hides settings that users are unlikely to change until users indicate that they want to change them. Implicit in this design are assumptions about which properties will be less frequently altered.

One place progressive disclosure is used is in property sheets. Some objects have a large number of properties, many of which are relevant only when other properties have certain values (see Figure 2). For example, on the page layout property sheet, there is no reason to display all of the properties for specifying running header content and position unless the user actually specifies that the document will have running headers.

Another example of progressive disclosure is the fact that property displays in Star are temporary, displayed on demand. In some systems, the properties of the current selection are displayed at all times, through codes embedded in the text or in an area of the screen reserved for that purpose, even though the user usually doesn't care.

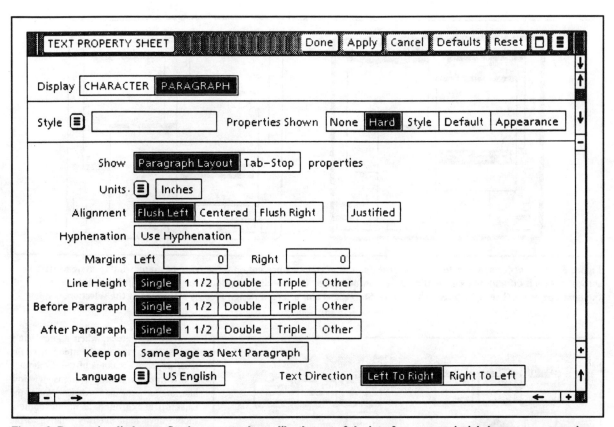

Figure 2. Progressive disclosure. Star's property sheets, like the rest of the interface, use a principle known as progressive disclosure to avoid overwhelming users with information. Usually, users don't need to see an object's properties: they only need to see and perhaps change its assigned style. Users see an object's properties only upon request. Also, even when a user sets a property sheet to show an object's properties, as shown here, some information remains hidden until the user asks to see it. For example, there is no need to clutter the property sheet here with boxes for entering numbers for "Other" values of Line Height, Spacing Before Paragraph, or Spacing After Paragraph until the user actually sets the property to "Other."

A highly refined manifestation of progressive disclosure recently added to ViewPoint is *styles*, which allows users to regard document content (such as a paragraph) as having a single style rule instead of a large number of properties. Thus, styles hide needless detail from users.

Consistency. Because Star and all of its applications were designed and developed in-house, its designers had more control over its user interface than is usually the case with computer systems. Because the designers paid close attention to detail, they achieved a very high degree of consistency. The left mouse button always selects; the right always extends the selection. Mouse-sensitive areas always give feedback when the left button goes down, but never take effect until the button comes up.

Emphasis on good graphic and screen design. Windows, icons, and property sheets are useless if users can't easily distinguish them from the background or each other, can't easily see which labels correspond to which objects, or can't cope with the visual clutter. To assure that Star presents information in a maximally perceivable and useful fashion, Xerox hired graphic designers to determine the appearance and placement of screen objects. These designers applied various written and unwritten principles to the design of the window headers and borders, the Desktop background, the command buttons, the pop-up menus, the property sheets, and the Desktop icons. The most important principles are

• The illusion of manipulable objects. One goal, fundamental to the notion of di-

rect manipulation, is to create the illusion of manipulable objects. It should be clear that objects can be selected and how to select them. It should be obvious when they are selected and that the next action will apply to them. Whereas the usual task of graphic designers is to present information for passive viewing, Star's designers had to figure out how to present information for manipulation as well. This shows most clearly in the Desktop icons, with their clear figure/ground relationship: the icons stand by themselves, with self-contained labels. Windows reveal in their borders the "handles" for scrolling, paging, window-specific commands, and pop-up menus.

• Visual order and user focus. One of the most obvious contributions of good graphic design is appropriate visual order and focus on the screen. For example, in-

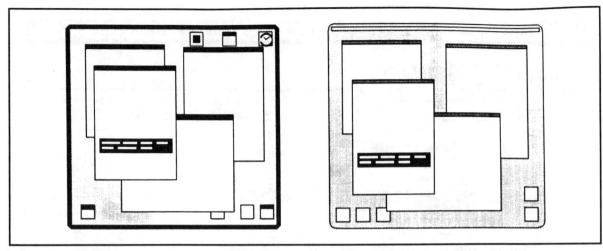

Figure 3. Visual order and user focus. The large amount of contrast present on the screens of many window systems (left screen) makes it difficult to focus on the relevant information. The selection should be the user's main focus: it is the object of the next operation. The right screen shows how Star/ViewPoint's screen design focuses attention on the selection.

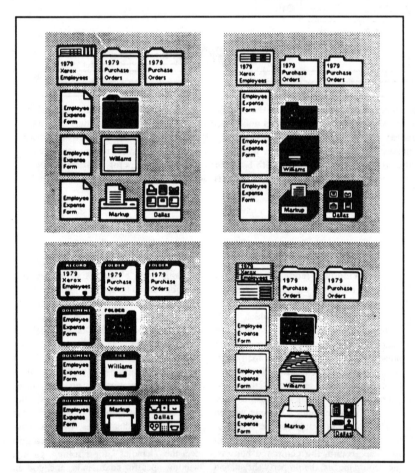

Figure 4. Visual order and user focus. Four candidate sets of icons were designed and tested for Star. A representative sample from each set is shown here. In Star, the icon selected by the user is indicated by inverting its image. Candidate icon sets in which the images are mostly white allow icons to stand out when selected. The set that best satisfies this criterion, the one on the upper left, was chosen.

tensity and contrast, when appropriately applied, draw the user's attention to the most important features of the display.

In some windowing systems, window interiors have the same (dark) color as the Desktop background. Window content should have high intensity relative to the Desktop, to draw attention to what is important on the screen. In Star, window content background is white, both for high contrast and to simulate paper.

Star keeps the amount of black on the screen to a minimum to make the selection stand out (see Figure 3). In most windowing systems, window headers and other areas of the screen are black, making the selection hard to find. This principle is so important that Star's designers made sure that the display hardware could fill the nonaddressable border of the screen with Desktop grey rather than leaving it black as in most systems. Star also uses icon images that turn from mostly white to mostly black when selected (see Figure 4) and allows at most one selection on the screen at a time.

• *Revealed structure.* Often, the more powerful the program used, the greater the distance between intention and effect. If only effect is displayed and not intention, the user's task of learning the connection is much more difficult. A good graphical interface can make apparent to the user these connections between intention and effect, that is, "revealed structure." For example, there are many ways to determine the position and length of a line of text on a page. It can be done with page margins, paragraph indentations, centering, tabs, blank lines, or spaces. The WYSIWYG, or "what you see is what you get," view of all these would be identical. That would be enough if all that mattered to the user was the final form on paper. But what will happen if characters are inserted? If the line is moved to another page, where will it land? WYSIWYG views are sometimes not enough.

Special views are one method of revealing structure. In Star, documents can show "Structure" and/or "Non-Printing Characters" if desired (see Figure 5). Another convenient means for revealing structure is to make it show up during selection. For example, when a rectangle is selected in a graphics frame, eight control points highlight it, any of which can attach to the cursor during Move or Copy and can land on grid points for precise alignment. The control point highlighting allows a user to distinguish a rectangle from four straight lines; both might produce the same printed effect but would respond differently to editing.

• Consistent and appropriate graphic vocabulary. Property sheets (see Figure 2) present a form-like display for the user to specify detailed property settings and arguments to commands. They were designed with a consistent graphic vocabulary. All of the user's targets are in boxes; unchangeable information such as a property name is not. Mutually exclusive values within choice parameters appear with boxes adjacent. Independent "on/off" or state parameters appear with boxes separated. The current settings are shown inverted. Some of the menus display graphic symbols rather than text. Finally, there are text parameters consisting of a box into which text or numbers can be typed, copied, or moved, and within which text editing functions are available.

• Match the medium. It is in this last principle that the sensitivities of a good graphic designer are most apparent. The goal is to create a consistent quality in the graphics that is appropriate to the product and makes the most of the given medium. Star has a large black and white display. The solutions the graphics designers devised might have been very different had the display had grey-scale or color pixels.

A common problem with raster displays is "jaggies": diagonal lines appearing as staircases. With careful design, jaggies can be avoided, for example, by using only vertical, horizontal, and 45-degree angles. Also important is controlling how the edges of the figures interact with the texture of the ground. Figure 6 shows how edges are carefully matched to the back-

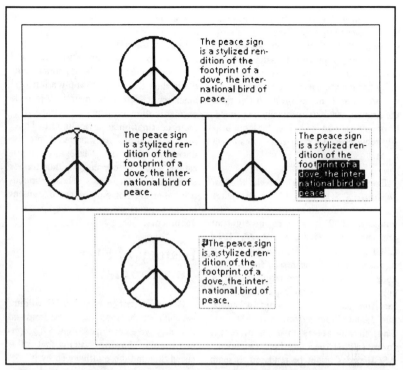

Figure 5. Revealed structure. At the top is the WYSIWYG view of mixed text and graphics. The middle two panels show that structure is revealed when an object is selected. When a line segment is selected, its control points are shown. When text is selected, the text string is revealed. The bottom panel shows the effect of the Show Structure and Show Non-Printing Characters commands, which is to reveal the location of embedded graphics and text frames (dotted lines) and "new paragraph" and Space characters.

ground texture so that they have a consistent quality appearance.

Document editor level. At the top level of Star's architecture are its applications, the most prominent of which is the document editor.

WYSIWYG document editor. Within the limits of screen resolution, Star documents are displayed as they will print, including typographic features such as boldface, italics, proportional spacing, variable font families, and superscripts, and layout features such as embedded graphics, page numbers, headers, and footers. This is commonly referred to as "what you see is what you get," or WYSIWYG.

Star adheres to this principle even in domains where other WYSIWYG document editors do not. For example, mathematical formulas are created and edited in documents using a WYSIWYG editor that has knowledge built into it about the appearance and layout of mathematical symbols. A square root sign has a slot for an

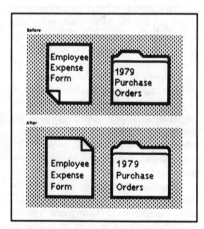

Figure 6. Match the medium. Many graphic refinements were made during the design process. For example, the turned corner of the document icon was moved to the top so that the three lines of label would line up with the labels of other icons. Also, icons were carefully sized and positioned against the gray background to create smoother lines.

expression and grows when the expression becomes large (see Figure 7). In most systems, mathematical formulas are created either by putting together special characters to make mathematical symbols or by using a special in-line notation (such as sqrt(sigma(1, n, (x*3)/2))) to represent the formula that will eventually be printed. Formulas created with such systems usually require several print-edit cycles to get right.

Extended character set for multilingual capability. Star uses 16-bit character codes, in contrast to most of the computer industry, which uses seven- or eight-bit character codes (for example, ASCII or EBCDIC). The Star character set is a superset of ASCII. The reason for a 16-bit code is a strong market requirement for enhanced multilingual capabilility coming from Xerox's subsidiaries in Europe and Japan. Most systems provide non-English characters through different fonts, so that the eight-bit "extended" ASCII codes might be rendered as math symbols in one font, Greek letters in another font, and Arabic in yet another. This has the effect that when any application loses track of font information while handling the text (which happens often in some systems), a paragraph of Arabic may turn into nonsensical Greek or math symbols or something else, and vice versa.

Star uses 16-bit character codes to permit the system to reliably handle European languages and Japanese, which uses many thousands of characters. All Star and ViewPoint systems have French, German, Italian, Spanish, and Russian language capabilities built in. The Japanese language capability was developed as part of the original Star design effort and released in Japan soon after Star's debut in the United States. Since that time, many more characters have been added, covering Chinese, Arabic, Hebrew, and nearly all European languages.

As explained in several articles by Joe Becker, the designer of Star's multilingual capabilities, handling many of the world's languages requires more than an expanded character set.[5] Clever typing schemes and sophisticated rendering algorithms are required to provide a multilingual capability that satisfies customers.

The document is the heart of the world and unifies it. Most personal computers and workstations give no special status to any particular application. Dozens of applications are available, most incompatible with each other in data format as well as user interface.

Star, in contrast, assumes that the primary use of the system is to create and maintain documents. The document editor is thus the primary application. All other applications exist mainly to provide or manipulate information whose ultimate destination is a document. Thus, most applications are integrated into the document editor (see "Integrated applications" above), operating within frames embedded in documents. Those applications that are not part of the document editor support transfer of their data to documents.

History of Star development

Having described Star and ViewPoint, we will describe where they came from and how they were developed. Figure 8 graphs this history, showing systems that influenced Star and those influenced by it.

Pre-Xerox. Although Star was conceived as a product in 1975 and was released in 1981, many of the ideas that went into it were born in projects dating back more than three decades.

Memex. The story starts in 1945, when Vannevar Bush, a designer of early calculators and one of President Franklin D. Roosevelt's science advisors, wrote an article describing his vision of the uses of electronics and information technology. At a time when computers were new, room-sized, and used only for military number-crunching, Bush envisioned a personal, desktop computer for non-numerical applications. He called it the Memex. Due to insufficient technology and insufficient imagination on the part of others, Bush's ideas languished for 15 years.

Sketchpad. In the sixties, people began to take interactive computing seriously. One such person was Ivan Sutherland. He built an interactive graphics system called Sketchpad that allowed a user to create graphical figures on a CRT display using a light pen. The geometric shapes users put on the screen were treated as objects: after being created, they could be moved, copied, shrunk, expanded, and rotated. They could also be joined together to make larger, more complex objects that could then be operated upon as units. Sketchpad

influenced Star's user interface as a whole as well as its graphics applications.

NLS. Also in the sixties, Douglas Engelbart established a research program at Stanford Research Institute (now called SRI International) for exploring the use of computers "to augment the knowledge worker" and human intellect in general. He and his collegues experimented with different types of displays and input devices (inventing the mouse when other pointing devices proved inadequate) and developed a system commonly known as NLS.*

NLS was unique in several respects. It used CRT displays when most computers used teletypes. It was interactive (i.e., on-line) when almost all computing was batch. It was full-screen-oriented when the few systems that were interactive were line-oriented. It used a mouse when all other graphic interactive systems used cursor keys, light pens, joysticks, or digitizing tablets. Finally, it was the first system to organize textual and graphical information in trees and networks. Today, it would be called an "idea processor" or a "hypertext system."

The Reactive Engine. While Engelbart et al. were developing ideas, some of which eventually found their way into Star, Alan Kay, then a graduate student, was doing likewise. His dissertation, *The Reactive Engine*, contained the seeds of many ideas that he and others later brought to fruition in the Smalltalk language and programming environment, which, in turn, influenced Star. Like the designers of NLS, Kay realized that interactive applications do not have to treat the display as a "glass teletype" and can share the screen with other programs.

Xerox PARC. In 1970, Xerox established a research center in Palo Alto to explore technologies that would be important not only for the further development of Xerox's then-existing product line (copiers), but also for Xerox's planned expansion into the office systems business. The Palo Alto Research Center was organized into several laboratories, each devoted to basic and applied research in a field related to the above goals. The names and organi-

---

*The actual name of the system was On-Line System. A second system called Off-Line System was abbreviated FLS, hence NLS's strange abbreviation. NLS is now marketed by McDonnell Douglas under the name Augment.

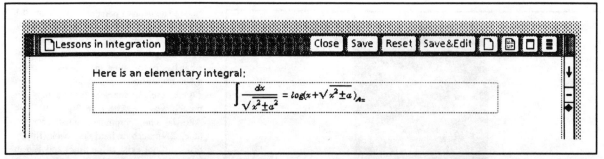

Figure 7. WYSIWYG formula editing. Mathematical formulas are edited in Star in a highly WYSIWYG fashion, in contrast to most systems, in which formulas are specified via in-line expressions or by constructing them from pieces in a special character font.

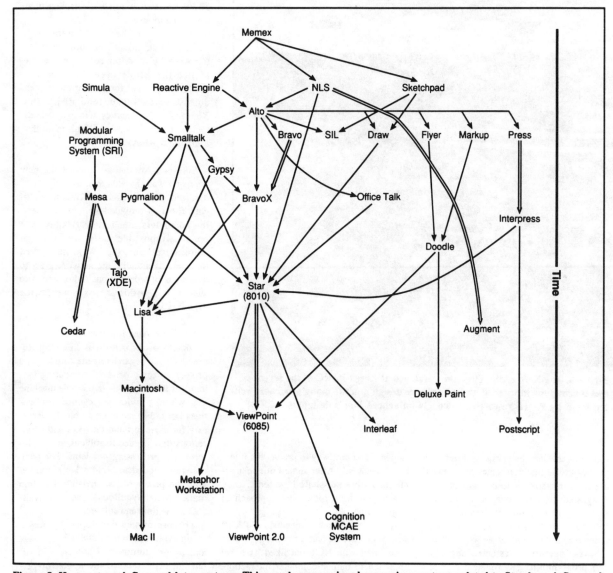

Figure 8. How systems influenced later systems. This graph summarizes how various systems related to Star have influenced one another over the years. Time progresses downwards. Double arrows indicate direct successors (i.e., follow-on versions). Many "influence arrows" are due to key designers changing jobs or applying concepts from their graduate research to products.

Figure 9. The Xerox Alto. The Alto, developed at Xerox PARC in the seventies, was a prototype for Star. Both its hardware design and the many programs written for it by PARC researchers strongly influenced Star's designers.

cated to a vision of personal computers in a distributed environment. In fact, they coined the term ''personal computer'' in 1973, long before microcomputers started what has been called the ''personal computer revolution.''

One result of the search for a new approach was the Alto (see Figure 9). The Alto was a minicomputer that had a removable, 2.5-megabyte hard disk pack (floppy disks did not exist at the time) and 128 to 256 kilobytes of memory. Unlike most machines of its day, the Alto also had a microprogrammable instruction set, a ''full-page'' (10½ × 8¼ inch, 600 × 800 pixel) bitmapped graphic display, about 50 kilobytes of high-speed display memory, and a mouse.

The first Alto became operational in 1972. At first, only a half-dozen or so Altos were built. After software that exploited the Alto's capabilities became available, demand for them grew tremendously, spreading beyond PARC into Xerox as a whole and even to external customers. Eventually, Xerox built more than a thousand Altos.

Ethernet. Another product of the new approach was the Ethernet. With its standardized, layered communications protocols, Ethernet provided a way of connecting computers much more flexibly than previously possible. Soon after the first Altos were built, they were networked together. Eventually, the network grew to thousands of workstations (Altos and Alto successors) within Xerox's worldwide organization.

Smalltalk. Alan Kay was one of the main advocates of the Alto. His Learning Research Group began using the Alto to build prototypes for a personal computing system ''of the future'' — a portable machine that would provide not canned applications but rather the building blocks necessary for users to build the tools and applications they needed to solve their own information processing problems. The technologies needed to build a lap computer with the power of the envisioned system (called the ''DynaBook'') were unavailable at the time and still are.

The prototypes developed by Kay's group evolved into the Smalltalk language and programming environment. Smalltalk further promoted the notion of personal computing; pioneered complete, interactive programming environments; and refined and solidified concepts of object-oriented programming that had been

zation of the labs have changed over the years, but the research topics have stayed the same: materials science, laser physics, integrated circuitry, computer-aided design and manufacturing, user interfaces (not necessarily to computers), and computer science (including networking, databases, operating systems, languages and programming environments, graphics, document production systems, and artificial intelligence).

Alto. PARC researchers were fond of the slogan ''The best way to predict the future is to invent it.'' After some initial experiments with time-shared systems, they began searching for a new approach to computing.

Among the founding members of PARC was Alan Kay. He and his colleagues were acquainted with NLS and liked its novel approach to human-computer interaction. Soon, PARC hired several people who had worked on NLS. In 1971, the center signed an agreement with SRI licensing Xerox to use the mouse. Kay and others were dedi-

extant only in vestigial forms in previous systems. Most importantly for Star, Smalltalk demonstrated the power of graphical, bitmapped displays; mouse-driven input; windows; and simultaneous applications. This is the most visible link between Smalltalk and Star, and is perhaps why many people wrongly believe that Star was written in Smalltalk.

Pygmalion. The first large program to be written in Smalltalk was Pygmalion, the doctoral thesis project of David C. Smith. One goal of Pygmalion was to show that programming a computer does not have to be primarily a textual activity. It can be accomplished, given the appropriate system, by interacting with graphical elements on a screen. A second goal was to show that computers can be programmed in the language of the user interface, that is, by demonstrating what you want done and having the computer remember and reproduce it. The idea of using icons — images that allow users to manipulate them and in so doing act upon the data they represent — came mainly from Pygmalion. After completing Pygmalion, Smith worked briefly on the NLS project at SRI before joining the Star development team at Xerox.

Bravo, Gypsy, and BravoX. At the same time that the Learning Research Group was developing Smalltalk for the Alto, others at PARC, mainly Charles Simonyi and Butler Lampson, were writing an advanced document editing system for it called Bravo. Because it made heavy use of the Alto's bitmapped screen, Bravo was unquestionably the most WYSIWYG text editor of its day, with on-screen underlining, boldface, italics, variable font families and sizes, and variable-width characters. It allowed the screen to be split, so different documents or different parts of the same document could be edited at once, but did not operate in a windowed environment as we use the term today. Bravo was widely used at PARC and in Xerox as a whole.

From 1976 to 1978, Simonyi and others rewrote Bravo, incorporating many of the new user-interface ideas floating around PARC at the time. One such idea was modelessness, promoted by Larry Tesler[3] and exemplified in Tesler's prototype text editor, Gypsy. Simonyi et al. also added styles, enhancing users' ability to control the appearance of their documents. The new version was called BravoX.

Shortly thereafter, Simonyi joined Microsoft, where he led the development of Microsoft Word, a direct descendent of BravoX. Another member of the BravoX team, Tom Malloy, went to Apple and wrote LisaWrite.

Draw, Sil, Markup, Flyer, and Doodle. Star's graphics capability (its provisions for users to create graphical images for incorporation into documents, as opposed to its graphical user interface) owes a great deal to several graphics editors written for the Alto and later machines.

Draw, by Patrick Beaudelaire and Bob Sproull, and Sil (for Simple Illustrator) were intellectual successors of Sutherland's Sketchpad (see above): graphical object editors that allowed users to construct figures out of selectable, movable, stretchable geometric forms and text. In turn, Star's graphic frames capability is in large measure an intellectual successor of Draw and Sil.

Markup was a bitmap graphics editor (that is, a paint program) written by William Newman for the Alto. Flyer was another paint program, written in Smalltalk for the Alto by Bob Flegel and Bill Bowman. These programs inspired Doodle, a paint program written for a later machine by Dan Silva. Doodle eventually evolved into ViewPoint's Free-Hand Drawing application. Silva went on to write DeluxePaint, a paint program for PCs.

Laser printing. Fancy graphics capabilities in a workstation are of little use without hard-copy capability to match it. Laser printing, invented at PARC, provided the necessary base capability, but computers needed a uniform way to describe output to laser printers. For this purpose, Bob Sproull developed the Press page-description language. Press was heavily used at PARC, then further developed into Interpress, Xerox's commercial page-description language and the language in which Star encodes printer output. Some of the developers of Interpress later formed Adobe Systems and developed Postscript, a popular page description language.

Laurel and Hardy. A network of personal workstations suggests electronic mail. Though electronic mail was not invented at PARC, PARC researchers (mainly Doug Brotz) made it more accessible to nonengineers by creating Laurel, a display-oriented tool for sending, receiving, and organizing e-mail. The experience of using Laurel inspired others to write Hardy for an Alto successor ma-chine. Laurel and Hardy were instrumental in getting nonengineers at Xerox to use e-mail. The use of e-mail spread further with the spread of Star and ViewPoint throughout Xerox.

OfficeTalk. One more Alto program that influenced Star was OfficeTalk, a prototype office automation system written by Clarence ("Skip") Ellis and Gary Nutt. OfficeTalk supported standard office automation tasks and tracked jobs as they went from person to person in an organization. Experience with OfficeTalk provided ideas for Star because of the two systems' similar target applications.

Summing up. The debt that Star owes to the Alto and its software is best summed up by quoting from the original designers, who wrote in 1982:

> Alto served as a valuable prototype for Star.... Alto users have had several thousand work-years of experience with them over a period of eight years, making Alto perhaps the largest prototyping effort in history. There were dozens of experimental programs written for the Alto by members of the Xerox Palo Alto Research Center. Without the creative ideas of the authors of these systems, Star in its present form would have been impossible.... In addition, we ourselves programmed various aspects of the Star design on the Alto ...

Star. To develop Star and other office systems products, Xerox created the Systems Development Department. SDD was staffed by transferring people from other parts of Xerox, including PARC, as well as by hiring from outside. Thus, contrary to what has often been stated in the industry press, Star was not developed at PARC, but rather in a separate product-development organization.

When SDD was formed, a decision was made to use Mesa, an "industrial-strength" dialect of Pascal conceived at SRI and further developed at PARC, as the primary product programming language. SDD took over development and maintenance of Mesa from the Computer Science Laboratory at PARC, freeing CSL to develop Mesa's research successor, Cedar.

Star hardware. Star is often discussed as if it were a computer. In fact, Star is a body of software.* However, using the

---

*The official name for Star was the Xerox 8010 Information System. The machine was called the 8000 Series Network Systems Processor. Originally, "Star" was only an internal name.

name Star to refer to the machine is understandable since the machine was designed in conjunction with the software to meet the needs of the software design. This is in sharp contrast to the usual approach, in which software is designed for existing computers.

The 8000 Series workstation was based upon a microcoded processor designed within Xerox especially to run the object code produced by the Mesa compiler. Besides being microprogrammed to run Mesa, the processor provided low-level operations for facilitating display operations. For example, the bitblt operation for manipulating rectangular arrays of screen pixels is implemented as a single instruction. As sold, the machine was configured with at least 384 kilobytes of real memory (expandable to 1.5 megabytes), a local hard disk (10, 29, or 40 megabytes), a 17-inch display, a mechanical mouse, an eight-inch floppy disk drive, and an Ethernet connection. The price was initially $16,500 with software.

Even though the machine was designed to run Star, it also ran other software. In addition to selling it as the 8010 "Star" workstation, Xerox sold it as a server machine and as an Interlisp and a Smalltalk workstation.

Star software. Although Star incorporated ideas from a number of predecessors, it still required a mammoth design effort to pull all of those ideas — as well as new ideas — together to produce a coherent design. According to the original designers, ". . . it was a real challenge to bring some order to the different user interfaces on the Alto."[1] About 30 person-years went into the design of the user interface, functionality, and hardware.

To foster uniformity of specifications as well as thoughtful and uniform design, Star's designers developed a strict format for specifications. Applications and system features were to be described in terms of the *objects* that users would manipulate with the software and the *actions* that the software provided for manipulating objects. This "objects and actions" analysis was supposed to occur at a fairly high level, without regard to how the objects would actually be presented or how the actions would actually be invoked by users. A full specification was then written from the "objects and actions" version. This approach forced designers to think clearly about the purpose of each application or feature and fostered recognition of similar operations across specifications, allowing what might have seemed like new operations to be handled by existing commands.

When SDD was formed, it was split between two locations: Southern California (El Segundo) and Northern California (Palo Alto). Few people were willing to transfer one way or the other, leaving SDD with the choice of losing many competent engineers or being creative. SDD's management took the creative route: they put the Ethernet to work, attaching the development machines at both sites to a network, connecting the two sites with a 56-kilobit-per-second leased line, encouraging heavy use of electronic mail for work-related communication, and developing tools for facilitating distributed, multi-party development.

As might be expected from Star's origins, most of the design and prototyping work was done in Palo Alto, whereas most of the implementation was done in El Segundo. Though this split was handled creatively, some of Star's designers now believe it caused problems not overcome by extensive use of e-mail. For example, the implementors did not benefit from much of the prototyping done at PARC.

The development process has been recounted in detail elsewhere[6] and will not be repeated here. Suffice it to say that the Star development effort

- involved developing new network protocols and data-encoding schemes when those used in PARC's research environment proved inadequate;
- involved a great deal of prototyping and user testing;
- included a late redesign of the processor;
- included several software redesigns, rewrites, and late additions, some based on results from user testing, some based on marketing considerations, and some based on systems considerations (see below);
- included a level of attention to the requirements of international customers unmatched in the industry; and
- left much of what was in the Star Functional Specification unimplemented.

Tajo/XDE. Since the machine upon which Star ran was developed in parallel with the software, it was not available early-on for use as a software development platform. Early prototyping and development was done on Altos and successor research machines developed at PARC. Though the Mesa language ran on these machines, development aids for Mesa programmers were lacking.

When the 8000 Series workstation became available, the systems group within SDD began working on a suitable development environment. Known internally as Tajo and externally as Xerox Development Environment (XDE), the completed development environment and the numerous tools written to run in it were quickly adopted by programmers throughout SDD. Star's later improvements adopted many good ideas from Tajo.

ViewPoint. Though Star's introduction at NCC '81 was lauded in the industry press, initial sales were not what had been hoped. Almost immediately, efforts were launched to improve its performance, extensibility, maintainability, and cost.

ViewPoint software. Even before Star was released, the implementors realized that it had serious problems from their point of view. Its high degree of integration and user-interface consistency had been achieved by making it monolithic: the system "knew" about all applications, and all parts of the system "knew" about all other parts. It was difficult to correct problems, add new features, and increase performance. The monolithic architecture also did not lend itself to distributed, multiparty development.

This created pressure to rewrite Star. Bob Ayers, who had been heavily involved in the development of Star, rewrote the infrastructure of the system according to the more flexible Tajo model. He built, on top of the operating system and low-level window manager, a "toolkit" for building Star-like applications.

In the new infrastructure, transfer of data between different applications was handled through strict protocols involving the user's selection, thus making applications independent from one another. The object-oriented user interface, which requires that the system associate applications with data files, was preserved by having applications register themselves with the system when started, telling it which type of data file they correspond to and registering procedures for handling keyboard and mouse events and generic commands. User-interface consistency was fostered by building many of the standards into the application toolkit. The development organization completed the toolkit and then ported or rewrote the existing applications and utilities to run on top of it.

Other software changes included

- the addition of several applications and utilities, including a Free-Hand Drawing program and an IBM PC emulation application;
- optional window tiling constraints, so that users can have overlapping windows if desired;
- redesigned screen graphics (icons, windows, property sheets, command buttons, and menus) to accommodate a smaller screen and to meet the demands of a more sophisticated public; and
- improved performance.

To underscore the fact that the new system was a substantial improvement over the old, the name was changed from Star to ViewPoint. ViewPoint 1.0 was released in 1985.

ViewPoint hardware. In addition to revising the software, Xerox brought the hardware up to date by designing a completely new vehicle for ViewPoint: the 6085 workstation. The new machine was designed to take advantage of advances in integrated circuitry, reductions in memory costs, new disk technologies, and new standards in keyboard design, as well as to provide IBM PC compatibility. The 6085 workstation has a Mesa processor plus an optional IBM-PC-compatible processor, one megabyte of real memory (expandable to 4 megabytes), a hard disk (10 to 80 megabytes), a choice of a 15- or a 19-inch display, an optical mouse, a new keyboard, a 5¼-inch floppy disk drive, and, of course, an Ethernet connection. The base cost was initially $6,340 with the ViewPoint software. Like the 8010, the 6085 is sold as a vehicle for Interlisp and Smalltalk as well as for ViewPoint.

Recent ViewPoint changes. The recently released ViewPoint 2.0 adds many features relevant to desktop publishing. These include

- Xerox ProIllustrator, a new vector graphics editing application designed mainly for professional illustrators;
- Shared Books, support for groups of users working on multipart documents;
- a Redlining feature, for tracking deletions and insertions in documents;
- cursor keys, for moving the insertion point during keyboard-intensive work; and

- stylesheets, for facilitating control of document appearance.

Lessons from experience

So what have we learned from all this? We believe, the following:

Pay attention to industry trends. Partly out of excitement over what they were doing, PARC researchers and Star's designers didn't pay enough attention to the "other" personal computer revolution occurring outside of Xerox. By the late seventies, Xerox had its own powerful technical tradition (mouse-driven, networked workstations with large bitmapped screens and multiple, simultaneous applications), blinding Star's designers to the need to approach the market with cheap, stand-alone PCs. The result was a product that was highly unfamiliar to its intended customers: businesses. Nowadays, of course, such systems are no longer unusual.

Developing Star and ViewPoint involved developing several enabling technologies, for networking, communicating with servers, describing pages to laser printers, and developing software. At the time they were developed, these technologies were unique in the industry. Xerox elected to keep them proprietary for fear of losing its competitive advantage. With hindsight, we can say that it might have been better to release these technologies into the public domain or to market them early, so that they might have become industry standards. Instead, alternative approaches developed at other companies have become the industry standards. Xerox's current participation in the development of various industry standards indicates its desire to reverse this trend.

Pay attention to what customers want. The personal computer revolution has shown the futility of trying to anticipate all of the applications that customers will want. Star should have been designed from the start to be open and extensible by users, as the Alto was. In hindsight, extensibility was one of the keys to the Alto's popularity. The problem wasn't that Star lacked functionality, it was that it didn't have the functionality customers wanted. An example is the initial lack of a spreadsheet application. The designers failed to appreciate the significance of this application, which may have been more important

than word-processing in expanding the personal computer revolution beyond engineers and hobbyists into business. Eventually realizing that Star's closedness was a problem, Xerox replaced it with ViewPoint, a more "open" system that allows users to pick and choose applications that they need, including a spreadsheet and IBM PC software. Apple Computer learned the same lesson with its Lisa computer and similarly replaced it with a cheaper one having a more open software architecture: the Macintosh.

Know your competition. Star's initial per-workstation price was near that of time-shared minicomputers, dedicated word-processors, and other shared computing facilities. Star was, however, competing for desktop space with microcomputer-based PCs. ViewPoint has corrected that problem: The 6085 costs about the same as its competition.

Establish firm performance goals. Star's designers should have established performance goals, documented them in the functional specifications, and stuck to them as they developed Star. Where performance goals couldn't be met, the corresponding functionality should have been cut.

In lieu of speed, the designers should have made the user interface more responsive. Designing systems to handle user input more intelligently can make them more responsive without necessarily making them execute functions faster. They can operate asynchronously with respect to user input, making use of background processes, keeping up with important user actions, delaying unimportant tasks (such as refreshing irrelevant areas of the screen) until time permits, and skipping tasks called for by early user actions but rendered moot by later ones. ViewPoint now makes use of background processes to increase its responsiveness.

Avoid geographically split development organizations. Having a development organization split between Palo Alto and El Segundo was probably a mistake, less for reasons of distance per se than for lack of shared background in "PARC-style" computing. However, the adverse effect of sheer distance on communication was certainly a factor.

Don't be dogmatic about the Desktop metaphor and direct manipulation. Direct manipulation and the Desktop meta-

279

phor aren't the best way to do everything. Remembering and typing is sometimes better than seeing and pointing. For example, if users want to open a file that is one of several hundred in a directory (folder), the system should let users type its name rather than forcing them to scroll through the directory trying to spot it so they can select it.

Many aspects of Star were correct. Though certain aspects of Star perhaps should have been done differently, most of the aspects of Star's design described at the beginning of this article have withstood the test of time. These include

- Iconic, direct-manipulation, object-oriented user interface. The days of cryptic command languages and scores of commands for users to remember (a la Unix and MS-DOS) should have passed long ago.
- Generic commands and consistency in general. Even Macintosh could use some lessons in this regard: the Duplicate command copies files within a disk, but users must drag icons to copy them across disks and must use Copy-Paste to copy anything else.
- Pointing device. Although cursor keys have some advantages and certainly would have enhanced Star's market appeal (as they have ViewPoint's), Star's designers stand by the system's primary reliance on the mouse. This does not imply a commitment to the mouse per se, but rather to any pointing device that allows quick pointing and selection. As interfaces evolve in the future, high-resolution touch screens and other more exotic devices may replace mice as the pointing devices of choice.
- High-resolution display. Memory is now cheap, so the justification for character displays is gone.
- Good graphic design. Screen graphics designed by computer programmers will not satisfy customers. The Star designers recognized their limitations in this regard and hired the right people for the job. As color displays gain market presence, the participation of graphic designers will become even more crucial.
- 16-bit character set. An eight-bit character set (such as ASCII) cannot accommodate international languages adequately. Star and ViewPoint's use of a 16-bit character set and of special typing and rendering algorithms for foreign languages is the correct approach.
- Distributed, personal computing.

Though the reorientation of the industry away from batch and time-shared computing toward personal computing had nothing to do with Xerox, PARC, or Star, it was an important part of the computing philosophy that led to Star.

Star has had an indisputable influence on the design of computer systems. For example, the Lisa and Macintosh might have been very different had Apple's designers not borrowed ideas from Star, as the following excerpt of a *Byte* magazine interview of Lisa's designers shows:

> Byte: Do you have a Xerox Star here that you work with?
> Tesler: No, we didn't have one here. We went to the NCC [National Computer Conference] when the Star was announced and looked at it. And in fact it did have an immediate impact. A few months after looking at it we made some changes to our user interface based on ideas that we got from it. For example, the desktop manager we had before was completely different; it didn't use icons at all, and we never liked it very much. We decided to change ours to the icon base. That was probably the only thing we got from Star, I think. Most of our Xerox inspiration was Smalltalk rather than Star.[7]

Elements of the Desktop metaphor approach also appear in many other systems.

The history presented here has shown, however, that Star's designers did not invent the system from nothingness. Just as it has influenced systems that came after it, Star was influenced by ideas and systems that came before it. It is difficult to inhibit the spread of good ideas once they are apparent to all, especially in this industry. Star was thus just one step in an evolutionary process that will continue both at Xerox and elsewhere. That is how it should be. □

Acknowledgments

When Star was announced, several articles on it appeared in trade magazines, journals, and at conferences. Many of these were reprinted in the Xerox publication *Office Systems Technology*.[8] Since then, several more articles have been published that are relevant to this retrospective. They include an article from MacWorld[9] that described the historical antecedents of Apple Computer's Lisa and Macintosh computers, which share much of Star's history. This retrospective owes a great deal to those previous writings. We also acknowledge the valuable contributions that Joe Becker, Bill Mallgren, Doug Carothers, Linda Bergsteinsson, and Randy Polen of Xerox, and Bob Ayers, Ralph Kimball, Dave Fylstra, and John Shoch made to this retrospective. Finally, we acknowledge the helpful suggestions made by the first and second authors' colleagues at US West Advanced Technologies and several anonymous reviewers to improve the quality of the article.

References

1. D.C. Smith et al., "The Star User Interface: An Overview," *Proc. AFIPS Nat'l Computer Conf.*, June 1982, pp. 515-528.

2. D.C. Smith, "Origins of the Desktop Metaphor: A Brief History," presented in a panel discussion, "The Desktop Metaphor as an Approach to User Interface Design," in *Proc. ACM Annual Conf.*, 1985, p. 548.

3. L. Tesler, "The Smalltalk Environment," *Byte*, Vol. 6, No. 8, Aug. 1981, pp. 90-147.

4. L. Winner, "Mythinformation," *Whole Earth Review*, No. 44, Jan. 1985.

5. J. Becker, "Multilingual Word Processing," *Scientific American*, Vol. 251, No. 1, July 1984, pp. 96-107. (See "Further reading" for other articles on Star's multilingual capability.)

6. E.F. Harslem and L.E. Nelson, "A Retrospective on the Development of Star," *Proc. Sixth Int'l Conf. on Software Engineering*, Sept. 1982, Tokyo, Japan. Reprinted in *Office Systems Technology*, OSD-R8203A, Xerox Corp., pp. 261-269.

7. G. Williams, "The Lisa Computer System," *Byte*, Vol. 8, No. 2, Feb. 1983, pp. 33-50.

8. *Office Systems Technology*, OSD-R8203A, Xerox Corp.

9. T. Nace, "The Macintosh Family Tree," *MacWorld*, Nov. 1984, pp. 134-141.

Further reading

For interested readers, we provide here a guide to further reading on Star and related topics. A more comprehensive and detailed version of this retrospective will appear in an upcoming Prentice-Hall book series. Also, the September issue of *IEEE Spectrum* includes an article, "Of Mice and Menus," on graphical user interfaces past and present. The authors of that article consulted several people who contributed to or are mentioned in this Star retrospective.

In the following bibliography, readings are categorized according to whether they pertain to work done prior to the establishment of Xerox PARC, to work done at PARC, to the original Star design done at Xerox SDD,[8] to enhancements to Star and ViewPoint, and to work on related topics.

Pre-Xerox

Bush, V., "As We May Think," *Atlantic Monthly*, Vol. 176, No. 1, July 1945, pp. 101-108.

Engelbart, D.C., and W.K. English, "A Research Center for Augmenting Human Intellect," *Proc. FJCC*, Vol. 33, AFIPS, 1968, pp. 395-410.

English, W.K., D.C. Engelbart, and M.L. Berman, "Display-Selection Techniques for Text Manipulation," *IEEE Trans. Human Factors in Electronics*, HFE-8, 1967, pp. 21-31.

Kay, A.C., *The Reactive Engine*, PhD thesis, University of Utah, Salt Lake City, 1969.

Sutherland, I.E., *Sketchpad: A Man-Machine Graphical Communications System*, PhD thesis, M.I.T., Cambridge, Mass., 1963.

Xerox pre-Star

Card, S., W.K. English, and B. Burr, "Evaluation of Mouse, Rate-Controlled Isometric Joystick, Step Keys, and Text Keys for Text Selection on a CRT," *Ergonomics*, Vol. 21, 1978, pp. 601-613.

Ellis, C., and G. Nutt, "Computer Science and Office Information Systems," Xerox PARC Tech. Report SSL-79-6, 1979.

Geschke, C.M., J.H. Morris, Jr., and E.H. Satterthwaite, "Early Experience with Mesa," *Comm. ACM*, Vol. 20, No. 8, 1977, pp. 540-553.

Ingalls, D.H., "The Smalltalk Graphics Kernel," *Byte*, Vol. 6, No. 8, Aug. 1981, pp. 168-194.

Kay, A.C., and A. Goldberg, "Personal Dynamic Media," *Computer*, Vol. 10, No. 3, March 1977, pp. 31-41.

Kay, A.C., "Microelectronics and the Personal Computer," *Scientific American*, Vol. 237, No. 3, Sept. 1977, pp. 230-244.

Smith, D.C., *Pygmalion: A Computer Program to Model and Simulate Creative Thought*, Birkhauser Verlag, Basel and Stuttgart, 1977.

Thacker, C.P., et al., "Alto: A Personal Computer," in *Computer Structures: Principles and Examples*, D. Siewioek, C.G. Bell, and A. Newell, eds., McGraw Hill, New York, 1982.

Star

Curry, G., et al., "Traits — An Approach to Multiple-Inheritance Subclassing," *Proc. ACM Conf. on Office Automation Systems (SIGOA)*, 1982.

Dalal, Y.K., "Use of Multiple Networks in the Xerox Network System," *Computer*, Vol. 15, No. 10, Oct. 1982, pp. 82-92.

Johnsson, R.K., and J.D. Wick, "An Overview of the Mesa Processor Architecture," *SIGPlan Notices*, Vol. 17, No. 4, 1982.

Lipkie, D.E., et al., "Star Graphics: An Object-Oriented Implementation," *Computer Graphics*, Vol. 16, No. 3, July 1982, pp. 115-124.

Shoch, J.F., et al., "Evolution of the Ethernet Local Computer Network," *Computer*, Vol. 15, No. 9, Aug. 1982, pp. 10-27.

Smith, D.C., et al., "Designing the Star User Interface," *Byte*, Vol. 7, No. 4, April 1982, pp. 242-282.

Sweet, R.E., and J.G. Sandman, Jr., "Empirical Analysis of the Mesa Instruction Set," *SIGPlan Notices*, Vol. 17, No. 4, 1982.

Star/ViewPoint enhancements

Becker, J., "Typing Chinese, Japanese, and Korean," *Computer*, Vol. 18, No. 1, Jan. 1985, pp. 27-34.

Becker, J., "Arabic Word Processing," *Comm. ACM*, Vol. 30, No. 7, July 1987, pp. 600-610.

Bewley, W.L., et al., "Human Factors Testing in the Design of Xerox's 8010 Star Office Workstation," *Proc. ACM Conf. on Human Factors in Computing Systems*, 1983, pp. 72-77.

Bushan, A., and M. Plass, "The Interpress Page and Document Description Language," *Computer*, Vol. 19, No. 6, June 1986, pp. 72-77.

Curry, G., and R. Ayers, "Experience with Traits in Star," *Programming Productivity: Issues for the Eighties*, IEEE Computer Society Press, Los Alamitos, Calif., 1986, Order #681.

Halbert, D., "Programming by Example," Xerox OSD Tech. Report OSD-T84-02, 1984.

Lewis, B., and J. Hodges, "Shared Books: Collaborative Publication Management for an Office Information System," *Proc. ACM Conf. on Office Information Systems*, 1988.

Miscellaneous

Bly, S., and J. Rosenberg, "A Comparison of Tiled and Overlapping Windows," *Proc. ACM Conf. on Computer-Human Interaction*, 1986, pp. 101-106.

Goldberg, A., *Smalltalk-80: The Interactive Programming Environment*, Addison-Wesley Publishing, Reading, Mass., 1984.

Goldberg, A., and D. Robson, *Smalltalk-80: The Language and its Implementation*, Addison-Wesley Publishing, Reading, Mass., 1984.

Halasz, F., and T. Moran, "Analogy Considered Harmful," *Proc. ACM Conf. on Human Factors in Computing Systems*, Gaithersburg, MD, 1982, pp. 383-386.

Houston, T., "The Allegory of Software: Beyond, Behind, and Beneath the Electronic Desk," *Byte*, Dec. 1983, pp. 210-214.

Johnson, J., "Calculator Functions on Bitmapped Computers," *SIGCHI Bulletin*, Vol. 17, No. 1, July 1985, pp. 23-28.

Johnson, J., "How Closely Should the Electronic Desktop Simulate the Real One?" *SIGCHI Bulletin*, Vol. 19, No. 2, Oct. 1987, pp. 21-25.

Johnson, J., "Modes in Non-Computer Devices," in press, *Int'l J. Man-Machine Studies*, 1989.

Johnson, J., and R. Beach, "Styles in Document Editing Systems," *Computer*, Vol. 21, No. 1, Jan. 1988, pp. 32-43.

Malone, T.W., "How Do People Organize Their Desks: Implications for the Design of Office Information Systems," *ACM Trans. on Office Information Systems*, Vol. 1, No. 1, 1983, pp. 99-112.

Rosenberg, J.K., and T.P. Moran, "Generic Commands," *Proc. First Int'l Conf. on Human-Computer Interaction (Interact-84)*, 1984, pp. 1,360-1,364.

Teitelman, W., "A Tour Through Cedar," *IEEE Software*, April 1984.

Whiteside, J., et al., "User Performance with Command, Menu, and Iconic Interfaces," *Proc. ACM SIGCHI '85*, 1985, pp. 185-191.

Jeff Johnson is a user-interface researcher at Hewlett-Packard Labs. While working on this article, he was a member of the Advanced User Interfaces Group of US West Advanced Technologies. Before that, he worked at Xerox designing and implementing enhancements to the Star/ViewPoint system, and at Cromemco as a software engineer and manager. He received BA and PhD degrees in cognitive psychology from Yale and Stanford universities, respectively.

Teresa L. Roberts is a user-interface researcher in the Advanced User Interfaces Group at US West Advanced Technologies. She spent 10 years at Xerox, designing and evaluating parts of the Star user interface. She received a PhD in computer science from Stanford University.

William Verplank is an interaction design consultant with IDTwo and a lecturer in human factors and design at Stanford University. He worked at Xerox from 1978 to 1986, doing user testing and user-interface design for Star and ViewPoint. He received a BS in mechanical engineering from Stanford University and MS and PhD degrees in man-machine systems from MIT.

David C. Smith received a PhD in Computer Science from Stanford University in 1975. He spent seven years at Xerox Office Systems Division as one of the principal designers of Star. After that, he was vice president of user communication at Cognition, Inc., an MCAE firm, and is now an advanced system designer at Apple Computer.

Charles H. Irby is vice president of Metaphor Computer Systems, Software Products Division. Previously, he managed the Advanced Development Group of Xerox Office Systems Division and in that capacity was one of the principal designers of Star. Prior to that, he worked with Douglas Engelbart at SRI developing the NLS system. He received a BA in physics and mathematics and an MS in computer science and electrical engineering from the University of California at Santa Barbara.

Marian Beard is director of release management at Metaphor Computer Systems. Before joining Metaphor, she managed user interface design for Xerox's 8000 and 6085 products, and was a member of the original Star design team. She received a BA in history from Stanford University and an MEd from the University of Missouri.

Kevin Mackey is a software engineer at Logitech. He worked at Xerox from 1982 to 1989, developing applications software for Star and View-Point, and in that capacity helped develop ViewPoint's PC-emulation facility. He received a BS in computer science from the University of California at Berkeley.

Readers may contact Jeff Johnson at Hewlett-Packard Labs, 1501 Page Mill Rd., 1AU, Palo Alto, CA 94303.

Rooms: The Use of Multiple Virtual Workspaces to Reduce Space Contention in a Window-Based Graphical User Interface

D. AUSTIN HENDERSON, JR., and STUART K. CARD
Xerox Palo Alto Research Center

A key constraint on the effectiveness of window-based human–computer interfaces is that the display screen is too small for many applications. This results in "window thrashing," in which the user must expend considerable effort to keep desired windows visible. *Rooms* is a window manager that overcomes small screen size by exploiting the statistics of window access, dividing the user's workspace into a suite of virtual workspaces with transitions among them. Mechanisms are described for solving the problems of navigation and simultaneous access to separated information that arise from multiple workspaces.

Categories and Subject Descriptors: D.4.2 [**Operating Systems**]: Storage Management—*virtual memory*; H.1.2 [**Models and Principles**]: User/Machine Systems—*human factors*; *human information processing*; I.3.6 [**Computer Graphics**]: Methodology and Technique—*ergonomics*; *interaction techniques*

General Terms: Design, Human Factors, Theory

Additional Key Words and Phrases: Bounded locality interval, desktop, locality set, project views, resource contention, Rooms, virtual workspace windows, window manager, working set

1. INTRODUCTION

The small size of computer screens is a more serious impediment for window-based workstations than is often appreciated. This paper presents a window manager design that effectively enlarges the user's screen. The design is based on an analysis of window usage.

Many potential knowledge-intensive computer applications require that the user interact with a moderately large number of objects. For example, paper materials, when used for writing a paper, may easily fill a dining-room table (Figure 1). Furthermore people tend to switch back and forth between parts of a project and among different activities [2, 21]. For example, a person writing a paper on a computer workstation may nonetheless read his or her electronic mail daily, answer letters, perform housekeeping on the computer files, and consult

This research was supported in part by NASA Ames under grant NAG 2-269.

Authors' address: Intelligent Systems Laboratory, Xerox Palo Alto Research Center, 3333 Coyote Hill Road, Palo Alto, CA 94304.

Fig. 1.   Dining-room table being used to manage a complex task by spreading out parts of the task in space so each part is quickly accessible. The large space simplifies the task.

with students. Each of these tasks has its own objects, such as electronic messages and file browsers, for the user to interact with. The result is many pieces of information for a user to look at, manipulate, and track.

When tasks are done with paper, current information is usually managed using a two-dimensional space in the form of a desk or often a dining table, on which papers are grouped and arranged meaningfully. This allows information needed for a task to be placed and ordered in temporary arrangements without the difficult and expensive effort of assigning formal codes or names. The visual availability of the papers in arrangement provides memory cues that organize and substantially ease the task. This natural use of space has been sought for computer systems in the "desktop metaphor" interface and its variants [1, 4, 24]. Unfortunately, any straightforward attempt to use computer display space in this fashion immediately confronts the problem that the display screen is often too small.

Computer displays are *much* smaller than desks or tables. Figure 2 compares the area outlines of different computer displays with those of a desktop and a dining table. A standard office desk has the area of 22 IBM PC screens, 46 Macintosh screens, or even 10 of the "large" 19-inch Xerox 1186 or Sun-3 screens. A dining table is the size of 57 PC screens, 119 Macintosh screens, or 27 19-inch screens. And, if one were to include the effects of resolution, gray scale, and color in the computation, the comparison would be even more extreme.

A number of techniques have been proposed for overcoming the small-screen problem. These can be roughly divided into four categories: (1) alternating screen

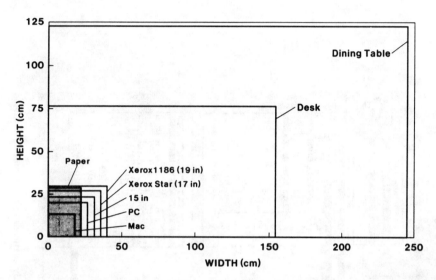

Fig. 2.   Superimposed outlines of different workspaces. The crosshatched area shows the size of an 8½-by-11-inch page. Desks and dining tables are very much larger than even large displays. If display resolution were taken into account, the comparisons would be much more extreme.

usage, (2) distorted views, (3) large virtual workspaces, and (4) multiple virtual workspaces.

Alternating screen usage. The user can simply switch the allocation of screen space from one application to another. The Xerox Star [24], for example, provides for storing documents in file drawers to be fetched and reopened as needed. The original Macintosh was a more extreme case, allowing only one application to be on the screen at a time.

Distorted views. Another way of gaining space is to distort the objects in the workspace. One of the oldest techniques for doing this, first appearing in Smalltalk, is the use of icons [23]: Windows are shrunk to small pictures that remind the user of the original window. Overlapping windows, also derived from Smalltalk [14], can be considered a distorting technique: Windows are allowed to cover each other leaving only a portion to remind the user of what lies behind. Icons and overlapping windows are probably responsible for making the electronic desktop metaphor possible at all. But, as Figure 3 shows, in many applications they are not enough. When the need for screen space outstrips the space available, overlapping windows can create an "electronic messy desk" in which the windows interfere with one another. More recently, "fish-eye" distortions have been explored by Furness [13] and Spence and Apperly [25]. The idea is to force all of the objects to fit into the screen space by allocating space to objects on the basis of their intrinsic importance and the user's current focus of attention. Parts of some objects may be clipped or their dimensions distorted to cause them to fit. The Boxer system [8] is a different sort of distorted-view system. A spatial box metaphor is used to represent many semantic notions of containment. The boxes

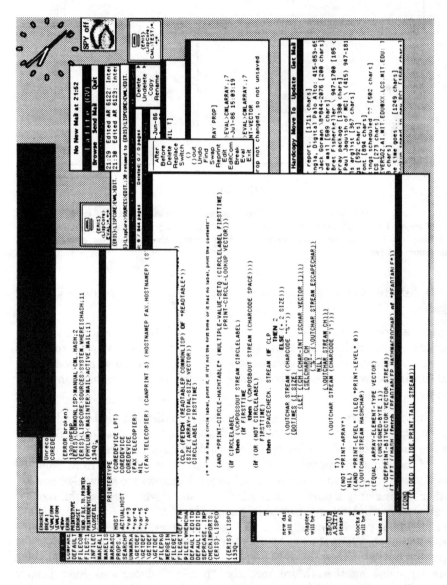

Fig. 3. Overlapped window display. Since the workspace is small, it is easily overloaded and becomes a cluttered desk.

are nested in a hierarchy. Individual boxes can either appear expanded or shrunk to a symbol, depending on where the user is in the hierarchy.

Large virtual workspaces. Instead of forcing all of the objects to fit on the screen, another technique is to arrange them in a single large virtual workspace much larger than the screen. The screen is treated as a movable viewport onto this space. Sketchpad [26] was one of the earliest graphical programs to use this technique. Many other systems have since developed their own versions. In Dataland [1], color pictorial and textual data are arranged in two dimensions. The user has three screens, one for an overview of the whole space, one for a detailed view of some portion of the space, and one touch screen for control. The user can translate or zoom his or her detailed view. As the user zooms closer to the data, more detail is revealed. In each of these systems, the data are passive—the user cannot interact with the data other than to view them. By contrast, the Cedar Whiteboard system [9] also provides translation and zooming over a large workspace, but individual data elements can lead to opening application windows. At the extreme of the virtual workspace systems are head-mounted displays (e.g., the NASA helmet [12]), which monitor user head and body movements to give the user a complete simulated 3D space.

Multiple virtual workspaces. The simulation of a single large workspace is natural, but carries over to the system some strong constraints of physical space—only a limited number of things can be adjacent to any object, for example, and the space required for the objects and their shapes puts strong constraints on how the space can be arranged and how densely it can be packed. An alternative to a single virtual workspace is to have multiple virtual workspaces, that is, geometrically oriented workspaces linked to each other, perhaps nonspatially. An example is Smalltalk Projects [14]. Each project contains a number of views and, when active, takes up the whole screen. Projects are arranged hierarchically, with subprojects represented in their parents as windows through which the projects can be entered: these windows are called ProjectViews, or (informally) doors. More direct access to all the projects can be created through browsers, which permit referencing by name all the projects at once. In the CCA system [1, 16] (a descendent of Dataland), whenever a user zooms close enough to a port, he or she is swept through into a subworkspace. Like Smalltalk Projects these subworkspaces are arranged hierarchically. A third example of multiple virtual workspaces is the Cedar programming environment multiple desktop overview [20]: 16 desktops are shown in miniature. The user selects which desktop to enter from this overview. Finally, in Chan's UNIX[1]-based Room[2] system [4], each workspace contains a set of collected icons that provide actions appropriate for carrying out a particular task: either to move to another workspace (doors) or to start a new process for the task the icon specifies. Moving to another workspace provides access to other icons.

---

[1] UNIX is a trademark of AT&T Bell Laboratories.

[2] We did not discover the existence of the similarly named system "Room" (Chan's Master's thesis at the University of Waterloo [4]) until after we had publicly demonstrated our Rooms system at the AAAI conference in August 1986. To avoid confusion in this paper, we refer to Chan's system as "Chan's Room system."

A more complex organization for multiple virtual workspaces than the tree-oriented systems described above is the Feiner et al. electronic book [11]. Pages in the book (each separate workspaces) are organized into subchapters and then chapters. Pages may contain pictures, any of which can be active in preset ways. Among other things, this provides single-action access to other pages of the book. Pictures can be used in different scales, another variant on the distortion technique.

At the extreme of increasing complexity of structure are the hypertext systems, characterized by small, often textual, networks of workspaces connected with arbitrary patterns of typed links. The earliest of these was NLS [10]. More recent examples are PROMIS [17], ZOG [22], and NoteCards [15]. PROMIS and ZOG display a single node at once; NLS provides access to a subtree of nodes, screen space permitting; and NoteCards provides access to any arbitrary set of nodes. Motion among the nodes is by traversing links.

The above techniques make progress toward solving the small-screen problem, but precipitate two new problems, which arise when not all the information is visible on the screen at once: (1) the problem of navigation (how to find objects in the workspace) and (2) the problem of arranging simultaneous access to separated information.

The problem of navigation. This is the user's problem of finding the way to information without getting lost. In large virtual workspaces with a strong physical model (Dataland, Whiteboard, etc.), the spatial analogy is a powerful space organizer. Thus these systems base much of their navigation on translating and zooming and may provide both global and local views [1]. As in unfamiliar cities, however, it may still be possible to get lost or not find what one is looking for. In systems with multiple virtual spaces (e.g., Cedar, Smalltalk Projects), an overview can also be provided if the number of virtual workspaces is not too large. In hypertext systems (e.g., Electronic Book, NoteCards) the task is harder. Here, the navigation issue is not aided by a strong physical model, and the separate nodes are related by a tangle of links. Visual presentation of the links may be more confusing than enlightening. One solution is presentations of local connectivity (Electronic Book, NoteCards); another is browser presentations of nodes (Smalltalk Project Browser, Electronic Book chapter structure, NoteCards Browser).

Simultaneous access to separated information. It is often necessary to bring together two or more pieces of information from separated parts of the workspace. In fact, the same piece of information may even be logically associated with more than one part of the workspace. In some systems, particularly those with a strong spatial model (e.g., Dataland), this presents the difficulty of having to destroy the old organization to gain the new. Of course, one can make copies, but copies have coordination difficulties if the information can change. Distortion (fish-eye views, icons, overlapped windows) provides another solution: The arrangement remains fixed, while the distortion can change to make the desired information simultaneously accessible. Sharing information (the same picture can be used on different pages in the Electronic Book) is another solution, one requiring more sophisticated information structuring. In the extreme, hypertext systems (e.g.,

NLS, NoteCards) provide for multiple linkings, which, in turn, provide multiple clusterings through separate views.

In the system we propose, our object is to prototype a workstation window manager that allows users to operate with larger collections of objects. Although a number of systems have developed techniques for mitigating the small-screen problem, no generally accepted framework for understanding the problem itself has yet emerged. As part of the process of advancing these techniques, we wish to begin building an understanding of the problem to aid us.

2. ANALYSIS OF DESKTOP INFORMATION USE

Instead of just developing another system to mitigate the small-screen problem, it is useful to construct some analytical understanding of the key constraints acting upon desktop information use. From this understanding we can gain abstractions with which to organize the design space and gain insight into promising regions of the design space for siting a design.

Basically, our analysis is that (1) the high overhead of moving and reshaping windows that users must often suffer with overlapped window systems derives from a severe screen-space resource contention lying just below the surface, but that (2) we can partially overcome this resource contention by designing a virtual workspace manager that exploits the statistics of window reference.

2.1 The Small-Screen Problem

Informally, the resource contention can be described by the following *gedanken* experiment: Imagine the task of writing a paper using a dining-room table. Drafts, figures, references, outlines, and notes can be spread on the table in a way that makes them easily accessible as the writer proceeds. Imagine the same task now done on an office desk. There is still considerable workspace, but perhaps some of the information must be piled together, necessitating occasional flipping through piles. Now imagine the task on a very tiny desk. Much of the writer's time must be devoted to thrashing about searching through papers: New papers dredged up top will cover other papers still in active use, and these, in turn, will need to be dredged up and will cover other papers in use. In addition to the immediate time consequence of thrashing, the ensuing chaos will tend to alter the task itself, pushing the writer toward more formal methods of accessing information, such as file folders and note cards, which have their own overheads: time to categorize, memory for categories, and conceptual ambiguities.

More formally, an analysis of resource contention leading to "thrashing" behavior is available from the study of virtual-memory operating systems [7], and we can apply some of its features to the small-screen problem. In a virtual-memory operating system, programs are run in a large, virtual-address space. This virtual-address space resides on some secondary storage medium, such as a rotating disk, much larger (and also much slower) than the physical address space available in the main computer. When reference is made to a page in virtual memory not actually resident in the computer's main memory, a "page fault" occurs: A page in physical memory is written back to disk if it has changed, and the referenced virtual-memory page is copied to main memory in the vacated slot.

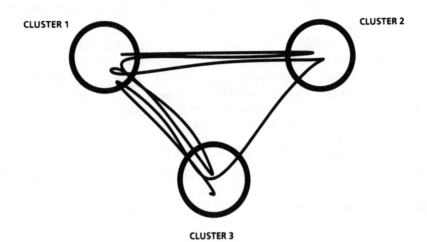

CLUSTER 1

CLUSTER 2

CLUSTER 3

Fig. 4. Locality sets and possible transitions between them. Each circle represents a cluster of page locations that tend to be referenced together in time. The line represents the locus of program control as it transitions back and forth between such clusters. Programs spend most of their time in clusters of page references, represented by the circles, and relatively little time (from 2 to 5 percent) in transitions between clusters, yet typically half of the page faults occur during the transitions. (After Madison [19, p. 26].)

Two principal factors determine the success of this scheme: (1) the size of the main memory available relative to the size of the program and (2) the statistical distribution of the program's references to virtual memory. With respect to the latter, a program that exhibits *locality of reference*, that is, a program whose references to virtual-memory page locations cluster together in time, causes fewer page faults and hence requires much less time to run (or much less main memory to run at a given speed) than one whose references are randomly distributed. Fortunately, most programs progress in distinct *locality phases* [7]: That is, most programs progress by making frequent references to a small set of virtual-memory locations (called a *locality set*) followed by transition to another small set of virtual-memory locations (Figure 4). Page faults tend to be relatively sparse within phases, but dense within transitions. For example, Kahn measured several programs [18, cited in 7] and found that the programs in his sample spent 98 percent of their time within some phase. But during the 2 percent of the time they were in transition, 40–50 percent of the page faults occurred [7, p. 72].

Reasons for locality in program reference behavior are not difficult to find. First, programs typically consist of blocks of memory that are executed more or less sequentially. Second, programs often have loops that iterate over the same locations. Finally, programs usually involve bursts of computations on related variables or data structures.

The reference characteristics of programs, then, essentially derive from two factors: (1) the sequential storage structure of most program code as assembled by a compiler and (2) the way in which references to the same variables tend to be clustered in time. It is important to note that locality of reference is strongly

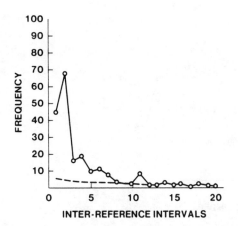

FREQUENCY

INTER-REFERENCE INTERVALS

Fig. 5. Window interreference interval distribution. The graph plots the frequency with which different numbers of window references intervening between references to the same window are observed. For example, there were 10 instances in which the same window appeared as the fifth window reference after it had previously appeared. The graph gives evidence for considerable locality in window references. If the references were uniformly random, the distribution would follow the dotted line. The actual distribution is heavily skewed toward short interreference intervals indicating locality. (From Card, Pavel, and Farrell [3].)

evident, even when this latter case of reference to variables is considered alone [7].

For virtual-memory operating systems, the size of main memory relative to the size of the virtual memory and the high cost of references to secondary memory are *key constraints* that drive the performance of the system. Main memory is a limited resource that is in contention. Operating-system algorithms attempt to exploit locality of reference in programs to reduce memory contention. Since memory contention is often a performance driver, reducing it can have a major impact on system performance as a whole.

For windows (as well as for paper-laden desks), the size of the available workspace relative to the needs of the task to be done is a key constraint that drives user performance on the task. Small display screens or desks are limited resources that are in contention. But, if users exhibit locality of window reference and a system can make explicit use of it, we can likely make a major improvement in window manipulation overheads that derive from the small-screen problem.

2.2 Window Locality Sets

Evidence for locality of window reference seems clear enough from protocols we have been able to examine of users interacting with an overlapped window system. In the first place we have informally observed such behavior: Users are often seen to use a group of windows for a while, then delete or shrink most of them, and then begin building another set. More systematically, the distribution of window interreference intervals (the number of window references between two references to the same window) is shifted heavily to the low end (compared with what would be expected for random window referencing), indicating that the user in this protocol often went back and forth among a small set (five or fewer) of windows (see Figure 5).

Other ways of looking at user window behavior suggest a similar conclusion. We can identify approximately the locality set of windows in active use at a given time by computing Denning's *working set* [5–7]. The working set consists of those windows referenced in the last T references. Figure 6 shows this metric computed for a user programming Interlisp-D on the basis of those window events detectable

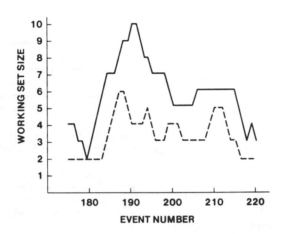

Fig. 6. Computation of Denning's working set for window references made by a user reading mail and programming in Interlisp-D: - - - -, $T = 6$; ———, $T = 14$. Computation is based on detectable system events. The waxing and waning of the number of windows in the computation interval T is clearly visible, but this way of estimating window locality sets does not show well the boundaries of the phase transitions. (From Card, Pavel, and Farrell [3].)

by the system. The figure shows a window working set varying between 2 and 10 windows for the fragment of behavior examined.

However, a better metric for our purpose is Madison's *bounded locality interval* (*BLI*) [19]. This metric overcomes two problems with the classical working-set measure: (1) that it depends on an arbitrary parameter T, the reference interval, and, more important, (2) that the interval size T is fixed, with the consequence that the boundaries between phases are not well defined [19]. The bounded locality interval is based on the top elements of an LRU (least recently used) stack that have all been referenced at least once since their formation (see [19]). The BLI metric has been shown by Madison to correspond well to intuitive notions of a phase. Figure 7 shows the BLI metric computed over 60 minutes of behavior on the Interlisp-D system. The computation indicates the existence of from zero to five windows in a locality set at any time for this fragment of user behavior. (Had the user referenced windows randomly, Figure 7 would be blank.)

These four indicators—simple observation, interreference interval, Denning's working set, and Madison's bounded locality interval—cannot yet be considered definitive pending further studies and refinements, but they do at this point all suggest in unison that users exhibit locality of window reference and that, therefore, as in the case of virtual-memory operating systems, mechanisms that exploit this statistical property of user behavior might be developed.

2.3 Tasks and Tools

It is not difficult to suggest reasons for the locality-of-window-reference behavior observed above. When there is some *task* to be done, such as reading mail, writing a paper, or creating a program, the user gathers a number of *tools* for doing it. In

292

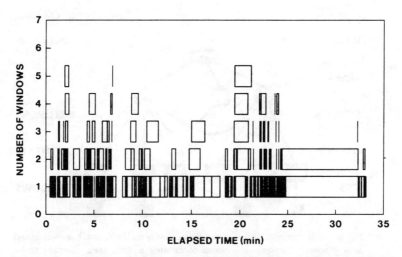

Fig. 7. Computation of the Madison's bounded locality interval (BLI) metric. The computation is based on a user programming Interlisp-D. In order to capture part of the user's visual reference to windows, windows in the enviornment have been programmed to "gray out," becoming barely readable after 10 s. The windows are instantly restored if the user selects them with the mouse or the system uses them. Each rectangle is a locality set plotted according to the number of windows in the set. The abscissa is time in milliseconds. If window references did not exhibit locality, there would be no rectangles. With this technique the boundaries of the window locality sets are easier to see. The technique shows promise, with refinement, for being able to describe complicated patterns of window use.

most window systems, these tools are each embedded in a window (e.g., mail-browser windows for mail; text-editor and file-browser windows for paper writing; program editors, debuggers, and measuring instruments for programming). As the user moves back and forth among these tools while doing the task, the tool windows form a locality set.

A task, from the point of view of the user, will therefore tend to correspond to a phase from the point of view of window reference statistics. Task switching will correspond to a transition, and we expect it to lead to heavy window faulting. The design of the Rooms system is based on the notion that, by giving the user an interface mechanism for letting the system know he or she is switching tasks, it can anticipate the set of tools/windows the user will reference and thus preload them together in a tiny fraction of the time the user would have required to open, close, and move windows or expand and shrink icons. A further benefit is that the set of windows preloaded on the screen will cue the user and help reestablish the mental context for the task. (We might even say that knowledge faulting in the user is thereby reduced.)

3. DESIGN OF THE ROOMS SYSTEM

The window-management system we describe provides the user with a suite of roughly screen-sized workspaces called *Rooms*. The overall scheme is shown schematically in Figure 8. Each Room contains a set of window *Placements*, each of which indicates a window, a shape, and other presentation information

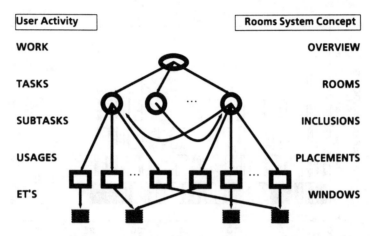

Fig. 8. Schematic structure of the Rooms system. Users' work is distributed among several Rooms, each Room containing a main task. Rooms can be included in other Rooms. Each Room contains a set of Placements. Placements indicate windows and Room-dependent presentation information for the window.

(i.e., how a given window is to appear in a particular Room). A key feature of Placements is that two Placements may refer to the same window, allowing windows to be shared among Rooms. Rooms may also be included in other Rooms as a mechanism for allowing the sharing of groups of windows among workspaces. Our system is implemented in Interlisp-D and uses the Interlisp-D window package for basic window manipulations.

Figure 9 shows two typical Rooms. The Room in Figure 9a has been laid out with mail-browsing windows and a mail-reader window. It has a prompt window for messages (the long black rectangle), two icons with controls for the mail system, a command typescript window for typing LISP functions, a clock, and *Doors* linking this Room directly with others. If the user selects the Door labeled PROG with the mouse, then the screen changes to the Room in Figure 9b; that is, the user has the illusion of moving to Room PROG. This latter Room is set up for doing programming and at the time of entering contains windows in which editing with the LISP structure editor is in progress. It also contains a *Back Door* (the Door in Figure 9b in reverse video) showing the Room from which the user came (and to which the user could return by means of a single mouse selection). To help the user navigate, the system has an *Overview* (Figure 10) that displays miniature versions of all the Rooms in the total user workspace. Any Room can be entered from the Overview, and indeed Placements can be copied, deleted, moved, shaped, and examined at full size from this Overview. Figure 11 shows the set of Rooms and direct Door links of an actual user workspace. The diagram has an obvious similarity to the phase and transition diagram of Figure 4.

The design for Rooms is based on our analysis of the key constraints on user window behavior as developed in the previous section. Since on present evidence much of the user housekeeping for an overlapped window system derives from contention for limited screen space, the design gives the user more virtual space. Since we expect the use of that space to be characterized by phases and transitions organized around tasks, this total virtual workspace is divided into multiple virtual subworkspaces through Doors (or the Overview). Our basic analysis, therefore, has helped suggest a promising position in the design space at which to site a design. But the design decisions to which we are thereby led have further entailments of their own. The design for Rooms reflects solutions that arise not only from the basic analysis, but also from these entailments—issues that may have little relation to the original problem that Rooms was designed to solve, but whose resolution is necessary for the system to be viable. As is the case for all systems in which information is not all visible on the screen at once, the Rooms system must face entailed issues that derive from (1) problems of navigation and (2) problems of arranging simultaneous access to separated information. A third group of entailed issues focuses around (3) simple user tailoring of system appearance and behavior. The major entailed design problems and their solutions are summarized in Table I. It is simplest to begin with problems of simultaneous access.

3.1 Simultaneous Access to Separated Information

Some windows, such as the invocation of a text editor on a particular file, are strongly associated with a particular task. Others, such as a clock or the command typescript window, are relatively independent of different tasks. Each Room tends to be organized around some dominant task, such as writing a paper or reading the mail. The windows contained in a Room provide the tools for the task and, indirectly, the material to which the tool is being applied (e.g., a window containing a text editor opened to a particular file). But tools and tasks can be combined in different ways. A single-purpose mail Room might have just mail-transport tools, mail files, and mail sorters in it, whereas a project Room might have a mail reader, a text-editor window, and a programming editor. So, although it is easy to recognize the global need for some sort of simultaneous access to the same windows across different Rooms, there are, in fact, a number of specific cases to be sorted out before sharing can actually be accomplished. These can be classified as (1) sharing tools across tasks, (2) workspace-dependent window presentations, (3) sharing collections of tools across tasks, and (4) carrying tools to another workspace.

3.1.1 *Sharing Tools across Tasks*

ISSUE 1 [*Multiple instances of windows*]. *Some windows need to appear in more than one workspace.*

DESIGN SOLUTION. *Multiple Placements of a window.*

The desire to have versions of the same window appearing in more than one Room forces us to the abstraction of a *Placement*. A Placement is a window together with location and presentation information.

Placement = Window + LocationInRoom + PresentationAttributes.

A Placement generalizes the concept of a window, separating the tool aspects of it (the fact that a particular set of editing commands work inside it) from its appearance on the screen.

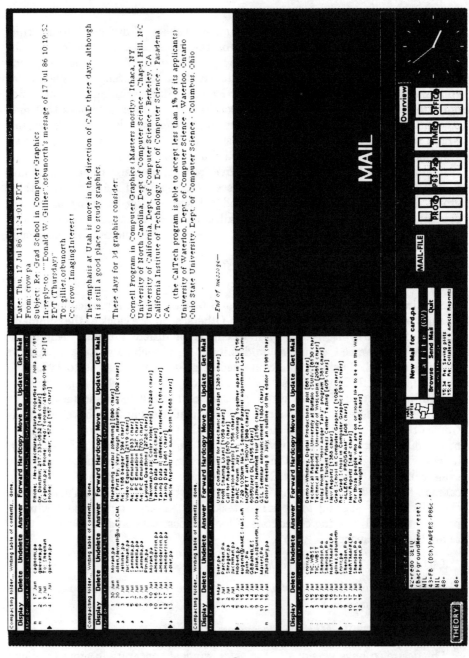

(a)

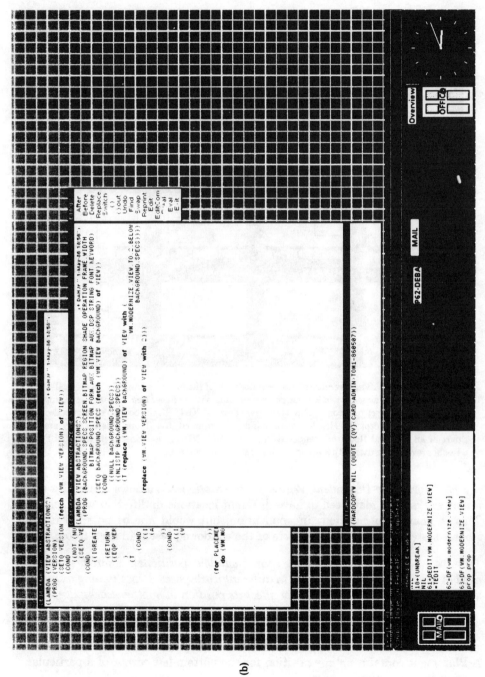

(b)

Fig. 9. Two examples of Rooms. Room (a) is used for reading mail; Room (b) for programming. In these Rooms both the panel door figures and the button-shaped figures (e.g., the one marked "Overview") are doors.

297

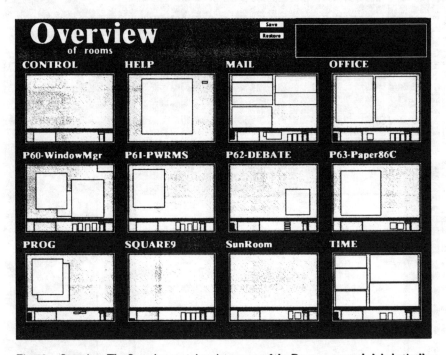

Fig. 10. Overview. The Overview contains pictograms of the Rooms arranged alphabetically. It also contains a message window for communicating with the user and buttons for saving and restoring the set of Rooms. This Overview shows a CONTROL Room that is included in every Room except the HELP Room. Windows contained in a Room because they are part of an included Room are rendered in gray. **EXPAND**ing the window in the HELP Room provides the user with a one-page illustrated system manual.

3.1.2 *Workspace-Dependent Window Presentations.* Windows shared by different workspaces may need to have different locations in different workspaces. This is immediately obvious in application, but would not be possible if the Rooms system merely contained lists of the windows present in each Room.

ISSUE 2 [*Workspace-dependent shared-window positions*]. *Shared windows need to have independent positions in different workspaces. Repositioning a shared window in one workspace should not affect its position in another workspace.*

DESIGN SOLUTION. *Position is part of a Placement, not a window.*

The independent location problem is also solved by the Placement mechanism. A Placement contains an x, y position for the bottom left corner of a particular window in the particular Room.

It is possible to go beyond the simple location of shared windows in the different Rooms to other aspects of presentation. For example, it may be desirable to have a text-editor window be large in one Room, but small in another. Or we may want the text-editor window to be squarish in one window, but tall and thin in another so as to fit into a differently arranged space. Or we may wish a window to have drop shadows in one Room, but not in another.

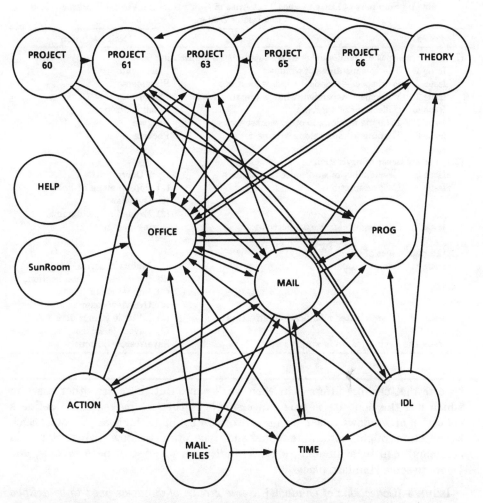

Fig. 11. Transitions among Rooms in a user's workspace. The diagram shows which Rooms have doors leading to other Rooms. It is an analog of Figure 4. Transitions through the Overview or pop-up menu are not shown.

ISSUE 3 [*Workspace-dependent shared-window presentation*]. *The shape, size, icon shrink location, drop-shadow attributes, and other aspects of the presentation of shared windows need to vary according to which Room the windows are in.*

DESIGN SOLUTION. *Presentation attributes are properties of Placements, not windows.*

Fortunately, the Placement mechanism is again a good solution to this issue. The Placement for each window in a Room contains slots for the presentation dimensions on which windows can vary.

3.1.3 *Sharing Collections of Tools across Tasks.* The issues above have derived from cases in which we want the same windows to have location and presentation

Table I.   Summary of Design Issues That Arise in Going from the Virtual Workspace Idea
to a Usable System

Issues		Design solution
(1) Interface issues of simultaneous access to separated information		
Issue 1	Multiple instances of windows	Placements
Issue 2	Workspace-dependent window locations	Placements
Issue 3	Workspace-dependent window presentations	Placements
Issue 4	Collections of windows	Room inclusion
Issue 5	Bringing windows to other workspaces	Baggage
Issue 6	Keeping windows along with user	Pockets
(2) Interface issues of navigation		
Issue 7	Reversibility of workspace transition	Back Doors
Issue 8	User orientation	(1) Pop-up menu of Rooms
		(2) Overview
		(3) Expanding pictograms
Issue 9	Showing workspace connectivity	Wiring diagrams
(3) Interface issues of tailorability		
Issue 11	Rooms redecoration	(1) Maintain normal LISP
		(2) Persistence of modifications
		(3) Pop-up menu
		(4) Overview commands
Issue 12	Unanticipated modifications structure	(1) Editable Rooms data
		(2) Layout language
Issue 13	Saving/restoring workspaces	Save/restore buttons

aspects that can be different in each workspace. But there are other cases in which just the opposite is true. An example is that we may wish to define a collection of windows to serve as a sort of control panel for many Rooms. Such a collection might contain a command typescript window (where typed-in commands can be evaluated), a clock, indicators for system performance, and Doors to some standard places.

ISSUE 4 [*Collections of windows*]. *Some groups of windows need to be defined as a collection whose location and positional attributes remain constant across workspaces. Changes to any of the windows need to be propagated to all workspaces containing them.*

DESIGN SOLUTION. *Room inclusion.*

Our solution to this problem is to allow Rooms to be included in other Rooms. A control panel is designed by making up a Room with the clock and other useful tools positioned together. We then make this Room an Inclusion of each Room that is to share the collection of windows. Resulting Rooms, when displayed to the user, will contain the combined set of windows. Figure 10 shows a control panel Room marked CONTROL that is contained in another Room. Figures 9a and b contain the windows in this control panel.

3.1.4 *Carrying Tools to Another Workspace.* So far we have not discussed how sharing of windows across workspaces arises. How can the user take a window that is in one workspace and carry it to another?

ISSUE 5 [*Carrying windows to other workspaces*]. *How can a set of windows be copied from one workspace to another?*

DESIGN SOLUTION 1. *Baggage.*

Our solution is to allow the user to carry some windows with him or her as the user transits to another workspace. The metaphor is that the user has Baggage that can be packed full of windows (actually, copies of Placements). The user presses a key while selecting a Door, which puts the user into a mode (with suitable feedback) in which he or she can point to all the windows wanted as Baggage. The Baggage goes through the Door with the user, and the windows assume their former positions, but in the new Room. The user can then reposition the windows in the new Room as desired.

DESIGN SOLUTION 2. *Overview move and copy commands.*

If the user is in the Overview or willing to go to the Overview, then the **MOVE** and **COPY** commands can be used to move or copy Placements rapidly from one Room to another.

Finally, there are applications in which the user wishes to define windows that are present no matter which workspace is used.

ISSUE 6 [*Keeping windows along*]. *In some applications windows need to be associated with the user rather than the workspace.*

DESIGN SOLUTION. *Pockets.*

The user can declare one Room to act as Pockets. This Room will be temporarily included in any Room the user enters. Thus, whichever windows are placed in the user's Pockets will be presented (at the same location and with the same presentation attributes) in all Rooms. A special application is that control panels can be included in a user's Pockets, if the user wants all Rooms to have the same control panel.

3.2 Interface Issues of Navigation

The Rooms system attempts to reduce space contention on the screen by distributing the user's windows into window locality sets in virtual workspaces. But this very fragmentation of the space creates a navigation problem: How can one keep track of the windows no longer visible and find one's way through the Rooms? If this challenge is not met, we shall only have replaced the electronic messy desk with an electronic maze. To keep the overall strategy viable, interface solutions must be found for this problem. Actually, the overall issue of navigation contains several subissues: (1) returning to a Room, (2) general orientation and finding other Rooms, (3) finding windows, and (4) finding which Rooms connect.

3.2.1 *Returning to a Room.* Frequently a user wishes to return from a present Room to the immediately prior Room. This can be a problem because Doors are one-way only. It can be even more of a problem if the user has forgotten the name of the previous Room or even what was being done before an interruption.

ISSUE 7 [*Reversibility of workspace transitions*]. *How can the user return to a previous workspace?*

DESIGN SOLUTION. *Back Doors.*

Each time a user enters a Room, a Door to the previously occupied Room is created and placed at a certain location. This Door is shown in reverse video to indicate that it is a Door back to the previous Room. An example is the reverse-video Door at the bottom left corner of Figure 9b. Further, the Door is destroyed after one use, and no Back Door is created when a Back Door is used to change Rooms. Back Doors reduce the task of returning to a previous Room from a major navigational undertaking to a trivial matter.

Other solutions are possible, but have disadvantages: All Doors could be bidirectional. The problem with this solution is that, when a Door is created in one Room, it would require placement of the Door in both the current visible Room and the indicated invisible Room. Either we would have to be willing to allow the new Door to appear over whatever happened to be in the other Room, or we would have to have an automatic window placement scheme (not a bad idea, but one beyond our current project). Also, Doors back to included Rooms would be conceptually obscure. Another problem with bidirectional Doors is that we want Back Doors to occur whether we entered the Room through a visible Door, through the pop-up menu, or through the Overview. In our system the Back Door is destroyed after one use because the meaning of Back Doors is to help the user return to where he or she just was, and multiple Back Doors would confuse this concept or complicate it with more interface mechanism.

3.2.2 *General Orientation and Finding Other Rooms.* A related problem is that the user can become disoriented. As the number of Rooms increases, the user can find it difficult to remember what Rooms exist. If there were to be a Door from every Room to every other Room, the Doors themselves would soon become unmanageable and consume inordinate amounts of screen space. Yet, without a fully connected topology, the space begins to become complex and difficult to remember—an electronic maze.

ISSUE 8 [*User orientation*]. *How can users remember (or discover) the route to particular workspaces?*

DESIGN SOLUTION 1. *Pop-up menu of Room names.*

The solution from within a Room is to have a pop-up menu that gives the names of the other Rooms (see Figure 12). The menu is a reminder of what Rooms exist, permitting selection of the one the user wants to go to. This solution is cheap in terms of response time, and, just as important, it is always available, even if the user deletes all the windows on the screen. However, it does not remind the user of the contents of the different Rooms.

DESIGN SOLUTION 2. *Overview.*

General orientation is achieved through the Overview. Figure 10 shows the Rooms Overview screen. The main feature of the Overview is a set of Room pictograms, reduced pictures of the Rooms, arranged in alphabetical order. All rooms are displayed, and the Room pictogram size is adjusted as Rooms are added and deleted. Windows within each Room are represented as rectangular window pictograms. From the Overview the user is reminded of the overall layout

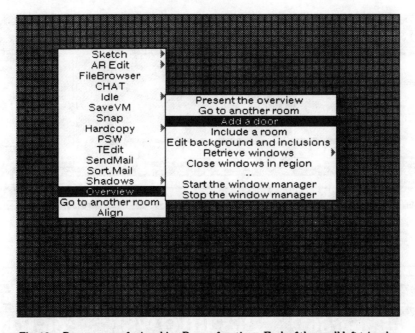

Fig. 12. Pop-up menu for invoking Rooms functions. Each of the small left triangles indicates where further expansion of the menu is possible (a standard Interlisp-D device). The menu has been expanded to show the main functions available through the menu. Since this menu is always available (by pressing the right mouse button when the cursor points to the screen background), the user is able to invoke Rooms commands even if all of the windows in a Room are deleted.

of a Room. The user can select a Room to enter by holding down the **OPEN** key while selecting a Room with the mouse. Design solution 1 (a pop-up menu) is fast, but gives only the names of the other Rooms. Design solution 2 (the Overview) takes a little longer, but gives the user much more information. The choice of one of these depends on the user's state of knowledge.

3.2.3 *Finding Windows.* Although the Room name and the shape and arrangement of window pictograms in the Overview definitely help the user's orientation, still more help is often needed to enable the user to locate particular windows or to be reminded of what particular pictograms mean.

ISSUE 9 [*Window identification*]. *How can the user identify particular windows in other Rooms from the Overview?*

DESIGN SOLUTION. *Expanding pictograms.*

The Rooms system permits the user to "expand in place" window pictograms pointed at by the mouse (Figure 13). It is worth noting that, whereas the Overview diagram is a space-multiplexed way of showing the whole view, the **EXPAND** key is a time-multiplexed technique. For reasons of speed, legibility, and versimilitude, the window is shown at full scale, as indicated by the selected Placement, instead of the information in the Room being scaled to fit the pictogram.

303

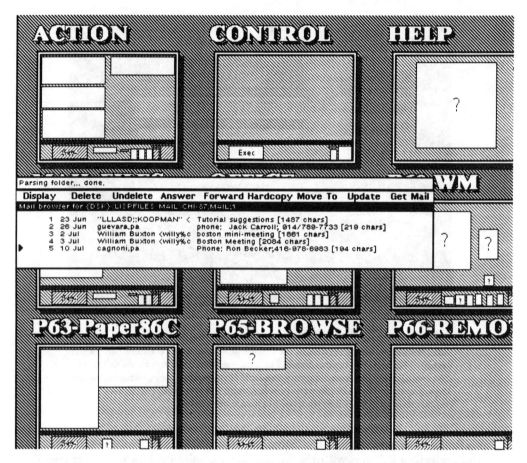

Fig. 13. Example of an **EXPAND**ed window. **EXPAND**ing windows is a time-multiplexed technique that allows the user to learn a large amount of information about the multiple workspaces in the system without crowding the display.

3.2.4 *Finding Which Rooms Connect.* From the Overview diagram, it is difficult to discover which Rooms have Doors to, or are included in, which other Rooms.

ISSUE 10 [*Workspace connectivity*]. *How can the user see the connections between Rooms?*

DESIGN SOLUTION. *Wiring diagrams.*

A solution to this problem is to trace out on the display a diagram showing the connections between Rooms. Figure 14 shows an example of such a diagram (**DOORS-OUT**, the set of Rooms to which the subject Room has Doors). Several such diagrams are available **DOORS-OUT, DOORS-IN, INCLUDES-ROOMS,** and **INCLUDED-IN-ROOMS.** Because of the complexity of the possible connections between Rooms and the desire not to rearrange the Overview display to simplify the connection lines (which would drastically decrease Room pictogram size), having the user interrogate one Room at a time is more successful

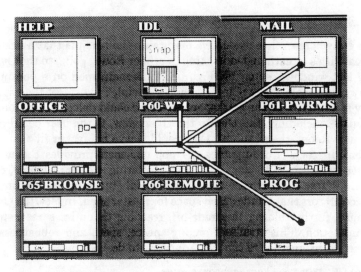

Fig. 14. Wiring diagrams. This is another time-multiplexed technique
that allows the user to see which windows are connected to which others.

than asking for all the connections simultaneously. This is another case in which
we fall back to the time-multiplexing of information, since showing all connections at the same time reduces the display to a tangle of lines.

3.3 Interface Issues of User Presentation Tailorability

User's workspaces change continually. Provision must therefore be made for
users to reconfigure their workspaces easily: altering windows; adding and deleting Doors; creating, deleting, and renaming Rooms. All these can be expected to
occur in the course of normal work.

3.3.1 Manipulating Rooms, Windows, and Doors

ISSUE 11 [*Room redecoration*]. *How can users manage the creation and deletion
of Rooms, windows, Doors, etc?*

DESIGN SOLUTION 1. *Maintain a normal Interlisp-D environment.*

The Rooms system is designed so that users have the illusion that they are in
a normal Interlisp-D window environment. Thus they can engage in all the
normal Interlisp-D window manipulations: creating, destroying, copying, and
moving windows or shrinking them into icons. Closing a window that exists in
more than one Room brings up a menu giving the user the choice of deleting
only this Placement or of deleting all Placements and closing the window itself.

DESIGN SOLUTION 2. *Persistence of window modifications.*

A related part of the design solution is that small changes users make in the
course of their work persist over entering and leaving Rooms. When reentering
a workspace, the user finds it arranged just as it was when he or she left it (the
contents of shared windows may well have changed, of course). Modifications to
a Room are accurately reflected in the Overview.

305

DESIGN SOLUTION 3. *Pop-up menu.*

Here, as elsewhere in the system, we maintain the principle that a basic set of system capabilities (creating Doors, going to other Rooms, going to the Overview, recovering lost windows, etc.) (see Figure 12) is maintained on a pop-up menu that is always available. One reason for this principle is to protect the user: Since completely free to design the workspace, the user could delete all the Doors from this workspace, including the Door to the Overview. Or the user could create a Door to a new Room, then enter it; this would leave him or her in a completely blank Room. In such circumstances the pop-up menu provides the user with adequate rescue controls. It does so without violating another principle, that the user should be free to determine the total physical appearance of a Room. Doors are thus accelerators that trade screen space for faster speed. In fact, the Overview just continues further along this trade-off, trading the entire screen space for rapid manipulation. This trade-off among space, speed, and robustness is the basic reason for having more than one solution to design issues.

DESIGN SOLUTION 4. *Overview commands.*

Some operations by users involve more than one Room, for example, moving windows from one Room to another or copying a Room. To make these easier, the Rooms system provides a set of commands available in the Overview (Table II). Generic commands (**COPY** and **DELETE**) can apply either to a Placement of a window in a Room or to a Room itself, according to which button on the mouse is used to select the object. Other commands (**MOVE, RESHAPE, RENAME**) apply only to one or the other.

An easy way to create a new Room, with a layout and Placements the user likes, is to press **COPY** and then select an existing Room. The system asks for the name of the new Room, then creates the new Room, and rearranges the Overview to show it (reducing the size of Room pictograms if necessary). The user could then delete any unwanted windows in the new Room by holding down **DELETE** while selecting the window pictogram with the mouse "Placement button" (left button). A similar mechanism can be used to include one Room in another.

3.3.2 *Extended Behavior and Appearance.* Although Rooms provides a number of single methods by which users can tailor their workspaces, we believe it is prudent to provide for a system's natural evolution by supplying escape hatches that enable more sophisticated and daring users to extend the system or modify it to serve their own purposes. Rooms descriptors are the mechanisms by which the advanced users in the community can achieve new effects and extensions quickly without rebuilding the system or understanding all its parts. Successful features are then given more general user interfaces.

ISSUE 12 [*Unanticipated modifications*]. *How can we provide a means for systems programmers to evolve the system by creating more complex effects?*

DESIGN SOLUTION. *Editing of Room descriptors.*

Each Room can have associated with it expressions that will be evaluated in conjunction with certain significant events (creating a Room, leaving a Room,

Table II.   Overview Commands

Command	Mode key(s)	Description
Overview commands for manipulating Placements[a]		
Move	**MOVE, M**	A Placement is moved within a Room or from one Room to another Room.
Shape	**SHAPE, S**	A Placement is reshaped within a Room or into another Room.
Copy	**COPY, C**	A copy of a Placement is made in another Room.
Delete	**DELETE, D**	A Placement is deleted from a Room.
Expand	**EXPAND, ?**	The window associated with a Placement can be temporarily viewed as the Placement indicates.
Overview commands for manipulating Rooms[b]		
Enter	**OPEN, O**	The Overview is left and the indicated Room entered.
New	**NEW, N**	A name is requested and the Room is renamed.
Edit	**EDIT, E**	A structural description of the Room is made available for editing. The changes take effect when the editing is finished. More than one Room may be modified at a time, permitting copying structure from one description to another.
Copy	**COPY, C**	A name is requested and a copy of the Room is made.
Rename	**RENAME, R**	A name is requested and the Room is renamed.
Delete	**DELETE,D**	The Room is deleted.
Doors-out	**DOORS-OUT**	The set of Rooms to which Doors in the indicated Room lead is displayed in Figure 14.
Doors-in	**DOORS-IN**	Like Doors-out, but the set of Rooms that have doors into the indicated Room is displayed.
Includes	**INCLUDES**	The set of Rooms that the indicated Room includes is displayed in a diagram similar to Figure 14.
Included-in	**INCLUDED-IN**	Like Includes, but the set of Rooms in which the indicated Room is included is displayed.
Overview commands for manipulating collections of Rooms[c]		
Save	**SAVE**	A set of Rooms is indicated by selecting maps (default is all the Rooms), a file name is requested, and a description of the set of Rooms is written onto the file.
Restore (Augment)	**RESTORE (AUGMENT)**	A file name is requested, and a set of Rooms is reconstituted from the descriptions on that file. The set of current Rooms is replaced (extended) with this reconstituted set.

[a] These commands are issued by depressing a mode key and buttoning the pictogram for the Placement with the left button on the mouse.
[b] These commands are issued by depressing a mode key and buttoning the map for the Room with the right button on the mouse.
[c] These commands are issued by selecting button-shaped windows appropriately labeled.

placing a window, hiding a window, saving a Room on a file, or restoring a Room). These are made available to the (advanced) user by making a descriptor of the editable Room through the normal structured program editor. A description of the background for the Room, an expression in a layout language (Table III), is

Table III. Layout Language for Rooms Background Graphics

Specification	Description
(WHOLEBACKGROUND shade)	Shades the whole background.
(WHOLEBACKGROUND bit map)	Tessellates the whole background with the bit map.
(BOX shade region operation)	Shades a region using the graphic operation. Graphics operations are replace, paint, erase, and invert.
(FRAME shade region width operation)	Frames a region with a shaded frame of a particular width using the graphic operation.
(BITMAP bit-map region operation)	Places the bit map clipped by the region using the graphic operation.
(TESSELLATE bit-map region operation)	Tessellates the region with the bit map using the graphic operation.
(TEXT string font position operation)	Places the text in the font starting at the position using the graphic operation. In this operation graphics operations include an extension for describing drop shadows and smearing.
(BORDER shade)	Sets the border region (from the edge of the screen to the bezel of the display) to be the shade.
(IF (condition spec ... spec) ...)	Carries out the specifications contained in the first clause whose condition is satisfied. Conditions are Interlisp-D forms treated as predicates.
(EVAL action)	Escape to Interlisp-D: Action is an Interlisp-D form that is evaluated, presumably for its graphic effect on the background.
(COMMENT ...)	A message to humans that has no effect on the background graphics.

Notes:

The background graphics for a Room is described by a list of graphic specifications that are executed in order, each affecting the results of the ones carried out before it.

All arguments can be either literal (for simple expression of the common cases) or forms to be evaluated (another escape clause to Interlisp-D).

also part of the Room descriptor. By holding down the **EDIT** key while pointing to a Room in the Overview, the user can "turn the pictogram of the Room around to reveal the clockwork mechanisms on the back" (Figure 15). On completion of editing, the system checks the structure of the Room descriptor to provide error protection before rendering the Room. This editing facility has been used to build elaborate graphical backgrounds and for other tasks, such as checking whether certain files are loaded before entering a Room.

3.3.3 *Saving and Restoring.* Finally, the system will not be successful unless it is possible to save, restore, and add to a user's suite of workspaces via information stored on files. If a system crash or reload/reinitialization means that the user must rebuild a suite of Rooms from scratch, few users will persist, and Rooms will not be successful in helping users to manage their screen space.

ISSUE 13 [*Saving/restoring workspaces*]. *How can a user save and restore workspace?*

DESIGN SOLUTION. *Save/restore buttons and Room descriptions.*

It should first be realized that a Room cannot be saved directly. Rooms contain complex structures including windows, large bit maps, file pointers, network

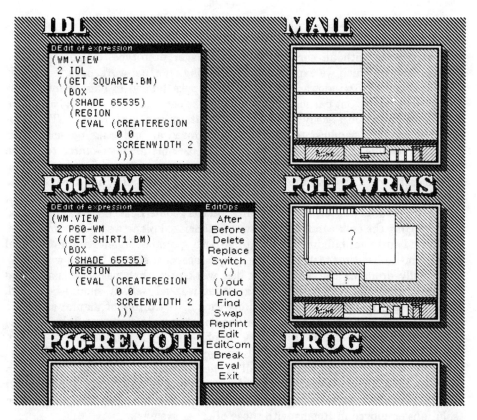

Fig. 15. Editing the Rooms description by "turning the window around to get at the clockwork on the back." Alterations to a Room will take effect as soon as the user exits from the editor for that Room.

streams, and other objects difficult to save. For this reason it is necessary to create an abstracted description of each Room such that the Room could be largely reconstructed from the description. Although the issues here are those farthest removed from the central mission of the Rooms system, they are also the most complex to program. Entries can be provided to users' initialization profiles so that, even when the user starts up a completely new system, the same Rooms structure will be created, complete with text editors open to the same files, etc. For the few cases in which this is not possible (e.g., an application not registered with the system), dummy windows still appear with indications of original titles to aid the user in remembering where he or she was. A facility is provided to allow users to save or load selected Rooms as a mechanism to enable them to design and exchange window designs and applications.

4. DISCUSSION

In Rooms, we adopted the multiple-virtual-workspace solution to the small-screen problem. This solution is used in conjunction with other techniques: Windows can be opened and closed, shrunk and overlapped, even moved off-screen within the same virtual workspace. In addition to the analysis presented above, our use of the multiple-virtual-workspace solution also reflects our experience with an earlier window manager prototype, called BigScreen (Figure 16), in which we explored the large single-virtual-workspace technique. We observed that windows laid out in this space tended to cluster into those necessary to carry out particular tasks, and that user movement quickly reduced to simple jumps into easily named areas on the plane (e.g., MAIL). To put it another way, the windows tended to get organized around tasks (generic tasks like mail reading or specific projects), and the user mainly just wanted to switch among familiar tasks. Task switching seemed to have a nonspatial representation in the user's mind: Tasks were easy to name ("read the mail"), but hard to locate in space (Is mail north or south of here?). In fact, the relative arrangement in space of the tasks was largely irrelevant, and the geometrical constraints entailed by arranging the task windows on a two-dimensional plane were just a nuisance. We found ourselves building accelerators (both spatial overviews and nonspatial pop-up menu lists) for task switching. The conceptual step to Rooms was small, essentially dropping the single extended workspace that was a nuisance and retaining the multiple spatial contexts that worked well. It should be noted, however, that there may be applications with a very different mental structure for the user (e.g., browsing unfamiliar documentation or computer-aided design) in which either the spatial proximity or physical analog properties of a large virtual workspace could be used to advantage.

As in other systems in which not all of the information is visible at any given moment, the Rooms system faced the questions of (1) navigation and (2) simultaneous access to separated information. We now contrast the design solutions employed in Rooms with those of other systems.

Navigation. Rooms provides a pop-up menu listing the Rooms and an Overview showing pictograms of all Rooms and their Placements. This is like the Smalltalk Project Browser or, more particularly, the Cedar desktop overview. Chin's Room system, by contrast, has no such Overview. Our experience suggests that navigation tends to be easier in a multiple-virtual-workspace system than in either a large single workspace or a hypertext system. In a large single workspace, an overview picture of the workspace tends to make the details of the overview picture too small to use. In a hypertext system, the workspace is fragmented into so many pieces that either the entire structure is too large to show, or, although it can be shown, the details of the overview graphics are too small to use or the user must settle for partial browsers (e.g., the user lays out the structure for one type of link). In a multiple-virtual-workspace system like Rooms, Smalltalk Projects, Cedar desktops, or CCA, the multiple workspaces provide a level of aggregation appropriate for overview displays.

Like hypertext systems, Rooms does provide (in the Overview) for querying the connectivity of the structure. Rooms also provides a trace of the user's motions through the space via its use of Back Doors. This is similar to the dynamic stack of Chin's Room system, but it has the advantage of not requiring any additional mechanism within the system, since Back Doors are Interlisp-D windows (and so can have actions associated with input events) just like any other Door. Finally, Rooms provides Doors, parallels for which exist in many

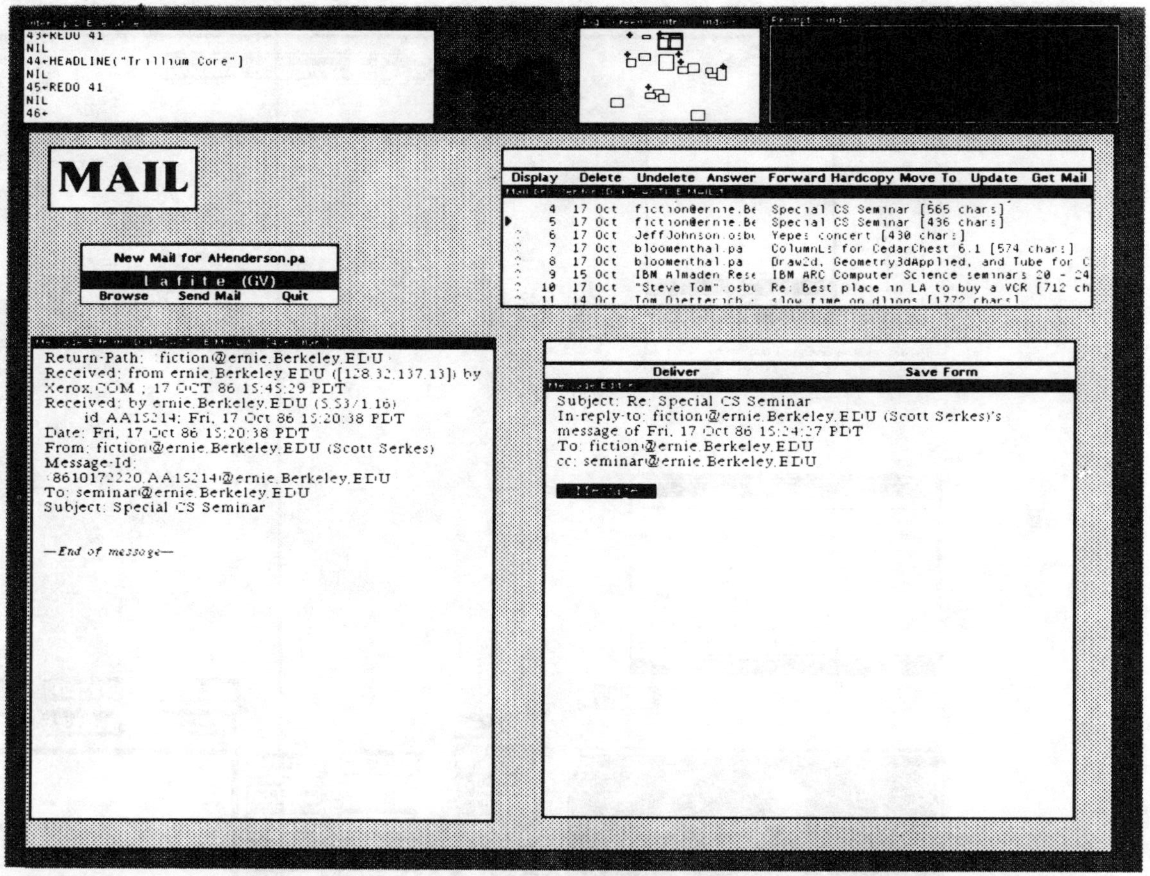

Fig. 16. BigScreen. This screen image from the BigScreen experimental system, a precursor to Rooms, shows a framed view of the mail area of a large virtual workspace. An overview of the workspace is presented in the control window (at top center). The overview contains pictograms of windows, named locations (marked with +), and the position of the current view (the heavy rectangle). The user moves the view either by selecting a named location (presaging Rooms) or by repositioning the view rectangle in the control window. Windows in the frame do not move (presaging Rooms's panels), and windows are used to identify named locations (presaging Rooms's background graphics). This system was considered unsatisfactory because of the need to have the same window in more than one location in the workspace.

311

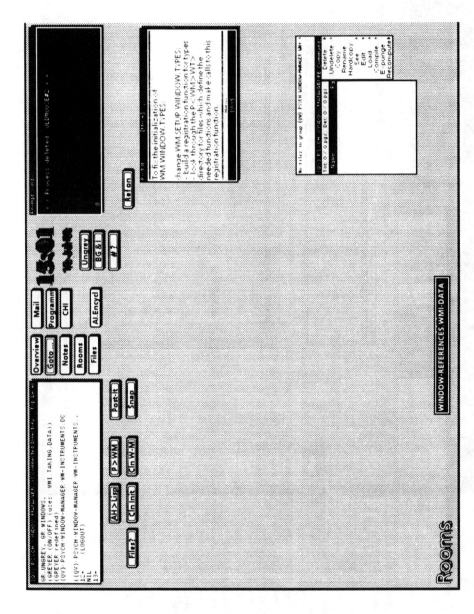

Fig. 17. Example of how the effective availability of more screen space enables a user to use the screen space for shortcuts. The buttons each call small programs for common tasks, such as connecting to a directory. This would be a lavish use of space without the Rooms system.

other systems (often even *named* "doors"). Some systems limit the functionality of these doors to motions within the structure of the system (in Smalltalk Projects and many others the doors move only up and down the hierarchy). In Rooms, doors support movement, as in hypertext systems, to any other Room and even to the Overview.

Simultaneous access to separate information. An advance of Rooms over previous systems is in the mechanisms worked out to share individual windows among workspaces through Placements and to share collections of windows through inclusion. In Smalltalk Projects, windows are partitioned among the workspaces. They cannot easily occur in several workspaces at the same time. Cedar multiple desktops does have a facility for allowing this, similar to our Placements, but the interface mechanisms that allow the user to take easy advantage of this facility are not developed. In large virtual-workspace systems, like Dataland, and in distortion systems, information can be moved among work areas, but only at the expense of destroying existing arrangements. This difficulty also appeared in our large virtual-workspace system BigScreen and was a factor in our progressing to the Rooms design.

Our early use of the Rooms system suggests the following ways in which it seems to impact the use of screen space: (1) A greater amount of information is kept in the total workspace (e.g., more windows and larger windows); (2) screens are less crowded (because information is distributed among workspaces, each related to a single task); and (3) users find new ways of consuming screen space for their convenience, particularly by using accelerators for common tasks.

With the pressure for screen space reduced, we have discovered a tendency to use some of this extra space to reduce the time required to do common tasks. Figure 9a shows one such use: a Room with several mail browsers already laid out. Normally, the user would reduce these browsers to icons or close them altogether. But, with a special mail Room, the browsers can be left open, ready for instant use, both saving considerable time and allowing the user to have a better overall picture of the incoming mail. Furthermore, because the layout will not be disturbed by the next task, the user can afford to spend more time carefully arranging the windows in the Room for maximum productivity. Another example is Figure 17. Here the user has created special "buttons" (icons that execute arbitrary code when selected) for a number of tasks. The buttons, which can be created in seconds, function like macrooperators and seem to boost user efficiency substantially.

5. CONCLUSION

We would argue that a major purpose of research into human–computer interaction is to discover and analyze *key constraints* that are the drivers of human performance and to use the representation of the problem gleaned from that analysis as tools for thought in design.

In the present case our analysis concludes that part of the "electronic messy-desk problem" derives from a screen-space resource contention. The severity of this contention depends on screen size and on the locality of window reference for the activities in which the user is engaged. We have attempted to use the representation of the problem provided by this analysis as the basis of a design for a virtual-workspace system Rooms. In the course of a design there arise a number of issues that must be faced in order to maintain the viability of the design. In Rooms these arise from navigation among workspaces, from simultaneous access to information in different workspaces, and in tailoring Rooms for particular application and appearance.

Complementing this derivation of design from theory are new perspectives on theory from experience with implementing and using designs. In the present case the emergent needs for sharing windows and sets of windows and the support needed for navigation have elaborated the structure of the phase-and-transition window faulting model. These insights, if not simply artifacts of the particular design, can offer new grist for our theoretical mill. We believe that these two processes, theory to design, design to theory, must complement one another for good design—or good theory.

ACKNOWLEDGMENTS

The resource-contention theory on which the design of Rooms is based derives from work done jointly with Misha Pavel and Joyce Farrell. The authors would like to thank Melissa Monty for discussions on the relevance of task switching to workspaces, John Maxwell and Dan Swinehart for discussions on Cedar windows, and Sue Booker for advice on graphics.

REFERENCES

1. BOLT, R. A. *The Human Interface*. Lifetime Learning Publications, Belmont, Calif., 1984.
2. CARD, S. K., AND HENDERSON, D. A., JR. A multiple virtual-workspace interface to support user task switching. In *CHI '87 Conference on Human Factors in Computing Systems* (Toronto, Canada, Apr. 6–9). ACM/SIGCHI, New York, 1987.
3. CARD, S. K., PAVEL, M., AND FARRELL, J. Window-based computer dialogues. In *Human-Computer Interaction—Interact '84*, B. Shackel, Ed. North-Holland, Amsterdam, 1985, pp. 239–243.
4. CHAN, P. P. Learning considerations in user interface design: The Room model. Tech. Rep. CS-84-16, Dept. of Computer Science, Univ. of Waterloo, Ontario, Canada, 1984.
5. DENNING, P. J. The working set model for program behavior. *Commun. ACM 11*, 5 (May 1968), 323–333.
6. DENNING, P. J. Virtual memory. *ACM Comput. Surv. 2*, 3 (Sept. 1970), 153–189.
7. DENNING, P. J. Working sets past and present. *IEEE Trans. Softw. Eng. SE-6*, 1 (Jan. 1980), 66–84.
8. DISESSA, A. A principled design for an integrated computational environment. *Hum.-Comput. Interaction 1*, 1 (Jan. 1985), 1–47.
9. DONAHUE, J., AND WIDOM, J. Whiteboards: A graphical database tool. *ACM Trans. Off. Inf. Syst. 4*, 1 (Jan. 1986), 24–41.
10. ENGELBART, D. C., AND ENGLISH, W. K. A research center for augmenting human intellect. In *Proceedings of the AFIPS Fall Joint Computer Conference*, vol. 33 (San Francisco, Calif., Dec. 9–11). AFIPS Press, Reston, Va., 1968, pp. 395–410.
11. FEINER, S., NAGY, S., AND VAN DAM, A. An experimental system for creating and presenting interactive graphical documents. *ACM Trans. Graph. 1*, 1 (Jan. 1982), 59–77.
12. FISHER, S. S., McGREEVY, M., HUMPHRIES, J., AND ROBINETT, W. Virtual environment display system. In *Proceedings of the 1986 Workshop on Interactive 3D Graphics*, F. Crow and S. M. Pizer, Eds. (Chapel Hill, N.C., Oct.). ACM, New York, 1986. To be published.
13. FURNESS, G. Generalized fisheye views. In *CHI '86 Conference on Human Factors in Computing Systems*, M. Mantei and P. Orbeton, Eds. (Boston, Mass., Apr. 14–18). ACM/SIGCHI, New York, 1986, pp. 16–23.

14. GOLDBERG, A. *Smalltalk-80: The Interactive Programming Environment.* Addison-Wesley, Reading, Mass., 1984.
15. HALASZ, F., MORAN, T., AND TRIGG, R. NoteCards in a nutshell. In *CHI '87 Conference on Human Factors in Computing Systems* (Toronto, Canada, Apr. 6–9). ACM/SIGCHI, New York, 1987.
16. HEROT, C. F. Spatial management of data. *ACM Trans. Database Syst. 5,* 4 (Dec. 1980), 493–514.
17. HURST, J., AND WALKER, K., EDS. *The Problem-Oriented System.* MEDCOM Press, New York, 1972.
18. KAHN, K. C. Program behavior and load dependent system performance. Ph.D. dissertation, Dept. of Computer Science, Purdue Univ., West Lafayette, Ind., Aug. 1976.
19. MADISON, A. W. *Characteristics of Program Localities.* University Microfilms International, Ann Arbor, Mich., 1982.
20. MCGREGOR, S. The viewer window package. In *The Cedar System: An Anthology of Documentation,* J. H. Horning, Ed. Tech. Rep. CSL-83-14, Xerox Palo Alto Research Center, Palo Alto, Calif., 1983.
21. MONTY, L. In *Human–Computer Interaction—Interact '84,* B. Shackel, Ed. North-Holland, Amsterdam, 1985, pp. 603–609.
22. ROBERTSON, G., NEWELL, A., AND RAMAKRISHNA, K. The ZOG approach to man–machine communication. *Int. J. Man–Machine Studies 14,* 4 (May 1981), 461–488.
23. SMITH, D. Pygmalion. Ph.D. dissertation, Dept. of Computer Science, Stanford Univ., Stanford, Calif., 1975.
24. SMITH, D. C., IRBY, C., KIMBALL, R., VERPLANK, W., AND HARSLEM, E. Designing the Star user interface. *Byte 7,* 4 (Apr. 1982), 242–282.
25. SPENCE, R., AND APPERLY, M. Data base navigation: An office environment for the professional. *Behav. Inf. Technol. 1,* 1 (Jan. 1982), 43–54.
26. SUTHERLAND, I. E. Sketchpad: A man–machine graphical communication system. In *AFIPS Spring Joint Computer Conference,* vol. 23, 1963, pp. 329–346.

Received July 1986; revised November 1986; accepted November 1986

Approaching Group Communication by Means of an Office Building Metaphor

Christian M. Madsen
Computer Science Department, Aarhus University
Ny Munkegade 116 - DK 8000 Aarhus C - Denmark
E-mail: cmm@daimi.aau.dk

ABSTRACT

This is a description of what one might call an environment for cooperative work. The work falls in two parts: First a conceptual framework for cooperative work is approached by way of the transaction cost theory of organizations [4]. The rest of the paper describes ideas for a system that supports cooperation as it is outlined in the first part.

1. Framework. A Transaction Cost Approach to Information Systems

Since the emergence of the term cooperative work a lot of consideration has been given to the question of what cooperative work is. It is not the aim of this work to contribute to this discussion. Rather the term cooperative work is used to describe work that goes on in organizations be it offices, firms, research laboratories or whatever. A very limited part of such work can be said to be totally individual. Even when an employee is writing a letter or a report he is building on a set of shared concepts, shared information within the organization which he is part of and thus in a sense he is cooperating. Thus in this paper the term cooperative work is given very wide limits.

One of the key issues in systems for support of cooperative work is communication. Sørgaard [16] operates with two forms of communication: Explicit - and by means of shared material. These two forms of communication work together, it is not a matter of one or the other. Also Thompson [17] emphasize the need to share information in order to be able to communicate. This implies that a communication system should not only support electronic mail, conference systems and other forms of explicit communication. Rather these should just be facilities in a system based on a shared and well-structured representation of all the information - all the shared material - of the organization. Thus an information system along these lines forms the basis of the environment system described later. Here cooperative work in terms of communication within an information system will be addressed.

A fundamental aspect of the theory of organizations is that people do not necessarily share goals and perspective, but rather opportunistic behavior must be anticipated (See [4] among others). No matter how broad or narrow one chooses to define the term cooperative work this element of opportunistic behavior among participators is inherent. One must be conscious of this fact when designing systems for cooperation, and when discussing a theoretic approach to cooperative work. To this end a theory of organizations that recognizes this opportunistic behavior must be employed in order to obtain a theoretical framework for cooperation. We have stopped at the transaction cost approach, because its classifications of organizations into market bureaucracy and clan correspond somewhat to the broad variety of different cooperative work settings, as will be further argued below.

Ciborra and others distinguishes between three mechanisms for controlling economic transactions: Market, Bureaucracy and Clan.

- A market is an assemblage of persons desirous of exchanging property, with prices serving both as incentives and coordinating guides to producers. Market requires very little know-ledge of the participants, i.e. their own needs and the prices, and no necessity for a central all-knowing authority.

- In a bureaucracy, market transactions are eliminated and in their place we find an entrepreneur-coordinator who is the authority.

"Approaching Group Communication by Means of an Office Building Metaphor" by C.M. Madsen, previously published in *First European Conference on Computer-Supported Cooperative Work*, September 1989, pages 449-460. Reprinted with permission of the author.

- Finally, there are situations where products and services are so complex, transactions so ambiguous that the parties involved in the exchanges have to trust each other and give up any attempt at a shortsighted calculation of the reciprocal cost and benefits acquiring from the exchange. In a clan networks of exchanges are governed in a stable manner by informal relationships of trust.

Transactions well suited for a market are characterized by low uncertainty and the market organization are able to tolerate a high degree of opportunistic behavior, whereas clans are vulnerable to opportunistic behavior and are better suited to control transactions with a high degree of uncertainty. Bureaucracies are characterized by a formal hierarchical organization enforcing control on information transactions. Thus a bureaucracy is able to cope with more complex patterns of transactions than can market type organizations, and are able to cope with opportunistic behavior by way of its formal rules and procedures.

As computer technology develops and more and more information processing power is made available to organizations, information is becoming the key asset of organizations. So what we want to look at is the transaction of information and the characteristics of the organizations controlling these transactions. In other words: In stead of viewing information as something that helps control transactions, information itself is viewed as the subject for transaction. Thus in the following, when clan, bureaucracy or market organization is mentioned, what is meant is that the organization controlling information transactions have clan, bureaucracy or market characteristics. Now, just as opportunistic behavior is realized in systems of economic transactions, conflicting interests of users of the information system is recognized as rational and legitimate.

Consider an information system controlled exclusively by market. A user of the system might for example have one or more of the following reasons for submitting a piece of information to the information system.

- He is explicitly asked to do so.
- He wants to express an opinion on a certain matter or in other ways influence other members of the organization.
- He wants to obtain recognition for a certain piece of work.
- He needs critique or other feedback on some work.

All these reasons give way for a relative straightforward - although not all that rational - cost benefit analysis for the persons submitting the information. "Considering my aim, is it worthwhile to make this contribution or not?" In the first case he will probably expect something in return for the information which he provides, and in the last three more or less explicit gains are acquired. Markets are characterized by allowing such simple cost benefit analyses.
In present information systems the amount of information produced is usually much larger than what one person can consume. Thus also in the consumption of information a clear cost benefit weighing must be utilized: Is the information worthwhile reading or not.
Several authors have discussed ways to overcome the ``information overload", eg. [11] and [13].

What has been described above is a rather simplified and idealistic picture of an information system. Often the organization in which the system is embedded has more or less formalized procedures for its use. Thus incentives for reading and submitting items in the system are guided by rules and requirements of the organization. Notice however that these rules are often outside the information system itself.
Take as an example a filing system for case files in a public administration office which has rules that prescribes workers to submit certain types of file for each case. There is no way to tailor a file cabinet or an electronic file server so that it demands journals of every case from the employees. In other words the formal organization or bureaucracy control of information transactions are implemented in the organization *surrounding* the information system, it is not directly supported in the system itself.

There are other types of motives for reading / submitting information in an information system. These are of a more irrational kind: Social connectivity, community feeling, mutual responsibility etc. These are not easy to calculate, and are certainly not base for any cost- benefit analysis. These are incentives that characterize a clan organization.

It is now clear to see in which type of organization opportunistic behavior is more common. In a market each individual can make his own cost-benefit analysis without concern of the ``common good". In bureaucracies this is in part prevented by the rules governing the transactions. In the ideal clan opportunistic behavior is in contrast to the incentives mentioned for reading and submitting information. Based on the above it is argued that information systems by them selves in general only support markets for information transactions, and that bureaucracy and clan characteristics are mainly implemented in the surrounding organization. This will be the case to a large extend no mater what information system is provided. In many conference systems aspects of clan organizations can be simulated by using a closed conference, but that does not create an actual working environment for clan work. It merely provides a shared space.

Below three examples of ways of cooperating are identified, one example of each sort of cooperation as classified above:

1. Actually working together on a task. A prototypical example of this kind of cooperation is two or more persons sitting and working together on the same material.
2. Divide and combine. Splitting a task into sub-tasks, performing these in parallel and combining the sub-tasks.
3. Using the work of others. Drawing on online or off-line sources when working on some tasks. Eg. citing published articles when writing a thesis.

These three reflect the different degrees of cooperation, from working very close together down to the point of cooperators not even being aware of each other or even of the fact that they are cooperating. Real cooperative work is often a combination of two or even all three of these modes.

Summary.

Above information transactions have been discussed in terms of the controlling organizations forms, and it has been established that current information systems only to a very low degree support clan and bureaucracy type organizations.

The point of this discussion was to make it clear that such distinctions are in fact relevant in the discussion of organizations. Whether the different formations and organizations of groups in organizations actually maps onto this theoretic description is a matter of dispute. The point to be used in the following is that organization members should be given the opportunity to self-organize into the kind of group structures that are relevant, not forcing a particular view on what such structures should look like.

A conceptual framework has now been established. This was done in three steps. First a number of theoretical issues were discussed and clarified, and it was made clear in what perspective this work is seen. Secondly some of the traditional features and system for communication in organizations were discussed briefly. Finally a concept of organization structures controlling information transactions were developed out of the transaction cost theory.

Out of this framework the following criterions can now be established for measuring how well an information system supports cooperative work:

- It should support both explicit communication and shared material, and the formation of a shared information space.

- It should be transparent both with regards to origin and context of information, but at the same time it should not violate the privacy of the individual, keeping in mind the possible lack of shared interests among members of organizations.

- It should support the formation of organizational structures not only for market- but also for clan and bureaucracy type organizations.

- It should provide support for a wide range of cooperative settings ranging form on line communication on multiple channels to accessing the work of other users.

318

2. Design

In the following a design of an information system to support the work processes that goes on in organizations along the lines of the presented framework will be described. The description is meant as a vision of a system more than a formal design description. Thus less concern is given to the problems of implementing such a system.

There are two cornerstones on which the design of the system rests: One is the concept of a shared information space represented by a hypertext system in which every information item in the organization is stored in order to support the information market present in the organization[1]. The implications of the hypertext representation will be discussed below.

The other cornerstone is the metaphor used for creating both the developers and the users conceptual view of the system.

The Office Building Metaphor.

A popular metaphor for designing office systems for individuals is the desktop. But when it comes to cooperative work this metaphor is no longer sufficient. In a way, it is not large enough. Instead the office building is chosen as a metaphor as it embraces the entire environment of office work. An office building contains, besides the offices of individuals, several rooms that are more or less shared amongst the "inhabitants": The Hallway, Conference rooms, Group working rooms, Library and Archives, Coffee-room or Canteen, Reception etc.

The concept of a room becomes central in the system.[2] The system contains a number of different classes of rooms, corresponding to the ones mentioned above. Each of these rooms corresponds to a "section" of the "information space" (These concepts will be explained later) and is equipped with facilities for information management and communication as well as the usual facilities available in office systems such as editors and other applications. Some rooms are shared by the entire organization, others are shared by a few people and jet others are private to one person.

Each **individual** has his own **room**, corresponding to the idea of an individual office, where the individual can keep his private documents. The private office room is the normal working environment of the individual.

A **group working room** is a construct that allows two or more people to share workspace and working environment. The members of the group can access all information present in the section of the group room and they are able to configure the room with a number of different tools for communication and information management. Some of these tools will be described in a later section; here is just a few examples of their implications. When one enters a group room, it is immediately visible if there are other persons present. If so, one is allowed to look at what the others are doing.

The group can define its own bulletin boards corresponding to closed conferences in a conference system, as well as mechanisms for handling incoming mail items. Eg. it should be possible to send a request for some action to a group who then internally decides who is going to carry it out On entering the group room all changes to the state of the rooms can be seen in a special window: New entrances to the bulletin boards, new nodes or links in the hypertext section, and other kinds of new objects in the room. The group members are able to work together by sharing screens.

Information is shared in a way that keeps the individual in charge of what information he allows the other group members to see. Thus the contents of the private rooms of the group members are not available to the group.

From outside a group looks the same as an individual; a section of the information space, and a mail address.

With this group construct it becomes possible to model organizational structures such as clans and bureaucracies. A clan structure is simply a group with probably no more than ten members. The group

----

1: This idea dates back to Vanever Bush in 1945 [3] and later Engelbart in his Augment system actually constructed something similar to this. [7] and [8]

2: The 1100 series of Xerox workstations runs a system called "Rooms". This does little more than just enable the user to shift between a number of work areas which are totally defined by himself. Although this system has served as an inspiration, the room concept described in this paper is quite different from Xerox "Rooms".

must be small enough to make formal structures unnecessary, and the members must in general know each other and share a certain amount of confidence, or at least be aware of each other's perspectives and intentions. The information transactions are organized by way of the configuration of the room (see below) and by the organization of the section of the hypertext system belonging to the group.

Likewise bureaucracies can be modeled by means of one or more group rooms and by using enforcing certain rules and procedures controlling information transactions.

The conference room is where electronic conferences and discussions take place. This corresponds to the open conferences of a conference system. The conference system contains a hierarchy of sub-conferences corresponding to a hierarchy of subsections of the information system. This is the structure of many conferencing systems eg. CONFER [9], Andrew [1].

Entrances to a conference are submitted by placing them in the conference section optionally linked to other objects in the conference, eg by one of the following link types: response, comment, agree, disagree, protest, continue, etc. It is also possible to enter an object by mailing it to the conference. Each subscriber has a facility by which links to new messages are kept. On entering a conference three windows appear (see fig 1): The browser of the conference section, The container of new messages and a display for reading. When a link is chosen from the container of new messages, the message appear in the display, and it is marked in the browser, in order to show the context.

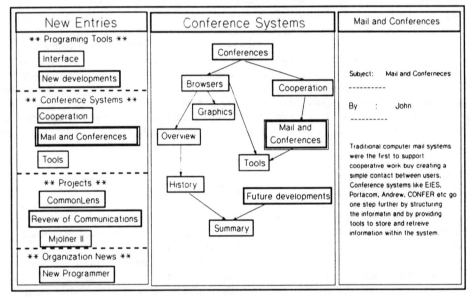

Figure 1. Conference participation. In the browser the titled rectangles refer to information items and the arrows represent links between them.

When the next item is chosen the former is automatically disappears from the display. This is similar to what most conference systems do, except that here the context of the items is visible in the browser.

Besides the conference system, there are three places for information shared by the entire local community: One is the Library where it is possible to retrieve information in a structured manner. The others are the Coffee room and the Hallway which contain information of a more informal or social character.

The **library** is the place where all publicly available information is stored.

In a library one expects to find information stored in a well-structured manner. When one wants to find a specific piece of information, the first thing to do is to go to the section of the library in which one expects go find the information. Further these sections are divided according to subjects and finally the publications are ordered by author or title. This ordering scheme is kept a long way down the road. The library section is divided into sub sections according to general areas such as person directory, accountancy, management and projects - these again subdivided according to different types of projects or other divisions appropriate for the particular organization. To find a particular item one uses a browser - these will be described below - or one can use various search facilities.

The **coffee room** is sort of a multiple talk facility. There is a window for everyone present where one can then just "type away". The topics are open, but a certain amount of etiquette should be followed. This facility enables people to catch bits of information at random. When a person leaves his window is closed after a few minutes.

The **hallway** has a similar function. To meet someone in the hallway means that a talk connection is established. When one is in the hallway, eg. in order to get from one room to another, other people are visible and may be addressed by establishing a talk connection. Root [15] describes a similar facility in which video connections are established as well.

These two facilities are not central to the system, and it is hard to tell whether they will be of any use and how they might be used. The value of such facilities will by nature be very hard to measure, and will probably differ greatly from one organization to the other.

On aspect to consider is one of peripheral versus central information[1]. By passing people in the hallway one gets a sense of which other people being around, and of the activity level even without consciously noticing these things. So by including a hallway concept it is hoped that parts of this level of information can be moved into the system.

Information Representation. A Hypertext System.

The advantages of hypertext systems are well recognized (see eg. [6]). Especially important in this connection are:

- Ease of creating and tracking cross references.

- Information structuring. Eg. for a software project, analysis documents, specifications, programs and documentation can be inter-linked in a logical and structured manner.

- Consistency of information. Updates to a document will only have to be made in one place. This is important because of the many different points of entry to the information system.

In this particular case the fact that all information is available from everywhere in the system but within different contexts becomes vital: For example a design document produced within some group space can be submitted to an electronic conference, and there be subject for discussion. Later this document can be inspected from either the group space or the conference space, in a combined context where both conference links and group- or project links are visible.

Sections

One of the fundamental problems of hypertext systems is the difficulty of retrieving relevant information due to the disorientation that easily occurs in an unstructured hypertext system [6]. Some sort of structure must be introduced to prevent this disorientation, and this is where the sections mentioned above come in. The organization of sections corresponds quite closely to the directory system of a conventional file system; A hierarchy of sections where a section can contain both subsections and other nodes of the system. However in this system a node can in general only be in one section at a time; the system does not allow multiple copies of the same node.

Thus we have two organizations of the information space which are independent of each other: the hierarchy of sections and the web of links and nodes. This structure gives us all the flexibility of the hypertext system, and all the order of the directory system, the best of both worlds. In addition people who are not familiar with the principles of hypertext can start using the system by just filing nodes in sections and subsections, and then start using links along the way. See figure 2 for a view of the structure.

In the hypertext system everything can be inter-linked, so in order to secure the privacy of the

----

1. This point was made by Liam Bannon.

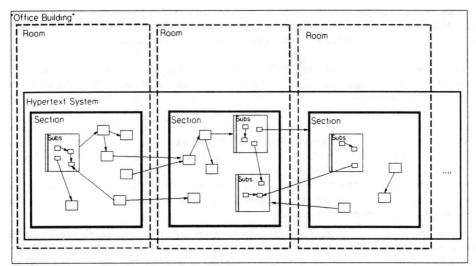

Figure 2. the Hypertext and Room Structure. The hypertext system is divided into a number of sections. These sections are contained in a Room. Furthermore the sections can contain subsections, thus forming a section hierarchy. The information items, here represented by the small rectangles, are placed in this hierarchy just like in a file system. The arrows represent links. These can go across any section boundary and between nodes and sections, thus forming a structure independent of the section hierarchy.

individuals and the groups the boundaries between the different "rooms" are made explicit by introducing a special linking convention: Links between different sections of the information space corresponds to submitting the linked-to item into the section from which the link was originated. The link is by default only visible from within that section. If, for instance, an individual creates a link from a conference to an item in his private section, this has the same effect as submitting this item to the conference, whereas if the link goes in the opposite direction, it serves merely as a private reference. By admitting access to an item in a private section permission is implicitly granted to follow the links from this item to other items as long as they belong to the same subsection. Thus one has to be a little cautious about which links are created into ones private area. On the other hand this provides the possibility of letting others view an item in its proper context rather than as an isolated message or text.

Electronic Mail.
The option to send any node to someone is always close by hand at the same level as "save" "close" or "print". There are two modes of sending a message, either sending the actual text or sending a link to the text. When sending a message one is prompted for the receiver and for the mode of sending. It is also possible to send a message to a conference, without going to the conference room.

Browsers
Maneuvering within the system is done by using the hypertext browser system and a overview of the available rooms. The latter will be described in the next section.

The browser system is connected to the system of sections, and thus is hierarchical in nature. A browser belongs to a room, and cannot show things outside the section of that room. When a browser of a room is initiated the top level of that section is shown, thus subsections are not expanded. This is just like the ls command in UNIX, except that the browsers show a graphical representation of the nodes and subsections. Furthermore the links between nodes are shown. Links between subsections are shown as one link and a number indicating the number of links between the subsections. Links out of the sections are shown with a line to the border of the browser, and the address of the other end. By clicking on a subsection with the mouse this subsection is displayed in the browser. An example of a browser is shown in fig. 3.[1]

----

1. Xerox Notecards which is a hypertext system running on the 1100 series of Xerox workstations [10] has a folder concept which is somewhat similar to the section. However, Notecards does not take advantage of the folder in its browser concept. An other important difference is that the folder is not independent of the web of nodes and links.

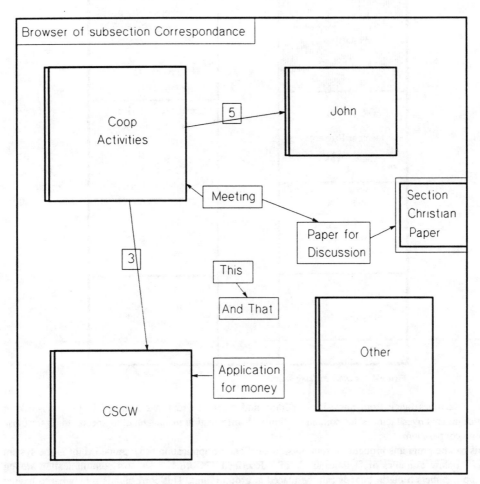

Figure 3. Browser of section. The large rectangles with a double line to the left represent subsections, the smaller rectangles represent information items, and the arrows represent links. The size and placement of the items are controlled by the user.

The office building map

For maneuvering between the rooms in the system a special browser is used which contains sort of a map of the organization. It can be individually designed in order to let the user create an individual understanding of the system and the organization. In addition to going from one room to another the browser can be used for obtaining information about the different rooms. Moving from one room to an other is done by a simple mouse click. One can either move directly between rooms or go via the hallway.

A simple example of an office building map is shown in fig. 4. Notice that it is possible to see how willing people are to be disturbed by how wide the doors to their offices are opened. This idea is widely used among the staff of this department (I do not know if it is more generally accepted). Whether such an unofficial, often unspoken convention can be meaningfully carried into a system like this remains to be seen.

Configuration of rooms.

The rooms described above fall in two groups. There are four rooms shared by the entire organization: Library, Hallway, Coffee room and Conference room. These are not tailorable to any note worthy degree. The other type of rooms are those that are open to certain people only. These are individual offices and group rooms. In fact these two types are quite similar; a room of an individual can be viewed as a group room with just one member. This type of rooms can be configured with a number of facilities for communication and cooperation to meet the needs of the owners.

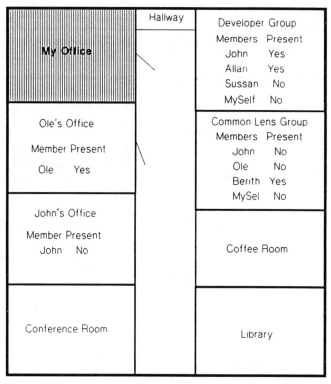

Figure 4. The Office Building Map

These facilities range from normal text editors and other programs well known in present working environments over facilities for communication and information management to special tools for close group cooperation.

This can be programs brought in from outside, or it can be application programmed right in the system itself. Below examples of facilities are briefly described. In order to support communication among group members **bulletin boards** can be placed in group rooms. This corresponds somewhat to having closed conferences in a conference system, where only members of the group can participate. A bulletin board may also be useful in the individual rooms as a personal reminder or referencer. In a conference system it is customary to have a facility that shows unread entrances. This facility is generalized into a **new-link container** so that it can be used both in the conference room and in other rooms such as the group room. Its function is quite simple; whenever an item is inserted in the section connected to the new-link container a link to this item is placed in the new-link container. Upon entering a room one may then check to see if any new items have been inserted. Afterwards the links may either be deleted or moved to appropriate places. The facility is often used in connection with a display in which the items are inspected, thus approaching the normal functions of a conference system.

Over the past few years attempts have been made to construct systems allowing rule based manipulation of information items within systems of different kinds. This approach encounter not only technical problems but also problems concerning what sort of such transactions can be usefully automated and questions concerning the sensibility of such an approach in the first place. Keeping this in mind, two concepts that might prove useful in some situations will now be presented. However, as these issues still need a great deal of investigations they will not be further pursued in this work.

Agents and **Communication structures** are user programmed features. Agents are inspired by Object Lens [12] and Communication structures by the COSMOS project ([2] and [18]) . Agents are for automatic object manipulation. The user can set up a number of rules that apply to objects in the system. When an object complies with a rule a certain action is carried out by the system. Typically the range of such an agent is a section of the information space. Agents are primarily used by individuals and to a certain extent by groups for managing the information system and the electronic communication items.

A Communication structure controls that a certain exchange of messages goes on in a certain order, and that no step is forgotten. In COSMOS a communication structure controlling a voting procedure is described. Another example could be a structure ensuring that every time a certain type of report was filed the superior was notified. Communication structures are more of a tool for modeling formal organizational structures.

A powerful tool for cooperation is a facility that allows one to link to another terminal and see what is on the other screen [5]. Such facilities come close to implementing a comprehensive shared workspace for participants. Below are some examples.

A **shared whiteboard** is a window shared by two or more screens in which two ore more people can write, draw and create images simultaneously. This can be used for close cooperation between members of a work group. The work is of course saved for later use.

Another facility that gives some of the same possibilities is the **group workspace**. The idea was developed in the SharedARK project [15]. When working with the group workspace the screen is split in two, an overview and a working area. The overview shows a map of the entire group workspace, which is much larger than one screen. The screens of everyone working on the group workspace is shown as small rectangles on the display. It is possible to move around in the workspace. In the working area one can perform all kinds of usual tasks. The objects that is being worked on stationary on the group workspace though, meaning that when one moves around, they stay. When two screens overlap in the overview the screen image that both see is the same. Thus two or more persons are able to collaborate.

In SharedARK both video and audio connection is provided in addition. A telephone line for audio communication would probably be sufficient for most purposes until the more advanced technology becomes generally affordable.

An example of a group workspace is shown in fig. 5.

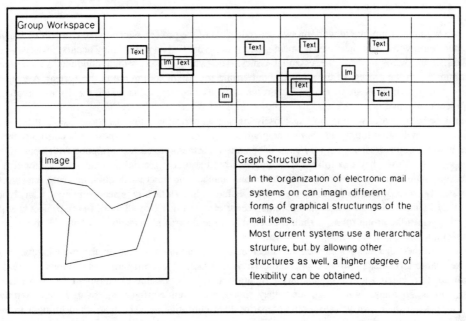

Figure 5, Group Workspace. The top part with the grid is the overview and below that is the working area. The small rectangles on the grid represent text and graphics items, the larger ones represent the screens of the users of the workspace.

These are just examples of facilities that might be useful. The question of which of them are actually workable and to any real use, and in what exact form, is left open, as no sufficient analysis of actual use of such facilities has been conducted as of yet.

Notice that it is left very much to the individual user organizations which kinds of programs and facilities they want to incorporate in the system.

Tailorability. The Object Hierarchy

Seen from an implementation point of view the system is a collection of objects, most of which are persistent, working together. Everything is represented as objects: Rooms, sections, nodes, links, text, messages, browsers, agents, etc. These are arranged in a class hierarchy.

One can create new instances of objects by selecting them from a special browser containing this class hierarchy, and then filing in its properties using an editor. In addition new classes can be created by editing one of the existing class definitions. In this way every aspect of the system can be tailored and further developed by advanced users and developers.[1]

3. Example.

The initial ideas of a system in support for communication and cooperation in organizations have now been presented.

In short, a system will consist of a collection of rooms configured with facilities for communication on different levels. The underlying structure is a hypertext system which has a section concept for building hierarchical structures.

A somewhat larger example of how the groups may be configured and used will now be presented. In an organization an analysis of, say, the communication structures is to be conducted. For this purpose a project organization is established which looks as follows:

- Group 1 consisting of one worker from each of the three departments of the organization to be investigated. They are picked because they have previously worked together and know each other quite well.

- Group 2 consisting of a representative for management and two from the local union.

- Project management group consisting of a worker, a manager and a consultant from outside of the organization

The two working groups are to work on two separate parts of the project, which in the end will be joined together. Meanwhile the project management group makes sure that no redundancy occurs, gives advice, and direct the work towards the essential issues. The whole project group conducts an ongoing discussion about the process of the project. Four Group rooms are configured in the system. A Project group room, of which all are members. This room contains a conference in which the discussion about the process takes place.

Group 1 decide that they want to work as closely together in performing their task as possible, they even want to help each other formulate central paragraphs of the report. For this purpose they configure their room with a group workspace for very close cooperation. Furthermore each is equipped with a container of new links, so that they can follow very closely what the others are doing. One bulletin board for discussing various parts of the work is installed and another for internal discussion about the work process. Also a scheduler for planning the work is included. Such a facility is needed in almost any kind of project. They decide that there should be no secrets amongst them, so all work in the project should be performed in the group room. It should be clear that the flow of information is controlled by a clan organization formed by the three group members.

Group 2 on the other hand recognize the inherent conflict of interests among the participants; they choose a more formalized form of cooperation. They want to be able to prepare contributions in privacy which are then entered into a preliminary structure where it is possible to comment on each others contributions. To comply with these needs they choose a different configuration of their work setting. They each sit in their own private rooms preparing their contributions. These are then brought to the group room and placed in the group section. The group members use a bulletin board for telling each others what they have contributed with and where they think it fits in with the rest. The others now have several options for commenting: They can do it on the bulletin board, they can link a comment to the contribution in the group section if it is the context of the contribution they are unhappy with, or they can send a message to the other two members arguing for changes.

The project management group need primarily a scheduler to help them control the progress of the work

----

1. Object Lens [12] has a similar method for creating new objects and object types.

and secure that deadlines are met. Bulletin boards for discussing individual pieces of work as well as the project in general are also necessary. The way in which they interact with the two groups differ significantly: Group 1 allow the management group free access to their section of the hypertext system by providing them with a link to the main section. This means that they are free to inspect the finished text nodes in there and create and inter-link comments. They cannot see unfinished nodes which are still at the group workspace.

Group 2 being more concerned with privacy will not allow this form of inspection. Instead they mail finished parts to the management group who in turn mail back their comments. For this purpose a formal procedures are set up which ensures that any piece sent off to the management group is in fact commented upon and that the comments are associated with the right piece.

At a certain point group 2 decide to send an enquiry to every member of the organization. They set up a voting structure to ensure that the results of the enquiry are collected and counted correctly and that the answers are anonymous. The structure sends the questions by e-mail to everyone in the organization and collects the answers from everyone. These are counted. As the enquiry is considered important and since it is anonymous, it is decided that everyone should answer the questions, and therefore people who delays their response receive reminders from the structure until their answer is received. Finally the results of the enquiry are sent to the working group who can then use them for further work.

At the end the two reports are merged together and the project management group write a short conclusionary report of the project. For this purpose they add a group workspace to their room, so that they can all work together on the report. It turns out that the report is very easy to write because any reference to the main report is just a matter of inserting a hypertext link. The entire work - the main report and the final, shorter report are now placed in the library section. In addition the shorter report is submitted to an appropriate conference in the conference system. People reading it there who want to look at the main report can find it by following the referential links within the submitted shorter report. As it is evident from this example the system support the formation of organizational structures to a much greater extent than traditional information systems. This example has included aspects of all three categories of organizing cooperative work: Group 1 was organized as a clan, group 2 and also the project group seen as a whole were more bureaucracy-like, although other aspects were involved as well, and finally, the information market was used during the enquiry and in the final publication of the work.

4. Conclusion

This paper sees cooperative work as processes characterized by communication and by opportunistic behavior among participators. In order to provide tools to cope with the opportunistic behavior the transaction cost theory (see [4] and others) is used to categorize organizations controlling information transactions.

A system is designed which among others things provides an environment in which communication - both explicit and in the form of shared material - is well supported as are both synchronous and asynchronous communication. For the design of the system a new design metaphor - the office building - is introduced, and the concept of users moving between different rooms of the system becomes central, thus providing users with a familiar conceptual understanding of the system. The hypertext system used for storing all information encourages people to make their work available to the public by linking it into the public area. A group construct is provided enabling the construction of bureaucracies and clans as information transaction control structures in addition to the market structure that is supported by the hypertext and conference system.

References

[1] Nathaniel S. Borenstein, Chris A. Thyberg : *Cooperative Work in the Andrew Message System*, Proceedings of the Second Conference on Computer Support for Cooperative Work 1988, Portland, Oregon.

[2] John Bowers and John Churcher : *Local and Global Structuring of Computer Mediated Communication. Developing Linguistic Perspectives on CSCW in COSMOS*, Proceedings of the Second International Conference on Computer Support for Cooperative Work 1988, Portland, Oregon.

[3] Vanever Bush : *As we may think,* Atlantic monthly 1945

[4] Claudio Ciborra : *Reframing the Role of Computers in Organizations. The Transaction Cost Approach,* Proceedings of the Sixth International Conference on Information Systems, 1985.

[5] Liam Bannon : *Extending the Design Boundaries of Human Computer Interaction,* ICS Technical Report 8505, 1985.

[6] Jeff Conklin : *Hypertext: An Introduction and Survey,* IEEE Computer, sept 1987, p.17-41.

[7] Douglas C. Engelbart, Richard W. Watson, James C. Norton : *The Augmented Knowledge Workshop,* Proceedings of AFIPS National Computer Conference, 42, p. 9-21. 1973.

[8] Douglas C. Englebart : *Authorship provision in Augment,* Compcon Digest, Proceedings of the 1984 Compcon Conference, San Francisco, Ca.

[9] Tony Fanning, Bert Raphael : *Computer Teleconferencing: Experience at Hewlett-Packard,* Proceedings of the First International Conference on Computer Support for Cooperative Work 1986, Austin, Texas

[10] Frank G. Halasz, Thomas P. Moran, Randall H. Trigg : *Notecard in a Nutshell,* Proceedings of the Second International Conference on Computer Support for Cooperative Work 1988, Portland, Oregon

[11] Starr Roxanne Hiltz and Murray Turroff : *Structuring Computer-Mediated Communication Systems to avoid Information Overload,* Communications of the ACM, July 1985, Vol. 28 nr.7.

[12] Kun-Yew Lai, Thommas W. Malone : *Object Lens : A ``Spreadsheet" for Cooperative Work,* Proceedings of the Second International Conference on Computer Support for Cooperative Work 1988, Portland, Oregon.

[13] Thomas W. Malone, Kenneth R Grant, Franklyn A. Turbak, Stephen A. Brobst, Michael D. Cohen: *Intelligent Information-Sharing System,* Communications of the ACM, May 1987 vol. 30 nr.5.

[14] Robert W. Root : *Design of a Multi-media Vihecle for Social Browsing,* Proceedings of the Second International Conference on Computer Support for Cooperative Work 1988, Portland, Oregon.

[15] Randall Schmidt, Tim O'Shea, Claire O'Malley, Eileen Scanlon, Josie Taylor : *Preliminary Experiments with a Distributed, Multi-Media, Problem Solving Environment,* Proceedings of the First European Conference on Computer Support for Cooperative Work 1989, Gatwick, UK.

[16] Pål Sørgaard : *A Cooperative Work Perspective on Use and Development of Computer Artifacts,* Daimi PB 234 nov. 1987.

[17] Gordon B. Thompson : *Information Technology: A Question of Perception,* Telesis, 11(2), 2-7. 1984.

[18] Robert E. Young (ed.) *Interim Report on the Cosmos Project,* Cosmos Coordinator's Office, Queen Mary College, London, 1987.

Chapter 6: Computer-Supported Meetings

Chapter 6: Computer-Supported Meetings

Computers have been in the workplace for more than 30 years. An anomaly exists, however: while computers are widely used, they are seldom involved in group work. Even more rare is the use of computers for meetings, whether they be face-to-face meetings or distributed meetings where people may be sitting at their desks or at home. Why is this so, and what value can computer technology bring to meetings?

This section presents several case studies that have explored the nature of human collaboration and cooperation during meetings. The articles cover (1) brainstorming, organizing, evaluating, prioritizing and voting on ideas; (2) proposing, arguing, and evaluating issues; (3) collaborative writing and policy development; (4) the benefits and drawbacks of anonymity during group work; (5) how group member proximity affects meetings; (6) meetings of groups of groups; and (7) the self-assessment that occurs in meetings.

Within this context of human interaction, the case studies describe how computers are used to support meetings. The articles present new technological challenges to develop software capabilities for meeting tasks, to fit computing technology into meeting rooms, to design meetings to support collaborative authoring, to share hardware in real-time work situations, and to support real-time distributed meetings.

Background: Computers as new media

Traditionally, people experience media such as overheads and flip charts as influencing a meeting, in terms of the way people communicate and how well they remember what was said. Yet few of us are conscious of this influence. This phenomenon might be due to the fact that meetings have, until recently, gone relatively unexamined. There is no theory of meetings within which groupware researchers can work and relevant results can be interpreted. Therefore, let us take the position that "meetings" are real-time work events, regardless of whether people are together or dispersed, and investigate how computers influence meetings.

Some early computer-supported meetings focused on how this technology, as a new medium, could benefit meeting practices. One insight was that meeting activities, which are hard or awkward for traditional media like flip charts and chalkboards, are easy for computers (for example, rearranging lists). A second insight was that traditional decision-support systems, because their underlying designs emphasized information management instead of collaboration support, are inconsistently effective in meetings.

Other efforts examined how technology impacts the behavior of people in meetings. They noted that technology intervenes in meetings (for example, by creating new power positions in the room, or causing a loss of privacy). In these cases, new meeting protocols had to be established for accessing and manipulating meeting information (to reestablish the team's work context), and existing software had to be adapted for specific meeting situations (so participants could run familiar software).

Thus, the evolution of electronic meeting support systems is socio-technical. On the one hand, there is the need to develop a system to support real-time communication (sharing displays of information, commitment tracking, collaborative authoring). On the other hand, there is also the need to develop stronger models to run effective meetings, especially those that take advantage of computing technology as a new medium.

Themes: Collaboration, interaction, distribution

We can classify meetings according to purpose: exploration, information sharing, brainstorming, presentation, problem solving, decision making, morale building, negotiating, planning, or social structuring. We can also classify meetings according to whether people are geographically together or dispersed. The diversity of meetings generates a wide range of issues: layout, capability, performance, connectivity, user interface, and so on. Following are some important themes for computer-supported meetings and electronic meeting support systems.

Face-to-face collaboration. Metaphors are extremely useful for designing meeting software. Stefik et al. employ the metaphor of the chalkboard, focusing on how this medium has traditionally been used in meetings, and how computer capabilities go beyond chalkboards. They extend the chalkboard metaphor to support meeting processes (task characteristics and expected outcomes), methods (ways of creating work artifacts), and environments (the rooms, hardware, how people organize themselves). They create this support by coordinating the simultaneous input from multiple, interconnected computers. They also suggest maximizing the advantage of a computer-supported meeting by observing the social norms that occur. For example:

(1) People always organize themselves, even in supposedly "unorganized" work, such as a brainstorming session.
(2) Unexpected joining of ideas and work products occurs in collaborative efforts, and this joining cannot be anticipated.
(3) It is often difficult to maintain a shared focus on the work, especially when parallel work is encouraged.
(4) Parallel work demands that meeting participants be aware of each other's work.

Stefik et al. close their discussion by stating that many technical issues need to be resolved before an adequate system-level software platform for groupware can be built. They cite the need for better shared-screen management, database replication across wide area networks, support for work partitioning and integration, timestamping transactions to ensure correct distributed-database changes, locking data during change transactions, a correct database-locking model, and a software clipboard transfer mechanism for pooling collaborative work results.

Group interaction tools. A key concept of computer-supported meetings is that they link meeting rooms with desktops. The outcome is that meetings fit directly into the continuum of work, instead of being outside the rhythm of the work flow. Nunamaker et al. suggest a seamless integration of software tools for accessing information throughout the work continuum. Their experience centers around decision making, and they strongly suggest designing software that focuses on supporting the entire decision-making process, instead of supporting isolated decision tasks. Nunamaker et al. demonstrate this concept by showing how integrating several tools can support a teamwork session. For example, consider the following meeting and how an integrated toolset can support the process that enables the team to work together towards a common result:

(1) The team brainstorms, recording words and ideas.
(2) They organize their ideas by linking them into sets.
(3) They link the sets into major points.
(4) The major points are evaluated and finalized.
(5) The team takes action on those points deemed most important.

Nunamaker et al. also describe an integrated toolset for the issue management process:

(1) An issue is proposed.
(2) Multiwindowed descriptions are created and linked.
(3) Team members argue their points.
(4) Pro/con statements are recorded and attached to the issue.
(5) Pro/con statements are evaluated.
(6) Assumptions, viewpoints, and beliefs are recorded.

(7) Decision-making criteria are formulated.

(8) A voting process results in a final decision.

The success of the tools just described requires considering the layout and dominance of computers in the meeting room, where people choose to sit, the sequencing of user participation during the meeting, the visual accoutrements of the room, the public displays of computer screens, and the general room ergonomics. For success factors, Nunamaker et al. describe four design parameters: group dynamics, size of the group, proximity of people, and time dispersion of the work.

Distributed meetings. Mantei et al. note that the design situation in meetings changes continually, rapidly, and sometimes dramatically and unexpectedly. Meetings affect their surroundings and vice versa. In fact, the design for a particular meeting becomes not only the hardware and software, but also the meeting process and even the room. In addition, the factors affecting the design of successful meetings are complicated when we have to consider people being geographically distributed.

Mantei et al. suggest that to support distributed meetings we must consider the technical media being used. First, media define new methods of communication, with novel and unforeseen uses and potentialities. Second, effective solutions require solving architectural and implementation problems in distributed computing. Third, group work environments contain a vast and rich collection of metaphors already built into the media. Last, the use of group communications media raises serious ethical issues of surveillance and privacy.

Mantei et al. describe their experiences in terms of the unexpected benefits they realized and the obstacles they encountered. The benefits they realized were meetings of groups of groups (as opposed to groups of individuals), created at no extra cost; improving communication skills by using the TV monitor to see each other; and monitoring their offices from other people's offices. The obstacles they encountered were: intolerable system response-time delays, ambient noise that degraded speech quality and sometimes interrupted ongoing discussions, audio speakers that did not localize sound to those who were speaking, and the "intelligent" lighting for cameras being problematic.

It is important to notice here how the introduction of new technology changes the social aspects of meetings in often dramatic ways. For Mantei et al., meetings were more difficult to manage because:

(1) People were more attentive to those with whom they were physically located;

(2) Gaze and eye contact were lost when people had to look into the TV monitors;

(3) Social relationships were altered with the loss of physical seating arrangements;

(4) They needed to generate entirely new sets of cues for speaking;

(5) Video image size distorted the perceived impact individuals had on the meeting and their social relationships to others; and

(6) Inadequate computer networking led some people to take increased security measures.

Mantei et al. close by stating a key groupware tenet: Groupware developers need to be sensitive to the changes in human interaction that occur when new technology is introduced in a meeting.

Futures: Better designed meetings that happen virtually anywhere

Media influence the course of meetings because they interact strongly with the participants' needs for communication, memory, and information sharing. The future will see more computerized meeting rooms and more offices being altered so their occupants can take part in distributed meetings. The design of these systems will have to consider room aesthetics, lighting, computer projection quality, and so on. Even with these considerations addressed, the design will not be complete without considering the social interactions and intentions for the specific meetings being supported.

The implications of electronic meeting support systems for distributed meetings and for organizations as a whole are very much an unknown at this time. However, some patterns are emerging. For example, computer-supported distributed meetings are proving that people can work together even though they are not face-to-face. This will produce some expected benefits (reduced travel, reduced task completion time, and reduced overall project completion time), and may create new and unexpected potential (increasing the number of people in a meeting, bringing the entire management spectrum into decision making).

Future computer-supported meeting systems are expected to develop through the cooperation of designers and users during actual meetings. New design metaphors will emerge so that the social norms of meetings are better supported. New designs may include software applications so highly customizable and usable that they span continuums of work tasks (reestablishing work context, coauthoring, brainstorming, decision making, collaborative problem solving), and augment traditional media (rearrangable lists, dynamically linked artifacts, navigable project archives).

Edgar H. Sibley
Panel Editor

Although individual use of computers is fairly widespread, in meetings we tend to leave them behind. At Xerox PARC, an experimental meeting room called the Colab has been created to study computer support of collaborative problem solving in face-to-face meetings. The long-term goal is to understand how to build computer tools to make meetings more effective.

BEYOND THE CHALKBOARD: COMPUTER SUPPORT FOR COLLABORATION AND PROBLEM SOLVING IN MEETINGS

MARK STEFIK, GREGG FOSTER, DANIEL G. BOBROW, KENNETH KAHN, STAN LANNING, and LUCY SUCHMAN

Meetings are used for virtually any intellectual task that requires the coordination or agreement of several people. Statistical studies suggest that office workers spend as much as 30–70 percent of their time in meetings [26]. Paradoxically, even with the widespread distribution of computers, most computer systems in use aid the work of separate individuals rather than their work in groups. In meetings, computers are typically left behind in favor of more passive media like chalkboards[1] and flip charts.

Media influence the course of a meeting because they interact strongly with participants' resources for communication and memory. Chalkboards, for example, provide a shared and focused memory for a meeting, allowing flexible placement of text and figures, which complements our human capabilities for manipulating spatial memories. However, space is limited and items disappear when that space is needed for something else, and rearranging items is inconvenient when they must be manually redrawn and then erased. Handwriting on a chalkboard can be illegible. Chalkboards are also unreliable for information storage: They are used in rooms shared by many groups, and text and figures created in one meeting may be erased during the next. If an issue requires several meetings, some other means must be found to save information in the interim.

Many of the functions that are awkward or impossible with chalkboards are implemented easily with computers. Window systems and drawing aids, for example, provide flexibility for rearranging text and figures, and text can be displayed in fonts that are crisp and reproducible. File systems make it possible to retrieve information generated from previous meetings, to revisit old arguments, to show the history of a series of arguments, and to resume discussions. Independent workstations allow meeting participants to share views, point to objects under discussion, and work on different aspects of a problem simultaneously, with the result that participation can feel less like being a member of a committee, and more like acting as a collaborator at a barn raising.

To explore these ideas, an experimental meeting room known as the Colab has been set up at Xerox PARC. In the Colab, computers support collaborative processes in face-to-face meetings. The Colab is de-

---

[1] The term *chalkboard* in this article refers to any of the wall-mounted erasable writing surfaces commonly used in meeting rooms, whether they are white, black, or some other color and whether the marks are made with chalk, crayon, or ink. We use this term to avoid misunderstandings about the word *blackboard*, which, among other things, can mean a commercially available teleconferencing product, or a programming organization for artificial-intelligence systems. We also avoid the term *whiteboard*, which can mean a white metal writing surface on which colored pens are used, or a specific graphical database tool developed at Xerox PARC [9].

signed for small working groups of two to six persons using personal computers connected over a local-area network (Figure 1). In our design, we have drawn on familiar elements from conventional meeting rooms. The focus of the Colab project is to make our own meetings among computer scientists more effective and to provide an opportunity for conducting more general research on how computer tools affect meeting processes.[2]

Much prior research has focused on the use of computer and communication technology to support teleconferencing [18, 19] and what is known as computer conferencing [16, 17], which emphasizes the use of computers to support asynchronous communication and discussion over a computer network. The Colab, on the other hand, focuses on problem solving in face-to-face meetings—the most common kind of meeting in our research group and our starting point.

In this article, we describe the meeting tools we have built so far as well as the computational underpinnings and language support we have developed for creating distributed software. Finally, we present some preliminary observations from our first Colab meetings and some of the research questions we are now pursuing.

TOOLS FOR COLLABORATION

An office worker using a computer will choose different programs to achieve different purposes. Completing a single project may involve the use of several different tools: a spreadsheet program, a text editor, and a sketching program. In a similar vein, activities arise in the course of a meeting that require different supporting programs. In this article, we use the term *meeting tools* to refer to programs that support group interaction and problem solving in meetings, and the term *Colab tools* to refer to meeting tools developed specifically for use in the Colab.

A fundamental requirement for meeting tools is that they provide a coordinated interface for all participants. Such a *multiuser* interface is intended to let meeting participants interact with each other easily and immediately through a computer medium.

The term *WYSIWYG* (what you see is what you get) is generally used to describe text editors in which text appears the same during editing as it will during printing. To describe an important abstraction for meeting tools, we have defined an analogous term: *WYSIWIS* (what you see is what I see—pronounced "whizzy whiz"), which refers to the presen-

The Colab is an experimental meeting room designed for typical use by two to six persons. Each person has a workstation connected to a personal computer. The computers are linked together over a local-area network (ethernet) that supports a distributed database. Besides the workstations, the room is equipped with a large touch-sensitive screen and a stand-up keyboard.

FIGURE 1. A View of the Colab

tation of consistent images of shared information to all participants. A meeting tool is *strictly* WYSIWIS if all meeting participants see exactly the same thing and where the others are pointing.

WYSIWIS creates the impression that members of a group are interacting with shared and tangible objects. It extends to a group conversation the kind of shared access to information that is experienced by two people sitting together over a sketch. WYSIWIS is the critical idea that makes possible the sense of teamwork illustrated in the barn-raising metaphor. It recognizes the importance of being able to see what work the other members have done and what work is in progress: to "see where their hands are." With meeting tools, this visual cue can be approximated by providing pointers to work in progress and by graying out objects that are being worked on.

Although *strict* WYSIWIS would give everyone the same image on their displays, in practice we have

[2] Lucy Suchman, the last author of the present article, is an anthropologist for whom the Colab represents part of a larger study of face-to-face collaboration and its technology.

found this too limiting and instead use relaxed versions of WYSIWIS [32]. For example, it can be useful to differentiate between *public* interactive windows that are accessible to the entire group, and private windows with limited access (e.g., for personal electronic mail). Private windows violate the concept of strict WYSIWIS, as does relaxation of pointer displays. Although pointing is an efficient way to refer to things in conversation, displaying the cursors of all active participants is usually too distracting. Making pointers visible only on request becomes an effective compromise. Another WYSIWIS relaxation permits public windows to appear at different places on different screens so that public pointers can be translated into window-relative coordinates. This sacrifices some ability to refer to things by screen position, but it does permit personalized screen layouts.

Meetings, like other processes, can be more efficient when several things are done at once. Since Colab tools support simultaneous action, a key issue in tool design is recognizing and supporting those activities that can be decomposed for parallel action. For parallel action, a task must be broken up into appropriately sized operations that can be executed more or less independently by different members of the group. If the operations are too small, they will be too interdependent, and interference will preclude any substantial parallelism. For example, to create a shared text, interactions should not be at the level of individual keystrokes. On the other hand, if operations are needlessly large, opportunities for synergy are lost.

The ability to act in parallel on shared objects also brings with it potential for conflict. Conflict resolution strategies will become necessary in some cases, but often we can rely on social constraints. A conflict detection system or "busy signal" graphically warns users that someone else is already editing or otherwise using an item; a busy item is grayed out on all screens.

Our initial goal was to create tools to support the kinds of meetings that our group has, which range from the informal to the formal. One of the informal meeting tools we have developed, Boardnoter, closely imitates the functionality of a chalkboard (Figure 2). It is intended for informal meetings that rely heavily on informal freestyle sketching. To draw with Boardnoter, one uses the "chalk," to erase one uses the "eraser," to type one uses the miniature "typewriter," and to point one uses the "pointer." To sketch a square with Boardnoter, one simply "picks up the chalk" and makes four strokes. A subsequent version of Boardnoter will go beyond the chalkboard by adding capabilities for copying, moving, resizing,

linking with rubber band lines, grouping, and smoothing (neatening), and for using and scaling selections from a set of predrawn images.

Other Colab tools are based on much more formal models of the meeting process. In this article, we focus our attention on two such tools: *Cognoter*, a tool for organizing ideas to plan a presentation; and *Argnoter*, a tool for considering and evaluating alternate proposals. Although both tools are intended to bring appropriate computational support to structured meeting processes, the contrast between the two processes will highlight the range of opportunities that exist for applying computer technology in this medium.

ORGANIZING IDEAS FOR A PRESENTATION USING COGNOTER

Cognoter[3] is a Colab tool used to prepare presentations collectively. Its output is an annotated outline of ideas and associated text. We have used Cognoter to prepare outlines for talks and papers, including this one. In some ways, it is similar to the Think-Tank, Freestyle [25], and NoteCards [34] programs. All are used to organize ideas, but Cognoter is unique in that it is intended for collective use by a group of people.

The Cognoter process imitates a meeting style for collaborative writing that we have used at Xerox PARC without computational support for several years. Usually, we begin with a clear slate: The ideas are in our heads and nothing is written down. The problem at this point is how to get started: It is not very helpful to begin by asking, "Well, we need an outline. What should we put in I.A.1?" Rather, planning a presentation requires that the group decide what the ideas are, which ideas go together, which ideas come first, the order of presentation, and, finally, which ideas warrant elimination.

Cognoter organizes a meeting into three distinct phases—*brainstorming*, *organizing*, and *evaluation*—each of which emphasizes a different set of activities. As the group advances through the respective phases, the set of possible actions is expanded: For instance, brainstorming, which is emphasized in the first phase, is still possible in the last phase. Groups that find the rigid enforcement of phases too prescriptive can skip immediately to the last phase where all the operations are possible. Our intention is to experiment with methods for encouraging particular meeting processes and styles of behavior without making the tools too inflexible and prescriptive.

---

[3] The name *Cognoter* comes from both *cog-noter* (a cognition noter) or *co-gno-ter* (knowing together).

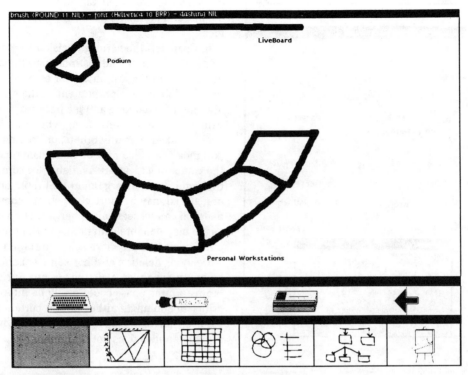

brush (ROUND 11 NIL) – font (Helvetica 10 BRR) – dashing NIL

LiveBoard

Podium

Personal Workstations

Note: The actual screen colors for the current version of Colab are black on white;
in Figures 2–6, the color green has been added for editorial emphasis—*Ed.*

The Boardnoter meeting tool in the Colab is operational but still in the early stages of development. A key feature is that it provides a large area for freestyle sketching. Below the writing area is a "chalk tray" containing several implements: a piece of chalk, an eraser, a miniature typewriter, and a pointer. To draw on the board, one picks up the chalk by clicking the mouse or pen over the chalk icon; to erase one picks up the eraser; to point one picks up the pointer. Since more than one boardful of information may be needed in the course of a meeting, the "stampsheet" of shrunken stamp-sized boards at the bottom makes it possible to obtain a fresh board or to switch back to a board created earlier.

FIGURE 2.   Screen Image of Boardnoter

Brainstorming

Since the brainstorming phase involves the initial generation of ideas used in the presentation, it is important to encourage synergy in group interactions and to not interfere with or inhibit the flow of ideas [10]. In Cognoter, therefore, ideas are not evaluated or eliminated in this phase, and little attention is given to their organization (see Figure 3, next page). Instead, there is one basic operation: A participant selects a free space in a public window and types in a catchword or catchphrase characterizing an idea. Participants may act simultaneously, adding idea items and supporting text at any time, but may not delete an item (even their own), although they can move them around. Supporting text is used to clarify the meaning of an item and to establish terminology for the presentation. Once entered, it can be publicly displayed or further edited by any participant. As the window fills up to encompass what

appears to be a jumble of ideas on different levels, begging for organization, pressure to move on to the next phase begins to mount.

Organizing

In the organizing phase, the group attempts to establish an order for the ideas generated in the brainstorming phase. With Cognoter, the order of ideas can be established incrementally by using two basic operations: linking ideas into presentation order and grouping ideas into subgroups. In addition, the item-moving operation allows these operations to be discussed prior to actually executing them by moving items near each other before clustering or linking.

The basic operation is to simply assert that one idea should come before another. Linking is usually accompanied by some verbal discussion: For example, a participant may say, "I'm putting *Colab tools* before *open issues* because you need to understand

337

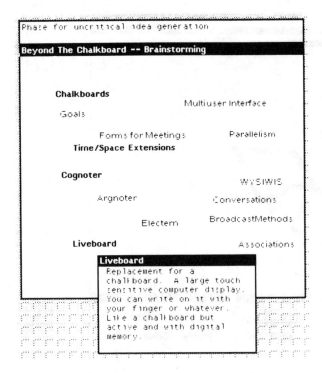

In the brainstorming phase, participants may add ideas and supporting text. Criticism or deletion of ideas is discouraged. Ideas are entered into the window by clicking the mouse in the background of the window and typing in a short title or phrase that stands for the idea. Text explaining the ideas in more detail is entered by selecting the item with a mouse and then using a text editor in a separate window.

FIGURE 3.   Brainstorming with Cognoter

what we have done before you can understand what comes next." The ordering is indicated visually by directed links between items as shown in Figure 4. The meaning of the links is transitive, meaning that, if X comes before Y, and Y comes before Z, then X must come before Z. The links are used collectively to determine a complete order of presentation. Items can also be clustered into groups and moved to their own windows as shown in Figure 5. When a group is formed, a bracketed item standing for the whole group is displayed in the window; the grouped items themselves are displayed in an associated window. Links are distributive across groups; a link to or from a bracketed item is treated like a link to or from the whole group. By these transitive and distributive operations, a small number of explicit links can highly constrain the total order of ideas.

Evaluation

The third phase, evaluation, determines the final form of the presentation. Participants review the

overall structure to reorganize ideas, fill in missing details, and eliminate peripheral and irrelevant ideas.

In Cognoter, the various decision-making processes are separate and distinct operations. Delaying deletion until the last phase, for example, provides a more visible basis for argument in the sense that an argument for deleting an idea because it is not relevant may be more convincing when that idea is not visibly linked with any others; or arguing the unimportance of an idea may be more convincing when the competing ideas are available for comparison. In the same sense, an argument that there is an excess of material may be more compelling when all the material can be seen, or a charge that an idea is vague may be more convincing in the presence of other ideas that are more fully substantiated.

Delaying deletion also has some beneficial effects on group dynamics: Deleting an idea during the brainstorming phase could easily be interpreted as criticism and might either inhibit certain participants or provoke tangential argument, whereas arguing that an idea does not fit or is insubstantial in the

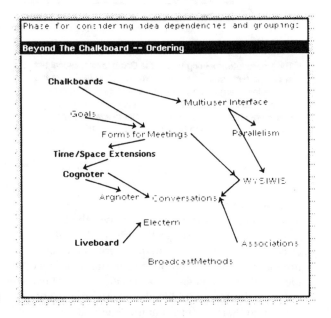

In Cognoter, the order of ideas is established incrementally. The basic operation is determining that one idea should come before another, which is indicated visually by directed links between items. The meaning is transitive, meaning that, if X comes before Y, and Y comes before Z, then X must come before Z. Collectively, the links determine the order of idea presentation. Links are added or removed by clicking the mouse on the desired items. Items will usually have one or more links to other items.

FIGURE 4.   Establishing the Order of Ideas

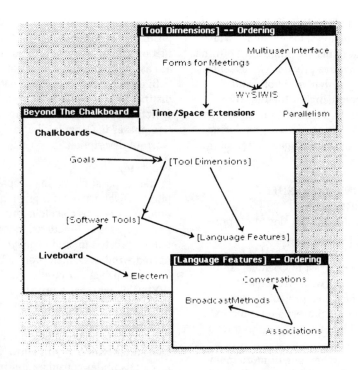

Items can be clustered into groups representing ideas that will be worked on together. Each group has an associated window for displaying its items. A group is named when it is formed, and that name appears as a bracketed item in the original window.

FIGURE 5. Grouping Items

evaluation phase may have the beneficial effect of prodding other group members to clarify or extend the idea.

Other operations besides deletion are also appropriately delayed until the evaluation phase. For example, arguing that an idea is misplaced is more compelling when alternate places to put it are visible; this is a good time to consider the reordering of ideas. Since the linking operation that takes place in the organizing phase is usually based on considerations local to two ideas, seeing the entire presentation, with most of the links in place, allows the user to appraise the overall structure and consider more global concerns, such as balance.

Cognoter provides a systematic process for answering the question, "What should we put in I.A.1?" Starting points for a presentation can be identified systematically: These are the items with no incoming links. Cognoter then helps in the final ordering of ideas by preparing an outline and indicating which ideas are ordered arbitrarily. By traversing the item graph, an outline is generated, with or without the attached text.

In many respects, Cognoter supports a process that is quite different from that underlying tools like ThinkTank. Beyond the most obvious difference, which is that Cognoter is designed for simultaneous use by multiple participants (although the process it embodies is also useful for single users), Cognoter also divides the thinking process into smaller and different kinds of steps that are incremental and efficient. In ThinkTank, ideas are always organized in an outline—there is no other place to put them— whereas Cognoter separates the tasks of idea generation and ordering. Cognoter also provides for incremental ordering through a link-forming operation whereby a partial ordering of ideas is refined stepwise toward a complete ordering. Transitivity and grouping operations make it possible to organize the ideas efficiently with a small number of links.

Some important parts of the presentation planning process are not explicit in Cognoter: For example, Cognoter does not inquire as to the audience, the appropriate technical level, the goals of the paper, or arguments for deleting or ordering ideas. Modifications to Cognoter could make such questions explicit, but they are now outside the scope of the current tool.

Cognoter is the first useful Colab tool developed and is still evolving. We are now experimenting with various relaxations of the WYSIWIS concept. In the current version of Cognoter, for example, windows showing links and items are public, but outline and item editing windows are private. The absence of visual cues indicating which are public and which private can be confusing for the first-time users. With several months experience using Cognoter's multiuser interface, we are actively exploring trade-offs in the design of the next generation of the tool [32].

AN ARGUMENTATION SPREADSHEET FOR PROPOSALS (ARGNOTER)

Argnoter,[4] the Colab tool being developed for presenting and evaluating proposals, is now in the early stages of design and implementation and is presented here chiefly as a contrast to Cognoter. Implementing and experimenting with Argnoter are now major focuses of the Colab project. As with Cognoter, the basic meeting process supported by Argnoter has been used by our group without computational aid for several years.

Proposal meetings start when one or more members of the group have a proposal for something to be done, typically a design for a program or a plan for a course of research. The goal of the meeting then becomes to pick the best proposal. The proposals are at least partially worked out before the meeting, as opposed to Cognoter meetings, which begin with a blank slate. Since Argnoter participants have already invested some energy in the creation of these proposals, the meetings have a greater potential for dispute and disagreement. Discovering, understanding, and evaluating disagreement are therefore essential parts of informed decision making in these meetings.

In developing a design—which is essentially a dialectic between goals and possibilities—designers usually begin without knowing exactly what is wanted or what is possible. They explore parts of the design space as driven by their current goals, and sharpen their goals as they learn what is possible. In collaborative design tasks, this interaction and tension between goals and alternatives must play itself out in the communications among collaborators. At the beginning, design goals are not necessarily shared; the elaboration of a common set of goals is part of the collaborative process and includes the incremental development and selection of design alternatives.

The intuition guiding the Argnoter process is the recognition that much of the dispute and misunderstanding that arise in meetings about design proposals are due to three major causes: *owned positions*, that is, personal attachment to certain positions; *un-*

stated assumptions; and *unstated criteria*. Hence, a major theme of Argnoter design is that alternatives be made explicit: Proposals themselves are explicit, as are assumptions and evaluation criteria.

In essence, the Argnoter meeting comprises three distinct phases—*proposing*, *arguing*, and *evaluating*—which in some respects are similar to the respective phases in Cognoter, but different enough to warrant description.

Proposing

In the proposal phase, the proposals are stated explicitly: Each proposal is given a short text description, and perhaps a sketch, and is named according to its features or functions. In Argnoter, a proposal will be created in, and displayed by, a set of connected windows called proposal "forms," which can be either private or public. Public proposal forms are WYSIWIS, whereas a private form appears only on the machine of the participant who controls it. Private forms ensure that every participant can view or create a new proposal without having to share its use. Other windows will allow viewing any of the proposals under consideration in the meeting. New proposals are created by modifying an existing one or combining features from two or more different ones. A new proposal automatically inherits text, sketches, and statements from its parent proposals.

Even with the high-resolution, wide-format displays used in the Colab, space for windows is limited: A proposal displayed with its text, sketch, and arguments occupies about one-fourth of the screen. The default configuration allows enough viewing space for two public proposal forms, one private form, and a variety of other forms. However, displays of the kind available on most personal computers would be inadequate for viewing even a single proposal and would not work well for most Colab tools.

Arguing

The next phase consists of presenting reasons for choosing or not choosing individual proposals. Reasons must be written down. On the chalkboard, the reasons are written as statements underneath the respective proposals. Each statement is identified as either pro or con and consists of a short text description like "very expensive" or "can't be done in less than six months." The structure of Argnoter encourages participants to write pro and con statements about all proposals, not just pro statements for the ones they are in favor of and con statements for the rest. Since the pro and con statements are there for all to see and contemplate, participants tend to take the time to formulate them carefully. Insubstantial statements like "I just don't like proposal X" will carry less weight than ones that are specific and focused.

---

[4] The name *Argnoter* is intended to suggest *argument noter*, that is, a tool to help organize and evaluate arguments.

This shared use of a chalkboard to present proposals and arguments has been used habitually and successfully by other groups that we know about. The following anecdote about another laboratory illustrates this:

> On any given morning at the Laboratory of Molecular Biology in Cambridge, England, the blackboard of Francis Crick or Sidney Brenner will commonly be found covered with logical trees. On the top line will be the hot new result just up from the laboratory or just in by letter or rumor. On the next line will be two or three alternative explanations, or a little list of "what he did wrong". Underneath will be a series of suggested experiments or controls that can reduce the number of possibilities. And so on. The tree grows during the day as one man or another comes in and argues about why one of the experiments wouldn't work, or how it should be changed. [27]

For comparative purposes, it is possible in the argument phase to categorize pro or con statements across proposals in terms of categories like compatibility, cost, development time, efficiency, feasibility, simplicity, and utility. With computational support, it is possible to automatically create auxiliary tables that compare proposals on the basis of these categories.

In the argument stage, participants can add statements or modify existing proposals. This tends to foster a synergy among ideas, joint contributions to proposals and reasons, and the systematic development of parallel reasoning across proposals. According to Platt [27], this kind of group participation in the articulation of *multiple* proposals and arguments often leads to a very productive decision-making process:

> The conflict and exclusion of alternatives that is necessary for sharp inductive inference has been all too often a conflict between men, each with his single Ruling Theory. But whenever each man begins to have multiple working hypotheses, it becomes purely a conflict between ideas. . . . In fact, when there are multiple hypotheses which are not anyone's "personal property" and when there are crucial experiments to test them, the daily life in the laboratory takes on an interest and excitement it never had, and the students can hardly wait to get to work to see how the detective story will come out.

The articulation of multiple proposals and their arguments leads naturally into the next phase—evaluation—in the sense that proposals are being evaluated *indirectly* by analyzing the reasons behind them. Moreover, this articulation encourages a style of decision making that separates arguments about evaluation criteria from arguments about the proposals themselves.

Evaluating

First, the evaluation considers the assumptions behind individual arguments. Assumptions in Argnoter are expressed as statements about statements: For example, the statement "this assumes that labor costs can be ignored" could refer to the statement "this proposal is inexpensive." Whereas historically we might have written such assumptions on the chalkboard next to the corresponding arguments, with Argnoter, we will ultimately provide facilities for viewing the structure of arguments in terms of the connections between these statements.

Meeting participants often disagree about the validity of statements: One person might believe that "sixteen million bit memory chips will be readily available in six months" and another may not. In Argnoter, we will try to model these differences with explicit "belief sets," a belief set being a mapping of a set of statements into valid (believed) or invalid (not believed) categories. This kind of modeling is something that cannot effectively be done on chalkboards.

The act of making belief sets explicit enables Argnoter to act as a kind of *argumentation spreadsheet* where a proposal is viewed and evaluated in relation to a specified set of beliefs. The proposal display is generated by stepping through the arguments about the proposal, looking up the assumptions, and then displaying those arguments that are supported in the specified belief set. Multiple belief sets may coexist, and any participant is able to create (or specialize) belief sets. The belief sets are intended to characterize different generic points of view (e.g., liberal versus conservative, marketing versus development).

Just as a numerical spreadsheet program provides a way of exploring entailments of hypothetical numerical relationships, an argumentation spreadsheet like Argnoter provides a way of exploring belief entailments. A numerical spreadsheet program provides no in-depth understanding of the meanings of interest rate, tax rate, or monthly income, but it does compute the necessary sums and display changes in the derived values when the input values are changed. In the same way, Argnoter need not understand the meanings of design proposals: It need only differentiate between proposals, arguments, assumptions, and belief sets, and compute the relevant logical support relationships. One should be able to change a belief assignment and then immediately see the relevant changes in the proposal display. Differences in point of view can also be highlighted (e.g., by displaying a proposal under different belief sets). Other evaluations, like sensitivity analyses, can be done using the same information.

Next, evaluation criteria are selected and ranked.

The values of specific criteria are often ranked differently by different participants: Feasibility, for example, is usually considered important, but there may be disagreements about trade-offs between cost versus utility or space versus time.

Evaluation criteria and beliefs represent different dimensions of the evaluation process. Two participants may agree that cost is a primary criterion, but disagree about whether a specific proposal is expensive; conversely, they might agree on the costs of different proposals, but disagree about the significance of cost as a criterion. Using Argnoter, we can experiment with different ways of ranking criteria and provide mechanisms for viewing proposals according to these rankings.

A major working hypothesis behind the design of Argnoter is that making the structure of arguments explicit facilitates consensus by reducing disagreement that arises from uncommunicated differences. Since participants using Argnoter first agree on criteria and then systematically apply those criteria to proposals, experiments suggest themselves as to whether in fact such behavior actually speeds consensus and to what extent Argnoter actually encourages such behavior.

In the process of making particular kinds of statements explicit and leaving other kinds implicit, Colab tool designers may inadvertently bias the meeting processes. In both Cognoter and Argnoter, the lack of an explicit representation of goals for the meetings may prejudice the discussion at particular times. Designers of Colab tools are therefore necessarily creating more than just tools: They are also designing and enforcing meeting processes. We see the Colab as a working laboratory for increasing our understanding of meeting processes and examining the effects of computational support tools on these processes.

PROGRAMMING ISSUES AND CONCEPTS

Two primary assumptions about the Colab's computing architecture were made: (1) Each meeting participant was to have a personal computer, and all the computers were to be connected together through a local-area network; and (2) all the computers were to run the same software. In retrospect, this approach has been workable and appears reasonable: It is also open-ended to the extent that processors can be added to the network to carry out special functions, and special software can be added to some of the computers.

Programs distributed over several machines are notoriously difficult to write and debug. This, combined with our need to experiment and change code frequently, motivated us to develop programming tools to simplify developing, testing, and revising. In

the balance of this section, we describe certain extensions to a programming language and environment we developed for the Colab, and how we have used them.

Colab tools enable people to share and jointly revise information presented in meeting situations. For this discussion, it is useful to think of this information as residing in a computer database that has certain properties. To this end, we leave the granularity of logical data items unspecified, although, in practice, grain size is determined by our intentions about the independence of the data items. The design of the database is a starting point for understanding the issues and programming techniques used in designing and executing Colab tools. The following goals arise naturally out of the Colab application and reflect as well general expectations about the use of personal computers:

- The delay in getting information should be very short. To generate complex information displays, the average retrieval time should be on the order of a few microseconds.

- The delay in changing information should be short. To avoid a feeling of sluggishness, it should usually be possible to change information in a fraction of a second.

- The database should converge quickly to a consistent state.

- The database should not be vulnerable to either the accidental actions of one participant or the failure in one participant's machine.

Maintaining the Database

To maintain the Colab database, we experimented with several control regimes: the centralized model, the centralized-lock model, the cooperative model, the dependency-detection model, and the roving-locks model.

Centralized Model. The straightforward centralized approach, which has been used successfully in other similar applications (e.g., [29, 30]), ensures that all participants use the same data: There is only one copy of the database, and concurrency control is straightforward. To coordinate simultaneous changes, database transaction mechanisms must be used. The centralized model was rejected out of hand for Colab purposes because we could not use these mechanisms to retrieve data fast enough to update our displays. Moreover, given our plan to use networked personal computers, we would incur the additional delay of network communication.

Centralized-Lock Model. The distributed model corrects the slow retrieval problem of the centralized model by caching data on each of the workstations.

Data for the visual display are always fetched directly from the cache and are updated whenever changes are received. Several variations on this approach are described in [2].

In this model, each computer has a copy of the database, but cannot make changes to an item until it obtains ownership of that item. To secure ownership of data means obtaining a lock from a centralized lock server. There can be one lock for the whole database, or separate locks for different parts of it. With multiple locks, changes to different parts of the database can proceed in parallel. When there is just one lock, only one participant at a time can make changes since any change requires locking the entire database. Another extreme is to have a separate lock for every datum.

Locks provide mutual exclusion for processes that write data, and changes to the database are serialized by the numbered sequences of lock owners. This ensures that machines will converge to the same state. If some transactions require ownership of more than one lock, the usual cautions and techniques for avoiding deadlock apply [7, 15] (e.g., transactions that require multiple locks must acquire them all at once).

Unfortunately, our implementation of this model has so far yielded unacceptable delays for obtaining locks; these delays can be traced to a limitation of the process scheduler in our programming environment, namely, that it is not preemptive. There is no way to guarantee limits on delays in our system since processes are not prioritized and can run an arbitrary amount of time without yielding.

Cooperative Model. In the cooperative model, the approach we are currently using, each machine has a copy of the database, and changes are installed by broadcasting the change without any synchronization. By itself, this approach entails the following inherent race conditions: If two participants make changes to the same data simultaneously, there is a race to see which change will take effect first, and the results can be different on different machines.

Two factors mitigate against these apparent shortcomings. The first is that most sequences of changes to our databases yield results that are independent of the order in which they are done. Moreover, Colab participants are aware of the problem and use verbal cues ("voice locks") to coordinate their behavior; it is therefore rare that participants will change the same data at the same time.

The second factor is that, quite apart from the mechanisms for ensuring integrity of the distributed database, in the Colab we need to provide mechanisms that coordinate the activities of the participants and support the social mechanisms for both

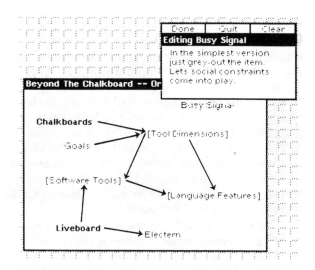

When multiple users interact with a shared object, conflicts can occur. An early conflict detection system—a busy signal—quickly warns users that someone else is already editing an item, and brings social constraints into play; one way to indicate a busy item is to gray it out.

FIGURE 6. A Busy Item

partitioning work and reaching agreement that meetings by their nature rely on. One such mechanism is the busy signal described earlier. By graying out screen items that are in use, the signal warns other collaborators not to change them (see Figure 6). But, because there is an inherent delay between the moment that someone starts working on an item and the time that the busy signal is propagated to others, it is possible that a second participant will begin an incompatible revision. In this case, the busy signal ensures that two participants will *quickly discover* that they are working in a conflicting way.

In total, we are not satisfied with the properties of the cooperative model and are planning to investigate several alternatives presented in [2] for using two-phased locking and time stamps. Since the immediate users of our database are all people in visual and verbal contact, we are willing to consider the need for manual intervention in occasional cases of synchronization failure (i.e., to make some sacrifices to achieve the desired performance levels). Two specific approaches that we are considering are the last two discussed here: the dependency-detection model and the roving-locks model.

Dependency-Detection Model. The dependency-detection model corrects some of the shortcomings of the cooperative model by annotating data with a stamp describing the author and time of the change. Every request to change data broadcasts several things: the new data, its stamp, and the stamp of the previous version of the data on the originating machine. When a machine receives a message requesting a change, it first checks whether the previous stamp in the request is the same as the stamp in its database. If they are different, a "dependency conflict" is signaled. The conflict is then resolved by a process that involves human intervention (at least to temporarily suspend activity), followed by propagation of the resolved values for data or the creation of multiple versions of the data.

The advantage of the dependency-detection approach is responsiveness. Changes to data do not first require serialization or the delay of obtaining a lock. The system assumes that a change can always be made, but it may have to fix things later if a conflict is detected.

Like the cooperative model, the dependency-detection model contains inherent race conditions, but it is able to detect them after the fact. If two participants change data at the same time, at least one of the machines will detect a dependency conflict as described above. However, it is possible to get "false alarms" if messages about changes to data from different sources arrive out of order; a dependency conflict would then be incorrectly signaled. Similarly, if two participants made a series of nearly simultaneous changes to a datum, multiple false alarms might be signaled. The ability to distinguish false alarms can be enhanced by keeping a longer history of changes. We do not yet have enough experience to decide whether the dependency-detection model (which is closely related to an approach called *certification* [2]) is necessary or practical.

Roving-Locks Model. The roving-locks model tries to reduce the delay in obtaining locks that is incurred with the centralized-lock model by distributing the lock-granting processes along with lock ownership. This is different than simply locating locks with the data; the intention here is to distribute control over specific data items to their last user, leading to a sort of "working set" [8] for locks. In this scenario, a participant's machine would tend to acquire the set of locks for that subset of the database on which it is actively working. Most lock requests would require no communication with other machines. After the first access, delay in getting a lock would be significant only in those cases where the lock is on a remote machine, that is, when two or more participants are actually competing for the same parts of the database.

Even if the working-set model is valid for locks, we suspect that the success of this model may de-

pend on its having a preemptive scheduler to bound the delays in obtaining remote locks. More experience with the model is needed to determine whether roving locks is a practical solution.

Language Support

Colab software is built on Xerox Lisp Machines connected by an Ethernet [23]. The software is written in Loops [4], an object-oriented extension of Lisp [28] that resembles Smalltalk-80 [14] in that programs are organized in terms of objects that can hold data. Computation proceeds as objects send messages to each other. Loops supports the notion of permanent objects whose identity is specified by a unique identifier that is guaranteed to be unique across machines. Versions of these permanent objects can exist on several machines simultaneously. An *association* is a set of representations on multiple machines that stand for the same object; the individual representations are called *associates* and have the same unique identifier.

In the Colab, we use the term *conversation* to refer to the combination of a set of machines, Colab tools, and participants working together to solve a problem. When a new participant is added to a conversation, all participants find out about the newcomer, and the newcomer finds out about the other participants; the newcomer's machine gets copies of the object that represent the database.

In a conversation, communication is implemented by a combination of system facilities and programming abstractions and is supported over the Ethernet by several layers of protocols. Our implementation rests on a protocol for remote procedure calls [3]. On top of this, we have added a mechanism for sending messages to an object on a remote machine, and another for sending messages to all the associates of an object in a conversation.

Colab tools communicate via a programming abstraction that we call *broadcast methods*. Broadcast methods extend the object-oriented notion of methods from a single machine to multiple machines in a conversation. When a method is annotated as being a broadcast method, invoking it on one machine means that it will be run on all machines in the conversation. For example, if *Move* is a broadcast method in a Cognoter window for moving an item in the window, and *item37* receives a *Move* message on one of the machines, then *item37*'s associates on all the other machines will also receive the same message. All the details of queueing and transmitting the message to the relevant machines are handled automatically without further specification by the programmer.

Broadcast methods provide a simple abstraction for organizing communication, and a mechanism for efficient communication about changes to the database. Colab tools assume that the software is loaded on the machines of all participants. In most cases, the bandwidth of network communication can be reduced by sending instructions rather than data.

Ideally, one should be able to take a program written for a single machine and change it into a distributed program by annotating some of the methods so that they will broadcast. In practice, this has worked out rather well. To support this facility, we have found it useful to establish a discipline for deciding which methods should be broadcast.

Methods are categorized roughly into three different sets that are treated differently with respect to conversion to broadcast methods: *user input, semantic actions*, and *display actions*. User-input methods control user interaction that specifies a change to be made to the database; they are run at the user's request (e.g., caused by mouse action) and are used to determine the nature and scope of a change. User-input methods are not made into broadcast methods because only the user initiating the change wants to engage in the interaction. The actual changes to the database are made by the semantic-action methods, which are broadcast so that the changes to the database will propagate to all machines containing the meeting database. Display-action methods update the displays and are not broadcast because the display is updated as a side effect of changing the database. If the image in more than one window depends on the value of a datum, then multiple display-action methods should be triggered by a single semantic-action method.

In some cases, the appropriate partitioning of methods into these categories can be subtle. For example, windows for displaying data can be parameterized (as in the case of proposal forms for Argnoter), thereby altering their display according to display parameters that specify belief sets or rankings of evaluation criteria. Maintaining WYSIWIS for these windows requires that changes to these parameters be considered part of the database and be broadcast as semantic actions; the subtlety arises to the extent that "display parameters" might be confused with display-action methods, which are not broadcast. Furthermore, when semantic actions can be derived from more primitive ones, only the primitive ones need be broadcast.

Support for Debugging
To make the debugging process more manageable, we have created tools for tracing and intercepting messages on the network. To monitor message transmission between machines, we use a conversation viewer. It works for all Colab tools, letting us monitor the broadcast queues and processes used to send messages between machines. The viewer shows when messages are queued, sent, and received, as well as the identity of the other machines. Using the viewer, we can often detect cases of unnecessary or incorrect message sending.

We have also developed tools for propagating program changes between machines. In debugging sessions, we have found it useful to make program changes on one machine and then to broadcast the changes to the other machines.

PRELIMINARY OBSERVATIONS AND RESEARCH QUESTIONS
If computers are to provide more effective meeting tools, we need a commensurately more adequate understanding of meeting processes. Although meetings are something that most of us know well, they come under the heading of those everyday activities that, because we know them so well, remain largely unexamined. Designing the Colab has required that we look again at the organization of meetings and meeting technology; at the same time, the Colab currently in place provides an experimental setting for pursuing these lines of research. In this section we present our preliminary observations about the Colab and describe the research issues that have been raised by these observations.

In their current form, Colab tools reflect our experience of, and ideas about, our own work processes, in particular those aimed at collaborative writing and argumentation. Our research strategy is to draw upon familiar practices first, and then to locate those practices within a wider range of face-to-face meetings in different settings and with different participants. The Colab was used early on to produce the present article, and even though the Colab was not yet fitted with audiovisual recording equipment or documenting software, these early sessions did provide a set of preliminary observations about the relationship between Cognoter tools and the writing process, and their relation to the process of collaborative writing.

The Structure of the Writing Process
The current Cognoter design reflects a set of conjectures regarding the writing process, from the early stage of idea generation and development through the generation of a path or outline for a final presentation. The actual use of Cognoter revealed not only the points of fit between design and process, but some subtle disjunctures as well.

For example, the design premise for Cognoter was that the brainstorming window be an unstructured repository for ideas. The availability of a public window, into which people could easily and spontaneously enter new text, would allow the group to put a large number of ideas "onto the table" without a great deal of discussion or negotiation. Ideally, this initial brainstorming phase is followed by an organizing phase, in which group members elaborate the relationships between ideas and debate their cogency. However, in early sessions with Cognoter, we found that even before moving on to the organizing phase, members began using spatial grouping in the brainstorming window to display relationships between ideas. Even after items were explicitly linked, the spatial cues helped to display the relationships between items; these spatial cues, in turn, were important to the elaboration of meaning.

The process of organizing and evaluation made it easier to see whether or not the set of ideas generated during brainstorming was complete. Although our initial design assumption was that use of the outlining tool would follow completion of the evaluation phase, in practice, participants found the outlining tool useful for displaying intermediate states of the emerging structure as well. These observations suggest slightly different "joints" in the process than we had originally assumed. In future sessions, we will look carefully at the natural organization of the group writing process, the way people use the available tools to see the developing structure of their collective argument, and the relationship between the initial design assumptions and the actual uses people make of the tools.

Maintaining the Collaboration
The Colab's starting premise was that serial access to problem-solving technology obstructs the kind of equal participation that ideally characterizes collaboration, particularly for an activity like writing, where collaboration seems ideally not to involve any predetermined or fixed division of labor among participants. The multiuser interface was designed to overcome this obstacle by letting participants act simultaneously, write independently, and enter new text into a shared database—virtually at the same time. By equalizing access of all participants to displays and shared data, the Colab's interface enhances flexibility as to roles and discourages control over the activity by any one participant.

However, our early sessions demonstrated that the constraints imposed by current technologies are not just a limitation on collaboration but in some ways a resource as well. In particular, the fact that a writing technology allows only one person to enter text at a time enforces a kind of shared focus (i.e., a focus on that person's actions) that maintains a common context for the group. Where only one person at a time has access to the writing technology, roles are in a very real sense visible at a glance; moreover, what is being done to the text is transparent in the actions of

whomever controls the writing technology. Many of the accompanying practices—rising to go to the chalkboard, taking over the keyboard—can also be viewed as resources for the participants in the sense of seeing what is going on and providing a basis for the smooth exchange of roles. The possibility of independent writing activity and simultaneous entry of new text brings new demands on participants to stay informed about what others are doing. Relaxing the requirements on turn taking by allowing parallel actions necessitates alternative ways of accomplishing what the turn-taking system accomplishes: namely, an orderly transition from one participant to the next, and an incremental, sequentially coherent development of the joint activity.

In early Cognoter meetings, the work of maintaining a shared focus was evident in the ebb and flow of meeting activity. During the ordering phase particularly, where ideas are elaborated, participants tended to interact verbally for a few minutes, explaining immediate goals and making short-term plans of action, after which the group settled into their "assignments," typing intently for a while. After a few minutes of parallel editing, people would lose track of what the others were doing and, therefore, of what to do next. The group would then stop interacting with the system and again discuss where they were and what they should do. These transitions between parallel and convergent activity sometimes required negotiation. In particular, individuals engaged in different activities might not arrive at transition places simultaneously and might not be equally interruptable at any given time. The early Cognoter sessions encompassed several such cycles of regrouping, summarization, joint planning, and then parallel action.

Along with personal interaction, shared focus is achieved by means of reference to common objects. Cognoter's goal, as with a chalkboard, is to enable participants to refer to common objects through various kinds of efficient reference such as deixis[5] and pointing. Although the WYSIWIS idealization recognizes that efficient reference depends on a common view of the work at hand, a distinctive problem arises in computer-based environments in that the boundary between logical and physical objects is blurred. This represents a tremendous advantage, on one level, in that relaxations of WYSIWIS allow participants to tailor their individual display of the shared view to their own specifications. However, it also means that, although people may be referring to the "same" piece of text, the text may be in an entirely different location on their respective displays. With the use of windows that can be moved, re-

---
[5] *Deixis* means referring to something either verbally (e.g., "the gray house across the street") or by pointing.

shaped, and scrolled, conventions are required to avoid situations in which one person tries to see some text at the top of a long passage while another tries to see text at the bottom, or one member of the group puts up a very large public window, obscuring everyone else's view (situations that we have informally dubbed "Scroll Wars" and "Window Wars").

As well as confirming the usefulness of a single view of the public record, our early experience with Cognoter identified a more subtle element of shared focus. With a single display device (e.g., a chalkboard or workstation), it is common for one person to be assigned the task of actually entering new text into the record; typically, not only the new text, but the writing activity itself, is visible to the other participants. In the current design of Cognoter, however, the actual editing is done in private windows, with only the finished text broadcast to coparticipants. This design decision, while encouraging parallel activity, poses some interesting new problems for the collaborative process. In particular, participants in the early sessions expressed frustration at not being able to see what the others were doing; specifically, at not being able to watch when others were engaged in writing. To an important degree, it seems that participants need access not only to the product of each others' writing, but to the writing process itself. The unanticipated usefulness of the video switch, which allows one to switch between displays,[6] underscores the importance of a shared view for maintaining the joint focus. User frustrations in this regard reopen the question as to the ideal grain size at which individual and group transactions take place, and the relationship between private and public views.

In general, these early observations were confirmed by a small set of controlled experiments run at UC Berkeley. In the trials, several pairs of student collaborators unfamiliar with the Colab used either Cognoter or a chalkboard to plan article outlines. The outcomes showed that the interface of Cognoter is complicated enough to require practice to be used effectively [13]. More extensive trials with larger groups will await the completion of video recording and meeting analysis tools that are now being created.

Research Questions

Our guiding question has been, What are the processes of collaboration for which the computer is an appropriate tool, and what particular Colab tools could be designed to support these processes? As a first approximation, Cognoter and Argnoter have as-

sumed two contrasting processes of collaborative writing and argumentation, both drawn from our own experience. Cognoter takes a joint presentation as its object and encourages consensus by supporting a single viewpoint, whereas Argnoter encourages competing proposals and delayed consensus by allowing the display and comparison of multiple views.

Having identified the collaborative processes and refined the associated tools, we need next to question the generality of our assumptions. To what extent do our work practices compare and contrast with other settings and other participants? Does a tool, by reifying a process and making it explicit, thereby also make it portable across groups? Or do we need a set of tools that can be customized to different users in different settings? Under what circumstances are explicit structures desirable, and under what circumstances do we want to minimize the amount of structure we build into our tools? These questions and others will be explored as we extend the design and experiment with its use.

RELATED WORK

The possibility that computers might be used to support group problem solving was appreciated by early visionaries long before it was practically feasible. In 1945, Bush presented a hypothetical system called a "Memex" that included an interactive database [6] by which associative "trails" of exploration could be saved to be recalled and retraced at a later time. Bush believed that a common encyclopedic database of information integrated from many areas of human activity would enhance the quality of societal problem solving.

In the 1960s, experimental systems like the NLS/AUGMENT [11, 12] began to use computers to support collaboration. The NLS/AUGMENT supported terminal linking, electronic mail, sharing of files, and "televiewing"—the ability to "pass the gavel" among several people working together at separate terminals. Englebart saw machines as providing an important medium for communication and was known for his development of novel user interfaces like the mouse. Englebart was also an early worker in hypertext, systems that organize fragments of text in annotated networks. This work has been pursued in several other systems including TEXTNET [33], Xanadu [24], NoteCards [34], and Annoland.

At a time when time-shared systems like TENEX [5] popularized electronic mail and shared files, some observers (e.g., Lederberg [21]) reported a qualitative difference in the ways they were interacting with colleagues. In the mid 1970s, researchers at the Stanford AI Lab built a video, audio, and keyboard

---

[6] The Colab video switch allows the content of any screen to be directed to another screen; it was originally designed to aid in debugging across multiple machines.

crossbar switch to allow users at multiple workstations to collaborate from separate workstations. At the same time, another line of work pursued the use of communications facilities to tie together people working at different locations. Known as *teleconferencing* [18, 19], this work eschewed much use of computers and has developed slowly, due largely to high communication costs for video images. Meanwhile, others have developed systems for remote conferencing that rely mostly on computers rather than video: Known as *computer conferencing*, these systems include electronic mail, editors, voting mechanisms, shared files, and archiving, but do not provide structure for the conferences based on any models of group problem-solving processes. In [16], Hiltz and Turoff review some of these systems and provide an extensive bibliography; prime examples are EIES [17] and some parts of NLS/AUGMENT [11].

Although computers have been used experimentally in meetings to support specialized problem-solving processes since at least 1972 [35], the impact has been much less dramatic than with other computer applications (see [20]). Most of these systems are organized around formal and mathematical models of decision making like multiattribute utility models and cost–benefit analyses. The Delphi method [22] and the Nominal Group method [20], for example, are techniques for structuring group problem solving that have been used with and without computer support. The Delphi model considered by Turoff [35] is designed for technological forecasting by a geographically dispersed group, while the Nominal Group represents a consensus-forming process for face-to-face meetings; both have been characterized as "rational but naive" [20]. Since we have little experience with them, we offer no independent assessment; however, we note that the meeting processes used in the Colab are similar to the meeting methods commonly taught in corporate training programs.

RTCAL/IOLC, a somewhat analogous system to the Colab that was developed at MIT by Sunil Sarin [30], allows a group of users to synchronously exchange information from personal calendar databases to schedule a future meeting. It differs from the Colab in particular trade-offs of computer communication (e.g., RTCAL has a centralized database management scheme) and the absence of process models for problem solving, but is similar in that it uses personal computers, works in real time, and maintains consistent views by message passing over a local network [29]. Another research project reported by Applegate, Konsynski, and Nunamaker [1] also resembles the Colab in that it provides personal computers to meeting participants around a conference table and uses a video projector to provide

large public views; it also provides tools for brainstorming and analysis. However, unlike the Colab, it is oriented around decision support models for planning and quantitative analysis. Also, since it is built using microcomputers with very limited display space, there has been little opportunity to experiment with private and public windows or multiuser interfaces.

Kraemer and King [20] observe that there are very few successful computer conference rooms, if any, and that even these systems have been plagued by hardware difficulties. As the primary obstacles to success, they cite inaccessibility of computing resources, unreliable video projectors, and limited graphics capabilities. However, they quite rightly note that in recent years computing and projection technology have become much more reliable and also less expensive. We agree with them that most of the activity with computer-supported conferences over the next three to four years will center on research and development.

In terms of technology, there have been several advances that will enable this work to proceed at a much more rapid pace: among them, more powerful personal workstations, local-area networks, advanced programming environments [31], distributed programming, and interface technology. These advances will make it possible to develop prototype systems quite rapidly and thus to experiment readily with new tools.

CONCLUSIONS

Focusing on developing and understanding "team computers" (i.e., collaborative systems for group meetings), the Colab project has produced a usable meeting room and several operational tools. The liveboard is operational but not fully integrated with our software. As we begin to use the Colab on a regular basis, it will afford a laboratory for studying the effects of the tools on collaborative meetings. The Colab meeting room is now being fitted with the video equipment necessary to record working Colab sessions. We will use the Colab to try to understand why collaborative problem solving is organized as it is, the relationship of that organization to existing technology, and the trade-offs involved in displacing old practices with new technology.

Upon hearing about the Colab, a manager from a large American corporation whose job it is to introduce appropriate computing technology at the executive staff level told us an interesting story. After working diligently for several months to bring things up-to-date and to revitalize operations with tools like electronic mail, document processing, databases, and automatic spreadsheets, he remained unsure about the degree of success he had achieved. One day, in a burst of frank evaluation, one of his charges told him that, despite the best intentions, he felt the computer was not making a difference and did not expect it to save him more than 30 minutes a day, even if he did learn how to use it. The reason was that this individual was not in his office for more than 30 minutes; he spent almost his entire day in meetings! *Moral: Office automation simply does not reach people who are away from their offices*, which brings us back to the premise of the Colab project: Meetings are important. They are at the core of the way most organizations do business. As such, tools like the Colab touch fundamentally the ways we meet and make decisions collectively.

Acknowledgments. This article has benefited greatly from the suggestions and criticisms of Agustin Araya, John Seely Brown, Richard Fateman, John Florentin, Mark D. Hill, Bernardo Huberman, Randy Katz, Mark Miller, Sanjay Mittal, Ted Selker, Jeff Shrager, and Mike Stonebraker.

Many thanks to Bill Volkers for creating the liveboard, and to Stu Card and Jeff Shrager for early ideas for the liveboard. We wish to acknowledge Ted Selker for his suggestions about many aspects of the Colab and for designing electronic chalk for the liveboard; Steve Osburn, Joan Osburn, Gene Hall, and Lee Anderson for creating the Colab physical setting; and Steven Levy for his contributions to the first implementations of Colab software.

Special thanks to John Seely Brown for his ideas, criticisms, and encouragement on the Colab project. Without his support, the project could never have been launched nor could the initial momentum have been sustained. Thanks also to Bill Spencer and George Pake for creating an environment at Xerox PARC that makes projects like this possible.

REFERENCES
1. Applegate, L.M., Konsynski, B.R., and Nunamaker, J.F. A group decision support system for idea generation and issue analysis in organizational planning. In *Proceedings of the Conference on Computer-Supported Cooperative Work* (Austin, Tex., Dec.). ACM, New York. To be published.
2. Bernstein, P.A., and Goodman, N. Concurrency control in distributed database systems. *ACM Comput. Surv. 13*, 2 (June 1981), 185–221.
3. Birrell, A.D., and Nelson, B.J. Implementing remote procedure calls. Tech. Note CSL-83-7, Xerox PARC, Palo Alto, Calif., Dec. 1983.
4. Bobrow, D.G., and Stefik, M.J. *The Loops Manual.* Xerox PARC, Palo Alto, Calif., 1983.
5. Bobrow, D.G., Burchfiel, J.D., Murphy, D.L., and Tomlinson, R.S. TENEX, a paged time-sharing system for the PDP-10. *Commun. ACM 15*, 3 (Mar. 1972), 135–143.
6. Bush, V. As we may think. *Atlantic Mon. 176*, 1 (June 1945), 101–108.
7. Coffman, E.G., Elphick, M.J., and Shoshani, A. System deadlocks. *ACM Comput. Surv. 3*, 2 (June 1971), 67–78.
8. Denning, P.J. Virtual memory. *ACM Comput. Surv. 2*, 3 (Sept. 1970), 153–189.
9. Donahue, J., and Widom, J. Whiteboards: A graphical database tool. *ACM Trans. Off. Inf. Syst. 4*, 1 (Jan. 1986), 24–41.
10. Doyle, M., and Straus, D. *How to Make Meetings Work.* Berkeley Publishing Group, New York, 1984.
11. Englebart, D.C. Collaboration support provisions in AUGMENT, OAC 84 digest. In *Proceedings of the 1984 AFIPS Office Automation Conference* (Los Angeles, Calif. Feb. 20–22). AFIPS, Reston, Va., 1984, pp. 51–58.
12. Englebart, D.C., and English, W.K. Research center for augmenting human intellect. In *Proceedings of the Fall Joint Computing Conference* (San Francisco, Calif., Dec. 9–11). AFIPS, Reston, Va., 1968, pp. 395–410.
13. Foster, G. Collaborative systems and multi-user interfaces: Computer-based tools for cooperative work. Doctoral dissertation, Computer Science Division, Univ. of California at Berkeley, Dec. 1986. To be published.
14. Goldberg, A., and Robson, D. *Smalltalk-80: The Language and Its Implementation.* Addison-Wesley, Reading, Mass., 1983.
15. Hansen, P.B. *Operating System Principles.* Prentice-Hall, Englewood Cliffs, N.J., 1973.
16. Hiltz, S.R., and Turoff, M. *The Network Nation: Human Communication via Computer.* Addison-Wesley, Reading, Mass., 1978.
17. Hiltz, S.R., and Turoff, M. The evolution of user behavior in a computerized conferencing system. *Commun. ACM 24*, 11 (Nov. 1981), 739–752.
18. Johansen, R. *Teleconferencing and Beyond: Communications in the Office of the Future.* McGraw-Hill, New York, 1984.
19. Johansen, R., Vallee, J., and Spangler, K. *Electronic Meetings: Technical Alternatives and Social Choices.* Addison-Wesley, Reading, Mass., 1979.
20. Kraemer, K.L., and King, J.L. Computer supported conference rooms: Final report of a state of the art study. Dept. of Information and Computer Science, Univ. of California, Irvine, Dec. 1983.
21. Lederberg, J. Digital communications and the conduct of science: The new literacy. *Proc. IEEE 66*, 11 (Nov. 1978), 1313–1319.
22. Linstone, H.A., and Turoff, M. *The Delphi Method: Techniques and Applications.* Addison-Wesley, Reading, Mass., 1975.
23. Metcalfe, R.M., and Boggs, D.R. Ethernet: Distributed packet switching for local computer networks. *Commun. ACM 19*, 7 (July 1976), 395–404.
24. Nelson, T. *Literary Machines.* Ted Nelson, Swarthmore, Pa., 1981.
25. O'Connor, R.J. Outline processors catch on. *InfoWorld* (July 2, 1984), 30–31.
26. Panko, R.R. Office work. *Off. Technol. People 2* (1964), 205–238.
27. Platt, J.R. Strong Inference. *Science 146*, 3642 (Oct. 1964), 347–353.
28. Sanella, M., et al. *Interlisp Reference Manual.* Xerox PARC, Palo Alto, Calif., 1983.
29. Sarin, S.K. Interactive on-line conferences. Ph.D. thesis MIT/LCS/TR-330, MIT, Cambridge, Mass., Dec. 1984.
30. Sarin, S., and Greif, I. Computer-based real-time conferencing systems. *Computer 18*, 10 (Oct. 1985), 33–45.
31. Sheil, B. Power tools for programmers. *Datamation* (Feb. 1983), 131–144.
32. Stefik, M., Foster, G., Lanning, S., and Tatar, D. The scope of WYSIWIS: Early experiences with multi-user interfaces. In *Proceedings of the Conference on Computer-Supported Cooperative Work* (Austin, Tex., Dec.). ACM, New York. To be published.
33. Trigg, R., and Weiser, M. TEXTNET: A network-based approach to text handling. *ACM Trans. Off. Inf. Syst. 4*, 1 (Jan. 1986), 1–23.
34. Trigg, R., Suchman, L., and Halasz, F. Supporting collaboration in NoteCards. In *Proceedings of the Conference on Computer-Supported Cooperative Work* (Austin, Tex., Dec.). ACM, New York. To be published.
35. Turoff, M. Delphi conferencing: Computer-based conferencing with anonymity. *Technol. Forecasting Soc. Change 3* (1972), 159–204.

CR Categories and Subject Descriptors: H.1.2 [**Models and Principles**]: User/Machine Systems—*human factors; human information processing*; H.2.4 [**Database Management**]: Systems—*distributed systems*; H.4.m [**Information Systems Applications**]: Miscellaneous
General Terms: Design, Human Factors, Languages
Additional Key Words and Phrases: Computer-supported collaboration, computer-supported groups, computer-supported meetings, multi-user interfaces

Received 1/85; accepted 7/86

Authors' Present Addresses: Mark Stefik, Daniel G. Bobrow, Kenneth Kahn, Stan Lanning, and Lucy Suchman, Intelligent Systems Laboratory, Xerox Palo Alto Research Center, 3333 Coyote Hill Road, Palo Alto, CA 94304; Gregg Foster, Computer Science Division, University of California, Berkeley, CA 94720.

ELECTRONIC MEETING SYSTEMS TO SUPPORT GROUP WORK

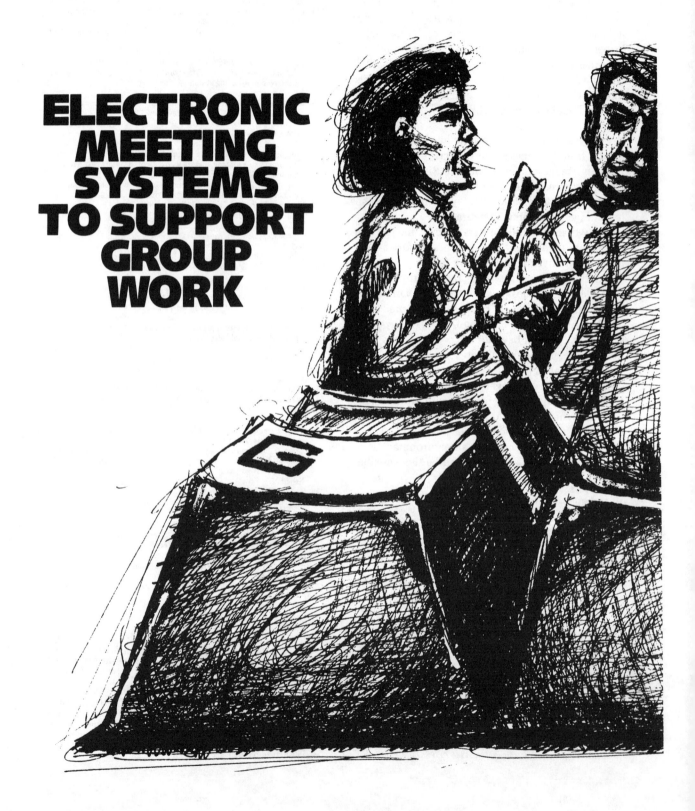

"Almost every time there is a genuinely important decision to be made in an organization, a group is assigned to make it—or at least to counsel and advise the individual who must make it." [21, p. 459]. No one works completely independently. Almost everyone is part of at least one group, typically several groups at any point in time.

Groups communicate, share information, generate ideas, organize ideas, draft policies and procedures, collaborate on the writing of reports, share a vision, build consensus, make decisions, and so on.

However, group meetings are often not as effective as they could be [42]. Meetings may lack a clear focus. Group members may not participate because they are apprehensive about how their ideas will be received or because a few members dominate discussions. Hidden agendas may promote political decisions that are not in the best interests of the organization. Meetings may end without a clear understanding or record of what was discussed. Yet in spite of these problems, little computer support is available for meetings—which is somewhat surprising given the ubiquitous nature of computer support in modern organizations.

A new form of meeting environment, which we term an Electronic Meeting System (EMS), has emerged which strives to make group meetings more productive by applying information technology. EMS technology is designed to directly impact and change the behavior of groups to improve group effectiveness, efficiency, and satisfaction. Our definition of a meeting is broad—including any activity where people come together, whether at the same place at the same time, or in different places at different times (see Figure 1) [5, 12].

The purpose of this article is to present the research conducted at the University of Arizona in developing and using same-time/same-place and same-time/different-place EMS technology.[1] The Arizona research program includes two types of research defined by Ackoff et al.[1]. The first type is developmental, which attempts to create improved work methods. The second type is empirical, which attempts to evaluate and understand them. The initial phase of the research program focused on the development of tools and techniques to support groups of analysts

J.F. Nunamaker
Alan R. Dennis
Joseph S. Valacich
Douglas R. Vogel
Joey F. George

PHOTO 1. The Collaborative Management Room at the University of Arizona

PHOTO 2. The Electronic Meeting Room at IBM Decision Support Center, Boulder, Colorado

and users in the construction of information systems. The second phase began in 1984 with the construction of a special-purpose meeting room to support the same-time/same-place meetings of these groups. This meeting room and the ones that followed are based on a series of networked microcomputer workstations arranged in a U-shape, around a table, or in tiered legislative style (see Photo 1). A large-screen video display is provided at the front of the room, from where the meeting leader/facilitator guides the meeting. Other audio-visual support is also available—typically white boards and overhead projectors [5, 36, 51, 53].

The realization that this technology enabled groups to perform many tasks beyond system development (e.g., strategic planning), led to the third phase which began in 1986 with the establishment of four major research projects with IBM. The number of EMS facilities at Arizona grew from one in 1985 to the three we have now. Four additional facilities are scheduled to open later this year. Each of these new facilities addresses a different cell in Figure 1; one is a large group meeting room, one is a small group meeting room, one supports distributed large groups, and the fourth is a meeting room-to-meeting room teleconferencing facility.

During this phase, new software was developed (University of Arizona GroupSystems[2]) and was installed at EMS facilities at more than 22 universities and 12 corpo-

[1]Much valuable EMS and related research has been conducted elsewhere. However, space limitations preclude us from discussing it, since an attempt to compare findings across different EMSs is appropriate only with a careful consideration of the different functions they provide. We encourage readers to examine the contributions made by other developers and empirical researchers (see [5, 39] for reviews of this work).

[2]GroupSystems evolved from the Plexsys Research Program.

[3]See "Strategy on the Screen," An Open University Videotape, Production Centre, British Broadcasting Corp., 1991.

rations, such as BellSouth and Greyhound Financial Corporation. IBM has built 36 GroupSystems facilities (e.g., see Photo 2), with an additional 20 scheduled to be operational by January 1992. More than 25,000 people have used GroupSystems within IBM; more than 3,000 others from 200 public and private organizations have used the Arizona GroupSystems facilities. Another 2,000 have used GroupSystems in more than 20 laboratory experiments and 15 doctoral dissertations that have been conducted at Arizona.

While GroupSystems supports a variety of different tasks, many groups follow a common sequence of use. The group leader meets with a GroupSystems meeting leader/facilitator, who assists in developing an agenda and selecting the GroupSystems tools to be used. Meetings typically begin with participants generating ideas (e.g., "How can we double our sales over the next four years?" see Figure 2). As they type their comments, the results are integrated and displayed on the large screens at the front of the room, as well as being available on each workstation. Everyone can see the comments of others, but without knowing who contributed what. Participants can build on each others' ideas, independent of any positive or negative bias about who contributed them—ideas are evaluated on their own merits, rather than on the basis of who contributed them. These ideas are then organized into a list of key issues (e.g., "Stronger ties with customers"), which the group can prioritize into a short list. Next, the group could generate ideas for action plans to accomplish the important issues, followed by more idea organization and prioritization, and so on. The result of the meeting is typically a large volume of input and ideas, and a group consensus for further action. In many cases, final decisions are not made during the meeting, but are made later by the group leader and/or other participants after considering all the in-

formation, knowledge and opinions shared. The EMS meeting can enable wide participation so that broad input has been obtained, ownership established, and consensus developed.

For example, Greyhound Financial Corporation has used GroupSystems on several occasions for a variety of tasks, including the development of a mission statement, strategy formulation, evaluations of senior managers, and information systems (IS) planning.[3] One meeting was a one-day session to develop proposals to create competitive advantage, in which 30 managers from all departments used a structured idea generation

process (a variant on the value chain technique) to develop proposals. On post-session questionnaires, 88% of participants reported that particular meeting was more effective than previous non-EMS meetings [7]. Said CEO S.L. Eichenfield: "I found that we accomplished 100% of our objectives. People usually reluctant to express themselves felt free to take part, and we were surprised by the number of new ideas expressed. We also reached conclusions far more rapidly."

The experience of this group is typical of the other groups in our field research. Our laboratory research generally supports our findings in the field. In this article we shall argue that EMS facilities can improve group work in many situations because it:

• enables all participants to work simultaneously (human parallel processing);
• provides an equal opportunity for participation;
• discourages behavior that can negatively impact meeting productivity;

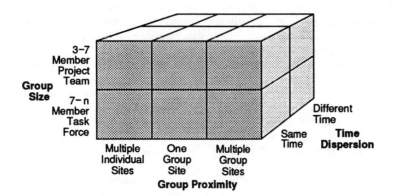

FIGURE 1. EMS Domain

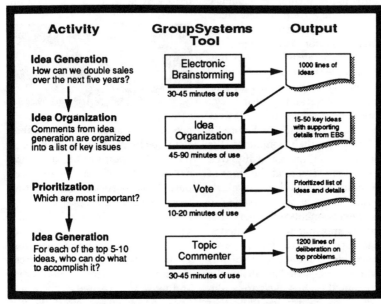

FIGURE 2. One Sequence of Use

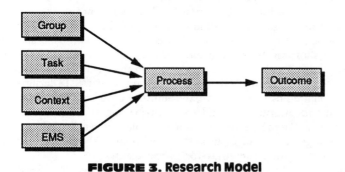

FIGURE 3. Research Model

- enables larger group meetings which can effectively bring more information, knowledge, and skills to bear on the task;
- permits the group to choose from a spectrum of structured or unstructured techniques and methods to perform the task;
- offers access to external information; and
- supports the development of an organizational memory from meeting to meeting.

We begin by discussing the theoretical foundations of Group-Systems. These foundations provide the basis for understanding the design and implementation of both our EMS software and facilities. We argue that EMS design is one of four contingencies, along with the group, the task, and the context, that affect the process of group meetings which in turn affects meeting outcomes [5]. We will then focus on the key elements in the design of GroupSystems, and how these elements interact with these contingencies. We examine one example of each type of contingency, using the findings from our empirical research to illustrate our arguments.

Theoretical Foundations

Prior research and theory with non-EMS-supported groups provides a rich starting point for EMS research. However, as information technology has the ability to profoundly affect the nature of group work [26], it becomes dangerous to generalize the *outcomes* or *conclusions* from research with non-supported groups to the EMS environment.[4] A better approach is to examine underlying theory that explains *why* these events occur and consider how EMS use and various situational characteristics may affect the theory to produce different outcomes.

---

[4]For example, such commonly accepted conclusions as larger groups are less satisfied than smaller groups, or that groups generate fewer ideas than the same number of individuals working separately (i.e., nominal groups [13, 27, 30] have been shown *not* to hold with EMS-supported groups [10, 11, 48, 49]).

Figure 3 presents a high-level view of the research model that has guided our work and has evolved with our research program. We contend that the effects of EMS use are contingent on a myriad of group, task, context and technology factors that differ from situation to situation [5]. Group characteristics that can affect processes and outcomes include (but are not limited to) group size, group proximity, group composition (peers or hierarchical), group cohesiveness, etc. Task characteristics include the activities required to accomplish the task (e.g., idea generation, decision choice), task complexity, etc. Context characteristics include organizational culture, time pressure, evaluative tone (e.g., critical or supportive), reward structure (e.g., none versus individual versus group), etc. Meeting outcomes (e.g., efficiency, effectiveness, satisfaction) depend upon the interaction within the meeting process of these group, task, and context factors with the EMS components the group uses (e.g., anonymity). Thus, it is inappropriate to say that EMS use "improves group task performance" or "reduces member satisfaction"; all statements must be qualified by the situation—the group, task, context and EMS to which they apply. One approach, then, is to conduct developmental research to build an EMS providing certain components that may improve meeting outcomes and empirical research to determine what effects these components have in what situations.

To understand these interactions, we need to examine group processes at a lower level of detail. Certain aspects of the meeting process improve outcomes (process gains) while others impair outcomes (process losses) relative to the efforts of the same individuals working by themselves or those of groups that do not experience them [22, 47]. Meeting outcomes are contingent upon the balance of these process gains and losses [3]. Situational characteristics (i.e., group,

task, and context) establish an initial balance, which the group may alter by using an EMS.

There are many different process gains and losses. Table 1 lists several important process gains and losses, but this list is by no means exhaustive. Each of these gains and losses vary in strength (or may not exist at all) depending upon the situation. For example, in a verbal meeting, losses due to *air time fragmentation*, the need to partition speaking time among members, depend upon group size [13, 27, 30]. Air time fragmentation is a greater problem for larger groups, as the available time must be rationed among more people. If everyone in a 3-member group contributed equally in a 60-minute meeting, each person would speak for 20 minutes, while each member of a 15-member group would speak for 4 minutes.

EMS Effects

There are at least four theoretical mechanisms by which the EMS can affect this balance of gains and losses: process support, process structure, task structure, and, task support (Figure 4). Process support refers to the communication infrastructure (media, channels, and devices, electronic or otherwise) that facilitates communication among members [12], such as an electronic communication channel or blackboard. Process structure refers to process techniques or rules that direct the pattern, timing or content of this communication [12], such as an agenda or process methodology such as Nominal Group Technique (NGT). Task support refers to the information and computation infrastructure for task-related activities [5], such as external data bases and pop-up calculators. Task structure refers to techniques, rules, or models for analyzing task-related information to gain new insight [12], such as those within computer models or Decision Support Systems (DSS).

For example, suppose a group was charged with generating a plan

to encourage more European tourists to visit the U.S. Providing each group member with a computer workstation that enabled him/her to exchange typed comments with other group members would be process support. Having each member take turns to contribute ideas (i.e., round-robin) or agreeing not to criticize the ideas of others would be process structure. Task support could include information on when, where and how many European tourists visited last year, or about tourist programs run by other governments. Task structure could include a framework encouraging the group to consider each U.S. region (e.g., New England,

California) or different types of tourists (e.g., tour clients, businessmen), or an economic model of potential impacts.

These four mechanisms are the fundamental means by which an EMS such as GroupSystems affects meetings. These mechanisms are not unique to EMS technology. The EMS is simply a convenient means by which to deliver process support, process structure, task support, and task structure. But in many cases, the EMS can provide a unique combination that is virtually impossible to provide otherwise. We hypothesize potential effects for each mechanism. These effects are those suggested most strongly by prior research, and again, this list is necessarily incomplete. As we will discuss, each mechanism can have many separate effects on process gains and losses, some positive, some negative. The combined effects are contingent on strength of the preexisting gains and losses and the strength of the EMS impact on them (e.g., if the EMS reduces a weak process loss, we would anticipate few effects on outcomes). For

TABLE 1.

Important Sources of Group Process Gains and Losses

Common Process Gains	
More Information:	A group as a whole has more information than any one member [30, 42, 47].
Synergy:	A member uses information in a way that the original holder did not, because that member has different information or skills [38].
More Objective Evaluation:	Groups are better at catching errors than are the individuals who proposed ideas [21, 22, 42].
Stimulation:	Working as part of a group may stimulate and encourage individuals to perform better [30, 42].
Learning:	Members may learn from and imitate more skilled members to improve performance [22].
Common Process Losses	
Air Time Fragmentation:	The group must partition available speaking time among members [13, 27, 30].
Attenuation Blocking:	This (and concentration blocking and attention blocking below) are subelements of "production blocking." Attenuation blocking occurs when members who are prevented from contributing comments as they occur, forget or suppress them later in the meeting, because they seem less original, relevant or important [13, 27, 30].
Concentration Blocking:	Fewer comments are made because members concentrate on remembering comments (rather than thinking of new ones) until they can contribute them [13, 27, 30].
Attention Blocking:	New comments are not generated because members must constantly listen to others speak and cannot pause to think [13, 27, 30].
Failure to Remember:	Members lack focus on communication, missing or forgetting the contributions of others [13, 27].
Conformance Pressure:	Members are reluctant to criticize the comments of others due to politeness or fear of reprisals [21, 42].
Evaluation Apprehension:	Fear of negative evaluation causes members to withhold ideas and comments [13, 27, 30].
Free Riding:	Members rely on others to accomplish goals, due to cognitive loafing, the need to compete for air time, or because they perceive their input to be unneeded [2, 13].
Cognitive Inertia:	Discussion moves along one train of thought without deviating, because group members refrain from contributing comments that are not directly related to the current discussion [27, 30].
Socializing:	Nontask discussion reduces task performance, although some socializing is usually necessary for effective functioning [42].
Domination:	Some group member(s) exercise undue influence or monopolize the group's time in an unproductive manner [27].
Information Overload:	Information is presented faster than it can be processed [23].
Coordination Problems:	Difficulty integrating members' contributions because the group does not have an appropriate strategy, which can lead to dysfunctional cycling or incomplete discussions resulting in premature decisions [21, 24].
Incomplete Use of Information:	Incomplete access to and use of information necessary for successful task completion [24, 34].
Incomplete Task Analysis:	Incomplete analysis and understanding of task resulting in superficial discussions [24].

simplicity, this discussion treats each mechanism separately; interactions are discussed later. This discussion assumes the group actually uses the mechanisms described; any mechanism that is provided by the EMS but is not used, obviously has few effects. In our discussion of these four mechanisms, the one that has been central to our research, process support, will be emphasized.

Task structure assists the group to better understand and analyze task information, and is one of the mechanisms by which DSS improve the performance of individual decision makers. Task structure may improve group performance by reducing losses due to incomplete task analysis or increasing process gains due to synergy, encouraging more information to be shared, promoting more objective evaluation or catching errors (by highlighting information). Methods of providing task structure include problem modeling, multicriteria decision making, etc. While task structure is often numeric in nature, it is not necessarily so. For example, Greyhound used a variant of the value chain technique. Many other non-numeric approaches to providing task structure are also available—e.g., stakeholder analysis [32].

Task support may reduce process losses due to incomplete use of information and incomplete task analysis, and may promote synergy and the use of more information by providing information and computation to the group (without providing additional structure). For example, groups may benefit from electronic access to information from previous meetings. While members could make notes of potentially useful information prior to the meeting, a more effective approach may be to provide access to the complete sources during the meeting itself. Computation support could include calculators or spreadsheets.

Task support is also important at an organizational level. Simon argues that technological support for organizational memory is an essential part of organizational functioning [45]. An EMS can assist in building this organizational memory by recording inputs, outputs and results in one repository for easy access for subsequent meetings. Although the importance of such an organizational memory has been recognized in system development (e.g., CASE tools), it has not yet been widely applied to other organizational activities.

Process structure has long been used by non-EMS groups to reduce process losses, although many researchers have reported that groups often do not follow the process structuring rules properly [21, 27]. Process structure may be global to the meeting, such as developing and following a strategy/agenda to perform the task, thereby reducing process losses due to coordination problems. The EMS can also provide process structure internal to a specific activity (local process structure) by determining who will talk next (e.g., talk queues) or by automating a formal methodology such as NGT. Different forms of local process structure will affect different process gains and losses. For example, the first phase of NGT requires individuals to work separately to reduce production blocking, free riding, and cognitive inertia, while subsequent phases (idea sharing and voting) use other techniques to affect other process gains and losses. Process structure has been found to improve, impair, and have no effect on group performance [cf. 21, 24, 42]. Its effects depend upon its fit with the situation and thus little can be said in general.

Process support can be provided by the EMS in at least three ways: parallel communication, group memory, and anonymity. With parallel communication, each member has a workstation that is connected to all other workstations, thus providing an electronic channel that enables everyone to communicate simultaneously and in parallel [5]. No one need wait for someone else to finish speaking. Process losses from air time fragmentation, attenuation blocking and concentration blocking should be significantly reduced. Free riding may be reduced as members no longer need to compete for air time. Domination may be reduced, as it becomes difficult for one member to preclude others from contributing. Electronic communication may also dampen dysfunctional socializing [54]. Parallel communication increases information overload (as every member can

contribute simultaneously). Process gains may be enhanced due to synergy and the use of more information. Increased interaction may also stimulate individuals and promote learning.

The EMS can provide a group memory by recording all electronic comments, which is typically done by many, but not all EMSs [e.g., 43]. Participants can de-couple themselves from the group to pause, think, type comments and then rejoin the "discussion" without missing anything. This should reduce failure to remember, attention blocking and incomplete use of information, and may promote synergy and more information. A group memory that enables members to queue and filter information may reduce information overload. A group memory is also useful should some members miss all or part of a meeting, or if the group is subjected to interruptions that require temporary suspension of the meeting [34]. The EMS may also provide other forms of group memory that do not capture all comments. An electronic black-

A group memory that enables members to queue and filter information may reduce information overload.

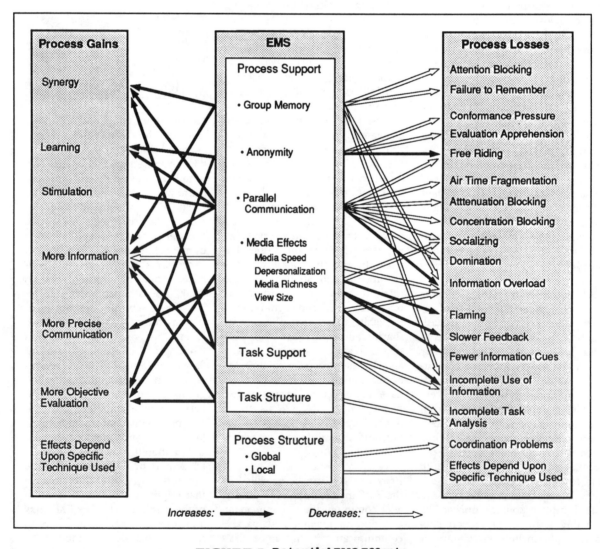

FIGURE 4. Potential EMS Effects

board, for example, may reduce failure to remember by presenting a summary of key information and reduce dysfunctional socializing by increasing task focus [46].

The electronic channel may provide some degree of anonymity. Anonymity may reduce the pressure to conform and evaluation apprehension, but may also increase free riding, as it is more difficult to determine when someone is free riding [2]. However, when the group meets at the same place and time, the lack of process anonymity (i.e., members can see who is and is not contributing) as opposed to content anonymity (i.e., members cannot easily attribute specific comments to individuals) may reduce free riding [50]. Anonymity may encourage members to challenge others, thereby increasing process gains by catching errors and a more objective evaluation. Anonymity may also provide a low-threat environment in which less skilled members can contribute and learn.

The use of electronic media may also introduce media effects that reflect inherent differences between verbal and electronic communication. These include *media speed, media richness, depersonalization/deindividuation* and *view size.* Media speed refers to the fact that typing comments to send electronically is slower than speaking (which can reduce the amount of information available to the group and introduce losses) while reading is generally faster than listening (gains) [54]. Electronic media are less rich than face-to-face verbal communication, as they provide fewer cues and slower feedback (losses), but typically promote more careful and precisely worded communication (gains) [4]. Depersonalization is the separation of people from comments, which may promote deindividuation, the loss of self- and group-awareness [54]. This may reduce socializing, and encourage more objective evaluation and more error catching—due to less negative reaction to criticism,

and increased group ownership of outcomes—(gains). But reduced socializing and more uninhibited comments like "flaming," may reduce group cohesiveness and satisfaction (losses). Workstations typically provide a small screen view for members (e.g., 24-line screen), which can encourage information chunking and reduce information overload (gains). But this can also cause members to lose a global view of the task [35, 36], increasing losses due to incomplete use of information.

The University of Arizona GroupSystems EMS

Here we summarize the developmental research conducted at Arizona. We have primarily focused on supporting large groups that meet at the same place and time—legislative sessions [5, 12]—although recent work has studied small project teams and distributed groups meeting at the same time in different places. This focus arose from our early work with a variety of organizations in which project teams of 10–20 members were typically assigned to address key issues.

What are the needs of large groups meeting at the same place and time? Research with non-EMS-supported groups has shown that larger groups have a greater need for process structure [42], particularly if members do not share the same information [21]. Large non-EMS-supported meetings are usually less effective and less satisfying than small group meetings [42], due to sharp increases in process losses as size increases [2, 47]. We concluded that, in general, high levels of global process structure and process support were appropriate.

Task structure and task support also depend on task characteristics. Since the groups with whom we worked often faced strategic issues, we developed several tools providing task structure and support for strategic planning (e.g., stakeholder analysis), as well as general-purpose tools capable of supporting a vari-

ety of task structure and support needs. As strategic tasks are often associated with political and highly competitive groups [32], process support components such as anonymity became important.

GroupSystems Architecture

The general design for Group-Systems builds on three basic concepts: an EMS meeting room, meeting facilitation, and a software toolkit. Although many different meeting room designs have been used, the minimum configuration provides a separate networked, hard disk-based, color graphics microcomputer workstation to each participant, with another one or

two workstations serving as the meeting leader/facilitator's console. A large-screen video display is provided as an electronic blackboard, with other audio-visual support also available (e.g., white boards and overhead projectors) [5, 36, 51, 53].

Meeting leader/facilitator: The person who chairs the meeting is the leader/facilitator. This person may be the group leader, another group member or, more commonly, a separate, neutral, individual who is not a group member. Using a nonmember enables all group members to actively participate, rather than losing one member as the chair. A nonmember can be a specialist in EMS and group work, but may lack the task and group knowledge of a regular member. The meeting leader/facilitator provides four functions. First, this person provides technical support by initiating and terminating specific software tools, and guiding the group through the technical aspects necessary to work on the task. This reduces the amount of training required of group members by re-

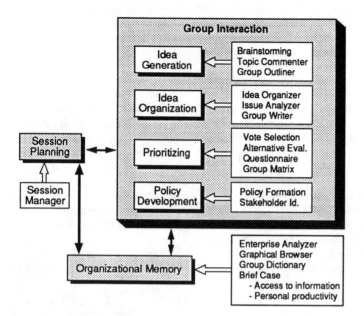

FIGURE 5. GroupSystems Tools

Chauffeured	Supported	Interactive
• One person enters group information	• All group members can enter comments	• All group members can enter comments
• Electronic black-board can provide group memory	• Electronic black-board can provide group memory	• All comments in group memory accessible via workstations
• Verbal communication predominates	• Both verbal and electronic communication	• Electronic communication predominates

FIGURE 6. Electronic Meeting Processes

moving one level of system complexity. In some cases, technical support is provided by an additional technical facilitator.

Second, the meeting leader/facilitator chairs the meeting, maintains the agenda and assesses the need for agenda changes. The meeting leader/facilitator may or may not take an active role in the meeting to improve group interaction by, for example, providing process structure in coordinating verbal discussion. This person also administers the group's knowledge. In EMSs designed without support for meeting leaders/facilitators, any member may change or delete the group memory. When disagreements occur, members' competition for control can become dysfunctional (e.g., "Scroll Wars" [46]). While this is manageable for small collaborative groups, it is much less so for larger groups with diverse membership, where competitive political motives and vested interests exist. With GroupSystems, members can view the group memory and add to it at their own workstation, but in general only the meeting leader/facilitator can modify and delete public information.

Third, the meeting leader/facilitator assists in agenda planning, by working with the group and/or group leader to highlight the principal meeting objectives and develop an agenda to accomplish them. Specific GroupSystems tools are then mapped to each activity. Finally, in on-going organizational settings where meeting leaders/facilitators are not group members, they provide organizational continuity by setting standards for use, developing training materials, maintaining the system, and acting as champion/sponsors, which is key to successful technology transfer [31]. The roles of the meeting leader/facilitator may also change over time. For example, after a group has some experience using EMS, the need for technical support and agenda planning advice may decrease.

Software toolkit: Many first-generation EMSs were task-driven, as defined by Huber [25], in that they were designed to support one single group task. Second-generation EMSs, such as GroupSystems, provide a software toolkit, similar to a DSS model base, which is a collection of generic tools for various group *activities* such as idea generation and voting rather than being one indivisible system to support the entire *task* like strategic planning. Such EMSs are activity driven.

The key advantage provided by a toolkit is flexibility. Each tool provides a different approach to support a particular activity, thus the EMS can provide various combinations and styles of process structure, process support, task structure and task support during any one meeting. Groups use many approaches and often do not proceed in a straightforward manner [40]. The tools can easily be mixed and matched and combined with non-EMS activities in whatever order the group believes is most effective. This philosophy also enables new tools to be easily added to the toolkit and existing tools to be customized to specific needs.

While flexibility is important, it is also important to restrict the number and type of functions available to participants [44]. Restrictiveness provides a more powerful intervention, increasing the liklihood that groups will use the EMS as intended by its designers; this has proved a problem with non-computerized techniques [21, 27]. Restrictiveness promotes the use of more effective techniques and prevents less effective ones, fosters learning, promotes consistency, and provides coordination to ensure that all group members are using the same tool at the same time. But it can also constrain creativity and exploration, limit the applicability of a system, promote user dissatisfaction, and be seen as manipulative, resulting in non-use of the system.

GroupSystems balances these is-sues by being both highly flexible *and* highly restrictive. The system is flexible in that a wide variety of tools are available, but each tool is locally restrictive so that users can perform only certain functions. The selection of which tools will be used for a specific meeting is done during a pre-meeting planning meeting. During the meeting itself, the system is restrictive, so that members use only those tools determined to be the most appropriate during pre-planning. While agendas sometimes change, it is the group leader or the group as a whole who makes changes, not individual members.

Development of GroupSystems tools has not followed either the Software Development Life Cycle model or the rapid prototyping model, although we do believe in prototyping as a means to determine requirements. GroupSystems tools have typically been "grown." The basic concept for a tool typically comes from prior group theory and research (e.g., NGT), from a specific task domain (e.g., stakeholder analysis [32]) or from our own experiences. The concept is first developed and tested within our research group, before being refined into an initial production version. This initial version is intentionally not a complete version of the tool, as it is difficult to determine exactly what functions are needed until the tool is actually used by groups. As the tool begins to be used, new functions are identified, and the capabilities of the tool grow. Significant changes are not unusual in the first few months after tools are added.

The GroupSystems toolkit provides tools in five areas:

1. session planning and management;
2. group interaction;
3. organizational memory;
4. individual work; and
5. research data collection.

Tools in the first three areas are discussed in Figure 5. Those in the latter two areas are not, because they are not central to our theme of improving group performance.

Tools for Session Planning and Management

The GroupSystems tool to support this activity, Session Manager (SM), has three components: pre-session planning, in-session management, and post-session organization. SM supports pre-session planning by providing an electronic questionnaire to ensure that important planning information is not overlooked, and an agenda tool to assist in agenda development. An expert system to assist this stage is currently under development. SM provides in-meeting management via

the control menu; all tools are initialized, started, and ended via SM. SM also provides a task assignment tool to record information about the tasks assigned to specific individuals. Members are provided read-only access to this list but only the facilitator is allowed to add to or modify its contents. Post-session organization involves the logical organization and physical storage of the session outputs as part of the organizational memory. Various components can be indexed and stored, task assignment reports generated and distributed, and paper printouts copied and distributed to better integrate information between this session and subsequent sessions.

Tools for Group Interaction

The purpose of these tools is to provide process structure, process support, task structure and task support for group interaction. While there are many possible combinations of the process support functions (i.e., parallel communication, group memory, anonymity), GroupSystems provides three dis-

361

As the tool begins
to be used,
new functions are identified
and the capabilities
of the tool grows.
Significant changes
are not unusual
in the first few months
after tools are added.

TABLE 2					
Group Interaction Tools					
	Activities Supported	**Process Support**	**Process Structure**	**Task Support**	**Task Structure**
Electronic Brainstorming	1,2	●	●	◑	○
Electronic Discussion*	1,2,3	●	○ to ●	◑	○
Topic Commenter	1	●	○	◑	●
Group Outliner	1,2	◑	○	◑	●
Idea Organizer	2,1	◑	◑	●	◑
Issue Analyzer	2	◑	●	●	◑
Group Writer	2,1	●	○	◑	○
Vote Selection	3	●	◑	◑	●
Alternative Evaluator	3	●	○	◑	●
Group Questionnaire	3	●	●	◑	●
Group Matrix	3	◑	○	◑	●
Stakeholder Identification	4	◑	●	◑	●
Policy Formation	4	◑	●	◑	●

Activities Supported:
1. Exploration and Idea Generation
2. Idea Organization
3. Prioritizing
4. Policy Development and Evaluation

*EDS is used for laboratory research only

Process & Task
Support & Structure
○ Low   ◑ Medium   ● High

tinct styles of process support which blend these functions with different amounts of electronic and verbal interaction: a *chauffeured* style, a *supported* style and an *interactive* style. These styles can be combined with each other and with non-EMS verbal discussion at different stages of any one meeting. We first describe these three styles (see Figure 6) and then consider the process gains and losses that each affects.

With a chauffeured style, only one person uses the EMS, either a group member or the meeting leader/facilitator. A workstation is connected to a public display screen, providing an electronic version of the traditional blackboard. The group verbally discusses the issues, with the electronic blackboard used as a group memory to record and structure information. A supported style is similar to a chauffeured style, but differs in that each member has a computer workstation that provides a parallel, anonymous electronic communication channel with a group memory. The meeting proceeds using a mixture of verbal and electronic interaction. The electronic blackboard is still used to present and structure information, but with each member able to add items. With an interactive style, the parallel, anonymous electronic communication channel with a group memory is used for almost all group communication. Virtually no one speaks. While an electronic blackboard may be provided, the group memory is typically too large to fit on a screen, and thus it is maintained so that all members can access it electronically at their workstations.

The interactive style is the strongest intervention (but not necessarily "the best") as it provides parallel communication, group memory and anonymity to reduce process losses due to air time fragmentation, attenuation blocking, concentration blocking, attention blocking, failure to remember, socializing, domination, interruptions, evaluation apprehension and conformance pressure. Informa-

tion overload may increase, and free riding may be reduced or increased. Process gains may be increased due to more information, synergy, catching errors, stimulation and learning. Media effects increase and decrease process gains and losses as noted previously.

The weakest intervention is the chauffeured style (but not necessarily "the worst"), for which the EMS does not provide a new communication channel, but rather addresses failure to remember by providing focus through a common group memory displayed on the electronic blackboard. An increased task focus promoted by this style may also reduce socializing. Few other process gains or losses are affected.

Between these styles is the supported style. When verbal interaction is used, the effects are similar to a chauffeured style; when electronic interaction is used, the effects are similar to an interactive style. But there are several important differences. First, while anonymity is possible with electronic communication, its effects on evaluation apprehension and conformance pressure are substantially reduced with the supported style because non-anonymous verbal communication occurs. Second, attention blocking (and possibly failure to remember and information overload) will be *increased* beyond that of a traditional meeting (or an interactive style) as members must simultaneously monitor and use both verbal and electronic communication channels. Third, process losses due to media speed, media richness and depersonalization will probably be less than with the interactive style, as members can switch media as needed (e.g., if media richness proves a problem when using the electronic channel, members can switch to verbal interaction).

Each GroupSystems tool was initially designed to use one of these meeting styles to support one specific type of group activity. There are many useful ways of classifying

group activities [42]. We use four categories. The first, exploration and idea generation, involves the development and exploration of issues relevant to the task. The second category, idea organization, involves the synthesizing, structuring, and organizing of ideas into specific alternatives which may follow the generation of ideas; if a group has previously discussed an issue, a meeting may begin with idea organization without idea generation. Tools in the third category, prioritizing, support the individual members in evaluating alternatives. The final category contains tools that provide formal methodologies to support policy development and

evaluation, such as stakeholder analysis. The tools may be used in whatever order the group chooses; there is no mandatory order, although many tasks follow a natural order of idea generation, idea synthesis, prioritizing, and exploration of important issues.

Table 2 summarizes the activities and process support, process structure, task support, and task structure of each group interaction tool. The levels of process support (low, medium, high) correspond to the three meeting styles (chauffeured, supported, interactive) respectively. While most tools can be used in chauffeured mode or in different ways according to the direction of the meeting leader/facilitator, they are described as they are normally used at Arizona. All tools provide at least a medium level of task support due to BriefCase, a memory resident organizational memory tool. For more information, see [7, 51].

Exploration and idea generation: The objective of these tools is to assist the group in exploring issues and generating ideas and alternatives.

Electronic Brainstorming (EBS) provides an interactive style in which participants enter comments into many separate discussions contained in separate files that are randomly shared throughout the group. The high degree of process structure from this random sharing of many discussions attempts to reduce cognitive inertia by precluding the group from focusing on one approach. Process support and structure are thus high, while task structure is low. Electronic Discussion System (EDS) was developed for laboratory research to support exploration and idea generation, idea organization and voting. Its support for exploration and idea generation works in a manner similar to EBS, except that it can also be configured to provide low process structure. All comments can be placed in one central file accessible by all participants at all times, thus providing only one discussion. Topic Commenter (TC), which uses an interactive style (high process support), provides a high level of task structure; comments are collected from participants using a task-specific framework. TC operates like a set of index cards, with each card having a name. Participants select a card, enter comments, and read comments entered by others. Group Outliner works similarly to TC, but enables the group to develop the set of cards (which may be hierarchically structured) using a supported style and then discuss them with an interactive style.

Idea organization: The purpose of idea organization is to identify, synthesize, formulate and consolidate ideas, proposals or alternatives—that is, to build a task structure for ideas. Idea Organizer (IO) provides a supported style, while Issue Analyzer (IA) provides a more structured two-phase approach that first *identifies* (via an interactive style) and then *consolidates* (i.e., achieves consensus on) ideas (via a chauffeured style). With both tools, each participant works separately to cre-

ate a private list of ideas which are submitted to the group. Comments from a previous idea generation activity may be available as task support and may be easily included. As the list grows, the meeting leader/facilitator assists the group in combining similar ideas to move to consensus. Group Writer is a multiuser word processor that enables a group to jointly write and organize documents. Most group interaction is electronic, but verbal communication is used to coordinate members' activities (e.g., who works on what).

Prioritizing: There are a variety of prioritizing methods available in Vote Selection (e.g., yes/no, multiple choice, 10-point scale rating or ranking in order), which employ an interactive style to collect votes, followed by a chauffeured style to discuss the results. Alternative Evaluator (AE) is a multicriteria decision-making tool that uses a similar interactive/chauffeured set of styles. With AE, the group rates each alternative on a 1-10 scale for each criterion. Criteria can be considered equally important, or can be assigned different weights. With Group Questionnaire each participant completes an electronic questionnaire, which may branch to different questions based on user responses. Group Matrix is a consensus-building tool that enables participants to dynamically enter and change numeric (or text) ratings in a two-dimensional matrix. Typically groups initially enter ratings with an alternative style. These ratings are then discussed and revised using a supported style.

Policy development and evaluation: Tools in this category implement formal methodologies to support policy development and evaluation. Stakeholder Identification and Assumption Surfacing (SIAS), based on the strategic assumption surfacing and testing techniques developed by Mason Mitroff [32], is used to assess the potential impact of a plan or policy by identifying those

individuals and organizations that affect (or are affected by) the plan (i.e., the "stakeholders"). SIAS provides a highly structured supported style, in which participants first identify stakeholders and then their assumptions, before rating assumptions for importance to the stakeholder and importance to the plan. Policy Formation (PF) provides a structured multi-phase supported style for reaching agreement in the exact wording of a policy statement. Each participant independently drafts one version of the policy, which is sent to the public screen at the front of the room. Each of the drafts is discussed verbally, and then the policy is sent out to be redrafted again by each participant.

Tools for Organizational Memory
The primary purpose of the organizational memory tools is to provide task structure and task support. Thus far, many EMSs have supported meetings as independent, autonomous events. GroupSystems views the meeting as one part of a larger whole. While improving meeting outcomes is important, it is also important to capture the additions to organizational memory and to provide access to them in subsequent meeting(s). The organizational memory tools provide this organizational memory. Some of the files it contains are knowledge bases in the artificial intelligence sense (e.g., semantic nets) while others are text files or databases.

Briefcase (BC), mentioned earlier, is a memory resident tool that provides immediate read-only access to any text file in the organizational memory at any point during the session. The user simply presses the appropriate keys and is presented with a menu describing each text file. BC also provides a calculator, notepad and calendar. Enterprise Analyzer (EA) facilitates the structuring and analysis of group information in a semantic net using a variety of user-defined modeling techniques (e.g., IBM's Business System Planning (BSP), Porter's

Value Chain). Information can be viewed in tabular form, or in graphical form with the Semantic Graphics Browser (SGB). SGB enables the user to move through the organizational memory and "zoom-in" on specific areas to view details, "zoom-out" to obtain a high-level view, or "explode" a view to display detail information under a node. Group Dictionary enables the group to develop and store formal definitions for use in current or subsequent meetings.

EMS In Practice: Lessons From Using GroupSystems

Our research strategy has been to build on theoretical foundations from prior research to develop EMS environments which are tested via empirical research. Our empirical research has included both laboratory experiments [e.g., 3, 10, 11, 14, 15, 18, 19, 28, 29, 48, 49, 50, 51, 55] and field research [e.g., 6, 7, 9, 20, 35, 36, 37, 51, 52], as we believe that both are important in understanding the impacts of EMS, and in developing the EMS components appropriate for various tasks, groups and organizations. While most studies have found EMS use to improve effectiveness, efficiency and satisfaction, they have also found different effects in different situations. Perhaps the most important conclusion is therefore that even within the same EMS, effects depend on the group, the task, the context, and the EMS components used. This should not be surprising; Figure 4 suggests that the effects depend on interactions among more than three dozen constructs in the meeting process.

We believe it will be difficult to find universal truths. In the meantime, we believe it is important to develop contingency theories to identify the best fit between specific EMS components and the specific group, task, and context characteristics. Isolating the individual effects of specific situational characteristics and EMS components is

difficult, as most studies have examined the combined effects of many factors simultaneously. In this section, we return to the contingency model in Figure 3, which hypothesizes that processes and outcomes depend upon the interaction of four sets of characteristics: context, group, task and EMS. There are dozens of potentially important contingencies. We consider only five: one from the set of EMS characteristics (anonymity), two from group characteristics (size and proximity), one from the context (evaluative tone) and one from task (task activities). For each, we present theoretical arguments and empirical evidence that lead us to hypothesize certain effects. In each case, however, more research is warranted.

Anonymity

Anonymity is possible in interactive styles and in the electronic component of supported styles, but not with the verbal component of supported and chauffeured styles. Anonymity can affect EMS use by reducing or eliminating evaluation apprehension and conformance pressure, as well as social cues. The reduction of evaluation apprehension and conformance pressure may encourage a more open, honest and free-wheeling discussion of key issues. However, the reduction of social cues can lead individuals to behave in ways that are outside of the realms of socially prescribed behavior. Some evidence of the de-individuation associated with the reduction of social cues has been found in some forms of computer-mediated communication, the most extreme form of which is "flaming" [cf. 43].

Changes in evaluation apprehension, conformance pressure and social cues brought about through anonymous communication should have some effect on the meeting process, which should in turn affect the meeting's outcomes. The relaxation of social cues in anonymous EMS groups has been found in varying degrees in five laboratory

experiments conducted at the University of Arizona. Groups using anonymous EMS have been found to generate more critical comments than groups using EMS where the author of each comment was identified [3, 28, 50]. Jessup and Tansik [29] also found that anonymous, non-proximate groups generated the most critical comments. However, only one of five experiments found anonymous groups to have increased performance compared to non-anonymous groups [3]; there were no performance differences in the other studies [19, 28, 29, 50].

Participants in field studies have usually reported that anonymity

was important, particularly in cases where there were power and status differences in the group (e.g., more than two management levels present) [6, 9, 35, 36]. We infer that student groups in the laboratory have lower evaluation apprehension and conformance pressure, and thus while anonymity may reduce these process losses, there are fewer noticeable effects on outcomes. In situations where evaluation apprehension and conformance pressure are high, anonymity appears to have a more significant impact on meeting outcomes.

In all of the laboratory studies referenced here, anonymity was treated as a discrete variable, i.e., communication was either anonymous or it was not. However, the Valacich, Dennis, and Nunamaker [50] study suggests that anonymity may be better thought of as a continuous variable—it may be more appropriate to think of degrees of anonymity. In this study, there were two independent variables, anonymity and group size. The small anonymous groups in this study were more critical than small identified groups, but there were no differences in the level of criticalness among small and large anonymous groups and large identified groups. Because the groups were composed of so many members, there was already a degree of anonymity built into the structure of the group. This was not the case in the smaller groups, where the relative intimacy of the group reinforced existing social cues.

fast with group size (see Figure 7). A supported style introduces more fixed process losses initially (e.g., media speed), but reduces the rate at which losses increase with group size. An interactive style addresses most losses (and thus they should increase very slowly with size) but introduces more fixed losses initially. Thus we hypothesize that interactive styles will be preferred for larger groups, and supported or

process losses may remain relatively constant as size increases. Other experiments have found outcome measures such as effectiveness and member satisfaction to *increase* with size for interactive styles [10, 11, 49]. Another laboratory experiment built, tested and confirmed a model of group performance which proposed process losses from interactive styles to be relatively constant across group size [49]. Our field studies also provide some support for these hypotheses. Participants in studies with larger groups (i.e., 12–20 group members) have reported that interactive styles were more important than supported styles [37].

FIGURE 7. Gains and Losses

Group Size

In general without EMS, process losses increase rapidly with group size [47]. Previous non-EMS research has concluded that in general, regardless of the task, context or group, the "optimal" group size is quite small, typically 3–5 members [42], because process losses quickly overtake any process gains from increased group size. Our EMS research draws a different conclusion: the optimal group size depends upon the situation (group, task, context, EMS), and in some cases may be quite large.

In theory, each of the three EMS styles (chauffeured, supported, interactive) can reduce or increase process losses in varying degrees. A chauffeured style reduces a few process losses. Thus compared to traditional non-EMS meetings, process losses do not increase quite as

chauffeured styles for smaller groups.

There is some empirical evidence to support these hypotheses. One measure of process losses is participation, as it is directly affected by air time fragmentation, production blocking, free riding, etc. A laboratory experiment with small groups found that participation was the same between groups using a chauffeured style and non-supported groups [14], suggesting few differences between the two styles. Another experiment found participation to be more equal in groups using an interactive style than in non-supported groups, suggesting differences between the two [19]. Experiments studying interactive styles have found per-person participation levels to remain constant regardless of the size of the group [10, 48, 50], suggesting that

Task Activities

The type of activities that must be performed to accomplish the task (e.g., idea generation) [42] has a significant impact on the balance of gains and losses. One primary goal of most group activities is the exchange of information among members [12], and thus the form of this information will have significant effects. Zack and McKenney [56] contrast three general states of information [also see 4]. Ambiguity exists when there is both a lack of information and a lack of a framework for interpreting that information. Uncertainty exists when a framework exists, but there is a lack of information. Equivocality exists when there are multiple (and possibly conflicting) interpretations for the information or the framework.

Equivocality requires negotiation among group members to converge to consensus on one interpretation, and media providing information richness are preferred [4]. In contrast, ambiguity and uncertainty require someone in the group (or the group as a whole) to provide, locate, or create the needed information or framework components. Thus the degree of media richness is unimportant; the ability of the group to rapidly gather information and framework components becomes paramount, especially if members of the group have different information, perceptions, and viewpoints.

Exploration and idea generation is more often a problem of ambiguity or uncertainty than of equivocality. It is a divergent activity, as members work individually to report information, propose elements of the framework, and respond to the comments of others. Prioritizing is also a divergent activity, as members work individually. In contrast, synthesizing and organizing ideas, building consensus on a framework, or interpreting the meaning of vote to achieve consensus are primarily problems of equivocality, as the group focuses on the same issues at the same time to resolve different viewpoints to converge on one interpretation.

Therefore, for divergent activities that are problems of uncertainty, such as idea generation, we hypothesize that an interactive style is more appropriate as its parallelism and anonymity facilitate rapid development of ideas. For convergent tasks that are problems of equivocality (such as synthesis and consensus building), process losses from reduced media richness in the interactive style increase dramatically. In this case, the relatively horizontal line for the interactive style in Figure 7 would move beyond the lines for supported and/or chauffeured styles for most group sizes, making them more appropriate.

Our laboratory and field research provide weak support for this hypothesis. A laboratory experiment of idea generation—a task of uncertainty—found groups using an interactive style to generate more ideas and be more satisfied than verbally interacting groups [18]. A similar study using GroupSystems at Indiana University had similar findings [16]. Experiments using purely interactive style for generating and choosing tasks (tasks which begin with ambiguity but evolve into equivocality) have found no performance or satisfaction differences compared to verbally interacting groups [19, 55]. The EMS groups in one of these

studies also required longer to reach consensus [19]. Groups in our field studies have typically used interactive styles to generate ideas, options, and analysis framework components, but used supported or chauffeured style to resolve equivocality.

Group Member Proximity

In our definition of an EMS [5], we note that groups may be distributed with respect to both space and time, although the majority of our research to date has focused on groups interacting in a single room at the same time. Other researchers have also argued that advanced computer-assisted communication and decision technologies, such as an EMS, can be important for project-oriented work groups and temporary task forces that may be distributed geographically and temporally throughout an organization [e.g., 26].

From a theoretical perspective, group process and performance for distributed groups may be substantially different from proximate groups. Social facilitation research has shown that the presence of others can improve a person's performance for easy tasks and hinder performance for more difficult tasks [57]. Remoteness may also foster increased anonymity, and increased anonymity may have several effects on the group, ranging from reduced apprehension to increased social loafing and deindividuated behavior as noted previously. Further, several small group researchers have found that close group proximity may foster liking and fondness among group members [57], and in EMS environments, proximate groups have been as satisfied [48] or more satisfied than distributed groups [29].

Our initial research in this area has built on our growing body of idea generation research (i.e., a problem of uncertainty not equivocality), where groups communicate only through electronic communication. One laboratory experiment found no difference in the number

of ideas generated between proximate and distributed groups, but found proximate groups to be more satisfied [29]. A second study using a similar research design found distributed groups to generate more ideas than proximate groups, with no satisfaction differences [48].

During these experiments, proximate groups were interrupted more often by disruptive movements or by laughter prompted by a humorous electronic comment. Social facilitation research suggests that such reaction will generally be stronger when a person is proximate to other group members than when working alone in a distrib-

uted group [57]. Thus, we believe that the primary explanation for these performance effects in the laboratory was that distributed groups remained more task-focused than proximate groups.

However, the effects of the proximity manipulation may have been different if this research had been conducted in the field. Our groups worked without outside interruptions. Yet, there are many potential interruptions for group members working alone in the privacy of their offices by events that cannot be helped (e.g., a call from the boss) or by purposely working on other tasks. As a result, distributed groups in the field may, or may not, be more task focused than groups working together in the same room, and thus may find different effects.

Evaluative Tone

Several researchers have advocated a supportive, non-judgmental atmosphere as a means to enhance group productivity by lowering evaluation apprehension and encouraging "freewheeling" stimulation. The withholding of criticism is a cornerstone of many idea generation techniques [38]. However, other researchers have proposed that group productivity may be stimulated by a more critical atmosphere where structured conflict (e.g., dialectical inquiry or devil's advocacy) is used to stimulate group members [e.g., 41]. In any event, there are two very distinct,

We are convinced that the use of EMS technology can improve group processes and outcomes in many cases...

and opposing, positions related to this construct.

Connolly, Jessup and Valacich [3] used a laboratory experiment which crossed anonymity (anonymous or identified groups) with the meeting tone (supportive or critical as manipulated by a confederate) to test whether the effects of evaluative tone were moderated by anonymity. Not surprisingly, anonymous groups and critical groups made more critical remarks than groups that were identified or supportive. Groups working anonymously and with a critical tone pro-

duced the greatest number of ideas of the highest quality. However, groups in supportive and identified conditions were typically more satisfied than groups in critical and anonymous conditions. This suggests that the combination of a critical tone and anonymity may improve idea generation, but also may lower satisfaction.

Observations from our field studies provide some insight into possible reasons for these effects. The anonymity may have encouraged group members to detach themselves from their ideas, allowing them to view criticism as a signal to suggest another idea:

"I noticed that if someone criticized an idea of mine, I didn't get emotional about it. I guess when you are face-to-face and everyone hears the boss say 'You are wrong' it's a slap to you, not necessarily the idea. . . . [Here] no one knows whose idea it is, so why be insulted? No one is picking on me. I think I'll just see why they don't agree with me." (manager, Hughes Aircraft).

This runs counter to the typical knee-jerk reaction that might occur in a traditional verbal meeting where a critical comment may be seen as directed at the contributor, not the idea (e.g., "I wasn't as uncomfortable when I saw someone being critical of someone else's idea, because I thought 'nobody's being embarrassed here at all.'" manager, Hughes Aircraft).

Conclusion
The Arizona EMS research program using the GroupSystems Concept has included both developmental and empirical research. Our developmental research has produced more than two dozen software tools currently in use at more than 70 EMS facilities worldwide. Our empirical research has studied EMS use in the laboratory and in the field by more than 30,000 individuals from more than 200 organizations. In this article, we have dis-

cussed several key aspects in the theoretical foundation of EMS, have illustrated how these aspects are reflected in the Arizona facility and software designs, and have highlighted the contingent nature of EMS effects. Nonetheless, much more research is needed to develop new group work methods embodied in facilities and software, and to empirically test the many contingencies involved in their use.

While still recognizing the need for future research, we are convinced that the use of EMS technology can significantly improve group processes and outcomes in many cases—but effects *are* contingent on the situation. For example, we would expect fewer benefits from EMS use for small cohesive groups in supportive contexts, as they face fewer process losses. Based on the theoretical foundation of process gains and losses, and our observations of EMS use in the field and the laboratory, we believe that EMS use may provide benefits because:

- Parallel communication promotes broader input into the meeting process and reduces the chance that a few people dominate the meeting;
- Anonymity mitigates evaluation apprehension and conformance pressure, so that issues are discussed more candidly;
- Group memory enables members to pause and reflect on information and opinions of others during the meeting and serves as a permanent record of what occurred;
- Process structure helps focus the group on key issues and discourages irrelevant digressions and unproductive behaviors; and
- Task support and structure provides information and approaches to analyze it.

We have drawn four general conclusions about conducting EMS developmental and empirical research. First, the effects of EMS use are contingent upon the situation. Thus we believe that it is critical to clearly document specifics about the group, task, context, and EMS in all research. Who were the group members and were they a cohesive team, strangers, or competitors? Exactly what did the task entail? Were group members motivated? What did the EMS provide at what points, and exactly how did the group use them? Without such detail, the contribution of a study cannot be clearly interpreted or extended.

Second, the results of any one study will not apply to all group work, so it is important to explicitly consider the bounds to which the findings can be generalized. Do they apply to large or small groups, chauffeured, supported or interactive styles, choice or idea generation activities, etc.? We agree with Huber [26] that even apparently subtle differences may have significant impacts. For example, in theory, slower system response time should increase process losses due to attenuation and concentration blocking; one experiment found groups using EBS with a few seconds slower response time to generate significantly fewer ideas than those using the standard version [17]. Only by carefully defining the scope of a study and interpreting the results within it can we extend our understanding of EMS effects.

Third, much EMS research to date has addressed the "what" of EMS technology; researchers have compared EMS and non-EMS groups to determine if there are differences between the two, which is typical of initial research into new technologies. From this research, we know that EMS and non-EMS meetings *are* different, but cannot completely explain *why*. While there is still a place for such research, we believe that it is now more important to understand why EMS encourages different effects in different situations. The research question becomes "does this factor explain why EMS use produces these results in this situation?" rather than "is there a difference?" To understand the "why," it is nec-

essary to compare situations that differ only in the one or two factors of interest. As EMS and non-EMS groups can differ in so many ways (e.g., production blocking, media richness), this research will typically not involve a comparison between EMS and non-EMS groups, as there are too many potential differences to draw conclusions. Field research presenting qualitative investigations of EMS effects on group process in different meeting situations and over the long term will also become important. Our future empirical research will continue to develop contingency models to isolate and explain why certain EMS features (i.e., types of process support, process structure, task support and task structure) are of value for certain groups, tasks and contexts.

Finally, we believe that in developing new EMS tools, it is important to strive to understand what EMS components are useful in what situations. A focus on these four mechanisms may help clarify the needs of specific situations. It will become increasingly important for developmental researchers to work closely with empirical researchers to best fit the components offered by different configurations of EMS technology to user needs. In the early years of EMS, there was little empirical research to guide developers. Developers built EMS environments, gave them to users to see what happened, and then redesigned them in an iterative cycle of design-test-redesign. Today, there is a growing base of empirical research, and while iterative development remains important, developers building on this empirical foundation can provide more successful initial environments requiring less redesign.

The study of EMS is still in its infancy. It is reminiscent of the early days of the automotive industry when a motor was put into a carriage giving the world a horseless carriage. We are now in the horseless carriage phase of EMS, having

installed computers into existing manual processes. We need to learn how best to support groups and group meeting processes, to build on these experiences to create systems that take better advantage of the abilities of technology and of groups. We may discover that many current EMS components (e.g., a facilitator) are the buggy whips of this horseless carriage phase. We are only beginning to discover what functions are robust and valuable, from which will emerge the next generation of EMS. Nonetheless, based upon research and experiences to date, we are convinced that this technology is fundamentally changing the nature of group work.

Acknowledgments
This research was partially supported by grants from IBM. Additional funding for several laboratory experiments was provided by the Social Sciences and Humanities Research Council of Canada. We would like to acknowledge the efforts of the following people who have been involved in the Group-Systems project: Erran Carmel, David Chappell, Kathy Chudoba, Bob Daniels, Mark Fuller, Glenda Hayes, Barbara Gutek, Bruce Herniter, Suzanne Iacono, Ben Martz, Jolene Morrison, Mike Morrison, David Paranka, Mark Pendergast, V. Ramesh, Ed Roberts, Bill Saints, Craig Tyran, Lee Walker, and Suzanne Weisband. We would like to thank Brent Gallupe, Karen Judson, the anonymous reviewers, and the editor for particularly helpful comments on earlier drafts of this article. ◀

References
1. Ackoff, R.L., Gupta, S.K. and Minas, J.S. *Scientific Method*, John Wiley & Sons, 1962.
2. Albanese, R. and Van Fleet, D.D. Rational behavior in groups: The

free riding tendency. *Academy of Management Review*, 10 (1985), 244–255.

3. Connolly, T., Jessup, L.M. and Valacich, J.S. Effects of anonymity and evaluative tone on idea generation in computer-mediated groups. *Management Science, 36,* 6 (1990), 689–703.

4. Daft, R.L. and Lengel, R.H. Organizational information requirements, media richness and structural design. *Management Science, 32,* 5 (1986), 554–571.

5. Dennis, A.R., George, J.F., Jessup, L.M., Nunamaker Jr., J.F. and Vogel, D.R. Information technology to support electronic meetings. *MIS Quarterly 12,* 4 (1988), 591–624.

6. Dennis, A.R., Heminger, A.R., Nunamaker Jr., J.F. and Vogel, D.R. Bringing automated support to large groups: The Burr-Brown Experience. *Information and Management, 18,* 3 (1990), 111–121.

7. Dennis, A.R., Nunamaker Jr., J.F. and Paranka, D. Supporting the search for competitive advantage. *Journal of MIS*, forthcoming.

8. Dennis, A.R., Nunamaker Jr., J.F. and Vogel, D.R. A comparison of laboratory experiments and field studies in the study of electronic meeting systems. *Journal of MIS, 7,* 2 (1991), 107–135.

9. Dennis, A.R., Tyran, C.K., Vogel, D.R. and Nunamaker Jr., J.F. An evaluation of electronic meeting support for strategic management. In *Proceedings of ICIS* (1990), 37–52.

10. Dennis, A.R., Valacich, J.S. and Nunamaker Jr., J.F. An experimental investigation of group size in an electronic meeting system environment. *IEEE Transactions on Systems, Man, and Cybernetics, 20,* 5 (1990), 1049–1057.

11. Dennis, A.R., Valacich, J.S. and Nunamaker Jr., J.F. Group, Subgroup and Nominal Group Idea Generation in an Electronic Meeting Environment, HICSS-24, 1991, III: 573–579.

12. DeSanctis, G. and Gallupe, R.B. A foundation for the study of group decision support systems. *Management Science, 33,* 5 (1987), 589–609.

13. Diehl, M. and Stroebe W. Productivity loss in brainstorming groups: Toward the solution of a riddle. *J. Personality and Social Psychology, 53,* 3 (1987), 497–509.

14. Easton, A.C., Vogel, D.R. and Nunamaker Jr., J.F. Stakeholder identification and assumption surfacing in small groups: An experimental study. HICSS-22, 1989, III 344–352.

15. Easton, G., George, J.F., Nunamaker Jr., J.F. and Pendergast, M.O. Using two different electronic meeting system tools for the same task: An experimental comparison. *J. of MIS, 7,* 1 (1990), 85–100.

16. Fellers, J.W. The effect of group size and computer support on group idea generation for creativity tasks: An experimental evaluation using a repeated measures design. Unpublished Ph.D. Thesis, Indiana University, 1989.

17. Gallupe, R.B., Cooper, W. and Bastianutti, L. Why is electronic brainstorming more productive than traditional brainstorming. Administrative Sciences Association of Canada Conference Proceedings, Information Systems Division (Whistler, Canada, 1990), 82–92.

18. Gallupe, R.B., Dennis, A.R., Cooper, W.H., Valacich, J.S., Nunamaker Jr., J.F., and Bastianutti, L. Group size and electronic brainstorming. Queen's University Working Paper, 1991.

19. George, J.F., Easton, G.K., Nunamaker Jr., J.F. and Northcraft, G.B. A study of collaborative group work with and without computer based support. *Inf. Syst. Res., 1,* 4 (1990), 394–415.

20. Grohowski, R.B., McGoff, C., Vogel, D.R., Martz, W.B. and Nunamaker Jr., J.F. Implementation of electronic meeting systems at IBM. *MIS Quarterly, 14,* 4 (1990), 369–383.

21. Hackman, J.R. and Kaplan, R.E. Interventions into group process: An approach to improving the effectiveness of groups. *Decision Sciences, 5* (1974), 459–480.

22. Hill, G.W. Group versus individual performance: Are N + 1 heads better than one? *Psychological Bulletin, 91,* 3 (1982), 517–539.

23. Hiltz, S.R. and Turoff, M. Structuring computer-mediated communication systems to avoid information overload. *Commun. ACM, 28,* 7 (1985), 680–689.

24. Hirokawa, R.Y. and Pace, R. A descriptive investigation of the possible communication based reasons for effective and ineffective group decision making. *Commun. Monographs,* 50 (1983), 363–379.

25. Huber, G.P. Issues in the design of group decision support systems. *MIS Quarterly,* (1984), 195–204.

26. Huber, G.P. A theory of the effects of advanced information technology on organizational design, intelligence, and decision making. *Acad. of Manag. Rev., 15,* 1 (1990), 47–71.

27. Jablin, F.M. and Seibold, D.R. Implications for problem solving groups of empirical research on 'brainstorming': A critical review of the literature. *The Southern States Speech Commun. J.,* 43 (Summer 1978), 327–356.

28. Jessup, L.M., Connolly, T. and Galegher, J. The effects of anonymity on group process in automated group problem solving. *MIS Quarterly, 14,* 3 (1990), 313–321.

29. Jessup, L.M. Tansik, D.A. and Lasse, T.D. Group problem solving in an automated environment: The effects of anonymity and proximity on group process and outcome with a GDSS. *Decision Sciences,* forthcoming.

30. Lamm, H. and Trommsdorff, G. Group versus individual performance on tasks requiring ideational proficiency (brainstorming): A review. *European J. of Soc. Psy.,* (1973), 361–387.

31. Maidique, M.A. Entrepreneurs, champions, and technological innovations. *Sloan Manag. Rev., 21,* 2 (1980), 59–76.

32. Mason, R.O. and Mitroff, I.I. *Challenging Strategic Planning Assumptions,* John Wiley & Sons, New York, 1981.

33. Miller, J.C. Information input overload and psychopathology. *J. of Psychiatry,* (Feb. 1960), 696–704.

34. Mintzberg, H., Raisinghani, D. and Theoret, A. The structure of 'unstructured' decision processes. *Administrative Sciences Quarterly,* 21 (1976), 246–275.

35. Nunamaker Jr., J.F., Applegate, L.M., and Konsynski, B.R. Facilitating group creativity with GDSS. *J. of MIS, 3,* 4 (1987), 5–19.

36. Nunamaker Jr., J.F., Applegate, L.M. and Konsynski, B.R. Computer-aided deliberation: Model management and group decision support. *J. of Operations Res., 36,* 6 (1988), 826–848.

37. Nunamaker Jr., J.F., Vogel, D., Heminger, A., Martz, B., Grohowski, R. and McGoff, C. Experiences at IBM with group sup-

port systems: A field study. *Decision Support Systems*, 5, 2 (1989), 183–196.

38. Osborn, A.F. *Applied Imagination: Principles and Procedures of Creative Thinking.* 2nd edition, Scribners, New York, 1957.

39. Pinsonnault, A. and Kraemar, K.L. The impact of technological support on groups: An assessment of the empirical research. *Decision Support Syst.*, 5, 2 (1989), 197–216.

40. Poole, M.S. Decision development in small groups II: A study of multiple sequences of decision making. *Communication Monographs*, 50 (1983), 206–232.

41. Schweiger, D.M., Sandberg, W.R., and Rechner, P.L. Experimental effects of dialectical inquiry, devil's advocacy, and consensus approaches to strategic decision making. *Academy of Management Review*, 32, 4 (1989), 745–772.

42. Shaw, M. *Group Dynamics: The Psychology of Small Group Behavior.* 3rd edition, McGraw-Hill, New York, 1981.

43. Siegel, J., Dubrovsky, V. Kiesler, S. and McGuire, T.W. Group processes in computer mediated communication. *Organizational Behavior and Human Decision Processes*, 37 (1986), 157–187.

44. Silver, M.S. Decision support systems: Directed and non-directed change. *Information Systems Research*, 1, 1 (1990), 47–70.

45. Simon, H.A. *Administrative Behavior.* 3rd edition, Free Press, 1976.

46. Stefik, M., Foster, G., Bobrow, D.G., Khan, K., Lanning, S., and Suchman, L. Beyond the chalkboard: Computer support for collaboration and problem solving in meetings. *Commun. ACM*, 30, 1 (1987), 33–47.

47. Steiner, I.D. *Group Process and Productivity.* Academic Press, New York, 1972.

48. Valacich, J.S. Group size and proximity effects on computer mediated generation: A laboratory investigation. Doctoral dissertation, University of Arizona, 1989.

49. Valacich, J.S., Dennis, A.R., George, J.F. and Nunamaker Jr., J.F. Electronic support for group idea generation: Shifting the balance of process gains and losses. Arizona working paper, 1991.

50. Valacich, J.S., Dennis, A.R., and Nunamaker Jr., J.F. Anonymity and group size effects on computer mediated idea generation. Proceedings of Academy of Mangagement Meeting, 1991, forthcoming.

51. Valacich, J.S., Dennis, A.R. and Nunamaker Jr., J.F. Electronic Meeting Support: The Group-Systems concept. *Intern. J. of Man Machine Studies*, forthcoming.

52. Vogel, D.R., Martz, W.B., Nunamaker Jr., J.F., Grohowski, R.B. and McGoff, C. Electronic meeting system experience at IBM. *J. of MIS*, 6, 3 (1990), 25–43.

53. Vogel, D.R., Nunamaker Jr., J.F., George, J.F. and Dennis, A.R. Group decision support systems: Evolution and status at the University of Arizona. In R.M. Lee, A.M. McCosh, and P. Migliarese Eds. *Organizational Decision Support Systems*, Proceedings of IFIP WG 8.3 Working Conference on Organizational DSS, North Holland, 1988, 287–305.

54. Williams, E. 1977. Experimental comparisons of face-to-face and mediated communication: A review. *Psychol. Bull.*, 84, 5, 963–976.

55. Winniford, M.A. The effect of electronic meeting support on large and small decision-making groups. Unpublished doctoral dissertation, University of Arizona, 1989.

56. Zack, M.H. and McKenney, J.L. Characteristics of organizational information domain: An organizational information processing perspective. Harvard Business School Working Paper 89-027, 1989.

57. Zajonc, R.B. Social facilitation. *Science*, 149 (1965), 269–274.

CR Categories and Subject Descriptors: H.1.2 [**Models and Principles**]: User/Machine Systems—*human information processing;* H.4.2 [**Information Systems Applications**]: Types of Systems—*decision support;* H.4.3 [**Information Systems Applications**]: Communications Applications—*computer conferencing and teleconferencing;* H.5.3 [**Information Interfaces and Presentations**]: Group and Organization Interfaces—*synchronous interfaces; theory and models;* J.1 [**Administrative Data Processing**]: General.

General Terms: Design

Additional Key Words and Phrases: Communication, computer-supportive cooperative work, electronic meeting systems, group decision support systems, groupware, group work, multiuser systems

About the Authors

J.F. NUNAMAKER heads the Department of MIS at the University of Arizona where he is a professor of MIS and Computer Science. His research interests include computer-aided support of systems analysis and design, and systems for management.

ALAN R. DENNIS is a doctoral candidate in MIS at the University of Arizona. His current research interests include electronic meeting systems, systems analysis and design, and business process re-engineering.

JOSEPH S. VALACICH is assistant professor of information systems at the University of Indiana. His current research interests include the design and investigation of communication and decision technologies to support collaborative group work, systems analysis and design, and group and organizational memory. **Authors' Present Address:** Decision and Information Systems Department, School of Business, Indiana University, Bloomington, IN 47405, valacich@iubacs.bitnet.

DOUGLAS R. VOGEL is an assistant professor of MIS at the University of Arizona. His research interests bridge the business and academic communities in addressing group support system development, implementation, and evaluation issues.

JOEY F. GEORGE is an assistant professor in the Department of MIS at the University of Arizona. His research interests focus on information technology in the work place, and currently include the study of group decision support systems.

Authors' Present Address for Nunamaker, Dennis, Vogel, and George: Department of MIS, Eller Graduate School of Management, University of Arizona, Tuscon, AZ 85721, nunamake@arizmis.bitnet, dennisa@arizmis.bitnet, vogel@arizmis.bitnet, george@arizmis.bitnet.

Experiences in the Use of a Media Space

Marilyn M. Mantei, Ronald M. Baecker, Abigail J. Sellen,
William A.S.Buxton, and Thomas Milligan

Department of Computer Science

Barry Wellman

Department of Sociology
University of Toronto
Toronto, Ontario M5S 1A4

ABSTRACT

A media space is a system that uses integrated video, audio, and computers to allow individuals and groups to work together despite being distributed spatially and temporally. Our media space, CAVECAT (Computer Audio Video Enhanced Collaboration And Telepresence), enables a small number of individuals or groups located in separate offices to engage in collaborative work without leaving their offices. This paper presents and summarizes our experiences during initial use of CAVECAT, including unsolved technological obstacles we have encountered, and the psychological and social impact of the technology. Where possible we discuss relevant findings from the psychological literature, and implications for design of the next-generation media space.

KEYWORDS
Computer-supported cooperative work, groupware, media spaces, desktop videoconferencing.

INTRODUCTION
Although Engelbart and English (1968) provided the first demonstration of a media space, the current wave of activity began with the Xerox PARC Portland Experiments (Goodman & Abel, 1986; Abel, 1990) and continued with recent developments including those at Xerox PARC (Stults, 1986, 1988; Bly & Minneman, 1990; Tang & Minneman, 1990), Bolt, Beranek and Newman (Thomas, Forsdick, Crowley, Schaaf, Tomlinson & Travers, 1988), Olivetti (Lantz, 1988), Bellcore (Root, 1988), and Rank Xerox EuroPARC (Buxton & Moran, 1990).

Despite marked differences in technology and approach, these experiments suggest common themes:

- Media spaces define new methods of communication, with novel and unforeseen uses and potentialities. Communication through a media space is more than

an approximation of face-to-face communication — it has a richness and complexity all its own.

- The effective realization of media spaces requires one to solve serious architectural and implementation problems in distributed computing.

- Group working environments contain an enormously rich collection of communication protocols. The subset of communication metaphors built into existing media spaces only begin to reflect the possibilities.

- Media spaces raise serious ethical issues such as those of surveillance and privacy.

We have constructed a media space that enables a small number of individuals and groups located in separate offices to meet and collaborate without leaving their offices. This paper presents initial observations based on several months use of the system. Our goal is to contribute to the emerging dialogue on the potential, appropriate design, impact, and implications of media spaces. After a brief introduction to our system, we present our observations organized in terms of unexpected affordances, technological obstacles, and social and psychological impact. Each of our observations is discussed in terms of applicable underlying theories and suggested design recommendations.

THE CAVECAT SYSTEM
The CAVECAT (Computer Audio Video Enhanced Collaboration And Telepresence) system consists of a number of enhanced workstations connected by a digital+audio+video network. Each workstation consists of a personal computer, a TV monitor, a TV camera, a pair of speakers, and a microphone. A 4 x 1 video board allows the display of composite images of up to 4 sites (Figure 1). In some locations, video boards can place a lower resolution video image directly on the workstation's screen so that a separate monitor is not necessary.

The heart of the system is the switching network (Figure 2), patterned after the IIIF Server developed at Rank Xerox EuroPARC (Buxton & Moran , 1990; Milligan, 1989). Audio and video transmission is analog, but is switched digitally by the IIIF Server software residing on a workstation. Personal workstations in each office send messages via Ethernet to the IIIF server requesting connections. The IIIF Server also examines privacy settings for each office to determine if requested access by another office is permissible.

Figure 1. Video image of a CAVECAT meeting.

A server agent resides on each personal workstation. The user interface to this agent permits each office occupant to select a variety of communication metaphors: task oriented, (e.g., calling a meeting); spatially oriented, (e.g., walking into someone's office); or object oriented, (e.g., turning off the microphone in your office) (Louie, Mantei & Buxton, 1990).

We are developing shared software to support the computer communication aspect of the media space. These packages include a shared drawing tool and a shared text editor. Until this software is in place, we are using commercial software such as Timbuktu (Farallon, 1989), and ShrEdit, an experimental shared editor (Olson,Olson, Mack & Wellner, 1990).

UNEXPECTED AFFORDANCES

In order to understand the impact of the media space on its users, we applied it to ourselves by setting up CAVECAT nodes linking two faculty offices, the system programmer's office, and a graduate student work area. For the communication interface, we used a spatial metaphor consisting of a layout of the offices involved. We digitized video images of the CAVECAT users and placed these miniaturized images inside their owners respective onscreen offices Moving one or more of these images from one virtual office into another establishes a visual and acoustic link with the office or offices of choice.

Meetings of groups of groups

We had intended our setup to work primarily as a communicating device for one person located in each office. Our camera setups and camera angles were not designed for video conference meetings. However, in reality there was a natural demand for such a facility and it was used in this way. Individual members of the group used CAVECAT to introduce their visitors to others without going through the effort of physically walking the visitor over to the other individual's office for a more time-consuming interruption.

Mirror function

Although the system was designed for displaying other meeting participants, unexpected benefits came from displaying oneself. We used this "mirror" facility to make sure we were properly framed in the camera. The mirror function was included automatically in the split-screen display of 4-way conversations (Figure 1).

Monitoring function

Another surprising use was for the purpose of being virtually in one's own office. Instead of using the media links to place oneself virtually in another's office, we could also use the links as windows into our own offices when we were not there. We could monitor who was looking for us and when the phone rang. We could also use the system for security.

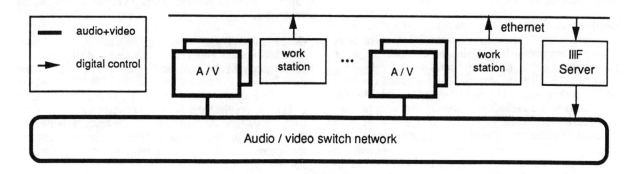

Figure 2 . Schematic diagram of the layout of the CAVECAT network.

TECHNOLOGICAL OBSTACLES

In our experience, a number of technological obstacles presented usability problems:

System response time delays

We initially built a prototype software package to run our virtual office connections. The time to establish a connection or to enter or leave an ongoing meeting was nearly two seconds. This delay quickly became intolerableAlthough system response times improved with a new version of the software, we must note that the two second wait time corresponds well with network switching and satellite delays for very long distance communications. This poses serious problems for the design of virtual offices spanning long distances.

Audio levels and noise

Ambient noise in the speakers' offices presented a major problem for sound quality. Different furniture arrangements, different numbers of people in the office, whether the office door was open or not, and where the office owner chose to sit in relation to speakers and microphones all had the potential to further degrade the quality of the sound. As a result, sound levels had to be continuously adjusted. When CAVECAT participants could not hear another participant, they tended to raise their voices, disturbing the audio levels more.

Obviously, it is inappropriate for us to tamper with the flexibility of individuals to decorate and move around their offices, nor do we have an intelligent device to automatically adjust levels. We are modifying the system by providing each participant with the ability to control their own audio, but we need to determine ways to make such adjustments easy and to guarantee that individual adjustments do not cause deterioration of the overall sound quality through feedback.

Sound localization

Participants of CAVECAT commented on how the sound in the shared communication seemed to come from "out of the air" rather than from the direction of the person speaking. When we had multiple participants communicating, the inability for participants to localize the sound sometimes made it difficult to determine who was speaking. Often, it was also difficult to know if one's phone was ringing, because of confusions with rings in other offices transmitted over the network.

Lighting and camera angles

The automatic light adjustments in our camera were intelligent but not intelligent enough. For example, some cameras were pointing at whiteboards located behind the occupants. The camera automatically adjusted for these white backgrounds, leaving the individuals in the foreground bathed in shadow. Some cameras were perched on bookshelves, while others sat on the side of their personal workstation. The location of the cameras, the lighting and color of the room's background, and the distance the individual chose to sit from the camera all affected the size and quality of the image transferred to the other offices.

Bad camera angles could distort impressions of speakers, which was particularly serious when one was not very familiar with a participant and when one was negotiating. Cameras with automatic focus continually zoomed in and out on the people moving about their offices, tending to make viewers in other offices slightly motion sick. It is clear that we need to consider carefully the placement of both camera and human, and to provide appropriate controls for presenting desirable video images.

PSYCHOLOGICAL AND SOCIAL IMPACT

Meetings between and within offices

Meetings of groups of groups of people were difficult to manage because people within an office were more "present" with each other than they were in the virtual office across the media. The physical closeness of people in the same office made them much more aware of their physical neighbors than of their video neighbors. This fact, combined with the poor acoustic quality across the network, encouraged people to address those in the same room rather than those in the other offices.

Two types of conversations often took place simultaneously. One conversation was public where people spoke to the camera. Private conversations were also being held among individuals in each office. Coordinating these two kinds of conversations and establishing the dominance of the public discussion when appropriate presented a challenge.

Another problem with such large meetings was that the displayed size of many individuals was so reduced that fine points of the interaction were often not visible. Facial expressions and nonverbal gestures were not as salient; interactions seemed less "real" than the ones taking place in the same room. When we switched from a meeting of multiple offices (a 2 x 2 video configuration of all participants) to a two-way communication (a single screen presentation of other participant), conversations again took place between offices rather than within offices.

Gaze and eye contact

Because participants were engaged in looking at the video image of their counterpart, they did not look directly into the TV camera. We did not use teleprompters or half-silvered mirrors to facilitate looking at the screen and the camera simultaneously. Thus eye contact was not established.

Gaze and mutual gaze are an important part of normal face-to-face communication. It is estimated that 61 percent of conversation involves gaze and 31 percent involves mutual gaze (Argyle, Ingham, Alkena & McCallin, 1973). Gaze serves at least five functions (Argyle et al., 1973; Exline, 1971): to regulate the flow of conversation; to provide feedback on how the communication is being perceived by the listener; to communicate emotions; to communicate the nature of the interpersonal relationship; and to reflect status relationships.

Rank Xerox EuroPARC (Buxton & Moran, 1990) used *video tunnels* — boxes containing cameras which pick up the video image of an individual via a half silvered mirror in front of their TV monitor. This solution makes it necessary for people to sit directly in front of big black boxes rather than in normal communicating positions within their office. EuroPARC has removed these video tunnels, but alternate solutions to achieving eye contact have not been devised. Hewlett-Packard embeds a miniature camera in the top of the workstation and uses on-screen video, but even this angle does not permit complete eye contact.

The best solution we have been able to achieve is produced by placing a camera with a wide-angle lens in front of and above the person and just above the monitor. The camera should not be very close to the person; zooming is used to make the person appear closer.

Status of meeting participants

Another interesting observation was that CAVECAT changed social status relationships due to the loss of the usual spatial and nonverbal cues which convey status information.

In face-to-face meetings, the seating of people in a room is usually indicative of a hierarchy with higher status people occupying more central positions or "head of the table" locations.

The design of CAVECAT unintentionally introduced its own social status cues. In meetings of four individuals, CAVECAT arbitrarily positioned participants' images in a 2 x 2 grid. CAVECAT also configured the video images for a meeting based on who requested the meeting. This meant that if meetings were reconvened after a short break by a different person, the result was a different image configuration. This was highly disconcerting to the participants. It was as if everyone had left the room and returned to take new positions around the table.

Meeting coordination

Our observed problems with loss of traditional status cues and generation of new cues speaks to the more general issue of control in discussions. When important cues are missing or degraded, there is a greater need for a moderator to control turn-taking and group decision processes. For example, people wanting to take control in conversations will often lean in to indicate their desire to speak. This cue is difficult to detect on video.

Our observation is that a moderator's success may depend on having "media presence" — a factor which does not necessarily come into play in face-to-face meetings.

Image size and personal impact

A participant's effectiveness within a conversation and the way each participant was perceived by others seemed to be, in part, determined by video image size. Participants with large images appeared to have more impact in the discussion. Participants with small images seemed distant and less effective in the conversation.

The size of the video image was determined by four factors: the screen size of the monitor, the distance of the viewer from the TV monitor, the distance of the person from the camera, and the zoom setting of the camera. Participants often had different sized images because these variables were rarely adjusted.

Video image and social distance

Image size and angle also interacted with people's perception of their social relationship to other participants. Inappropriate image size sometimes gave the sense of people being too personal or too impersonal in the conversation.

These observations are consistent with the social psychology literature which finds that interpersonal physical distance is predictive of relationships between people (Argyle & Dean, 1965). People who are only casually acquainted tend to maintain a distance of about 4 to 12 feet between them while interacting. Distances from 1 1/2 to 4 feet tend to be maintained for friends, while distances of less than 1 1/2 feet are reserved for intimate relationships. It is well established that people quickly become uncomfortable if the distance between them is perceived to be inappropriate for the relationship. Too close, and people feel their space is being violated. Too far, and people are also uncomfortable.

In the media space, what is relevant is the "perceived" interpersonal distance, a virtual distance rather than a physical one. Observation suggests that video images may be viewed as less personal and intrusive in general. In one hot summer's day usage, the participants talked freely with each other over the media space, but one individual immediately donned a lab coat to cover her shorts and tank top when meeting face-to-face with the same individual. One the other hand, occasionally a meeting participant reached for a book from a shelf or stood up, creating views several inches from the participant's neck or stomach, making an onlooker uncomfortable.

What is also unusual about a media space is that the interpersonal distance may be simultaneously different for any member of the group communicating. This is not the case for physical distance where distances between people are, in a sense, negotiated and shared. In CAVECAT, a participant's personal space can be invaded without the invader being aware of this.

Privacy and surveillance

When we first put the system in place, any node on the network could immediately connect with any other node via video and audio. The system was kept running semi-continuously because of the need to troubleshoot startup problems. This lack of privacy led to very strong protection behaviors on the part of two participants — one who was negotiating the secret sale of a company, and another who was negotiating problems in a personal relationship. The first individual unplugged or shut off all CAVECAT connections while the second worked shorter hours.

It became clear very early that "knowing" when you were connected to another office and being able to inhibit the connection were critical and necessary features. The media space, as it was, did not provide enough feedback to indicate that others were suddenly present in your office. In addition, although available, the privacy setting features in the IIIF Server were too complicated for easy use. One good approach to the provision of adequate feedback is through the use of non-speech audio cues (Buxton & Moran, 1990; Gaver & Smith, 1990).

IMPLICATIONS FOR FUTURE DESIGN

Our experiences begin to illustrate how technology can significantly alter the nature of human communication patterns. One important conclusion is that many of the cues implicit in face-to-face communication situations need to be taken into account and provided for in the design of the interface.

There are many communication variables that we had not considered in our original design. It is easy to take for granted aspects implicit in face-to-face communication such as the physical presence of someone in an office implying a desire to communicate, or nonverbal gestures of individuals in a meeting.

Another implication of our observations is that it is important to provide easy-to-use features that place some of the system variables under user control. For example, because there are many aspects of the visual image which affect the way participants perceive each other and interact, it is important that users are able to adjust for viewing and being viewed.

We have a number of specific plans based on our experiences to date:

- We are developing metaphors for communication and privacy protection that follow accepted communication practice. These metaphors consist of interface selections that allow the user to: (1) wait to see someone who is busy talking to someone else; (2) drop by to ask a quick question; (3) shut one's door partially or wholly; or (4) whisper something to a co-worker at a meeting. We are working with variables such as video image size, blurriness of the video image, duration of the video/audio connection and verbal and non-speech audio cues to create these communication protocols.

- We are building an underlying visual language for manipulating the parameters of the system so that its users can build their own protocols for adjusting the media space parameters.

- We are putting in new basic functionalities such as individual control of audio and comparative viewing of video images. We are also trying out automatic audio switching so that the person speaking in a meeting becomes the single image presented to all participants. This avoids our image size problems but may create new problems associated with not being able to view everyone in the meeting.

Despite our current problems, our media space has proved to be a successful tool for collaborative communication. We find that it is used extensively for communicating about software development. The system not only allows an approximation to face-to-face communication, but also confers many new advantages upon its users. We can have virtual open offices with the bad effects of continuous noise and disturbance removed and the good effects of proximity enhanced. Meantime we are continuing the process of iterative design in order to minimize the problems and capitalize on the advantages discussed in this paper.

ACKNOWLEDGEMENTS

For research support, the authors are indebted to the Natural Sciences and Engineering Research Council of Canada, the Information Technology Research Centre of Ontario, Apple Computer, Digital Equipment Corporation, IBM Canada and particularly to Rank Xerox EuroPARC, which contributed the code for the IIIF Server. In addition, we are grateful to the University of Michigan, which loaned us the object code for their shared editor. We also wish to thank the many students who have worked long hours on CAVECAT: Beverly Harrison, Jeffrey Lee, Gifford Louie, Iva Lu, Kelly Mawby, Tracy Narine, Ilona Posner, Michael Sheasby, and Ian Small.

REFERENCES

Abel, M.J,. Experiences in an exploratory distributed organization. In Galegher, Kraut & Egido (Eds), *Intellectual Teamwork: Social and Technological Foundations of Cooperative Work*, Lawrence Erlbaum Associates, 489-510.

Argyle, M. and Dean, J. (1965) Eye contact, distance, and affiliation. *Sociometry*, 28, 289-304.

Argyle, M., Ingham, R., Alkena, F. and McCallin, M. (1973). The different functions of gaze. *Semiotica*, 7, 10-32.

Bly, S.A. and Minneman, S.L. (1990). Commune: a shared drawing surface. In *Proceedings of the Conference of Office Information Systems*, Cambridge, MA, April 1990. 184-192.

Engelbart, D. and English, W.K. (1968). A research center for augmenting human intellect. In Greif, I. (Ed.) . *Computer-Supported Cooperative Work: A Book of Readings*, Morgan Kaufmann Publishers, San Mateo, Calif., 81-105.

Exline, R.V. (1971). Visual interaction: The glances of power and preference. In J. K. Cole (Ed.) *Nebraska Symposium on Motivation* Vol. 19, 163-206, University of Nebraska Press.

Farallon Computing, Inc. (1989). *Timbuktu*. 2201 Dwight Way, Berkeley, CA, 94704 USA.

Gaver, W.W. and Smith, R.B. (1990). Auditory icons in large-scale collaborative environments. In Diaper, D., Gilmore, D. Cockton, G. and Shackel, B. (Eds) *Proceedings of Human-Compuer Interaction, INTERACT'90*, Cambridge, England, August 27-31, 1990, 735-740.

Goodman, G. and Abel, M. (1986). Collaboration research in SCL. In *Proceedings of the First Conference on Computer Supported Cooperative Work*, Austin, TX, December 86.

Lantz, K.A. (1988). An experiment in integrated multimedia conferencing. In Greif, I. (Ed.) . *Computer-Supported Cooperative Work: A Book of Readings*, Morgan Kaufmann Publishers, San Mateo, Calif., 533-552.

Louie, G., Mantei, M. and Buxton, W.A.S.(1990) Making contact in a multi-media environment. HCI Consortium on CSCW, Ann Arbor, MI., February 1991.

Milligan, T. (1989). IIIF: The Integrated Interactive Intermedia Facility design report - Revision 3 January 1989. Rank Xerox EuroPARC working paper.

Buxton, W.A.S. and Moran, T (1990). EuroPARC's Integrated Interactive Intermedia facility (IIIF): Early Experiences. *Proceedings of the IFIP WG8.4 Conference on Multi-user Interfaces and Applications*, Heraklion, Crete, September 1990. 24pp.

Olson, J.R., Olson, G.M., Mack, L.A. and Wellner, P. (1990). Concurrent editing: the group's interface. In Diaper, D., Gilmore, D. Cockton, G. and Shackel, B. (Eds), *Proceedings of Human-Compuer Interaction, INTERACT'90*, Cambridge, England, August 27-31, 1990, 835-840.

Root, R.W. (1988). Design of a multi-media vehicle for social browsing. In *Proceedings of the Second Conference on Computer-Supported Cooperative Work*, Portland, OR, September 1989, 25-38.

Stults, R. (1986). Media space. Xerox PARC technical report. 20 pp.

Stults, R. (1988). Experimental uses of video to support design activities. Xerox PARC technical report SSL-89-19.

Tang, J.C. and Minneman, S.L. (1990). VideoDraw: a video interface for collaborative drawing. *Proceedings of CHI '90*, 313-320.

Thomas, R.H., Forsdick, H.C., Crowley, T.R., Schaaf, R.W., Tomlinson, R.S., and Travers, V.M. (1988). Diamond: a multimedia message system built on a distributed architecture. In Greif, I. (Ed.) *Computer-Supported Cooperative Work: A Book of Readings*, Morgan Kaufmann Publishers, San Mateo, Calif., 509-532.

Chapter 7:
Bridging Time and Space

Chapter 7: Bridging Time and Space

People interact with one another in various ways: face-to-face, at a distance, at the same time, at different times. Networked systems make remote communication nearly instantaneous, enabling people to bridge time and space, facilitating access to vast stores of information and to correspondence among many individuals. But easy access to information does not necessarily mean appropriate access.

It is essential to understand why people want to exchange information and relate to one another in the first place. How can groupware systems augment the ways people work by enabling them to span time and distance barriers? What are key problems and issues for designing effective solutions that facilitate communication, coordination, and collaboration across time and space?

This section describes software systems designed from a group perspective seeking to improve communication, enhance coordination, and foster collaboration among work groups or task teams. Going considerably beyond patterns of interpersonal communications, these systems have the potential to enable work groups to evolve new business practices.

Background: Mail and fax

Exchanging documents is a fundamental component of group work. As an eighteenth-century American entrepreneur and social theorist, Benjamin Franklin recognized the central importance of mail services for business communications when he organized one of the first postal systems in the Colonies. Over the years we have extended this concept by inventing various artifacts to define and describe the nature of electronic communication (transmitting the information contained on a piece of paper without physically transmitting the paper itself). The telegraph, telephone, and telex are among the earliest examples. They represent different communications paradigms, and are the combination of technological infrastructures and people's imaginations.

In the 1970s and 1980s, the speed and reliability of computer networks changed the nature of electronic information exchange. Advances in information systems technologies have enhanced communication among individuals and groups. It is essential to understand the consequences of two contemporary artifacts, electronic mail and fax (facsimile transmission).

Electronic mail promotes interpersonal communication (one-to-one or one-to-many) through the process of composing, sending, receiving, and storing messages. Users can transmit messages almost as easily as talking to one another, and in asynchronous (or delayed) time, as if speaking to a telephone answering machine (which receivers can then hear at their convenience). One person can quickly broadcast a message to many; another can engage in multiple conversations, gathering facts and opinions from disparate sources; a third can send documents to others for review and comments.

Fax provides an important variation to traditional electronic mail. The connection may be slower, but it is more robust and considerably more pervasive. With fax, it takes longer to "mail" a document from one place to another (typically just under a minute per page, depending on the quality of the hardware and connection). Nevertheless, people simply use telephone lines, so there are no special wiring, addressing, or networking requirements. Another telephone number will suffice. Moreover, the receiver gets an exact copy of what is sent, including text, penmarks, sketches or whatever, without getting into issues of formatting and conversion.

Based on traditional (hard copy) models for business communication, electronic mail and fax enable rapid transmission of electronic documents, regardless of the distances involved. The obvious benefits derive from shortening delivery times. This creates the possibility that individuals might work together more expeditiously, and perhaps more effectively. In theory, people in a work group or task team would benefit from improved communications. Nevertheless, each person has the responsibility for sending and receiving individual messages, and for managing his or her own collections of stored documents; improved organizational effectiveness is not guaranteed.

Enabling the free flow of information is a principle component for groupware, but one that opens Pandora's box. By itself, interpersonal communication is primarily a one-to-one activity. Simply sending and receiving electronic documents does not automatically enhance group effectiveness.

On the contrary, many people frequently identify "information overload" as one of the unanticipated consequences of information-rich environments. Users do not necessarily take advantage of the flexibility and power provided by the electronic exchange of information. New information systems can provide many different ways to improve traditional models for business communication, but when people have ready access to all kinds of information, they need tools and techniques to find the *right information just in time*.

It is important to consider communication and coordination from a group perspective. Groupware that bridges time and space can help support group-level tasks and improve group-level patterns of interaction.

Themes: Improving group communications

While people identify information overload as a problem, designers and developers work to provide solutions, based on varied underlying metaphors about the users' intended tasks, how they want to access shared information, and how they might better communicate with one another. Designers and developers also have different assumptions about features and functionality of the enabling hardware, software, and networking environments.

Computer-mediated communication systems. Hiltz and Turoff describe how simply structuring shared information might improve the nature of communications among groups of people. They present their experiences with computer conferencing, designed to facilitate communication through the process of posting information on a shared bulletin board and engaging in group discussions.

Often termed "many-to-many" communication, this allows people to discuss common topics by putting electronic messages in a shared file or central repository, in effect, conducting an electronic meeting. Like being in a business meeting, classroom, or social gathering, participants discuss and debate, cajole and inform one another by sending messages to a shared location, and by reading other people's ideas. The rules of participation may vary, depending on the nature of the discussions and the facilities of the conferencing system. Participants access a shared environment, in effect, talking to one another at their own convenience.

An individual topic or note begins a conversation, followed by a series of comments or replies as rejoinders. All participants have the personal responsibility to track conversations in a conference and to initiate their own comments on the subjects at hand. The conferencing system might provide a number of features to assist participation: mechanisms for filtering, indexing, and scanning comments; limiting the length of replies; providing voting structures for group decision making; or enabling designated people to moderate conversations. Moderators' roles are often crucial for the success of a computer conference in an organization or work group.

Maintaining mutual intelligibility. Trigg, Suchman, and Halasz propose a different metaphor, NoteCards, which seeks to support collaboration by striving to maintain the mutual intelligibility (or shared understanding) of the work at hand. There are different kinds of conversations, depending on the context. Some are substantive, focusing on the actual work being done; others are annotative, providing commentary on the work at hand; still others are procedural, discussing the process of performing work-related tasks.

For instance, the processes of coauthoring and coediting raise many issues of mutual intelligibility when authors share information by circulating a draft document. People comment on each other's work, ask one another probing questions, and suggest changes. NoteCards, as a prototype groupware environment, distinguishes between annotative comments and substantive changes, and maintains a trail of questions, answers, actual changes, and suggestions.

Going considerably beyond the comments and replies of a computer-conferencing system, a groupware environment such as NoteCards might help coauthors and coeditors manage their interactions. This can be as simple as coordinating asynchronous revision cycles, so that one person after another receives a revised and annotated draft, and all comments or suggestions are uniquely identified. Or this may entail a more complex series of interactions in which many people work on a document at the same time.

Synchronous coauthoring and coediting environments envisioned by NoteCards present a set of particularly thorny problems. Users expect the environment to coordinate revision cycles and mediate conflicts so that they do not lose information and are made aware of one another's modifications. This requires solutions for access contention and real-time update notification. The environment must provide special information management and user interface mechanisms to facilitate synchronous collaboration: shared write access, section interlocking, techniques for lock passing, and conventions for indicating modified information.

Diversity in the use of electronic mail. Mackay identifies two basic patterns for use of electronic mail and describes how simple tools such as electronic mail filters might considerably improve individual and group communication.

Part of the structure of electronic information, sometimes termed a message header, is initially required by the system for transmitting mail from one user to another. This structure might be something as simple as a user's address (as understood by an electronic mail application), and perhaps a date field. Or it may have a more complex set of conventions specified by an international standard (such as X.400 for electronic mail), or conventions from common practice (such as the tagged fields from a newswire service).

Mackay describes how groups might use semistructured messages to capitalize on existing group norms and improve intragroup communications. Often groups have developed their own jargon in their ongoing relationships. Users in a work group might define additional fields in semistructured messages to signal explicit meaning. To the extent that users can agree upon a common vocabulary they can better coordinate their activities, and the system can then directly support their interactions.

Once the knowledge of relevant terms is disseminated within a work group, semistructured messages can be used for (1) composing messages to be sent; (2) selecting, sorting, and prioritizing received messages; (3) responding automatically to messages received; and (4) suggesting likely responses to received messages. Rule-based agents for filtering semistructured messages vary widely. Some are primarily *prioritizers*, seeking to order and process electronic mail upon arrival, anticipating likely actions and scenarios. Others are primarily *archivers*, seeking system assistance to manage read mail for subsequent retrieval. Individual mail users are extremely diverse and exhibit different usage patterns.

Objects and agents for group work. Lai, Malone, and Yu propose a new metaphor for defining a groupware environment. Object Lens is a "spreadsheet" for cooperative work. Effective group work applications should provide mechanisms for information sharing and coordination, combining capabilities of semistructured messages, intelligent agents, object-oriented representation of information, and hypertext linkages. With an object-oriented approach, the abstract things in the system closely correspond to the real world things in the work environment. Groupings of semistructured fields and lists of valid values can be passed from general to more specific objects.

For instance, Object Lens might define people, meetings, tasks, and work-related activities in terms of semistructured objects. These objects might inherit attributes in a hierarchical fashion (for example, a "student" would include additional attributes, beyond simply those of a "person"). Object Lens can group objects into varied collections (a team of people, a project composed of interrelated tasks, etc.) and display them in "containers" or "folders." Users can view these collections of objects in many different ways, depending on their immediate tasks and intentions. They can share the same information, yet organize it in different ways appropriate to their own unique tasks at hand.

Semiautonomous agents can perform functions according to predefined criteria, whenever specific conditions are met. Potential groupware includes task-tracking applications that support project planning and are capable of sending automatic reminders when deadlines approach, and coordination applications capable of automating work processes according to well-defined information flows.

Futures: Towards collaborative systems

The future evolution of groupware that bridges time and space will proceed along three dimensions simultaneously. Getting the *right information, just in time* will continue to gain importance as work groups are increasingly likely to function across time and space. Going beyond semistructured information and simple information filters, groups will seek to interrelate time and task activities, and many other kinds of information objects, so that "intelligent assistants" will be able to coordinate schedules and work flows based on adaptive, easily modifiable criteria. (We will describe some of the underlying theories of coordination technologies in Section 8.) Groups will interact with one another through highly visual displays so that the information users view and the activities they are likely to perform correspond closely to their underlying cognitive models of the tasks at hand.

We will begin to describe these group-oriented environments as "collaborative systems." They will use more than personal artifacts such as electronic mail, fax, or an electronic desktop. Users will rely on the systems not only to support their interpersonal communications (the processes by which they send and receive information) but also to coordinate various kinds of work tasks and group activities.

STRUCTURING COMPUTER-MEDIATED COMMUNICATION SYSTEMS TO AVOID INFORMATION OVERLOAD

Unless computer-mediated communication systems are structured, users will be overloaded with information. But structure should be imposed by individuals and user groups according to their needs and abilities, rather than through general software features.

STARR ROXANNE HILTZ and MURRAY TUROFF

"Structuring Computer-Mediated Communication Systems to Avoid Information Overload" by S.R. Hiltz and M. Turoff from *Communications of the ACM*, Vol. 28, No. 7, July 1985, pages 680-689. Copyright © 1985, Association for Computing Machinery, Inc., reprinted with permission.

OVERVIEW

Computer-mediated communication systems (CMCS's) use computers and telecommunications networks to compose, store, deliver, and process communication. Among the types of systems that come under this heading are electronic mail, computerized conferencing, and bulletin-board systems. CMCS's can provide sufficient speed and volume for effective communication flow within and between groups and organizations. However, this "solution" to constrictions on the flow of information and communication is not without cost, in a behavioral as well as an economic sense. Computers and related "office-automation" technology can often create as many problems for an organization as they solve. As Kerr and Hiltz have put it,

> The volume and pace of information can become overwhelming, especially since messages are not necessarily sequential and multiple topic threads are common, resulting in information overload [13, 30]. Information overload presents itself first as a problem, then as a constant challenge to be overcome. Intensive interaction with a large number of communication partners results in the mushrooming of the absolute amount of information and the number of simultaneous discussions, conferences, and other activities, that goes well beyond normal coping abilities. [15]

Denning [2] cogently characterizes one contributing factor to information overload as "electronic junk"—frequent CMCS users can expect to be imposed on by unwanted and useless messages. This problem is becoming worse as more systems, and therefore more users, are interconnected by networks like CSNET, USENET, and MAILNET.

The research on which this paper is based was partially supported by grants from the National Science Foundation (NSF) (NSF-MCS-00519, MCS-77-27813, and MCS 812865). The opinions and conclusions are solely those of the authors and do not necessarily represent those of the NSF.

Portions of this paper were presented at the 16th Hawaii International Conference on System Sciences.

However, on the basis of several years of observing users of these systems, we must disagree with Denning's prescription for this problem, that "the research community must study traditional (nonelectronic) communications paths in existing organizations" and "abstract the key properties of successful communications and replicate them electronically" [2]. This premise takes computer-mediated systems as automated versions of off-line media. CMCS's are a new medium with their own advantages, disadvantages, social dynamics, problems, and opportunities. For instance, putting the computer into the communication loop makes new information filtering and handling techniques possible. Indeed, the automation of communication practices developed for nonelectronic media may actually counteract some of the potential benefits of CMCS's.

In this article we present our current thinking on desirable design options and implementation strategies for CMCS's, and consider information overload, communication filtering, and the total productivity of information workers. It may seem that we are only discussing the subset of CMCS's known as conferencing systems, but that is not the case. Although most of our examples are drawn from conferencing systems, we believe that many of the distinctions between "simple" store-and-forward message systems and group-communication-oriented conferencing systems will become negligible as CMCS's take on more of the features of full-scale conferencing systems. Among the authors who have dealt with such prospects are Tsichritzis et al., who state,

> In current message systems, the messages remain uninterpreted .... The system delivers the message but does not manage the messages .... In order to enhance their functionality, message systems have to interpret, at least partially, the messages they handle .... [26]

Our argument is that the computer must play a more

active role in filtering and structuring communication. Palme puts it this way:

> Systems are often designed to give the sender too much control of the communication process, and the receiver too little control .... Electronic mail systems thus need to be more database oriented, like some computer conference systems already are. [20]

We would add that CMCS's should also be designed to foster the emergence of cohesive groups that can exert social control over members' behavior. In addition to active software roles, there are active human roles that can be played; these roles can to a certain extent be built into the software in the form of special privileges and functions.

The body of literature applicable to the topic spans computer and information science, human-factors engineering, management science, and the social sciences. A complete review would constitute a lengthy treatise, and so we restrict ourselves to selected literature on specific points.

One study relevant to our topic comes from a surprising source: an examination of crowded dormitory living situations [1] "characterized by frequent unwanted or unmediated social interaction." A CMCS, like a crowded dormitory, can subject individuals to an excess of communication stimuli by dramatically increasing "social density" or "connectivity." Overload and the stress it causes can be mitigated if certain structural design aspects of the interaction space are optimized. In dormitories, designs that cluster residents in short hallways (with 20 people or less) were found to be less stressful than those that put larger numbers of residents into a common interaction space: Small groups developed, "residents knew more of their neighbors, and interaction with them was more predictable." With long-corridor designs, there was "a surfeit of unwanted interaction" and "a lack of protective group structure." Thus architecture was a key to structuring social interaction to make a densely occupied space feel more like a set of small communities. Analogously, we believe that one of the basic principles of CMCS design should be to encourage relatively small task-oriented groups and communities of interest.

The dormitory study also drew on earlier work by Mehrabian [17] and supported his finding that successful coping with high social density is related to personal "screening" skills:

> Screeners ... effectively reduce the stress of numerous inputs by constructing a priority-based pattern of attention to information (i.e., by disregarding low-priority inputs). [They] cope with the high rate of social interaction in the environment in a deliberate and organized manner .... Nonscreeners are more likely to become overaroused in situations characterized by high rates of information and are prone to fatigue and psychosomatic components in such settings. [1]

In order to cope successfully with high social density, then, people must be able to screen incoming information. Computer-mediated interaction environments should provide tools that can help users to organize information and set priorities.

Our tentative conclusions are based on observations, user surveys, and controlled experiments [5, 6, 7, 11], as well as a review of the literature. They can be summarized as follows:

1. Perceptions of information overload peak at intermediate levels of CMCS use, when communications volume has built up but users have not had a chance to develop screening skills.
2. To inhibit the flow of "useless junk" is to risk the loss of one of the most valuable impacts of CMCS's—the flow of potentially useful information and ideas among persons with no previous or off-line communications links. These systems greatly increase the number of individuals with whom a person can stay in regular contact and the number of activities a person can monitor. For an individual to make an optimal transition from current communication habits to what is possible electronically requires some exposure to the risks of overload.
3. To automate procedures that work for traditional forms of communication, like the telephone or the internal memo, is to ignore the basic fact that computer-mediated communication offers new potentials for filtering and ordering information. Moreover, it is to ignore the strong role that emergent social norms can play in preventing undesirable behavior. To design a CMCS is ultimately to alter a social system.
4. Individuals learn to *self-organize* communication flows that might initially seem overwhelming. Moreover, different individuals have different needs and preferences. Systems should offer a number of options for information organization and handling, instead of imposing a single solution for all users. Any method for filtering or reducing overload should allow individuals or groups to select their own criteria for valuable communications.
5. Careful evaluation and feedback from users are necessary for gaining an understanding of the kinds of structures or features that are useful for various

sizes of communication nets and various types of tasks. Users, as individuals and as groups, evolve in their use of CMCS's. In evaluating the usefulness of possible features for avoiding information overload, we must consider the long-term effects on the social cohesion and productivity of information-exchange networks that the system fosters, and not just the immediate and short-term convenience of individual group members. An organization's ultimate success with a system is likely to reflect the degree to which the system is tailored to the requirements of experienced users.

In the remainder of this article, we expand the first three of these points. The main empirical basis for our assertions is surveys, experiments, and observations of users of the Electronic Information Exchange System (EIES), a computerized conferencing system operated by the New Jersey Institute of Technology that is devoted to the design and evaluation of alternative structures for computerized human communication. We have also looked at other CMCS's, surveyed their users on a more casual basis, and attempted to distill our observations into generalizations for this entire class of computer systems.

PERCEPTIONS OF INFORMATION OVERLOAD
Information overload has traditionally been defined as "information presented at a rate too fast for a person to process" [23]. Perhaps we should invent a new term to describe what information overload means in the context of CMCS's, because here the term refers first to the delivery of too many communications and to an increase in social density that gives individuals access to more communications than they can easily respond to, and second to what might be termed *information entropy*, whereby incoming messages are not sufficiently organized by topic or content to be easily recognized as important or as part of the history of communication on a given topic. For either the traditional or the electronic context though, the basic responses are the same. Individuals might

1. fail to respond to certain inputs,
2. respond less accurately than they would otherwise,
3. respond incorrectly,
4. store inputs and then respond to them as time permitted,
5. systematically ignore (i.e., filter) some features of the input,
6. recode the inputs in a more compact or effective form, or
7. quit (in extreme cases) [23].

Miller [19] found that individuals tend to focus on filtering and omitting (ignoring) information as the primary effective ways of coping at high rates of information overload. So, from a totally different research tradition, we come to the same conclusion as the sociologist who studied social density in dormitories: The need is for structures that will distinguish communications that are probably of interest from those that are proba-

bly *not* of interest; these structures must also be useful for compacting, condensing, and organizing information.

Software is only part of the solution, though. Individuals must learn screening skills and develop shared norms about sending behavior so as not to impose unwanted material on others. In one of our longitudinal studies of EIES users, we asked, "Thinking back over your experiences with the system, how frequently have you felt overloaded with information?" The question and scale were chosen to match an earlier study of PLANET users by Vallee et al. [30], so that the results could be compared. This question was asked three to six months after users first signed on line. As Table I shows, the average EIES user "sometimes" feels overloaded. The means obtained for a second sample of EIES users and for users of other systems who answered at a similar cumulative activity level are comparable. Thus, information overload would seem to be a serious and common problem, but not one which is immobilizing for most users.

However, these studies also indicate that users learn to cope with information overload after they gain sufficient experience with a system. Individuals in the intermediate ranges of cumulative use would seem to be most susceptible. Among the first sample of EIES users, reported in Table I, 31 percent of those with 20–49 on-line hours reported "almost always" experiencing information overload, whereas 100 percent of those with 100 hours or more reported feeling overloaded only "sometimes," "almost never," or "never."[1] The same strong pattern of association with activity level persists for the results of the second through the fifth samples. The modal cumulative time category is included in Table I as a reminder that overload is strongly correlated with usage level.

Apparently, experienced users develop effective ways of coping with what may initially seem to be an "overload" of communications. (Of course, without longitudinal data, we cannot be sure that there is not an alternative explanation for the observed curvilinear pattern of association between overload and on-line hours; specifically, that users who almost always experience overload quit before becoming experienced users.)

The corollary is that beginners tend to overextend themselves, not so much by reading junk mail as by trying to be fully informed on a multitude of activities. This phenomenon is most pronounced in a conference structure, where beginners tend to join all the conferences that sound interesting. When they reach overload, they begin to withdraw from some of the discussions and make use of more sophisticated options for limiting the amount of material they receive.

Users can also take advantage of the storage capacity of the computer to arrange for an optimal number of transactions per session. In a prior paper [9], we pointed out that users seem to be driven to sign on often enough to keep their per-session transactions (individ-

[1] Unless otherwise specified, subsequent data about EIES users or references to the "EIES sample" are from this first sample.

TABLE I. User's Reported Overload Experience

Responses are to the question, "Thinking back over your experiences with the system, how frequently have you felt overloaded with information?"

System	Responses (by percent)					Mean*	Modal use
	Always	Almost always	Sometimes	Almost never	Never		
EIES1	4	18	55	16	6	3.0	20–49 hours 35%
EIES 2	6	23	42	20	9	3.0	10–49 hours 62%
COM	3	16	43	32	5	3.2	<10 hours 57%
PARTI	7	17	48	23	5	3.0	20–49 hours 48%
INTMAIL	2	5	25	45	23	3.9	5–9 hours 43%
PLANET	3	6	44	24	22	3.6	

Sources: EIES1—follow-up questionnaire three to four months after the beginning of system use; 110 scientific and professional users; EIES2—four-month follow-up survey of new users (1983), responses from 140 managers and professionals; COM—four-month follow-up survey of new users (1983), 37 responses; PARTICIPATE (on the Source)—sample of 100 new users (1983–1984); INTMAIL—follow-up at four months of internal corporate users of a commercial mail system, 60 responses from managerial users; PLANET—percentages and means computed from raw data reported in [30, p. 182], 115 scientific and professional users.

Note on use categories: Cumulative time on line at end of four months was arranged into four categories—less than 4 hours, 5–19 hours, 20–49 hours, and 50 or more hours. The modal category and percentage in that category are shown as a rough guide to the typical activity level of respondents.

* The mean is determined by responses from 1 for "always" to 5 for "never."

ual text items they receive or compose) down to about five [18]. Three years later, a sample of 273,000 usage hours continues to support this conclusion. The current average number of transactions handled per session on EIES is four; we cannot, however, accurately measure the delivery of text items virtually addressed by other text items, which would add to this total.

As Rouse has pointed out [22], the human-factors literature supports the view that human performance deteriorates when the work load is too great or too small. There is therefore an optimal loading rate for phenomena such as communications. This is how we interpret the sign-on rate as a function of the number of transactions.

The observation that intermediate users seem to suffer the most from information overload is consistent with some experiments that have been done on management information systems [3]. Individuals in decision-making situations seem to do just as well using summary data as raw data, but their confidence in the results is not as high. We suspect that intermediate CMCS users feel compelled to observe all the communications they can access in order to maintain confidence that nothing relevant is being overlooked. More experienced users are confident enough to use keywords and other filtering mechanisms. They develop more trust in the summary mechanisms associated with filtering.

INFORMATION OVERLOAD VERSUS UNANTICIPATED SYNERGY
The popularity of garage sales and flea markets demonstrates how one person's junk can be another's collect-

ibles. This is also true with information and ideas. For this reason, we believe that no automated routine can simultaneously filter out all useless and irrelevant communications for addressees, and at the same time assure their receipt of all communications that may be of value to them. This is especially true since what may be irrelevant when it arrives can become valuable once a user's tasks or interests change.

EIES users seem to recognize that communications on unexpected topics and from unexpected sources may increase their effectiveness, even as they decrease immediate efficiency. Some of the completely open public conferences do indeed seem a bit like intellectual flea markets. But like flea markets, they are well attended and of interest to their participants.

One of Denning's suggestions for filtering communications was to impose an organizational hierarchy on sending privileges: "Access among mailboxes can be restricted to persons authorized by an organization's normal communications paths. Users cannot send to arbitrary mailboxes" [2]. Although it is true that the imposition of such a hierarchy would reduce message traffic in the short run, it is also likely to make the transmission of new information, "bad news," or other kinds of organizational intelligence unlikely. Wilensky notes that

In reporting at every level, a hierarchy is conducive to concealment and misrepresentation. Subordinates are asked to transmit information that can be used to evaluate their performance. Their motive for "making it look good" is obvious . . . . In addition . . . middle-level managers, and even lower level employees, sometimes have a near monopoly on insight into feasible alternatives . . . . Whatever the shape of

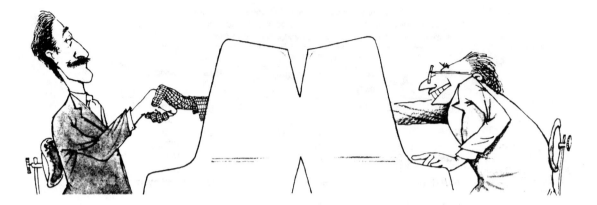

the hierarchy, to extract information from those who have it typically requires bypassing conventional ranking systems. [31]

The problem of balancing the value of open communication channels with the cost of information overload is expressed by users when they name the least and most valuable aspects of communicating on the EIES system. The feature cited as "most useless or distracting" was annoyance with members who sent "junk messages" or made "off-the-wall comments" or "cute remarks," rather than problems with any software features.

In describing the most valuable feature of the system, users frequently cited the flexibility it allowed them; one user, for instance, refers to the "self-organization" of information. Among the most frequently reported productivity-related impacts are that EIES has increased the "stock of ideas" that might be useful in future work (this was reported by 71 percent of all users and 90 percent of users with 100 or more hours on line); and provided "leads, references, and other information useful in my work" (79 percent of all users, 95 percent of heavy users). The strongest predictor of these productivity-related benefits is how many new people a user as "met" on line and begun to communicate with [6]. To restrict communications to preauthorized partners would cut off the most valuable of the perceived benefits of system use.

STRUCTURES AND PROCESSES FOR MINIMIZING OVERLOAD

Although restricting CMCS communications to certain channels goes against our strategy, there are some specific situations where it may be useful. In his study of communication and organizational control, for instance, Hage [4] identifies two basic alternative mechanisms: "programming with sanctions" and "high feedback with socialization." For centralized organizations with personnel performing routine (programmed) tasks, efficiency might be increased by restricting information to official channels. Conversely, for professionals performing complex, diverse, and nonroutine tasks, high feedback with much horizontal and out-of-hierarchy communication may produce the best results.

In general, though, such restrictions are not advised.

The basic problem is the whole "mailbox" analogy, in which control resides with the sender. With message groups and conference structures, where membership is self-selected by topic or interest and recipients can screen incoming communications, we believe individuals should be allowed to discover and implement the devices that work best for them, and to change them as needs and the volume of communications change.

Users vary a great deal in terms of their previous experience with interactive computer systems, their level of CMCS use, their cumulative experience with a particular system, and the number of partners and topics they are involved with. This is why we believe there can be no single design that will optimize the trade-offs between useful information from unanticipated sources and information overload. For example, EIES users can set options for automatic delivery of waiting messages, for delivery on request, or for delivery of complete items for certain conferences and headers (e.g., author, keywords, and date entered) for others. A default option would be appropriate for new users, of course, since they would be unable to make intelligent choices about options before they had gained some experience with a system.

The secret of designing on-line communication systems is sticking with process options—nothing should be content dependent. Designers should not try to impose specific organization structures, but should give individuals options for filtering out material. Users will use process options to control content as they see fit.

Within the context of a single organization using a CMCS, there are process options that are not appropriate to a public system like EIES, which has members from scores of different organizations. One example is the incorporation of user roles or multiple subidentities that would correspond to organizational functions. An individual in an organization may be a worker on one project, a manager on another, a coordinator on a third, etc. This individual may have to deal with both personal matters and group matters. Within a single organization, it might be appropriate to identify a number of common organizational roles and to ask message senders to address their messages accordingly. This would self-organize incoming message traffic. The concept of using roles as a sending category index is actually a psychologically appropriate approach in that it is easier for users to adapt to than some of the standard database approaches.

Software design based on the systematic analysis of the behavior and practices of experienced users as they organize and filter their communications to prevent overload is more likely to be useful than design based only on casual observation and intuition. There is a high degree of unpredictability in determining which communications might interest a user. Interests may also be strongly time dependent or change with fluctuating situations in a group or an organization.

As users become familiar with computer-communication technology, they begin, at a group level, to evolve their own norms for communication behavior. There are precedents for this process: As children we go through a learning process for using the telephone and for understanding the norms of behavior that have evolved for telephone conversations. These norms do not, however, prevent us from getting a certain number of nuisance calls. When we get a number of such calls from the same person, we tell that person to stop phoning us or we refuse to talk to them if they persist. Directed junk communications are a human problem more than they are a computer problem, the side effect of an on-line social system, rather than of any particular computer system.

Huber [12] distinguishes two basic processes for increasing the organizational efficiency of information systems: *message routing* and *message summarizing*. Message routing need not be determined by the sender. Software can sort communications into categories based on conference structures and interest groups with self-selected memberships, for instance, or can permit recipients to route or filter them by topic. Message summarizing, or condensation, can be accomplished by structuring the form of inputs. Senders might, for instance, be required to adhere to length limitations, or to use votes or other numeric estimates instead of full messages. Summarizing can also be performed by human "digesters"—some bulletin-board operators, for instance, read incoming items, discard irrelevant ones, and summarize others before posting them on a bulletin board. We can also add a third to Huber's two efficiency-increasing processes—social organization and social pressure can be used to regulate communication and make it more efficient.

Routing Information via a Conference Structure

By a computerized-conferencing system, we mean software that supports on-line group interaction and task completion. The communications being generated and exchanged may include data and graphics as well as text. All of the conferencing systems we know of use the computer to keep a marker for each individual member, so that attention can be called to new items each time a particular member rejoins the conference.

In a message system, communications from all sources and on all topics tend to get mixed together. By routing communications into topic-oriented discussion

spaces, we make a quantum leap in screening capabilities and facilitate the emergence of on-line social groups with strong norms.

There is a problem with finding appropriate terminology and metaphors for describing this concept in general terms, rather than as a package of specific implementations. Stevens [24] uses the term "many-to-many communication," while the American Productivity Center has suggested "computer networking." However, the former term does not make it clear that the process is computer based, and the latter might be interpreted as communication between computers rather than among groups of people using computers.

A conference is simply a topic-oriented discussion or information-exchange space. Individuals can belong to as many conferences on as many different subjects or tasks as they wish. All communications on a specific task or subject are collected together in a space that can be accessed by members at any time. For instance, automatic routines can be set to pick up the full text of all new items for a conference of high interest, while selecting only "headlines" from new items in other conferences. Conference structures are unlike the "distribution lists" employed by many electronic mail systems in that it is the receiver, rather than the sender, who decides when and if to receive communications on a given topic. Often, special software routines for voting structures and other options are operative within a conference; such structures usually require a human moderator with the authority to add or remove members and add or change keywords. Conferences usually also have a member-status list showing conference membership, who has read what, and who is on line at any given time. Though conference software is most often operative on a single central computer, some systems, such as IBM's internal EQUAL system and the EIES2 system, now under development, are distributed among many constantly or frequently updated computers in a network.

When conference structures exist, discussions assume shape, continuity, and social order. Social pressure is often exerted to encourage members to put everything except urgent or personal communications into the structure so that members are not inundated with messages on subjects not of immediate interest. Members can also let each other know when entries seem completely "off the subject."

When a conference system is coupled with a message system, the flow of unwanted messages is greatly reduced. Messages tend to be used more for transitory things and short announcements of one sort or another. Personal notebooks or files facilitate the conference process by allowing members to draft and polish items before distributing them to the group. An analog to a conferencing structure is created by some receiving nodes in distributed message systems when they filter out messages addressed to a message list and place them on separate bulletin boards or in separate files (by the name of the distribution list), rather than in any individual's private message queue.

As more communication options become available,

problems with junk mail and overload begin to decrease. Indeed, overload becomes no more than a transitory learning problem in a "rich" system environment. The key, as we see it, is that strategies allowing users to structure communications are intrinsically better suited to alleviating these problems than strategies based on nonautomated communication systems. This freedom does have its price, however, since users will need to learn some complex system features beyond simple sending and receiving operations.

Filtering and Scanning Features
David Morris, one of the principal designers of EQUAL, an IBM internal conferencing system, asserts that "An effective method of presenting each user with an overview of what is available and letting them pick what is of interest to pursue further is the single most important capability a CMCS can provide" (personal communication). Within a conference structure for a small group discussing a narrowly defined topic or working on a task, filtering and selection devices other than the conference structure itself may actually be detrimental to the group's ability to accomplish its goal. For a large group, a complex task, or a broad conference topic, however, some additional mechanisms for skimming and filtering may be necessary.

Some systems allow users to scan limited portions of communications and then to decide which items and how much of each item to retrieve. For instance, EIES includes keywords for each item, and PARTICIPATE includes an "About" line in the header. EQUAL requires an abstract to be entered with each item and displays the abstracts when a user enters a conference, using the highlighting available on a full-screen terminal to call attention to new items. On the COM system, a user can set a "scan" command to print out only the first N lines of pending items. Users can then enter the command "read the rest" if they want to see the remainder of the entry, or "mark" the item for later reading [21]. One problem with this approach is that the writer will not know how many lines the reader will be scanning: The first two lines, for instance, might not summarize the subject sufficiently. If a scan command worked in a standard way for each recipient, by printing the first three lines, for instance, writers would learn to include a kind of abstract in that amount of space. They could also be prompted to provide a three-line abstract at the beginning of each item for particular conferences when a scanning convention has been adopted.

Conferences can organize themselves if users specify keywords and associations to other items. A reader can then use search and retrieval functions to ask for items with a particular key, or a series of items associated with one another as a kind of subtopic or discussion thread in a conference structure. Automatic indexing routines can then be used on this information to produce conference outlines. An individual sitting at a meeting cannot extract all the statements dealing with a particular topic or relating to a comment made earlier in the meeting, but must listen to everything in order to hear the relevant information. Within a conference structure, though, information can be organized in such unique and convenient ways.

As software and user behavior can be used in combination to filter communications by topic, filters can also be imposed on individuals in a conference structure. Members whose contributions are not desired for one reason or another can be restricted to a "read only" status, or even excluded from the group. Similarly, if a particular sender is responsible for an inordinate number of useless communications, future messages from that sender can be screened out by receivers, with or without notification to the sender. On one conferencing system, there were problems with anonymous messages of an unpleasant nature for some of the female members. Software was implemented so that a recipient could block anonymous messages without blocking signed messages. The real issue with such options is social etiquette. Messages like "Sorry, you do not have the privilege of sending messages to (name)" might come into vogue.

Length Limitations
The permitted length of individual items can be limited in order to ensure that communications are concise. Different lengths may be suitable for different functions and different groups. In EIES, for instance, it was initially decided to limit individual messages and conference entries to 57 lines (although items in reports or personal notebooks could be up to 400 lines long). On the EMISARI crisis-management system, items were limited to 9 lines [27]. This prevents some of the more bureaucratic users from using messages as internal memos. Although a few individuals initially protested loudly, the complaints began to disappear as the volume on the system began to increase.

Length limitations on EIES were set by a group of about 75 legislative science advisers and their resources persons, who created a TOPICS system to limit the length of inquiry items that could be broadcast to the entire group to only three lines [14]. The group discussed and agreed on this limitation before the software was implemented. Recipients had to actively "select" an inquiry in order to access the often voluminous material associated with it.

It is important that groups new to this technology be encouraged to discuss the norms they wish to adopt. It is also quite common for such norms to change as a result of experience and later discussion. The presence of a leader or group member with experience in the technology can be helpful for pointing out the need for discussions as problems like overload arise.

Users can circumvent length limitations by stringing several short items that are really only one long item together. Despite this loophole, however, limitations do exert pressure on users to keep communications within the limit; social pressure helps to reinforce this subtle guidance.

There are various options for allowing users to create short items that reference longer items. For instance, it is possible to virtually reference text in such a way that the computer can check whether the item in question has already been seen by the reader; if so, the computer will not print it out, but will inform the reader that the particular item has been referenced. A given message will thus have different lengths for different receivers, depending on whether they have already seen parts of it or not. Other devices, such as process keys (SUMMARY, DETAIL, ELABORATION, etc.) can also be used to determine which part of a particular item a particular user sees.

Delphi and Other Voting Structures
A larger number of users can exchange information in a more concise and precise way when numerical responses are used in place of conventional text responses. The computer can be used to average, analyze, and display results for a given issue. The PARTICIPATE system refers to this capability as *dialogue balloting*, which is explained as "polling not to elect or to sample but to facilitate participation" [24]. Such procedures can take the form of scales that indicate, for instance, the degree of agreement on a statement or proposal on a one-to-five or a one-to-ten scale, numerical estimates of items such as the proportion of a budget to be devoted to research and development or advertising, or the rank ordering of alternatives.

With the Delphi technique, communication structures are designed to allow knowledgeable individuals to efficiently pool or compare information on complex problems [16]. The technique is traditionally implemented with pen and paper over several rounds. Analysis and feedback are provided to the respondents between rounds, allowing them to expand and/or change their original views. EIES provides some nine different Delphi-like voting scales that can be attached to conference comments. For example, an individual proposing a project modification can attach voting scales for "desirability" and "feasibility." The computer would then collect the votes and provide a display of the resulting distribution. This is a highly efficient way of discovering if the group already agrees with a proposal and avoiding what may be a lot of unnecessary communication. Considering a series of items in this manner allows a group to make a quick determination of the issues on which they need to focus discussion. There are literally hundreds of potential communication structures in the Delphi literature; many of these lend themselves to implementation in a computerized-conferencing environment. For example, for controversial proposals a structure can be implemented to collect pro and con arguments, organize them according to matching counterarguments, and then solicit evaluation votes from the group as the arguments are presented. The merger of Delphi concepts and computerized conferencing can greatly minimize the amount of communication necessary for groups carrying out various planning functions. In fact, it provides a kind of group-oriented decision support system.

A system was developed for a standards group on EIES to allow individuals to propose an alternative definition (standard) for a phrase. The system then col-

lected votes on any such proposed revision. A proposed standard would be issued only if the agreement was unanimous. This rather simple software modification speeded up the group's work considerably by keeping members up-to-date on the relative acceptance of all the proposed alternatives. As in any Delphi-like voting process, voters could change their votes at any time. The voting process and the associated structures for relating complex information devised in Delphi designs represent a highly condensed form of human communication allowing extremely efficient transmission of a great deal of information. It is the merger of these techniques into CMCS structures that will allow geographically dispersed groups to work as teams dealing with complex problems on a day-to-day basis.

Leaders or Moderators
When activity is routed into topic-oriented conferences, software support can be provided for leadership or information-management functions. For instance, conference leaders are called "coordinators" on COM and "moderators" on EIES. Our controlled experiments with problem-solving discussions have demonstrated that a designated human leader for a computerized conference can help a group to accomplish its task [7]. Software support may empower a leader or moderator to edit items or keywords for clarity, or to delete or move inappropriate or out-of-date items. More importantly, a specified leadership role usually entitles an individual to make organizing suggestions that can help to limit irrelevant communications. Some bulletin boards also have moderators or "sysops" who play an active role in filtering and managing information. Among the ARPANET boards, for example, INFO IBMPC and AILIST are organized by moderators.

Pen Names and Anonymity
We have mentioned the role that social pressure by group members can play in enforcing the use of conventions like conference structures and length limitations. Sometimes such norms are stated and stressed by the leader or manager of an on-line group. Often, though, group members collectively sanction an errant member. This can be done, of course, with signed messages or conference comments, but only at the cost of considerable strain on the social fabric of the group. If pen names are used or anonymity is maintained, individuals can vote to sanction or criticize errant members without embarrassing themselves. For example, one EIES entry entered anonymously read, "Joe, please remember that 57 lines is a maximum, not a minimum." A second chimed in with an anonymous "Amen." Subsequently, "Joe's" entries became noticeably shorter.

Other Features for Minimizing Overload
There are other computer-mediated communications-handling techniques that have no direct counterparts in nonelectronic media:

Purges and Discouraged Sending. Messages and documents can be sent with a "self-destruct" date, or a system default can be set to automatically purge old items. For instance, the ONTYME message system purges undelivered items after about four weeks. Although these procedures may indeed protect receivers from "out-of-date" communications, they unfortunately also prevent users who may have been unable to sign on for one reason or another from receiving items that might still be of interest. A more adaptive feature incorporated into some systems (e.g., COM) informs would-be senders when intended recipients have been off line for a significant interval. EIES includes a convention that notifies members when an intended recipient is to be away for a certain length of time.

Alarms and Reminders.   Features that allow system users to communicate with themselves can be useful for remembering and organizing information. For instance, EIES has a personal "reminder file" that stacks references to unanswered messages or other items. Individuals can remind themselves with "alarms" that send them messages at prespecified times. These features, sometimes called "tickler files," can be very helpful on busy systems.

Notifications.   On EIES an individual can edit a message or conference comment. All receivers who had already read the original would then be sent a notification that the item had been modified. The receiver could then decide whether or not to retrieve the new version. Notifications can also be sent to writers of private messages to alert them when receipt occurs. This allows a sender to pace additional communications to a particular receiver. In a conference, notification is also available, on demand, of a conferee status list indicating what different members have and have not read. These signals are very important for allowing individuals to regulate the flow of traffic in a meaningful manner.

Costs.   For an organization having problems with electronic junk mail, the ultimate remedy might be the imposition of charges on a per-transaction basis. If senders are charged according to the number of recipients, the number of messages sent to many individuals is bound to drop. This approach is not recommended unless other techniques have failed. A more sophisticated approach is to charge senders according to both the size of the message and the salary of the recipient [28, 29].

CONCLUSION: SUPERCONNECTIVITY AND THE ELECTROPOLIS

The most fundamental impact of a CMCS is to increase the social connectivity of users (i.e., the number of people in regular communication) by about tenfold. We use the term *superconnectivity* to capture the essence of this order-of-magnitude change. Joining the "electropolis" of an active CMCS can be stressful in the short term, but should also significantly increase opportunities for fruitful interaction.

It is very difficult for individuals to adapt to such a new communications paradigm. It is far easier to think of computer-mediated communication in terms of preexisting systems, like the telephone or the postal system. It is also easier to market such systems as cheaper but equivalent alternatives to conventional communications structures. People are not easily sold on anything that promises change in cognitive processes and organizational social structure. The majority of the activity to date with CMCS's has therefore been in simple "electronic mail" and "message" systems. Furthermore, it is difficult to take the significant long-term impacts of CMCS's into account in the justification and planning process. Fortunately, professionals in the field do realize that the automation of conventional manual systems has often been the wrong way to go, historically, and that, although such efforts can sometimes boost efficiency, they can rarely boost effectiveness. In the computer-mediated environment, overload is as much an important motivational factor for encouraging users to develop systems skills as it is a problem. Different individuals are overloaded at different levels as a function of how much information they can perceive and deal with cognitively. The real problem is understanding the group and organizational objectives and providing the tools that allow individuals and groups to structure their own communications. Any process that limits overload by structuring content will also destroy many potential benefits. Tools for limiting overload should be based on structuring processes and should allow individuals to control content.

With a variety of software tools for managing communication and information, users can not only adapt to high levels of information input, but can actually thrive. For instance, Tapscott observed the following in his study of pilot users of a rich system:

> It was hypothesized that the disparity between perceived "information needed" and perceived "information received," noted at the time of the pretest, would decrease for the pilot group. This did not occur. There *were* a number of improvements between the pretest and posttest in the "information received." However, the perceived findings suggest that as access to information improved, so did expectations regarding what is possible and perceived requirements regarding what is necessary. [25]

In any organization there are formal and informal communications. In a sense this is analogous to the "structured" and "unstructured" dichotomy in decision support systems. Computer-mediated communication systems allow informal communication that is semi-structured and highly adaptive in nature. By increasing the number of individuals who can be involved in informal information flows, we offer them more of an opportunity to pool their talents and expertise, and facilitate the lateral movement of information in organizations. Productivity-increasing concepts like matrix management (i.e., the assignment of personnel resources to task teams on a project-by-project basis) and lateral task groups become more feasible. To miss these opportunities by trying to impose the formal hierarchical communication rules that are traditional for internal memorandums would be the height of folly.

Overload, within the context of an organization, is essentially a behavioral phenomenon. It makes more sense to address inappropriate behavior through social norms and sanctions than to obscure the problem with software. It is very easy on many message systems to accept a message, look at its title, and then delete it. This action would not be reported back to the sender, who would assume that the message was received and read. In a formal structure, this is clearly a conscious risk decision for the receiver. In an informal one, it is a more serious violation of the cooperative relationship between sender and receiver, comparable to not returning telephone calls. If CMCS's are to accommodate and expand the informal exchange process in organizations, junk mail will have to be dealt with by social sanctions, since attempts to deal with junk mail and other negative aspects of information overload entirely by technological means or by the imposition of a formal hierarchical structure would compromise the utility of the system for improving informal communication exchange.

Acknowledgments. We are grateful to all of the staff and associates of the Computerized Conferencing and Communications Center at NJIT for their participation in the research projects whose results are described in this paper. Jacob Palme facilitated access to COM and surveys of its users, Harry Stevens and Christine Bullen assisted with access to PARTI users, and David Morris provided access to IBM's EQUAL and its documentation. Elaine Kerr collaborated in the surveys. Elizabeth Rumics and the reference staff at the Upsala Library assisted with obtaining many of the publications cited. We would also like to thank Ray Panko, Rob Kling, and our anonymous ACM reviewers for their helpful comments.

REFERENCES

1. Baum, A., Calesnick, L., Davis, G., and Gatchel, R. Individual differences in coping with crowding: Stimulus screening and social overload. *J. Pers. Soc. Psychol. 43*, 4 (Oct. 1982), 821–830.
2. Denning, P. Electronic junk. *Commun. ACM 25*, 3 (Mar. 1982), 163–165.
3. Dickson, G.W., Senn, J.A., and Chervany, N.L. Research in management information systems: The Minnesota experiments. *Manage. Sci. 23*, 9 (Mar. 1977), 913–921.
4. Hage, J. *Communication and Organizational Control: Cybernetics in Health and Welfare Settings.* Wiley, New York, 1974.
5. Hiltz, S.R. The impact of a computerized conferencing system on scientific research communities. Res. Rep. 15, Computerized Conferencing and Communications Center, New Jersey Institute of Technology, Newark, 1981.
6. Hiltz, S.R. *Online Communities: A Case Study of the Office of the Future.* Ablex, Norwood, N.J., 1984.
7. Hiltz, S.R., Johnson, K., and Turoff, M. The effects of formal human leadership and computer-generated decision aids on problem solving via computer: A controlled experiment. Res. Rep. 18, Computerized Conferencing and Communications Center, New Jersey Institute of Technology, Newark, 1982.
8. Hiltz, S.R., and Turoff, M. *The Network Nation: Human Communication via Computer.* Addison-Wesley, Reading, Mass., 1978.
9. Hiltz, S.R., and Turoff, M. The evolution of user behavior in a computerized conferencing system. *Commun. ACM 24*, 11 (Nov. 1981), 739–751.
10. Hiltz, S.R., and Turoff, M. Office augmentation systems: The case for evolutionary design. In *Proceedings of the 15th Hawaii International Conference on System Sciences*, Vol. 1 (Honolulu, Hawaii, Jan.). Univ. of Hawaii, 1982, pp. 737–749.
11. Hiltz, S.R., Turoff, M., and Johnson, K. Mode of communication and the risky shift: A controlled experiment with computerized conferencing and anonymity in a large corporation. Res. Rep. 21, Computerized Conferencing and Communications Center, New Jersey Institute of Technology, Newark, 1985.
12. Huber, G. Organizational information systems: Determinants of their performance and behavior. *Manage. Sci. 28*, 2 (Feb. 1982), 138–153.
13. Johansen, R., Vallee, J., and Spangler, K. *Electronic Meetings: Technological Alternatives and Social Choices.* Addison-Wesley, Reading, Mass., 1979.
14. Johnson-Lenz, P., and Johnson-Lenz, T. The evolution of a tailored communications structure: The topics system. Res. Rep. 14, Computerized Conferencing and Communications Center, New Jersey Institute of Technology, Newark, 1981.
15. Kerr, E.B., and Hiltz, S.R. *Computer-Mediated Communication Systems: Status and Evaluation.* Academic Press, New York, 1982.
16. Linstone, H., and Turoff, M. *The Delphi Method: Techniques and Application.* Addison-Wesley, Reading, Mass., 1975.
17. Mehrabian, A. A questionnaire measure of individual differences in stimulus screening and associated differences in arousal. *Environ. Psychol. Nonverbal Behav. 1*, 2 (Spring 1977), 89–103.
18. Miller, G.A. The magic number seven plus or minus two: Some limits on our capacity for processing information. *Psychol. Rev. 63*, 2 (Mar. 1956), 81–97.
19. Miller, G.A. Information input overload. In *Proceedings of the Conference on Self-Organizing Systems*, M.C. Yovits, G.T. Jacobi, and G.D. Goldstein, Eds. Spartan Books, Washington, 1962.
20. Palme, J. You have 134 unread mail! Do you want to read them now? In *Computer-Based Message Services*, H.T. Smith, Ed. IFIP Proceedings, Elsevier North-Holland, New York, 1984, pp. 175–184.
21. Palme, J., and Albertson, E. COM-teleconferencing system—Advanced manual. C10157E, Stockholm University Computing Center, Sweden, 1983.
22. Rouse, W.B. Design of man-computer interfaces for on-line interactive systems. *Proc. IEEE 63*, 6 (June 1975), 847–857.
23. Sheridan, T.B., and Ferrell, W.R. *Man-Machine Systems: Information, Control, and Decision Models of Human Performance.* MIT Press, Cambridge, Mass., 1974.
24. Stevens, C.H. Many-to-many communication. CISR 72, Center for Information Systems Research, MIT, Cambridge, Mass., 1981.
25. Tapscott, D. Research on the impact of office information communication systems. In *Computer Message Systems*, R.P. Uhlig, Ed. North-Holland, Amsterdam, 1981, pp. 395–409.
26. Tsichritzis, D., Rabitti, F.A., Gibbs, S., Nierstasz, O., and Hogg, J. A system for managing structured messages. *IEEE Trans. Commun. COM-30*, 1 (Jan. 1982), 66–73.
27. Turoff, M. Party-line and discussion: Computerized conferencing systems. In *Proceedings of the 1st International Conference on Computer Communications* (Washington, D.C., Oct. 24–26). ACM, New York, 1972, pp. 161–171.
28. Turoff, M. Information and value: The internal information marketplace. *Technol. Forecasting Soc. Change.* To be published.
29. Turoff, M., and Chinai, J.S. The design of an information marketplace. *Computer Networks.* To be published.
30. Vallee, J., Johansen, R., Randolph, R., and Hastings, A. *Group Communication through Computers.* Vol. 4, *Social, Managerial, and Economic Issues.* Institute for the Future, Menlo Park, Calif., 1978.
31. Wilensky, H.L. *Organizational Intelligence: Knowledge and Policy in Government and Industry.* Basic Books, New York, 1967.

CR Categories and Subject Descriptors: H.4.3 [**Information Systems**]: Communication Applications; K.4.3 [**Computers and Society**]: Organizational Impacts
General Terms: Design, Human Factors
Additional Key Words and Phrases: computerized conferencing, filters, information overload

Authors' Present Address: Starr Roxanne Hiltz and Murray Turoff, Computerized Conferencing and Communications Center, New Jersey Institute of Technology, Newark, NJ 07102.

SUPPORTING COLLABORATION IN NOTECARDS

Randall H. Trigg

Lucy A. Suchman

Frank G. Halasz *

Intelligent Systems Laboratory

Xerox Palo Alto Research Center

3333 Coyote Hill Road

Palo Alto, CA 94304

"Supporting Collaboration in Notecards" by R.H. Trigg, L.A. Suchman, and F.G. Halasz, previously published in *First Conference on Computer-Supported Cooperative Work*, December 1986, pages 153-162. Reprinted with permission of the authors.

Abstract

This paper describes a project underway to investigate computer support for collaboration. In particular, we focus on experience with and extensions to NoteCards, a hypertext-based idea structuring system. The forms of collaboration discussed include draft-passing, simultaneous sharing and online presentations. The requirement that mutual intelligibility be maintained between collaborators leads to the need for support of annotative and procedural as well as substantive activities.

Introduction

In the Intelligent Systems Lab (ISL) at Xerox PARC, we are engaged in a two-part project to study collaboration in naturally occurring research settings and to design technology that better supports it. This paper focuses on supporting collaboration in NoteCards, a hypertext-based idea structuring system. The work examining collaboration is described in [Suchman&Trigg 86].

The term *hypertext* describes any system employing non-linear structuring of text, graphics, and other media. Hypertext systems are often implemented using linked network structures with data (usually text or graphics) at the nodes and occasionally typing information on the links. (See [Delisle&Schwartz 86] and [Yankelovich et al 85] for overviews of existing hypertext systems.) For the most part, these systems have been single-user. A few have supported shared *Idea Bases* (to use a term coined by Norman Meyrowitz), but none, to our knowledge, have provided tools that deal explicitly with the social interactions arising in collaborative settings. Instead, most of the work in multi-user environments has focused on system level support for capabilities such as simultaneous access to distributed databases. This paper directly addresses system supported collaboration at the social interaction level. Rather than presenting a finished product that fully meets the needs of collaborators, we describe preliminary work done with a particular idea structuring system.

Hypertext systems can be broadly classified into those designed to support browsing of existing databases and those designed to support creation and modification. *Idea structuring* systems are examples of the latter. They are designed to support the early

_____

* Frank Halasz, MCC, Kaleido #2, 9390 Research Blvd, Austin, Texas 78759.

stages of idea generation, development and organization, as well as later document preparation. Such systems are becoming prevalent not only in research environments, but in the personal computing market as well. They have been applied in areas as diverse as education, writing and software management.

NoteCards [Halasz et al 87] is an idea structuring hypertext system. It was not initially designed with collaboration in mind, yet there were times when users had to work together in NoteCards. Their experiences coercing NoteCards into supporting collaboration provide valuable insight into capabilities lacking in NoteCards and eventually, perhaps, into general requirements for collaborative idea structuring systems.

The following sections introduce the notion of *mutual intelligibility* and discuss techniques designed to help NoteCards users maintain the mutual intelligibility of their work over the course of a collaboration. We restrict our focus to three modes of collaboration: draft passing, simultaneous sharing and online presentation.

Mutual intelligibility

A crucial requirement of collaboration is that the participants find ways to make their work mutually intelligible. Along with the production of substantive work, participants in a collaboration engage in activities done expressly to maintain the coherence of their interaction.

Consider the following scenario. Two researchers share an office, but work different shifts and so are never there at the same time. They decide to work collaboratively on a project using the office whiteboard as a shared project notebook. Very soon, they realize that in the absence of other forms of communication, the whiteboard will have to contain discussion *about* their work at the board as well as the substance of the work. In part, this discussion includes commentary and annotations on one another's work. But in addition, it includes communication about conventions for use of the medium, for example, which color marker or portion of the whiteboard to reserve for which subject area. Such meta-communication makes the substantive work intelligible to each of the participants.

This scenario illustrates three kinds of activities occuring in collaboration: *substantive*, *annotative* and *procedural*. Substantive activities are those that constitute the work at hand. When writing a paper, the substance of the work is the ideas expressed in the paper's actual text. In design, the substance is the plan and implementation of the artifact, in research discussions the problem or topic of interest.

The mutual intelligibility of the substantive work is supported through annotative and procedural activities. Annotative activities are *about* the work and include commenting, critiquing, questioning and otherwise annotating the work itself. There are a few systems that explicitly support these activities. For example, Annoland (designed by Richard Burton and described in [Brown 85]) is a window-based system that allows the attachment of pieces of text to an existing document. The user interface includes a graph-based browser of annotations organized according to time of creation.

Procedural activities include discussions about conventions for use of the medium or technology, logistics of turn-taking, record keeping, etc. No systems that we know of adequately support these activities. However, many hypertext systems, by their very nature, are well suited to providing such support. The requirement here is that the information base being created be able to include procedural discussion along with substance and annotations. Furthermore the procedural discussion should be linked to the relevant parts of the substance.

Use of a whiteboard in a draft-passing setting bears some similarity to collaborative use of an online hypertext system. Both share the qualities of non-linearity and novelty. Whiteboards are almost always used as a resource in face-to-face conversations where the collaborators rely on other communication channels. Similarly, we've had very little experience with hypertext systems as the sole media for collaboration. Because of this, collaborators using hypertext systems will have to discuss and adopt various conventions regarding use of the medium. Ideally, these discussions should go on within the medium, especially in the absence of other communication channels.

NoteCards

There are several reasons for our decision to use NoteCards as the environment for testing our ideas on computer support for collaboration: (1) NoteCards is a fairly stable system that is being used widely in our lab, (2) the tailorable nature of NoteCards makes it particularly well suited to incremental extensions in support of collaboration and (3) the members of the collaboration project include one NoteCards designer and one experienced user. (2) and (3) make it convenient for us to design prototype collaborative tools in NoteCards while (1) makes it likely that these tools will have a user community.

The basic object in NoteCards is an electronic notecard containing text, graphics, images, etc. Different kinds of notecards are defined in an inheritance hierarchy of notecard types (e.g., text cards, sketch cards, query cards, etc.). On the screen, multiple cards can be simultaneously displayed, each one in a separate window having an underlying editor appropriate to the card type. Individual notecards can be connected to other notecards by arbitrarily typed links, forming networks of related cards. It is up to each user to utilize the link types to organize the notecard network. Individual links are represented by link icons (usually boxed titles) in the card's substance.

NoteCards also includes a filing mechanism (implemented by the FileBox notecard type) for building hierarchical structures using system-defined card and link types. There are also Browser cards containing node-link diagrams (i.e., maps) of arbitrary pieces of the notecard network and Sketch cards for spatially organizing information in the form of drawings, text and links.

All of the functionality in NoteCards is accessible through a set of well-documented Lisp functions, allowing the programming user to create new types of notecards, develop programs that monitor or process the notecard network, and/or integrate other programs into the NoteCards environment. A complete description of NoteCards can be found in [Halasz et al 87].

There are other hypertext systems similarly well-suited to supporting collaboration. The Neptune system [Delisle&Schwartz 86] has functionality that overlaps to a large degree with that of NoteCards and is being used in multi-user computer aided design and software management tasks. Other hypertext systems that have attempted to support collaboration are Intermedia at Brown University [Yankelovich et al 85], Xanadu [Nelson 81] and Textnet [Trigg&Weiser 86]. The Augment system conceived by Doug Engelbart in the 60's was perhaps not strictly hypertext, but nonetheless made impressive strides in collaborative authoring and teleconferencing [Engelbart 84]. Finally, support for hypertext versioning; the storing, maintaining and accessing of prior versions of nodes and links, can be found in systems like

Neptune and PIE [Goldstein&Bobrow 81].

Draft passing

The most prevalent form of collaboration in NoteCards to date is draft passing. This is because NoteCards currently does not allow multiple users to simultaneously access a notefile (but see the description of simultaneous sharing in the next section). Thus, collaborators sharing a notefile agree to take turns. Often, this involves file copying between servers and workstations coordinated through electronic mail. The amount of time any one user holds onto a notefile tends to vary from several hours to several days.

In this section, we focus on a particular draft-passing collaboration centering around a NoteCards notefile belonging to two of the authors (Trigg and Suchman). At the substantive level, this notefile serves as a project notebook. In the project, we are engaged in a study of collaboration in the research lab, as well as in an ongoing discussion of how NoteCards might support collaboration. The notefile provides a medium for documenting the study of collaboration and for project plans and directions. It includes a dialogue on ideas, slides for talks, drafts of papers, the results of interviews, etc. Figure 1 shows a NoteCards screen snapshot of the collaboration project notefile. The top level filebox for the notefile is called "Contents" and contains sub-fileboxes corresponding to various projects, topic categories, mechanisms and activities happening in the notefile.

In using the notefile as a project notebook, we have discovered several techniques that support our annotative and procedural activities as well. Our most common annotative activity is commenting on each other's work. Initially, we inserted comments directly into the card being critiqued. In order to distinguish comment from substance, we used different fonts. In the

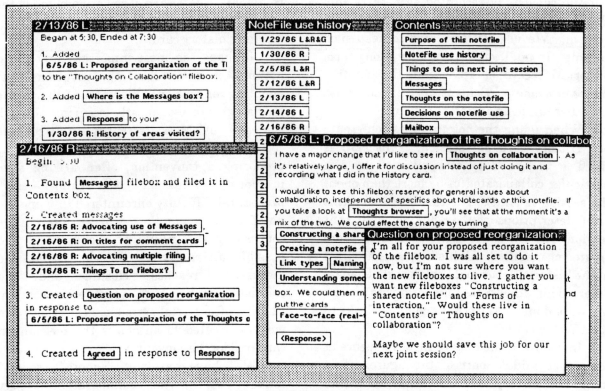

Figure 1: The collaboration project notefile.

limit, however, this leads to either proliferating fonts or confusion over the historical order of annotations. Currently, we create all annotations in separate cards and link them to the cards being annotated with the link icon at the appropriate place. This provides both distinction of comment from substance and a history of commentary creation. Furthermore, annotation cards have titles describing their substance, while link types are used to capture the relation between the annotation card and the card annotated. (Annotative link types include Comment, Response and Argument.) In Figure 1, for example, the comment card "Question on proposed reorganization" is linked from "6/5/86 L: Proposed reorganization ..." via a "Response" link which appears as a link icon at the bottom of the card.

Procedural activities include record keeping, message posting and convention adoption. Record keeping in the project notefile consists of recording each entry into the notefile and the changes made during that session. We use *History* cards to keep such records. In addition to providing a long term historical record of activity in the notefile, they allow one participant to easily see what the other has done during a session.

When using the notefile, we each create one History card per session. This card is titled with the date and initialed by the particular collaborator (or by more than one if the session is joint). The card's text contains brief descriptions of the work done in that session and links to the cards that were created or modified. All history cards are filed in the history filebox and kept in chronological order. This allows one collaborator to review the work done by the other and follow links to the affected cards.

In Figure 1, the history filebox appears in the upper middle part of the figure. Two individual history cards are displayed on the left. Notice that the various cards created

during a session are linked from the session's history card. For example, the session of 2/13/86 contains a link to "6/5/86 L: Proposed reorganization ...", a card created during that session. In a later session, the response to that proposal was captured in "Question on proposed reorganization." Again, notice that the entire interchange is recorded via links and descriptive text in the session history cards.

Another procedural activity involves message posting. We occasionally need to direct a question or suggestion directly to the other collaborator. This is the kind of communication that happens routinely in face to face collaboration, but that we also want to be supported online and within the medium. We do this through *Message* cards. These resemble notes left on a bulletin board, waiting to be read by the recipient the next time he or she visits the notefile. In Figure 1, the Message card "2/16/86 R: On titles for comment cards" is one of several created in the session of 2/16/86 and linked from that session's history card.

Perhaps the most important procedural activity involves creating, proposing and adopting conventions. We've found this to be a four-stage process, mostly occuring through the use of Message cards. First, one collaborator begins the discussion by proposing a convention, often arising from previous discussion concerning some procedural difficulty encountered in using the notefile. This is followed by an interchange concerning the merits of the proposal and possible alternatives. At some point, the discussion reaches closure and the collaborators agree to adopt a convention. Finally, after a trial period, a piece of software may be created to automate the mechanism captured by the convention.

We have already adopted several conventions in the collaboration project notefile. In one case, one of us proposed that different fonts be used in our text cards so that we could easily ascertain a card's author. After some discussion, we settled on three fonts, one each for our individual sessions and one for those times that we work on the notefile together (sharing a terminal). A tool to support this could simply set the default text card font based on the identity of the user when the notefile is opened.

In another case, we discussed the issue of when it was reasonable for one person to reshape another's card. The decision in this case was to adopt *no* convention. That is, we would reshape cards at will.

It should be noted that there are certain procedural matters that cannot currently be accomodated within the shared notefile. For example, the logistics of turn taking for use of the notefile is coordinated via real time conversations or electronic mail.

Simultaneous sharing

In simultaneous sharing, several collaborators work contemporaneously on a single notefile. Simultaneous sharing is similar to draft passing in the substantive, annotative, and procedural activities that can occur. However, simultaneous sharing highlights three additional procedural issues regarding support for collaborative interactions.

Access contention. Access to information stored in a draft passing notefile can be restrictive. In particular, the mechanics of draft passing prevents collaborators from simultaneously working on a single notefile, even if the sets of cards that they need to access are entirely disjoint. Simultaneous sharing changes the nature of access contention, moving the contention from the level of the whole notefile to some finer-grained level.

Real-time monitoring. Because draft-passing collaborators are not working contemporaneously, each collaborator usually does a substantial amount of work before passing the "draft" off to the other collaborators. During this period, the other collaborators cannot review the ongoing work, and hence cannot affect or modify its real-time progress. In a setting of simultaneous shared access, real-time monitoring is possible. Note, however, that special mechanisms need to be designed into any system intended to support such monitoring.

Real-time communication. The communication between draft-passing collaborators occurs by placing information in the shared notefile and expecting the other collaborators to locate and read this information at some later point in time. This communication occurs across time and space with consequent loss of mutual context, timeliness, etc. Simultaneous information space sharing allows for the possibility of remote real-time communication between collaborators, thereby changing the nature of their communications. Again, special mechanisms beyond simple simultaneous access are required to support such communication.

In order to study collaboration through simultaneous access to a shared information space, we have designed and are currently implementing a distributed version of NoteCards. Distributed NoteCards will allow users simultaneous shared access from their workstation to the notefiles residing on any machine attached to the same local-area network.

Distributed NoteCards provides contention resolution at the level of individual cards. The system allows any number of users simultaneously to read and display a given card. However, permission to make modifications to the card is restricted to one user at a time. All readers of the card are notified when certain modification events occur. Following [Stefik et al 87] we notify readers as soon as possible that a card they are accessing may be changed. Readers are provided with three levels of modification notices. First, when one person requests write permission for a card, all readers of that card are notified that someone has declared an intention to modify the card. Second, when the writer actually writes the modified card onto the shared notefile, all readers of the card receive a notification that the card they see is now out-of-date. Finally, when a writer deletes a card, all readers of the card receive notification that the card has been deleted. NoteCards prevents any further operations using the card, but users can continue to examine the card displayed on the screen.

Distributed NoteCards provides no special mechanism for dealing with access collisions at the individual card level; exclusive write permission is simply allocated for an unlimited period of time on a first-come, first-served basis. The expectation is that users sharing a notefile will in general be working in different regions of the network and hence will not be subject to access contention at the individual card level. This situation may in fact occur frequently when the system is being used by a group of collaborators focused on a common task, as often occurs in face-to-face meetings. In this case, the users could devise some form of draft passing convention for individual cards. Note, however, that preliminary observations of the Colab in [Stefik et al 87] suggest that participants may sometimes need to monitor modifications below the card level as they occur in real-time.

The primary goal of the Distributed NoteCards project is to eliminate some of the more tedious *mechanical* aspects of sharing notefiles and to move access contention from entire notefiles down to the more natural level of individual cards. In its present design, Distributed NoteCards does not address in detail the issue of real-time collaborative interactions. The notification procedure built into the system provides a very minimal monitoring tool; users know when a card on the screen is about to be modified or has been modified. This was intended more as a way of marking outdated information than as a tool for monitoring the activities of other users. As a result, there is no monitoring of read accesses to cards, and there is no tool for monitoring modifications to cards not on the screen. A more sophisticated monitoring tool might, for example, provide an overview browser of some user determined subnetwork in the notefile. Cards about to be modified or recently modified (or read) could be highlighted on this browser.

Distributed NoteCards also does not specifically address the problem of communication between collaborators. The tools and techniques available for such communication are the same as those described in the draft passing section above; there is no special communications channel for simultaneous users of a notefile. However, future plans call for a Talk card in which all of the current users of a notefile could carry on (as well as record) a real-time written conversation.

Since Distributed NoteCards is still being implemented, we have no observations on its use. Like draft passing, we expect that using a simultaneously shared notefile will require the development of conventions, methods, and further tools to adequately support collaborative work. In particular, we expect the need for better monitoring facilities and for better communications channels to become apparent as people try to use Distributed NoteCards for real collaborative activities.

Online presentation

Though online presentations are not usually thought of as collaborative, their support imposes requirements similar to those outlined above for draft passing and simultaneous sharing. In online presentations, the author has to make his or her work intelligible to a future, often unknown reader. The system must provide means for the author to document conventions adopted in the presentation in order that the substance of the presentation be intelligible.

Documentation can be either at the annotative level, and thus about the substance, or at the procedural level, about using the medium. For example, the text in a "README" card filed in a filebox might describe the contents of that filebox and thus provide annotative documentation. A separate card instructing the reader to always look first for "README" cards when bringing up a filebox would be an example of procedural documentation.

A more dynamic form of documentation might be called a *guided tour*. Guided tours are created by the notefile's author and used by the reader. They provide paths that visit certain landmark cards in a notefile. Figure 2 shows part of a tutorial notefile. Novice users learn about NoteCards by reading the cards found along documented paths through this notefile. The documentation takes the form of text surrounding each link icon (many resembling small buttons) representing the tour's links.

We imagine future guided tours being tailored according to the reader of the notefile. For example, users might choose different tours based on their expertise in the area or on the time they have available. At any point during the tour, the reader could venture off the path to inspect cards of interest.

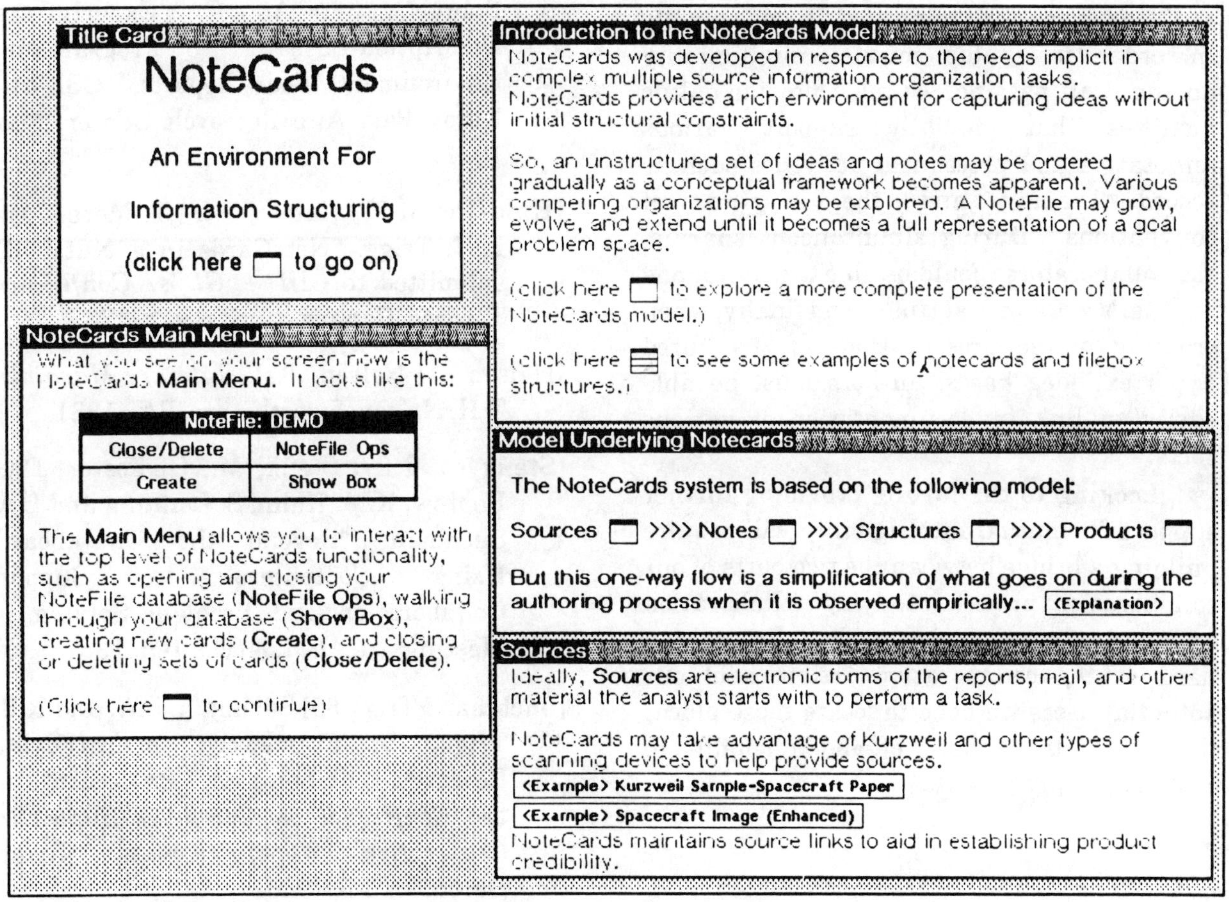

Figure 2: A tutorial notefile.

Concluding remarks

In order for people to collaborate, they must be able to make their work mutually intelligible. This requires annotative and procedural discussion as well as substantive work. Ideally, computer systems designed to support collaboration should capture both sorts of discussion and store them in the same medium as the work itself.

Hypertext systems, by nature, provide a good starting point. For example, NoteCards can contain multiple interlocking hierarchies allowing users to maintain different organizations of the shared information simultaneously (as opposed to a single outline, say, when writing a paper). Furthermore, annotative and procedural discussion can be linked to the appropriate parts of the work.

However, pure hypertext is not enough. In order to enable mutual intelligibility during draft passing, we must provide online facilities that specially support various annotative and procedural activities such as record keeping and the adoption of conventions. During simultaneous sharing, the collaborators should be able to monitor one another's work in real time. And finally, when creating online presentations of structured hypertext idea bases, authors must be able easily to link in documentation of various sorts.

Looking to the future, providing further support for mutual intelligibility will require building a bridge between the two parts of our collaboration project; studying collaboration and designing computer tools. By looking hard at the collaborative activities of our potential users we hope to locate those places that are both in need of and amenable to computer support.

References

[Brown 85] Brown, J.S., "Process versus Product: A Perspective on Tools for Communal and Informal Electronic Learning," *Journal of Educational Computing Research*, 1 (2), 1985, 179-201.

[Delisle&Schwartz 86] Delisle, N. and M. Schwartz, "Neptune: a Hypertext System for CAD Applications," *Proceedings of ACM SIGMOD '86*, Washington, D.C., May 28-30, 1986, 132-142.

[Engelbart 84] Engelbart, D.C., "Authorship Provisions in Augment," *IEEE 1984 COMPCOM Proceedings*, Spring 1984, 465-472.

[Goldstein&Bobrow 81] Goldstein, I. and D. Bobrow, "An Experimental Description-Based Programming Environment: Four Reports," CSL-81-3 Xerox Palo Alto Research Center, Mar. 1981.

[Halasz et al 87] Halasz, F.G., T. Moran, and R.H. Trigg, "NoteCards in a Nutshell," submitted to *CHI + GI '87 Conference*, Toronto, Canada, April 5-9, 1987.

[Nelson 81] Nelson, T.H., *Literary Machines*, T.H. Nelson, Swarthmore, PA., 1981.

[Stefik et al 87] Stefik, M., G. Foster, D.G. Bobrow, K.M. Kahn, S. Lanning and L.A. Suchman, "Beyond the Chalkboard: Using Computers to Support Collaboration and Problem Solving in Meetings," *CACM*, 30 (1), Jan. 1987.

[Suchman&Trigg 86] Suchman, L.A. and R.H. Trigg, "A Framework for Studying Research Collaboration," Proceedings of the *Conference on Computer Supported Cooperative Work*, Austin, Texas, December 3-5, 1986.

[Trigg&Weiser 86] Trigg, R.H. and M. Weiser, "TEXTNET: A Network-Based Approach to Text Handling," *ACM Transactions on Office Information Systems*, **4** (1), Jan. 1986.

[Yankelovich et al 85] Yankelovich, N., N. Meyrowitz, and A. van Dam, "Reading and Writing the Electronic Book," *Computer* **18** (10), Oct. 1985, 15-30.

Diversity in the Use of Electronic Mail:
A Preliminary Inquiry

WENDY E. MACKAY
Massachusetts Institute of Technology

This paper describes a series of interviews that examine the ways that professional office workers use electronic mail to manage their daily work. The purpose is to generate hypotheses for future research. A number of implications for the design of flexible mail systems are discussed.

Two principal claims are made. First, the use of electronic mail is strikingly diverse, although not infinitely so. Individuals vary both in objective measures of mail use and in preferred strategies for managing work electronically. Feelings of control are similarly diverse and are related to the size of the user's inbox, numbers of folders, and subscriptions to distribution lists. This diversity implies that one's own experiences with electronic mail are unlikely to provide sufficient understanding of other's uses of mail. Mail designers should thus seek flexible primitives that capture the important dimensions of use and provide flexibility for a wide range of users.

The second claim is that electronic mail is more than just a communication system. Users archive messages for subject retrieval, prioritize messages to sequence work activities, and delegate tasks via mail. A taxonomy of work management is proposed in which mail is used for information management, time management, and task management activities. Directions for future research are suggested.

Categories and Subject Descriptors: H.4.3 [**Information Systems Applications**]: Electronic Mail

General Terms: Human Factors, Management

Additional Key Words and Phrases: Computer-supported cooperative work, electronic mail, information filtering, information lens, task management, time management

1. INTRODUCTION

In a growing number of corporations, electronic mail has become an essential form of communication. As the number of people with access to electronic mail increases, the benefits to individuals increase accordingly. Now that several organizations have more than a decade of experience with electronic mail, it is useful to examine how mail use has evolved and what additional capabilities would best support the needs of users.

Other studies have already demonstrated a number of substantial effects of electronic mail. It can solve certain kinds of problems such as increase the speed of decision making [4] or enable the exchange of new information [7, 14].

Author's address: Massachusetts Institute of Technology, Project Athena, Amherst St., Cambridge, Mass. 02139.

"Diversity in the Use of Electronic Mail: A Preliminary Inquiry" by W.E. Mackay from *ACM Transactions on Office Information Systems*, Vol. 6, No. 4, October 1988, pages 380-397. Copyright © 1988, Association for Computing Machinery, Inc., reprinted with permission.

Electronic mail can also create new problems, most notably "information over-load" [6, 8, 12]. Sometimes there are both positive and negative effects such as changes in organizational structure [5, 15].

What is the total effect of the introduction of electronic mail? Do organizations with extensive experience with electronic mail evolve new patterns of use that extend beyond the exchange of informal messages? When presented with the opportunity both to address problems created by mail and to use mail to solve other problems, what do users do? When presented with a system such as the Information Lens [13], which provides users with the ability to write personal rules for managing electronic mail messages, what kinds of rules do people choose to write? How do these rules reflect the ways in which people use mail in their work?

This paper describes a series of interviews that identify existing patterns of electronic mail use within an organization. It is hoped that investigation of mail use within a mature electronic mail environment will help us to better understand how to expand the capabilities of electronic communication within organizations and lead to systems that better facilitate collaborative work.

This is a qualitative study. The purpose is to closely observe a small group of experienced electronic mail users and identify characteristic patterns of mail use. The data consist of snapshots of existing mail use, for example, daily quantity of messages sent and received, and interviews about subjective impressions of electronic mail. Participants were asked how they would like to improve their own management of mail and their use of mail to accomplish other tasks. Limited quantitative and qualitative analyses of these data are used to help generate hypotheses that provide the basis for future research. It is important to emphasize that the sample size here is small, and the addition or deletion of one or two individuals would have a large effect on these results. The data presented raise new questions rather than answer old ones.

2. DESCRIPTION OF THE STUDY

Members of a large research laboratory (approximately 60 people) within a major corporation were informed about a study of the Information Lens. Because I was interested only in active users of electronic mail, I described the study and solicited participation via electronic mail. This paper describes the interviews conducted with members of this laboratory and is primarily concerned with current and desired uses of electronic mail. These interviews were conducted just prior to the introduction of Lens; the study of how people actually use Lens is still in progress.

The Information Lens is a prototype electronic mail system which was developed at MIT and designed primarily to help users filter and organize electronic mail [13]. Lens uses semistructured messages which have predefined fields, such as DATE: or MEETING LOCATION:, as well as open-ended text areas. Users can create their own sets of IF-THEN rules, and Lens processes incoming messages according to those rules. The rules can perform various operations such as moving a message to a mail folder or adding information to a calendar program. Lens rules can also be used to identify characteristics of "interesting messages." One individual may write a rule that fires if a particular message meets certain criteria. If another person creates such a message and addresses it to "anyone," the first user receives it automatically.

It is important to point out that the description of Lens affected the ways in which people thought about and described their use of electronic mail. It encouraged them to think about the rules they currently use to manage their mail and what it would take to automate them. It also focused attention on certain kinds of problems and provided scenarios for their solution. Individuals were attracted to different features of Lens, and the overall explanation of Lens provided a common ground for discussion.

2.1 Participants

The 23 individuals who were interviewed for this study were selected because they are all extremely active electronic mail users. Some limit their use of the computer to electronic mail and writing activities, whereas others are full-time computer programmers. Participants have a wide range of jobs within the research laboratory. Eighteen decided to try Lens; 5 did not. Of the 18, 15 are full-time researchers, and 3 are managers. Six of the researchers were trained as computer scientists, and 9 were trained in physics, psychology, anthropology, or sociology. The 5 participants who chose not to use Lens included 3 administrators, 1 computer scientist, and 1 manager. The reasons for failure to participate included reluctance to use a prototype mail system, satisfaction with current mail use, and use of an incompatible workstation.

All of those interviewed work in an environment that has supported mail for over a decade. All rely on mail for both formal and informal communication. Their existing mail system operates in a networked workstation environment which permits the use of separate windows for composing, reading, and browsing messages or folders. Messages can be marked with system-defined characteristics, such as moved or deleted, or with characteristics specified by the user. Users can create and name as many folders as they like. The Lens prototype was designed to enhance rather than replace this system; potential participants were told they could choose any or none of the new Lens features, as desired.

2.2 Interview Procedure

The first interviews were scheduled just after the general electronic mail announcement of the Lens study. Several weeks later, my colleagues and I demonstrated Lens at an open meeting, and we invited people to try it. Those who chose to participate in the Lens study were interviewed again, just prior to installing Lens on their machines. Thus, the data reported include one interview for some people and two interviews for others, separated by several weeks.

I scheduled all interviews for one hour in the participant's office. I asked each person to save the current day's mail and delete confidential messages. (No one actually deleted any messages.) I was able to examine the participant's mail messages, inbox, and mail folders and used this information to check the participant's perception of mail use.

After answering general questions about the study, I asked a series of specific as well as open-ended questions. Participants were asked to estimate the daily numbers of messages sent and received, the number of mail folders, the size of the inbox, and the number of distribution list subscriptions.[1] These answers were checked against the actual numbers for the day and participants were asked if the day was typical. Participants were also asked open-ended questions about major problems and successes with electronic mail. They used this as an opportunity to describe their current communication patterns, successful mail management strategies, problems that needed to be addressed, and whether or not particular Lens features would be expected to help. The actual questions are listed in the Appendix.

3. THREE EXAMPLES

Before examining the overall results of the study, it is instructive to look at three individual cases. These cases have been selected to represent extremes in the use of electronic mail, rather than to identify "typical" users. In order to disguise the identities of the interviewees, their names and some of their personal characteristics have been changed.

3.1 A Classic "Prioritizer"

Mary is a research scientist with a very active personal network. She estimates that she receives over 30 electronic mail messages per day and receives a large number of telephone calls as well. Many of these interactions take the form of personal requests that require her time, for example, reviewing papers, serving on program committees, and offering advice to people at other sites. Other people have become resigned to the fact that she will not always answer her electronic mail or return phone calls; they often find this quite frustrating.

From her perspective, electronic mail is an essential communication medium which also threatens to dictate her life. As a result, she has devised a set of schemes to prioritize her mail to ensure that she sees and responds to correspondence that is important to her. "My goal is to read as little as possible. I try not to read mail more than once a day; I budget my time." In this case, mail is both part of the problem and part of the solution. Because the cost is low for others to reach her electronically, she is inundated with requests, and it is simply not possible for her to respond to all of them. She does not have a secretary or people working for her to whom she can delegate tasks, so she must prioritize them herself.

She is willing to occasionally miss important messages (assuming, perhaps, that people will telephone or get to her somehow if it is *really* important). She has no desire to see unimportant messages. She identifies several categories of electronic mail. Priority 0 requires immediate attention. Priorities 1 and 2 are categorized by sender and only include messages addressed to her personally. Priority 3 consists of bulk mailings, which she browses every couple of months. She sees mail as a way to maintain her large personal network of research colleagues and wants help identifying the most important messages. She feels as if she is on the edge of losing control of her mail.

---

[1] Estimates of mail use are more relevant than actual numbers in determining the *perceived* feelings of control.

3.2 An Overwhelmed "Archiver"

Ralph is a computer scientist who is responsible for obtaining information from a wide variety of sources and applying it to specific problems. He has hundreds of messages in his inbox and is afraid to delete them because "there might be something important . . . What percent of the ocean don't you like?" Some of these messages are from personal friends and require lengthy correspondence, some are requests for information or other kinds of action, and others contain information that "may be useful someday" but can not be immediately categorized. Many messages require some form of action on his part and cannot simply be deleted. His meetings and other work prevent him from reading mail on a regular basis. As a result, he often reads only a fraction of his new messages and reserves the rest for "later." His inbox is always a jumbled mix of unseen messages, unclassified messages, and messages that remind him to do something. He is wary of getting help to do this because it would increase his feelings of lack of control.

One of his most pressing problems is trying to organize his messages in such a way that he can find them again. "I don't always delete messages after printing them; they're a reminder in case it gets lost." His strategy is to delete clearly unimportant messages, leaving the rest in his inbox as a reminder of what remains to be done. He keeps a large number of different mail folders and transfers messages into them on an ad hoc basis. He wants to be able to automatically identify different characteristics of messages once they have been acted upon so that he can use these characteristics to retrieve messages again. He also wants some sort of automatic reminder facility to help him keep track of messages that he still must process.

In general, he views mail as an absolutely essential communication medium for both his job and his personal life. It creates problems because of the volume of messages (he usually has over 600 messages in his inbox and maintains over 40 mail folders), and he feels as if the situation is completely out of control.

3.3 A Manager–Secretary Team

Ann is a manager who is responsible for a group of researchers. Unlike the previous users, she does not use mail to maintain a network of colleagues. She talks to most of her group face-to-face on a regular basis. Instead, mail is an efficient way to keep informed about events in the lab, provides a record of interactions, and is an efficient way to communicate when she is traveling. "If I'm on the road, I use mail for almost everything."

Her primary problem is managing the volume of mail. Members of her group send her copies of many messages to keep her informed. She would like to offload the management of these messages to her secretary. To be worthwhile, this delegation process must be faster than doing it herself. "I can't afford to spend more than half an hour a day on mail; it's an inefficient use of my time."

Ann and her secretary have developed a shorthand for exchanging and processing mail. Ann flags messages with one of five different actions for her secretary: "please file," "take some action," "please reply to," "for your information," and "remind me." The secretary can easily prioritize and handle the messages without going back to Ann for clarification. Note that this classification scheme is not based on the content of the messages, but rather on the actions the manager chooses to take. Ann wants help in automating this system to avoid the redundancy of copying messages back and forth and to save them both time.

3.4 Analysis of the Cases

These three users exhibit a striking diversity in their patterns of mail use. One user is always "on the edge" of losing control of mail, another is completely overwhelmed, and the third feels very much in control of her mail. As might be predicted, the person who feels most in control receives the fewest messages, keeps the fewest mail folders, and subscribes to the fewest distribution lists. On the other hand, the person who is "on the edge" actually has a significantly smaller inbox than the other two and has the highest number of subscriptions to distribution lists. The perceived level of control does not correspond directly with the objective measures of mail use.

These three users choose to process and organize mail differently and describe the function of mail in very different ways. One person wants help archiving and retrieving messages and views mail as an information management tool. One person wants help prioritizing incoming messages for later action and views it as a time-management tool. The third person uses it effectively to delegate tasks and views it as a task-management tool.

This level of diversity has been reported in other aspects of work, including different writing strategies using NoteCards [17], different desk organization techniques [11], and different styles of information exchange [2]. Although these patterns of use are diverse, they do not appear to be infinitely so. Individuals tend to cluster in their views of mail and the kinds of problems they want it to address. The next section describes the patterns of mail use found in the entire group.

4. PATTERNS OF ELECTRONIC MAIL USE

Participants estimated the daily numbers of messages sent and received and average numbers of mail folders, sizes of mail inboxes, and numbers of distribution lists. These numbers were then checked against the current day's mail, and the user stated whether or not the day was typical. When a range was given, the midpoint of the range was chosen. These estimates, as well as the actual numbers of mail folders and distribution lists, and the user's reported rates of reading mail, are presented in Table I.[2]

---

[2] The mail system in this organization does not explicitly provide electronic conferencing but instead has a very sophisticated distribution list system. These lists are "owned" by someone in the organization who decides whether or not others can add themselves. Some lists are mandatory such as corporate-wide lists. Others are restricted to members of a particular group. Still others are voluntary and include everything from information for users of prototype software to nonwork-related topics (want ads, political action, local entertainment, etc.). When asked to estimate the number of distribution lists, some people answered verbally (e.g., "few"), others guessed a number, and several did both.

Table I

	Messages Sent (Estimate)	Messages Received (Estimate)	Mail Folders (Actual)	Messages in Inbox (Estimate)	Distribution Lists (Estimate)	Distribution Lists (Actual)	Reading Rate Messages per day (Estimate)
Managers:							
Sr A	8	30	29	200	12	29	Constantly
Sr B	6	20	6	250	10	21	Once
Sr C		25	15	100	few	37	Intervals
Computer Scientists:							
Sr D	17	75	38	41	many	93	Constantly
Jr E	2	50	26	204	many	75	Constantly
Jr F	10	50	30	85	many	26	Intervals
Jr G	4	40	46	100	many	68	Constantly
Jr H	4	50	89	500	10	46	Constantly
Jr I	7	50	42	600	10	33	Intervals
Other Researchers:							
Sr J	6	30	29	7	36	52	Once
Sr K	6	35	63	450	10	41	Constantly
Sr L	10	50	49	600	20	85	Constantly
Jr M	4	12	8	15	10	19	Constantly
Jr N	5	35	12	80	15	22	Intervals
Jr O	10	35	23	15	10	51	Intervals
Jr P	10	50	20	450	30	36	Intervals
Jr Q	1	17	9	85	7	9	Constantly
Jr R	4	30	22	250	18	43	Constantly
NonLens Users:							
Jr S	30	75	40	10	few	56	Constantly
Jr T	3	20	few	100	11	46	Constantly
Jr U	5	23	100	1,350	10	68	Constantly
Sr V	3	35	11	1,350	6	84	Intervals
Jr W	8	50	15		15		Constantly
Means:	7	39	33	311	14	47	
Ranges:	(1–30)	(12–75)	(6–100)	(7–1,350)	(6–36)	(9–93)	

Most users vary somewhat in their estimates of messages they send (1–10) and receive (12–50) per day. One user, a senior administrator, handles significantly more than anyone else. She sends 30 messages and receives 75 per day.

Users of this mail system can create mail folders in which to store mail messages. Here, the variability among users is much greater ranging from 9 to 100 folders. All job categories show this variability, indicating that job requirements are not the primary determinant of number of folders.

Messages first arrive in a special folder called the inbox. The sizes of inboxes vary greatly, ranging from a low of 10 to a high of 1,350. Those with small inboxes often make a point of clearing them out on a regular basis. Note that small inboxes are not necessarily associated with a low volume of mail. The administrator with the highest volume of mail has the smallest average inbox size. Another administrator with a low volume of mail has one of the largest inboxes.

Users have very different attitudes towards distribution lists. First, nobody has an accurate idea of how many they are subscribed to. Everybody underestimates the number, probably because it is easy to forget about low-volume lists, and people are placed on some lists automatically. Second, some users choose to subscribe to many lists, while others remove themselves from as many as possible. Those in the first category "do not want to miss anything" and are willing to put up with the extra volume of junk mail. Four of the six computer scientists and one researcher placed themselves in this group. Those in the second category are willing to risk missing mail. All of the managers and administrators, most of the researchers (5 out of 9), and one computer scientist are in this category. The remaining people feel that they subscribe to a moderate (and reasonable) number of distribution lists.

The diversity of mail use found in the three examples described earlier is also apparent in these data. While message traffic is somewhat similar, there are large differences in the numbers of messages kept in inboxes and numbers of distribution lists. The difference between the lowest and highest value is at least an order of magnitude in all but the number of messages received. This variability obtains within job categories as well as among them. Note that these items are not all independent of each other because people influence their use of mail. For example, reducing the number of distribution lists directly reduces the number of messages actually received. Similarly, people who do not like clutter may continually delete messages from their inboxes and also maintain a small number of folders.

The size of the inbox also contributes to whether or not users feel in control of mail. Those with very small inboxes are far less likely to feel overwhelmed than those with hundreds of messages. Most people treat the inbox as an on-line "to do" list. "My inbox also holds unclassified mail. It acts as a reminder that something needs to be done." Not only is it more difficult to find messages in a large inbox, but the very size contributes to feelings that there's an overwhelming amount of work left to be done.

Users have several ways to limit inboxes. One is to get off voluntary distribution lists and simply never receive a large number of mail messages. Some people are quite willing to do this ("after awhile you get tired of all the junk"), while others are not ("it's worth it to have to delete 90 percent if 10 percent is interesting").

One researcher said "I get off as many distribution lists as possible; then I make friends with people who filter them!"

Another way to reduce inboxes is to systematically delete messages after they have been read or skimmed. Some people do this regularly ("I like to prune my mail"), and others let it get out of hand ("If there's a lot of new mail, I do the easiest thing and don't delete. So the garbage builds up."). Several people said that when the inbox gets too big, they copy it to a mail folder, date the folder, and start over.

Preferred frequency of reading mail varies considerably. Two people are very careful to limit mail reading to once a day, usually for a specified period of time. One-third of the people in each job group limit their mail reading to two or three times per day. They allow mail to accumulate and read it only when convenient. The rest of the people read mail as soon as it arrives. This "constant" reading of mail refers only to the time people spend at their desks.

Subjective reports about feelings of control sometimes refer to rates of reading mail. Some feel that mail is seductive and carefully restrict their mail reading, either by limiting the actual time spent or by restricting the number of times mail is retrieved per day. Others treat the appearance of a "new mail" message as if it were a telephone call; they retrieve mail as soon as it arrives. Those who feel out of control are often those whose jobs do not require immediate responses to mail but feel they can not stop themselves from reading it anyway.

5. SUBJECTIVE VIEWS OF MAIL

The next two sections present data that result from an exploratory analysis of users' subjective views of mail based on the open-ended interview questions. Two observations emerged during the early interviews. First, individuals differ greatly in their feelings of control over their mail. Second, individuals either ask for help prioritizing their incoming messages or in archiving them for later retrieval. (A few users requested both.) I was interested in how these categories correspond to different patterns of mail use.

Individuals interviewed in the latter part of the study were explicitly asked to rate their feelings of control over mail and specify a preference with respect to prioritizing or archiving mail. For those who did not provide an explicit categorization, I made subjective judgements based on the following criteria: I rated users as "OK" if they did not report difficulty finding messages, read as much of their mail as they felt was important, and felt they had effective strategies for managing their inboxes. I rated users as "overwhelmed" if they reported serious problems finding messages, were unable to read all of their mail, and were unable to manage the mail in their inboxes. I rated users as "on the edge" if they reported some success in these areas but were not satisfied with their ability to manage their mail.

Similarly, I rated users as prioritizers if they specified that they were interested in rules that ran before reading their mail or if they maintained one or more folders for "high priority" activities. I rated users as archivers if they explicitly refused to run rules prior to reading mail and also maintained a large number of subject-based folders but no "priority" folders. Users were designated as both if they wanted rules to run in both occasions and maintained both kinds of folders.

Table II. Feelings of Control over Electronic Mail

Feelings of Control	Messages Sent	Messages Received	Total Folders	Inbox Size	Distribution Lists	Interview Data
"OK"	n = 8					
Mean	8.29	30.50	21.00	84.38	38.38	3 Senior
Standard Deviation	9.98	20.23	16.15	78.67	20.52	5 Junior
Range	1–30	12–75	6–46	10–250	9–68	
"On the Edge"	n = 8					
Mean	7.5	44.38	32.50	407.43	65.57	6 Senior
Standard Deviation	4.66	15.22	17.19	466.61	24.78	2 Junior
Range	2–17	30–75	11–63	7–1,350	29–93	
"Overwhelmed"	n = 7					
Mean	6.43	41.14	45.00	473.57	39.14	0 Senior
Standard Deviation	2.64	11.58	35.21	436.13	15.32	7 Junior
Range	4–10	12–100	12–100	80–1,350	26–68	7 Archive

Table III. Prioritizing Versus Archiving Electronic Mail

Processing Patterns	Messages Sent	Messages Received	Total Folders	Inbox Size	Distribution Lists	Interview Data
Prioritize	n = 7					
Mean	9.83	32.00	21.86	61.71	36.14	5 OK
Standard Deviation	10.36	20.58	11.81	72.07	18.02	2 On Edge
Range	1–30	12–75	9–40	7–200	9–56	0 Overwhelmed
Archive	n = 13					
Mean	7.23	49.92	40.85	502.17	50.69	6 Overwhelmed
Standard Deviation	3.83	14.59	29.00	440.85	26.05	5 On Edge
Range	4–17	20–75	6–100	41–1,350	15–93	2 OK

I then compared the patterns of use for each category described above. These data are summarized in Tables II and III. Because of the small sample sizes, most of the differences between groups are not statistically significant.

5.1 A Methodological Note

It is important to emphasize that this approach is designed to generate testable hypotheses, rather than to draw conclusions about the validity or generality of those hypotheses. These hypotheses are derived from one part of the data and are examined with respect to the whole group. They have a theoretical basis and fit the current set of data. Additional tests with a larger number of users from a different population are necessary to determine whether or not these patterns of use are generalizable.

5.2 Feelings of Control: Does the User Manage Mail or Does Mail Manage the User?

Subjective views of mail also reveal diversity in perceptions of mail use. Differences in feelings of control over mail are particularly interesting because they do not always correspond to more objective measures of mail volume. For example, one person felt that 36 distribution lists was "a few," while another felt that

20 was "a lot." One person felt in control with 75 messages a day, while another felt overwhelmed with 23. This section suggests factors that may influence these feelings of control and hypothesizes about how they relate to different strategies of work management.

Some people seem quite content with their electronic mail and feel that they use mail successfully in their jobs. ("I trim my inbox and don't hoard things. I don't have trouble finding things.") These people have been categorized as "OK". They

(1) do not try to read all of their mail messages.
(2) remove themselves from voluntary distribution lists.
(3) keep their inboxes small.
(4) keep a small number of folders.

Other people describe themselves as out of control ("I an overwhelmed by mail") and constantly feel that they are missing information and forgetting to do things because of it. ("I don't read all my mail. There's too much. I sometimes miss meetings and things because I didn't see the message.") These people have been categorized as "overwhelmed". They

(1) read mail at irregular intervals or constantly.
(2) try to read all of their mail but do not always succeed.
(3) keep hundreds of messages in their inboxes.
(4) often do not get to the bottom of an inbox.
(5) want to save a large percentage of their mail.
(6) maintain many mail folders on diverse topics.
(7) have difficulty finding messages.

A third group describe themselves as barely able to maintain control over their mail. ("I intend to read all my mail ... someday!") These people have been categorized as "on the edge." They

(1) read mail at irregular intervals or constantly.
(2) try to read all of their mail but do not always succeed.
(3) keep hundreds of messages in their inboxes.
(4) have difficulty finding messages.
(5) subscribe to many distribution lists.

Table II shows how the patterns of mail use differ among these three categories. Interestingly, individuals in the "on the edge" category do not appear to be simply at an intermediate point between "OK" and "overwhelmed." They maintain an intermediate number of folders, but their inboxes are roughly the same size as those in the "overwhelmed" category, and they receive similar numbers of messages. They are markedly different with respect to distribution lists, subscribing to twice as many as people in the other two categories (who are roughly equivalent). Essentially, the "on the edge" group deals with the same volume of mail as the "overwhelmed" group but appears to manage it more effectively.

One possible explanation for the differences between "overwhelmed" and "on the edge" users may be related to seniority in the lab. All of those in the "overwhelmed" category are junior members of the laboratory, whereas almost all of those in the "on the edge" category are senior members. On the other hand, seniority is not sufficient to determine feelings of control because equal numbers of junior and senior lab members appear in the "OK" category. Job responsibilities were evenly distributed across the three categories.

The data here suggest that users differ significantly in their feelings of control over their electronic mail. Those in the "overwhelmed" category appear to be experiencing "information overload," an increasingly common problem [1]. Weick [20] claims that information overload relates to the one-to-one correspondence between input and output of messages, electronic or otherwise. Such predictions become relatively easy to test when studying which factors increase or decrease perceptions of information overload with electronic mail.

Another question is how feelings of control over mail relate to feelings of control over work in general. These may be the same or may differ on the basis of the percentage of work that is received electronically as opposed to via other means. Presumably junior members of the lab receive a greater percentage of their work electronically, which matches the general findings. Additional research is necessary to understand how mail use changes with respect to this factor.

5.3 Mail Handling Strategies: Prioritizers and Archivers

During the open-ended section of the interviews, I asked users what kinds of rules they would like to apply to their mail. It quickly became apparent that the specification of rules was dependent upon *when* the user intended the rules to be run. This distinction affected the content of the rules requested and the kinds of work problems the user wanted to address.

Subjective views of mail also reveal diversity in mail handling strategies. Some people want a system that manages their mail before they see it. Others are adamant about reading all of their incoming mail first but want subsequent help to store and later retrieve messages.

I classified individuals with the first preference as *prioritizers*. These people are interested in limiting the time spent with mail and maximizing efficiency. They want help in selecting important messages for immediate viewing, deleting unimportant ones, and organizing the rest for efficient handling later. They are willing to risk the possibility of missing an important message in exchange for increased efficiency in managing their mail. These individuals

(1) do not read all of their mail.
(2) limit the number of times they read mail per day.
(3) reduce mail volume by getting off distribution lists.
(4) keep fewer messages in their inboxes.
(5) keep fewer mail folders.

People interested in prioritizing their mail were not necessarily more successful at managing their time than other people. They were, however, more likely to describe time management as a salient issue in their current work. Differences reported in how messages are perceived over time were consistent with research in the perception of time [3, 9].

I classified individuals with the second preference as *archivers*. These people want to ensure that they see all incoming messages and are willing to spend the extra time necessary to avoid the possibility of missing something important.

They want help in categorizing and storing messages and want better tools for subsequently finding them. These individuals

(1) increase mail volume by subscribing to voluntary distribution lists.
(2) save a large percentage of their mail messages.
(3) maintain a large number of mail folders.
(4) tend to read all of their mail or try to.
(5) have difficulty finding mail that has been filed.

Archivers are not necessarily pack rats who can not bear to throw anything away. Instead, they identify the gathering, digesting, and distributing of information as an important part of their jobs. They do not view eliminating "unimportant" messages as particularly useful. "I don't trust a formula for sorting mail before I see it. I'm afraid it will get sorted and I'll never look at it again. I prefer to read it manually and then have it sorted for me." Because they feel they have to process everything anyway, they want tools that help them classify interesting messages. They also want a consistent scheme for storing messages to facilitate later retrieval. Some of these people are very organized and have developed efficient filing systems for their messages. Richer retrieval mechanisms and faster access times would be appreciated but would probably not fundamentally change their jobs. Others are very disorganized and have a difficult time finding anything. These people probably need help with time management as much as help with archiving.

Table III shows the differences between those who prefer rules for prioritizing their messages and those who prefer rules for archiving their messages. "Prioritizing" and "archiving" are not mutually exclusive, although people in this study tend to have a preference for one or the other. Those interested in both or neither are not included in the table.

As with Table II, this table is generated from the interview data and is not the result of testing a hypothesis. With this caveat in mind, it is interesting to note that those who want to prioritize their mail manage to maintain much smaller inboxes and are more likely to feel in control of their electronic mail ("OK") as opposed to "on the edge" or "overwhelmed." Preference for prioritizing also appears to correspond with fewer folders and subscription to fewer distribution lists. These results are consistent with the interviews. No programmers appear in the prioritizing category, although other job categories, both junior and senior, appear in both. Rates of reading mail are evenly distributed between the two groups.

Senior members of the lab do not differ much from junior members in terms of messages sent and received, rates of reading mail, or categorization as prioritizer or archiver. Among senior members, managers have significantly larger inboxes than their senior research colleagues (mean = 475 versus 225). Senior members of the lab are less likely to describe managing information as a major problem in their work and state that they rely on junior members of the lab for this function. On the other hand, junior members of the lab appear to be less experienced at managing their time and far less willing to delegate the problem to others. They tend to be less likely to request rules that help them manage time spent reading mail or accomplishing tasks delegated electronically. Future studies are necessary to see whether time management and information tools will blur these distinctions.

5.4 Delegating Tasks by Mail

Researchers have examined the process of delegating tasks within an organization [10, 21]. This study suggests that mail is also an effective medium for delegating tasks. Managers and secretaries establish patterns that facilitate the exchange of tasks. Members of groups use mail as an efficient way to allocate tasks to the individual who is least busy or most competent to handle a particular problem.

The burden of handling electronically assigned tasks is often distributed disproportionately throughout the organization. In some sense, any request for action is a delegation of a task. On the other hand, the significance of the tasks delegated varies significantly across job responsibilities. Some people, particularly managers and high-level administrators, request more tasks. Others, usually individual contributors and secretaries, more often respond to these requests. Senior researchers appear to fall between the two extremes.

Senior members of the organization should, presumably, feel less overwhelmed by mail than their more junior colleagues. Not only do they receive a relatively smaller percentage of their work load via electronic mail, but electronic mail also provides an efficient mechanism for further delegating tasks. Junior members of the organization may be unable to refuse or delegate tasks they receive electronically, which would increase their feelings of being overwhelmed. In contrast, senior researchers may receive a similar number of requests but be able to refuse them or more easily hand them to someone else. This may be another explanation for the differences between the "overwhelmed" and the "on the edge" groups.

6. A TAXONOMY OF WORK FUNCTIONS ACCOMPLISHED WITH MAIL

Studies of organizations have identified and investigated characteristic patterns of work and how people manage their time. For example, Webber [19] categorizes activities in terms of order of arrival, level of urgency, and importance. Trickett [16] identifies four continua of work activities: intrinsic importance, urgency, delegation, and visitations. I have argued that electronic mail contributes to at least three functions of work: information management, time management, and task management. The specification of these functions emerged from the requests people made for rules to help manage their electronic mail. They are not mutually exclusive, although individuals usually choose mail handling strategies that support only one or two of these views of work.

The effectiveness of different mail handling strategies is influenced by job requirements and status within the laboratory. For example, some people who feel overwhelmed with too many messages can reduce the number of distribution lists they subscribe to. However, those whose jobs involve tracking information cannot simply remove themselves from distribution lists. They must actively manage the information that comes in via mail and archive it in such a way that they can retrieve it when it becomes relevant. These users view mail in terms of *information management* and use it to manage large quantities of information.

Some people receive a large percentage of their work assignments via mail, which creates a choice about when these tasks will be done. People who feel overwhelmed by mail often allow the order in which messages are received dictate the order in which tasks are performed. Individuals with jobs that require immediate responses, such as fixing broken equipment, often have no other choice. However, of those who can afford to wait before responding to any particular request, those who actively prioritize feel in greater control of their mail. These users view mail in terms of *time management* and use it to identify tasks and prioritize them.

The third work function that emerged was the delegation of tasks, both large and small, via electronic mail. One of the functions of electronic mail is to lower the cost of deciding who should perform which task. Some delegation patterns are easy to examine such as those between a manager and a secretary. Others are more complex, such as deciding which member of a software development group should fix a particular "bug." New bug fix requests come into the group via a distribution list, and the appropriate member of the group either accepts the task or uses mail to request help from other members. These users view mail in terms of *task management* and use it to allocate tasks among group members.

These work functions can be summarized as follows:

(1) *Information Management.* Especially relevant to individuals responsible for gathering information, digesting it, and providing it to others. Electronic mail is both a source and a repository of information.
(2) *Time Management.* Relevant to everyone, especially those who perform a high number of electronically assigned tasks. Strategies for ordering tasks range from performing them in the order they arrive to complex organizations of priority folders.
(3) *Task Management.* Relevant to everyone, especially those who perform a large percentage of their work electronically. Task exchanges are established among small work groups and pairs.

7. IMPLICATIONS FOR THE DESIGN OF ELECTRONIC MAIL SYSTEMS

The observation that users perform different work functions with electronic mail has important implications for the design of mail systems. Comments such as "Mail is my lifeblood" indicate the level of importance of mail in this organization. Because everyone can be assured that everyone else has regular access to electronic mail, these people have adapted mail to support different kinds of work. Examining these "lead users" of mail [18] can inform the design of future mail systems in several ways. Not only will it help identify limitations in current mail systems, but it may also challenge assumptions about the purpose of mail systems and suggest new approaches that support diverse uses of mail.

The level of diversity found within this small group argues against searching for a single correct mail strategy. Instead, it is important to look for powerful primitives that support the flexible extension of mail to aid different kinds of individual and group work. Because no single set of rules is likely to be useful for everyone, providing users with the ability to write their own personal rules should be an effective solution.

Groups should benefit from tools that help distribute tasks throughout an organization. A number of users in this study requested special types of messages and rules for this purpose. Two managers want to establish routine communication between themselves and their secretaries. Another is interested in creating "organizational processes for handling short-lived groups." Others are members of existing groups that handle routine requests from the outside, mostly bug fixes and requests for information. They are interested in rules that can help them allocate tasks among themselves.

The information management function needs an improved system of classifying and retrieving messages. Combining semistructured messages and intelligent information retrieval techniques may prove both practical and powerful. The time management function needs better ways of identifying and sequencing important messages. The importance of a message has as much to do with the current state of the user as the content. Effective time management tools must provide ways for the user to include information about context when processing the content of messages. For example, rules for handling messages should vary according to how busy the user is. The task management function needs better ways to determine who is best suited to perform a particular task and assign it accordingly. "Best suited" must include some indication of the current workload of the performer of the task to prevent people from becoming overwhelmed.

This study indicates that no individual is likely to have experienced the range of mail handling strategies possible, nor be aware of all of the different work functions that mail is routinely used for. Thus, it is important that ideas such as those raised in this paper be systematically tested with large groups of mail users, both to better understand how people in organizations use electronic mail to perform work and to generate ideas for improving future mail systems.

8. SUMMARY AND SUGGESTIONS FOR FUTURE RESEARCH

The most striking result of this study is the level of diversity in patterns of mail use. Basic mail functions, such as numbers of mail folders, numbers of distribution lists, and sizes of inboxes, vary by at least an order of magnitude. Individuals also vary greatly in their feelings of control over their mail, ranging from completely in control to totally overwhelmed. Much of this diversity can be explained by the differences in people's work and how that affects their views of mail.

In this organization, mail has evolved beyond a passive communication system. Because everyone can assume that everyone else has access to mail, mail has become an integral part of everyone's work. Mail is both a source of additional work and a tool for managing work. It should not be surprising that mail has come to reflect the diversity found in that work.

Three major forms of work management have been identified: information management, time management, and task management. Those who view mail as a time management tool, called prioritizers, are most interested in identifying and prioritizing important messages. Those who view mail as an information management system, called archivers, are most interested in sorting and retrieving messages. Those who use mail for task management, are most interested in assigning tasks to those who can perform them most efficiently.

Viewing mail as support for different kinds of work can help in the design of successful mail systems. An important lesson here is that an individual designer's own experience with mail is unlikely to provide sufficient understanding of how other people want to use mail. Mail systems should be designed to accommodate diversity. Rather than searching for an optimal set of functions, designers should seek primitives that provide both power and flexibility. With these features, mail can be more than just a communication system: It can be a sophisticated tool for accomplishing a wide variety of individual and group work.

APPENDIX: Interview Questions

Participants were asked the following sets of questions:

A. Descriptions of Electronic Mail Use

(1) How many messages did you send today?
(2) How many messages did you receive today?
(3) Is this a typical day?
(4) How many mail folders do you have?
(5) How many messages are in your inbox?
(6) Is this typical?
(7) How many distribution lists do you subscribe to?
(8) How often do you read your mail?
(9) Do you read all of your mail?
(10) What percentage of messages do you wish you had never seen?

B. A Subset of the Open-Ended Questions

(1) Describe how you use mail.
(2) In what categories do you place your mail messages?
(3) Can you think of times in the past week in which you needed technical information? What did you do?
(4) Can you think of times in the past month when you have looked at a previously filed message? Describe the procedure you used to find it.
(5) What kinds of rules would you like to process your mail?

ACKNOWLEDGMENTS

I would like to thank Tom Malone for his extensive comments on early drafts of the paper and support of the project. I would also like to thank Stu Card, Kevin Crowston, Ramana Rao, David Rosenblitt, and Deborah Tatar for their work on the study and insightful ideas. Finally, I would like to thank Lotte Bailyn, Geoff Bock, Jintae Lee, Steve Poltrock, Jane Salk, and the participants in the study for their thoughtful comments and willingness to discuss their different strategies for managing electronic mail.

REFERENCES

1. ABELSON, P. H. Coping with the information explosion. *Science* (1966), 75.
2. ALLEN, T. J. *Managing the Flow of Technology*. The MIT Press, Cambridge, Massachusetts, 1986.
3. COTTLE, T. J. *Perceiving Time*. Wiley and Sons, New York, 1976.
4. CRAWFORD, A. Corporate electronic mail—A communication-intensive application of information technology. *MIS Quarterly* (Sept. 1982), 1–13.

5. CROWSTON, K., MALONE, T., AND LIN, F.   Cognitive science and organizational design: A case study of computer conferencing. *Human-Computer Interaction 3* (1988), 59–85.

6. DENNING, P.   Electronic junk. *Commun. ACM 23*, 3 (Mar. 1982), 163–165.

7. FELDMAN, M.   Constraints on communication and electronic messaging. In *Proceedings of the Conference for Computer-Supported Cooperative Work* (Austin, Tex., Dec. 3–5). ACM, New York, 1986, pp. 73–90.

8. HILTZ, S. R., AND TUROFF, M.   Structuring computer-mediated communication systems to avoid information overload. *Commun. ACM 28*, 7 (7), (July 1985), 680–689.

9. KOEHLER, J. W., ANATOL, K. W., AND APPLEBAUM, R. L.   *Organizational Communication: Behavioral Perspectives*. Holt, Rinehart, and Winston, New York, 1976.

10. MACKENZIE, R. A.   *The Time Trap*. Amacom, New York, 1972.

11. MALONE, T. W.   How do people organize their desks? Implications for the design of office information systems. *ACM Trans. Off. Inf. Syst. 1*, 1 (Jan. 1983), 99–112.

12. MALONE, T. W., GRANT, K. R., LAI, K. Y., RAO, R., AND ROSENBLITT, D. R.   Semistructured messages are surprisingly useful for computer-supported coordination. *ACM Trans. Off. Inf. Syst. 5*, 2 (Apr. 1987), 115–131.

13. MALONE, T. W., GRANT, K. R., TURBAK, R. A., BROBST, S. A., AND COHEN, M.D.   Intelligent information-sharing systems. *Commun. ACM 30* (June 1987), 484–497.

14. SPROULL, L., AND KIESLER, S.   Reducing social context cues: Electronic mail in organizational communication. *Manage. Sci. 32*, 11 (1986) 1492–1512.

15. STASZ, C., AND BIKSON, T.   Computer-supported cooperative work: Examples and issues in one federal agency. In *Proceedings of the Conference for Computer-Supported Cooperative Work* (Austin, Tex., Dec. 3–5). ACM, New York, 1986, pp. 318–324.

16. TRICKETT, J. M.   A more effective use of time. *California Management Review 4*, 4, 1962.

17. TRIGG, R. H., AND IRISH, P. M.   Hypertext habitats: Experiences of writers in NoteCards. In *Proceedings of Hypertext '87* (Chapel Hill, N.C., Nov. 13–15). ACM Press, New York, 1987.

18. VON HIPPEL, E.   Lead users: A source of novel product concepts. *Manage. Sci. 32*, 7 (1986), 791–805.

19. WEBBER, R. A.   *Time and Management*. Van Nostrand Rineholt, New York, 1972.

20. WEICK, K. E.   The twigging of overload. In *People and Information*, H. B. Pepinsky, Ed., Pergamon, New York, 1970.

21. WILSON, G. L., GOODALL, H. L., AND WAAGEN, C. L.   *Organizational Communication*. Harper and Row, New York, 1986.

Received June 1988; revised September 1988; accepted October 1988

Object Lens: A "Spreadsheet" for Cooperative Work

KUM-YEW LAI, THOMAS W. MALONE, and KEH-CHIANG YU
Massachusetts Institute of Technology

Object Lens allows unsophisticated computer users to create their own cooperative work applications using a set of simple, but powerful, building blocks. By defining and modifying templates for various semistructured objects, users can represent information about people, tasks, products, messages, and many other kinds of information in a form that can be processed intelligently by both people and their computers. By collecting these objects in customizable folders, users can create their own displays which summarize selected information from the objects in table or tree formats. Finally, by creating semiautonomous agents, users can specify rules for automatically processing this information in different ways at different times.

The combination of these primitives provides a single consistent interface that integrates facilities for object-oriented databases, hypertext, electronic messaging, and rule-based intelligent agents. To illustrate the power of this combined approach, we describe several simple examples of applications (such as task tracking, intelligent message routing, and database retrieval) that we have developed in this framework.

Categories and Subject Descriptors: H.1.2 [**Models and Principles**]: User/Machine Systems; H.2.1 [**Database Management**]: Logical Design—*data models*; *schema and subschema*; H.2.3 [**Database Management**]: Languages—*data description languages (DDL)*; H.2.4 [**Database Management**]: Systems—*distributed systems*; H.3.1 [**Information Storage and Retrieval**]: Content Analysis and Indexing; H.3.4 [**Information Storage and Retrieval**]: Systems and Software; H.4.1 [**Information Systems Applications**]: Office Automation; H.4.3 [**Information Systems Applications**]: Communications Applications; I.2.1 [**Artificial Intelligence**]: Applications and Expert Systems—*office automation*; I.2.4 [**Artificial Intelligence**]: Knowledge Representation Formalisms and Methods—*frames and scripts*; *representations*; I.7.2 [**Text Processing**]: Document Preparation—*format and notation*

General Terms: Design, Economics, Human Factors, Management

Additional Key Words and Phrases: Computer-supported cooperative work, hypertext, information lens, intelligent agents, object-oriented databases, semiformal systems

1. INTRODUCTION

It is common in the computer industry today to talk about the "next spreadsheet"—to claim that a particular application will be the "next spreadsheet" or to wonder what the "next spreadsheet" will be (e.g., [7]). Usually the term

The work described in this paper was supported, in part, by Wang Laboratories, Xerox Corporation, General Motors/Electronic Data Systems, Bankers Trust Company, the Development Bank of Singapore, and the Management in the 1990s Research Program at the Sloan School of Management, MIT.

Authors' current addresses: K.-Y. Lai, 10-174 Block 129, Bukit Merah View, Singapore 0315, Republic of Singapore; T. W. Malone and K.-C. Yu, Sloan School of Management (E53-333), Massachusetts Institute of Technology, Cambridge, Mass. 02139.

"spreadsheet" is used in this context simply to connote a product that embodies some kind of design breakthrough and is very successful.

We will focus here on a more specific property of spreadsheet programs: They make a restricted, but nevertheless, very flexible and useful, set of computational capabilities extremely easy to use. It is, of course, possible to do any computation a spreadsheet can do in a general purpose programming language. But because doing these things with a spreadsheet program is so much more convenient, the number of people who can use computers to do them increases by orders of magnitude.

In this paper, we describe an early prototype of a system, called Object Lens, which we believe shares this property of spreadsheets: It makes accessible to unsophisticated computer users a set of computational and communications capabilities that, although limited, are quite flexible and useful for supporting a wide variety of cooperative work activities. In other words, we use the term "spreadsheet" here, not to connote financial modeling or constraint languages, but to connote a flexible infrastructure in which people who are not professional programmers can create or modify their own computer applications.

In the remainder of this paper we (1) describe the key ideas used in the design of Object Lens, (2) show how these ideas are realized in Object Lens features, and (3) illustrate the flexibility and usefulness of these ideas in several examples of cooperative work.

1.1 Three Views of Object Lens

Before proceeding, it is useful to point out three ways of viewing the Object Lens system.

(1) *Object Lens is the "second generation" of the Information Lens system.* Object Lens is based on our experience with using and enhancing the Information Lens [13, 14], an intelligent system for information sharing and coordination. A very large number of the enhancements that we and others have suggested for the Information Lens are included in Object Lens. Like the Information Lens, Object Lens uses ideas from artificial intelligence and user interface design to represent knowledge in such a way that both people and their computational agents can process it intelligently. Object Lens, however, is a significant generalization of the Information Lens. It potentially goes far beyond the Information Lens in the kinds of knowledge that can be represented and the ways that information can be manipulated.

(2) *Object Lens is a user interface that integrates hypertext, object-oriented databases, electronic messaging, and rule-based intelligent agents.* Object Lens does not include all the capabilities of all these different classes of systems, but we have been surprised at how cleanly a large portion of these diverse capabilities can be integrated. The key contribution of Object Lens is thus not the completeness of its implementation, but the integration of its user interface. Since the capabilities of these different kinds of systems are no longer separate applications, each capability is more useful than it would be alone, and the resulting system is unusually flexible.

(3) *Object Lens is a knowledge-based environment for developing cooperative work applications.* In the original Information Lens system, we developed specific

applications for information sharing, meeting scheduling, project management, and computer conferencing. From the viewpoint of knowledge-based systems, these applications only included knowledge about different types of messages: the kinds of information the messages contained and the kinds of actions they could evoke. Object Lens, by contrast, can include explicit knowledge about many other kinds of objects such as people, tasks, meetings, products, and companies. We expect that the flexible tools Object Lens provides for dealing with these diverse kinds of knowledge will significantly increase the ease of developing a much wider range of applications. This last view of Object Lens, which emphasizes its flexibility, is our primary focus in this paper.

2. KEY IDEAS

One of the most important characteristics of Object Lens is that it is a *semiformal system*. We define a semiformal system as a computer system that has the following three properties: (1) it represents and automatically processes certain information in formally specified ways; (2) it represents and makes it easy for humans to process the same or other information in ways that are not formally specified; and (3) it allows the boundary between formal processing by computers and informal processing by people to be easily changed.

Semiformal systems are most useful when we understand enough to formalize in a computer system some, but not all, of the knowledge relevant to acting in a given situation. Such systems are often useful in supporting individual work, and we believe they are especially important in supporting cooperative work where there are usually some well-understood patterns in people's behavior and also a very large amount of other knowledge that is potentially relevant but difficult to specify.

In order to create such a flexible semiformal system, the knowledge embodied in the system must be exposed to users in a way that is both *visible* and *changeable* (cf., [20]). That is, users must be able to easily see and change the information and the processing rules included in the system. In Object Lens, there are three key ideas about how to represent and expose knowledge to users:

(1) "Passive" information is represented in *semistructured objects* with template-based interfaces;
(2) "Aggregate" information from collections of objects is summarized in *customizable folders*; and
(3) "Active" rules for processing information are represented in *semiautonomous agents*.

In the remainder of Section 2, we provide an overview of how these three components allow us to expose knowledge to users in a way that is both visible and changeable. Detailed descriptions of the system features are in Section 3.

2.1 Semistructured Objects

Users of the Object Lens system can create, modify, retrieve, and display objects that represent many physically or conceptually familiar things such as messages, people, meetings, tasks, manufactured parts, and software bugs. The system provides an interface to an object-oriented database in the sense that (1) each object includes a collection of fields and field values, (2) each object type has a set of actions that can be performed upon it, and (3) the objects are arranged in a hierarchy of increasingly specialized types with each object type "inheriting" fields, actions, and other properties from its "parents" [4, 16, 17]. For example, a TASK object may have fields like Requestor, Performer, Description, and Deadline; a PERSON object may have fields like Name, Phone, Address, and Job title; and a STUDENT object may add fields like Year and Advisor to the fields present in all PERSON objects. Some objects (e.g., MESSAGES) have specialized actions defined for them (e.g., Answer and Forward). As described in more detail below, we have provided rudimentary facilities for saving and sharing objects, and we are currently exploring ways to link our interface to remote databases.

The objects in Object Lens, like messages in the Information Lens, are *semistructured* in the sense that users can fill in as much or as little information in different fields as they desire, and the information in a field is not necessarily of any specific type (e.g., it may be free text such as "I don't know").

2.1.1 *Template-Based User Interfaces.* Users can see and change objects through a particularly natural form of template-based user interface. These interfaces have a number of virtues. For instance: (1) they resemble forms, with which users are already familiar; (2) they conveniently inform users about the fields contained in an object and about other information such as the likely alternatives for different fields; and (3) their use is consistent across many different kinds of objects. We discuss later how this interface approach, which was used for messages and rules in the Information Lens, can be easily generalized to many different kinds of objects.

2.1.2 *Relationships Among Objects.* Users can easily see and change the relationships among objects by inserting and deleting *links* between the objects. For instance, the Requestor and Performer fields of a Task object might contain links to the Person objects that represent, respectively, the person who requested that the task be done and the person who performs the task. Then, for instance, when the user looks at the Task object, it is easy to get more information (e.g., the phone numbers) about the people involved with the task. We discuss later how this capability of linking objects to each other provides a rudimentary *hypertext* system as a special case (see [1] for an extensive review of hypertext systems). We also show how it is also possible for an object, to which a link appears, to be displayed as an *embedded template* inside the original template.

2.1.3 *Tailorable Display Formats.* Users have several options for changing the ways they see objects. For instance, they can easily (1) select which fields are to be shown and which are to be suppressed, (2) rename selected fields, and (3) specify the default and alternative values the system presents for individual fields.

2.1.4 *Inheritance Hierarchy for Objects.* The creation and modification of type definitions is simplified by arranging object types in an inheritance hierarchy (e.g., [17]). New types of objects are defined as specializations of existing object types, and they automatically "inherit" all properties of the existing objects except those which are specifically "overridden." Since most of the information about new object types can thus be "inherited" from existing types, rather than having to be reentered each time, creating new object types becomes simpler. Also, when an object type definition is changed later, the changes are automatically "inherited" by the specializations of that object type.

2.2 Customizable Folders

Users of Object Lens can group collections of objects together into special kinds of objects called Folders. For instance, folders can be created for groups of people (e.g., project teams, company directory), tasks (e.g., those completed, those to be done by you, those to be done by others), messages (grouped according to topic or urgency), and so forth. Users can also easily customize their own displays to summarize the contents of objects in a folder. For instance, they can select certain fields to be displayed in a *table* with each row representing an object in the folder and each column representing a field. They can also select fields from which the links between objects can be used to create a *tree* (or graph) display with each object represented as a node in the tree and each link in the selected field represented as a line between nodes.

2.3 Semiautonomous Agents

Users of the Object Lens system can create rule-based "agents" that process information automatically on behalf of their users (see [2] for an extended discussion of agents). These agents provide a natural way of partitioning the tasks performed automatically by the system. As discussed later, agents can be "triggered" by events such as the arrival of new mail, the appearance of a new object in a specified folder, the arrival of a prespecified time, or an explicit selection by the user. When an agent is triggered, it applies a set of rules to a specified collection of objects. If an object satisfies the criteria specified in a rule, the rule performs some prespecified action. These actions can be general actions such as retrieving, classifying, mailing, and deleting objects or object-specific actions such as loading files or adding events to a calendar.

The agents in Object Lens are *autonomous* in the sense that once they have been created, they can take actions without the explicit attention of a human user. They are only *semiautonomous*, however, in the sense that (a) they are always controlled by a human user (that is, all their rules can be easily seen and changed by their human user), and (b) they may often "refer" objects to their human user for action (e.g., by leaving the object in the user's inbox) instead of taking any actions on their own.

2.3.1 *Descriptions.* Since agents and rules are themselves objects, users can see and modify them with the same template-based user interface that is used for all other kinds of objects. To specify the criteria for when rules should act upon a given object, users create *descriptions* of the objects to which the rules apply. A description is simply a partially filled-in template for an object of a particular type. Descriptions can also include *embedded descriptions* that specify characteristics that must be satisfied by objects to which the original object is linked. For instance, a description of a Task might include an embedded description of the person who performs the task. These embedded descriptions (like those in the Rabbit system [19]), allow users to easily specify object retrieval operations that are equivalent to "joins" followed by "selects" in a relational database.

3. SYSTEM FEATURES

In this section, we describe in more detail the basic system features of Object Lens and illustrate them with simple examples (see [10] for more details about an earlier version of the system). The Object Lens system is implemented in Interlisp-D on Xerox 1100 series workstations connected by an Ethernet. The system makes heavy use of the object-oriented programming environment provided by Loops and the built-in text editor, Tedit. Except where otherwise noted, everything described here has been implemented, but many features have not yet been extensively tested. As of this writing, the basic mail handling capabilities have been used regularly by two people in our development group for about six months, and the other facilities have received limited testing.

3.1 Terminology: Objects and Templates

Before proceeding it is helpful to clarify some terminology concerning objects and templates. First, we distinguish between *object types* (or "classes") and specific *object instances* (e.g., see [5]). We use the term *object type* to refer to a kind of object (such as Person or Task) and the term *object instance* (or simply "instance") to refer to a specific example of one of these object types (e.g., "Joe Smith" or "Task No. 17"). In contexts in which the distinction between object types and object instances is not critical, we use the term *objects* to include both.

We also use the term *template* in two ways. First, in a general sense, we use the term *template* to mean any semistructured collection of fields and field contents. Most of a user's interactions with Object Lens are based on such templates. Second, in the Object Lens screen displays, we use the word Template to mean object type definition. (When we use Template in this specialized sense, we always capitalize it.) For instance, users can change the display format for all Person objects by editing the Template that defines the Person object type.

3.2 Editing Instances

Figure 1 shows a template for an instance of a Person. Using the built-in text editor, users can insert text or bitmaps in any field. In addition, when users click on a field name with the mouse, a list of likely alternative values for that field appears in a pop-up menu. The alternatives may be links to other objects or just text strings. Selecting one of these alternatives causes the alternative to be automatically inserted in the field. For instance, the figure contains a link to the Person object representing Kum-Yew Lai's supervisor. To insert links to objects that are not in the alternatives list, the user (a) positions the cursor at the place in the template where the link is to be inserted, (b) selects the Add Link option from the menu at the top of the window, and then (c) points to the object to which the link should be made. After a link is inserted, clicking on it with the mouse causes the object it points to to appear on the screen.

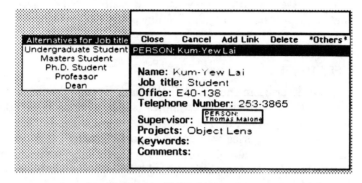

Fig. 1. Objects can be edited with a simple template editor. Fields can include text, graphics, or links to other objects.

In the current version of Object Lens, users can insert any combination of text, numbers, links, and bitmaps in any field. Then, in some cases, type checking is done when the editing window for the instance is closed or when certain kinds of processing are done. For instance, the To and cc fields are checked for valid addresses before sending messages and the "move to" field in rule actions is checked for valid folders (see Sections 3.5 and 3.7 for descriptions of rules and folders). In future versions of Object Lens, we may experiment with more restrictive type enforcement in certain fields. For instance, it should probably be impossible to even insert something other than a folder in the "move to" field of a rule action.

Figure 2 shows a slightly more complex template; this one is for a Bug Fix Request message. One of the fields of this template is the Bug to be fixed, and the value of this field is a link to a Bug object. In this case, instead of simply showing a link to the Bug object, the template contains an *embedded template* for the Bug object itself. The fields in this embedded template can be edited just like the rest of the fields in the template. We later discuss how users can specify whether links to other objects should be displayed as *link icons* (as in Figure 1) or as *embedded templates* (as in Figure 2).

3.3 Creating New Instances

To create and display a new instance of an object type that already exists, users click with the mouse on the definition (i.e., the Template) for that object type. Figure 3 shows the Templates currently included in our system. For instance, to send a new message, users click on the Template for the type of message they want to create; to create a new person object, users click on the Person Template. Then an object instance, like those shown in Figures 1 and 2, appear, and the user can fill it in.

3.4 Creating New Object Types

To create a new object type, users click (with both mouse buttons instead of the left one) on the Template for the "parent" object type (see Figure 3). This causes a menu to appear showing alternative actions that can be performed on a Template. One of these actions is to Create a subtemplate. When the

428

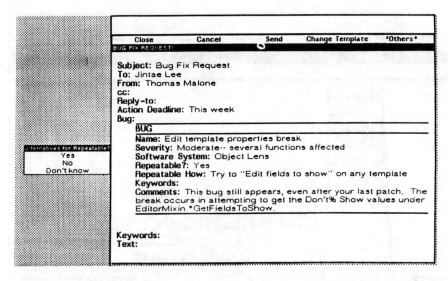

Fig. 2. Embedded templates allow related objects to be viewed and edited simultaneously.

user selects this action, a new `Template` is created with all the fields and
properties of its "parent." Then users can add fields to the new Template or
change its display format and other properties.

In the current version of Object Lens, all `Things` have three fields: `Name`,
`Keywords`, and `Comments`. All objects inherit these fields, though as discussed
below, some objects rename these fields or suppress their display. For instance,
`Messages`, rename the `Name` field to be `Subject` and the `Comments` field to
be `Text`.

3.5 Changing the Display Format and Other Properties of Object Types

To change the display format or other properties of an object type, users "edit"
the `Template` that defines the object type. Users make these changes by
selecting actions from the menu that appears when they click on the `Template`
(as shown in Figure 3) with both mouse buttons. In this way, users can change
(a) which fields of the objects are actually displayed, (b) the names of the fields
that are displayed, (c) the alternative values that are displayed for each field, (d)
the default values that are displayed in each field when new instances are created,
and (e) whether the links in a field should be shown as link icons (see Figure 1)
or as embedded templates (see Figure 2). In this mode, users can also add or
delete fields from a template. All the changes made to a template are applied to
old instances of an object type as well as to newly created ones. For example, if
a user changes the name of a field, then the new name is shown when any old
instances are redisplayed.

We anticipate that this system will be used with a core set of object types
shared by the users in a group, and that the fields in these types will be modified
only by an "authorized view administrator." Other users will be able to change
the display format of these types (e.g., suppress the display of a field or change
its name), but they would not be able to delete or add fields to these "official"

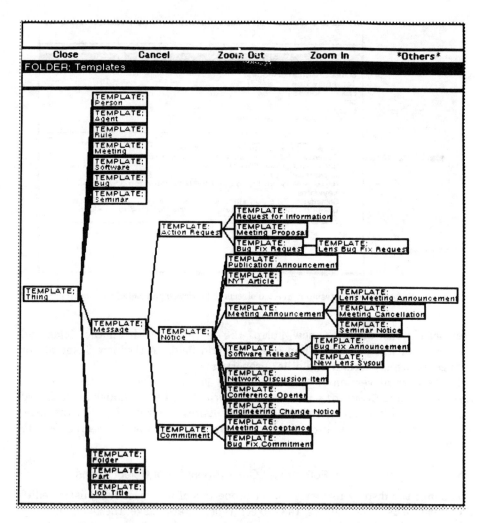

Fig. 3. Object types are defined by a set of Templates.

types. All users would, however, be able to create their own types as specializations of the official types, and for these types they could add and delete new fields as desired. Elsewhere [11, 12], we have proposed a scheme for letting an arbitrarily large number of groups share partially overlapping sets of type definitions in arbitrary ways. One of the key ideas of this scheme is that specialized types created by one group can be interpreted by members of another group as instances of the most specific "ancestor" type that both groups share. For instance, a "Student" object created by one group might be interpreted as a "Person" object by another group that does not have a definition for "Student."

3.6 Folders

As previously noted, Object Lens users can group collections of objects together into special kinds of objects called Folders (see Figure 4). An object can be

430

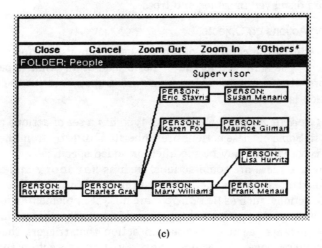

Fig. 4. Users can select which fields to display in tables that summarize a collection of objects.

added to a folder in two ways: (1) automatically, as the result of a rule action, or (2) manually using the Add Link action from the *Others* submenu on the folder. In both cases, the folders contain links to the objects, not the objects themselves. Therefore, the same object can appear in more than one folder. Other actions for moving, copying, and deleting both objects and links are described in Section 3.7.

Object Lens currently provides two formats for displaying the contents of folders: *tables* and *trees*. Tables show the values of selected fields from the objects contained in the folder. For instance, Figure 4(a) shows a folder that contains objects representing people with the fields for a simple office directory displayed. Users can easily tailor the format of these displays by selecting from a menu the fields they want to have included in the table. For instance, Figure 4(b) shows the same folder, but with the display format changed to include a different set of fields.

Trees are graphs that show the objects in a folder and the links that connect these objects. Just as users can select the fields to be shown in a table, they can also select the fields from which links are shown. For instance, Figure 4(c) shows the same folder again, but this time in tree format with the "Supervisor" field selected as the one from which links are displayed. In this case, the display resembles a simple organization chart. In the current version of Object Lens, only the links in one field at a time can be displayed in a tree. In future versions, we plan to allow links from multiple fields to be shown with the links from different fields being displayed as different types of lines (e.g., solid, dotted).

When a new folder is created, the user is asked to select the default object type to be contained in the folder. The user is then allowed to choose from the fields of this default object type when selecting the fields to show in a table or when selecting the fields from which links are to be shown in a tree. Even though all folders have default object types, no strict type checking is enforced. If an object of an unexpected type is inserted into a folder, only the fields it shares with the default type are displayed in tables and trees.

3.7 Performing Actions on Objects

In addition to editing the contents of objects, users can also perform predefined actions on them. The actions that can be performed at any time depend on two primary factors: (1) the type of object being acted upon, and (2) the context in which the action is invoked.

3.7.1 *Object Specific Actions.* Each object type has a set of actions that can be performed on it. Some of these actions are "inherited" directly from the "parents" of the object type. Others may be modified or added specifically for this object type. For instance, there are some actions, such as Hardcopy and Save, that can be performed on all objects (i.e., all instances of Thing and all its subtypes). (Some of these actions, such as Hardcopy, are not yet implemented for all object types.) In addition, more specialized types of objects have other actions defined for them. For instance, agents have a Run action that triggers them to start running, and folders have a Change Display Format action that changes them from table format to tree format or vice versa.

In a few cases, the object specific actions depend, not just on the type of the object, but also on its state. For instance, messages created on the local workstation have a Send action, and messages received from elsewhere have actions such as Answer and Forward. So far these state-specific actions on objects are implemented as special cases. However, we would like to experiment with a more general mechanism for representing state-specific actions and perhaps making this representation accessible to users. In some ways, this mechanism would be a generalization of the conversation manager in the Coordinator [21], which restricts the types of messages that a user can send at a given point in a conversation on the basis of the conversation state.

3.7.2 *Context Specific Actions.* There are some actions that can be applied to any kind of object but which can be invoked only from certain contexts. The primary contexts are (1) from an editor (like the one in Figure 1), (2) from a folder that contains the object, (3) from a rule operating on the object, and (4) from a link icon for the object.

For instance, when an object is being displayed in an editor, there are several kinds of actions, such as Close, Move, and Shape, that apply to the editing window. Other actions in an editor include (a) Add Link (insert at the current cursor position a link to another object selected by the user) and (b) Cancel (close the window without saving any of the changes made since the window was last opened).

When an object is displayed in a folder, other context-specific actions can be applied to it such as (a) Show (open an editor on the object) and (b) Select (select the item for some later folder action such as Delete Selection).

The actions that can be applied to an object by rules are discussed in Section 3.8. The actions that can be applied to link icons include Show (open an editor on the object) and Delete (delete this link to the object).

3.7.3 *Displaying and Invoking Actions.* Users invoke the above actions in slightly different ways depending on the context in which the object is displayed. If the object is displayed in an editor (like the one in Figure 1), then several of its most common actions are shown across the top of the editor, and all the other actions are shown in a menu that pops up when the *Others* action is selected.

When a link to an object is displayed (either as a link icon or as a row in a table), users can invoke actions in two ways. First, if users click on the link with both mouse buttons, a menu pops up showing all possible actions on the object. In addition, simply clicking on the link with the left mouse button invokes the most common action. For instance, clicking with the left button on a row in a table Selects the object for subsequent folder actions, whereas clicking with the left button on a link icon inside an editor Shows the object in another window on the screen.

3.8 Creating Agents and Rules

In some cases, agents can take actions automatically on behalf of their users. For instance, Figure 5 shows an example of a simple agent designed to help a user process incoming mail. When an agent is triggered, it applies a set of rules to a collection of objects in a folder. The agent in Figure 5 is applied to objects in the New Mail folder and is triggered by the arrival of new mail. That is, when mail is brought to the workstation, the mail program automatically inserts links to the new messages into the user's New Mail folder, and these New Links trigger the agent. In the current version of Object Lens, two other kinds of automatic triggers are available: Daily at Midnight and On the Hour.

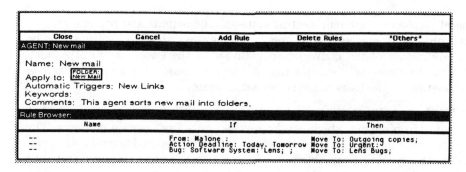

Fig. 5. Agents include a collection of rules and specifications for when and where to apply them.

The agent shown in Figure 5 includes several rules, one of which is shown in Figure 6. A rule contains an IF field (predicate) and a THEN field (action). Both parts of the rule contain links to other objects which are shown as embedded templates. The IF part of the rule is a *description*, a special kind of template that describes a set of instances in terms of the values of their fields. The THEN part of the rule is an Action object.

To construct the IF part of a rule, a user (a) clicks on the IF field with the middle mouse button, (b) selects "Descriptions" from the menu presented, and then (c) selects an object type from the tree of object types presented. This causes a description of the appropriate type to be inserted in the rule as an embedded template, and the user can then fill in the fields in this description to specify the values that must appear in particular fields for an object to satisfy the rule. As in the Information Lens, more complex specifications for a field can be constructed by combining strings with *and, or, not*, and parentheses (i.e., arbitrary Boolean combinations are possible within a field). If specifications appear in more than one field, then all specifications must be satisfied at once for the rule to succeed (i.e., specifications in different fields are implicitly *and*-ed). As in the other template-based editors in Object Lens, pop-up menus listing likely alternatives for a field are available in editing descriptions.

To specify the THEN part of a rule, a user simply clicks on the THEN field and selects an action from the menu of alternatives presented. These actions are applied to the *current object* (the object matched by the IF part of the rule) in the context of the *current folder* (the folder specified in the "Apply to" field of the agent). In some cases (such as the "Move" action shown here), the user also needs to fill in some fields in the embedded template for the action (e.g., the field specifying where the object is to be moved). The actions currently implemented in rules include the following: copy (add the current object to a different folder without removing it from the current folder), move (add the current object to a different folder and delete it from the current folder), delete (remove the object from the current folder), and add keyword (add the specified keyword to the Keywords field of the object). In addition, rules can invoke object specific actions, including the actions that apply to all objects such as hardcopy and save. We view the addition of more rule actions (and possibly the refinement of the rule syntax) as one of the important directions for our ongoing research.

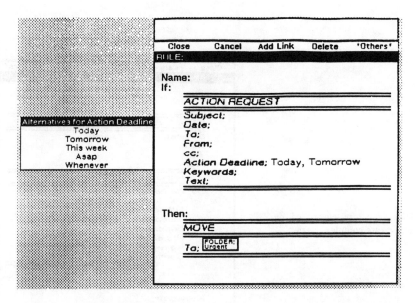

Fig. 6. Rules describe the objects that satisfy them and specify what action to perform on those objects.

The rules are applied in the order in which they appear in the agent's rule folder. Users can create extended reasoning chains by having some rules set characteristics of objects (using the Add Keyword action) which other rules test (by checking the Keyword field).

3.8.1 *Embedded Descriptions.* With the capabilities we have described so far, all rules must depend only on information contained in the objects to which they are being applied. For instance, a rule about a message can depend only on information contained in the message itself. It is often desirable, however, to be able to specify rules that also depend on other information contained elsewhere in the knowledge base. For instance, in the Information Lens system, if a user wanted to specify a rule that applied to all messages from vice presidents, the rule would have to include the names of all the vice presidents in the From field.

In Object Lens, it is possible to draw upon other information by having descriptions embedded within other descriptions. For instance, the rule shown in Figure 7 is satisfied if the message is from any person with a job title that includes "vice president." To apply this rule, the system checks to see whether the string in the From field of the message is the same as the Name of any Person object in the knowledge base that satisfies the description.

3.9 Navigating Through the System

The starting point for navigation through the Object Lens system is the Object Lens Icon, a window that shows whether the user has new mail waiting and includes a menu item to Show Basics (show the basic folders included in the system). The system folders accessible through the Show Basics action include (1) a folder containing all the other folders in the system, (2) a folder containing all the Templates defined in the system (Figure 3), (3) a folder containing all

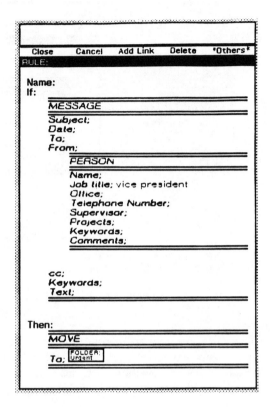

Fig. 7. Rules can use embedded descriptions to create complex queries.

the agents defined in the system, (4) a folder for each object type containing all the instances of that type in the system, and (5) the New Mail folder, into which new mail retrieved from the mail server is automatically inserted. In addition, we have designed but not fully implemented two other folders: (6) Everything, a virtual folder containing all objects in the system, and (7) Orphans, a virtual folder containing all objects to which no links exist.

These basic folders provide users with convenient starting points for locating any object in the system. In relatively small systems, users can browse through these folders directly. In larger systems, we expect users to let their agents search through the system folders to find objects that meet certain criteria. It is also possible for (a) individual users to create their own customized directory folders that contain the folders and other objects they most often use, and (b) application developers to create folders containing the objects used in their application.

3.10 Saving and Sharing Knowledge

One of the important research directions we plan to pursue in the Object Lens system involves different ways for people to save and share the kinds of knowledge described above. For instance, we are currently experimenting with linking Object Lens to a remote database server which contains large shared relational databases. This work is still at an early stage, but it is clear that the usefulness of Object Lens is significantly enhanced if it includes access to shared databases.

436

In the current version of Object Lens, we have preliminary solutions to the problems of saving and sharing knowledge that meet some, but not all, of the needs people have in this area.

3.10.1 *Saving Knowledge.* Users can save an object (or a collection of objects in a folder) at any time by performing the Save action on the object (or the folder). This action uses the file package commands from the underlying Loops and Lisp systems to store the objects in permanent files in a form that can be reloaded at any time. There is also a Save action on the main Object Lens icon that saves all the instances in the workstation.

The potential disadvantages of this approach to saving knowledge are that (1) it requires explicit user actions to save objects in permanent storage and (2) it requires all knowledge used by the system to be loaded onto the local workstation. Sharing remote databases, of course, helps solve these problems, but we expect that systems like Object Lens can be of value even without shared databases. For example, many users are already accustomed to explicitly saving their work in applications such as word processing, and even this task can be simplified by creating agents to run periodically (e.g., every night) and do automatic backups of selected objects.

3.10.2 *Sharing Knowledge by Sending Messages.* There are two ways users of Object Lens can share objects with each other: (1) by sending messages, and (2) by transferring files. In this subsection, we discuss sending messages; in the next, we discuss transferring files. When an Object Lens user sends a message, the message object is converted into text and sent via the existing mail system. Any connected electronic mail users can receive and read this textual message. When an Object Lens user receives the message, it is added as a new object in the receiver's knowledge base.

When a user sends a message containing an embedded object that is expanded (as in Figure 2), the embedded object is converted into (indented) text in the message in a form that (a) can be easily read by any receivers who are not using Object Lens, and (b) is reconverted into another embedded object when it is received by Object Lens users. When a user sends a message containing embedded objects that are *not* expanded (e.g., that are shown only as link icons), the names of the objects are included in the message in place of the link icons, but these names are not resolved back into link icons at the receiver's end.

One intriguing research direction here involves how to communicate embedded objects in such a way that they can be resolved into preexisting objects at the receiver's end. For example, if the sender's message contains a link to a person object, it would be nice for the receiver's system to be able to automatically resolve this link into the receiver's object representing the same person.

3.10.3 *Sharing Knowledge by Transferring Files.* The second way for users to share objects is by transferring files. As described above, it is easy for users to store on a file server the current state of a set of objects. Other users can then load these files to create (or update) the objects in their own workstations. Saving and loading these files can often be done automatically. For example, we expect that a common way for users to keep current versions of shared information such as names, addresses, and job titles of people in their organization is to have someone maintain the official version of this information and periodically distribute updates to other users in the organization. Distributing these updates could be done in several ways: (1) the maintainer could have automatic agents that periodically store the current versions on a file server, and the other users could have automatic agents that periodically load the most recent versions, or (2) the maintainer could explicitly send out messages announcing the availability of files containing updated objects, and the other users could have agents that automatically load the files announced in such messages (e.g., a rule might load all files specified in "Official file update" messages from the official maintainer).

One potential problem with this approach is that any changes users have made to their local copies of objects (e.g., any notes they had added in the Comments field) are lost when a new version of the object is loaded. To help solve this problem, we are currently investigating more specialized updating actions for agents to use. With this approach, the official maintainer will be able to distribute update messages that specify changes in particular fields of particular objects. Users can then set up agents that make these updates automatically under most conditions, but under certain conditions the user might be notified before the update is made (e.g., if the field about to be modified has previously been changed by the user). In some cases, the user might want to have the change made automatically but also want to be notified (e.g., if someone in the user's group is changing phone numbers).

4. OTHER APPLICATIONS

In this section, we give more examples of how the above features can be combined to create a variety of cooperative work applications.

4.1 Task Tracking

One frequently mentioned capability for cooperative work applications is the ability to keep track of the tasks people are supposed to do (e.g, [18, 22]). For instance, such systems can help answer questions like: What tasks have other people requested me to do? Are any of these tasks overdue? What tasks have I requested other people to do for me?

Supporting capabilities like this in Object Lens is a straightforward matter. For instance, the system already includes message types for action requests and commitments. Even in the Information Lens, it was possible to automatically sort these messages into folders according to who is to perform the task, which project it involves, and so forth. In the Information Lens, however, the summary display of a folder's contents shows only the standard message header fields: From, Date, and Subject. To see more about the tasks, individual messages have to be displayed, one at a time. In Object Lens, the messages within a folder can easily be summarized by displaying whatever fields the user chooses. For example, Figure 8 shows a table display of action request messages that includes the action deadline.

4.2 Intelligent Message Sorting: Engineering Change Notices

As we have described in more detail elsewhere [15], an intriguing example of a cooperative work problem involves disseminating information about changes in

438

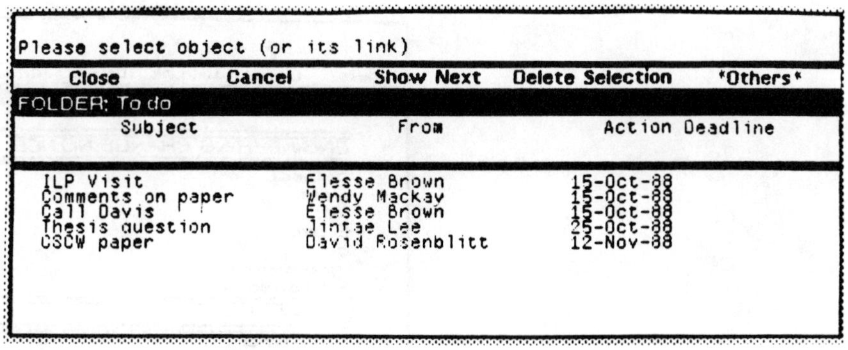

```
Please select object (or its link)
  Close          Cancel        Show Next   Delete Selection   *Others*
FOLDER: To do
          Subject                 From                Action Deadline

  ILP Visit                Elesse Brown           15-Oct-88
  Comments on paper        Wendy Mackay           15-Oct-88
  Call Davis               Elesse Brown           15-Oct-88
  Thesis question          Jintae Lee             25-Oct-88
  CSCW paper               David Rosenblitt       12-Nov-88
```

Fig. 8. Tables can be used to summarize selected fields from Action Request messages.

product specifications (often called "engineering change notices") to the appropriate people in an organization. It was already possible in the Information Lens to sort engineering change notices according to the contents of fields such as Part Affected, Type of Change, and Severity. In Object Lens, it is possible to use additional knowledge to do even more intelligent sorting. For instance, Figure 9 shows a rule that uses a doubly embedded description to select all change notices that involve parts for which anyone reporting to a particular manager is responsible.

4.3 Database Retrieval

There are clearly many cases in both individual and cooperative work when it is useful to be able to automatically retrieve objects that satisfy certain conditions from a database. Object Lens provides a simple way to perform database queries: Users can simply create agents that scan the objects in one folder and insert links to selected objects into another folder. The rules in the agents specify the criteria for selecting objects.

For instance, suppose you wanted to find all the technical staff members who were assigned to both the project code-named "Dragon" and the one code-named "Lancelot." Figure 10 shows a rule that would retrieve all such people. Instead of listing all the technical job titles by name ("software engineer," "systems programmer," etc.), the rule includes an embedded description to determine whether a particular job title is on the technical, as opposed to the managerial or administrative, career ladder.

In addition to this general interface for database retrieval, we have also implemented a specialized feature in Object Lens for determining the recipients of messages. With this feature, descriptions (like that shown in the IF field of Figure 10) can be embedded in the To and cc fields of a message. Then, when the message is sent, these descriptions are automatically applied to all the Person objects in the local knowledge base, and the resulting people are inserted in the To and cc fields. This feature allows senders to create distribution lists that are dynamically computed at message-sending time on the basis of current information about people in their database (see [23] for a similar capability).

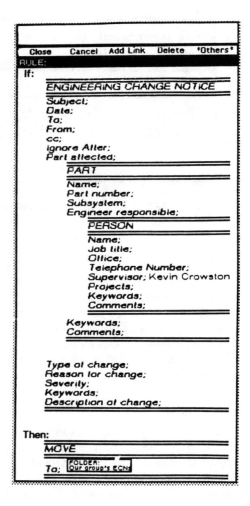

Fig. 9. Rules can include multiple levels of embedded descriptions that refer to linked objects throughout the knowledge base.

4.4 Hypertext

As noted above, it is a straightforward matter to use many of the features of a hypertext system in Object Lens (e.g., [3, 6, 9]). For instance, our system currently contains an object type called Text that displays only two fields: Name and Text. The Text field of a Text object can contain links to as many other objects as desired. For example, Figure 11 shows a sample Text object that contains links to people and bibliographic citations as well as to another Text object.

In addition to the usual benefits of hypertext systems, Object Lens derives additional benefits from its integration of hypertext with other database, messaging, and computational capabilities. For instance, in order to insert a link to another node in a hypertext system, a user must first find the node to which the link will be made. In Object Lens, the database retrieval capabilities described above can be used to automatically find objects (such as people or bibliographic citations) that satisfy certain criteria. Then links to these objects can be inserted into the text. One desirable feature found in some hypertext systems that is not yet included in Object Lens is the ability to show and follow the incoming links

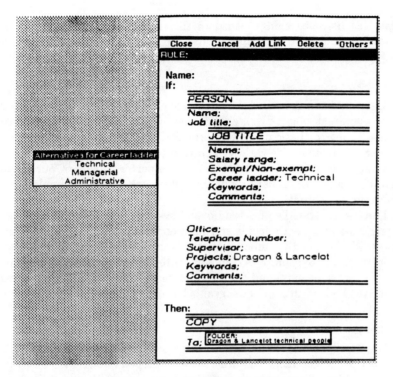

Fig. 10.   Agents can retrieve all the objects from a database that satisfy certain criteria.

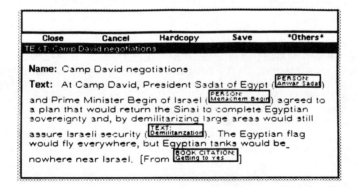

Fig. 11.   Hypertext documents can include links, not only to other text passages, but also to other object types such as people and bibliographic citations.

to an object. We would like to implement this capability as another action available on all objects.

Even though the relationship between Object Lens and previous hypertext systems is not the primary focus of this paper, it is interesting to observe that Object Lens appears to have some functionality in at least four of the seven areas that Halasz [8] listed as being needed in the next generation of hypermedia systems (search and query, computational engines, collaborative work, and tailorability).

5. CONCLUSION

In this paper, we have described a system called Object Lens that integrates facilities for hypertext, object-oriented databases, electronic messaging, and rule-based agents. Using the basic primitives provided by this system, we believe it is relatively easy to create a wide variety of cooperative work applications. We have shown several such applications here, and an important focus of our ongoing research will be to test the generality of the framework further by implementing more applications within it.

Object Lens is an example of a semiformal system, a system that represents knowledge in a way that both people and their computational agents can process intelligently. We believe that much of the power and flexibility of this system results from its choice of primitives (semistructured objects, customizable folders, and semiautonomous agents) and from the template-based interfaces that make these primitives both visible and changeable by inexperienced computer users.

ACKNOWLEDGMENTS

We would especially like to thank Ken Grant who suggested some of the earliest ideas that led to Object Lens and Jin Lee who helped debug the most recent version. The Object Lens system and this paper have also benefited from conversations with Cheryl Clark, Kevin Crowston, Randy Davis, Frank Halasz, Mitch Kapor, Stan Lanning, Wendy Mackay, Ramana Rao, Randy Trigg, David Rosenblitt, and Franklyn Turbak.

REFERENCES

1. CONKLIN, J. Hypertext: An introduction and survey. *IEEE Computer 20*, 9 (1987), 17–41.
2. CROWSTON, K., AND MALONE, T. W. Computational agents to support cooperative work. Working Paper No. 2008-88, Center for Information Systems Research, Massachusetts Institute of Technology, Cambridge, Mass., 1988.
3. DELISLE, N., AND SCHWARTZ, M. Contexts—a partitioning concept for hypertext. *ACM Trans. Off. Inf. Syst. 5*, 2 (Apr. 1987), 168–186.
4. DITTRICH, D., AND DAYAL, U., Eds. In *Proceedings of the International Workshop on Object-Oriented Database Systems* (Asilomar, Calif., Sept. 23–26). IEEE Computer Society, Washington, D.C., 1986.
5. FIKES, R., AND KEHLER, T. The role of frame-based representation in reasoning. *Commun. ACM 28*, 9 (Sept. 1985), 904.
6. GARRETT, L. N., SMITH, K. E., AND MEYROWITZ, N. Intermedia: Issues, strategies, and tactics in the design of a hypermedia document system. In *Proceedings of the Conference on Computer-Supported Cooperative Work* (Austin, Tex., Dec. 3–5). ACM, New York, 1986, 163–174.
7. GREIF, I. Computer-supported cooperative work: Breakthroughs for user acceptance (Panel description). In *Proceedings of the ACM Conference on Human Factors in Computing Systems (CHI '88)* (Washington, D.C., May 16–19). ACM, New York, 1988, pp. 113–114.
8. HALASZ, F. G. Reflections on NoteCards: Seven issues for the next generation of hypermedia systems. *Commun. ACM 31*, 7 (July 1987), 836–855.
9. HALASZ, F. G., MORAN, T. P., AND TRIGG, R. H. NoteCards in a nutshell. In *Proceedings of the 1987 ACM Conference on Human Factors in Computer Systems (CHI + GI '87)* (Toronto, Ontario, Apr. 5–9). ACM, New York, 45–52.

10. LAI, K. Y. Essays on Object Lens: A tool for supporting information sharing. Master's thesis, Sloan School of Management, Massachusetts Institute of Technology, Cambridge, Mass., 1987.
11. LEE, J., AND MALONE, T. W. How can groups communicate when they use different languages? Translating between partially shared type hierarchies. In *Proceedings of the ACM Conference on Office Information Systems* (Palo Alto, Calif., Mar. 23–25). ACM, New York, 1988, pp. 22–29.
12. LEE, J., AND MALONE, T. W. Partially shared views: A scheme for communicating among groups that use different type hierarchies. Sloan School of Management Working Paper, Massachusetts Institute of Technology, Cambridge, Mass., Sept., 1988.
13. MALONE, T. W., GRANT, K. R., LAI, K.-Y., RAO, R., AND ROSENBLITT, D. Semistructured messages are surprisingly useful for computer-supported coordination. *ACM Trans. Off. Syst. 5*, 2 (Apr. 1987), 115–131.
14. MALONE, T. W., GRANT, K. R., TURBAK, F. A., BROBST, S. A., AND COHEN, M. D. Intelligent information-sharing systems. *Commun. ACM 30*, 5 (May 1987), 390–402.
15. MALONE, T. W., GRANT, K. R., LAI, K.-Y., RAO, R., AND ROSENBLITT, D. The Information Lens: An intelligent system for information sharing and coordination. In *Technological Support for Work Group Collaboration*, M. H. Olson, Ed. Lawrence Erlbaum, Hillsdale, N.J., 1989.
16. SHRIVER, B., AND WEGNER, P. *Research Directions in Object-Oriented Programming*. MIT Press, Cambridge, Mass., 1987.
17. STEFIK, M., AND BOBROW, D. G. Object-oriented programming: Themes and variations. *AI Magazine* (Spring 1986), 40–62.
18. SLUIZER, S., AND CASHMAN, P. M. XCP: An experimental tool for supporting office procedures. In *IEEE 1984 Proceedings of the 1st International Conference on Office Automation* (Silver Spring, Md.). IEEE Computer Society, Washington, D.C., 1984, pp. 73–80.
19. TOU, F. N., WILLIAMS, M. D., FIKES, R. E., HENDERSON, D. A., AND MALONE, T. W. RABBIT: An intelligent database assistant. In *Proceedings of the National Conference of the American Association for Artificial Intelligence* (Pittsburgh, Pa., Aug. 18–20). American Association for Artificial Intelligence, Philadelphia, Pa., 1982, pp. 314–318.
20. TURBAK, F. A. Grasp: A visible and manipulable model for procedural programs. Master's thesis, Department of Electrical Engineering and Computer Science, Massachusetts Institute of Technology, Cambridge, Mass., 1986.
21. WINOGRAD, T. A language/action perspective on the design of cooperative work. *Human Computer Interaction 3*, 1 (1988), 3–30.
22. WINOGRAD, T., AND FLORES, F. *Understanding Computers and Cognition: A New Foundation For Design*. Ablex, Norwood, NJ, 1986.
23. ZLOOF, M. M. QBE/OBE: A language for office and business automation. *IEEE Computer 14*, 5 (May 1981), 13–22.

Received June 1988; revised October 1988; accepted October 1988

Chapter 8:
Coordinators

Chapter 8: Coordinators

Coordination differs from all other human endeavors for three reasons. First, it is a requirement not in itself, but because other work is involved. Second, everyone, without exception, coordinates. Third, coordination creates relationships among people (as opposed to creating artifacts). In fact, coordination typically goes unnoticed until its absence or a flaw negatively impacts the ongoing work. Can something so pervasive and yet so intangible as coordination be supported by computers?

This section presents four systems explicitly designed to help coordinate human activity: DIPLANS is a language for describing coordination, CHAOS contains an exhaustive petri-net model of conversations, COSMOS encapsulates actions and message exchanges, and STRUDEL implements conversation types and moves. These systems are commonly called coordination programs, or coordinators for short. Two other coordinators, CONTRACT and The Coordinator, are described in Chapter 3, "Design Methods."

Background: communicational and conversational frameworks

One historical avenue for coordinators started from the perspective that communication occurs in organizations of people. This led to the development of software for reducing the transaction costs of coordinating by focusing on its information processing aspects. The tradition behind this software sees computers as devices that manipulate information. Thus, the *communication framework* led to coordinators built on such concepts as agents that perform activities according to goals, message passing among agents, and permitting specific activities only when a person is assuming a particular role. These early coordinators directly implemented work task sequencing and fixed work terminology, which made them inflexible and nontransferable.

This leads us to the second historical avenue for coordinators, the perspective that says language is a design center. In this *conversational framework*, spoken language is seen as continually designing organizations. (Please refer to Chapter 3 for more details.) This approach, commonly called the language/action perspective, sees coordinators based on a theory of linguistic commitment and completion of conversation. The tradition behind this software sees computers as artifacts that can preserve conversations, allowing them to be reinterpreted when situations in the workplace change. This software has a user interface designed to fit into the social norms and the everyday speaking of the workplace.

Themes: Language, protocols, structures, toolkits

At the present time, the communicational and conversational frameworks create numerous differences in the implementation and use of coordinators. Some coordinators are designed from the communication mechanisms the software can provide, while other coordinators are designed from an understanding of the process by which speaking occurs. Here are some themes that have emerged from the communicational and conversational frameworks.

Coordination language. Holt puts forth a theory of coordination centered around constituent responsibilities and a work arena. Bodies exist in the work arena, operations are performed on bodies, and there are restricted views on both bodies and operations. From these concepts come other coordination primitives such as consuming, producing, safekeeping, synchronization, transfer, and acceptance. All these primitives are then used to control work from coordination centers, which optimize the maintenance and execution of work plans and interactions.

Holt implements his theory with a language he calls DIPLANS, in which graphic symbols represent bodies and operations, lines represent involvement and aspect, and arrows represent activities such as consuming and producing. The relevance of DIPLANS is that people can more easily express what they do at work, in a form that can correctly control computers to help coordinate that work. This can enable the creation of a coordination base, an operating system capable of executing human work plans (as opposed to executing software).

Petri-net formalisms. DeCindio et al. have developed a coordinator based on the rules for two-party negotiation. The basic negotiation process is represented with two very detailed petri-net models. The first model represents the "asker", the person who initially requests that something be done. The second model represents the "doer", the person who initially promises to do the work.

To accomplish this, DeCindio et al. start with the socio-linguistic and organizational rules as the constitutive rules of the negotiation process. They then employ Searle's speech acts for the transitions between states in the petri-net model. The CHAOS system was given the ability to create and execute these models, to maintain negotiation status and history, and to interlink commitments. Groupware developers can learn from the CHAOS experience, especially with regard to implementing a complete model of speech acts using petri-net formalisms.

Communication structures. Bowers asserts that exhaustive speech act models cannot fully address cooperative work. His argument is based on studying the adjacency pairs of speech that come into existence when two speakers issue a related pair of utterances in adjacent turns. Such a conversation, he says, is locally managed by the two people. Global conversation management happens when, for example, two different kinds of organizational working practices coexist alongside each other. During cooperative work, both local and global conversation management occur simultaneously, and each affects the other. Thus, Bowers says, it may not be possible to fully model every possible communication situation.

Bowers demonstrates this theory with a system that supports communicative actions without explicitly binding those actions with speech acts. His COSMOS system is built on the primitives of actions, objects, roles, rules, contextual conditions, and temporal orderings. Actions are work tasks. Objects define work products. Roles limit who can work on which objects. Rules and contextual conditions specify group interactions. Temporal orderings define action sequences. Groupware developers can use Bowers' approach to create a system by evolving a model of conditions and expected actions within those conditions.

Conversation toolkits. Shepherd et al. noticed that technology may be particularly useful at capturing and structuring the work conversations for work groups engaged in *specialized recurring conversations*. In particular, the concepts of conversation, task, message, and action item can be used to represent these specialized group work situations. The authors use these primitives to build specific conversational structures for electronic mail, enabling the members of a group to carry out their tasks more effectively.

What is unique about their STRUDEL system is how it compliments the basic coordination mechanisms with semistructured messages for each step in a standardized work discourse, allowing people to create an entire discourse by simply threading together step messages. Groupware developers can use this alternative way of implementing the state-to-state transitions of a discourse to build systems that are extremely customizable and easy to maintain.

Futures: Primitives, models, architecture, personalization

The future will see the maturing of coordinators. For example, these systems will be developed from generalized coordination primitives; models for representing the doing and speaking that occur in the workplace; and methods for translating different group work terminology. Future coordinators will also allow higher degrees of customization and personalization to individual work styles.

The future may also see a two-tier architecture for coordinators, with the conversational framework used to accurately describe office work, and the communication framework used to implement primitives. This architecture will occur if groupware developers can successfully design both the social and technical aspects of people's work into their systems. If successful, the resulting systems will assist in the parallel evolution of human skills and computer capabilities.

Diplans: A New Language for the Study and Implementation of Coordination

ANATOL W. HOLT

Coordination Technology, Inc.

In this paper the reader is introduced to coordination in the workplace as an object of scientific study and computer automation. *Diplans* are the expressions of a new graphical language used to describe plans of operation in human organizations. With diplans, systems of constraint, which may or may not take the form of procedure definitions, can be specified. Among the special strengths of diplans is their ability to render explicit the interactive aspects of complex work distributed over many people and places—in other words, coordination. Diplans are central to coordination technology, a new approach to developing support for cooperative work on heterogeneous computer networks.

Categories and Subject Descriptors: C.2.4 [**Computer-Communication Networks**]: Distributed Systems; H.4.1 [**Information Systems Applications**]: Office Automation; H.4.3 [**Information Systems Applications**]: Communications Applications; K.4.3 [**Computers and Society**]: Organizational Impacts

General Terms: Design, Theory

1. INTRODUCTION

Coordination is an elusive concept. We know it well, yet do not know it at all. It involves and surrounds everyone all the time. It brings to mind a dancer, birds heading south, an orchestra, a modern airport, a business enterprise.

There is nothing elusive about coordination when it fails for people at work. Waiting increases; so does misunderstanding, searching, frustration, and error. Management effort goes up while output goes down.

Just like any other defined task, coordination takes effort. Yet coordination is not just another task. Here are some important differences:

—Coordination is a requirement not in itself but because other tasks are required.

—Everyone, without exception, takes part in the coordination effort.

—Coordination has no product. Instead it serves to establish *relationships* between tasks and their products. Coordination has no independent purpose; it is a prerequisite for the accomplishment of other purposes.

Coordination, as we see, is a kind of "dynamic glue" that binds tasks together into larger, meaningful wholes.

Author's address: Coordination Technology, Inc., 35 Corporate Drive, Trumbull, CT 06611.

Coordination has an intimate relationship to *organization*. Organizing is what people do so that coordination will function. There are two major aspects to organizing considered in this light:

(1) specifying a subdivision of a total enterprise into constituent responsibilities,
(2) creating a properly equipped and properly stocked work arena.

The work arena may spread over many media: office space and factory floors, document pages, telephones wires, computer memories, and so forth. In short-hand, we may refer to the first aspect of organizing as *logical*, and the second as *physical*. Each of these aspects conditions the other; both are indispensable to coordination.

Coordination as just described is an aspect of human social behavior of great practical importance, particularly since the advent of contemporary computer and communications technology—easily the most powerful tool for organizing and coordinating (as well as misorganizing and miscoordinating) ever created.

In social organizations unaided by modern technology, people achieve very high levels of wonderfully adaptable coordination, without the benefit of conscious understanding. Indeed, conscious understanding tends to inhibit the process. "If the centipede had to think about how to coordinate his legs he would never move," people say. Indeed, in most work situations, we do not think about *how* the content and timing of our actions affect our coordination partners. To do so would interfere with working. But this unconscious knowledge is *medium dependent*. It works when people affect one another in ordinary physical space. It does not automatically transfer to computers. To make this new medium conform better to human coordination habits requires a new understanding of how these habits function in the preelectronic environment.

The goal of turning linked computers into a powerful medium to support coordinated work became a motivating force some 25 years ago for the development of a new exact-scientific approach to coordination, now called *coordination mechanics*. Not coincidentally, the first decade of coordination mechanics research was also the first decade of Petri net research. In that decade these two endeavors exerted a great influence on one another. Two years ago a company called Coordination Technology, Inc. was organized to turn linked computers into coordination engines by turning coordination mechanics into technology and technology into product.

The aim of this paper is more modest than the above introduction might suggest. It focuses on a new graphical "planning language"—the language of *diplans*—which bears the same relationship to coordination mechanics that the language of chemical equations bears to chemistry. Diplans describe the logical as well as the physical organization of coordinated human activity.

This paper has the following objectives:

(1) To rouse an interest in diplans among those who have practical needs that might be described as "managing coordination." (It is clear that planning instruments generally have that purpose.) We shall illustrate how diplans provide new help with projecting resource requirements, dealing with reality constraints, and working out plan alternatives. This new help has to do mainly with coordination.

(2) To explain the role that diplans may play in the utilization of computers, especially networked computers.

(3) To indicate how Coordination Technology, Inc. builds the bridge from theory to practice.

2. DIPLAN SEMANTICS

The diplan language is a formal graphical language for expressing plans. The principal new attribute of diplans is the scope of reality which they address.

In everyday language the word "plan" has two rather different meanings, as illustrated by "the plan of the building" and "the plan of the project." The one deals with physical relations in space, the other with effort relations in time. Without some new source of insight, these two uses of the word do not seem much related. By far the greatest difficulty in understanding diplans is that they amalgamate these two classes of meaning. The most direct path to understanding how diplans do this is *to conceptualize an active organized work arena as an "organization machine."* The activity of this "machine" is nothing other than the coordinated conduct of the work to which the work arena is dedicated.

"Organization machines" are in some ways similar to and in other ways different from other typical machines. Like all ordinary machines, organization machines really are physically organized utilitarian structures, with static as well as moving parts. Their parts are described in terms that the work participants understand, such as "the conference room," "the Xerox machine," "Building 20," "parking lot B," "the mechanical drawings," and "my memo." Unlike most other machines, their users are *in them* instead of *outside of them*. Also unlike most other machines, they are not normally operated by one user but by many users in concert and/or in conflict.

When the work is performed, the machine runs. As it runs, its various parts change state relative to one another, as in the case of any machine. The users who are in the "machine" participate in its operations and therefore participate in the state changes. Whatever else may or may not change, each operation performed certainly changes some participants' states of work-related expectation. These state changes are a part of the machine's operation. In this sense people do not so much "use" organization machines as "take a part" in them.

Another unusual feature of organization machines as compared with other typical machines is that organization machines are normally modified without being stopped. Very often, in fact, a significant part of the structure of such machines is devoted to enabling maintenance, growth, and modification without global disruption of operation.

Diplans describe organization machines. This always requires the descriptions of "bodies," that is, physical components of such machines, and "operations" in which these bodies are involved. Multiple bodies interact to produce coordinated behavior. These bodies always include the people "on location." Only the state changes directly relevant to the intended work in progress are observed and described.

Diplans are normally written by someone who—like a manager—is trying to have an effect on an organization machine. Such a person, when performing a job, must take a part in this machine. Otherwise the phenomena of concern are not accessible to observation, let alone control.

It is always true that descriptions of a machine in motion entail some level of architectural description. Conversely, the description of a machine architecture has implications for its motions. As shown below, diplans make these connections explicit.

3. THE DIPLAN GRAPHICAL LANGUAGE

3.1 A Preliminary Example

Consider a small project plan. Three parts are to be made, one of them in two versions. Then two assemblies are made, as indicated in the critical path method (CPM) diagram of Figure 1. In this diagram tasks are named by their key output, for example, task A produces part A. Task 2C produces 2 copies (or versions) of part C, destined for incorporation into two assemblies, AC and BC. These two assemblies, taken as a pair, constitute the end of the project.

This diagram, representing the "3 parts, 2 assemblies" project, may be put to various uses, for example, to develop a resource schedule and to consider the effect of alternatives on project goals. In so doing, all resource requirements and costs are accounted to the tasks.

Before showing what a *diplanner* would draw when driven by the same planning interest, we describe the basic terms and graphic representation of diplans.

3.2 Diplans Terms and General Meanings

Figure 2 displays the basic terms of diplans and their graphical representation. The following notes clarify the somewhat specialized meanings of these terms in the context of diplans.

(1) *Bodies* refer to identifiable parts of an organized work arena distinguished in their properties *insofar as relevant to the work*. *Operations* refer to the identifiable units of effort. The entire physical volume of the work arena and its associated "state space" is covered by its constituent bodies. Its entire running time is covered by its operations. Typically, its bodies are rooms, documents, material packages, machines, persons, and storage compartments. Its operations will be transfers, transforms, imports, exports, productions, consumptions, maintenances, and so forth, of bodies.

(2) A body is *involved* in an operation if it is directly necessary to it and significantly affected by it, that is, "significant" by the standards of the work that the plan describes.

(3) Any restricted view of a body is an *aspect* of it. Certainly a body part in the conventional sense might be an aspect. However, only operationally significant restricted views appear explicitly as aspects in a diplan. Similarly, any restricted view of an operation is an aspect of it.

Figure 3 displays two specializations of the involvement relation which we also need to build our examples. The notes to Figure 3 follow.

(4) A body is *consumed* in an operation if its going out of existence is a necessary manifestation of the operation; it is *produced* by an operation if its coming into existence is a necessary manifestation of the operation. No body can be involved in both of these ways in any given operation.

451

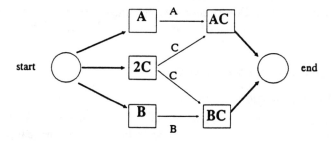

Fig. 1.   3 parts, 2 assemblies.

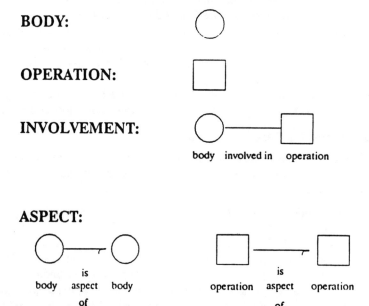

Fig. 2.   Diplan basic terms and graphic representations.

(5) In the context of diplans, we treat input and output as operation-relative terms: Inputs are bodies that it consumes; outputs are bodies that it produces.

3.3 Working the Example

We are now ready to sketch a diplanner's approach to the "3 parts, 2 assemblies" example. The purposes are

—To illustrate in this familiar setting how "organization machine thinking" applies.

—To distill coordination effort in pure form out of this plan by capturing a small quantity of that "elusive something" mentioned in the Introduction.

—To illustrate improved ability to express what matters.

452

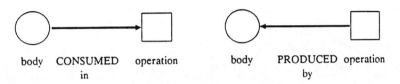

body   CONSUMED   operation   body   PRODUCED   operation
          in   by

Fig. 3. Production/consumption: a specialization of the involvement relation. Note that the arrow is to be seen as composed of a "shaft" and a "point": the shaft signifies the involvement relation; the point qualifies the involvement relation.

The diplanner's first thought in considering the 3 + 2 tasks in the example is how they may be spatially located relative to one another. Certainly the diplan will be different if they are scattered over five continents than if they are colocated on a single factory floor. The producer of the CPM diagram in Figure 1 must also have been influenced by this issue, even though personal assumptions cannot be read unambiguously out of the resulting diagram. To match the diplanner's frame of mind, we now assume that all five tasks are near to each other.

The diplan will also reflect assumptions about the gross scales of these tasks relative to one another, as measured in space, time, personnel requirements, and so forth. Once again, Figure 1 suggests that the planner was thinking of tasks of comparable magnitude, but the diagram does not say so explicitly.

Figure 4 shows an allocation of the five tasks to "rooms" in a manner that will make the diplan to be constructed look as much as possible like the CPM diagram in Figure 1. Notes to this figure follow.

—The passages 2C-to-A and 2C-to-B are necessary because the C parts must be transferred from the site of their construction to the assembly sites. The three passages to the outside are only relevant to beginning and ending the project. (The parts in Room 2C could be transported via the "Outside," but that would enlarge the work arena covered by the plan.)

—The intention of the CPM diagram cannot be carried out at all without a minimum of three rooms. This follows from the fact that the plan calls for the *independent, not mutually interfering, execution of the three tasks.*

—Notice that the two drawings of the CPM and the floor plan constitute two parts of a single plan.

Figure 5 shows the diplan result.

In this diplan all bodies that are aspects of Room A are indicated by a bold-faced A exterior to the circle symbol; similarly for rooms B and 2C. All the elements of the CPM diagram reappear in the diplan. These are indicated in bold outlines. The additional elements enter the picture because of the mechanics of coordinating.

A series of questions and answers about Figure 5 follows:

What is body S?

It includes all that is involved in beginning the project. In particular, three *aspects* of it are the three rooms initialized for the project. This initialization

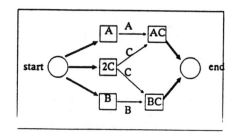

Fig. 4. A minimal organization of "Rooms" to support the "3 parts, 2 assemblies" plan.

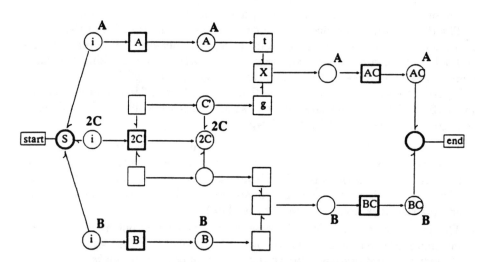

Fig. 5. The diplan that expresses the plan in Figure 4.

includes the persons responsible being ready to go. (Recall that the organization machine includes the people.)

What are the bodies 2C and C'?

Body 2C is Room 2C upon completion of Task 2C, with the person responsible knowing that the task is accomplished. In other planning approaches, the output of Task 2C would be viewed in a more restricted manner as consisting of the two copies of part C without regard to location and person states.

Body C' is an aspect of body 2C, an aspect that includes one of the two copies of part C under someone's responsibility in Room 2C. The content of this responsibility is analyzed below. This aspect will have been consumed (i.e., will no longer exist) by the time Task AC is about to begin.

What does operation X include? Who is responsible?

Operation X is the transfer of part C′ from Room 2C to Room A. It begins whenever Task A or Task 2C ends, whichever is sooner. Before it has completed, it will have covered the following efforts:

—*Safekeeping.* Suppose Task 2C ends before Task A. Upon ending, the person responsible, is satisfied that the product meets requirements for the next step. The effort of safekeeping is to maintain the part with no loss of these required properties. The greater the time difference between task completions, and the harder it is to keep the part safe, the greater the safekeeping effort. Barring other arrangements for responsibility transfer, the person responsible for Task 2C will have to carry this burden if the task is done before Task A.

—*Synchronization and Transfer.* Upon conclusion of the later of the two tasks, the part from Room 2C must be transferred to Room A. The less time there is to be lost, the more effort it costs both persons responsible, particularly in checking that the transfer can be started.

—*Acceptance.* To be protected, the person responsible for Task AC will have to be satisfied that the part received meets his or her requirements. The person responsible for Task 2C will have to remain "on line" until acceptance is complete.

Each of these three efforts will place some burden on both persons responsible. These efforts are explicitly represented in the diplan as aspects of Operation X: "g" for give and "t" for take.

There follows next a series of observations about the diplan and its interpretation:

—Operation X is coordination effort in pure form. It has all of the characteristics of such efforts described at the beginning of the Introduction. Operation X is indeed the "dynamic glue" between primary tasks.

—The two persons responsible must charge more time than required by the primary tasks they perform. They are both necessarily involved in Operation X.

—The two pure coordination tasks in the diplan could dominate the total cost of its execution.

—The transfer of anything from one responsibility to another always entails all three of the coordination efforts just described. (Although these are facts of *human coordination*, they are also relevant to a hardware or software engineer implementing the transfer of information from one storage medium to another.)

—The diplanner is forced into noticing Operation X because of an early concern with the spatial allocation of tasks. Since, according to plan, Task 2C is confined to Room 2C and Task AC is confined to Room A, there is no way to connect them without another operation. The semantics of the involvement relation (see point 2, Section 3.2) makes this mandatory.

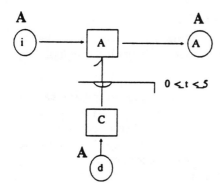

Fig. 6. Repeated Room A cleanup as part of Task A.

3.4 An Elaboration of the Example

We next illustrate how the diplan in Figure 5 might be elaborated by the addition of detail. In the process we also introduce one more diplan construct.

—There are two new diplan elements in Figure 6: body *d* and operation C. Body d is Room A in dirty state during Task A. If this aspect of Room A comes into being, Operation C, cleanup, "consumes" it, that is, results in its ceasing to exist.

—In Figure 6 there is also a new diplan construct, a graphical "quantifier." It asserts that, for each instance of Operation A, there are at most five instances of Operation C and associated bodies d, and possibly none at all.

—The graphical quantifier is noncommittal as to whether the possibly multiple operations C are sequential or concurrent, or some of each. Note that with regard to the total effort expended on cleanup, this distribution in time and space is irrelevant.

—The entire cleanup construct is noncommittal about the control relationship between cleanup and the rest of Task A. All, some, or possibly none of the other work of the task may be interrupted in order to allow cleanup to go forward.

—What can we tell from the diplan about the cause of the dirty condition (body d)? If we assume that when Room A is involved in Task A it is involved in nothing else, then the dirty condition must arise from the execution of this task. Neither this assumption nor its contrary is expressed in the diplan as written.

Figure 7 augments the diplan in Figure 6 by including Room A explicitly. It also shows Task A as capable of multiple performances in any given instantiation of Room A. Assuming that a given performance of Task A requires the whole room, these performances would have to be sequential repetitions. This construct is noncommittal as to whether the possibly multiple operations CL are sequential or concurrent, or some of each. When the concern is total effort put into cleanup, this distribution in time and space does not matter.

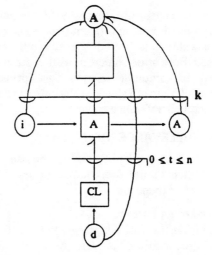

Fig. 7.   Room A added to Figure 6.

$0 \leq t \leq n$

Table I

Diplan structural parts described as sets	Undirected Petri net parts as carryovers from diplans
1. A set of elements, B	Carried over
2. A set of elements, O, disjoint from B	Carried over
3. A relation i with domain $(i) = B$ and range $(i) = O$	Carried over
4. A relation a with $a = O \times O \cup B \times B$	Deleted

3.5 Diplans and Petri Nets

We close this section with a brief note about the relationship of diplans to Petri nets.

As explained above, diplans are expressions in a graphical language specifically developed for thinking about organized human activity in "physical" terms. Petri nets, on the other hand, have been understood as a type of abstract mathematical structure for a much wider class of applications. Therefore there already exist condition/event nets, place/transition nets, office/channel nets, structure/constraint nets, timed nets, and more. In this regard diplans and Petri nets are different in kind.

However, *abstract diplans* and undirected Petri nets are obviously relatives. Leaving the graphical quantifier construct out of consideration, we have the structural comparison detailed in Table I.

Abstract diplans without aspect in which every involvement is a production or consumption are equivalent to directed Petri nets. When Petri nets have been used to model concurrent processes in computer science, the interpretation of the net elements and their relations to one another is at odds with diplan semantics.

Two differences of interpretation are salient. In computer science, state hold-ings account for all significant process durations; the changes of state are viewed as "instantaneous" for all practical purposes. In the context of diplans this is reversed. Both state change as well as state maintenance are viewed as operations. Second, in computer science, descriptions of concurrent processes make no explicit reference to spatial relations or to the role of human will; diplans always make explicit reference to both.

4. THE RELEVANCE OF DIPLANS TO COMPUTER USE

There are numerous obstacles to the use of computers by people in any walk of life, whether or not the computers are networked together. Some of the most important of these are

—the learning barrier,
—the barrier against adapting what is offered to one's own needs,
—the discontinuity between the electronic world and the rest of one's work world,
—the discontinuities from one computer application to the next,
—the danger of placing reliance on machines one does not understand and cannot control.

Computer networks will aggravate rather than ameliorate these problems. In addition to providing better access to distributed resources, the new connectivity also spreads the effects of error and malevolence in ways that are very difficult to track.

In substantial part the difficulties just enumerated are traceable to a single cause: the "disconnect" between the act of programming and the end user's practical intentions. There was no such disconnect to speak of when computers mainly served "computers," that is, people like accountants, statisticians, and physicists, whose work demands significant computing efforts. Most people's work demands few, if any, such efforts. By contrast, almost everyone's work demands coordinating and organizing on large or small scales.

It was true when computers began—and it is still true today—that program-ming is suited to expressing exactly prescribed procedures, and nothing else. This is as true of high-level languages as it is of low-level ones and is what gives rise to the above-mentioned disconnect.

Most of the useful computer applications today have nothing to do with the execution of user-prescribed exact procedures. The user wants to write a docu-ment, do a spreadsheet, get stock information, keep airplanes from colliding, and so on. But before such applications can be realized, a programmer will have to prescribe *an exact procedure*, that is, write the application. What exact procedure "translates" the user's needs? Programmer and ultimate client must slowly develop a common understanding through trial and error. The resulting connec-tion between the wishes and the procedure is tenuous at best. Therefore many client needs are met badly, and many others, theoretically amenable to "computer solution," are not met at all.

How many diplans contribute to the solution of this problem? Given appropriate interpreters, "diplanning" represents an alternative approach to programming as a means of connecting users' intentions to computer operation. This alternative has the following key features:

—Diplans express what people and computers do together, not only what computers can do alone.

—Diplans were specifically developed for expressing, organizing, and coordinating the activity of people, rather than only expressing automatable procedures. Above all else, it is in organizing and coordinating that computing and communications technology can be most helpful to the majority of people.

—Diplans explicitly deal with spatial relations. This allows users to deal with a fundamentally important class of constraints on their organized activities, including computer network topology when appropriate.

—Diplans not only describe organizationally distributed operations—true of every multiperson organized activity, no matter how centrally controlled—but *diplan descriptions can be evolved and maintained in a distributed manner.* Once again, with appropriate interpreters, the processes of developing these descriptions can be smoothly meshed with the execution of the processes that they govern.

—Very useful starter skills can be acquired by anyone who can learn elementary algebra. Indeed, doing "word problems" in diplanning should be easier than the algebra equivalent.

5. FROM THEORY TO PRACTICE

Coordination technology puts theory to practice. Coordination technology's problem is how to turn networks of computers into coordination utilities. Like telephones today, these networks should enter into the day-to-day conduct of most people's business. In addition, when one considers that telephone networks today already are computer networks, it is not hard to imagine that the distinction between the two will disappear.

The coordination technology approach calls for a new type of system software package called a *coordination base*. It is added to the standard complement of system software packages widely assumed today: an operating system, communications, and windows. The coordination base resides on every machine of a network and creates a coordination environment among many machines.

One can think of a coordination base as a higher level operating system. Today's operating systems are concerned with the problem of program execution. They, just like a coordination base, must coordinate the utilization of resources that programs require, such as data, I/O devices, and CPU time. But coordination bases deal with the problem of executing (human) work plans. The resources to be coordinated are scattered over a network, and directly involve not just CPU time but *people's* time.

Very few work plans resemble programs. Some work plans say as little as "we will accomplish X together, within some general time frame"; some say "we will relate to one another in manner X, until further notice." But work plans can also become arbitrarily detailed in prescribing procedures, as do computer programs.

Work plans are always conditioned by how the people involved are physically located relative to one another, what resources are available to them, and what authority relationships exist among them. As partially illustrated in earlier sections of this paper, diplans deal with all of these dimensions explicitly.

Just as operating systems "understand" programs and program relationships, so coordination bases "understand" diplans and diplan relationships. There follows a brief description of the structures with which coordination bases deal in order to make the execution of work plans in the electronic medium possible.

5.1 Coordination Environments and Organizations

The largest unit that a coordination base understands is a so-called coordination environment (CE). It is an "electronic territory" under unified administration in which work communities and their constituent organizations, teams, and work groups can set up to conduct business electronically.

This functional description also applies to many systems, for example, a UNIX-based[1] time-sharing system or a local-area network (LAN). But these systems mostly deal with *persons at workstations* (or terminals) and very little with *organizations on networks*. Cooperating groups will certainly form in a time-sharing system or a LAN, but they will receive little special support from the system for the accomplishment of their joint business. There may be e-mail and "servers" in a generalized sense, and little more. As explained below, a coordination base provides powerful support for (a) the formation of work groups at various hierarchic levels, and (b) the subsequent ongoing coordination effort involved within these groups.

5.2 Centers

Just as a LAN consists of interconnected machines, so an organization established in a CE consists of interconnected centers. One of these centers serves as a control point for the organization as a whole. These centers are "soft structures," as is true of directories under MS-DOS. The centers of some organizations may be confined to a single machine or may be spread over many machines.

Each center is created to support a work mission. Within it, all materials dedicated to the mission are aggregated and organized; within it, one person performs the mission in concert with others, as further described. A single person's work is likely to be housed in about 3 to 30 centers possibly related to missions of different organizations. All CE-supported communications are center to center. Figure 8 is a diplan about CEs, centers, and machines (organization groupings are not represented).

5.3 Center Work Plans and Interactions

The overall work plan of an organization ultimately expresses itself in a collection of work plans carried out by individuals. At some stage of subdivision, these become work plans associated with centers in a CE. The numerous plans at the center level must mesh loosely or tightly with one another, depending on the nature of the mission-to-mission relationships. Another way of saying this is that the planned tasks must coordinate with one another, in loosely or rigidly controlled patterns of interaction. Depending on many factors, such as assurance

---

[1] UNIX is a trademark of AT&T Bell Laboratories.

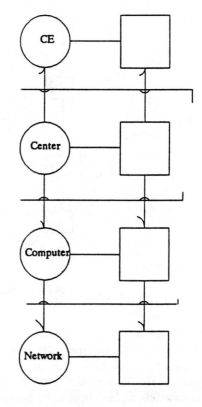

Fig. 8.   A coordination environment on a network.

requirements, bandwidth, time, distance, and people involvement, different interactions will require very different quantities and types of coordination effort. (Some of the effort types involved were detailed in the discussion of what Operation X includes in Section 3.3.) A small example follows.

A work group might be established in a CE to carry on a "3 parts, 2 assemblies" production project, as diplanned in Figure 5. The rooms A, B, and 2C may then be electronic centers. Figure 9 depicts a simplified diplan for a "Room 2C" center, assuming its function to be as in Figure 5.

Room 2C is shown as being involved in three general classes of interaction: with room A, with room B, and with "the rest of the world." The part of Figure 9 in bold might already serve as a diplan for a center called 2C. In this diplan, centers A and B are distinguished from one another and from the rest of the world because, presumably, from 2C's point of view there are three distinct interaction requirements. The coordination base is prepared to "understand" local descriptions of interaction requirements and to generate significant amounts of coordination support.

And now the "3 parts, 2 assemblies" plan becomes embedded in the more general plan just discussed. The specific steps and interactions that it calls for will take place in a context of interactive relations that the more general plan provides, such as message and package interchanges of a nonspecialized sort. In this context, for example, the inputs needed to make the parts C need not be

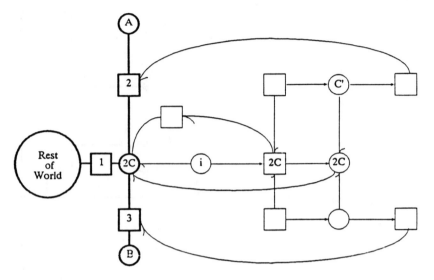

Fig. 9. Diplan for a "Room 2C" center.

limited to what exists in Room 2C when the production begins. Some of them may, in fact, be acquired from the rest of the world in the course of production.

In a coordination environment, the diplan just discussed would be encoded as part of the "Room 2C" soft structure. Clearly, it cannot be executed without compatible diplans in centers corresponding to rooms A and B. Such compatibility may have been achieved through negotiations between preexisting centers which, after the negotiations, will be set up (diplanned) to be rooms A, B, and 2C. Or, it may be achieved through organizational planning at a higher level. The higher level plan would then be implemented by allocating the component tasks to existing centers or creating new ones for this purpose.

Of course the "rest of the world" must also be compatible with the interaction requirements of operation 1 in Figure 9. What guarantees this compatibility depends on how much "world" is encompassed. If it is the whole coordination environment, then the coordination base guarantees it; if it is restricted to a particular organization of which the "3 parts, 2 assemblies" is a part, then it is this organization that provides the compatibility guarantees.

The example just described exhibits, in a microcosm, some of the important principles of a coordination environment. By dynamically interpreting centers and their interdependent work plans, a coordination base shifts coordination effort from the shoulders of participating people onto computer-programmed mechanisms. For participating people the result is as follows:

—There is less to remember and less to think about in order to keep coordinated with one another.

—The routine aspects of working yield to mechanization, leaving the nonroutine to personal management. Since what is routine and what is nonroutine changes over time (sometimes rapidly), adaptability is an essential feature.

—There is greatly improved contextual information to guide what one chooses to do.

—A uniform operating style prevails encompassing wide domains of work performed at computers—all of this in the context of physically distributed organizations using a physically distributed medium.

The interdependent work plans interpreted by a coordination base evolve under the direct control of the work community instead of being products of system builders. Various evolutionary paths exist: adding a new negotiated agreement or a new centrally controlled plan to already ongoing operations; generating a whole new organizational unit or only modifying parts of an old one. This is how functionality enhancements and adaptations develop in the nonelectronic human work world. In the absence of coordination technology, users have not had the means of achieving similar patterns of function evolution within the electronic medium.

6. SUMMARY AND CONCLUSION

Coordination is an elusive subject. It is as hard to notice and understand as gravity and air were in their day. Perhaps computers, and above all computer networks, are pushing this mysterious and ubiquitous aspect of social behavior into consciousness.

As in other cases in scientific history, the emergence of the new understanding is impeded by deeply entrenched habits of thought—notably the habit of distinguishing the logical from the physical spheres of consideration. In the computer field this has expressed itself in the manner in which we distinguish between problem specification and problem implementation, the former being treated as a "logical" problem and the latter as a "physical" one. (Witness the numerous attempts at the use of formal logic for system specification.)

In this paper we introduced a new formal graphical "language of plans," called diplans, whose newness lies in the meanings it brings to consciousness, rather than in its encoding of meanings already there. These new meanings, body and operation, amalgamate the physical and the logical, the spatial and the temporal, the forces of mechanisms and the forces of will. The paper suggests that this new language is necessary if coordination is to be understood and today's electronic technology harnessed in its service.

Much of the diplan presentation was built around a small project plan example ("3 parts, 2 assemblies"). The main purpose of the exercise was to show how diplans make coordination effort explicit. Diplans achieve this precisely because they lead their users to take the physical and responsibility aspects of human work into account.

After some discussion of the relationship between diplanning and programming, we sketched the coordination technology approach to supporting group effort with computer and communications power. Coordination Technology, Inc. is now developing a product based on this approach. The company expects that coordination technology will make a significant contribution to the productivity of work communities while keeping them adaptable to the rapidly changing conditions of today's economic life.

BIBLIOGRAPHY

HOLT, A. W. Introduction to occurrence systems. In *Associative Information Techniques*, E. L. Jacks, Ed. Elsevier, New York, 1971, pp. 175–203.

HOLT, A. W. Coordination technology and Petri nets. In *Advances in Petri Nets*, Lecture Notes in Computer Science, No. 222. G. Rozenberg, Ed. Springer-Verlag, Berlin, 1985.

HOLT, A. W., AND CASHMAN, P. Designing systems to support cooperative activity: An example from software management. In *Proceedings of IEEE Computer Society's 5th International Computer Software and Applications Conference* (Nov.). IEEE Computer Society, Los Alamitos, Calif., 1981, pp. 184–190.

HOLT, A. W., RAMSEY, H. R., AND GRIMES, J. D. Coordination system technology as the basis for a programming environment. *Electr. Commun. 77*, 4 (1983), 307–313.

MELDMAN, J. A., AND HOLT, A. W. Petri nets and legal systems. *Jurimetrics J. 12*, 2 (1971), 65–75.

PETRI, C. A. Kommunikation mit automaten. *Schriften des Rheinisch-Westfaelischen Institutes fuer Instrumentelle Mathematik and der Universitaet Bonn*, no. 2, E. Peschi and H. Unger, Eds. Univ. of Bonn, Bonn, West Germany, 1962.

PETRI, C. A. Introduction to general net theory: Net theory and applications. In Lecture Notes in Computer Science, vol. 84., W. Brauer, Ed. Springer-Verlag, Berlin, 1984, pp. 1–9.

Received January 1988; revised March 1988; accepted May 1988

The Communication Disciplines of CHAOS

F. De Cindio, G. De Michelis, C. Simone
Dipartimento di Scienze dell'Informazione
Università di Milano

Abstract

Although Petri's Communication Disciplines have little influenced the scientific community till now, they offer a powerful theoretical framework for dealing with the pragmatics of human communication.

In particular theoretically founded Communication Disciplines can be effectively embodied in Office Computer-Based Tools improving the flexibility of the communication protocols and their adaptability to changes in the office structure.

The paper discusses this claim by presenting CHAOS (Commitment Handling Active Office System), an 'intelligent' system supporting the coordination of activities inside the office, and its Communication Disciplines.

I. Introduction

Carl Adam Petri wrote his papers on Communication Disciplines in 1977 [Pet77a], [Pet77b] and [Pet79]. Up to now they have remained widely unknown, or at least little studied and considered, although in the same period Petri Nets became very popular in the Computer Science community.

It is our opinion that there is no specific reason for this negligence, and that, on the contrary, Communication Disciplines offer an original and effective framework for dealing with the problems of system design in the area of computer support of cooperative work. In this paper we aim to show how Communication Disciplines have contributed to the development of a software package whose purpose is to coordinate office work.

Human communication pragmatics can be the framework within which co-operation between human beings can be fully understood in all its main features. Within this framework, many efforts have been made recently to analyse organizational systems (mainly offices) and, as a result, new computer-based tools have been proposed (see, for example, the Proceedings of the CSCW (Computer-Supported Cooperative Work) Conference recently held in Austin, USA [CSCW86]).

Two are the main points of view from which human communication pragmatics has been characterized within offices.

1) By focusing on the mutual commitments office members make coordinating their work.

From one hand, when the attention is focused on the way mutual commitments are made, the Speech Acts Theory developed by Austin [Aus62] and Searle [Sea69], [Sea79] can be the basis for commitments analysis. In his well known work, Searle gives a taxonomy of speech acts (Assertives, Directives, Commissives, Declarations, Expressives) from the point of view of their illocutionary point, i.e., in terms of the (commitment-) relationships they create between the two involed interlocutors. For example, "John, can you give me your pencil ?" cannot be characterized by its propositional content. Its illocutionary point, in that a directive, characterizes the relationship between the speaker and the hearer it creates. Flores [FL81] and Winograd [WF86], [Win86] apply Searle's Speech Acts Theory to office work and design a package for office conversations handling: the Coordinator [AT84].

From the other one, when the attention is focused on the way coordination integrates roles and activities, the basis is the analysis of task assignment. Holt [Hol79], [Hol86] and Cashman [CH80], [SC84] characterize the coordination as it is performed by task distribution and integration.

In this tradition, our main endeavour is to analyse organizational systems in terms of the rules their members follow by mutually inter-acting in the linguistic domain. The characterization of offices as linguistic games (see Wittgenstein [Wit53]) has been the main result of our research [DDS85], [DDS86a]. The game rules of an office define the possible speech acts each member, depending on her/his role, can do at any moment within the conversations s/he is involved in. In turn the speech acts performed by the office members induce (in a perturbation-compensation mode) a change in the office rules. This basic circularity in office life allows one to consider the office as a particular type of closed, autonomous system [MV80], i.e., a living social system, organizationally closed, which maintains its identity by changing its structure (its rules) in order to compensate for the perturbations (the speech acts of its members) its structure is able to distinguish [DeM86].

2) By focusing on the communication disciplines the office members follow in their inter-action.

The above mentioned pioneeristic work by Carl Adam Petri moving the observer of organizational systems from outside to inside the system opened a new perspective in the analysis of human communication. As Petri claims in [Pet77b] communication disciplines are disciplines in both its senses: "that of schema of the same science" and that of "restraint of behavior". While in the second sense any organization disciplines communication, it is necessary a research effort in order to develop the theoretical framework of the communication disciplines and to transform the verbal description of any theoretically founded piece of a communication discipline into a mathematical theory. In this direction Richter and Voss [RV86] use net models to integrate information and resources management within the office; Holt [Hol86] bases on the Role/Center model his Coordination Technology, an office system supporting the coordination of tasks within the organizations; through the definition of GAMERU [DDS87] and the design of the CHAOS system [DDS86] we are developing a system-theoretical approach to organization behaviour.

The two points of view give different, although strictly related, images of the organizational systems and of the inter-actions between their members: in short, the first one emphasizes communication as a sense-making activity, while the second one emphasizes communication as a socially disciplined activity.

It is our opinion that they offer complementary, mutually influencing insights on organizational behaviour. In fact, the rules of organizational games are necessarily implemented by using a well-defined set of rules within each communication disciplines, and therefore the rules determine how the organizational game rules are actually followed in any organizational system.

Changes in the organizational rules induce changes in the rules within the communication disciplines since the former become ineffective in supporting the organization behaviour; e.g., the growth of an organizational system can induce more formal communication protocols, as the rather informal previous protocols become more and more ineffective. In turn, changes in the rules within the communication disciplines induce changes in the organization rules since office members experiment how new comunication patterns can be effectively used; e.g., the introduction of an efficient and well designed PABX can induce new communicative behaviours of the office members, and through them, the creation of new organizational rules.

As this last example shows, the rules within the communication disciplines of an organizational system can be (partially) embodied in a set of tools: e.g., some rules of the addressing discipline can be embodied in the Telephon Index, in the Yellow Pages, and in a personal address book together with the Public Telephone System; some rules of the synchronization discipline can be (partially) embodied in the telephon system with automatic secretaries.

It is important to emphasize that the embodiment of the rules of the communication disciplines in a set of tools is effective as well as those communication disciplines are based on well defined theories. The embodiment in a tool of a purely heuristic rule introduces rigidities in the organization from two points of view: on the one hand, the communicative behaviors of the organization members are restrained to the most frequent observed protocols; on the other one, the rules of the communication disciplines embodied in the tools can be modified only after the heuristic identification of the emerging communication protocols. On the contrary, as far as the communication disciplines have a theoratical foundation the disciplines themselves can be embodied in the tools avoiding the two above mentioned drawbacks.

The information techonologies offer to communication disciplines a wide range of possibilities, largely un-exploited till now, of being embodied. The recent efforts in the area of computer support of cooperative work (see [DJM86], [MGL86], [Win86] in the already mentioned [CSCW86]) show some interesting steps in this direction. Furthermore they make clear that the focus in the pragmatics of human communication is fundamental to the design of effective communication disciplines rules, and to their embodiment in computer systems.

Since 1980 we have been working in the area of organizational systems analysis and design, along the above proposed lines.

First, we developed the GAMERU language for the analysis and design of the organizational processes [DDS87]. GAMERU is based on a class of Petri Nets, namely Superposed Automata Nets [DDPS82], and supports the representation of the Game Rules of organizational systems, i.e., of the rules that define the domain of the possible speech acts te members of the organization can do within the conversations they play with their colleagues.

Secondly, we proposed [DDS85], [DeM86] a characterization of organizational systems as closed autonomous systems, i.e., as systems modifying their structure (their rules) to compensate for the commitments their members make within them. The CHAOS (Commitments Handling Active Office System) project currently under development at the Dipartimento di Scienze dell'Informazione of the Universita' degli Studi di Milano by a research group composed by the authors together with Raffaela Vassallo and Annamaria Zanaboni, is aimed at the development of a tool that supports office coordination [DDS86].

CHAOS is designed as a model of the above mentioned basic circularity of organizational systems. Its rules have been specified by means of GAMERU models. CHAOS design has been for the authors the occasion to investigate practically the relations between office game rules and the rules within communication disciplines.

The paper is organized as follows: after a short presentation of the CHAOS project, the communication disciplines it embodies are presented. A conclusive section discusses the missing disciplines and the problems their absence leaves open.

2. CHAOS: Commitment Handling Active Office Systems

CHAOS is the name of a family of office support systems, presently under development, aimed at supporting the network of conversations occuring inside an office, more in general inside an organization, and, in particular, aimed at supporting the network of commitments mutually undertaken by the office members through these conversations.

In this section first a short presentation of the approach is given (2.1) for introducing the basic terminology. Then the main modeling (2.2) and architectural (2.3) characteristics of the implemented package are briefly summarized. A more detailed presentation of the package can be found in [DDS86].

2.1 Conversing in the Offices

While performing their work people spend the most of their time communicating, more precisely developing conversations with people both inside and outside their office in order to make commitments for an effective coordination of the activities. Coordinating means opening new conversations to deal with the breakdowns affecting both the activities the office members are involved in and the conversations that are going on in the office. From this point of view, the office is a network of conversations for future possibilities and/or committed activities.

A conversation between A and B is a sequence of related utterances. The utterances within a conversation cannot be characterized in semantic terms (what is the meaning of a request? is it true or false?), but can be classified from the pragmatic point of view in some basic categories of Speech Acts [Aus62], [Sea69] on the basis of their illocutionary point [Sea79]: namely, directives (e.g. Requests, Acceptance or Rejecting of a Promise), commissives (e.g. Promises, Counter-offers, Acceptance or Rejecting of a Request), declaratives (e.g. Withdrawing of a Commitment, Declaration of new fileds of activitiy, Delegation of responsibility).

CHAOS conversations occur between an Actor, i.e., the person who opens the conversation, and a Partner, her/his interlocutor. Other members can be involved in some subconversation of the main one if, due to the declared responsibilities, they are asked to approve the commitment between the Actor and the Partner. There are two main types of Conversation occurring in any office.

The first is the Conversation for Action, characterized by the (possibly unsuccessful) definition of a commitment for doing an action. There are, for instance, conversations opened by a Cooperation request, where the actor asks the partner for some activity. The partner has, in general, various reply possibilites: to accept the request, to renege it, or to make a counter-offer. The conversation proceeds through a negotiation between the two interlocutors until one of them closes it in a negative way or they find an agreement. In this second case the conversation is still open until the negotiated action is accomplished or the commitment is revoked. Conversations for Action can embed subconversations, e.g., when the person responsible for an area of activity is asked to give his/her approval about a commitment concerning that area.

The second is the <u>Conversation for Possibilities,</u> where the two interlocutors discuss new possibilities for the office, in terms of its structure, responsibilities distribution, subjects of interest and the like. These conversations are effective, i.e., actually modify the relationships between the members of the office and their domain of possibilities, when they end with a declaration which reflects an agreement about its content among the members of the office involved in the conversation. This is, for instance, the case of the delegation of a responsibility to some office member by someone having the authority for performing the delegation: it is effective only if the candidate accepts taking the new responsibility upon her/himeself and if the other members involved through subconversations give their approval.

Let us note that both Conversations for Action and for Possibilities are positively closed if the interlocutors find a mutual agreement. The accent we put on the need of agreement is aimed to improve organization liveliness and transparency. In fact, declarations performed on the basis of the necessary authority but without consensus give rise to a gap between the declared responsibility structure and the responsibility roles actually played. In an analogous way, task attribution without consensus will probably give rise to quantitative (e.g. delays) and qualitative problems.

Both Conversations for Actions and for Possibilities can either concern areas of already structured acitivities or not. In this second case the patterns of conversations model the protocols (or better the rules of the linguistic game) followed by human beings when involved in conversations in whatever social systemwithout any regard to their role.

For instance Fig. 2 in the next section models a conversations opened by a "generic" cooperation request. Here "generic" means that the Actor has not associated the conversation to any field of responsibility and therefore no approvals must be obtained for taking the commitment.

On the contrary the first case concerns conversations associated to structured areas of activity. Here the patterns of conversations characterize the roles played by the different interlocutors inside the organization. That is, they depend on the particular role distribution determined both by the effective declarations closing conversations for possibilites and by the commitment taken within conversation for action and then fulfilled or currently under fulfillment.

For instance, if the chief of a software research laboratory, by a declaration which closes a Conversation for Possibilities, attributes to a system designer, say X, the responsibility upon A.I. activities and the designer accepts, then a rule is created such that any commitment in the A.I. field taken by any laboratory member is subject to X's approval, so that X's role acquires a new characterization in terms of responsibility in the A.I. field.

If a software designer, say Y, is making, inside a Conversation for Action, the commitment of designing in Common Lisp a new shell ("A.I." being the area of responsibility and "Common Lisp" the area of expertise characterizing that commitment), since the commitment falls into the "A.I." area of responsibility, Y must ask the approval of X as "A.I." responsible. If X gives the ok and Y then fulfill the taken commitment, then a rule is created such that Y gives, sooner or later, an answer to any information request concerning Common Lisp, so that her/his role acquires a new caracterization in term of expertise in this subject.

CHAOS embeds a characterization of office roles, based on a distinction between responsibility and expertise. Fields of responsibility, such as areas of activity, customers, people and groups of people, must be explicitly declared and then other declarations can attribute to a person a responsibility role in the field. Expertise in a field is acquired in the actual fulfillment of a commitment which requires this expertise in the associated field (see next section).

On the basis of this distinction, CHAOS characterizes three roles of responsibility:
-    The role of supervisor is characterized by the fact that the supervisor of a field is the only one having the authority (authorized) to issue effective declarations concerning the field, such as: declaring a new subfield; re-structuring some subfields.
-    The role of (control) manager implies the responsibility of a close control over the commitments concerning the field. This means that if the manager of a field is declared, then, before a commitment in the field is made inside a Conversation for Action, her/his approval must be obtained.
-    The role of operative is characterized by the fact of being a privileged executor of tasks concerning the field. This implies that if one looks for cooperation in a field without explicitly indicating the partner, CHAOS identifies as partner one of the operatives on the field, if s/he exists (see section 3.5).

Furthermore, CHAOS identifies the role of expert of a field, which belongs to those who have made and fulfilled commitments in the field. If one looks for cooperation in a field without explicitly indicating the partner and an operative on the field has not been declared, then CHAOS addresses the request to the most expert in the field.

2.2 Conversations Models

In order to support people conversing and making commitments in the offices, CHAOS supports various kinds of Conversations for Action and of Conversation for Possibilites (see Fig.1).

CONVERSATIONS FOR ACTION
- two types of conversations opened by a Request:
  - Cooperation Request;
  - Information Request;
- two types of conversation opened by a (conditional) Promise:
  - Cooperation Offer;
  - Offer to oneself.

CONVERSATIONS FOR POSSIBILITES
- conversations for delegating responsibility by declaring a supervisor, a manager, an operative in a field of responsibility;
- conversations for revoking responsibility;
- conversations for declaring a new member;
- conversations for creating a new field of responsibility
- conversations for re-structuring fields of responsibility

Fig. 1

Each type of conversation is modeled by a Gameru model [DDS87] which represents the combination of elementary speech acts it consist of (see Fig. 2a and Fig. 2b). The transitions enabled under the current marking give the set of speech acts open to each interlocutor at a particular moment in whatever conversation of each type.

The choice of representing conversations by means of Gameru models fits the need for having models which represent the set of the possible behaviours of the various members involved in conversations and subconversations without forcing constraints on their behaviour [DDS85].

In addition, CHAOS structures the content of each speech act inside a Conversation for Action in terms of:
- the <u>illocutionary point</u>, which expresses the type of the speech act in accordance with Searle's Speach Act Taxonomy (Assertives, Directives, Commissives, Declarations, Expressives) in terms of the relationship it creates between the two involed interlocutors;
- the <u>propositional content</u>, in turn given by: the *action* to be performed, augmented by some information characterizing it: e.g., an action of selling a product can be detailed by specifying the related 'contract' and 'customer'; the field(s) of *responsibility* and the field(s) of *expertise* to which the action belongs;
- <u>the satisfaction conditions</u>, in particular:
  - a) the *expiration time* indicating the time-out for waiting for an answer;

CONVERSATION OPENED BY A COOPERATION REQUEST

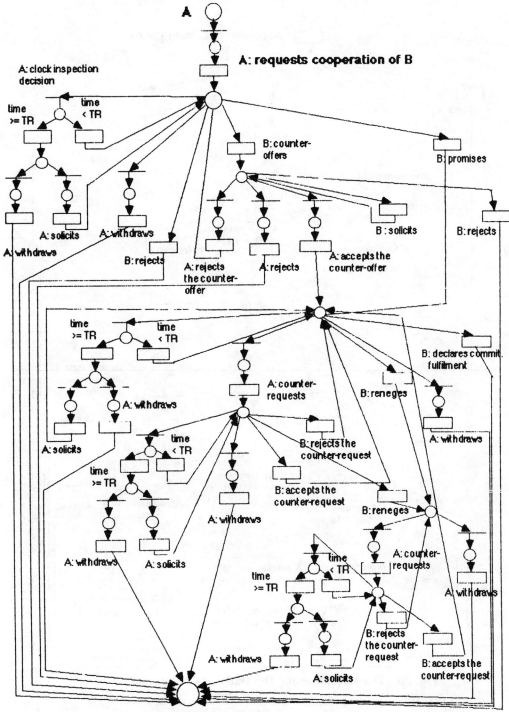

Fig. 2a: The Net modeling the Actor's behaviour

CONVERSATION OPENED BY A COOPERATION REQUEST

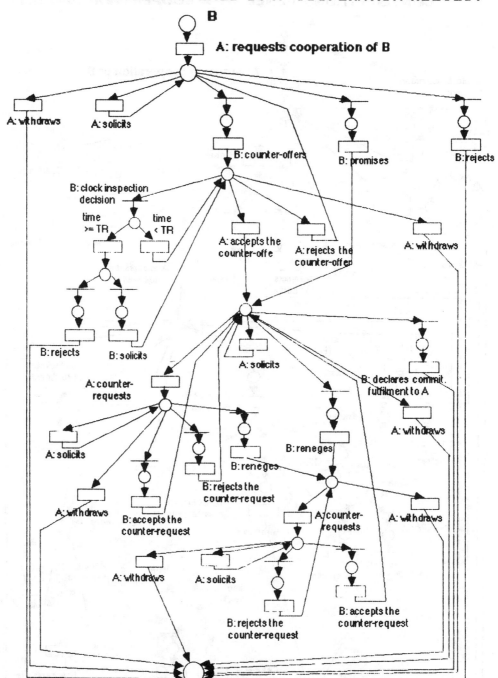

Fig. 2b : The Net modeling the Partner's behaviour

LEGENDA: each unlabelled transition represents the decision which
precedes the interaction represented by the subsequent transition

474

b) the *environment conditions* declaring if the action is *part of* another action; if the action has one or more *precondition*, i.e. if it can start only after some other actions are finished,

c) the *completion times* indicating:
   - the beginning time, when the action cannot start before a given date;
   - the time-out for the final fulfillment of the commitment;
   - the overall time required for accomplishing the action;

- some <u>comments.</u>

The structure of speech acts contained inside a Conversation for Possibilites is analogous, except for the propositional content which depends on the particular conversation.

If we consider a Petri Net as an object, each particular conversation of a given type is represented by an instance of that object. The set of possible speech acts open to each partner at a particular moment in a conversation of a given type, is given by the status (marking) of the corresponding conversation instance (see Fig. 3).

===

CONVERSATION FOR ACTION

- ACTOR
- PARTNER
- TYPE OF CONVERSATION
- STATUS OF THE CONVERSATION
- HISTORY (the sequence of the performed speech acts)

===

SPEECH ACT (of a Conversation for Action)

- ILLOCUTIONARY POINT
- PROPOSITIONAL CONTENT
  - ☐ ACTION
  - ☐ FIELD(S) OF RESPONSIBILITY
  - ☐ FIELD(S) OF EXPERTISE
- SATISFACTION CONDITIONS
  - ☐ EXPIRATION TIME
  - ☐ ENVIRONMENT CONDITIONS
  - ☐ COMPLETION TIMES
- COMMENTS

===

Fig. 3

2.3 CHAOS Architecture

The CHAOS family is currently under development. The first prototype, called CHAOS-1, runs on the VAX 750 under Unix® Operating System and is written in FranzLisp plus Pearl [DFW82]. We presently are developing a new release which overcomes some of the CHAOS-1 limits: in fact, it deals with the responsibility structure by handling the Conversations for Possibilities; with the commitments structure by handling the mutual relationships between conversations; and with a more flexible user interface by allowing a disciplined use of a semi- structured messages in natural language. Till now, all the topics concerning communication/distribution of the application are neglected and simulated by means of shared data.

The focus is here on the overall CHAOS architecture which consists of three main modules:

- the User Interface Module;
- the Conversations Handler Module;
- the Knowledge Builder.

They are briefly sketched here below.

The User Interface module

The User Interface allows the user to:

a) perform speech acts, consistent with the set of speech acts available to her/him in the current state of the selected conversation. Once the user has selected one of her/his possibilities among the ones displayed on the screen, the User Interface guides her/him to express in a structured way the speech actcontent, following the pattern shown in Fig.3. Since the 'action' is described in a semi-natural language, the User Interface invokes the Knowledge Builder for its interpretation.

b) select a subset of all her/his conversations which satisfy certain properties: for instance, the conversations in which the user is waiting for an answer, the conversations having a certain partner, the converstions in which the user is waited for a commitment completion, an other ones.

c) execute some operations on a specific conversation such as: to read from her/his own mailbox (buffer) the messages carrying a speech act already arrived, but not yet consumed; to visualize or verify some properties on it; to continue the conversation, possibly after the buffer contents have been visualized. All these operation requests are passed to the Conversations Handler which retrieves the suitable data, and returns them back to the User Interface for displaying.

The Conversation Handler

The Conversations Handler handles conversations by sending, receiving, storing and retrieving the speech acts they consist of.

Every time a user opens a conversation, the Conversations Handler creates an instance of the object corresponding to the conversation type (a CONVERSATION INSTANCE) and stores it into the user database. If the partner is partially specified, the Conversation Handler calls the Knowledge Builder to identify the appropriate destination.

Every time a user performs a speech act inside a conversation, the Conversations Handler updates the current status of the corresponding CONVERSATION INSTANCE and calls the Knowledge Builder in order to update the Knowledge Base with the new information contained in the performed speech act.

Furthermore, the Conversation Handler is activated by the User Interface every time a user asks to continue a conversation, and every time the User Interface needs information about the conversations (status, contents, properties) or about the messages not yet consumed by the user.

The Knowledge Builder

CHAOS does not require *ad hoc* input by its users, but derives knowledge automatically by the conversations it handles. The Knowledge Builder "observes" each speech act in a conversation and uses the information contained in the speech act to update the Knowledge Base. This latter contains:

● The Responsibility Structure of the organization, i.e., the set of declared responsibility fields together with the relationships connecting them expressed in terms of the relationship "is subfield of";

● The Expertise Distribution inside the organization consisting of a set of facts which correlate organization members to fields of expertise by keeping track of the degree of expertise the various members have in the different fields and by associating to each area the set of members having expertise in it.

● A Dictionary containing the definition of the objects and actions referred to during conversations, in terms of their attributes; a Thesaurus containing the relationships between them [Sco86]: specifically in the case of the actions, the two above mentioned relationships of being 'precondition' or 'part of' another action.

● The Committed Action Network which keeps track of the relationships among different actions committed inside interrelated conversations together with the completion times.

This Knowledge Base, updated by the Knowledge Builder by "observing" the conversations occurring in the office, is used for supporting and disciplining communication inside the organization, as it will be shown in the next section.

3. How CHAOS learns from conversations and disciplines communication

The communication disciplines embodied in CHAOS are based on a theory, presently under development |DeM86|, which considers organizations as closed autonomous systems in the linguistic domain. In this frame the events relevant inside an organization are the agreements reached within conversations by the organization members, both at the commitments and at the commitment satisfaction level. The rules within communication disciplines are derived from the conversations in a formal and unambiguous way, fully described in the specifications of the new CHAOS release. Hints about this are presented in the following subsections in an intuitive way.

First of all, when conversations for possibilities are considered, the declaratives which close their successful termination modify the domain of possibilities open to the office members, possibly changing role distribution, introducing new areas of activities, and the like. Mainly involved here are the disciplines of <u>authorization</u> and <u>delegation</u>.

Secondly, when conversations for action are considered, the specific issue are the commitments, how they are interrelated both from the viewpoint of the authority structure and of the use of resources. Mainly involved here are the disciplines of <u>authorization</u> and <u>synchronization</u>.

Thirdly, the professional language characterizing the office work is shown in the action part of any speech act occurring in both kinds of conversations. In this framework, the linguistic games binding the office members can be analyzed in order to understand how names are given to objects and to activities manipulating them. Then, the discipline of <u>naming</u> is involved here.

As a nice consequence of how all the previous communication aspects are disciplined, both sources and destinations inside communications can be understood and properly connected even in presence of partially specified information. These aspects refer to the disciplines of <u>identification</u> and <u>addressing</u>.

Finally, the way in which CHAOS supports the organizational changes defines a discipline of <u>reorganization</u>, in accordance with the organizational analysis approach underlying the proposed technology.

In the following subsections all the quotations are taken from Petri's [Pet77b].

3.1 Delegation

"<u>Delegation</u>: this means the delegation of tasks from one agency to another... If somebody delegates something, this has, of course, formally comprehensible consequences for synchronization, addressing and other disciplines."

478

Applying this perspective to offices, CHAOS disciplines delegation on the basis of the roles characterization presented in Section 2.1. CHAOS supports delegation of responsibilities and delegation of tasks in the way sketched in Fig. 4.

Any delegation attributes to the delegated member a well defined role which s/he then plays inside the subsequent Conversations for Action and Conversations for Possibilities, as described more in detail in the following Sections.

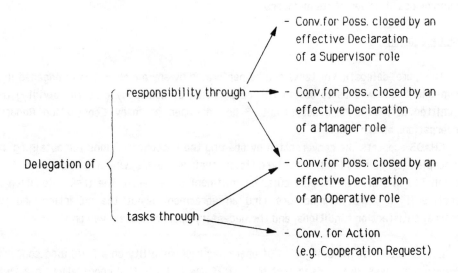

Fig. 4

Responsibility Delegation

Only the Supervisors have the authority to delegate whatever responsibility on the field of their competence. More precisely, the supervisor A of field F has the authority:
- to delegate supervision responsibility, i.e., to declare a new supervisor, on subfields of F, but not on the whole F. The only one who has the authority to perform such declaration is the supervisor of the field which has F as its subfield;
- to delegate responsibility of lower degree, i.e. to attribute to someone the role of manager or operative, both on the whole field F and on any of its subfields.

For delegating a role of responsibility to an office member B the competent supervisor A (called "the Delegating") opens a Conversation for Possibilities with B (called "the Delegated"). CHAOS supports the conversation by opening the subconversations for obtaining by other supervisors and managers their approvals which are necessary for making the specific delegation effective.

For instance, if A is the supervisor of the area of activity "SHELLS" with subfields "ART" and "KEE", and wants to delegate supervision responsibility to B who was before just control manager of the field 'Kee', then A must obtain the agreement of B and the approval of the supervisor of area "A.I.", which has "SHELLS" as its subfield.

If the necessary approvals are given and B accepts, either immediately or after some counter-offer cycle, to take upon her/himself the responsibility, then A closes the conversation by an effective declaration, i.e., by a declaration which is accepted by the organization, or better, by its involved part, and which therefore actually changes the domain of possibilities of its members.

Task Delegation

The "pure" delegation of tasks can be performed by any member who is engaged in a commitment, and wishes to obtain the cooperation of somebody else for dividing the committed action in more subactions. S/he can open as many Cooperation Request Conversations as s/he needs.

CHAOS supports the conversation by opening the subconversations for obtaining, by the people responsibles for the involved fields, their approvals, which are necessary (see section 3.2) in order for the particular commitment to be taken. The task delegation is effective if the two interlocutors find an agreement about the subaction and its temporal satisfaction conditions, and the necessary approvals are given on it.

Let us note that the delegation of operative responsibility on a field also concerns delegation of tasks. In fact (see section 3.5), if one looks to find cooperation in a field and does not indicate the partner, CHAOS adresses the request to the declared Operative responsible, if s/he exists . In other words, the Operative Responsible is the preferential partner in Cooperation Request Conversations.

3.2 Authorization

"Authorization: this discipline is concerned not only with assigning and schematically representing access rights but also with scheduling obligations which are consistently connected with access rights and authorizations for issuing directives, and with the rules for an adequate basis of supervision."...

CHAOS disciplines authorization by defining how the office members who have a delegated responsibility perform their role inside Conversations for Action and Conversations for Possibilities.

We have seen in the previous section that only the Supervisors have the authority to open Conversations for Possibilities finalized at responsibility delegation, and we have also mentioned that managers can be asked for approving commitments and declarations which fall in their field of competence. We can now be more precise.

Supervisor S of field F:

   a)   authorizes declarations concerning the field which are not performed by her/himself, as in the situation described in the previous section concerning delegation of supervision responsibility on the field 'KEE';

   b)   exercises a form of weak control inside Conversation for Action concerning field F . S/he is made aware by the system of the conversations which discuss commitments concerning the field and has access right into these conversations. If s/he does not exercise this right within a fixed amount of time, then "by default" her/his authorization to make the commitment is assumed.

Manager M of the field F:

   a)   authorizes the making of commitments concerning field F, i.e., having F indicated as field of responsibility inside the speech act (see Fig. 3). S/he can execise this control in different ways, from the strongest one, in which M makes directly any commitment concerning F, to the weakest one, in which M is asked for the approval when all negotiation about the commitment is successfully finished. Let us note that in this last case if the two interlocutors do not reach an agreement, the manager remains completely in the dark about the conversation concerning field F.

   b)   is asked for her/his opinion about declarations concerning field F. For instance, if supervisor S of F wants to open a new subfield of F, s/he asks the opinion of M to obtain her/his consensus since afterward M exercises control also over the new subfield.

   Note that, beyond the different formulation, the essence of the two situations is the same, and is therefore correct to speak of authorization in both cases. In fact, M can always reject the proposal: in one case, by denying approval; in the other, by giving a negative opinion. As said in section 2.1, goal of CHAOS is to enhance organization liveliness by supporting negotiation within conversations for action and for possibilities until an agreement is found, and by allowing all the people involved in it because of their role of responsibility to deny authorization. Nevertheless the possibility of dealing with (persistent) authorization refusals is preserved. In the above mentioned situation, if M continues to reject any proposal of adding subfields to F, then supervisor S can revoke the control responsibility of M.

3.3 Synchronization

   "This discipline is concerned with getting proper timing restraints for different activities. In some cases, the use of clocks may serve for synchronizing all activities. But what should we generally understand by the term 'synchronization' ? My answer is that the precise definition of the term should be based upon the partial ordering in terms of causality as opposed to an ordering in terms of time."

481

Here we have to distinguish between two different orders of questions. The first one concerns synchronization among the different speech acts constituting a conversation. This synchronization is naturally disciplined in CHAOS, where the models of conversations as combination of elementary speech acts are expressed in terms of Gameru models, i.e., Petri net, models. Therefore, only a partial ordering among speech acts is assumed.

Furthermore, also the relationships among the actions committed in different but related conversations are expressed in terms of a casual relation. We have already mentioned that for indicating, for instance, that action A, say coding, cannot start before another action, say specification, is finished, the user must indicate as environment condition: B is-pre- of A. Therefore, only a partial ordering among actions is assumed.

Nevertheless, inside organizations, as Petri himself observes, "In some cases, the use of clocks may serve for synchronizing all activities". CHAOS assumes a time scale common to the whole organization in order to give a way for indicating time constraints, namely, the *expiration time* associated to any speech act and the *completion times* of the overall commitment (see Fig. 3).

This allow CHAOS to support a further kind of synchronization among interrelated activities which must be accomplished in order to fulfill a commitment. In fact, on the basis of precondition relations among actions and of the completion times of each one of them, the system is able to derive a PERT of the related activities and to support the handling of the consequences of the possible delay in the fulfillment of some of them.

3.4 Naming.

Naming "is conceived as the act of giving names, and will be subject to a discipline because not everybody may arbitrarily name entities ... A typical question would be: how can we understand the incompatible naming of files in different computer systems as a consequence of only one naming discipline? .... exactly how much freedom exists when names are given? ..."

Inside an office the questions can be specified as follows:
1)   how new names and relations among them and with the old ones are created and possibly shared?
2)   when and how names used by any two ineterlocutors inside a conversation have to be compatible with the names shared between (any group of) office members?
3)   to what extent ambiguities arising in conversations should be avoided and office members helped in solving them?

Let us explain naming discipline of CHAOS by trying to answer these questions.

1) Since professional languages are involved [Nyg84] , a set of basic names can be defined to build an <u>initial dictionary</u>. For example, let's take the software production process as a possible linguistic domain. In this domain concepts such as project, module, requirements, programming language, coding, testing, and the like can be defined, using suitable attributes (frames) to capture their overall meaning. Furthermore, these concepts can be linked together to construct <u>an initial thesaurus</u>, using some relationships as: part of, precondition of, and the like [Sco86].

<u>New</u> objects with their <u>names and relations</u> with other objects are introduced in the dictionary and in the thesaurus, and then become knowledge shared among the office members, at three moments in office life:

- when a commitment concerning an action is made, all the names and relations defining its propositional content (in our domain, they generally define projects or subprojects) enter the shared knowledge, following the rules implied by the authority structure;

- when a report is done an analogous process takes place: the propositional content of the fulfilled commitment becomes a common experience. Notice that in general the content of a commitment and of the related report can differ due to possible negotiations after the commitment definition.

- finally, upon declarations of new objects, such as new fields of responsibility, areas of activities and the like.

In such a way as the professional languages evolve as professions do, the dictionary and the thesaurus are updated accordingly, by means of functions as: creation, enrichment, specialization, and the like. For example, prototyping, software production techniques derived from the use of AI tools modify the relationships between the production steps also depending on the kind of project under consideration. Old methodologies have to coexist with new ones.

2) The (possible) conflict between a shared lexicon and the linguistic conventions used by two interlocutors is handled in CHAOS on the basis of the following principles:

• at any speech act occurring inside a conversation, CHAOS keeps track of any (new) relationship between objects or activities created by the ineterlocutors. This is considered as a local convention, valid as far as these two ineterlocutors are concerned. For example, A and B may agree that 'design of CHAOS' means the detailed specification of data and fuctions before the implementation, while inside the organization 'design of something' means the overall production process involving this 'something'.

• this freedom can be limited only when names have to be used in different contexts: e.g., inside a diagram describing a project activities scheduling which is handled by another office member, let's say the project responsible. In this case, an inconsistency is signalled. The two interlocutors either accept the lexicon shared inside the organization: in the previous example A and B do not use improperly the word 'design'. Or define suitable synonyms (aliasing): in the example, the local name 'design' is considered as synonim of the shared name 'detailed architecture'.

3)   The acceptability of any support to human communication depends on a reasonably free use of language, with ambiguities arising from anaphores of different kinds. CHAOS aims at solving these situations for two kinds of reasons: from the system point of view, the necessity of 'understanding' in order to learn from what is going on in view of future inquiry (selection and updating of conversations); from the user point of view, the possibility of reducing the amount of communication necessary to solve ambiguities between any two interlocutors, by providing upon request the intended meaning of ambiguous sentences.

This is done by a process which incrementally uses some specialized views of what CHAOS learns during the conversations: first, by considering the knowledge collected during the conversation containing the ambiguous sentence; secondly, by considering the knowledge collected during past conversations between the two members; thirdly, by doing the same on conversations between the actor or the partner with any other office member in similar circumstances. In the last two cases, a user model is needed, in order to use the formalized knowledge the interlocutors of the conversation have mutually constructed in the past (communicated knowledge). This knowledge consists of shared partial views of the dictionaries and of information (beliefs and suppositions) deduced by means of a set of inference rules based on the structure of the conversations and on the type of speech acts they have done.

The final result of the process, possibly its failure, is (generally) shown to the user for an acknowledgement or for a more precise specification, which becomes part of the system and can be provided at any time.

3.5 Identification and Addressing

Identification "involves demonstrating the identity of the source and destination of phenomena .....covers the question of pattern recognition as well as problems of proving the competences of agencies with regard to certain actions."

Addressing is the "description of routes or system paths through a net of channels and agencies".

These two disciplines are obviously strictly related to one another: if the source or destination is not identified, any addressing is impossible; once the source or destination is identified, the message has indeed to be properly addressed.

CHAOS disciplines identification and addressing on the basis of the following principles.
•   Since any speech act occurs inside a specific (sub-)conversation and is univocally positioned inside it (i.e., it corresponds to a unique transition in the net which models the (sub-)conversation), the identification of source and destination   follows

automatically, since they are known after the opening speech act, and cannot change during the conversation.

● CHAOS allows any actor to partially define the destination of the message in the speech act opening the conversation without affecting the previous point, since it is able to retrieve the complete information from the knowledge base (the responsibility structure, the committed actions network, the expertise distribution, the dictionary and thesaurus). For example, the user can indicate as destination 'an expert of the area Common Lisp', 'the person responsible for the project CHAOS', 'who will implement procedure Search of the module User Interface', and the like. CHAOS is not only able to identify the correct partner but also delivers to him/her the appropriate messages.

● CHAOS supports the user in the identification of the office members whose approval is necessary about a commitment under discussion. In fact, when the two interlocuotrs reach an agreement about it, the user who actually takes the commitment can simply express his/her willingness to prosecute the conversation and the system, on the basis of the model of the authority structure governing the commitments making and fulfillment shows which subconversation has to be opened and with whom (see the examples in 3.1).

It is worth noting that CHAOS disciplines addressing at the 'people' level by helping the office members to follow the office game rules. In regard to addressing at the 'message' level, CHAOS rests on the rules embodied in the underlying mail/communication system. It is not difficult to imagine an integration toward a system which is able to reach the partner also in the case of his/her dynamic location, once the system is informed about the new one (possibly using the flexibility provided by the information contained in the Knowledge Base: e.g., 'I'm going to the boss', 'I'm moving to implement the User Interface Module', 'I'm looking for authorization to start project CHAOS').

3.6 Reorganization

"Suppose you have a system of pipes and tubes in a chemical factory, and that you wish to attach a new tube to the system. A specification that a certain subset of valves must be closed in order to cut off flow from the part of the system that is being altered is inadequate; it must also be specified that while the new tube is being fitted the valves must remain under control in order that nobody can open them, that is, that no other independent activity be allowed to interfere disastrously."

The discipline of reorganization is the one that is at the deepest level influenced by the theoretical approach underlying CHAOS.

As it has been sketched above, we consider any organizational system as a linguistic game, i.e., as a closed social system whose structure defines the space of possibility (in terms of speech acts) of the members within it, compensating the perturbations (the speech acts) its members actually perform according to its structure, by means of a modification of its structure itself, reorganizing itself. There is therefore a basic circularity in the organizational systems between structure and behavior, and this circularity disciplines the reorganization of each organizational system.

CHAOS embodies a model of this basic circularity, appearing to its users as a self-reorganizing system. In fact, CHAOS reorganizes itself by compensating for the perturbations that are the mutual commitments of its members w.r.t. the actions to perform and/or the new possibilities to experiment in terms of responsibility delegation, and modifies its rules so that they embody the derived expertise and authority distribution.

The reorganization discipline of CHAOS emulates in a partial way the basic circularity between organizational rules and conversations which characterizes the organizations as social systems, by reducing it to the two-level hierarchy of facts and inference rules in its Knowledge Base. This is the reason why CHAOS shows differences w.r.t. Petri's guidelines, which suggest to consider reoganization as an intervention by an external agent.

4. The missing disciplines

Copying, cancellation and composition are disciplines which consider objects flowing in the office as "documents" and define the rules for handling them: they are naturally related to authorization and delegation, which state who, when and how is allowed to manipulate any kind of office documents.

Up to now CHAOS has not dealt with these problems, since its attention is concentrated on the commitments made by its members, and not on the actions those commitments refer to. Two are the major reasons for this choice.

From one point of view, the disciplines of document handling have up till now been defined on an empirical basis, and lack a sound theoretical foundation. Their integration in CHAOS is made difficult by this situation, because the architecture of CHAOS is based on a sound and coherent theoretical framework.

From another point of view, the extension of CHAOS to document handling is logically subsequent to the full development of its commitments handling kernel. In fact, the disciplines of copying, cancellation and composition contribute to a richer characterization of office roles, but do not change the linguistic essence of the basic circularity of the office, through which roles are attributed and changed.

In regard to valuation discipline, which Petri claims "must treat the exchangeability of resources and its modalities", we agree with Petri that it "is perhaps the most important one since we know least about it, compared with others". We are now investigating if it has not as its primary concern the implementation issues in a communication system. Any scheduling algorithm in a distributed system, in fact, defines implicitly a valuation of the scheduled processes. From this point of view the current implementation of CHAOS embodies some rules of the valuation discipline w.r.t. the expertises , the degrees of responsibility, etc.

In [Pet77b] C. A. Petri claims that "modelling is done according to a scheme which normally has come into existence through a historical process running independent of conscious methodical technology". This is the very situation in which CHAOS has been developed: it reflects part of its environment since it is a model of the basic circularity of the office, but it is not based on any general schema for deriving models from systems. It is therefore not possible to claim that CHAOS embodies in any sense *the rules of* the discipline of modelling.

5. Acknowledgements

Many persons have contributed to project CHAOS. Among them, we would like in particular mention Raffaela Vassallo and Annamaria Zanaboni, who have participated in the development of CHAOS from its very beginning. Giacomo Ferrari is helping us in respect to the linguistic aspects of CHAOS with discussions, suggestions and criticisms. Alfonso Gerevini and Alessandro Bottarelli are deeply involved in the project, on which they are preparing their Masters theses. Klaus Voss provided useful suggestions, in particular for what concerns the distinction between communication disciplines and their rules.

This research has been supported by Ministero Della Pubblica Istruzione on a national contract.

6. References

[AT84]   Action Technologies Inc., *Coordinator - User Manual and Report*, San Francisco, 1984

[Aus62]   J. Austin, *How to do Things with Words*, Oxford University Press, London, 1962

[CH80]   P.M. Cashman, A.W. Holt, A communication-oriented approach to structuring the software maintenance environment, *ACM SIGSOFT, Software Engineering Notes*, 5:1, january, 1980

[CSCW86] CSCW'86, *Proceedings of the Conference on Computer-Supported Cooperative*

[DDPS82] F. De Cindio, G. De Michelis, L. Pomello, C. Simone, Superposed Automata Nets, in: *Application and Theory of Petri Nets,* IFB 52, Springer-Verlag, Berlin, 1982

[DDS85] F. De Cindio, G. De Michelis, C. Simone, Formal Computer systems in social organizations, in: *Proc. Working Conference on Development and Use of Computer-based Systems and Tools,* Aarhus, 1985

[DDS86] F. De Cindio, G. De Michelis, C. Simone, R. Vassallo, A. Zanaboni, CHAOS as a Coordination Technology, in [CSCW86]

[DDS87] F. De Cindio, G. De Michelis, C. Simone, GAMERU: a language for analysis and design of human communication pragmatics within organizational systems, in: *Advances in Petri Nets 1986,* LNCS, Springer-Verlag, Berlin, 1987 (to appear)

[DeM86] G. De Michelis, Sistemi autopoietici del terzo ordine: il caso degli uffici, *Metamorfosi* 2, 1986

[DFW82] M. Deering, J. Faletti, R. Wilensky, *Using PEARL AI Package,* Computer Science Div. EECS Dept, University of California, 1982

[DJM86] R. Dunham, B. M. Johnson, G. McGonagill, M. Olson, G. M. Weaver, Using a Computer Based Tool to Support Collaboration: A Field Experiment, in [CSCW86]

[FL81] C.F. Flores, J.J. Ludlow, Doing and Speaking in: the Office, in F. Fish, R. Sprague (eds.), *DSS: Issues and Challenges,* Pergamon, New York, 1981

[Hol79] A. W. Holt, Net Models of Organizational Systems, in Theory and Practise, in C. A. Petri (ed.), *Ansätze zur Organizationstheorie Rechnergestutzer Informationssysteme,* Oldenburg, Munchen, 1979

[Hol86] A. W. Holt, Coordination Technology and Petri Nets, in *Advances in Petri Nets 1985,* LNCS 222, Springer-Verlag, Berlin, 1986

[MGL86] T. W. Malone, K. R. Grant, K-Y. Lai, R. Rao, D. Rosenblitt, Semi-structured messages are surprisingly useful for Computer-supported Coordination, in [CSCW86]

[MV80] H. Maturana, F. Varela, *Autopoiesis and Cognition,* Reidel, Dordrecht, 1980

[Nyg84] K. Nygaard, Profession Oriented Languages, in *Proc. Medinfo Europe 84,* Bressels, 1984

[Pet77a]   C. A. Petri, Modelling as a Communication Discipline, in: H. Beilner, E. Gelenbe (eds.) *Measuring, modelling and evaluating computer systems*, North Holland, New York, 1977

[Pet77b]   C. A. Petri, Communication Disciplines, in: B. Shaw (ed.), *Proc. of the Joint IBM-Univ. of Newcastle upon Tyne Seminar*, Univ. of Newcastle upon Tyne Computing Lab., 1977

[Pet79]   C. A. Petri, Kommunicationsdisziplinen, in C. A. Petri (ed.), *Ansätze zur Organizationstheorie Rechnergestutzer Informationssysteme*, Oldenburg, Munchen, 1979

[RV86]   G. Richter, K. Voss, Toward a comprehensive Office Model integrating Information and Resources, in *Advances in Petri Nets 1985*, LNCS 222, Springer Verlag, Berlin, 1986

[Sco86]   D.S.Scott, Capturing concepts with Data Structures, [preliminary version, paper to be revised], Dept. of Computer Science, CMU, nov. 86

[SC84]   S. Sluzier, P.M. Cashman, XCP : An experimental tool for supporting office procedures, *IEEE 1984 Proceedings of the First International Conference on Office Automation*, Silver Spring, MD:IEEE Computer Society, 1984

[Sea69]   J.R. Searle, *Speech Acts : An essay in the philosophy of language*, Cambridge University Press, Cambridge, 1969

[Sea79]   J.R. Searle, A Taxonomy of Illocutionary Acts, in: J.R. Searle (ed.) *Expression and Meaning: Studies in the Theory of Speech Acts*, Cambridge University Press, Cambridge, 1979

[Win86]   T. Winograd, A Language Perspective on the Design of Cooperative Work, in: [CSCW86]

[WF86]   T. Winograd, C. F. Flores, *Understanding Computers and Cognition*, Ablex, Norwood, 1986

[Wit53]   L. Wittgenstein, *Philosophische Untersuchungen*, Blackwell, Oxford, 1953

Local and Global Structuring of Computer Mediated Communication: Developing Linguistic Perspectives On CSCW in COSMOS

John Bowers
Department of Experimental Psychology
University of Oxford
U.K.

John Churcher
Department of Psychology
University of Manchester
U.K.

ABSTRACT: This paper is concerned with the development of a language/action perspective in the Cosmos project. We emphasise the importance of seeing cooperative work in terms of participants' communicative actions. In contrast to some explorations of speech act theory, we argue that communicative actions should be seen as essentially embedded in dialogical contexts. In particular, we attempt to show the relevance of concepts derived from the analysis of actually occurring conversations, for computer mediated communication in general and cooperative work in particular. We distinguish between local and global structuring of communication and argue that many group working situations combine both sorts. These observations have influenced our work in the Cosmos project on the design of a structure definition language (SDL) by means of which users can configure their computer mediated communication environment. We describe SDL and show how its interpretation is influenced by our conversation analytic approach. We illustrate our arguments with an example of cooperative document preparation.

1 INTRODUCTION

A new communications technology does not leave the social world as it was. Marshall McLuhan's famous dictum, "the medium is the message", should alert us to the determining effect any communication medium has upon the messages it can support. As McLuhan [1] illustrated in analyses of print, telegraphy, radio, television and other media, each technology has made possible new messages, new "patternings of human association", new meanings, new forms of life (*and* death). Media are not socially or politically neutral, and the designers and engineers of a new medium bear responsibility for the way it changes the social world. For McLuhan, the "electronic age" demanded new languages and concepts with which to articulate and confront the problems that its media present.

In this paper we are concerned with computer-based message systems (CBMSs) and computer-mediated communication (CMC), a technology and a form of communication which have developed since McLuhan's best known works. There already exists a considerable variety of CBMS applications [2, 3], and because of the inherent flexibility of the technology, the potential variety of its applications is immense, particularly in the area of computer-supported cooperative work (CSCW). Cosmos,[1] an interdisciplinary research project in the U.K. funded under the Alvey programme for advanced information technology, is developing the specification for an advanced CBMS which recognises this potential variety.

Cosmos is designed to support historically changing communicative practices. The concept of a *practice* is inherently social and historical; it cannot be reduced to a set of individuals together with their respective beliefs, habits, desires, etc., nor can it be removed from historical context. However, just as in linguistics it is possible, for the purposes of analysis, to identify abstract grammatical structures corresponding to relatively stable patterns of usage (e.g. 'sentence', 'noun phrase'), so can we identify forms of communicative practices (e.g. 'committee', 'voting by secret ballot'). Such abstract forms of communicative practice are referred to in Cosmos as *Communication Structures* (CSs), and they include all the familiar kinds of applications of CBMSs (bulletin boards, computer conferences etc.) some of the less familiar ones (remote tutoring, various group working support facilities) and still others yet to be thought of.

The functionality of a Cosmos system will be determined by the CSs represented in it. As it has to allow for change in the practices it supports, it must provide users with some instrument for modifying or augmenting its CSs in new ways. The most powerful solution would be a means of producing, for any CS, an interpretable description which uniquely specifies it. Cosmos provides this in the form of SDL, a structure definition language, which is made available to all users, and whose well-formed expressions are the structure definitions.

In the first part of this paper, we address the specific properties of CMC as a form of communication and in particular we assess and develop the "language/action perspective" on CSCW [4], drawing on work in speech act theory [5, 6] and, especially, conversation analysis e.g. [7]. In the second part, we show how these considerations have influenced the design and intended

---

[1]COnfigurable Structured Message Oriented System

interpretation of SDL. By providing both a theoretical perspective and a formal language we hope to help users and designers to articulate and confront some of the problems presented by CBMSs in the CSCW context.

2 LANGUAGE AS ACTION

2.1 Speech Act Theory and Conversations for Action: A Critical Discussion

Much recent theoretical work in CSCW has been influenced by speech act theory [4, 8, 9, 10]. The central insight of speech act theory is easily summarised: *to speak is to do*. That is, speaking (and by extension all forms of communication) are species of action. This thesis is largely due to J. L. Austin [5] who was concerned to draw attention to sentences such as:

I bet you six pence it will rain tomorrow.
I declare war on Zanzibar.
I dub thee Sir Walter.

According to Austin, these sentences are not being used *declaratively* to describe states of affairs in the world, rather they are being used to *do* things. Said by the appropriate person at the right time, the world will be *changed* by such sentences in substantial ways. Acts like dubbing, requesting, promising, asserting, expressing etc., which are performed *in* speech, Austin called *illocutionary acts*.

Since Austin, the development of speech act theory has largely been associated with Searle [6, 11]. Searle has been at pains to formalise the notions introduced by Austin, to classify the conditions under which different kinds of speech act can be appropriately ("felicitously") issued, and to explicate a typology of illocutionary acts. It is Searle's work which has proved particularly influential in CSCW.

The original contribution made to speech act theory by Winograd and Flores [4, 9]goes beyond a consideration of isolated utterances and addresses the orders of illocutionary acts found in conversational structures. It is these larger structures which they see as comprising an important part of cooperative work. In the form of a transition network, Figure 1 shows the orders of acts that Winograd and Flores regard as appropriate for a kind of conversation they claim is central to cooperative work, *conversations for action* or CfAs.

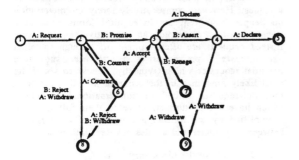

Figure 1: The Basic Conversation for Action (from Winograd [4])

Winograd [4, p206] elucidates the diagram in the following way:

> In a simple *conversation for action*, one party (A) makes a request to another (B). The request is interpreted by each party as having certain *conditions of satisfaction*, which characterize a future course of actions by B. After the initial utterance (the request), B can accept (and thereby commit to satisfy the conditions); reject (and thereby end the conversation); or counter-offer with alternative conditions. Each of these in turn has its own possible continuations (e.g., after a counter-offer, A can accept, reject, or counter-offer again)...... This diagram is not a model of the mental state of a speaker or hearer, but shows the conversation as a 'dance', in which the acts generate the structure of *completion* of the conversation.

This extension of speech act theory into conversation is of interest both theoretically (it implicitly makes a number of claims about the nature of conversation) and in terms of advanced CBMSs (networks like Figure 1 underlie the design of COORDINATOR, the commercially available system associated with Flores, and CHAOS, the commitment-handling system developed by DeCindio et al. [10]). Here we detail some criticisms of this work because they are instructive for the general relevance of speech act theory for system design and will set up our developments of the language action perspective for CSCW.

First, it is customary for speech act theorists to suppose that utterances (message-texts) can be mapped onto illocutionary acts in a one-to-one fashion. That is, the issuance of an utterance will *count as* a request, counter, rejection or whatever. This makes it possible to think of a conversation as a *chain* of illocutionary acts and legitimates system designs where senders of messages classify their message-texts by selecting a category of act presented, say, on a menu of possible options.

However, it is questionable whether, in conversations, utterances (message-texts) can be mapped on to illocutionary acts in this simple fashion. As Austin was well aware (but his followers less so), many utterances require *uptake* for an illocutionary act to be secured. For example, *I bet you six pence it will rain tomorrow* can scarcely be considered to perform the act of betting unless the addressee responds with some ratification like *You're on!* Without this signal the illocutionary act has not been accomplished, the bet-offer 'hangs'. Similarly, as Levinson [12] argues, a promise requires uptake for the commitments and expectations associated with promising to be secured. If I promise to pay you back for the meal you just bought, does what I said still stand as a promise if you tell me not to (*it was nothing!*)? Furthermore, sometimes addressees can intervene and renegotiate promises, thus:

A: I'll bring back the book I borrowed from you tomorrow.
B: No, that's okay. You can keep it until the weekend.
A: Thanks.

In this conversation, A's initial offer is 'deflected' by B's response. This shows that the lone utterance of *I'll bring back the book I borrowed from you tomorrow* is not sufficient for A to be committed to the future course of action you might expect from, say, Searle's [6] list of felicity conditions for promising. B's response overturns A's initial promise. And the response in turn elicits a *Thanks* from A which constitutes her acceptance of the offer. As a result of this dialogue, A and B have entered into an agreement in which they understand A to be obliged to return the book at around about the weekend. However, at no stage did A utter *I hereby promise you to bring back at the weekend the book I borrowed*, nor did B utter *I hereby request you to bring back at the weekend the book you borrowed* (or anything like it), which would be the standard ways in which A's obligation could have been secured on orthodox speech act theory accounts. It seems more sensitive to claim that, very often in actual conversation, the commitments and reciprocal agreements which speech act theory associates with the issuance of single utterances or message-texts emerge from processes of negotiation and/or disputation between participants - processes which are distributed over several turns [13].

Conversely, one utterance can be used to perform many acts. Consider the first utterance in the following interchange [14]:

A: Would you like another drink?
B: Yes I would, thank you, but make it a small one.

A's utterance seems to be both a question and an offer, and it is taken up by B in this way.

Further objections can be lodged against the idea that conversations can be captured as chains of illocutions for other action-oriented aspects of an utterance can also be addressed in conversation. Levinson [14] asks us to imagine hearing A (being bored) say to his party-companion B:

A: It's getting late, Mildred.
B: a. But I'm having such a good time.
   b. Do you want to go?
   c. Aren't you enjoying yourself, dear?

Any of the three responses is quite plausible but none of them addresses the illocutionary act A has performed (*stating* that it's getting late). Rather, they concern possible *perlocutionary aims*, intents pursued *through* speech which are specific to the occasion of utterance and not conventionally tied to utterance forms as illocutionary acts are [5]. In much recent work on speech acts the distinction between illocutionary acts and perlocutionary aims and effects is often elided (e.g. Allen [15] who conflates the two when coining the term "illocutionary effects").

The objections outlined so far concern general problems with speech act models of conversation. However, Winograd and Flores' contribution has some other problems which are worth bringing out. Consider the horizontal line of transitions across the top of Figure 1. This represents the minimal path through the network leading to successful completion. We can rewrite this path as:

A: Request.
B: Promise.
B: Assert [that conditions of satisfaction are met].
A: Declare [that conditions of satisfaction are met].

However, actual conversational sequences which involve the minimal bringing off of requests are almost *never* structured in this way. Rather, requests are often brought off in two-part interchange like:

Doctor: Say "Ahhh"
Patient: Ahhh

Sequences like this, where two speakers issue a related pair of utterances in adjacent turns, are known as *adjacency pairs* and have been the subject of much research by conversation analysts, e.g. [16]. Goffman [17] and Coulthard [18] amongst others have claimed that adjacency pairs constitute the fundamental units of conversational organisation. The adjacency pair of which 'request' forms the first part typically has 'compliance' or 'rejection' as the second. It seems odd that Winograd and Flores do not recognise 'compliance' as a legitimate follow-up to a request. Rather, they seem to believe that addressees have to issue a promise to advance the conversation towards completion. However, addressees can proceed straightaway to the requested action if they see fit. Indeed, there is evidence (see [14] for a review) that responses to a request *other than compliance* are linguistically marked or signaled as unusual or *dispreferred*. This is not to say it is impossible or illformed to follow-up a request with a promise but rather this sequence should not be given special status over what is preferred in actual conversation, a request-compliance pair.

It must be admitted that Winograd makes some qualifications to the CfA network, in one of which he notes that "the actual doing of whatever is needed to meet the conditions of satisfaction lies outside of the conversation structure" [4, p207]. On this view, perhaps compliance need not be represented in the CfA network, but this underplays the central and important insight of speech act theory. For speech act theorists, speaking should be seen as part of a general theory of action and, indeed, some recent developments in speech act theory have been consistent with this. For example, see the attempts to relate speech acts to context-change in Gazdar [19]. Why, then, treat compliance as external to the CfA network?

Indeed, we can query the Winograd and Flores term *conversations for action* and ask why they should distinguish them from *conversations for clarification, possibilities and orientation*. If conversations are always already sites for action, why speak of conversations *for* action? Furthermore, to distinguish these different kinds of conversation is to underestimate how they often intertwine seamlessly. To see this, consider again the CfA network. Its point of entry involves the issuance of a request. However, comparatively rarely in conversation do people issue requests in explicit forms such as *I request you to....* or employ an imperative sentence-type. Instead, requests are often brought off through so-called *pre-requests*. A pre-request is an utterance issued by a potential requester which (typically) checks to see if the most likely hindrance to the requestable action exists or not. Pre-requests embed in conversational sequences which have a four turn structure in their full form, as exemplified by the following fragment of conversation between a customer and a sales assistant [20, p324]:

A: Do you have the blackberry jam?
B: Yes.
A: Okay. Can I have half a pint then?
B: Sure. (*turns to get*)

However, issuing a pre-request does not always initiate a sequence like this, for sometimes the request need never be explicitly articulated if its addressee can pre-empt it and respond with an offer instead [20, p324]:

A: Do you have pecan Danish today?
B: Yes we do. Would you like one of those?
A: Yes please.
B: Okay. (*turns to get*)

Indeed, it can be possible to carry the 'veiling' of a request further and proceed directly from the pre-request to the requested action. Truncated sequences like this are ubiquitous as the following two examples show [21, p60 and p68]:

A: Have you got Embassy Gold please?
B: Yes dear. (*provides*)

A: Can I have two pints of Abbott and a grapefruit and whisky?
B: Sure. (*turns to get*)

These two examples illustrate another feature of pre-requests: they are often constructed specifically to obtain a requested action immediately rather than a response which requires the subsequent request/response adjacency pair. Both involve pre-requests which contain enough information to specify the kind of action that would subsequently be requested. When feasible, truncated sequences are likely to be preferred over pre-emptive offers which are, in turn, preferred over full four turn sequences.

From this discussion of pre-requests, a number of points can be made which are relevant to speech act theory in general and Winograd and Flores' use of it in particular.

First, requests are often brought off without the explicit issuance of a request at all. Often conversants proceed from a pre-request straightaway to compliance. Thus, what - for Winograd and Flores - is the point of entry to a CfA can be bypassed altogether. Indeed, as the execution of the requested action is not represented in their network, the most preferred way to bring off a request will involve actions *none of which* are to be found in a CfA! This anomaly is a consequence of treating requested actions and pre-condition checks as *external* to the "central fabric" made up of CfA. It must also give us further reasons to doubt whether the structure of request-based sequences is captured by the CfA network.

It should be noted that speech act theorists have often seen utterances like *Can I have two pints of Abbott and a grapefruit and a whisky?* and *Have you got Embassy Gold?* as so-called *indirect* speech acts and have sought mechanisms by which speakers and hearers might derive an underlying direct form from them typically by a process of inference [22]. On this view, it might seem appropriate to modify the entry conditions on a CfA by allowing indirect requests along with direct forms. However, when we inspect how such forms are used in actual conversation, it seems that they are or become *indirect* through their *position in extended discourse sequences*. Compare the two interchanges below:

(i)
A: Do you stock Philip Morris?
B: Yes dear. (*provides*)

(ii)
A: Do you stock Philip Morris?
B: Yes dear.
A: A crush proof pack, please.
B: Here you are. (*provides*)

If A's *Do you stock Philip Morris?* is taken to be an indirect request as sequence (i) suggests it might be, what are we to make of sequence (ii)? Does A issue two requests in this sequence? And thereby initiate two separate CfA? Surely not. This would miss the fact that *Do you stock Philip Morris?* is a *preparatory* move in (ii): it lays the way for the third turn request *A crush proof pack, please.* Alternatively, if a speech act theorist were to claim that *Do you stock Philip Morris?* is an indirect request in (i) but a preparatory question in (ii), all hope for a systematic account of how explicit forms connect with underlying illocutions would have been forfeited. Surely, identical forms cannot be different acts in response to a speech act theorist's say-so.

To escape from this dilemma, we have to contextualise *Do you stock Philip Morris?* in the entire strip of talk in which we find it. In particular, we must not neglect what follows next, its uptake. In (i), it meets with *Yes dear* plus (*provides*) whereas in (ii), just *Yes dear* comes in response. In (i), a preferred anticipation of the request is made whereas in (ii), the request has to be made explicit. If we are to retain speech act terminology to describe such states of affairs, we need to say that *t h e illocutionary act of an utterance is indeterminate until we know how it has been taken up.*

If this is correct, illocutionary acts are social accomplishments and not individual performances [23]. We need to understand illocutions *dialogically*, as at least in part determined by their *uptake*. A CBMS in which the senders of messages fix the classification of their turn by selecting from a set of illocutionary options will not respect this. A general point can be made: the tendency to see illocutions only monologically in terms of relations between utterance forms, utterer's intentions and the world is endemic to many forms of speech act theory. Perhaps, rather than start with the isolated utterance as our datum, we should consider whole strips of conversation. This is the approach of the conversation analysts, whose work we have already made use of and which we shall develop further below.

2.2 Local and Global Management and the Limits of Prospective Representation

We have emphasised uptake in understanding the organisation of conversation. This relates to a general and important feature of conversation: it is *locally managed* [7]. Many aspects of ordinary face-to-face conversation operate on a turn-by-turn basis with just a single transition organised at a time. As Sacks et al. have shown, the rules which determine turn-taking allocate turns to speakers locally, concerning (typically) only the *very next* turn. For example, issuing the first pair part of an adjacency pair (a question, say) makes its second (an answer) *expectable* at the very next turn. If an answer is returned, it fulfils the expectation and retrospectively confirms the appropriateness of the question.

However, departures from strict adjacency are possible, as exemplified below:

A: What's the time? (Q1)
B: Why do you want to know? (Q2)
A: I have a train to catch. (A2)
B: It's 5.30 (A1)

Here, one question-answer pair is embedded in another. Schegloff [24] calls such embedded utterances *insertion sequences*.

Strict adjacency also breaks down when the second part is not forthcoming. The absence of a second can itself be significant; for example, an unanswered question can sometimes be taken as evidence that the intended answerer does not know or does know but would be committing herself to something that she wishes to avoid etc. etc. depending on other factors.

Phenomena such as the 'notable absence' of second parts and insertion sequences suggest to Schegloff [24] that strict adjacency should be qualified by the notion of *conditional relevance*. Thus, given a first part, a second is immediately relevant and predictable, but if it fails to occur, and, say, some other first part occurs in its place, then that will be heard, where possible, as some preliminary to the doing of the second part, the relevance of which is locally maintained on a turn-by-turn basis until it is either directly attended to or aborted by the announced failure to provide some preliminary action. If it is not possible to interpret the non-expected response as a preliminary, the responder may find herself accountable for specific inferences that her behaviour will have generated [14, p321, note 16]. Schegloff's [24] distinction between *location* - i.e. the sequential locus of a turn - and *position* - its relation to some prior but not necessarily adjacent pair - is useful here. In an adjacency pair with a question-answer sequence inserted between the two parts, the second part still occupies the second position though the insertion sequence entails it being located fourth. Thus, adjacency pairs retain a local management of *position* even if the first and second parts may be separated.

A consequence of local management in conversation is that it is hard to sustain any more than locally operating predictions as to how a conversation will proceed. Thus, whether a request takes two turns to bring off or requires a longer sequence depends upon how participants respond to a succession of local considerations regarding the turns available to them at each stage. The localism and situatedness [25, p73-83] of conversation is somewhat missed by network models of conversation where only certain options are represented at particular junctures as an extended non-locally managed representation unfolds. No matter how exhaustive the network-modeller thinks she has been, *other* actions can always be executed by participants for reasons which may be highly specific to the particular situation of utterance and relate to the inferences participants are willing to be held accountable for. Indeed, the localism and situatedness of conversation calls into question the utility if not the *very possibility* of a prospective representation of its structure, even for apparently more 'specialised' conversations like those surrounding requests.

We want to assert the relevance of conversation analysis for understanding the kinds of communication that takes place in group working situations and for its automated support. To show this, we shall attempt two things. First, we shall indicate that the concepts associated with conversation analysis - developed in face-to-face settings - have applicability for the analysis

of the asynchronous communication which characterises the most challenging applications of CBMSs in CSCW. Secondly, we shall investigate how far and in what sense group working activities exemplify the localism and situatedness which we claim characterise conversations.

2.2.1 Conversation Analysis and Asynchronous Computer Mediated Communication

Although CBMSs can be employed to communicate in real-time, it is perhaps their use in supporting asynchronous communication which raises the most novel problems. Most conversation analytic work has centred on face-to-face conversation, communication under the "full conditions of co-presence" [26]. A number of researchers - for various, different reasons - have denied the relevance of this area for asynchronous media or attempted to show significant differences [27, 28]. However, it is our contention that - when understood appropriately - conversation analytic concepts do provide insights into the nature of communication when spatio-temporal co-presence of participants is not demanded.

Under asynchronous conditions, there are at least three (dis)junctures at which sets of actions synchronised in co-present conversation need not be in CMC. Consider the actions involved in the creation, transmission and receipt of a standard electronic mail message. We identify the following Asynchronies:

Asynchrony 1: between the time of message-creation and the time of transmission. The message-author can go back over the text, amend and append sections etc. before transmitting. By contrast, in conversations under co-presence, the creation and transmission of an utterance are simultaneous processes.

Asynchrony 2: between the time of transmission and the time of receipt by the addressee ('receipt' here means the time the addressee first inspects the message). No detachment exists at the analogous moment in co-present conversation; the utterance is heard (received) as it is transmitted.

Asynchrony 3: between the time of receipt (inspection) and the time of response. Recipients are under no obligation to respond immediately. Between receipt and future response, other actions of greater, lesser or no relevance to responding can intervene. As we have seen with conversation, the addressee's following actions are conditionally relevant to what has gone before and absences can be significant.[1]

The existence of these Asynchronies has doubtless led many researchers to suppose that they make many of the findings of conversation analysis irrelevant to CMC. For example, Hiltz [28] - largely through focussing on Asynchrony 1 and emphasising the freedoms participants enjoy when not competing for the floor - has claimed that turn-taking has little influence on computer-conferencing. However, a careful examination of the corpora of messages collected by Black et al. [27] and Severinson Eklundh [29] should indicate otherwise.

In her study of "letters" in the COM system, Severinson Eklundh found many examples of two turn

---

[1]There is direct evidence from construct studies carried out in the Cosmos project that participants are aware of the three Asynchronies we have laid out and see them as constitutive of the differences between CMC and other forms of communication [48].

494

structures, particularly involving questions as first parts, e.g. [29, p52]:

A: Subject: OSIS meeting in London (TURN 1)
   What did your man think?
B. Subject: OSIS meeting in London (TURN 2)
   He seemed positive. David had advertised us well, so he found himself representing the whole banking world. Next meeting will be in Stockholm, I think, and then we shall come up with a lot of expertise. He thinks that we might be interested in an even larger field than information services (He is going to start running COM himself in connection with the implementation of VAX: es at our subsidiaries.)

This is an exemplary question-answer adjacency pair. The question is topicalised by the subject header and followed up by an answer yoked to the same header.

Severinson Eklundh found the modal length of asynchronous dialogues with an initial turn containing a question to be two turns, the vast majority of second turns being in answer to the first turn. However, sometimes the basic two-part structure was augmented by a third turn giving feedback. In the above example the sender of the first part followed up with:

A: Subject: OSIS meeting in London (TURN 3)
   That's great.

Severinson Eklundh [29, p43-4] tries to argue that such three-part sequences often constitute the fundamental structural unit or "minimal interaction" in CMC. However, her own data suggest two-part sequences to be empirically more common and three-part sequences may only be the dominant "minimal interaction" when it is thought legitimate for one party to have both the first and the last words (e.g. in teaching settings, [30]). It seems more appropriate to analyse the *OSIS meeting* sequence as an adjacency pair in which the second part is not only an answer but also sets a context for a following 'agreement' in an 'assessment/agreement' structure [31]. This suggests that turns can be *multifunctional* in that they can contain coexisting 'elements' serving different discursive functions.

Both Severinson Eklundh's and Black et al.'s corpora contain many examples of multifunctional turns (or "connectives" in Black et al.'s terms). Below, three questions are issued in a single message and all are answered in a single reply [29, p50]:

A: Subject: Report C 123660
   The above mentioned report is out of stock. The remaining ones are C 12366 + C 123660. What to do? Reprint? In that case, do you have any changes to suggest?
B: Subject: Report C 123660
   I do have changes that I want to make. But there is no time to make them right now. So I suggest that you print a new version which will be enough for the period up to next summer or so. Then I'll perhaps get the time to do the improvements I want. In other words, use the old text for a reprint now!

Similarly [27, p68-9]:

Marti: Subject: amount time on system
   how does a student determine the amount of

time thats/he has spent on the system. At the logout portion of the system it tells you the amount of time and money spent for that particular entry. what about all my entries taken together. als to use a question mark within a message (im afraid that it will give me all the commands)
Levin: Re: amount of time on system
   Yes, ? is ok within a message. Anything is ok, except for control D at the beginning of a line.We will get printouts at the end of each week week telling you how much each account spent so far, so check with Bud if you want.
   jal

Here Marti poses two questions (one in two different ways) and both are taken up by Levin in a single reply. Although dialogues of this sort *can* be found in conversational discourse, multifunctionality is particularly prominent in CMC where participants can autonomously determine exactly how a turn is constructed. Asynchrony 1 allows authors to compress into one turn as many actions requiring response as is desired [32].

In the last two examples, several adjacency pairs were compressed into two turns. However, it is possible to find sequences in which a number of questions, say, appear in one turn but they are answered in more than one turn in reply, for example [29, p53]:

A: Subject: SIGSIM meeting
   Are you going to Linkoping tomorrow?
   In that case when are you leaving?
   Does SIGSIM pay for the trip or what?
B: Subject: SIGSIM meeting
   I thought of leaving around 0822. Although I will be somewhat late then...
B: Subject: SIGSIM meeting
   Yes, SIGSIM pays for the fare (2:nd class).

Severinson Eklundh [29, p53] conjectures that B forgot to reply to A's question concerning who pays and sent a second message (third turn) as an afterthought. However, in CMC, absences and delays do not admit of unambiguous interpretation [33] and it is equally possible that, say, B did not know who pays when sending the first reply but, sometime thereafter, checked the details of the meeting before sending the second reply. Of course, this is only one further interpretation amongst many possibilities but it indicates that a user can *stagger* her responses to turns containing several actions, dealing with each as and when she can.

The converse is also to be found in Severinson Eklundh's corpus. In the following, in a single reply, actions appearing in more than one prior message are dealt with [29, p54]:

A: Subject: DSK:COMPTY.REL<12,345>
   Why has it been removed, but not ATR 7 SIM?
A: Subject: DSK:COMPTY.REL<12,345>
   It is easier for me if you recompile, then I won't have to change the search list in the code.
B: Subject: DSK:COMPTY.REL<12,345>
   I have no idea! Perhaps QZ has shifted some files onto tapes?
   I will recompile.

Here, A's initial question was supplemented with a second turn statement before B replied by taking A's two turns together in a single multifunctional turn in the third location.

The last few examples illustrate two discourse phenomena that are comparatively rare (but not non-existent) in face-to-face conversation: (i) *multifunctionality* - a turn can contain several actions; (ii) *staggering* - a multifunctional turn can meet with several turns in reply, or a single multifunctional turn can serve as a reply to several prior turns. These phenomena indicate that turns have a more oblique relation to actions and discourse structuring than in co-present conversation. Indeed, given the data presented and these novel phenomena, one might query whether the concept of an adjacency pair is appropriate to CMC at all. We believe that it is provided that some important qualifications are noted.

First, we must re-iterate our earlier observation that strict adjacency is too strong and that the first part of an adjacency pair establishes the *conditional relevance* of whatever it is that serves as a response to it. Indeed, as strict adjacency is not an organising principle of conversation, it is unfair to make out a conversation/CMC difference by demonstrating that strict adjacency does not obtain in CMC, *pace* [27].

Secondly, we must not necessarily make the action performed by the issuance of a first or second pair part coextensive with a single turn - a turn (message) can contain a number of first parts or second parts (or other actions) coexisting alongside each other. Such multifunctionality does not seem to be allowed for in conversational networks like the CfA presented in Figure 1.

Thirdly, because of Asynchronies 1, 2 and 3, between an agent's turn containing a first part action and her receipt of a conditionally relevant response, *any number of other turns* related to other sequences may be formulated, transmitted and/or received. Thus CMC discourse sequences can complexly *intertwine* in a way that is not readily possible in co-present conversation, where - typically - only one conversation at a time can be adequately attended to per agent and only one speaker holds the floor at any moment [27].

None of this is to say that structuring breaks down in CMC. There are still local constraints on action order. The second parts of adjacency pairs can only *follow* their firsts. We can still define temporal regions in which a turn containing certain action(s) will be conditionally relevant and expectable. Thus, for CMC, we need a concept of the *relative temporal precedence* of actions. This we shall develop more formally in 3.2.5 below.

2.2.2 Group Working as Communication Manifesting Local and Global Structuring

We have been at pains to emphasise that conversational interactions in CBMSs are locally managed and structured around adjacency pairs. This should indicate the utility of conversation analysis for understanding asynchronous CMC and should underline the importance of respecting the localism of conversation in any CBMS which offers automated support for such interactions. However, it must be recognised that not all interaction is conversational.

According to Sacks et al. [7], conversations, being locally structured, lie at one extreme of a 'dimension' of *pre-allocation*. In conversation, only the turn in the next position is allocated to a speaker and constrained in advance with respect to its expectable content. At the other extreme, lie other "speech-exchange systems" in which all (from first to last) turns are pre-allocated. Sacks et al. give the example of a 'ceremony' or 'ritual' as located at or near this extreme. In ceremonies (or at least in typical ones) all turns are pre-allocated. At any given turn, you will know who will be speaking (and, usually for that matter, what they'll be saying). By contrast to Sacks et al.'s local management notion, we can say that such communication activities are subject to *global management systems*.

If conversation is a 'pure' example of local structuring and ritual a 'pure' example of global structuring, we believe that many kinds of interaction involve *combined local/global structuring*. Consider speech exchange in a medical encounter, a physician being visited by a patient. Often, such interactions can be analysed into the following episodes: beginning of consultation, patient's narrative, questioning led by the physician, (optionally) physical examination, specifying treatment and (optionally) issuing prescription, leave-taking. An organisation of this sort can be subject to many situated variations but captures the episodic structure of many consultations, especially those with doctors who try to maintain short turn round times. The transitions from episode to episode will usually be determined by the physician and will often be marked by issuing pragmatic particles such as *Now..., So...* or *Well...* together with making explicit the content of the next episode: *Well, I think I ought to examine you, would you mind coming over to the couch?* Within episodes, communication is conversation like and locally managed, though typically the physician will control the topicalisation of the talk (at least after the initial narrative) and will sometimes initiate *three* part structures resembling adjacency pairs but with a follow up comment as third. The episodic structure allows a number of non-local projections concerning the course of future interaction; yet within episodes, local projections may be all that is possible (or relevant for participants). (Our discussion here is based on work by amongst others: [34, 35, 36, 37]). Similar organisational principles - locally managed interactions within a globally structured activity - also characterises communication in many "scripted" situations [38], instructional settings [30] and interviews [37].

Local and global structuring also coexist in many group working tasks. As part of the COSMOS project Paul Buckley has analysed transcripts of interviews with the officers of a British local government department, who periodically produce reports which are eventually combined in a document known as an Agenda, which is then presented to a committee of elected councillors [39].

The process of report production and Agenda compilation is complex and involves several scheduled meetings and often unscheduled ones as well. It is striking how often the informants allude to unscheduled meetings and conversations in their descriptions of their working practices. For example, one officer reveals that weekly scheduled meetings with the Chair can be supplemented by "chats" when necessary. Similarly, locally instigated conversations may come into existence if some matter has not been covered adequately in a scheduled meeting or if there is insufficient time to call another. The content of such meetings is decided locally and situatedly by its participants and tends simply to be about "items that have cropped up".

Regular scheduled meetings are also often depicted by interviewees as having a discussive or conversational microstructure, though it may be nested within a recurrent form. The content of such meetings, that is, what topicalises the talk within them, can often be only locally decided even if the meetings have a 'formal' procedure or order of business.

Even who attends a meeting can be situatedly determined; whether an officer attends a particular meeting may depend on what is to be discussed that day, the officer's current priorities etc. Many of the 'roles' or 'responsibilities' of the officers are in reality fluid and negotiable in the light of the specificity of situations that arise.

The pervasive impression gained from Buckley's transcripts is of a department continually engaged in many local situated negotiations of role, responsibility and work content. However, at the same time, many aspects of the working practices are somewhat more fixed. For example, authors must append a background documents list to their report to permit any reader (including members of the public) to check on the report's sources. This requirement is fixed *by statute* as are many of the responsibilities of the Council Officers.

Similarly, the process of report production and Agenda creation takes place within a time schedule which is fixed by the regular occurrence of public Committee Meetings with an order and frequency again fixed in part by statute. Indeed, the imminent occurrence of such a Meeting can affect the extent to which locally negotiated commitments become supplanted by other more formal responsibilities.

This is not to say that the existence or structure of Committee Meetings or the nature of people's responsibilities with respect to them are unchangeable or non-negotiable. Even legal statutes can be made the subject of discussion and debate and changed accordingly, even if for the most part this possibility may not affect an officer's diurnal conduct. The point is that two different kinds of organisation of working practices coexist alongside each other. This is reflected in the nature of the communications which take place in the department and how they unfold over time. Alongside the formal procedures associated with certain kinds of meeting, there exists a manifold of unscheduled conversational activity which both determines and is determined by the content and temporal proximity of scheduled meetings. To focus exclusively on the scheduled meetings and events associated with them (like deadlines) would present an idealised view of the temporal patterning of communication and the nature of responsibility. Winograd [4] makes a similar point in his discussion of Kaasboll's [40] work on the activities associated with a hospital ward: we must not ignore *conversational* activity. But equally, we must not over-extend the scope of conversations. Communication also occurs in a form which involves the non-local patternings of events, in which more distal projections are possible. These two forms can coexist. Accordingly, any approach to group working which attempts to provide automated support for such situations must be tolerant of both the local and global structuring of work and the communication which surrounds and penetrates it.

3 THE STRUCTURE DEFINITION LANGUAGE (SDL) IN THE COSMOS PROJECT

3.1 Communication Structures and the functional requirements of a Structure Definition Language

SDL has been designed to meet certain requirements many of which emerge from our considerations of CSCW through a conversation analytic development of the language/action perspective. Fundamentally, we see the characterisation of a CS to involve the definition of a set of *expectable communicative actions* and a set of constraints over their *temporal orders* and *contexts of realisation*. To define a CS can be thought of as a process of answering two kinds of question: *what sorts of actions are there?* and *when are they expected to occur?* Following from our criticism of the more rigidified forms of speech act theory, we want to insist on a *dialogical* model of communication which emphasises *interaction* among participants, and not merely the separate 'transmission' and 'reception' of messages between an active Sender and a passive Receiver. As we shall see, this leads us to a particular conceptualisation of the relation between moments of information passing (messages or turns) and the accomplishment of communicative actions. Typically, we see the accomplishment of communicative action as a locally managed affair, even though such (inter)actions may be embedded in more globally structured communication for which a prospective representation can be given in SDL.

3.2 The Structure Definition Language

Figure 2 depicts the conceptual framework which underlies SDL at its current stage of development. The encircled concepts can be thought of as the 'primitives' of SDL.

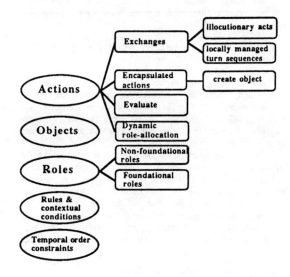

Figure 2: SDL Conceptual Framework

3.2.1 Actions

We recognise several kinds of action but a fundamental distinction is made between *encapsulated actions* and *exchanges*. An encapsulated action (EA) involves the creation of some object which is typically exchanged on completion. To define an EA requires the specification of the role associated with the creation of the object, the object's name and any other (pre-existing) objects that the new object is created from or based upon. The syntactic form of an EA in SDL is as follows:[1]

[role_name] **create** [object_name] {**from** [object_name]...}

In 3.2.6, we present a definition in SDL of a REPORT_WRITING_CS drawn from our work characterising the report writing practices discussed above. The following fragments are taken from that definition and exhibit the EA notation:

Author **create** *report*
Interested_others **create** *comments* **from** *report*
Author **create** *backgound_documents_list* **from** report

Exchanges are the elementary communicative acts and involve at least two roles and typically one object. The simplest syntactic form of an exchange in SDL is as follows:

[object] [role_name] [role_name]

and the following fragments exemplify this form:

report Author Line_manager
report_summary Author Director

The order of the role names is significant. The first role is the initiator of the exchange. Initiating an exchange involves sending the object stipulated to the other role(s) who serve(s) as recipient(s).

The form for an exchange can be expanded to allow the specification of the illocutionary act performed in the exchange, together with any other actions or exchangeable entities that are predicted or pre-supposed, thus:

invitation [**for** comments] report Author Interested_others

Here, sending the report from the 'Author' to the 'Interested_others' is classified as an invitation which renders expectable the future existence of an object (or objects) called 'comments'. This enables SDL users to express some of the dependencies which exist between actions in a CS definition.

It is in recognition of Asynchrony 1 that we make the distinction between those aspects of communicative action which are relatively encapsulated (i.e. do not require reference to other roles) and those moments where two or more roles become related by means of an exchange occurring (and encapsulation breaking down). Accordingly, to permit the representation of these features of the time-course of asynchronous

communication, we distinguish between the process of object creation and the moment of exchange.

Due to the dialogical nature of the accomplishment of speech acts, an exchange need not correspond to just a single moment of information passing, but can be distributed over several turns. Thus, the sending of a report from an Author to a Line Manager may involve a single turn if the report is transmitted in one go, or several turns may be implicated if the report is presented to the Line Manger in sections. These are local considerations about which no stipulations are made in SDL. Similarly, the presence of an exchange from role A to role B in a definition does not rule out the possibility that information can be passed from B to A. Exchanges mark the sites of locally managed interactions which are initiated by the sender of the specified object. They need not stop upon the transmission of the object if participants wish to enter into an extended interaction. In this way, any illocutionary act associated with an exchange is permitted to emerge over the course of several turns.

3.2.2 Objects and their Individuation
An object is any kind of entity which can be created and exchanged. It could be a text-file, a program, a graphics file or some combination or whatever. In the REPORT_WRITING_CS, we identify the following objects:

report
comments
background_documents_list
report_summary
rejection
authorisation

Many CSs are characterised as having objects which appear in many different versions; for example, a paper before and after revision. For a variety of reasons, it can be convenient to give the same name to a number of different versions of an object. It is important, then, that SDL should have the means to refer to objects both generically (all version of object, O) and individually (e.g. version n of object, O). SDL offers two means for achieving this.

The first way is to use integer indices as subscripts and allow various computational operations be defined on them. This method is familiar from programming languages and algebraic methods. We shall not discuss it further here.

The second way is to refer to object versions by history. This involves specifying one or more 'contexts of prior appearance' Thus, following the object name, there can appear a list of prior contexts which pick out the object version which is to be referred to. For example, to individuate the 'paper which A sent to B' we can write:

paper /*paper* A B/

Here, the object name 'paper' is modified by reference to its prior appearance in the exchange 'paper A B'. Now, in case there have been several exchanges of the form 'paper A B', we make the default assumption that it is the last of these that is being referred to. However, if, instead, we want to refer to all the papers which have appeared in a 'paper A B' exchange we write:

paper.. /*paper* A B/

---

[1] In this presentation of SDL, the 'keywords' of the language and any other stipulated syntactic device that promotes parsability are emboldened. Also, optional parts are placed within curly brackets. In the example and the fragments cited, objects appear italicised.

A number of different SDL concepts can appear modifying an object name. For example, encapsulated actions can be listed to individuate object versions. Similarly, we can list CS names if we wish to individuate an object version which appeared in another CS, an example of which can be seen in the REPORT_WRITING_CS in 3.2.6.

3.2.3 Roles
In SDL, roles are the agents and patients of action, without prejudice to what kind of real world entity might correspond to a particular role as identified in an SDL expression; it might correspond to an individual human user, to some kind of collective person, or even an automated process. SDL is neutral with respect to the ontological status of the entities which may become associated with roles. Thus, we use the role concept to drive a wedge between an 'abstract' description of action coordination of the sort expressions in SDL provide and proper-named entities which can be pointed out and individuated in the 'real world'. It provides a way of expressing the actions associated with a CS without reference to actually existing entities which on the occasion of a particular instantiation of a structure might become associated with those roles identified in the CS.

This approach has a number of consequences. First, there need be no match between the criteria by which roles are individuated in SDL and the criteria by which entities are individuated in the 'real world'. Thus, we might count x roles in an SDL definition without thinking that we should be able to enumerate x entities on any particular occasion of use of the CS. Secondly, on this approach, defining a role is not to be seen as providing a fixed set of responsibilities or any other kind of moral injunction. Defining a role falls out of the definition of a structure in SDL and involves associating names with actions. We do not want the departure by any real-world agent from the set of actions associated with their role name to be crudely taken as a ground for praise or blame, for such departures are often made for important and legitimate situated reasons.

Instantiation of a CS as an 'activity' in a Cosmos system is the process by which roles get associated with proper names. However, just as many human individuals may share a user name (e.g. the use of "guest" or "user" on some systems), the process of instantiation need not involve picking out human individuals. What it does involve is association of a set of role names with a set of proper names although, as we shall shortly see, it is not the case that all the role names that appear in a structure definition have to be associated with proper names.

SDL provides two means for defining relations between roles: canplay and allocate. The concept of canplay has been adopted from the work of Tschritzis and Gibbs [41]. As we have understood roles as (merely) an assemblage of actions, in SDL X canplay Y should be understood as "the actions that are associated with Y become associated with X". That is, for all members of the set of actions involving reference to Y, Y can be substituted with X. Consistent with our general understanding of SDL, it is role names (and not proper names) which stand in the X and Y positions.

canplay can be used for a number of purposes in CS definitions, not least of which is to set up a name which can be used to substitute a list of role names which if repeated on each occasion of appearance would make the SDL expressions unwieldy. In general, when canplay is used in this fashion, it will denote those junctures where, on instantiation, facilities will be required akin to distribution lists. canplay can also be used dynamically within a CS. That is, role relations established by the canplay relation can come into existence or be redefined at specifiable moments.

allocate is used when one role determines which agents should become related to a particular role name. Thus, X allocate Y means that X decides which agents become associated with the role name Y. The choice of term 'agent' is deliberate here for role allocation may involve the player of X during run time associating role names or proper names with Y. That is, role allocation may involve an already instantiated role instantiating another by associating a proper name with a role name.

The important difference between canplay and allocate concerns whether the agents denoted by a particular role name can be determined prospectively (i.e. prior to running an instance of the CS) or whether a particular role player has to make a local situated decision. Thus, in the REPORT_WRITING_CS, we find the following two actions:

Author allocate Interested_others,
invitation [for *comments*] *report* Author Interested_others

Here, the Author determines who constitute the 'Interested_others' on the basis of local considerations (perhaps related to the content of the paper, who is available, has already expressed an interest or whatever).

As remarked earlier, not all roles will be associated with proper names at run time. Indeed, we make a distinction between *foundational* and *non-foundational* roles in terms of the former and not the latter being those requiring association with proper names during the instantiation process. Formally, we can take those roles which nowhere in the definition appear after canplay as foundational.

The notion of a foundational role enables us to tell where to look during run time for 'contact with the outside world'. For example, an exchange between two roles will ultimately be resolved so that each of the roles related by means of the exchange are foundational. By definition, this involves the recovery of the proper names of the users or whatever entities are filling the foundational roles in question.

3.2.4 Rules and Contextual Conditions
Exchanges and other actions can be clustered together by means of a rule facility. A rule brings together related actions and ties them to a contextual condition which specifies the circumstances under which they are expected. In this way, a set of rules can represent the episodic organisation of a CS and capture its globally managed aspect.

Typically, SDL rules have the form of a left hand side (LHS) made up of a rule name and a contextual condition and a right hand side (RHS) which is a list of actions. Broadly speaking, a contextual condition is any statement which can be evaluated as true or false. As such SDL's rules can be thought of as productions [42]. In contrast to some realisations of the production rule concept, we allow more than one action to appear on the RHS of a rule. However, RHSs are interpreted as unordered sets of actions; i.e. no significance - temporal or otherwise - is attributed to the order in which actions appear. We also allow rule names to appear on the RHS.

We distinguish between rules which are active and rules which are not (i.e. that are non-active or 'asleep'). Just how a rule becomes active, we shall discuss shortly. Each active rule is tested to see if its contextual condition has turned true. If the contextual condition has turned true, the rule is 'triggered'. When the rule is triggered, the actions on the RHS are expectable. Thus, a production rule system enables us to represent the contexts in which actions become expectable, their actual execution being a matter of local situated determination.

Typically, a rule is activated when some other rule on the RHS of which its name appears is triggered. An example. Consider the following rule pair (rule names are in blocks, contextual conditions embedded in square brackets, LHSs and RHSs separated by an arrow):

REPORT_WRITING_ SENIOR [Author **evaluate** "The Author is a Senior Management Team member"] ->
Author **create** *report*,
OBTAIN_COMMENTS,
CHANGE_REPORT,
SUMMARY_FOR_DIRECTOR,
BACKGROUND_DOCUMENTATION

SUMMARY_FOR_DIRECTOR [Author **evaluate** "Report requires a summary for the Director"] ->
Author **create** *report_summary* **from** *report*,
report_summary Author Director

Assume that REPORT_WRITING_ SENIOR is active and its condition turns true through the Author evaluating "The Author is a Senior Management Team member" as true. This triggers the RHS. The encapsulated action on the RHS now becomes expectable and in addition the four rules listed are made active. Consider the one of these cited, SUMMARY_FOR_DIRECTOR. This has two actions on its RHS, an encapsulated action and an exchange. These are not necessarily expectable yet. That only occurs when that rule's condition becomes true in its turn, i.e. when the Author evaluates "Report requires a summary for the Director" as true.

This fragment of the REPORT_WRITING_CS exhibits two other properties of SDL which are worth noting. The first concerns the global structuring of communication in report writing as we have characterised it in this CS. We can read the REPORT_WRITING_SENIOR rule as informing us of the global structure of the activity. According to this rule, report writing for a senior author involves creating a report, obtaining comments (on it), revising it (in the light of comments), creating the Director's summary (if necessary) and creating a background documents list. Ultimately, these rules break down into locally managed actions. Secondly, it is worth noting the presence of the **evaluate** expressions. These allow role players to make local situated decisions regarding the appropriateness of actions which will be triggered if they evaluate the expressions to true. Thus, the truth values of some contextual conditions can be decided by people (if people are filling the designated roles). In a significant sense, some aspects of SDL need not be machine interpretable. We insist on this not through an antipathy regarding automation but because of our recognition of the importance of situated knowledge as underlying at least some of the decisions required on particular occasions of use.

3.2.5 Temporal Order Constraints

We have remarked already that several actions can appear on the RHS of an SDL rule without prejudice concerning their order of occurrence. This is because SDL makes a strict separation between a rule component and a temporal order component. The rule component contains the set of SDL rules and the temporal order component contains a set of expressions which determine the legitimate orders in which actions defined in the rule component can occur. In this way, SDL maintains a strict distinction between a component which reveals the *constituent structure* of a CS and a component which reveals *temporal precedence*. This is motivated by arguments concerning the representational flexibility of Generalised Phrase Structure Grammars where a similar distinction is made (see the exposition of the "ID/LP" format in [43]).

As discussed in 2.2.1, CMC is characterised by the breakdown of temporal orders which require strict adjacency and yet this does not entail the elimination of all constraint on action order. Similarly, group working - as revealed in the interviews we have discussed - may often involve deterministic orders (e.g. a fixed order of business) and less (or un-) constrained orders (e.g. when situated decisions are made regarding the exact order in which a number of independent tasks may be executed). The advantage of dealing with temporal order in a separate component is that such orders can be notated independent of considerations as to the constituent (or episodic) structure of a CS.

Order Constraint (OC) statements make up SDL's temporal order component and they relate actions in one of two basic ways:

[action1] < [action2]

meaning "action1 (if it occurs) occurs before action2 (if it occurs)"; and:

[action1], [action2]

meaning that [action1] and [action2] can occur in either order. It is important to note that an OC statement like [action1] < [action2] means [action1] precedes [action2] without making any assumptions about actions which might occur between the two: strict adjacency is not assumed.

Although the forms above express < and , as binary relations, it is readily possible to give unambiguous interpretations to chains of actions related by < or ,. For example, here is an OC statement from the REPORT_WRITING_CS:

Author **create** *report*,
Author **allocate** Interested_others
< **request** [**for** *comments*] *report* Author Interested_others
< Interested_others **create** *comments* **from** *report*
<*comments* Interested_others Author
< Author **create** *report* **from** *report comments*..
< *report* Author Line_manager
< Line_manager **create** *rejection* , Line_manager **create** *authorisation*
< *rejection* Line_manager Author,
authorisation Line_manager Author

Note that no stipulation is made here concerning the order in which the Author creates the report or decides who are the Interested_others who shall receive it for comments. This seems appropriate because, depending on situated factors, the Author may or may not know in advance of writing the report who would be interested in its content. In contrast, many of the other order constraints are derived from a priori considerations. For example, the Interested_others cannot receive the report (i.e. enter into an exchange with the Author) until after the report has been created. Ongoing research in COSMOS is developing 'inferencing schemata' [33] which will give a generic characterisation to such relations and permit automated derivation of otherwise unstated actions and/or temporal relations between them. A set of inferencing schemata could be embedded in a 'structure editor' which would assist an SDL user in constructing well formed and maximally expressive CS definitions.

3.2.6 Putting a Well Formed CS Definition Together: An Example

A well formed CS definition consists of a triple: a CS name, a rule component and a temporal order component. The CS name is simply a character string which serves to individuate the definition from others in the COSMOS environment. The rule component is a set of production rules of the form we have described subject to the constraint that one of them should have the CS name as its name and should, accordingly, be regarded as the 'start' rule. The temporal order component consists of a (possibly empty) set of OC statements.

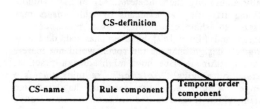

Figure 3: Components of a CS-definition

We present below a well formed CS definition in SDL which is supposed to capture many aspects of report writing as practiced in the local authority department we have been studying. The entire report writing and Agenda creation activity we model as a number of CSs which are interrelated in ways which we shall not discuss in this paper. The CS below is intended to provide some representation of the global organisation of that part of the activity which concerns the initial authorship of reports and how this can be decomposed into locally organised communicative actions. Of course, it does not (cannot) represent all aspects of the work involved; the point is rather to give an impression of what CS definitions in SDL are like. The CS name appears first followed by the rule component which is followed by the temporal order component. It will be noted that there are two different "tracks" [38] through the CS depending on whether the report Author is a senior manger or a junior Officer, the latter requiring 'line authorisation' for her work.

REPORT_WRITING_CS

REPORT_WRITING_CS ->
REPORT_WRITING_JUNIOR,
REPORT_WRITING_SENIOR

REPORT_WRITING_JUNIOR [Author **evaluate** "The Author is not a Senior Management Team member"]
->
Author **create** *report*,
Author **allocate** Line_manager,
OBTAIN_COMMENTS,
CHANGE_REPORT,
LINE_AUTHORISATION,
REVISE_REPORT,
SUMMARY_FOR_DIRECTOR,
BACKGROUND_DOCUMENTATION

REPORT_WRITING_ SENIOR [Author **evaluate** "The Author is a Senior Management Team member"] ->
Author **create** *report*,
OBTAIN_COMMENTS,
CHANGE_REPORT,
SUMMARY_FOR_DIRECTOR,
BACKGROUND_DOCUMENTATION

OBTAIN_COMMENTS ->
can (Author **allocate** Interested_others &
invitation [for *comments*] *report* Author
Interested_others),
can (Interested_others **create** *comments* from
report & *comments* Interested_others Author)

CHANGE_REPORT ->
Author **create** *report* from *report comments..*,
LINE_AUTHORISATION [Author **evaluate** "Line authorisation is now required"] ->
report Author Line_manager,
(Line_manager **create** *rejection* & *rejection*
Line_manager Author)
or (Line_manager **create** *authorisation* &
authorisation Line_manager Author)

REVISE_REPORT [on *rejection* Line_manager
Author] ->
CHANGE_REPORT,
LINE_AUTHORISATION

SUMMARY_FOR_DIRECTOR [Author **evaluate**
"Report requires a summary for the Director"] ->
Author **create** *report_summary* from *report*,
report_summary Author Director

BACKGROUND_DOCUMENTATION ->
Author **create** *backgound_documents_list* from
report,
backgound_documents_list Author Proper_Officer

REWRITING_REPORT [on *rejection*
Senior_Management_Team /CS:
SMT_AUTHORISATION_CS/ Author **or** *rejection*
Senior_Management_Team Line_manager] ->
REPORT_WRITING

Author **create** *report,*
Author **allocate** Interested_others
< **request** [**for** *comments*] *report* Author
Interested_others
< Interested_others **create** *comments* **from** *report*
<*comments* Interested_others Author
< Author **create** *report* **from** *report comments..*
<*report* Author Line_manager
< Line_manager **create** *rejection,*
Line_manager **create** *authorisation*
< *rejection* Line_manager Author,
authorisation Line_manager Author;

Author **allocate** Line_manager
< *report* Author Line_manager;

Author **create** *report_summary* **from** *report*
< *report_summary* Author Director;

Author **create** *backgound_documents_list*
from report
< *backgound_documents_list* Author Proper_officer

3.3 Implementing SDL in a Cosmos CBMS

In Cosmos, SDL is to be implemented by translating it into a language called KSDL (for Kernel Structure Definition Language) which is then mechanically interpretable. Thus, SDL is interpretable indirectly through its translation into KSDL. The reasons for this and other KSDL design decisions will not be the subject of this paper but see [44], [45] and [33].

There are two important differences between KSDL and SDL which are worth noting. First, KSDL is machine-oriented in its design whereas SDL is intended to be available to users of the Cosmos system, either directly or by means of a graphical editing environment within the 'structure editor' [33, 45]. A full KSDL representation of a CS is considerably less readable than SDL, giving little impression of the constituent structure of the CS and including much redundancy. Second, whereas SDL represents a CS in its entirety, KSDL partitions the actions expressed in SDL into scripts. There is a script for each role defined in SDL and all the actions associated with a role are represented in the appropriate script. The sequencing of the actions in each KSDL script is derived from SDL's OC statements and the coordination between scripts is sustained through message passing. Script partitioning has a number of consequences; for example, what for SDL is a single exchange becomes represented in KSDL twice or more, once in the script corresponding to the initiating role and once in each of the scripts corresponding to the recipient roles.

KSDL is currently being developed by Tim Roberts, Jean Dollimore and George Coulouris at Queen Mary College, London and a working prototype Cosmos system will be undergoing testbed evaluation this year. It is hoped that the prototype will implement most features of SDL and the SDL/KSDL conversion process.

4. CONCLUSION

Throughout this paper we have emphasised the importance of the localism and situatedness of many aspects of communication and group working, and we have suggested that interaction in CSCW is often characterised by combined local/global structuring. We have indicated some scepticism concerning the possibility in principle of constructing a model of the control of such communication which exhaustively represents possible interactions in advance of their situated realisation in practice.

In our presentation of SDL, we have insisted on exchanges as marking the sites of locally managed communicative action. On this view exchanges, and therefore illocutionary acts, do not necessarily stand in a one-to-one correspondence with turns (moments of message passing); although an exchange can be initiated through the transmission of some object, further interaction may ensue before it is completed. *Prima facie*, such flexibility in the representation of exchanges, seems to leave it indeterminate when an action is completed and hence unclear when any events contingent on the completion of an action become expectable. If it's always possible for situated reasons to 're-open' an exchange, how is a CBMS implementing SDL going to be able to follow what's going on?

We believe this is a radical indeterminacy, in the same sense as Quine [46] once argued for the notorious case of radical translation, and that it cannot be ignored by designers of systems for CSCW without unwittingly coercing their users. We are currently exploring ways of formally addressing such indeterminacy in SDL without sacrificing its utility as a means by which users may represent to themselves their own practices. As Winograd and Flores [47] have emphasised, design is ontological: design changes the social world not merely the tools within it. But how might design practices negotiate ontological *violence*? We think this is a challenge to CSCW researchers generally: how to design a system which facilitates and enhances communicative action by capturing some of the richness of its texture, without artificially limiting its openness to local and global change.

ACKNOWLEDGMENTS

We wish to thank the Cosmos team and in particular Susan Ormrod, for tireless assistance, Robert Young, for many small acts of kindness, and Tim Roberts, who will recognise his influence on this paper. Paul Wilson has been a constant source of enthusiasm. Address for correspondence: Dr. J. M. Bowers, The Queen's College, Oxford, OX1 4AW, U. K. or email: churcher@uk.ac.man.psy or bowers@uk.ac.oxford.vax or bowers@uk.ac.man.psy (JANET network).

REFERENCES

[1] McLuhan, M. (1964) *Understanding media.* London: Routledge and Keegan Paul.

[2] Wilson, P. (1988) Key research in computer-supported cooperative work (CSCW). In Speth, R. (ed.) *EUTECO '88: Research into networks and distributed applications.* North Holland: Elsevier/Commission of European Communities.

[3] AMIGO Advanced Group Communication Project. (forthcoming) *AMIGO group communication model for a computer based communication environment.*

[4] Winograd, T. (1986) A language/action perspective on the design of cooperative work. In *CSCW '86: Conference on computer-supported cooperative work.* Austin: ACM.

[5] Austin, J. L. (1962) *How to do things with words.* Oxford: Clarendon Press.

[6] Searle, J. R. (1969) *Speech acts.* Cambridge: Cambridge University Press.

[7] Sacks, H., Schegloff, E. and Jefferson, G. (1974) A simplest systematics for the organization of turn-taking in conversation. *Language,* 50, 696-735.

[8] Cashman, P. and Holt, A. W. (1980) A communication-oriented approach to structuring the software maintenance environment. *ACM SIGSOFT: Software engineering note,* 5: 1 (January).

[9] Flores, C. F. (1981) *Management and communication in the office of the future.* Doctoral dissertation, University of California at Berkeley.

[10] DeCindio, F., DeMichaelis, G. and Simone, C. (1988) Computer based tools in the language/action perspective. In Speth, R. (ed.) *EUTECO '88: Research into networks and distributed applications.* North Holland: Elsevier/Commission of European Communities.

[11] Searle, J. R. and Vanderveken, P. (1985) *A Logic of Illocutionary Acts.* Cambridge: Cambridge University Press.

[12] Levinson, S. C. (1981) The essential inadequacies of speech act models of dialogue. In Parret, H., Sbisa, M. and Verschuren, J. (eds.) *Possibilities and limitations of pragmatics: Procedings of the conference on pragmatics at Urbino, July 8-14, 1979.* Amsterdam: Benjamins

[13] Leudar, I. and Antaki, C. (forthcoming) Completion and dynamics in explanation seeking. In Antaki, C. (ed.) *Analysing everyday explanation: A casebook of methods.* London: Sage.

[14] Levinson, S. C. (1983) *Pragmatics.* Cambridge: Cambridge University Press.

[15] Allen, J. (1983) Recognizing intentions from natural language utterances. In Brady, M. and Berwick, R. (eds.) *Computational models of discourse.* Cambridge, MA: MIT Press.

[16] Schegloff, E. A. and H. Sacks (1973) Opening up closings. *Semiotica,* 7.4, 289-327.

[17] Goffman, E. (1976) Replies and responses. *Language in Society,* 5, 257-313.

[18] Coulthard, M. (1977) *An Introduction to Discourse Analysis.* London: Longman.

[19] Gazdar, G. (1981) Speech-act assignment. In Joshi, A. K., Webber, B. L. and Sag, I. A. (eds.) *Elements of discourse understanding.* Cambridge: Cambridge University Press.

[20] Merritt, M. (1976) On questions following questions (in service encounters). *Language in Society,* 5.3, 315-57.

[21] Sinclair, A. (1976) *The sociolinguistic significance of the form of requests used in service encounters.* Unpublished Diploma dissertation, University of Cambridge.

[22] Searle, J. R. (1975) Indirect speech acts. In P. Cole and J. L. Morgan (eds.) *Syntax and semantics 3: Speech acts.* New York: Academic Press.

[23] Habermas, J. (1984) *The theory of communicative action, volume 1: Reason and the rationalization of society.* Boston: Beacon Press.

[24] Schegloff, E. A. (1972) Notes on conversational practice: formulating place. In Giglioli, P. P. (ed.) *Language and social context.* Harmondsworth: Penguin.

[25] Suchman, L. (1987) *Plans and situated actions: The problem of human-machine communication.* Cambridge: Cambridge University Press.

[26] Goffman, E. (1972) *Interaction ritual.* London: Allen Lane.

[27] Black, S. D., Levin, J. A., Mehan, H. and Quinn, C. N. (1983) Real and non-real time interaction: Unraveling multiple threads of discourse. *Discourse Processes,* 6, 59-76.

[28] Hiltz, S. R. (1977) Computer conferencin: assessing the social impact of a new communications medium. *Technological Forecasting and Social Change,* 10, 225-238.g

[29] Severinson Eklundh, K. (1986) *Dialogue Processes in Computer-Mediated Communication: A Study of Letters in the COM System.* Linkoping: Linkoping Studies in Arts and Science.

[30] Sinclair, J. M. and Coulthard, R. M. (1975) *Towards an analysis of discourse: the English used by teachers and pupils.* London: Oxford University Press.

[31] Pomerantz, A. (1978) Compliment responses: notes on the co-operation of multiple constraints. In Schenkein, J.(ed.) *Studies in the organization of conversational interaction.* London: Academic Press.

[32] Bowers, J. M. (1987) *Discourse analysis, speech act theory and computer mediated communication: An introductory review.* COSMOS Document number 42.2. Department of Psychology, University of Manchester.

[33] Bowers, J. M., Churcher, J., and Roberts, T. (1988) Structuring computer-mediated communication in COSMOS. In Speth, R. (ed.) *EUTECO '88: Research into networks and distributed applications.* North Holland: Elsevier/Commission of European Communities.

[34] Goffman, E. (1959) *The Presentation of Self in Everyday Life.* New York: Doubleday.

[35] Fisher, S. (1984) Institutional authority and the structure of discourse. *Discourse Processes,* 7, 201-224.

[36] Heath, C. (1986) *Speech and body movement in medical interaction.* Cambridge: Cambridge University Press.

[37] Labov, W. and Fanshel, D. (1977) *Therapeutic discourse: Psychotherapy as conversation.* New York: Academic Press.

[38] Schank, R. and Abelson, R. (1977) *Scripts, plans, goals and understanding.* Hillsdale: Erlbaum.

[39] Buckley, P. (1988) *Group working in a local government department: Task analysis report.* COSMOS Document number 47.1. Department of Computer Science, Queen Mary College, University of London.

[40] Kaasboll, J. (1986) *Observation of people working with information: A case study.* Draft dated Jan 7, 1986.

[41] Tschritzis, D. and Gibbs, S. J. (1985) Etiquette specification in message systems. In Tsichritzis, D. C. (ed.) *Office automation: Concepts and tools.* Berlin: Springer Verlag.

[42] Newell, A. and Simon, H. (1972) *Human problem solving.* Englewood Cliffs: Prentice Hall.

[43] Gazdar, G., Pullum, G., Klein, E. and Sag, I. (1985) *Generalised phrase structure grammar.* Oxford: Blackwell.

[44] Coulouris, G., Dollimore, J., and Roberts, T., (1987) *The script technique for modelling communication structures,* COSMOS Document number 19.1. Department of Computer Science, Queen Mary College, University of London.

[45] Young, R. (ed) (1988), *Interim report on the Cosmos Project.* COSMOS Document number 45.4. Queen Mary College, University of London.

[46] Quine, W. v. O. (1960) *Word and object.* Cambridge: Cambridge University Press.

[47] Winograd, T., and Flores, F. (1986) *Understanding computers and cognition.* New Jersey: Erlbaum.

[48] Lea, M. (forthcoming) *Users' perceptions of electronic mail in comparison with other communication media: a repertory grid study.* Department of Psychology, University of Manchester.

Strudel - An Extensible Electronic Conversation Toolkit

Allan Shepherd, Niels Mayer, Allan Kuchinsky
Hewlett-Packard Laboratories

March 5, 1990

Abstract

This paper describes the conceptual model of *Strudel*, a toolkit of generic components for conversation and action management. To empower work groups to more effectively conduct their computer-based communication, coordination, and information sharing activities, *Strudel* packages within a simple model of task and action the semi-structured message, active message and conversation management paradigms. To facilitate acceptance and use within varying work cultures, we define this model in terms of a set of extensible components, which are implemented as a prototype software toolkit that is efficient, portable, customizable, and extensible. Issues considered briefly in this paper include threading in conversations that are converging or multi-party, and interoperability between active message systems.

1 Introduction

Our project is investigating the potential for achieving better management of computer-based conversations in work groups through technologies that enable teams to capture and structure discourse. We believe this to be useful for work groups engaged in specialized, recurring conversations, where building specific conversational structures for certain tasks allows them to more effectively coordinate their activities when carrying out these tasks. Examples of such specialized conversations include coordination of software engineering activities and deliberation of system design issues.

Many work groups within Hewlett-Packard routinely use computer-based conversations to deliberate on design decisions, track and follow up on negotiations and agreements, and to schedule their activities. These work groups have evolved ad hoc structures and conventions to carry out specialized conversations, which include the use of specialized mail templates and incorporation of the mail system within applications – e.g. to send notification messages in a software defect tracking system.

To enable users to more easily integrate the usage of computer-based conversations into other electronically supported work, we are exploring more systematic mechanisms for structuring computer-based conversations.

1.1 Overview of the Technical Approach

Strudel provides a toolkit of components for end-users to manage email-based conversations and action items. This paper describes *Strudel*'s conceptual model and the design of the toolkit components, with examples from the current prototype.

To facilitate acceptance within varying work cultures, the toolkit emphasizes standards, user-extensibility of toolkit components, interoperability with existing applications, and good run-time performance on widely installed platforms. It is compatible with existing practice, for example it has a similar look and feel to existing e-mail user agents. It is aimed at producing a small, fast and portable C-implemented platform that enables delivery of groupware applications on relatively low-cost graphics workstations running industry standard software — *UNIX*[1], X11 Windows [16] and ARPA Internet mail [14]. User-acceptance of *Strudel* is further addressed through its use of the graphical interface provided by the OSF Motif UI Toolkit [13]. To support tailoring, Strudel provides an extension language which is based on *WINTERP* [12][2]. An early experimental prototype of *Strudel* was demonstrated at the IFIP Groupware Technology Workshop last year [17].

As a starting point we have integrated the main features of other conversation management systems into a simple conceptual model. This builds upon work in email user-agents that support message filtering [15, 1], and work on semi-structured message systems [11], and conversation management [19, 2, 4, 18, 6]. *Strudel* contains a library of components, which include user-customizable definitions for conversations, conversational moves, and actions, and for tasks, action items and notifications. Presenters allow viewing, editing and navigating among these objects.

Previous work [11] has focussed on making the flood of incoming email manageable through support for the rules that filter messages into message classes for presentation in browsers[3], and for actions that can be applied to messages in a class, such as "forward all messages from X to Y". *Strudel* complements this work by focussing on facilities that will help users (within groups) add partial structure and actions to messages while messages are being composed. *Strudel* supports this addition of structure to messages during composition by providing a library facility in which user-extensible types for message and conversation components are managed.

In *Strudel*, messages can contain actions. For example, a message could contain an "Add to To-Do list" action. Messages can contain typed *conversational moves*[4], such as a "Request", as in Conversations for Action[19]. A move may have fields, as in semi-structured messages, in which case specialized actions may access these. For example, a "Request Meeting" move may have an action "Add to Calendar" (that accesses date, location, topic fields, etc.). Users draft messages by selecting a move from a top-level menu, or via buttons, menu, or list items displayed in previous

---

[1]UNIX is a trademark of AT&T.

[2] *WINTERP* was released on the X11r4 tape – it provides an interactive object-oriented interface to the OSF/Motif UI Toolkit, using XLisp's light-weight interpreter and object system.

[3]This filtering is based either on explicit message typing, or some pattern matching with the content of message fields. The effectiveness of these systems depends on their ability to classify incoming messages. In semi-structured message systems, the sub-structure in the message body is used to simplify how the user defines predicate matching. It is also used to allow actions on the messages to interpret particular fields. The utility of these systems is determined by the actions that can be applied to the classes and to the messages in the classes.

[4]We use the name conversational move, rather than message "type", since messages are allowed to contain more than one such "move", and to emphasize that each move may suggest next moves that are typically taken by other parties in a conversation.

messages.

Messages are collected into conversations based on the threading between successive conversational moves. Conventional email messages and *Strudel* messages may be freely inter-threaded within conversations. Conventional email messages are traced to a predecessor message using existing "In-reply-to:" or "Subject:" field entries where possible. Pseudo-conversations [2], i.e. collections of messages with the same topic, or sender, etc, will be supported. Actions can be applied to messages classified into pseudo-conversations, for example, an action "request an item from library" may be defined for a class of messages that contain lists of new library aquisitions.

Strudel differs from previous approaches in that users can dynamically evolve conversational move and conversation type definitions. For example a user may create a new conversational move type "Ask who is responsible for repairing a medical instrument defect". They may then specify this as an initial move type in a "Medical Instrument Defect Repair" conversation type. However there is currently little support for integrating new definitions of moves or conversations into a centralized library, as would be necessary to support COSMOS style scripts. Unlike more complex office procedure and task modelling systems [3, 5, 7], *Strudel* currently plans support for only simple scripts to help end-users select and draft next moves in conversations and tasks[5].

Since conversation and move types can be evolved by users, these can be made task specific. Similarly, the actions supported on messages and other objects can also be made task specific. To allow users to tie the message system into the state of their tasks, users can create *action items* in Strudel. Action items are memos created by a user to describe an activity they intend to carry out, and the status of that activity. For example, a software development engineer may create an action item to note an intended defect repair, its priority, etc. Analogous to messages in conversations, action items are represented as semi-structured typed forms and threaded into *tasks*.

An interface to other tools is supported so that actions specified within conversation and task objects can initiate operations on objects managed by other tools. In particular, simple programmatic interfaces to general purpose applications such as a room reservation system, and to domain specific coordination tools such as software maintenance and defect tracking systems can be defined. For example, a "Request meeting" message may have an action "Make room reservation" – this action could invoke an operation in a room reservation application. In addition, to inform Strudel users of an event in a foreign tool, a special kind of action item, named a *notification*, can be created by a call from the tool.

The evolution of message and conversation types is decentralized and done by individual users, but is expected to be mediated through a group's discussion and acceptance of modified types. Thus as groups adopt methodology or protocols for their work process, they may choose to represent some conversation and task activities in *Strudel*. *Strudel* does not advocate particular protocols but rather tries to provide ways for groups to support their protocols of choice, and to allow groups to informally integrate and then specialize these. *Strudel* conversation types do not restrict the types of next moves that can be made, thus different conversation types can be freely initiated at any point in a conversation. For example, a "Request meeting" or a "Post design issue" move can be sent in response to a "Defect notification" received in the defect resolution conversation.

---

[5]Expert users can define complex task actions in *Strudel* by writing interpreted procedures [12].

1.2 Example of Usage

Detailed application scenarios have been developed with potential users. To support the scenarios prototyped so far, several *conversation types* have been defined in the library. These include a conversational IBIS[6] used for design issues discussion, a Conversation for Action [19], meeting scheduling, and software defect tracking and repair.

Throughout the paper, a defect resolution scenario is used to give examples. In this scenario, a software build system notifies a *Strudel* server that a defect in a product assembly was found. A software technician responsible for the build process uses *Strudel* to read pending notification reports. The defect notification is presented as a graphical form. Buttons on the form allow the software technician to draft and send specific types of messages, for example, a message to ask several development engineers if they know who is responsible for handling the defect. One development engineer responds to this message, by sending a message agreeing to "own" the defect. The development engineer also starts the repair process by pressing another button on the message form to create an initial action item form for the repair task. Later the development engineer starts a related conversation by posting to other engineers a message that raises a design issue concerning the reported defect. From the action item form the engineer may access copies of related defect notifications from the software build system, other mail messages concerning the defect, and the status of the defect repair (as communicated to *Strudel* by the software maintenance tools).

2 Conceptual Model

The basic types in *Strudel*'s abstract computational model are described in this section, first in overview, then in more detail. *Conversations* and *tasks* are composed of collections of *messages* and *action items*, respectively. A message can be used to carry *conversational moves*, for example a "Request to repair a defect". Conversational moves typically suggest next conversational moves, for example to "Agree to repair a defect", and they present *actions* that can be executed by the message's reader, for example to start to repair a defect. *Conversation types* and *task types* can be defined to guide the way that conversations and tasks are started, developed and ended. For example, a defect resolution conversation is started by either a "Request to repair a defect" or a question asking "Are you the right person to handle this defect?". A defect tracking task is started when a *notification* of a defect is reported to *Strudel* by a foreign tool, such as a product build system. Figures 1 and 2 sketch the basic relations between these abstract types, with example moves from a defect resolution conversation.

The basic types *conversational-move*, *action-item* and *notification* are subclasses of a root type, namely *task-move*. Instance of these types have a title, optional fields, and actions that the user can apply in the context of the move. Figure 3 shows an example Motif form for a simplified "Repair Defect" action item. Figure 4 shows the type definition for this action item. The type definition in the user's local library supplies default field and action information when the action item is instantiated by the user. *Notifications* are treated as pseudo action-items in that they are

---

[6]We introduce a conversation type based on the Issue Based Information System (IBIS) methodology [8], in which the Issues and Positions are sent as specialized messages to others in the design team rather than being added to an argumentation database.

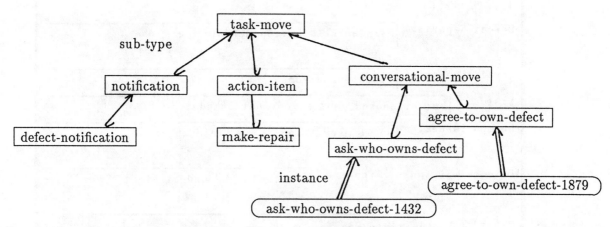

Figure 1: Move types

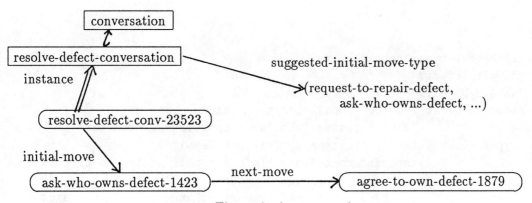

Figure 2: A conversation type

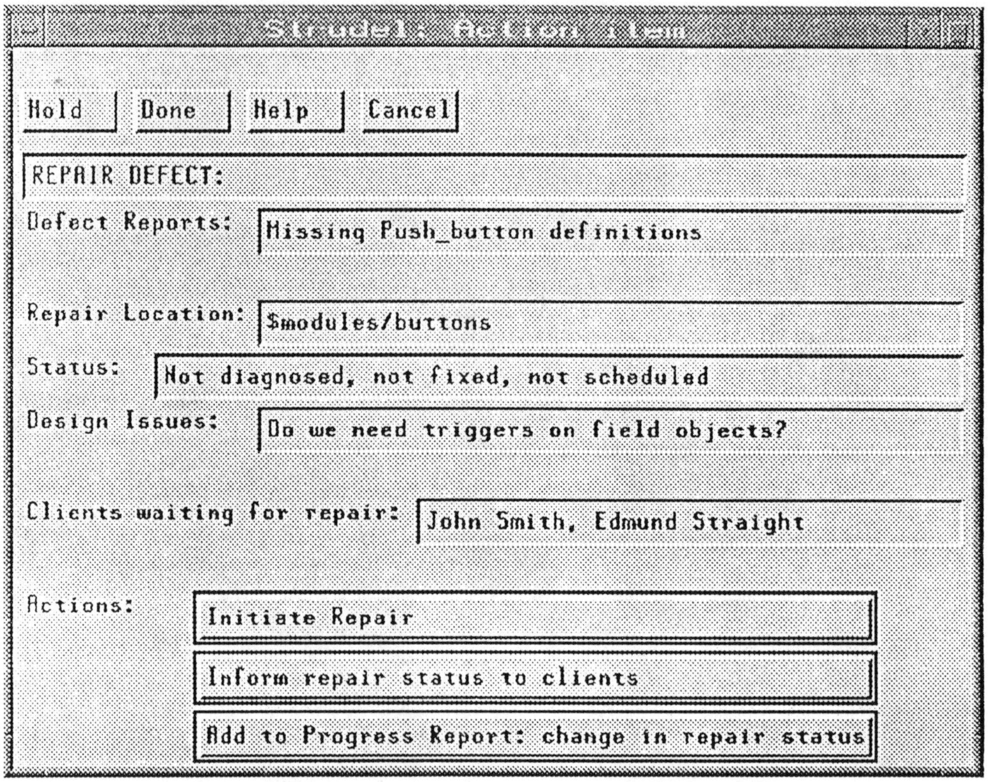

```
 ┌───────────────────────────────────────────────────────┐
 │                    Strudel: Action item                │
 ├───────────────────────────────────────────────────────┤
 │  ┌──────┐ ┌──────┐ ┌──────┐ ┌────────┐                 │
 │  │ Hold │ │ Done │ │ Help │ │ Cancel │                 │
 │  └──────┘ └──────┘ └──────┘ └────────┘                 │
 │  REPAIR DEFECT:                                         │
 │  Defect Reports:  ┌──────────────────────────────────┐ │
 │                   │ Missing Push_button definitions   │ │
 │                   └──────────────────────────────────┘ │
 │  Repair Location: ┌──────────────────────────────────┐ │
 │                   │ $modules/buttons                  │ │
 │  Status:          ├──────────────────────────────────┤ │
 │                   │ Not diagnosed, not fixed, not scheduled │
 │  Design Issues:   ├──────────────────────────────────┤ │
 │                   │ Do we need triggers on field objects? │
 │                   └──────────────────────────────────┘ │
 │  Clients waiting for repair: ┌─────────────────────────┐│
 │                              │ John Smith, Edmund Straight │
 │                              └─────────────────────────┘│
 │  Actions:   ┌─────────────────────────────────────────┐ │
 │             │ Initiate Repair                         │ │
 │             ├─────────────────────────────────────────┤ │
 │             │ Inform repair status to clients         │ │
 │             ├─────────────────────────────────────────┤ │
 │             │ Add to Progress Report: change in repair status │
 │             └─────────────────────────────────────────┘ │
 └───────────────────────────────────────────────────────┘
```

Figure 3: Drafting an action item

```
(register-task-move-type 'make-repair
  :title "Repair Defect"
  :intro "REPAIR DEFECT:"
  :field-sequence (list 'review 'repair-location 'cause  'status
                        'design-issues 'who 'who-reporting-to 'comment)
  :action-types (list (list 'start-repair "Initiate Repair")
                      (list 'inform-clients "Inform repair status to clients")
                      (list 'note-in-progress-report
                            "Add to Progress Report: change in repair status")))
```

Figure 4: An action item type definition

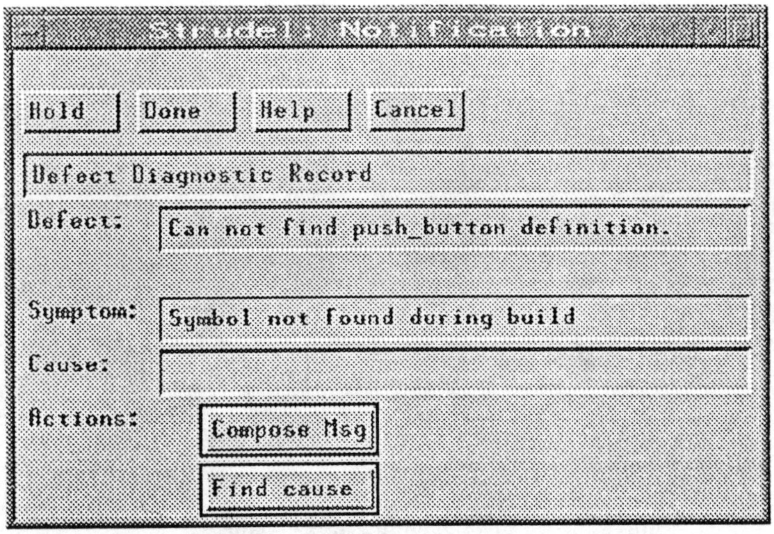

Figure 5: A received notification

not instantiated by users but in response to a call from an application; otherwise they have the same properties as action items. Figure 5 shows an example notification created by a call from a software build tool to inform the user of a defect.

Actions that are specific to a move type can defined[7]. These are attached to buttons when the move is presented, for example the "Initiate repair" button in Figure 3. Depending on whether a move is being drafted or read, different actions may be presented as specified in the move's type definition. For example the draft message in Figure 6 has actions specific to the move, whereas the same message presented to the recipient has several, as shown in Figure 7. Actions defined for current moves can be used, for example, to draft action items or next conversational moves. Actions defined on fields can be used for example to confirm that a time is free in a calendar or schedule. Actions can also be user-defined to invoke task specific operations on task domain objects. For example an action that posts an engineering change order to the design history of a product may be implemented by calling an interface to an inventory management tool[8]. An action to retrieve a defective software module may be implemented by a call to a software maintenance tool.

Conversational moves may be semi-structured[9]. When drafted they are inserted into an email message to be sent to other users. A message may contain several moves. A type definition for a conversational move can specify an explicit sequence of suggested next conversational move types, and a preferred or default one. For example, in the message shown in Figure 7 the user is presented with the choices "I am", etc. Figure 8 shows the type for this move.

Messages are threaded into one or more *conversations*. A conversation consists of an opening and the successor messages to the initial message. The opening specifies the participants, the initial message, and so forth. A user starts a new conversation by selecting a conversational move type

---

[7] For convenience, conversational moves, action items, and notifications are referred to as moves or task moves (as instances of the *task-move* type).

[8] These actions are specified as *WINTERP* procedures.

[9] By semi-structured, we mean containing fields of unstructured text or other information.

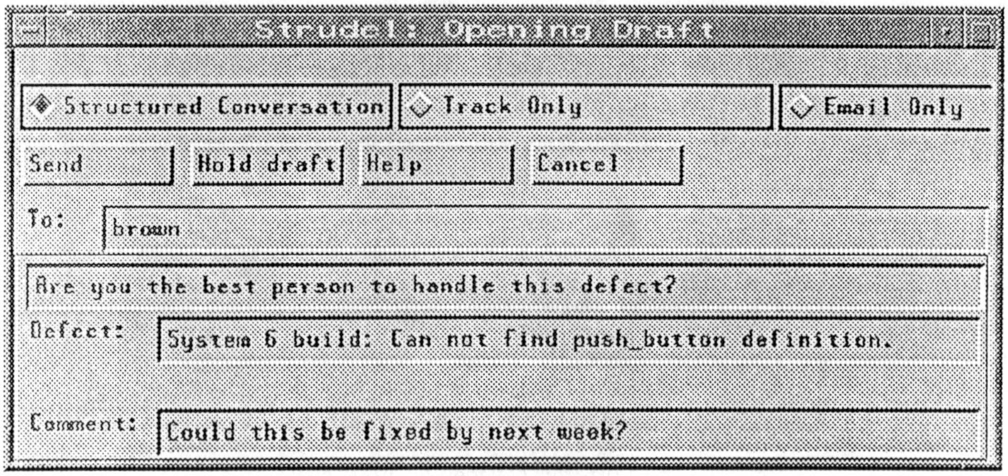

Figure 6: A draft conversational move

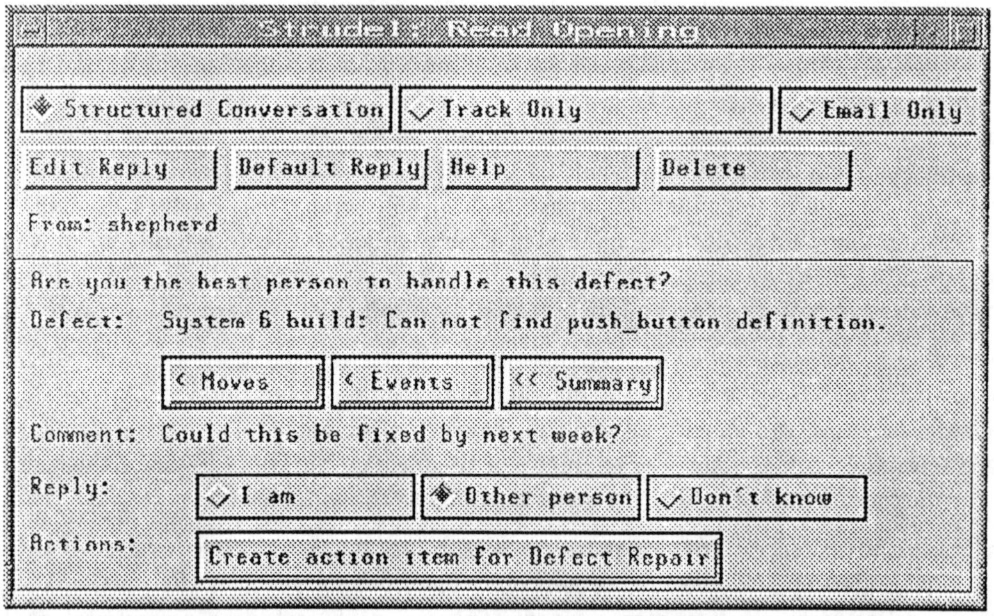

Figure 7: A received conversational move

```
(register-conversational-move-type 'who-will-handle-defect
    :title "Defect owner?"
    :intro "Are you the best person to handle this defect?"
    :utterance-sequence  (list 'defect 'comment)
    :preferred-response-action-type 'other-may-handle
    :next-conv-move-types (list (list 'i-will-handle-defect   "I am")
                                (list 'other-may-handle       "Other person")
                                (list 'do-not-know            "Don't know"))
    :action-types   (list (list 'make-repair-action   "Make Repair")))

(send who-will-handle-defect :set-field 'defect
        :label "Defect"
        :presentation (list 'string 80 50)
        :presentation-default <defect description>
        :read-actions (list 'prev-move 'prev-event 'summary))
```

Figure 8: A conversational move type definition

to instantiate. This selection is made either from the "Start conversation" top-level menu, or in the context of an existing action item or notification. For example, the initial move who-will-handle-defect (shown in Figure 6) is selected from a menu on the "Compose msg" button in the notification shown in Figure 5. The user then edits and sends the message. In responding to a message, users send successor moves thus extending the conversation. A conversation is just this collection of successor messages and the opening descriptor[10]. Users may copy and join the conversation, and can navigate between the messages and to linked action items and notifications. When a message is reviewed, actions on the message can be invoked by the recipient, for example to add a meeting announcement to a calendar, or in the case of Figure 7, to draft or retrieve an action item with the "Action item for Defect Repair" button. Definitions for these actions are given in the recipients library, or a definition of the action is sent in the message (in this sense messages are self-describing)[11]. Other specialized actions for a conversational move allow a user to navigate to the previous and predecessor moves in the conversation[12]. With the ability to navigate, a graphical network of the moves in a conversation can be displayed. Figure 9 shows some of the moves in the defect resolution scenario – the highlighted moves were made; dashed links connect these to moves that could have been made.

A *task*, analogous to a *conversation*, is a collection of action items or notifications that is generated from the initial action item or notification of the task. A conversation is treated as a specialized task. *Conversation types* and *task types* specify a set of initial move types. For example, the IBIS

---

[10]In the current prototype, *Strudel* implements the conversation opening by including a conversation id in the message with the initial conversational move. This id is quoted in responding messages.

[11]If an action definition is not present locally, *Strudel* will request a copy of the action definition from the message's sender or from the groups' server.

[12]To allow users to navigate to a previous message which has been lost or deleted, a control move can request a copy of a message to be forwarded, as in Dragon.

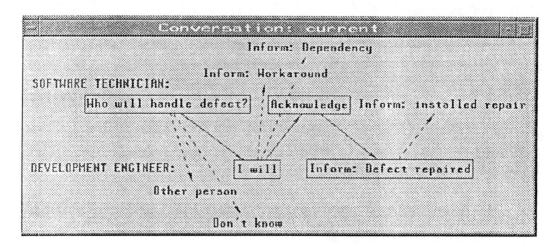

Figure 9: Conversation graph

conversation type has the initial conversational move "Post issue". Menus of the initial move types declared in conversation and task types are currently used to start new conversations and tasks. A task type may also specify how next moves are to be drafted, as described in Section 2.1.

Several default presentations of tasks and conversations are provided, including list browsers for various classes of action items, notifications, and messages. A simple message browser, which resembles current email browsers, allows conventional email messages, Strudel messages and telephone messages to be presented. To present Calendar and "To-Do list" views, browsers that list action items will allow users to sort, filter, group, etc, based on relations for time and keyword matches. Browsers for messages are treated as specialized browsers of action items. For example, messages can be sorted by time sent, grouped by participants, etc. Conversation browsers allow users to navigate within conversations, to archive conversations, etc.

Users can define *overview* presentations for conversations and tasks. Defaults will be simple graphs or indented outlines showing the ordering of moves taken and available, as in Figure 9. Particularly within a typed conversation or task, a procedure can draft a simplistic specialized *summary* of the conversation or task, for example by assembling from specific fields in several messages a draft of a project's progress report, or the minutes or agenda of a meeting. In the defect-resolution scenario, a summary form links related defect reports, a repair status summary, clients waiting for the repair, and so forth.

2.1 Drafting Messages

The current focus of *Strudel* is on how users can interactively carry the state of each conversation or task forward, rather than on automated response to events; for example when a user replies to a message, or marks an action item in a task as "Done".

When a user reads a message containing a conversational move, the user can draft a next conversational move, based on the type and content of a predecessor move. The user chooses a next move type from those suggested in the current move or from other library-defined types, or can send a message containing an untyped move, or can create a new type to use. Conversation types are extended on the fly by users defining new move types as "next-conv-move-types" in existing move types. In a similar way task types may be defined and evolved.

In the current interface to *Strudel*, the possible next move types are presented via buttons or menus. When reading a received message, the user presses a button to select a next move type. In the defect resolution scenario, Figure 7 shows buttons labelled "I am", "Other person", etc. A default next move type can be set by the sender of the message, perhaps to indicate a preferred choice which may express a methodology or policy, or just to set a default focus of the discourse. The user chooses either to edit the next move, or to send a default move of the selected type. This next move is "in response to" the current move. This is analogous to the threading created by conventional "in-reply-to" email messages, however the "in response to" move may be addressed to anyone, thus allowing other parties to be entered into the conversation at that point[13]. For example, on receiving a problem description, a user may ask for separate solutions to the problem by sending separate requests to distinct parties.

In order to support drafting of messages using the content of several previous messages, as when summarizing or comparing the content of several previous moves (perhaps from different parties), a message can contain a move which may be "in response to" several moves in several predecessor messages. For example, a "Request to meet" may include agenda items derived from design issues raised in several previous messages. We will need to provide ways for users to at least manually reorder and merge fields in the newly drafted message, in much the same way as users currently cut and paste text when summarizing several previous messages in current interfaces.

2.2 Issues

The computational context in which a next conversational move is drafted is dominated by the conversational model. At first glance it appears necessary to support a context containing multiple immediate predecessor moves, in order to thread converging conversations. In order to develop as simple a model as possible, we provided in the current prototype a drafting context that contains only a single immediate predecessor move – the move that the new move is explicitly "in response to". In drafting new moves, only data in this context is usually accessed, for example in copying the topic of an agenda item or the date of a meeting into a next move. A draft could reflect the state of other moves in the conversation, since other moves can be retrieved given the current move. However, also in order to keep the model simple, the state of moves in each conversation is currently represented only in each move's state, it is not represented in any global state for the conversation or specific to the conversation type. In our limited use of the initial prototype, when drafting moves, we did not find cases in which these simplifying constraints were too restrictive.

In conventional office forms systems, the text labels on fields and buttons are fixed. In *Strudel*, users

---

[13]Making a particular move "in response to" a move in a conversation does not prevent the user from making other moves also "in response to" the move. However, the subsequent moves are made "within the sequence of" previously made moves, as in Dragon.

can easily change the surface text of labels and the default field contents, for example to change the formality of the displayed introductory text. A number of issues arise with this flexibility. The advantage that fixed forms can be scanned quickly by the reader is lost. Misunderstandings may be caused by small changes made by a sender since there is the same lack of cues as in conventional email.

An important issue is the development of a framework for interoperability among conversation management systems and coordination systems[9]. Our initial practical approach to this problem has been to design *Strudel* to permit experimental interoperation with conventional "unstructured" email, and other prototype conversation management, active message or coordination systems[14]. We have defined conversational move typing, semi-structuring and actions orthogonally to each other. This will allow *Strudel* to experimentally interpret messages from other systems that may support one or more of these features. For example, a particular application may send only semi-structured messages, or only unstructured typed messages such as a "Request", or active structured messages. A key issue is providing interoperable references to and descriptions of actions (in messages). For example, if there is a meeting-date field in a message, users would like to be able to apply their local definition of an Add-to-Calendar action so that appropriate entries are made in a local calendar, irrespective of the source of the meeting announcement.

3   Conclusion

We have described the conceptual model of the initial *Strudel* toolkit, and its approach to user extensibility of conversation and task objects.

We expect the prototype to be deployed for further development with actual users within Hewlett-Packard by the time of the Conference. We intend for *Strudel* to gradually evolve groupware extensions to their current work practices by adding semi-structured messages, active messages and conversation management tools as features available in a system that "feels" like a traditional email user agent.

The prototype demonstrates that the basic functionality of *Strudel* can be provided in a small, fast package that is portable, customizable and extensible. With this we will be able to investigate the value to actual user groups of this approach to extensible conversation structuring. Design and usability issues that we are exploring include the ease of adoption of conversation structuring by work groups, identification of the appropriate "units" of conversation to support, striking the proper balance between user-driven and technology-driven design, integration of computer-based conversations with other collaboration and communication mechanisms in work groups, and identification of classes of conversations most appropriate for machine support.

4   Acknowledgements

Thanks to Susan Brennan, Mark Corscadden, Martin Griss, Lars-Erik Hammarin, Nancy Kendzierski, Scott McGregor, Steve Whittaker and David Williams for helpful discussions.

---

[14]Lee discusses this from the perspective of communication using typed messages[10].

References

[1] Nathaniel S. Borenstein and Chris A. Thyberg. Cooperative work in the Andrew message system. In *Conf. on Computer-Supported Cooperative Work*, 1988.

[2] D. Comer and L. Peterson. Conversation-based mail. *ACM Transactions on Computer Systems*, 4(4):299–319, November 1986.

[3] F. De Cindio, G. De Michelis, C. Simone, R. Vassallo, and A. Zaboni. CHAOS as coordination technology. In *Conf. on Computer-Supported Cooperative Work*, 1986.

[4] Jean Dollimore and Sylvia Wilbur. Experiences in building a configurable CSCW system. In *Proc. 1st European Conf. on CSCW*, pages 215–225, September 1989.

[5] Hiroshi Ishii and Kazunari Kubota. Office procedure knowledge base for organizational office work support. In B. Pernici and A. A. Verrijn-Stuart, editors, *Office Information Systems: The Design Process*. Elsevier, 1989.

[6] Simon Kaplan. COED: A conversation-oriented tool for coordinated design work. In *Proc. IFIP Int. Workshop on Human Factors in Information Systems*, June 1990.

[7] T. Kreifelts, F. Victor, G. Woetzel, and M. Woitass. A design tool for autonomous group agents. In *Proc. 1st European Conf. on CSCW*, pages 204–214, September 1989.

[8] Werner Kunz and Horst Rittel. Issues as elements of information systems. Technical report, Inst. of Urban and Regional Development, Univ. California, Berkeley, July 1970. Working Paper No. 131.

[9] Kum-Yew Lai and T. Malone. Object-Lens: A spreadsheet for cooperative work. In *Conf. on Computer-Supported Cooperative Work*, September 1988.

[10] Jintae Lee. How can groups communicate when they use different languages? Translating between partially shared type hierarchies. Technical Report SSM WP #3076-89-MS, MIT, September 1989.

[11] T. Malone, K. Grant, K. Lai, R. Rao, and D. Rosenblitt. Semi-structured messages are surprisingly useful for computer-supported coordination. In *Conf. on Computer-Supported Cooperative Work*, pages 102–114, December 1986.

[12] Niels Mayer. WINTERP: An object-oriented rapid prototyping, development and delivery environment for building user-customizable applications with the OSF Motif UI Toolkit. Technical Report in print, Hewlett-Packard Labs, Palo Alto, California 94303, August 1990.

[13] Open Software Foundation. *OSF/Motif Series (5 volumes)*, 1990. Prentice-Hall.

[14] J. B. Postel. Standard for the format of ARPA Internet text messages, requests for comments 822. Technical Report SRI-NIC RFC-822, Stanford Research Institute, August 1982.

[15] M. T. Rose and J. L. Romine. *The Rand MH message handling system: User's manual, UCI Version 6.5 #12*. University of California, December 1986.

[16] Robert Scheifler and Jim Gettys. The X Window System. *ACM Transactions on Graphics*, 5(2):79–109, April 1986.

[17] Allan Shepherd, Niels Mayer, and Allan Kuchinsky. Strudel: An electronic conversation toolkit. Technical Report STL-89-04, Hewlett-Packard Labs, Palo Alto, CA 94303, August 1989.

[18] Reijo Sulonen and Panu Pietikainen. Forget-Me-Not - Controlling intercompany operations by intelligent mail. In *Proc. 23rd Annual Hawaii Int. Conf. on Systems Sciences*, pages 428–435, 1990.

[19] T. Winograd. A language/action perspective on the design of cooperative work. Technical Report STAN-CS-87-1158, or CSLI-87-98, Stanford University, 1987.

Chapter 9:
What Makes
Systems Effective?

Chapter 9: What Makes Systems Effective?

Groupware developers can neither rely on their intuitions nor fully predict user intentions or reactions for several reasons. First, the "user" is actually a group of people; second, only direct experience can accurately communicate a group's social norms and shared work practices; and third, the results of an evaluation of the system are elusive because the work context continually changes. Given these factors, what can developers do to create effective groupware systems?

This section presents several case studies, each evaluating the effectiveness of a groupware technology or system. Some successes and some failures in developing and using groupware systems in real work situations are examined. The studies contain interpretations of system usability, ranging from very positive to somewhat negative, from which extremely important principles can be gleaned. (Review the primer on groupware dynamics in Chapter 1 for other important principles.)

Background: An awareness that groupware is a shared technology

Early groupware applications failed for several reasons. First, they required some people to do additional work while receiving no benefit. Second, the designers' intuitions about how computers are used did not translate to real group situations. Third, experience with group application development could not be generalized. For example, video conferencing in the 1970s and 1980s failed because people assumed that the technology could support face-to-face meetings, even though it could not replicate the psychological and social factors occurring in those meetings. In addition, video conferencing systems were typically installed without prior needs assessment.

Upon investigation, researchers found task analysis, design, and evaluation to be considerably more difficult for groupware applications than for single-user applications. Motivational, economic, and political factors affect a group's success with a *shared* technology. To complicate matters, the situation surrounding a particular success is very difficult, if not impossible to replicate. Also, traditional practice lacks evaluations that can (1) measure which network structures and human interaction patterns are influenced by new technology, and (2) measure them against the ongoing social relationships, task differences, and so on.

Themes: Involvement, cooperation, disparity

Groupware does not necessarily help in the situation where the owner of a problem is not the person who has the information to solve it. For example, if the electronic calendars of managers are maintained by their secretaries while other workers voluntarily maintain their own calendars, a system for electronic meeting scheduling may not be effective in that organization. In other words, the complexity and uniqueness of group work makes developing effective groupware systems difficult. Here are some themes for achieving effectiveness.

Increased user involvement. Eason and Harker note an increasing focus on the end user. They give the following evidence for this phenomenon: (1) purchasers of computing solutions are now end users, as opposed to being just data processing managers; (2) the maturing of computing technology opens up new markets; (3) competitive advantage now comes from usability, not from having the most functionality; and (4) users are demanding systems that can be used by groups and entire organizations (organizational software systems).

Given this business context, software suppliers are transitioning to design methods that actively engage the user. Their strategy is to form new relationships between designers and end users, such as establishing usability labs, holding user group meetings, modeling user groups, making users part of the design team, visiting user sites, studying in-house groups who are similar to end users, and enrolling technical groups in the users' organization.

Eason and Harker note that suppliers are improving their user contacts, but are failing to simultaneously improve their methods. They cite the need for better techniques throughout the software development cycle. In particular, they suggest that (1) analysis must address user tasks and organizational behavior, (2) specifications must accurately represent human endeavors, (3) designs must be flexible and easy to prototype, (4) system delivery must emphasize customization and training, and (5) system use must include ongoing support and usability testing. Groupware developers can use these points to change the software development process in their own organizations.

Cooperative application development. Nardi and Miller present a startling observation: spreadsheets are viewed as single-user programs, yet they provide strong support for cooperative application development. The authors' studies reveal that spreadsheet use in the workplace often results in collaboration between people with different levels of programming and domain expertise. They offer two supporting arguments for this phenomenon. First, the division of spreadsheets into two distinct programming layers allows programming tasks to be distributed. Second, the spreadsheet's strong visual format allows domain knowledge to be shared.

Nardi and Miller challenge our existing notions about spreadsheets by noting that spreadsheet codevelopment is the rule, not the exception, and that spreadsheet formats support the sharing of both programming expertise and domain knowledge. In support of these claims, they cite their field study results:

(1) People share programming expertise by exchanging spreadsheet code.
(2) People transfer domain knowledge via spreadsheet templates.
(3) People debug spreadsheets cooperatively.
(4) People use spreadsheets cooperatively in group settings.
(5) People train each other in new spreadsheet techniques.

Nardi and Miller close with two major implications for groupware developers. First, as users gain more control over computational resources through end-user programming systems, system designers should anticipate and take advantage of these cooperative work practices. Second, a fundamental reason to engage in cooperative work is to share domain knowledge, and software that provides strong visual formats will encourage this cooperative learning.

No disparity between end users. Grudin discovered three dynamics common to the current practice of groupware application development. First, disparity occurs when those who support an application are not the ones who benefit from it. Second, when managers lack intuition about groupware systems, they make poor decisions during software development. Third, the extreme difficulty in evaluating groupware inhibits learning and generalizing from user experiences.

Grudin cites the situation in which managers sponsored the development of an electronic meeting scheduling system, thinking that everyone used the electronic calendar the same way they did. However, the managers had their secretaries maintain their calendars, while everyone else had to personally maintain their own calendars. This set up an enormous disparity between the managers and the rest of the organization. The result: the meeting scheduling system was built and installed, but never used.

Note that while the automatic meeting scheduling system is a small case, the same phenomenon can be found in other software application areas, such as digitized voice applications, project management systems, natural language interfaces to databases, and group decision support systems. Grudin closes by noting that, as a computing profession, we have an imbalance in experience. For example, system designers have less experience with multiuser applications than with multiuser systems, less experience with multiuser applications than with single-user applications, and less experience redesigning people's jobs than redesigning technology. Groupware developers are becoming aware that they must grow their experience base to produce effective systems.

Futures: New assumptions, intuitions, and investigations

Groupware is built on assumptions about social interactions. For example, the very few early video conferencing successes had a common theme: highly involved user participation during system specification, design and installation. The future success of groupware systems relies on increased user involvement to achieve a match between the work needs and the recommended technological solution.

Traditionally we have drawn on intuition created from our experiences with single-user applications. This phenomenon leads to conclusions like "What works for me should work for you," "No extra work for me means no extra work for you," and "I accept this tool so you should, too." The future will have to see a fostering of new intuitions about group work and about how computers are to be used by groups before groupware systems enjoy wide success.

Only field experiments have the immediacy and the richness needed for evaluating group work situations. Successful field experiments for investigating group work probably require an intervention of roughly one year, a strong mission focus for all those involved, and physically dispersed groups of individuals who come from the same work culture, share the same work concerns, and have a reason for working together. The future will see groupware developers spending more time planning and doing these kinds of field experiments.

The Supplier's Role in the Design of Products for Organisations

K.D. EASON AND SUSAN HARKER

HUSAT Research Centre, Department of Human Sciences, University of Technology, Loughborough, Lancastershire LE11 3TU

A survey of design processes in the United Kingdom demonstrates that suppliers of all kinds are showing an increasing concern for the requirements of user organisations. This paper examines the reasons for this development. It then reviews the many relationships between user organisations and suppliers that can be fostered during the design process in order to promote the development of systems that meet organisational needs. Finally, it examines a variety of techniques which can be used during the design process to enable designers and users to work together.

Received May 1988

1. INTRODUCTION

The early development of information technology products can be classified under two broad headings: the creation of generic functional products and the bespoke development of applications. In the former case the supplier of the technology created general-purpose products, which were programmed for use by a wide variety of user organisations for a limited sub-set of tasks. In the latter case applications technologists would take the general-purpose product and build specific software applications which would satisfy the needs of specialist users with specialist tasks. While big systems were sometimes developed by the IT supplier companies on this basis, for example, in the military systems field, the most usual sources of specific applications development were the data processing departments inside organisations and the software houses.

This separation of responsibility for meeting specific user needs is becoming increasingly untenable and we now find suppliers of all kinds who are preoccupied by the needs of specific user groups as part of their product development process. This paper seeks to review the structures and mechanisms which have to be established if suppliers are to be able to deliver products into the organisational environment which will satisfy the demands that now exist.

The data which have been used as the primary basis of this paper come from an analysis of design activities in a range of U.K. IT supplier and user organisations, undertaken as part of the Alvey programme of information technology research, Harker *et al.*[1] For reasons of confidentiality it is not possible to provide specific examples, and the data have been analyzed to allow description of the broad trends which emerge.

2. THE TREND TOWARDS AN INCREASING FOCUS ON THE END USER

As a way of explaining the increasing preoccupation with user needs it is instructive to look at what is happening in supplier companies which have been primarily technology driven, i.e. those which have previously seen their business as the production ad sale of 'boxes' which are faster, more powerful or cheaper than the competition. Four kinds of change appear to be influencing these companies in terms of their policies with regard to end use.

2.1 A change in the buyer

Traditionally the purchasers of computer equipment were technical specialists, for example, data processing managers, who were primarily concerned with technical and economic criteria and who expected to deal with application issues themselves. As technology has become cheaper and its potential more widely appreciated, the range of purchasers has expanded enormously. Not only do D.P. Managers buy IT products but user department managers, office managers and, in many instances, the end user him or herself. The technology has moved into the mass market. Few of these buyers are technical specialists and they expect to be able to purchase systems which can match their particular requirements without significant implications for their own learning and development.

2.2 A shift towards a market orientation

The maturation of the technology means that an enormous range of products is now feasible. It is now possible to put a tremendous range of functionality into even a relatively cheap product. The technology is not the constraint it was. As the suppliers in the survey reported, the problem is not what you can make but what there is a market for. Consequently, analysis of market requirements is assuming an increasingly significant role in product development. Market analysis of new opportunities tends to reveal quite specific market segments with a limited array of applications in a particular type of business.

2.3 Functionality and usability

Many suppliers have hitherto operated on the basis that they should 'match the functionality of their competitors and then add some'. Many research studies, e.g. Stevens,[2] Eason,[3] have shown that the pursuit of maximum functionality leads to perplexed users who employ only a small fraction of the facilities available. This has resulted in a growing awareness that it is necessary to provide an appropriate level of functionality which can only be determined by understanding the requirements of target groups of users. Similarly the realisation that end users are no longer technical specialists has led to the recognition of the competitive advantage which can come from ensuring products are usable as well as functional. Shackel[4] illustrates the way in which this kind of thinking has emerged in the policies of IBM. Usability also depends on understanding the characteristics of the target users and their tasks.

2.4 Demand for shared systems

A more recent development has been the recognition that, within organisations, work is shared between many different people. Thus, as the application of IT systems spreads, there is an increasing demand for multi-user systems which will support the need to share information and facilities. Early generic products, such as word processing and spread sheets, were essentially concerned to support the work of a single user. The tasks which they supported were also very similar across many organisations. Now suppliers are designing systems to serve groups of users. To achieve this successfully the design team needs to understand the interdependencies of the people between whom the work is divided. This will include how control and co-organisation may be exercised in user organisations, and the different ways in which these processes may be manifested in different organisations. Grudin[5] offers an instructive analysis of why many early multi-user products failed, for example, products designed for diary co-ordination. The designers do not appear to have been conscious of the organisational framework within which these products would need to fit if they were to be acceptable and productive. Such failures are hardly surprising when the study of organisational issues plays no part in the training of IT systems designers and there is no explicit recognition of the need to determine organisational requirements within the design cycle.

The result of these trends is that an increasingly large proportion of the IT product market is concerned with the delivery of complete systems for use in specific applications domains.

3. ACHIEVING THE TRANSITION TO A USER-ORIENTED APPROACH TO DESIGN

Suppliers working on bespoke developments have long worked in close relations with their client organisation. Our concern here is to examine the situation when the supplier is developing a generic product which it hopes to sell to many organisations. From our investigations of design processes it is apparent that the trends identified above are having an effect upon policies, structures and methods of work within the supplier companies. In many suppliers there are attempts to find new forms of organisation to match the new demands. For example development teams may be charged with responsibility for a particular application domain rather than with a technology domain. Changes in working practice may introduce procedures, techniques and tools to support a more user-oriented approach to design. One example is the development of usability laboratories in which product testing can be extended to cover the user's ability to work with the product and the product's acceptability.

The survey has revealed a wide range of changes that are taking place so that suppliers are more market- or user-oriented In many ways it reveals an emerging 'good practice' for this user-oriented approach. It is evident that it has not yet penetrated all the levels of the design process and that while companies are exploring different

ideas and trying out different methods, they have not yet established integrated strategies which will lead to products which have utility, usability and acceptability for target organisations. Clearly further work is required in this area and indeed this forms part of the ongoing programme for work of the ESPRIT HUFIT project (Russell and Galer).[6]

One major organisational feature of this approach is the development of new ways for suppliers and users to relate to each other. The requirement to match complex organisational realities makes it necessary to establish much closer relations than was hitherto necessary. In the next section the variety of approaches which we found in the survey is presented and the utility of each approach examined.

4. ESTABLISHING RELATIONS BETWEEN SUPPLIERS AND USER ORGANISATIONS

In order to demonstrate the kind of changes which are occurring it is useful to begin by characterising the nature of the relationships which have been typical up to now. While there are specific variations, most larger suppliers of generic products have maintained their contact with the user organisations who are their customers through the technical specialists in charge of centralised computing facilities in those organisations, who are the 'buyers' of computing equipment. The staff of the supplier organisations involved have usually been members of sales teams, although maintenance staff and training staff may also be involved. This contact has principally supported the flow of information from supplier to user, although marketing information and technical 'bug' reports may feed back to the supplier. However, from our investigations, it appears that very little information about the behaviour and needs of end users flows via this route into the design teams developing the next generation of products. This feedback could most obviously be used in the planning of product enhancements, but even here it is more likely that the view of the d.p. 'buyer' will be conveyed rather than the needs of the end user.

To improve the knowledge available to design teams about the user world a number of strategies are being employed. One strategy attempts to build formalised models of users which can be used as frames of reference for design teams. These models take knowledge about relevant tasks, user and organisational behaviour and build up a picture for a specified set of circumstances, for example, generic users such as secretaries, or relevant work processes such as order entry. If these models prove valid they will provide much valuable design guidance. They are best suited to those aspects of the user's world which can be generalized across organisations, i.e. common characteristics of human beings and perhaps aspects of technology-oriented tasks, such as file retrieval and editing. They cannot be complete because there are many user aspects which are dependent on task characteristics peculiar to the application and to user and culture characteristics which vary greatly from one organisational setting to another.

If there is a need to study the specific requirements of a particular type of user or organisation, an obvious route is to link the design team with relevant users.

A number of supplier organisations have adopted a strategy of employing people from user organisations so that their knowledge may be utilised in the development process. This can be a very effective way of bringing user insight and expertise into the design team itself. This is likely to be most useful when the former 'user' is new to the supplier organisation but the phenomenon of 'going native', which is known to occur quite quickly once the user identifies with the design team, limits its long term utility. The 'user' will need to renew his knowledge of the user world by continually revisiting user sites.

A slightly different kind of relationship which is sometimes adopted as a way of recruiting knowledge which directly reflects end-user needs is to bring typical users into the supplier organisation on a temporary basis as sources of data about the specific requirements. Halasz[7] reports a development in which a history graduate student worked in the design team to enable the designers to understand how he undertook his tasks. This has useful features because it provides direct evidence of how users engage in their tasks and enables the design team to test prototypes and check how useful and usable they are. A small number of users, however, offers only limited opportunities to identify user variability, and where the work is usually done with others, a single user's behaviour may be further distorted by his isolation from the normal work group, an important consideration for multi-user systems.

One strategy designed to overcome this involves the use of a team of 'visiting' users which is an approach widely adopted in the development of military systems designed on a bespoke basis for a particular customer. The nature of the relationships in such bespoke systems development are carefully specified and usually figure as a formal commitment within the terms of the contract. Thus this model is not directly applicable to design activities aimed at the production of 'off-the-shelf' products.

A somewhat analogous strategy which some suppliers have adopted as a means of dealing with generic products is to study appropriate user groups within their own organisations. Thus secretaries, personnel managers, accountants etc. become the models for the large user population in those occupations. Two problems arise in relation to this approach. Firstly, the people studied may not be typical of the wider population and the extent of variation remains to be determined in some way. Secondly, it can only be used for those functions which exist 'in-house'. Thus it will not be possible to gain access to users who have other specialized functions, for example, the medical team in a hospital or the clerical staff of a government department.

A direct and enduring link is formed when the supplier engages in some more or less formal relationship with a 'favoured customer' with a view to developing a system. This relationship may simply be based on an agreement that the user organisation will accept products for testing before they are released for general distribution, or it may involve a relationship which extends from the start of the design process. While the most obvious example of the latter case may be development of a bespoke system at the behest of the user organisation there is evidence that some suppliers are keen to initiate such collaborative arrangements with a view to creating a product which can subsequently be extended to form a generic product for that application domain. In this situation, suppliers like to work with a market leader in the application domain, in order to identify the issues which are at the leading edge of development. This also offers the advantage that if the product proves highly acceptable and is adopted for widespread use within a market leader, it creates a market pull for other customers within the same area. The main difficulty with this approach is that the concentration on one customer can mislead the designers into thinking that unique characteristics within one organisation are in fact typical. They may then find that the product cannot be generalised in the way that had been anticipated.

The national and international Research and Development programmes, such as Alvey, ESPRIT and EUREKA, have offered the opportunity to establish a broader-based linking of user organisations and suppliers. In the Alvey programme, for example, the Large Scale Demonstrator Projects bring together suppliers, users and University research teams with the aim of creating a pre-competitive demonstration product which could be exploited in an application marketplace. When these products involve more than one user organisation they provide more generalisable evidence in relation to the field of application. There is, however, considerable evidence, Eason,[8] that relations within the consortia require very careful negotiation and management if the end result is to be judged as beneficial by all those involved. For example, user organisations may expect to receive solutions within short time-scales which meet their immediate and specific needs, while suppliers may see the user organisations as a field laboratory through which to develop a family of products in the long term. A clear understanding of the implication of the proposed programme of work and commitment to its objectives is an essential requirement for such relationships. It may be necessary for the different partners to agree to the delivery of additional services which, while not central to their own view of the work, give it a focus which is valued from the perspective of others.

5. THE DEVELOPMENT OF TECHNIQUES TO SUPPORT USER-ORIENTED DESIGN

Whatever the extent and the form of engagement between supplier and user organisation, it is necessary to have techniques for analysis and design which will make the best use of the opportunities that present themselves. One of the major conclusions to emerge from the studies which have been conducted is that even when suppliers have good contact with users they rarely have techniques available which they can use effectively. This is not really surprising since development work has typically been driven by technological innovation, and the specification of user requirements on the basis of the functionality which the technology can support. Techniques for investigating human and organisational behaviour are not part of the designer's repertoire. The demand for increased attention to these issues, which accompanies the maturation of the technology, has led to the identification of the gap which needs to be filled.

It is instructive to look at the techniques that are required in terms of the product design and development cycle and a simplified version of this cycle is presented in figure 1.

Each stage of the design process creates specific demands for techniques which will serve to establish the relevant knowledge about users. Such techniques have been established in the context of application developments within organisations placing a strong emphasis on user participation; see, for example, the ETHICS methodology developed by Mumford.[9] What is required is to develop the principles involved to suit the situation where suppliers are working to develop products to support a variety of users and organisations. The implications of this for the various stages will be discussed briefly.

Development cycle   Activity

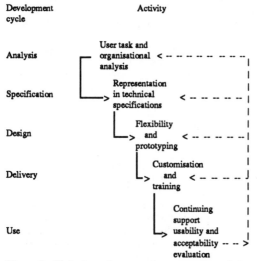

Figure 1. Techniques to support user-supplier relations at different stages in the design process.

In the analysis phase what are required are forms of user, task and organisational analysis which will accurately describe the user's situation and reveal what is common across functionally similar organisations. They should conversely reveal what differences arise because of the unique character of each organisation. Eason[10] reviews these methods and they have been incorporated in a design methodology known as DIADEM, which is in use in a number of major systems developments, Damodaran.[11] One technique for checking the generality of conclusions is described in Gower and Eason.[12] This involves a detailed study in one organisational setting followed by limited studies in other comparable settings where the existence of general properties is checked.

If the information gathered from these analyses is to be used effectively in the specification phase it has to be translated into a form with which the designers can work. The User Skills and Task Match methodology developed by Hutt et al.[13] offers an example of a procedure for building this kind of information into the specification processes of design teams developing generic products.

The design process needs to be informed by the many guidelines and standards that now exist in relation to the design of human-computer systems, but there are two features of the design phase which require specific attention if the products are to serve complex organisa-

tional tasks. The first is that they must embody a level of flexibility which is commensurate with the variety of ways in which organisations undertake the work associated with their goals. If design teams make assumptions about the viability of a single way of undertaking complex processes in which the staff of the user organisations are experts, the products will almost certainly be deemed unacceptable. No user organisation can afford to become tied to a particular way of undertaking a critical work process as defined by a supplier. The user organisation must always be given the functionality it needs to undertake the work and the potential for implementing it in a flexible way, which can be moulded to local requirements and can change where appropriate. The other requirement is to ensure that proposed forms of design are tested before the decision to confirm them is finally made. Early testing of prototype or pilot systems is an important mechanism for ensuring that task and user needs are met. However, the creation of prototype environments which adequately reflect the organisational context in which the products are to be used requires careful planning, Harker.[14]

The delivery process is usually associated with the provision of documentation, training and technical support but, if complex organisational products are to be implemented, user organisations will need help which stretches beyond these areas. They will need help to use the flexibility in the system to adapt it to their specific requirements. Many current products have facilities to allow customisation, but this potential is often not realised because user organisations lack the skill to do the necessary work. If suppliers offer support for this process users should be able to make much more successful use of products. User organisations also need help in coping with the implication that major technical advances will require commensurate organisational and procedural change. A user organisation which engages in a single implementation will have little evidence on which to base its planning. A supplier implementing similar systems in a number of organisations will build up an awareness of the issues and should be in a position to offer information and advice about the process of change and how to handle it effectively.

A further consideration affects the continuing relationship which may exist once the system is in use. All the evidence from studies of the information technology implementation process demonstrates that successful take-up is an evolutionary process in which the staff of the organisation steadily become more sophisticated with respect to the technology and are thus able to cope with progressively more advanced systems. The acceptance of this approach will mean that suppliers must be prepared to offer on-going support rather than offering a one-shot implementation.

The existence of the system in use creates one more demand on the supplier-user relationship. Suppliers need to gain information about the usability and acceptability of the products they have designed. These evaluations will show whether the assumptions made in design were valid and indicate directions for future design work. To get this information, suppliers may need to offer users advice, and even support, in monitoring and evaluating the impact of the technology. In this way they will add to the creation of more user-led developments.

6. CONCLUSIONS

In the design processs we have studied some of the structures and techniques described above are already established, but there is no case where a complete set is in place. The result is that products show some movement towards satisfying the requirements of user organisations, but still fail to provide a good match to organisational reality.

It will be clear that embracing the kinds of user-supplier relations which are required to design complex organisational products will place considerable demands upon both supplier and user organisations. We have identified some of the changes in design practice and new methods which need to be adopted. However, there is one further comment which must be made here. Commercial confidentiality and competitive advantage mean that suppliers are often reluctant to discuss their development plans and the sales organisation keeps a careful eye on who has contact with clients and what issues are discussed. The resolution of the conflict between maintaining commercial confidentiality and making information freely available for the purpose of new product development becomes a critical issue in the establishment of a relationship and a set of methods which will foster user-centered design.

It takes two sides to create a relationship, and there are also considerable implications for the user organisations. The research evidence shows that a number of user organisations tend to define their requirements and then to examine the market expecting to find just what they need. There is also resistance to entering a relationship with a supplier to create generic products when the organisation wants products which are tailor-made to its specification. It is necessary to encourage the recognition that it is in the long term interests of user organisations to be open to examination and debate, because it is only in this way that suppliers can develop the knowledge to create the appropriate ranges of products.

It is in the nature of all organisations to take a self-centered view of relations with others and a considerable amount of exploration and experimentation of the suitability of various strategies will be required in order to establish the credibility and value of the structures and techniques described in the eyes of the parties involved. It is particularly important, therefore, that there remain programmes of Government support which will foster the establishment of these relations and offer the opportunity to develop the full range of methods and techniques which are required.

Acknowledgements

We wish to acknowledge the support of the Alvey Directorate and the Science and Engineering Research Council for funding Alvey project MMI 080, which enabled the collection of data for this paper. We are indebted to our co-workers, David Poulson, Helen Maskery and Andrew Parkes for their work on the cases. Finally, no information about design processes can be obtained without the co-operation of designers and users, and we gratefully thank the many companies and organisations who have provided assistance.

REFERENCES

1. S.D.P Harker, K.D. Eason, D.F. Poulson and A. Parkes. Classifying the target for human factors outputs. Paper to the Annual Alvey Conference, UMIST. Manchester, July 1987.
2. G.C. Stevens. User-friendly systems? A critical examination of the concept. *Behaviour and Information Technology* 2 (1) 3-16 (1983).
3. K.D. Eason. Patterns of usage of a flexible information system. In *The Application of Information Technology*, edited S.D.P. Harker and K.D. Eason. Taylor and Francis, London (1988).
4. B. Shackel. IBM makes usability as important as functionality. *The Computer Journal* 29 (3) (1986).
5. J. Grudin. Social evaluation of the user interface; Who does the work and who gets the benefit? In *Human-Computer Interaction, INTERACT '87*, edited H.-J. Bullinger and B. Shackel. Elsevier North-Holland, Amsterdam (1987).
6. A.J. Russell and M.D. Galer. Designing human factors design aids for designers. In *Cognitive Engineering in the Design of Human-Computer Interaction and Expert Systems*, edited by G. Salvendy. Elsevier, Amsterdam (1987).
7. F.G. Halasz, T.P. Moran ad R.H. Trigg, NoteCards in a nutshell. In *Conference Proceedings of CHI 87*, edited J.M. Carroll and P.P. Tanner. Toronto, Canada (1987).
8. K.D. Eason. *Information Technology and Organisational Change*. Taylor and Francis, London (1988).
9. E. Mumford. *Designing Human Systems for New Technology; The ETHICS Method*. Manchester Business School (1983).
10. K.D. Eason. The human interface; the need for bridge building. Paper to the Annual Alvey Conference, UMIST. Manchester, July 1987.
11. L. Damodaran. Creating a human factors strategy for I.T. systems. *Proceedings of the CREST Course 'Human Factors for Informatics: Usability'* Loughborough University, December 1986.
12. J.C. Gower and K.D. Eason. Defining information technology systems for electricity supply distribution. In *Human-Computer Interaction INTERACT '84*, edited B. Shackel. Elsevier North-Holland, Amsterdam (1985).
13. A. Hutt, L. Macaulay and C. Fowler. The user skills task match methodology for introducing human factors into the I.T. product specification process. *Proceedings of HCI 86*, University of York (1986).
14. S.D.P. Harker. The role of user prototyping in the system design process. In *Work With Display Units 86*, edited B. Knave and P.-G. Wildeback. North-Holland, Amsterdam (1986).

Twinkling lights and nested loops: distributed problem solving and spreadsheet development

Bonnie A. Nardi and James R. Miller

Hewlett-Packard Laboratories, Human-Computer Interaction Department, 1501 Page Mill Road, Palo Alto, CA 94304 USA

(Received April 1990 and accepted in revised form August 1990)

In contrast to the common view of spreadsheets as "single-user" programs, we have found that spreadsheets offer surprisingly strong support for cooperative development of a wide variety of applications. Ethnographic interviews with spreadsheet users showed that nearly all of the spreadsheets used in the work environments studied were the result of collaborative work by people with different levels of programming and domain expertise. We describe how spreadsheet users cooperate in developing, debugging and using spreadsheets. We examine the properties of spreadsheet software that enable cooperation, arguing that: (1) the division of the spreadsheet into two distinct programming layers permits effective distribution of computational tasks across users with different levels of programming skill; and (2) the spreadsheet's strong visual format for structuring and presenting data supports sharing of domain knowledge among co-workers.

1. Introduction

People organize themselves and their work so that problems can be solved collectively (Vygotsky, 1979; Bosk, 1980; Lave, 1988; Newman, 1989; Seifert & Hutchins, 1989). We are interested in the artifacts that support and encourage this collective problem solving. A spreadsheet is a "cognitive artifact" (Norman, unpublished manuscript; Chandrasekaran, 1981; Holland & Valsiner, 1988; Norman & Hutchins, 1988) that can be understood and shared by a group of people, providing a point of cognitive contact that mediates cooperative work. In this paper we examine the shared development of spreadsheet applications. We report the results of our ethnographic study of spreadsheet use in which we found that users with different levels of programming skill and domain knowledge collaborate informally to produce spreadsheet applications. In the first part of the paper we present a descriptive, empirical report of collaborative work practices, documenting the kinds of cooperation found among spreadsheet users, and the ways in which problem solving is distributed across users with different skills and interests. In the second part of the paper we describe and analyse the characteristics of spreadsheet software that support cooperative work.

In contrast to studies of computer-supported cooperative work (CSCW) that focus on software systems specifically designed to support cooperative work within an organization (Grudin, 1988), we address how a certain class of traditional personal computer applications—spreadsheets—function as *de facto* cooperative work environments. We describe how spreadsheet users work together, even though spreadsheets lack "designed-in" technological support for cooperative work.

We use the term "cooperative work" in the general sense of "multiple persons working together to produce a product or service" (Bannon & Schmidt, 1989). In this paper we want to draw attention to a form of cooperative computing already well established in office environments. As we will describe, spreadsheets emerge as the product of several people working together, through not in formally designated teams, task forces, or committees. On the contrary, spreadsheet work flows across different users in fluid, informal ways, and cooperation among spreadsheet users has a spontaneous, self-directed character.

Our research highlights two forms of cooperative work that are central to computer-based work and that have received little attention in the CSCW community: the sharing of programming expertise and the sharing of domain knowledge. Because of the CSCW emphasis on computer systems that enhance interpersonal communication (e.g. e-mail, remote conferencing, shared white-boards), the importance of collaboration in programming itself has been over-looked. The current interest in "empowering users" through participatory design methods (Bjerknes, Ehn & Kyng, 1987) and end user programming systems (Panko, 1988) will, we believe, begin to draw attention to collaborative programming practices of the kind we describe in this paper. The sharing of domain knowledge has been only implicitly recognized in CSCW research; studies tend to focus on communication techniques themselves, rather than on what is being communicated. In this paper we discuss the implications of the particular visual representation of the spreadsheet for communicating analyses based on numeric data.

Since 1986 about five million spreadsheet programs have been sold to personal computer users, second in number only to text editors, and far ahead of any other kind of software (Alsop, 1989). Spreadsheets deserve our interest as the only widely used end user programming environment; text editing and drawing packages are used by many, but involve no programming. With spreadsheets, even unsophisti-cated users can write programs in the form of formulas that establish numerical relations between data values. Users who show no particular interest in computers *per se* voluntarily write their own spreadsheet programs, motivated by interests beyond or completely unrelated to job requirements—a claim that cannot be made for any other kind of software that we know of. In large part this is because the spreadsheet's "twinkling lights"†—the automatically updating cell values—prove irresistible. Spreadsheet users experience a real sense of computational power as their modifications to data values and formulas appear instantly and visibly in the spreadsheet.

Despite the prevalence of spreadsheets in the personal computing world, spreadsheets have not been widely studied. Kay (1984), Hutchins, Hollan and Norman (1986), and Lewis and Olson (1987) enumerated some of the benefits of spreadsheets which include a concrete, visible representation of data values, immediate feedback to the user, and the ability to apply formulas to blocks of cells. There are some experimental studies of spreadsheet use that focused on small aspects of the user interface; for example, Olson and Nilsen (1987) contrasted the methods by which subjects entered formulas in two different spreadsheet products. (See also Brown & Gould, 1987; Napier, Lane, Batsell & Guadango, 1989.) In

† We are indebted to Ralph Kimball of Application Design Incorporated of Los Gatos, California for this turn of phrase.

another type of study, Doyle (1990) reported his experiences of teaching students to use Lotus 1-2-3,† though most of his observations could apply to any kind of software (e.g. inconsistencies in file naming conventions). Other researchers have used spreadsheets as a model for various kinds of programming environments (Van Emden, Ohki & Takeuchi, 1985; Piersol, 1986; Lewis & Olson, 1987; Spenke & Beilken, 1989).

Our study began with the traditional "single-user application" perspective. We were (and still are) interested in spreadsheets as computational devices, and wanted to learn more about how spreadsheets users take the basic structure of a spreadsheet and mould it into an application that addresses some specific need. In particular, we were interested in the success *non-programmers* have had in building spreadsheet applications. We saw no reason to dispute Grudin's (1988) comments that spreadsheets are "single-user applications" in which "an individual's success . . . is not likely to be affected by the backgrounds of other group members", and that "motivational and political factors" are unimportant for spreadsheet users. However, as the study progressed, we were struck by two things:

- **Spreadsheet co-development is the rule, not the exception.** In the office environments we studied, most spreadsheets come about through the efforts of more than one person. The feeling of co-development is very strong; people regularly spoke of how "we" built a spreadsheet, and were very aware of the cooperative nature of the development process.
- **Spreadsheets support the sharing of both programming and domain expertise.** Because of our focus on end-user programming, we soon noticed that one reason spreadsheet users are so productive is that they successfully enlist the help of other, more knowledgeable users in constructing their spreadsheets. In the same way, experienced co-workers share domain knowledge with less experienced colleagues, using the spreadsheet as a medium of communication.

We do not mean to suggest that spreadsheets are never developed by individual users working completely independently. But presupposing that spreadsheets are "single-user" applications, blinds us to seeing the cooperative use of spreadsheets of which we found much evidence in our study. We will describe how spreadsheet users:

(1) share programming expertise through exchanges of code;
(2) transfer domain knowledge via spreadsheet templates and the direct editing of spreadsheets;
(3) debug spreadsheets cooperatively;
(4) use spreadsheets for cooperative work in meetings and other group settings; and
(5) train each other in new spreadsheet techniques.

We will elaborate these activities via ethnographic examples from the research.

2. Methods and informants

The ideas presented in this paper are based on our ethnographic research including extensive interviewing of spreadsheet users, and analysis of some of their spread-

---

† Lotus and 1-2-3 are registered trademarks of Lotus Development Corporation.

sheets which we collected during the course of interviewing. We have chosen to study a small number of people in some depth to learn how they construct, debug and use spreadsheets. We are interested in the kinds of problems for which people use spreadsheets and how they themselves structure the problem solving process—topics that by their very nature cannot be studied under the controlled conditions of the laboratory. We have also examined and worked with several different spreadsheet products including VisiCalc (the original personal computer spreadsheet), Lotus 1-2-3 and Microsoft Excel.†

For the field research we interviewed and tape recorded conversations with spreadsheet users in their offices and homes.‡ Our informants were found through an informal process of referral. We told them that we were interested in software for users with little formal programming education and that we wanted to talk to people actively using spreadsheets. The interviews were conversational in style, intended to capture users' experiences in their own words. A fixed set of open-ended questions was asked of each user (see the appendix for the list of questions), though the questions were asked as they arose naturally in the context of the conversation, not necessarily in the order in which they appear in the appendix. During the interview sessions we viewed users' spreadsheets on-line, and sometimes in paper form, and discussed the uses and construction of the spreadsheets. The material in this paper is based on about 350 pages of transcribed interviews with 11 users, though we focus on a smaller subset here to provide ethnographic detail.

Informants in the study were college-educated people employed in diverse companies, from small start-ups to large corporations of several thousand employees. Informants had varying degrees of computer experience ranging from someone who had only recently learned to use a computer to professional programmers. Most were non-programmers with three to five years experience with spreadsheets. Informant names used here are fictitious. Five sets of spreadsheet users illustrate the cooperative nature of spreadsheet development:

- *Betty and Buzz* run a start-up company with eight employees. Betty is the chief financial officer of the company and Buzz a developer of the product the company produces. Betty does not have a technical background though she has acquired substantial computer knowledge on her own, largely through using spreadsheets. Buzz is a professional programmer. They use spreadsheets for their customer lists, prospective customer lists, product sales, evaluation units, tradeshow activity and accounts receivable.
- *Ray* manages a finance department for a large corporation and has a large staff. He has an engineering degree and an MBA, and some limited programming experience. He uses spreadsheets to plan budget allocations across several different departments, to track departmental expenses and headcounts, and to forecast future budgetary needs.
- *Louis,* in his seventies, is semi-retired and works as an engineering consultant about two hours a day for a large manufacturing corporation. He has been working with Lotus 1-2-3§ for about a year, and has no other computer experience of any kind (he uses Lotus as his word processor). Louis's main application is analysing test data from his engineering simulations of radar designs. He learned Lotus with the help of his son Peter, an architectural engineer.

† Microsoft and Excel are registered trademarks of Microsoft Corporation.

‡ The interviews were conducted by the first author. We use the plural "we" here for expository ease.

§ All those in our study use either Lotus 1-2-3 or Microsoft Excel.

531

- *Laura and Jeremy* work for a medium size high tech equipment manufacturer. Laura is an accountant, the controller of the company. She directs a staff of eight, all of whom use spreadsheets. Laura is knowledgeable about spreadsheets but has no programming experience. Jeremy, Laura's manager, is the chief financial officer of the company. He is skilled at spreadsheet macro and template development.
- *Jennifer* is an accountant in a rapidly growing telecommunications company. She works closely with the chief financial officer of the company. Jennifer has been working with speadsheets for about five years. She took a course in BASIC in college but has no other computer science education.

Segments from the interviews will be presented at some length as we feel it is most convincing to let users speak for themselves. The segments are verbatim transcriptions.

3. Cooperative development of spreadsheets

3.1. BRIDGING DIFFERENCES IN PROGRAMMING EXPERTISE

Spreadsheets support cooperative work among people with different levels of programming skill. We have found it useful to break the continuum of skill level into three groups: non-programmers, local developers and programmers. Non-programmers have little or no formal training or experience in programming. Local developers have substantial experience with some applications, and often much more willingness to read manuals. Programmers have a thorough grasp of at least one general programming language and a broad, general understanding of computing. Local developers typically serve as consultants for non-programmers in their work environments. Local developers may in turn seek assistance from programmers.

It is also important to note that the three kinds of users vary along another related dimension: *interest in computing*. In some cases non-programmers may be budding hackers, but many are simply neutral towards computers, regarding them as a means to an end rather than objects of intrinsic interest. A key to understanding non-programmers' interaction with computers is to recognize that they are not simply under-skilled programmers who need assistance learning the complexities of programming. Rather, they are not programmers at all. They are business professionals or scientists or other kinds of domain specialists whose jobs involve computational tasks. In contrast, local developers show a direct interest in computing, though their skills may be limited in comparison to programmers as a result of other demands on their time.

Betty and Buzz's work on spreadsheets for their company's finances offers a good example of cooperation among spreadsheet users with different levels of programming skill. As individuals, Betty and Buzz are quite different. Betty has a strong focus on her work as chief financial officer, and claims few programming skills. She has limited knowledge of the more sophisticated capabilities of the spreadsheet product she uses, knows little about the features of competing spreadsheets, and relies on Buzz and other more experienced users for assistance with difficult programming tasks, training, and consulting. In contrast, Buzz has a clear technical focus and strong programming skills. He is well-informed about the capabilities of the spreadsheet product in use in the company and of other competing products, and provides Betty with the technical expertise she needs.

From this perspective, then, Betty and Buzz seem to be the stereotypical end-user/developer pair, and it is easy to imagine their development of a spreadsheet to be equally stereotypical: Betty specifies what the spreadsheet should do based on her knowledge of the domain, and Buzz implements it. *This is not the case.* Their cooperative spreadsheet development departs from this scenario in two important ways:

(1) Betty constructs her basic spreadsheets *without assistance from Buzz*. She programs the parameters, data values and formulas into her models. In addition, Betty is completely responsible for the design and implementation of the user interface. She makes effective use of color, shading, fonts, outlines, and blank cells to structure and highlight the information in her spreadsheets.

(2) When Buzz helps Betty with a complex part of the spreadsheet such as graphing or a complex formula, his work is expressed in terms of Betty's original work. He adds small, more advanced pieces of code to Betty's basic spreadsheet; Betty is the main developer and he plays an adjunct role as consultant.

This is an important shift in the responsibility of system design and implementation. Non-programmers can be responsible for most of the development of a spreadsheet, implementing large applications that they would not undertake if they had to use conventional programming techniques. Non-programmers may never learn to program recursive functions and nested loops, but they can be extremely productive with spreadsheets. Because less experienced spreadsheet users become engaged and involved with their spreadsheets, they are motivated to reach out to more experienced users when they find themselves approaching the limits of their understanding of, or interest in, more sophisticated programming techniques.

Non-programming spreadsheet users benefit from the knowledge of local developers and programmers in two ways:

(1) Local developers and programmers *contribute code* to the spreadsheets of less experienced users. Their contributions may include: macros; the development of sophisticated graphs and charts; custom presentation formats, such as a new format for displaying cell values; formulas with advanced spreadsheet functions such as date-time operations; and complex formulas, such as a formula with many levels of nested conditionals.

(2) Experienced users *teach less experienced users* about advanced spreadsheet features. This teaching occurs informally, not in training classes. Often a user will see a feature in someone else's spreadsheet that they would like to have, and he or she simply asks how to use it.

As shown in the way Betty and Buzz divide up spreadsheet tasks, the problem solving needed to produce a spreadsheet is distributed across a person who knows the domain well and can build most of the model, and more sophisticated users whose advanced knowledge is used to enhance the spreadsheet model, or to help the less experienced user improve spreadsheet skills. Compare this division of labor with traditional computing which requires the services of a data processing department, or expert system development in which knowledge engineers are necessary. In these cases, the domain specialist has no role as a developer, and domain knowledge must first be filtered through a systems analyst, programmer, or knowledge engineer before it is formulated into a program.

Our interview with Ray offers another example of co-development. Ray is a local developer who makes use of programmers for some aspects of spreadsheet development. As with Betty and Buzz, the chief difference between the spreadsheet environment and traditional programming is that more experienced users develop only specific pieces of the spreadsheet program, working directly off the basic work done by the original user. For example, Ray recently commissioned a set of Lotus macros for custom menus to guide data input for the spreadsheets used by his staff. He prefers to concentrate on using spreadsheets for forecasting future trends and allocating money among the departments he serves—his real work. Ray is not interested in becoming an expert macro writer, even though he has taken an advanced Lotus 1-2-3 class where macros were covered. In the following exchange we are looking at the custom menus:

Interviewer: . . . [these menus] look like they'd be pretty useful. And who developed those for you?
Ray: A programmer down in Customer Support.
Interviewer: Okay, not somebody in your group. You just sent out the work, and . . .
Ray: Yeah, well, essentially, you know, I came at it conceptually, this is what I'd like to see, and they developed it. So [the programmer] made [the menus] interactive, set up the customized use.

Ray has reached the limits of his interest in programming advanced spreadsheet features himself. But he is not limited to spreadsheets without these features; he distributes the work to someone who has more interest in such things. This task distribution is similar to traditional software development in that a user provides a specification to a developer for implementation. The difference, however, is that here the user has constructed the program into which the contributed code fits. In some sense, the roles of user and "chief programmer" (Brooks, 1975) have been merged.

Spreadsheets also support cooperation between users with different programming expertise via tutoring and consulting exchanges. For example, Louis has learned almost everything he knows about Lotus 1-2-3 from his son Peter. He avoids the manual, finding it easier to be tutored by Peter. Louis's spreadsheet use, highlights an important feature of the cooperative development of spreadsheets: because the initial effort to build something really useful is relatively small, less experienced users, having had the reward of actually developing a real application, are motivated to continue to learn more, at least up to a point. Louis is starting to have Peter teach him about controlling the presentation format; for the first several months of use he concentrated only on creating basic models of parameters, data values and formulas. In general, users like Louis successfully engage other, more experienced users in the development of their spreadsheet models. They make use of problem-solving resources—i.e. more experienced users—in a very productive manner, building on their existing knowledge in a self-paced way, as they feel ready to advance.

Distributing tasks across different users and sharing programming expertise are characteristic of many programming environments—programming in Pascal or Lisp or C would almost certainly involve such collaboration. However, with spreadsheets the collaboration is specified quite differently: the end user, usually relegated to "naive user" status in traditional software development, comes center stage, appearing in the role of main developer. Spreadsheets have been successful because they give real computational power to non-programmers. Accountants and biologists and engineers who may never have taken a computer science course build useful, often complex spreadsheet applications (Arganbright, 1986). Spreadsheet users are not "naive users" or "novices"; they command knowledge of both their domain of interest and the programming techniques necessary to analyse problems in their domain. With spreadsheets, problem solving is distributed such that end users do not rely on programmers as the indispensable implementers of a set of specifications; instead end users are *assisted by* programmers who supply them with small pieces of complex code, or with training in advance features, as they build their own applications.

4. Bridging differences in domain expertise

An important aspect of cooperative work is the sharing of domain knowledge. Because spreadsheet users build their own applications, spreadsheets allow the direct transfer of domain expertise between co-workers, obviating the need to include a programmer or other outside specialist in the development cycle. Domain knowledge flows from manager to staff since managers tend to be more experienced than those they supervise, and also from staff to manager, as staff members often have specialized local knowledge needed by managers. This direct transfer of domain expertise provides efficient knowledge sharing and helps co-workers learn from one another. Instead of transferring domain expertise to a programmer or systems analyst or knowledge engineer who may never need it again, less experienced workers directly benefit from the knowledge of co-workers.

Spreadsheets mediate collaborative work by providing a physical medium in which users share domain knowledge. Spreadsheet users distribute domain expertise by directly editing each other's spreadsheets, and by sharing templates. For example, Laura works very closely with Jeremy, her manager, in developing spreadsheets. Jeremy happens to be a skilled spreadsheet user who provides macros and tutoring that Laura and her staff use. However, the more interesting distinction to be drawn here is centered around Jeremy's greater experience with their company, its manufacturing and marketing procedures, and its managerial and budgeting practices. Spreadsheets provide a foundation for thinking about different aspects of the budgeting process and for controlling budgeting activity. In the annual "Budget Estimates" spreadsheet that Laura is responsible for, many critical data values are based on assumptions about product sales, costs of production, headcounts, and other variables that must be estimated accurately for the spreadsheet to produce valid results. Through a series of direct edits to the spreadsheet, Laura and Jeremy fine-tune the structure and data values in "Budget Estimates". Laura describes this process:

Interviewer: Now when you say you and your boss work on this thing [the spreadsheet] together, what does that mean? Does he take piece A and you take piece B—how do you divide up [the work]?
Laura: How did we divide it up? It wasn't quite like that. I think more . . . not so much that we divided things up and said, "OK, you do this page and you do this section of the spreadsheet and I'll do that section," it was more . . . I did the majority of the input and first round of looking at things for reasonableness. Reasonableness means, "What does the bottom line look like?" When you look at the 12 months in the year, do you have some

funny swings that you could smooth out? Because you want it to be a little bit smoother. So what can you do for that? Or, if you do have some funny spikes or troughs, can you explain them? For example, there's one really big trade show that everybody in the industry goes to . . . So our sales that month are typically low and our expenses are high. This trade show is very, very expensive . . .

Interviewer: So there's a spike in your [expenses and a trough in sales] . . .

Laura: Yeah. So as long as you can *explain* it, then that's OK. So what my boss did was, I would do the first round of things and then I would give him the floppy or the print-outs and I'd say, "Well this looks funny to me. I don't know, is that OK, is it normal? Should we try to do something about it?" And so what he did was he took the spreadsheets and then he would just make minor adjustments.

Interviewer: Now was he adjusting formulas or data or . . . ?

Laura: Data.

. . .

Interviewer: . . . So it was a process of fine tuning the basic model that you had developed. And then you of course had to get his changes back, and look at them and understand them.

Laura: Yes. And one thing he did do, was, he added another section to the model, just another higher level of analysis where he compared it to our estimate for this year. He basically just created another page in the model—he added that on.

In preparing a budget that involves guesswork about critical variables, Laura is able to benefit from her manager's experience. They communicate via the spreadsheet as he literally takes her spreadsheet and makes changes directly to the model. She has laid the groundwork, provided the first line of defense in the "reasonableness" checking; Jeremy then adjusts values to conform to his more experienced view of what a good estimate looks like. Jeremy also made a major structural change to the spreadsheet, adding another level of analysis that he felt would provide a useful comparison. The spreadsheet was cooperatively constructed, though not in a simple division of tasks; instead the model emerged in successive approximations as Laura and Jeremy passed it back and forth for incremental refinement.

Spreadsheet users often exchange templates as a way of distributing domain expertise. Jeremy, for example, prepares budget templates used by Laura and her staff. They contain formulas and a basic structure for data that he works out because of his greater knowledge of the business. Laura and her staff fill in the templates according to their knowledge of their individual areas. Laura and her staff are doing more than "data entry"; as in the "Budget Estimates" spreadsheet, estimates requiring an understanding of many factors often make up a significant aspect of a spreadsheet, and deriving these estimates demands thought. Users such as Laura may also specialize a template if their particular area requires additional information, such as another budget line item. The use of templates takes advantage of domain expertise at local levels, such as that of Laura and her staff, and higher levels, such as Jeremy's.

Ray's work with spreadsheets provides another example of how users share spreadsheet templates. Ray prepared "targeting templates" for his staff in order to standardize the process of targeting expenses. Because of his wider perspective looking across several departments, Ray is in the best position to develop a standard. The templates also contain the custom menus that facilitate data input. Each staff member builds the spreadsheet for his or her area on top of the template, insuring that minimum requirements for data collection and analysis are met, and

536

insuring that the best possible information at the local level goes into the spreadsheets. Ray links them together. In these spreadsheets, problem solving is distributed over users who vary in both level of programming skill and domain knowledge: Ray, a local developer with domain expertise, provided the basic template; a programmer created the menus constructed of macros; and Ray's staff members, domain experts in their departments, supply data values for their respective areas.

5. Cooperative use

Many spreadsheets are destined from the start for the boardroom or the boss's desk or the auditor's file. In our study, spreadsheet users were very aware of the importance of presenting their spreadsheets to others—Laura stated, "I usually think in terms of my stuff [her spreadsheets] as being used by somebody else"—and users constructed spreadsheets with effective presentation in mind.

Spreadsheets are a common sight at meetings and in informal exchanges between co-workers—usually in paper copy or slide format. The use of paper copies and slides of spreadsheets is another means by which co-workers share domain knowledge. Some workers work with spreadsheets exclusively in hardcopy form and are not users of the software—for example executives who analyse and modify paper copies of spreadsheet models prepared by their staff members, and who present spreadsheets on slides and handouts at meetings.

In the following exchange we are discussing a budgeting spreadsheet Jennifer created for her company's chief financial officer. She condensed 43 pages of data from a mainframe application (prepared by the MIS department) into one summary page. We begin by looking at the MIS data:

Jennifer: These are the budget numbers. And then it shows the detail of what was purchased against those budget numbers, and when and how much month-to-date and year-to-date against those. And it shows the actual [amount] spent and variance from the budget.
Interviewer: And this really does have a lot of detail—it's down to the fabric on the chains.
Jennifer: Uh huh, ha! . . . everybody wants to know what we spent our money on, and, "How much do we have left?"
Interviewer: Now what do you do with this information?
Jennifer: . . . we have a presentation for the Board of Directors and the CFO [Chief Financial Officer] makes, but I prepare all this information for him. I compile this. I condense it onto a spreadsheet. . . . So I summarize the larger items, say, you know, the H-P 3000 [a Hewlett-Packard computer recently purchased by her company] for example. That's one of the big items that I pull out. . . . The Board of Directors does not want to see [a lot of] detail—they just want something very summarized. . . . So now it's down from 43 pages to one page. So mine shows the year-to-date budget . . . but it's all summarized into large dollar value items within each functional area.
. . .
Interviewer: Now what happens . . . when they go into the meeting and the CFO presents it? Does he explain it to the Board of Directors, or just put it up on a slide, or, what do they do with this?
Jennifer: . . . he hands out a copy to everybody, and then he puts it up on a slide, and he goes through each of the areas where they are going to be over [-budget]. And he was also presenting this so he could get approval for next quarter's budget. . . . he was showing them the . . . Q3 [Third Quarter] forecast column, and saying, "Okay, that is how much we need to approve it." And, "Where are we going from here?" Also, "What are we anticipating?"

The spreadsheet artifact is used by the CFO to organize and stimulate discussion in the Board of Directors meeting. The structures and cell values of the spreadsheet are meaningful to the board members; for example, the CFO points to the "Q3 forecast column" and individual data values such as the number showing "how much we need to approve (the Q3 budget)." Larger issues, e.g. "Where are we going from here?" are also introduced in the context of viewing the spreadsheet in the meeting.

Later in the interview Jennifer describes how the summary spreadsheet was created. The creation of this spreadsheet is an example of cooperative development; we include it here to show how development and use flow together as users collaborate in creating a spreadsheet whose ultimate purpose is a presentation to others. The final spreadsheet presented to the Board was the result of quite a multi-media production: Jennifer created the original spreadsheet in Excel, gave a paper copy to the CFO for his input, made pencil annotations on another paper copy because the CFO's changes came back via voice mail, and finally updated the on-line spreadsheet:

Interviewer: . . . What are your little pencil scribbles on here [a paper copy of the one-page spreadsheet]?
Jennifer: Oh, this is what I gave to the CFO at first, just comparing Q2 year-to-date budget to Q2 year-to-date actuals. And he said, "Well, for the board meeting I want [some other things]". Every time you do this he wants it differently. So I can't anticipate it. I just give him what I think [he wants] and then he says, "Ah, no, well, I want to have projected Q3 and projected Q4, and then total projected, and then have the whole year's plan on there". So that is what I was scribbling on here.
Interviewer: Was this in a meeting with him where he was telling you?
Jennifer: Actually he sent me a voice mail message. So that is why I take notes and go back and listen to the message again and say, "Now did I write this down right?"

Laura also described the use of spreadsheets in meetings. Her comments show that the spreadsheet organizes discussion, as we have seen in the preceding example. She notes the clarifications required to reveal assumptions underlying the spreadsheet models. Making such clarifications is often a part of meetings where spreadsheets are presented. Some spreadsheet users, including Laura, attach memos which list their assumptions (e.g. a budget allocation is based on department revenue not headcount). In the following discussion Laura describes a meeting she attended where executives are poring over spreadsheets and memos:

Laura: . . . So he [the president of the company] is sitting there and he's looking at [the spreadsheets and memos], and you're just kind of sitting there [she mimics slumping over in boredom, waiting for the president to ask a question] and he refers back and forth to various pages, whether he's looking at the budget [a spreadsheet] or whether he's looking at the last year's actuals [a spreadsheet] or he's looking at a list of assumptions.
Interviewer: So he looks at all of them?
Laura: That's right Yeah . . . And occasionally he asks a question and you say, "Oh, okay, that's this here. [She points to an imaginary spot of importance on the spreadsheet.] And you know here's this and this. And *this* was the [she waves her hand indicating a phrase like "such-and-such"] and *that* was because of [another gesture], or, "Oh, I didn't think about that!"

Laura explains how spreadsheets are used in distributed locations:

Laura: . . . And also another thing that's really classic, I mean I've experienced this before [at other jobs], is you do about as much as you can . . . and then he [the executive] gets on the airplane to go to England [or wherever] and he's on a plane for 10 or 12 hours and he looks at [the spreadsheets] again. And he's totally uninterrupted. . . . And he probably has more space up there than he does in his office! And then . . . they'll get where they are [going] and either phone call or fax.

Interviewer: To ask you a question?

Laura: Yeah. To get an explanation, or more detail, or "What did you say here? What did you assume there?"

. . .

Laura: . . . [Last year my boss and I spent a lot of time on a large spreadsheet that had to be faxed.] . . . We had to make some modifications in the spreadsheet . . . to add more types of expenses, or break things out into more detail. And we sat there together sort of hunched around the screen. We had to fax about 40 [pages of print-out]. No, it was more than that. We faxed a hundred pages to England one night . . . because they had to have it. They needed to have it prior to the meetings.

Interviewer: Wow.

Laura: So they would have an opportunity to digest it and come up with their list of questions.

As the descriptions show, though the spreadsheet provides a great deal of useful data, and is meaningful to the executives and others who use them, it does not fully expose all the assumptions in a model. However, the necessary verbal explanations are quickly produced (as in the faxed spreadsheet followed up by phone calls) because the spreadsheet developers are also the domain experts—there is no need to involve programmers or MIS personnel. While spreadsheets could benefit by better facilities for exposing assumptions, the spreadsheet artifact works as well as it does because users themselves control the process of putting information into spreadsheet models. Problem solving is handled locally, without requiring the intervention of personnel from other work groups—especially valuable, as Laura described, in fighting last minute fires.

A rather emblematic example of the cooperative use of spreadsheets is provided by Louis's meticulous black binder of spreadsheet print-outs that he carries between home (where his computer is) and office (where he has meetings). Although Louis's current spreadsheets contain none of the advanced presentation features provided by spreadsheet products (because he is just learning them), the simple print-outs are a regular feature of Louis's meetings with his colleagues as they discuss new designs for radar. It is a major benefit for Louis, an unsophisticated spreadsheet user, that the development environment and the presentation environment are the same in spreadsheets; once Louis has programmed his model, he has also created an effective presentation for group discussions, with no additional work.

Though users developing spreadsheets sometimes viewed each other's spread-sheets on-line, we found no extended examples of cooperative use of on-line spreadsheets, e.g. for the duration of a meeting. Hardcopies were virtually always used, and seemed to work well since the contents of the spreadsheet were being studied not manipulated. Productive uses of on-line spreadsheets are easily imagined, e.g. organizing a meeting around trying out different what-if scenarios and projecting the spreadsheet views overhead.

6. Cooperative debugging

In an experiment, Brown and Gould (1987) found that almost half of all spreadsheets constructed by experienced spreadsheet users contained errors. Most errors were in the formulas. Formula errors were most commonly caused by inserting erroneous cell references into formulas (pointing to the wrong cell or typing the wrong cell reference); incorrectly copying a formula so that the new formula got erroneous cell references; and putting the wrong item in a column. It is difficult to know how representative these specific types of errors are because the data consisted of only 11 formula errors, out of a total of 17 errors across the nine subjects in the study (each subject committed at least one error in at least one of the three spreadsheets they constructed for the study). It does seem likely that formula errors are more common than data entry errors since much more can go wrong in a formula.

While Brown and Gould's finding seems generally valid, if it were taken out of context—that is, out of the context of the experimenter's laboratory—it could be misinterpreted to suggest that spreadsheets in actual use are full of errors. In our study we found that users devote considerable effort to debugging their spreadsheet models—they are very self-conscious about the probability of error and routinely track down errors before they can do any real harm. Spreadsheet users specifically look for those errors that could have serious consequences. For example, a spreadsheet model with a value for department headcount that is off by one would probably have some budgetary or political implications, whereas being off by one in a forecast of annual budget dollars would not.

Debugging is a task that is distributed across the group—in particular, managers monitor their staffs' spreadsheets. Cooperation is valuable in error correction tasks (in many settings) as errors that become, through over-familiarity, invisible to their authors, are readily apparent when subject to the fresh scrutiny of new viewers.

In the following exchange we are discussing sources of error in the spreadsheets prepared by Ray's staff. Ray checks these spreadsheets himself. He uses "reason-ableness checks" (inspecting values to see that they fall within reasonable ranges); footing and cross-footing;† spot checking values with a calculator; and examining formulas, recording the results of the formula checking with pencil and paper:

Interviewer: [Are the staff errors] usually in the data entry of the formulas, or does it vary?
Ray: It's mostly in the formulas. Because I think everybody is careful about making sure they have tie numbers‡ so that you can get the data in. I'm not saying it doesn't happen in data entry, but I think usually it's the formulas that are suspect. Either it's a question of the right kind of formula, or it's a situation where they weren't really careful in terms of . . . what comes first, and link it to what, and that sort of thing, they've got to be careful in that.
Interviewer: [It sounds like] you guys are pretty careful about checking things.
Ray: Yeah, we're pretty careful. Where I think it can get a little difficult is when you have a really large spreadsheet—it's a big model or something—and sometimes it's difficult to check, you know, a pretty extensive spreadsheet.
Interviewer: You mean because of the volume of data, or volume of formulas? What is it about the size that makes it harder?
Ray: You got a tremendous amount of formulas in there that are pointing all kinds of different directions, and you know, it's a pretty big pass to kind of walk back through the whole thing. So you have to be very careful.

† Making sure that the sum of row totals matches the sum of column totals.

‡ A tie number is a known quantity; it provides a sort of anchor within the spreadsheet. If a tie number is incorrect, dependent values are sure to be wrong (unless, by rare chance, incorrect values cancel each other out).

Here Ray noted the difficulty of tracing relations through large spreadsheets ("formulas that are pointing all kinds of different directions"). He finds that while his analysts are generally careful, there is room for error, so he does some checking.

Other informants described similar procedures for catching errors. Laura, for example, described how she verifies cell references in formulas by writing them down and tracing them to their origin in the spreadsheet. Like Ray, she noted that a major source of errors in spreadsheets is complex formulas in large spreadsheets.

Norman (1987) and Seifert and Hutchins (1989) argue that error in the real world is inevitable. Seifert and Hutchins (1989) studied cooperative error correction on board large ships, finding that virtually all navigational errors were "detected and corrected within the navigation team." The errors in spreadsheets could be at least a little less "inevitable" with improvements to spreadsheet software such as views showing cell relations more clearly (perhaps through the use of color, highlighting and filtering), and mechanisms to constrain cell values to allow range and bounds checking. Even with improvements, however, there would still be need for vigilance to eliminate errors, which are, as Norman, Seifert and Hutchins point out, inevitable in the real world. For spreadsheet debugging, as for tasks in other rather different domains (such as navigating large ships), a key part of the error correction solution lies in distributing the work across a group.

7. How spreadsheets support cooperative work practices

We have documented in some detail how spreadsheet users develop, debug and use spreadsheets cooperatively. We now examine the spreadsheet itself, focusing on the support for cooperative work implicit in its design. Though spreadsheets were not deliberately designed to support cooperative work, they nevertheless have two key characteristics that enable collaboration:

(1) Spreadsheet functionality is divided into two distinct programming layers—a *fundamental layer* and an *advanced layer*—that provide a basis for cooperative programming. By cleanly separating basic development tasks from more advanced functionality, the spreadsheet permits a distribution of tasks in which end users accomplish the basic implementation of a spreadsheet model, and those with more sophisticated programming knowledge provide smaller, more advanced contributions in the form of code and training. The notion of "layers" is intended to capture the different aspects of spreadsheet functionality as they relate to the user's tasks of *learning and using spreadsheets.*†

(2) The visual clarity of the spreadsheet *table* exposes the structure and intent of users' models, encouraging the sharing of domain knowledge across users with different levels and kinds of domain knowledge.

7.1. THE SPREADSHEET'S PROGRAMMING LAYERS

How do spreadsheets both meet the needs of the non-programmer and allow for the development of sophisticated applications? The answer lies in the articulation of the two programming layers: the fundamental layer, sufficient for constructing basic

† The layers do not map onto any aspect of the implementation of a spreadsheet product, or a manufacturer's description of a product.

programs, is completely self-contained and independent from the advanced layer of more sophisticated features.

The fundamental layer allows users to build basic spreadsheet models that solve real problems in their domain of interest. Users who know nothing about the advanced layer can create spreadsheets. In our study, Louis was such a user; his work was accomplished entirely within the fundamental layer, and he was just beginning to explore the advanced layer. Once users have grasped the fundamental layer, they learn the advanced layer. The advanced layer is composed of a variety of individual features that can be learned and used separately. Progress in learning advanced spreadsheet features may be very fast or very slow, depending on the user.

Because the features of the fundamental and advanced layers are independent and separately manipulated, the end user can proceed with the main programming of a spreadsheet, leaving more advanced development to local developers or programmers, or learning advanced features when they are needed. We have seen how Ray drew the line at writing macros for data entry, assigning the task to a programmer.

We now look in more detail at the fundamental and advanced layers.

7.1.1. The fundamental layer

To solve a problem with a spreadsheet, the user requires facilities for *computation, presentation* and *modeling*. The fundamental layer meets these needs. It is composed of two parts: the *formula language*† which enables computation; and the spreadsheet *table* which provides both a means of structuring data into a model, and a presentation format.

The formula language allows users to compute values in their models by expressing relations among cell values. Each cell value may be a constant or a derived value. A formula is associated with the individual cell whose value it computes. The formula language offers a basic set of arithmetic, financial, statistical and logical functions. To use the formula language, the user must master only two concepts: cells as variables, and functions as relations between variables. The simple algebraic syntax of the formula language is easy to write and understand.

In our study we found that most users normally use fewer than 10 functions in their formulas. Users employ those functions pertinent to their domain (e.g. financial analysis) and do not have need for other functions. Spreadsheet users are productive with a small number of functions because the functions provide *high-level, task-specific operations that do not have to be built up from lower level primitives*. For example, a common spreadsheet operation is to sum the values of a range of cells within a column. The user writes a simple formula that specifies the sum operation and the cells that contain the values to be summed. The cell range is specified compactly by its first and last cell; e.g. SUM(C1:C8) sums cells 1–8 in Column C. In a general programming language, computing this sum would require at least writing a loop iterating through elements of an array, and creating variable names for the loop counter and summation variable. Spreadsheet functions obviate the need to create variable names (cells are named by their position in the grid), and

---

† We refer to "the formula language" because most spreadsheet products have nearly identical languages which differ only in small syntactic details.

the need to create intermediate variables to hold results—non task-related actions that many users find confusing and tiresome (Lewis & Olson, 1987).

Once the user has created some variables and established their relations in formulas, the spreadsheet takes care of the rest. It is responsible for automatically updating dependent values as independent values change. There is no programming effort necessary on the part of the user to make this happen. The spreadsheet user's task is to write a series of small formulas, each associated with an individual cell, rather than the more difficult task of specifying the full control loop of a program as a set of procedures.

The spreadsheet table solves the presentation problems of the basic spreadsheet application. The cells of the table are used to present data values, labels and annotations. In the process of developing the spreadsheet, i.e. entering the data, labels and annotations into the table, the user is at the same time creating the user interface, at no additional development cost. Even a very simple table with no use of color or shading or variable fonts for cell entries is an effective visual format for data presentation (Jarvenpaa & Dickson, 1988; Cameron, 1989; Hoadley, 1990; Nardi & Miller, 1990.

Spreadsheet users must be able to represent the structure of the problem they are trying to solve. The spreadsheet table is a structuring device: the main parameters of a problem are organized into the rows and columns of the spreadsheet, and constants and calculated values are placed in cells. Rows and columns are used to represent the main parameters of a problem. Users know that related things go in rows and columns, and spreadsheet applications take advantage of the simple but powerful semantics provided by the row/column convention. Each cell represents and displays one variable. For calculated values, the spreadsheet associates a visual object, the cell itself, with a small program, the formula. Program code is this distributed over a visual grid, providing a system of compact, comprehensible, easily located program modules (Nardi & Miller, 1990).

What distinguishes the fundamental layer of spreadsheets from the operations a beginner user might learn in a general programming language? First, the high-level facilities for computation, modeling and presentation that we have described shield users from the necessity of working with lower level programming primitives. Users can concentrate more fully on understanding and solving their problems, with much less cognitive overhead devoted to the distraction of coping with the mechanics of the software itself.

Second, because the spreadsheet has so much "built-in" functionality (automatic update, the table as a presentation device), and a high-level language (the formula language), it takes only a few hours for non-programmers to learn to build simple spreadsheet models that solve a real problem in their domain of interest. After a small investment of time, the beginning spreadsheet user has a functioning program of real use (not a toy program or completed exercise), and also an effective visual representation of the application. The spreadsheet user's first efforts yield a complete application, rather than the partial solution that would result from writing the same application in a general programming language. The fast, early success spreadsheet users' experience motivates them to continue to use the software (Nardi & Miller, 1990; Warner, 1990; also Brock, personal communication; Flystra, personal communication).

7.1.2. The advanced layer

The advanced layer of the spreadsheet provides functionality that is unnecessary for constructing a basic spreadsheet model. We call its features "advanced" because basic work proceeds without them, not because they are necessarily difficult to learn.

The features of the advanced layer are inessential for basic work, but very useful. They are: conditional and iterative control constructs; macros; advanced functions such as database, date-time, and error trapping functions; graphs and charts; and a user interface toolkit. Each part may be learned and used completely independently of any other part. Some of the advanced capabilities are very easy to learn, such as how to change column width (the first thing Louis was learning), and others are more difficult, such as the use of macros (well-understood by Buzz and Jeremy, used in simple form by Jennifer, understood but avoided by Ray, and not known by Louis, Betty and Laura).

Users learn selected parts of the advanced layer as they need them, and as they feel ready to. Some users in our study could build a spreadsheet and significantly modify the user interface after a day-long training class, and others did nothing but build basic spreadsheets using only the formula language and modeling capabilities of the spreadsheet for several months before learning anything else. Most users do not know all the aspects of the advanced layer.†

The control constructs in the advanced layer of the spreadsheet are simple but useful. They allow users to write IF-THEN-ELSE statements within an individual formula, and to iterate functions over a cell range (a rectangular group of contiguous cells).

The user interface toolkit gives users control over column width, row height, fonts, shading, outlining, color and formatting of cell values (though not all spreadsheet products provide all of these capabilities). Spreadsheets allow users to split the screen so that non-contiguous portions of a spreadsheet may be viewed at once. The graphing and charting capabilities provide graphic views of the individual data values in the cells of the spreadsheet table. Macros allow users to reuse sequences of keystokes. "Advanced" macros provide more general facilities for data and file manipulation, screen control and controlling inter-action with the user during macro execution (e.g. in Lotus 1-2-3, the macro command "GETLABEL" displays a prompt in a control panel, waits for the response to the prompt, and enters the response as a label in a cell). The advanced macros are much like traditional programming functions, but they are stored, loaded, edited and manipulated like other spreadsheet macros.

As we have noted, advanced spreadsheet features often find their way into the spreadsheets of non-programmers as code written by more skilled users. Many users reach the limits of their interest in learning advanced features, at least certain ones such as macros, and do not learn to use them. But spreadsheets also provide a growth path for those interested in continuing to learn. Because the individual features of the advanced layer are independent of one another, users can selectively

---

† We had the fun of stumping Buzz, during an interview, with our knowledge of the IRR—internal rate of return—function in Excel.

learn them when they wish to. Very slow progress in learning features of the advanced layer does not impede the user's ability to do constructive work. Spreadsheets provide a self-paced course of study because the features of the advanced layer are inessential for basic application development and independent of other functionality.

Over time, the distribution of problem solving tasks of an individual user changes; users take on new development tasks as they acquire knowledge of additional spreadsheet functionality. For example, Jeremy described how he "discovered" macro programming. Jeremy is an executive—the chief financial officer of his company—and has never taken a computer science class. He received his MBA from Harvard Business School just prior to the time when quantitative methods (including mandatory instruction in the use of spreadsheets) were introduced into the curriculum. In the following discussion Jeremy explains how he learned about macros from reading the Lotus 1-2-3 manual and talking to programmers. We are examining one of his macros that selects files for printing and sets up printing parameters. The macro utilizes a counter, branching, and binary variables that can have 0 or 1 as values. We have been looking at each line of the macro in detail:

Jeremy: . . . And then [the macro] compares [this variable] with the counter over here.
Interviewer: So this is real programming, basically.
Jeremy: Yes, right! And unfortunately that's what I had to do for me to be able to do this. It is exactly—a program. . . . I found that out later. I didn't realize [that I was programming]. I thought I was being very clever—I was inventing something new!
Interviewer: How did you find out later? Talking to other programmers?
Jeremy: Yeah, well, exactly. I was talking to our programmer, he came over and I showed him, "Look what I've done!" And he looked at me and he says, "Well, any time you want to be a rookie programmer on my staff, you just passed, you just made the grade".
Interviewer: But you were actually able to figure out how to do this by looking at examples in the manual?
Jeremy: That's right. Yeah, because I just mapped out: What is it that I want to do? . . . What I would like to do is to have a series of instructions and have the macro search for those instructions, and based on certain yes/no conditions either perform the operation or go to the next step. That's really all I'm after. And so I kept on looking for [branching mechanisms], and once I found them in the book I found so many different places where I could use them.

There is a gradual tendency for end users to include more complex features in their spreadsheets and to utilize local developers and programmers less. It should be remembered however, that this process may be very gradual, and would not happen at all for many users if they did not have an easy route of entry through the fundamental layer. In contrast, many students resist the frustration and tedium of learning general programming languages and do not become adept at programming in them.

In our study, spreadsheet users most commonly learnt new spreadsheet functionality in collaboration with other users. The non-programmers were extremely resistant to reading manuals (in contrast to local developers like Jeremy who kept searching the manual till he found what he wanted). Non-programmers commented that the manuals often did not explain everything they needed to know to actually use the feature they were trying to learn about. Since this meant that they would have to ask someone to supply the missing information anyway, it seemed easier to ask at the outset.†

Several users in the study, even after learning many aspects of the advanced layer, still relied on more experienced users to show them how to do new things.

7.2. THE SPREADSHEET TABLE

The strong visual representation of an application embedded in the spreadsheet table allows users to directly share domain knowledge through templates and direct edits to the spreadsheets of others, and to collectively use spreadsheets in meetings and other exchanges. Users are able to understand and interpret each other's models with relative ease because the tabular format of the spreadsheet presents such a clear depiction of the parameters and data values in spreadsheet applications.

Spreadsheets have done well at data display by borrowing a commonly used display format—that of the table. Cameron (1989) pointed out that tables have been in use for 5000 years. Inventory tables, multiplication tables and tables of reciprocal values have been found by archaeologists excavating Middle Eastern cultures. Ptolemy, Copernicus, Kepler, Euler, and Gauss used tables. Modern times brought us VisiCalc, in tabular format. VisiCalc was modeled directly on the tabular grid of accountants' columnar paper which contains numbered rows and columns. Today's spreadsheets, while much enhanced in functionality, have not changed the basic VisiCalc format in the smallest detail. A tabular grid in which rows are labeled with numbers and columns are labeled with letters characterizes all commercially available spreadsheets.

Tables excel at showing a large amount of data in a small space and in helping users to identify individual data values (Jarvenpaa & Dickson, 1988; Cameron, 1989)—precisely what is needed for spreadsheet applications because they contain many numeric values, each of which may be important to understanding an application. The perceptual reasons that tables so effectively display discrete data items are not well understood. Cleveland suggests that the notion of "clustering"—the ability to hold a collection of objects in short-term memory and carry out further visual and mental processing—applies to many visual forms (Cleveland, Unpublished data), and it seems relevant to tables. The arrangement of data items in rows and columns appears to permit efficient clustering as users can remember the values in a row or column and then perform other cognitive tasks that involve the values.

The semantics of rows, columns and cells are agreed upon and well understood by spreadsheet users. Because tables are so commonly used to display data of many kinds, most spreadsheet users are already familiar with them. Jarvenpaa and Dickson (1988) noted that many people must be taught to correctly interpret

† Manuals may be confusing at a more fundamental level. Louis gave up completely on manual reading (getting his son Peter to tutor him instead) when he could not figure out the sense in which the word "default" was being used in his Lotus 1-2-3 documentation. (Louis had a rather old copy of the manual, and the newer Lotus 1-2-3 manuals may be less confusing.) The meaning did not jibe with what he understood "default" to mean, nor with the dictionary definition, which, puzzling over the manual, he looked up. During our interview he showed us the definition. Webster's Ninth New Collegiate Dictionary defines default as "failure to do something required by duty or law"; also failure to appear in court, to pay a debt, meet a contract, or agreement, or failure to compete in or finish an appointed contest. Louis' confusion is understandable.

plotted line graphs, but most people are already practised at understanding tables. Users readily comprehend that in a spreadsheet, rows and columns are used to represent the main parameters of a model, and each cell represents and displays one variable. In looking at the spreadsheets of co-workers, the conventions of rows, columns and cells permit users to interpret the intentions of the developer.

Spreadsheets fare less well at clearly exposing the formulas underlying the cell values in the table. As we described in our discussion of debugging, checking a formula from a co-worker's spreadsheet (or from one's own spreadsheet for that matter) involves an awkward pencil and paper procedure of tracking down and verifying cell references in the formulas.† In our study we found that users do follow the pencil and paper procedures to ensure that formulas are correct, but many users cited the necessity of doing this as their main complaint about spreadsheets.

8. Implications for computer supported cooperative work

Our research focused on a single cognitive artifact—the spreadsheet. In the course of examining its structure, following it into meetings, finding out how people use it to solve certain kinds of problems, we learned two things of broad interest to CSCW research:

(1) As users gain more control over computational resources through the use of end user programming systems, cooperative work practices should be anticipated and taken advantage of by designers of such systems. Users will inevitably vary in their skill level, and computational tasks can be distributed over users with different skills through the sharing of code and training.

(2) One of the most fundamental reasons to engage in any kind of cooperative work is to share domain knowledge. Software systems that provide a strong visual format which exposes the structure and data of users' problem-solving models will support and encourage the exchange of domain knowledge.

End user software systems must provide basic development capabilities for non-programmers—what has made spreadsheets so successful is putting computational power into the hands of domain experts. In this distribution of computing tasks, development is shifted away from programmers; they supply limited but technically advanced assistance to developer/domain experts.

The layered design of spreadsheet software seems a good model for other software systems—the ability to build complete, if simple, models with basic, easily learned functionality is the key to getting users off to a quick, rewarding start. The spreadsheet provides for distributed programming by separating the basic functionality of the fundamental layer from the useful but unnecessary features of the advanced layer. End user programming systems should take advantage of the fact that local developers and programmers can reinforce and extend the programs of non-programmers through cooperative work practices—users need not be limited by their lack of programming sophistication.

Non-programmers attain rapid proficiency with the functionality of the fundamental layer because its operations are high-level and task-specific. This implies

---

† Some spreadsheet products provide views of the table in which the formulas are shown instead of cell values. This has its uses, but is not sufficient for formula verification because the cell values are no longer visible, and long formulas are truncated.

547

that end user programming systems must develop rather domain specific languages and interaction techniques whose operations will make sense to some particular set of users. The requirement that user programming languages be task-specific, contrasts sharply with the commonly advocated proposal to empower end users by helping them acquire competence in using general programming languages (Lewis & Olson, 1987; Maulsby & Witten, 1989; Neal, 1989). In general, we feel that users should be supported at their level of interest, which for many is to perform specific computational tasks within their own specialized domain, not to become computer programmers.

Just as spreadsheets distribute problem solving tasks *across* users differently than traditional computing, there is a different temporal distribution of tasks taken on by an individual user. Some users go on, over time, to learn and use new spreadsheet features (often very slowly)—in contrast to those who completely give up on general programming languages. Once users have successfully developed their own applications, they can begin to add new software techniques to their repertoire as they are ready. Through collaborations with more experienced users, spreadsheet users progress into the advanced layer. It is precisely because users have been supported by a high-level, task-specific software system that allowed them to get their work done and to experience a sense of accomplishment that they can then make progress, if they choose, in learning more general techniques. When spreadsheet users learn macros or the use of conditional and iterative facilities or formatting tricks, they venture into the realm of general programming. Such learning may occur in glacial time from the perspective of an experienced programmer, but perhaps that is appropriate for users whose primary accomplishments lie outside the field of programming.

Spreadsheets succeed because they combine an expressive high level programming language with a powerful visual format to organize and display data. Because the spreadsheet table so clearly exposes the structure and content of spreadsheet applications, co-workers easily and directly exchange domain knowledge. The shared semantics of the table facilitate knowledge transfer between co-workers; the very structure of the rows, columns and cells of the table transmits a great deal of information.

The lesson to be learned from the tabular structure of the spreadsheet is that simple, familiar visual notations form a good backbone for many kinds of scientific, engineering and business applications. Visual notations are based on human visual abilities such as detecting linear patterns or enclosure, that people perform almost effortlessly. Many diagrammatic visual notations such as tables, graphs, plots, panels and maps have been refined over hundreds if not thousands of years (Tufte, 1983; Cameron, 1989). They are capable of showing a large quantity of data in a small space, and of representing semantic information about relations among data. Like the spreadsheet table, these visual notations are simple but expressive, compact but rich in information.

We expect to see computer-based versions of tables, graphs, plots, panels and maps evolve into more sophisticated visual/semantic mechanisms, utilizing knowledge-based representations and interactive editing and browsing techniques such as filtering and fish-eye views (Furnas, 1986; Ciccarelli & Nardi, 1988). Today, visual notations are commonly used for display purposes, but it is less common for users to be able to manipulate their components—to be able to ask about the values behind a point on a plot, for example, or to expand a region on a map to show more detail. It is even less common for these displays and their components to possess any semantic information about their relationships to other displays or components—for example, constraints between specific values, or the mapping from one notation to another.

Visual notations with well-defined semantics for expressing relations will provide useful reusable computational structures. Filling a middle ground between the expressivity of general programming languages and the particular semantics of specific applications, they represent a fairly generic set of semantic relations, applicable across a wide variety of domains. New visual notations are possible and useful as Harel (1988) has shown with his work on statecharts. Statecharts formally describe a collection of sets and the relationships between them. Although Harel's work is quite new, Bear, Coleman and Hayes (1989) have already created an interesting extension to statecharts called object charts, for use in designing object-oriented software systems. Heydon, Maimone, Tygard, Wing and Zaremski (1989) used statecharts to model a language for specifying operation system security configurations.

As we have tried to show in our discussion of cooperative work practices among spreadsheet users, spreadsheets support an informal but effective interchange of programming expertise and domain knowledge. Spreadsheets achieve the distribution of cognitive tasks across different kinds of users in a highly congenial way; sojourners of the twinkling lights mix it up with crafters of nested loops—and all with software for which no explicit design attention was given to "cooperative use".

Many thanks to Lucy Berlin, Susan Brennan, Dave Duis, Danielle Fafchamps, Martin Griss, Jeff Johnson, Nancy Kendzierski, Robin Jeffries, Jasmina Pavlin and Craig Zarmer for helpful discussions and comments on earlier drafts of this paper. Thanks also to our informants, who showed great generosity in taking the time to talk to us, and provided careful explanations of their work with spreadsheets.

References

ALSOP, S. (1989). Q & A: Quindlen and Alsop: Spreadsheet users seem satisfied with what they already have. *InfoWorld,* September 11, 102–103.

ARGANBRIGHT, D. (1986). Mathematical modeling with spreadsheets. *Abacus,* **3,** 18–31.

BANNON, L. & SCHMIDT, K. (1989). CSCW: Four characters in search of a context. *Proceedings of the First European Conference on Computer Supported Cooperative Work EC-CSCW'89,* September 13–15, Gatwick, London, pp. 358–372.

BEAR, S., COLEMAN, D. & HAYES, F. (1989). *Introducing Objectcharts, or How to Use Statecharts in Object-oriented Design,* HPL-Report-ISC-TM-89-167. Bristol, England: Hewlett-Packard Laboratories.

BJERKNES, G., EHN, P. & KYNG, M. (1987). *Computers and Democracy: A Scandinavian Challenge.* Brookfield, Vermont: Gower Publishing Company.

BOSK, C. (1980). Occupational rituals in patient management. *New England Journal of Medicine,* **303,** 71–76.

BROOKS, F. (1975). *The Mythical Man Month: Essays on Software Engineering.* Reading, MA: Addison-Wesley.

BROWN, P. & GOULD, J. D. (1987). How people create spreadsheets. *ACM Transactions on Office Information Systems,* **5,** 258–272.

CHANDRASEKARAN, B. (1981). Natural and social system metaphors for distributed problem solving: Introduction to the issue. *IEEE Transactions on Systems, Man and Cybernetics*, **SMC-11**, 1–5.

CAMERON (1989). *A Cognitive Model for Tabular Editing*, OSO-CISRC Research Report, Ohio State University.

CICCARELLI, E. & NARDI, B. (1988). Browsing schematics: Query-filtered graphs with context nodes. In *Proceedings of the Second Annual Workshop on Space Operations, Automation and Robotics (SOAR'88)*, July 20–23, Dayton, Ohio, pp. 193–204.

DOYLE, J. R. (1990). Naive users and the Lotus interface: A field study. *Behavior and Information Technology*, **9**, 81–89.

FURNAS, G. (1986). Generalized fisheye views. *Proceedings of CHI'86, Conference on Human Factors in Computing Systems*, April 13–17, Boston, pp. 16–23.

GRUDIN, J. (1988). Why CSCW applications fail: Problems in the design and evaluation of organizational interfaces. In *CSCW'88: Proceedings of the Conference on Computer Supported Cooperative Work*. September 26–28, 1988, Portland, Oregon, pp. 85–93.

HAREL, D. (1988). On visual formalisms. *Communications of the ACM*, **31**, 514–520.

HEYDON, A., MAIMONE, M., TYGAR, J., WING, J. & ZAREMSKI, A. (1989). Constraining pictures with pictures. In *Proceedings of IFIPS'89*, August, San Francisco, pp. 157–162.

HOADLEY, E. (1990). Investigating the effects of color. *Communications of the ACM*, **33**, 120–125.

HOLLAND, D. & VALSINER, J. (1988). Cognition, symbols and Vygotskty's developmental psychology. *Ethos*, **16**, 247–272.

HUTCHINS, E., HOLLAN, J. & NORMAN, D. (1986). Direct manipulation interfaces. In D. Norman & S. Draper, Eds. *User Centered System Design*. pp. 87–124. Hillsdale, NJ.: Erlbaum Publishers.

JARVENPANA & DICKSON (1988). Graphics and managerial decision making: Research based guidelines. *Communications of the ACM*, **31**, 764–744.

KAY, A. (1984). Computer software. *Scientific American*, **5**, 53–59.

LAVE, J. (1988). *Cognition in Practice: Mind, Mathematics and Culture in Everyday Life*. Cambridge: Cambridge University Press.

LEWIS, G. & OLSON, G. (1987). Can principles of cognition lower the barriers to programming? *Empirical Studies of Programmers: Second Workshop*. pp. 248–263. Norwood, NJ: Ablex Publishing.

MAULSBY, D. & WITTEN, I. (1989). Inducing programs in a direct-manipulation environment. In *Proceedings of CHI'89, Conference on Human Factors in Computing Systems*. April 30–May 4, 1989. Austin, Texas. pp. 57–62.

NAPIER, H., LANE, D., BATSELL, R. & GUADANGO, N. (1989). Impact of a restricted natural language interface on ease of learning and productivity. *Communications of the ACM*, **32**, 1190–1198.

NARDI, B. & MILLER, J. R. (1990). The spreadsheet interface: A basis for end user programming. In *Proceedings of Interact '90*, 27–31 August, Cambridge, UK, pp. 977–983.

NEAL, L. (1989). A system for example-based programming. In *Proceedings of CHI'89, Conference on Human Factors in Computing Systems*, April 30–May 4, Austin, Texas.

NEWMAN, D. (1989). Apprenticeship or tutorial: Models for interaction with an intelligent instructional system. *Proceedings of the Eleventh Annual Conference of the Cognitive Science Society*, August 16–19, Ann Arbor, Michigan, pp. 781–788.

NORMAN, D. (1987). *The Psychology of Everyday Things*. New York: Basic Books.

NORMAN, D. & HUTCHINS, E. (1988). *Computation via Direct Manipulation*, Final Report to Office of Naval Research, Contract No. N00014-85-C-0133. University of California, San Diego.

OLSON, J. & NILSEN, E. (1987). Analysis of the cognition involved in spreadsheet software interaction. *Human–Computer Interaction*, **3**, 309–349.

PANKO, R. (1988). *End User Computing; Management, Applications, and Technology*. New York: John Wiley and Sons.

PIERSOL, K. (1986). Object-oriented spreadsheets: The analytic spreadsheet package. In *Proceedings of OOPSLA'86*, September, pp. 385–390.

SEIFERT, C. & HUTCHINS, E. (1989). Learning from error. In *Proceedings of the Eleventh Annual Conference of the Cognitive Science Society*, August 16–19, Ann Arbor, Michigan, pp. 42–49.
SPENKE, M. & BEILKEN, C. (1989). A spreadsheet interface for logic programming. In *Proceedings of CHI'89 Conference on Human Factors in Computing Systems*, April 30–May 4, Austin, Texas, pp. 75–83.
TUFTE, E. (1983). *The Visual Display of Quantitative Information*. Cheshire, CT: Graphics Press.
VAN EMDEN, M., OHKI, M. & TAKEUCHI, A. (1985). *Spreadsheets with Incremental Queries as a User Interface for Logic Programming*, ICOT Technical Report TR–144.
VYGOTSKY, L. S. (1979). *Thought and Language*. Cambridge, MA: MIT Press.
WARNER, J. (1990). Visual data analysis into the '90s. *Pixel*, **1**, 40–44.

Appendix: Spreadsheet study questions

(1) What do you do here (i.e. what are the tasks of your job)?
(2) What do you do with spreadsheets? (This question involved looking at actual spreadsheets on-line and/or in paper copy. We looked at spreadsheet structure, the use of annotations and labels, formula complexity, how spreadsheets are used during meetings, etc. as part of this question.)
(3) Who else uses this spreadsheet (i.e. of those we talk about in Question 2)?
(4) How did you create this spreadsheet (i.e. of those we talk about in Question 2)? Or alternatively, who created it and who else uses it?
(5) How accurate is your spreadsheet? How do you know?
(6) How do you find errors?
(7) How do you fix errors?
(8) Are there any problems you tried to solve with spreadsheets where the spreadsheet approach didn't work? If so, what are they and what were the problems?
(9) What is your educational background?
(10) What do you like about spreadsheets?
(11) What do you dislike about spreadsheets?
(12) What would make spreadsheets easier to use?
(13) What else would you like spreadsheets to do?

WHY CSCW APPLICATIONS FAIL: PROBLEMS IN THE DESIGN AND EVALUATION OF ORGANIZATIONAL INTERFACES

Jonathan Grudin

MCC
3500 West Balcones Center Drive
Austin, Texas 78759

Abstract.

Many systems, applications, and features that support cooperative work share two characteristics: A significant investment has been made in their development, and their successes have consistently fallen far short of expectations. Examination of several application areas reveals a common dynamic: 1) A factor contributing to the application's failure is the disparity between those who will benefit from an application and those who must do additional work to support it. 2) A factor contributing to the decision-making failure that leads to ill-fated development efforts is the unique lack of management intuition for CSCW applications. 3) A factor contributing to the failure to learn from experience is the extreme difficulty of evaluating these applications. These three problem areas escape adequate notice due to two natural but ultimately misleading analogies: the analogy between multi-user application programs and multi-user computer systems, and the analogy between multi-user applications and single-user applications. These analogies influence the way we think about cooperative work applications and designers and decision-makers fail to recognize their limits. Several CSCW application areas are examined in some detail.

Introduction. An illustrative example: automatic meeting scheduling.

Where electronic calendars are in use on a large or networked system, an automatic meeting scheduling feature is often provided (e.g., Ehrlich, 1987a, 1987b). The concept that underlies automatic meeting scheduling is simple: The person scheduling the meeting specifies a distribution list and the system checks the calendar for each person, finding a time convenient for all. The system then notifies all involved of the tentative schedule.

For automatic meeting scheduling to work efficiently, everyone involved must maintain a personal calendar and be willing to let the computer schedule their free time more often than not. Data reported by Ehrlich (1987a, 1987b) suggest that neither of these requirements is generally satisfied.

Electronic calendars are *not* electronic versions of paper calendars. They serve communication functions, primarily for managers and executives with personal secretaries who maintain the calendars. An electronic calendar may be used simultaneously by the secretary for scheduling, the manager for reviewing, and other group members for locating or planning. Ehrlich describes the successful use of the electronic calendar in detail; a key point is that "the secretary's role is critical"; those who do not have a secretary are much less likely to maintain an electronic calendar. Another relevant finding is that for managers, "free time is never really free." Unauthorized scheduling of a manager's apparently open time "can be sufficient motivation for total rejection of the system by the manager."

Thus, electronic calendars are voluntarily maintained primarily by managers and executives (or their secretaries). This has dire consequences for automatic meeting scheduling. If a manager wants to meet with non-management subordinates, few of the latter are likely to maintain electronic calendars. The scheduling program will find all times open, schedule a meeting, and conflicts will ensue. "In order to take full advantage of an electronic calendar, all members of a group must commit to using this medium," (Ehrlich, 1987b). If managers or executives keeping on-line calendars wish to meet among themselves, automatic scheduling could work. But as noted above, free time is often not truly free for such managers; it would be wise to consult with their secretaries anyway. Thus, automatic meeting scheduling may rarely be used in this situation, either.

The simple meeting scheduling feature previews the pattern that emerges from the major applications discussed later. Who would benefit from automatic meeting scheduling? The person who calls the meeting: in general, a manager would benefit. But who would have to do *additional* work to make the application succeed? The subordinates, who would have to maintain electronic calendars that they would not otherwise use. The application might be made to work through persuading or ordering employees to maintain calendars, and replacing people who won't, but automatic meeting scheduling is not perceived to be of great enough collective benefit to warrant such measures.

Why design and implement a feature that is unlikely to be used? The managers who make the final design decisions may see the personal benefit of automatic meeting scheduling to managers such as themselves, without noticing that those users who would be forced to do extra work to support the feature would not benefit from it. (Other reasons for adding this feature might be a potential marketing benefit or simply the ease of implementing it.)

As with the more complex cases described later, the conclusion is not entirely negative. Automatic meeting scheduling could be targeted to environments or groups making the most uniform use of electronic calendars. Their value can be enhanced by adding conference room and equipment scheduling. Individual use of calendars to support the feature might increase if the perceived collective benefit were higher; that is, if organizations recognized how much they may be losing through inefficient meeting scheduling (Ehrlich, 1987b).

Problems in the design and evaluation of organizational interfaces.

Several major CSCW application areas have attracted significant investments of capital and labor over many years, with results that have uniformly fallen far short of expectations. These include the areas of digitized voice, group decision support, natural language interface to shared databases, and project management. The preceding example, automatic meeting scheduling, is a simple and relatively inexpensive feature. Its problems are easily identified, however, and can then be seen as common to many CSCW applications and as key factors in the their disappointing performance. The problems are:

- The application fails because it requires that some people do additional work, while those people are *not* the ones who perceive a direct benefit from the use of the application.

- The design process fails because our intuitions are poor for multi-user applications -- decision-makers see the potential benefits for people similar to themselves, but don't see the implications of the fact that extra work will be required of others.

- We fail to learn from experience because these complex applications introduce almost insurmountable obstacles to meaningful, generalizable analysis and evaluation.

These problems have received altogether inadequate attention given their impact on CSCW applications. This may be due to two powerful, natural analogues to CSCW applications for which these problems are in general less severe: multi-user *systems* (such as management information systems, computer-integrated manufacturing, order-and-inventory-control systems), and *single-user* applications. Our possible unconscious use of the analogies and

the danger of failing to identify where they break down are discussed below and explored in more detail in two appendices.

The paper concludes with detailed "case studies" of four CSCW application areas. While the focus is on their problems, all of these areas are important and may lead to significant advances. It sometimes appears that in striving toward very ambitious goals we are taking turns beating our heads against the same wall, but pointing to the wall is not intended to devalue the goals. There are ways to get over the wall -- to build successful CSCW applications. Investing resources adequate to the solution of the problems, developing the appropriate research and development methodologies, finding niches where the problems don't arise or where applications will succeed in spite of them, and adequately preparing users for the introduction of the applications are all approaches that may lead to success. The first step is to see the problems clearly.

Problem 1. The disparity between who does the work and who gets the benefit.

The immediate beneficiary of the automatic meeting scheduler is the manager (or secretary) who initiates a typical meeting. Successful use of the feature in a typical environment would require additional work for other group members, most of whom would have to maintain electronic calendars when they would not otherwise do so. Not all CSCW applications introduce such a disparity -- with electronic mail, for example, everyone generally shares the benefits and burdens equally. But electronic mail may turn out to be more the exception than the rule, unless greater care is taken to distribute the benefit in other CSCW applications.

Can a CSCW application succeed if doing the extra work is left to individual discretion? Unfortunately, probably not. Communication, at the heart of most CSCW applications, will break down without relatively uniform use. If a substantial number of people do not maintain their calendars, the meeting scheduler is pointless. In this respect, the single-user application is a misleading model. In many environments, there is no harm if different users choose to use different editors, for example; but an application designed to support the entire group must be used by everyone in the group. "A critical mass of users is essential for the success of any communication system" (Ehrlich, 1987b).

Can a CSCW application be made to succeed by mandating that those who need to do the extra work do so? Even setting aside the implications of coercion (which are discussed in the final appendix), this is complicated. This traditional approach, changing existing job descriptions or inventing new ones, is widely used when CSCW *systems* are introduced (Cherns, 1980; Rowe, 1985). Word processing skills become a job requirement for secretaries, the new job of database administrator is created, and so forth. However, the multi-user system -- multi-user application analogy breaks down. An organization invests a large amount in introducing a *system* and is usually willing to reorganize to make it succeed, retraining, transferring, or dismissing people as deemed necessary. This will not be done for each CSCW *application* that arrives -- the cost will outweigh the benefit. Maintaining a personal calendar in order to support automatic meeting scheduling is unlikely to become a job requirement. In general, *the organization may adapt to the computer system, but an application program must adapt to the organization.*

What if the application really might provide a collective benefit to the group or organization? Of course, measuring a "collective benefit" may be hard. If maintaining the application requires an hour per week from each group member, and its benefit is to save just one person an hour per week, is it worth it? What if the one person is the group manager? What if it is the Vice President of Research & Development? But assuming that a collective benefit has been determined, education and leadership may be critical. If it is demonstrated that inefficiency in scheduling meetings is costly to the group and that maintaining calendars to support the scheduling feature is the best solution, people may be willing to do the extra work.

However, the best solution is to try to insure that everyone benefits directly from using the application. This may mean building in additional features. It certainly means eliminating or minimizing the extra work required of anyone, or rewarding them for doing it. (This includes minimizing the training needed; Carasik and Grantham, 1988, attribute a rejection of The Coordinator, a CSCW application, in large part to the effort required to learn it.) User interfaces must be provided that vary appropriately with a user's background, job, and preferences. This is a substantial undertaking, but there may be no other option.

Problem 2. The breakdown of intuitive decision-making.

Why was the problem with the automatic meeting scheduler not anticipated? More generally, we need to understand why thousands of developer-years and hundreds of millions of dollars have been committed to various CSCW application areas despite little or no return. In most instances of failure, a substantial and timely return on investment was certainly anticipated; the decision-makers were not in business to throw away money.

Decision-makers in a position to commit the resources to application development projects rely heavily on intuition (see e.g. Butler, Bennett, & Whiteside, 1987). The experience, and very likely the track record, of a development manager considering a CSCW application is generally based on single-user applications. Intuition may be a far more reliable guide to single-user applications -- a manager with good intuition may quickly get a feel for the user's experience with a word processor, spreadsheet, or so forth. But a typical CSCW application will be used by a range of user types -- people with different backgrounds and job descriptions, *all of whom* may have to participate in one way or another for the application to succeed. The decision-maker's intuition will fail when an appreciation of the intricate dynamics of such a situation is missing.

Not surprisingly, the decision-maker is drawn to applications that selectively benefit one subset of the user population: managers. Intuitions about what will be useful to people similar to ourselves are generally good. Managers

tend to overlook or underestimate the down side, the extra work that might be required of other users to maintain the application; extra work that might not be forthcoming in most environments, subjecting the application to neglect or sabotage. The decision-makers may also fail to appreciate the difficulty of producing and evaluating this new type of application, as described in the next section. The converse possibility also exists: the decision-maker may not see the value in applications or features that will primarily benefit other categories of user, even where they would provide a collective benefit to the organization. This would be particularly true for features that might undercut or create additional work for the manager.

Intuition may be less unreliable for applications directed at smaller or more homogenous groups. In particular, there may be less bias when only peer-peer communication is involved than when the communication moves vertically through the organizational hierarchy. Beyond that, education seems to be called for -- general education about groupware, the risks involved, and the resources and approaches required to minimize the risk; specific research on the application area at hand. Education is needed, and vigilance.

Problem 3. The underestimated difficulty of evaluating CSCW applications.

Task analysis, design, and evaluation are never easy, but they are considerably more difficult for CSCW applications than for single-user applications. An individual's success with a particular spreadsheet or word processor is not likely to be affected by the backgrounds of other group members or by administrative or personality dynamics within the group. These factors are, however, quite likely to affect applications intended to support an entire group, where motivational, economic, and political factors come to the fore (Malone, 1985).

Evaluation of CSCW applications requires a very different approach, based on the methodologies of social psychology and anthropology. This may not be news to those who have been monitoring the field of CSCW very closely, but the skills are largely absent in development and many research environments, where human factors engineers and cognitive psychologists are only starting to be accepted. And the required methods are generally more expensive, more time-consuming, and less precise.

It is relatively easy to bring a single user into a lab to be tested on the perceptual, cognitive, and motor variables that have been the focus for single-user applications. But it is difficult or impossible to create a group in the lab that will reflect the social, motivational, economic, and political factors that are central to group performance (Malone, 1985). In addition, group observation must extend over a longer period of time. Much of a person's use of a spreadsheet might be observed in a single hour, for example, but group interactions typically unfold over days or weeks.

Evaluation of groupware "in the field" is remarkably complex due to the number of people to observe at each site, the wide variability that may be found in group composition, and the range of environmental factors that play a role in determining acceptance, such as user training, management buy-in, and vendor follow-through (e.g., Lucas, 1976; Gaffney, 1985; White, 1985; Ehrlich, 1987b). Establishing success or failure will be easier than establishing the underlying factors that brought it about.

Finally, the difficulty of evaluation is increased dramatically by the importance of providing features and interfaces that vary according to a user's job, background, and preferences, as mentioned above. A single-user application may get away with appealing to a kind of "lowest common denominator." CSCW applications will often have to appeal to every possible denominator.

As with the other problems, evaluation may be less difficult if the application supports a smaller or more homogeneous group than if the target user population involves individuals distributed across an organization. But it will still be substantial, and management must be aware from the start of the skills and the time that will be required.

Case 1. Digitized voice applications.

At a conference panel titled "Voice: Technology searching for communication needs" it was noted that after 25 years of research, no company specializing in voice technology has become profitable, and that projected sales of voice products have recently been revised downward sharply (Aucella, 1987). Eventual success of voice technology may require an understanding of the exaggerated forecasts and the relative failures to date. Here only the use of voice in computer-mediated communication is considered, as in computer-based voice messaging or voice annotation to documents. (Voice is also used for input only -- speech recognition -- and for output only -- e.g., speech synthesis.)

The advantages of digitized voice as a computer-based communication medium. Almost everyone can speak, while many people cannot type fluently. Moderately paced speech is much faster than even the fastest typing. Speech can readily convey emotion and subtle nuance. Voice messages can be sent or received by telephone when away from the computer. Voice annotation can be added without cluttering or overloading a visual display.

The disadvantages of digitized voice. It can be more difficult to understand than "live" speech, because stereophony and lip movements are absent and the speaker cannot be asked to clarify inaudible or unclear passages. Speaking may be faster than typing, but reading is faster than listening to speech. A digitized voice message cannot be scanned (by computer or human) as written text can -- the only way to be sure there is nothing of interest in a message is to listen to the whole thing. Similarly, the receiver cannot review a voice message later as easily as a written message. If suggested document changes or additions are contained in a voice annotation, the receiver must type those changes into the document. For the speaker, reviewing and correcting a spoken message is more difficult; hence, voice messages may be more likely to contain errors. A recipient cannot edit a voice message and must forward the entire message or none at all, which can be inconvenient (or even embarrassing to the originator; Ehrlich, 1987a, 1987b). Voice mail with no accompa-

nying visual display has only the transient auditory channel for presenting and explaining options, leading to serious user interface challenges (see Aucella and Ehrlich, 1986). Finally, digitized voice requires a lot of disk space. (See Newell, 1984, for a broader discussion.)

The pattern. The advantages of digitized voice over typed input are almost all advantages for the speaker: Speech is faster to produce, conveys emotion and nuance easily, and may be available without access to a computer terminal. The disadvantages to digitized voice, however, are overwhelmingly problems for the listener. It is harder to understand, slower to take in, not easily scanned or reviewed, more likely to contain errors, and more difficult to manipulate.

To succeed, voice systems require that everyone in an environment use them. If some people do not use voice mail, time is wasted trying to reach them and group distribution lists won't work. If some people do not listen to their voice mail frequently enough, calls won't be returned promptly and use of the system may dwindle and die.

The speaker benefits from voice applications, and the listener does additional work. When will it be acceptable for speakers to thus burden listeners? One such time is when all users are both speakers and listeners in equal measure, thus sharing the benefits and costs, which is generally true of voice mail systems. In some cases, there may be no alternative -- a sales force on the road may have no electronic mail option, and for such users voice mail has proven particularly successful (Ehrlich, 1987a). Similarly, voice may be the best recourse for a user whose hands are necessarily busy. A disparity may also be acceptable when the speaker is of higher status than the listener, although this may be unpredictable.

Some past failures of voice technology are no doubt due to technical problems and storage requirements. Digitized voice messaging has proven successful given the right environment and implementation (Ehrlich, 1987a, 1987b). Voice may succeed more generally where its potential collective benefit is conveyed through high-level support and action (Ehrlich, 1987a, 1987b). In one case, a voice messaging system that failed initially succeeded when the alternative, telephone receptionists, was removed.

But, in general, the disparity between who is inconvenienced and who gets direct benefit from digitized voice may work against its adoption in situations where sender and receiver are of comparable status -- the imposition it makes upon the receiver may be unacceptable. Voice annotation may be unacceptable in most environments, where the authorial and editorial roles are rarely evenly shared. Voice annotation particularly benefits those who don't type or who are more likely to act in an editorial than in an authorial role. These are characteristics of managers and executives. Because of their status, they may not be concerned by the inconvenience of voice for others -- dictaphones are used. But the manager-secretary gulf is a particularly wide one; the danger is that decision-makers will support the development of voice applications that appeal to them but that will fail because their use will be onerous to other categories of user.

Case 2. Project management applications.

A project management application running on a distributed system might be the best demonstration of the potential of computer-supported cooperative work -- a major advance over the currently available single-user work management applications. A distributed project management application would cover the scheduling and chronicling of activities, the creation and evaluation of plans and schedules, the management of product versions and changes, and the monitoring of resources and responsibilities (Sathi, Morton, and Roth, 1986). Milestone completions might be signaled, documents routed to appropriate recipients, problems identified early and communicated to those who can help solve them, delays in critical path activities flagged, costs calculated, and so forth. Some people have felt that such an application will be the next major commercial success, "the next spreadsheet."

Cooperative work management applications are being developed. "Callisto: an intelligent project management system" (Sathi et al., 1986; reprinted in Greif, 1988), is a thorough description of a project begun in 1981. It is clear that in this area, it is crucial to ask who is the immediate beneficiary, who will be asked to take on additional work to make the application succeed, and what will be the incentive to do this extra work. The principal beneficiaries are clear: project managers. It is also clear that the success of such an application will be contingent on *all* group members keeping the information base current. This includes updating significant developments that occur around, rather than through, the system: in meetings, telephone conversations, and so forth. The project management application may also require that critical information that is usually unstated be made electronically accessible, such as a secretary's awareness of a manager's priorities (Ehrlich, 1987b).

The greatest user interface challenges will be on the side of information input -- reducing the additional effort to a bare minimum, allowing information to be entered in a manner comfortable to each worker, providing compensatory benefits to those who must take on the additional effort of maintaining the on-line database or knowledge base. But that is not where attention is being directed. It is being directed toward information display, toward the user interface for the principle beneficiary, the manager. "Managers must know what information is needed, where to locate it, and how to interpret and use it. Equally important is that they be able to do so without great effort" (Sathi et al., 1986). This is not unimportant, but exclusive focus on improving the system for the person already its principal beneficiary seems ill-advised, although it might appeal to the manager sponsoring such a project.

This is reflected in experience with management information systems. In one example, a ten year development project culminated in a "computer-assisted management system" installed on an aircraft carrier, "its primary purpose to help the Commanding Officer and his department heads administer the ship" (McCracken and Akscyn, 1984). While numerous factors contributed to its eventual replacement by a system that lacked manage-ment features, one reported reason for the failure of the management system was the difficulty of getting everyone to use it (Kling, 1987).

Worse fates than neglect may confront a project management application if monitoring and reporting are not carefully handled. In one implemented system, an employee who reported identifying a priority problem began receiving system-generated requests for progress reports to be forwarded to the Chief Executive Officer! This quickly led to the end of priority problem reporting. The vigilant system noted that employees had stopped using the system, and alerted the administrator. The employees dealt with the resulting complaints by writing programs that periodically opened files and changed dates, which satisfied the watchful, automatic monitor. Thus "sabotaged," the work management application was of little use, and was eventually quietly withdrawn. (Carroll Hall, personal communication.)

Case 3. Natural language interfaces to shared databases.

Natural language is not usually included in treatments of CSCW, but it is typically described as an interface style that by virtue of familiarity will appeal to subsets of users -- novice and "casual" or intermittent users -- with other interfaces available for heavy users (Rich, 1984; Shneiderman, 1987). Thus, it is in fact portrayed as useful in group work settings, and will seem more attractive as we address the problems of designing interfaces that must appeal to almost all users. As computer systems offer more capability, casual use of a given feature will increase, perhaps become the norm. Within a group, frequency of use of a CSCW application will inevitably be uneven; natural language could make it easier for some users to enter and retrieve information.

Database access seems a logical target application: the domain is circumscribed, much of the necessary vocabulary is explicitly set down in the database field and record labels, and the interaction -- user query followed by system response -- is predictable and limited. Natural language interfaces to databases have been available for several years.

Over the last ten years, most major developers of office systems have undertaken natural language projects and over fifty software companies have entered the field (Foley, 1986). While absorbing 1000 developers and hundreds of millions of dollars, none of these ventures had been profitable by 1985 (Johnson, 1985). (While one or two companies marketing databases with natural language interface options have since reported profitability, surveys have shown that the natural language feature was not responsible; Paul Martin, personal communication, 1988.) A survey of the natural language industry concluded "its story is not the stuff of which venture capitalists' dreams are made," (Johnson, 1985).

We need to understand two things: why has natural language failed to meet expectations and how has it attracted such high levels of support?

Problems of natural language interfaces to databases. Natural language understanding is incredibly complex: there is not yet a complete theory of syntax and semantics and pragmatics may be even more difficult. While a database interface based even on primitive linguistic approaches can correctly respond to a high percentage of the limited range of queries it encounters, it is not clear how an occasional error will affect the user's overall confidence in the system. If you ask for the average secretary's salary at the U.N. and are told $50K because it has averaged in the General Secretary of the U.N., you may cease to trust the system (Paul Martin, personal communication).

Another potential problem is coverage. People rely on a huge, structured knowledge acquired over years in order to understand simple things, more than existing systems can hope to incorporate (see e.g., Bobrow et al., 1977). A related problem is that users may expect an application that handles English to exhibit broad human intelligence and be disappointed when it does not (Rich, 1984). Rich also notes that the natural language user must do a lot of typing, although users can and do develop truncated "pidgin languages" that may end up more concise than complex queries in a formal query language. And one must also consider the conservatism of the database market and the need to develop appropriate marketing strategies as contributing factors to the poor reception for natural language interfaces.

Finally and more speculatively, natural language may not be matched to the tasks for which computers are used. In human interactions, we gravitate toward more formal language when we are uncertain of our audience, when we will get minimal feedback and opportunity to correct misinterpretations, and when we desire precise responses by the listener. All of these are characteristic of human–computer interaction. Perhaps if neural net or connectionist systems succeed in giving computers a more "fuzzy," human–like intelligence, natural language will be a good match.

The attraction of a natural language interface to databases. Perhaps more important than the circumscribed domain of a database and the explicit, built-in terminology are the problems outlined in this paper. The casual database user is the beneficiary of the natural language interface. The heavy user pays the price of additional keystrokes and reduced precision. The truly heavy user may work primarily by creating and modifying command files for frequently-issued complex queries in the formal query language. The heavy user always retains the option of using the formal query language that accompanies the natural language interface, but if that query language is not the best available formal interface, the heavy user would pay a price to use the system.

The manager and executive can envision themselves as casual users of a shared database, with others delegated to enter the data and carry out routine queries. Thus, natural language interfaces may appeal to decision-makers. But once again, decision-making intuition has failed if frequent users, the principal users of databases, prefer not to do the extra work that choosing such a system may entail.

Case 4. Group decision support systems.

The many efforts to develop computer support for group decision-making have generally produced systems, but it is clear that group decision support will benefit considerably by integrating with the systems people use for other aspects of their work and will thus become a CSCW application area. Such applications are already under development. At CSCW'86, Kraemer and King reviewed a large number of group decision support systems and concluded that their current reality is "far less than might be expected given their need and promise," and that "although some for-profit companies have undertaken to build (group decision support systems), they are not yet making much money," (Kraemer and King, 1986).

While they vary considerably in character, group decision support systems are highly susceptible to the problems outlined in this paper. They are expressly designed to be of principal benefit to decision-makers, insofar as one person is primarily responsible for the outcome of a meeting or a group decision process (undoubtedly the norm in our culture). The amount of work required of others to learn and use the system may vary. If use of the system requires significant learning, requires putting information on-line to make it publicly available, records information that a participant would prefer not to leave the meeting, blocks other means to influence decision-making (such as private lobbying), or undermines management authority, then the system may encounter resistance.

Conclusion.

Computer support for the activities of individuals in their group and organizational contexts will unquestionably change the way people live in significant ways. It is difficult to imagine anything more important or fascinating than trying to understand and guide that change. The analyses in this paper suggest that we are just beginning. Progress has been technology-driven to a surprising degree -- technologies searching for needs, as one panel organizer described it (Aucella, 1987). Many of us are aware of this general problem, pointed out by Engelbart (1982, 1985) and others, but its specific manifestations may continue to elude analysis, much less solution.

We need to have a better understanding of how groups and organizations function and evolve than is reflected in most of the systems that have been developed. At the same time, we also need to know more about individual differences in responding to technology if we are to develop systems that can support entire groups. One approach may be the contextual research of John Whiteside and his colleagues (Whiteside, Bennett, and Holtzblatt, 1987). Another is that used at Aarhus University in Denmark: "The Aarhus people start out with a problem situation defined by workers, and work beside them a long time in order to develop a new system that is "owned" by the workers... This is very different from traditional systems development, as you can imagine, and you can't simply package a set of techniques to do the job...see Ehn and King (1987)." (Liam Bannon, personal communication).

We must also develop a better behavioral understanding of our own decision-making processes as researchers and developers. The intuitions that have guided us in the past are breaking down. If we are going to support groups that include any diversity at all, we will have to learn much more about how different kinds of people work. Very frequently we see researchers studying other researchers, developers building systems because the technology exists, and managers supporting the development of systems that will appeal to other managers. We must make a strong effort to broaden our intuitions because experiments in the cooperative work area are so expensive and time-consuming.

Appendices.

Analogy 1. Multi-user systems and multi-user applications.

Most of our experience with computer support for group activity is based on the introduction of entire *systems* into an organization. I do not intend "multi-user system" to include a central, timesharing computer that essentially supports several individuals using individual applications, but rather a system that includes hardware and software developed to support group activity, such as a management information system, a computer-integrated manufacturing system, or an inventory control system. Multi-user *application* refers to software (and possibly minor hardware) acquired with the intent of integrating it into an existing computer system, such as a co-authoring program.

Computer support of group activity has typically required the acquisition or development of an entire system because the prerequisites -- multi-tasking, networking, interactive interfaces, and computer literacy -- were not in place. But as more advanced environments become widespread and people are comfortable with the terminal, PC, or workstation on their desk, systems will have to give way to applications. Today, an entire work management *system* might be installed, replacing or absorbing existing technology, but tomorrow a work or project management *application* will be sought, to run on an existing system. Cooperative applications that are appearing include co-authoring aids, sophisticated mail and time management, voice applications, shared databases, shared financial analysis packages, etc.

Our experience with multi-user systems, whether direct or through the literature, may influence our approach to multi-user applications. They have similarities -- they may serve the same purpose and behave much the same. But there are critical differences, particularly at the time of introduction: the system has a much higher cost, greater visibility, and stronger commitment of upper management. As a result, a new system brings with it the expectation of organizational change. While an organization will also adapt or evolve following the introduction of a CSCW application, the far less expensive application will not carry the same visibility, commitment, and expectation of change. From the perspective of the user, the introduction of the application must be smoother. This makes the job of the designer and implementer more difficult (see Pew, 1986).

The strong management commitment to ensuring the success of a new system means that a) the *collective* benefit of the system is recognized to be high; b) the organization may create new jobs to achieve success, if necessary; c) if a few important individuals will not or cannot use the system (the manager who won't use a terminal, for example), ways to work around them may be found; d) pressure from management to try the system may be high (whether through leadership and positive example or through more coercive approaches). Even with these forces working to the advantage of the system, we know that successful implementation is difficult. Introducing CSCW applications without this backing, all else being equal, will be *more* difficult. Better design and implementation are ways to ensure that all else isn't equal. (The application may have the advantage of finding a higher level of computer literacy, since a system is already in place.)

The much less expensive application program is likely to provide a smaller or uncertain collective benefit and won't have the same degree of management commitment. The organization cannot restructure itself around each new application, nor will management be likely to work as hard to ensure full participation. To a greater degree, the application must fit into existing work patterns and appeal to all the people needed to support it. For many of these communication-centered applications, this may be everyone: The application program may require full group participation without the advantage that a system often has of choosing or defining its users.

Analogy 2. Single-user applications and multi-user applications.

Whether we are researchers, designers, implementers, users, evaluators, or managers, most of our computer experience has almost certainly been with single-user applications. This experience has inevitably influenced the skills we have acquired, the intuitions we have developed, and the way we view our work. When we find ourselves thinking about or working with a CSCW application, it is useful to examine our approach carefully with this in mind, as many of our skills, intuitions, and outlooks will not help us in this different domain.

One effect of working with single-user applications is that we do not train ourselves to think extensively in terms of the disparity between the benefit obtained by and the work required of different user categories. We do of course give some consideration to the novice, casual user, heavy user distinctions, but in general, we can rely on feedback from a few "typical users." This experience may lead us to be unaware that we are only viewing a CSCW application from the perspective of the primary intended user, the user who obtains the most direct benefit. For managers, this may have the effect of biasing their judgment regarding the CSCW application. A manager with good intuition might look at the design of an editor and correctly surmise "I would like these features and I think most users would." Looking at a CSCW application, the manager might surmise "I would like these features and I think most users would," but only be correct insofar as the other users are also managers. The single-user application does not train us to consider users of the same product who have a crucial but entirely different engagement with it.

Another effect of working with single-user applications is that we do not acquire the very different evaluative skills that CSCW applications will require. Most human factors engineers and other user interface specialists are versed primarily in applying techniques from perceptual, cognitive, and motor psychology to study phenomena of relatively brief duration. The one-hour experiment is still typical, and a study involving even a few sessions over several days is rare. But the group processes that will influence and be influenced by the use of CSCW applications bring social, motivational, economic, and political factors into prominence, and the temporal granularity required to understand such dynamics is much larger.

When is job redesign justifiable?

Central to this paper is the point that many CSCW applications will directly benefit certain users, often managers, while requiring additional work from others. A traditional method of coping with such a problem is to create new jobs or "redesign" existing jobs -- in short, to require people to do the additional work. Technology and organizational change is covered in depth elsewhere (e.g., Kraut, 1987a, 1987b; Crowston and Malone, 1987). This paper comments more on how things are than on how they might be, so I will limit myself to a few observations.

First, as noted in the paper, CSCW applications will not have recourse to changing job requirements to the degree that often occurs when entire systems are installed. The investment and commitment are smaller and the organization won't tolerate significant disruption for each new application acquired. CSCW applications will have to be more "group-friendly" than systems have been. They will change the organization, but more gradually. For this reason, the focus of CSCW will shift to user interface issues to minimize the disruption and additional work required of *any* user of the application.

Second, there may be a shift toward greater egalitarianism in the workplace (see e.g. Cherns, 1980), some of it surface and some of it perhaps a deeper emphasis on managing by building consensus. Therefore, it may be more difficult for management to mandate participation in new applications unless the collective benefit is very evident.

Third, when the collective benefit of using an application *does* appear great enough to warrant requiring some people to accept new or different tasks -- and measurements of collective benefit are of course difficult -- management has several options. Educating all users to the collective benefit may create a willingness to do the work. Inspiring through example or positive leadership is another approach. And, of course, improving the user interface to minimize the work or providing compensatory benefits in another area will help.

Finally, in some cases the work *will* be made part of the job. Setting aside tasks that most people would agree *no one* should be asked to do, the discomfort from job redesign is often transitory: Those hired with an understanding of the new requirements will be less uncomfortable with them than those living through the change.

Consider the example of programmer documentation of software code. Twenty years ago programmers writing entirely undocumented code might have been unhappy if forced to change for the collective benefit to the company of having maintainable software. But today more programmers are educated and socialized to accept this as part of their work; it is written into job descriptions, those taking the job are reasonably content to do it.

This is a cursory treatment of a difficult ethical topic, but anything more is, as they say, beyond the scope of this paper.

Acknowledgment.

This paper owes a lot to published and personal communications of Susan F. Ehrlich and to Liam Bannon's insightful comments. Clarence Ellis, Don Gentner, Donald A. Norman, Gail Rein, and Elaine Rich also contributed useful comments and encouragement. I am especially grateful for conversations on specific issues with Carroll Hall, Paul Martin, and Steven Roth. Clarence Ellis, Simon Gibbs, Bill Kuhlman, Steve Poltrock, Gail Rein, and I explored the significance of a group's position on the continuum from a small, homogeneous team to a large, heterogeneous organization using GROVE, a CSCW application developed by the MCC Software Technology Program to support brainstorming, leading to my greater appreciation for the importance of this factor. Many of the ideas in this paper were developed from a paper delivered at Interact'87 (Grudin, 1987).

References.

Aucella, A.F. (moderator), 1987. Voice: Technology searching for communication needs. In *Proc. CHI+GI '87 Human Factors in Computing Systems (Toronto, April 5-9, 1987)*, pp. 41-44.

Aucella, A.F. and Ehrlich, S.F., 1986. Voice messaging: Enhancing the user interface based on field performance. In *Proc. CHI '86 Human Factors in Computing Systems (Boston, April 13-17, 1986)*, pp. 156-161.

Bobrow, D.G., Kaplan, R.M., Kay, M., Norman, D.A., Thompson, H., and Winograd, T., 1987. Gus, a frame-driven dialog system, *Artificial Intelligence, 8*, pp. 155-173.

Butler, K., Bennett, J., and Whiteside, J., 1987. Engineering objectives for usability. Tutorial presented at CHI+GI '87 Human Factors in Computing Systems (Toronto, April 5-9, 1987).

Carasik, R.P. and Grantham, C.E., 1988. A case study of computer-supported cooperative work in a dispersed organization. In *Proc. CHI '88 Human Factors in Computing Systems (Washington D.C., May 15-19, 1988)*, pp. 61-66.

Cherns, A.B., 1980. Speculations on the social effects of new microelectronics technology. *International Labour Review, 119, 6*, pp. 705-721.

Crowston, K. and Malone, T.W., 1987. Information technology and work organization. CISR WP No. 165. Cambridge, MA: MIT Sloan School of Management.

Ehn, P., and Kyng, M., 1987. The collective resource approach to systems design. In Bjerknes, G., Ehn, P., and Kyng, M. (Eds.) Computers and democracy - a Scandinavian challenge. Aldershot, UK: Gower.

Ehrlich, S.F., 1987a. Social and psychological factors influencing the design of office communication systems. In *Proc. CHI+GI '87 Human Factors in Computing Systems (Toronto, April 5-9, 1987)*, pp. 323-329.

Ehrlich, S.F., 1987b. Strategies for encouraging successful adoption of office communication systems. *ACM TOOIS, 5*, pp. 340-357.

Engelbart, D.C., 1982. Towards high-performance knowledge workers. OAC 82. Reprinted in Greif, 1988.

Engelbart, D.C., 1985. Plenary address, CHI '85 Human Factors in Computing Systems (San Francisco, April 18, 1985).

Foley, M.J., 1986. Teaching computers plain English. *High Technology*, May, 1986.

Gaffney, C.T., 1985. Avoiding the "seven deadly sins" of OA implementation. In *Proc. Syntopican XIII Making Business Systems Effective* (Washington, D.C., June 17-20, 1985), pp. 241-254.

Greif, I. (Ed.), 1988. *Computer-supported cooperative work: a book of readings*. San Mateo: Morgan Kaufmann.

Grudin, J., 1986. Designing in the dark: Logics that compete with the user. In *Proc. CHI '86 Human Factors in Computing Systems (Boston, April 13-17, 1986)*, pp. 281-284.

Grudin, J., 1987. Social evaluation of the user interface: Who does the work and who gets the benefit? In *Proc. INTERACT'87 (Stuttgart, September 1-4, 1987)*, pp. 805-811.

Johnson, T., 1985. *Natural language computing: the commercial applications*. London: Ovum Ltd.

Kling, R., 1987. The social dimensions of computerization. Plenary address given at CHI+GI '87 Human Factors in Computing Systems (Toronto, April 5-9, 1987).

Kraemer, K. and King, J., 1986. Computer-based systems for group decision support: Status of use and problems of development. In *Proc. CSCW Conference on Computer-Supported Cooperative Work*, (Austin, December 3-5, 1986), pp. 353-375.

Kraut, R.E. (Ed.), 1987a. *Technology and the transformation of white-collar work*. Hillsdale: Lawrence Erlbaum Associates.

Kraut, R.E., 1987b. Social issues and white-collar technology: an overview. In Kraut (1987a), pp. 1-21.

Lucas, H.C., Jr., 1976. *The analysis, design and implementation of information systems*. New York: McGraw-Hill.

Malone, T.W., 1985. Designing organizational interfaces. In *Proc. CHI '85 Human Factors in Computing Systems (San Francisco, April 14-18, 1985)*, pp. 66-71.

McCracken, D.L. and Akscyn, R.M., 1984. Experience with the ZOG human-computer interface system. *Int. J. Man-Machine Studies, 21*, pp. 293-310.

Newell, A.F., 1984. Speech -- the natural modality for man-machine interaction? In *Proc. INTERACT '84 IFIP Conference on Human-Computer Interaction*, (London, September 4-7, 1984), pp. 231-235.

Pew, R. (moderator), 1986. Socio-tech: What is it (and why should we care)? In *Proc. CHI '86 Human Factors in Computing Systems (Boston, April 13-17, 1986)*, pp. 129-130.

Rich, E., 1984. Natural-language interfaces. *Computer*, September, 1984, pp. 39-47.

Rowe, C.J., 1985. Identifying causes of failure: a case study in computerized stock control. *Behaviour and Information Technology, 4*, pp. 63-72.

Sathi, A., Morton, T.E., and Roth, S.F., 1986. Callisto: An intelligent project management system. AI Magazine, Winter, 1986, pp. 34-52. Reprinted in Greif (1988), pp. 269-309.

Shneiderman, B., 1987. *Designing the user interface*. Reading: Addison-Wesley.

White, K.B., 1985. Socio-technical task team design. In *Proc. Syntopican XIII Making Business Systems Effective* (Washington, D.C., June 17-20, 1985), pp. 32-35.

Whiteside, J., Bennett, J., and Holtzblatt, K., 1988. Usability engineering: our experience and evolution. In M. Helander (Ed.), Handbook of human-computer interaction. Amsterdam: North-Holland, *in press*.

Selected Bibliography

The following references were used to develop the chapter introductions for this tutorial. Since many influenced more than one chapter, they were compiled into this one section for brevity. We encourage those seeking a more in-depth understanding of groupware to consider sampling these works.

References marked with an asterisk are from the 1984 Workshop on Computer Supported Cooperative Work — an event sponsored by Digital Equipment Corporation, which was a catalyst for the CSCW field. Those references marked with a plus sign are additional works cited in Saul Greenberg's "Annotated Bibliography of Computer Supported Cooperative Work," *ACM SIGCHI Bulletin*, Volume 23, Number 3, July 1991.

Abdel-Hamid, T., and S. Madnick, "Lessons Learned from Modeling the Dynamics of Software Development," *Comm. ACM*, Vol. 32, No. 12, Dec. 1989.

+ Abel, M., "Experiences in an Exploratory Distributed Organization," in *Intellectual Teamwork: Social Foundations of Cooperative Work*, R. Galegher, R. Kraut, and C. Egido, eds., Lawrence Erlbaum Assoc., 1990.

+ Abel, M., et al., "The US West Advanced Technologies TeleCollaboration Research Project," in *Computer Augmented Teamwork*, G. Wagner, ed., Van Nostrand Reinhold, 1989.

+ Abel, M., and G. Rein, "Report on the Collaborative Technology Developers' Workshop," *ACM SIGCHI Bulletin*, Vol. 20, No. 1, Jan. 1989.

Adams, J., *The Care And Feeding of Ideas: A Guide to Encouraging Creativity*, Addison-Wesley Publishing Co., 1986.

+ Adrianson, L., and E. Hjelmquist, "Group Processes in Face-to-Face and Computer-Mediated Communication," internal report, University of Gotenborg, Dept. of Psychology, n.d.

Agresti, W., ed, *New Paradigms for Software Development*, IEEE Tutorial No. 707, 1986.

Ahuja, S., J. Ensor, and S. Lucco, "A Comparison of Application-Sharing Mechanisms in Real-Time Desktop Conferencing Systems," *Proc. Office Information Systems*, Apr. 1990.

Ahuja, S., et al., "Network Support for Distributed Collaboration," *Proc. Groupware Technology Workshop*, Aug. 1989

Aiken, M., O. Sheng, and D. Vogel, "Integrating Expert Systems With Group Decision Support Systems," *ACM Trans. Information Systems*, Vol. 9, No. 1, Jan. 1991.

Akscyn, R., D. McCracken, and E. Yoder, "KMS: A Distributed Hypermedia System for Managing Knowledge in Organizations," *Comm. ACM*, Vol. 31, No. 7, July 1988.

+ Allen, R., "User Models: Theory, Method, Practice," *Int'l J. of Man-Machine Studies*, Vol. 32, No. 5, May 1990.

Alexander, C., *Notes on the Synthesis of Form*, Harvard University Press, 1964.

Alexander, C., *A Pattern Language*, Oxford University Press, 1978.

Allam, A., and G. White, "Expertnet: A Cooperative Problem Solver," *Proc. Groupware Technology Workshop*, Aug. 1989.

+ Ancona, D., and C. Caldwell, "Information Technology And Work Groups," in *Intellectual Teamwork: Social Foundations of Cooperative Work*, R. Galegher, R. Kraut, and C. Egido, eds., Lawrence Erlbaum Assoc., 1990.

Andersen, P., and K. Madsen, "Design And Professional Languages," Report DAIMAPB-244, Aarhus University, Mar. 1988.

Applegate, L., "Technology Support for Cooperative Work: A Framework for Studying Introduction and Assimilation in Organization," *Organizational Computing*, 1990.

Applegate, L., and B. Konsynski, "A Group Decision Support System for Idea Generation and Issue Analysis in Organization Planning," *Proc. CSCW*, Dec. 1986.

+ Attewell, P., and J. Rule, "Computing and Organizations: What We Know and What We Don't Know" *Comm. ACM*, Vol. 27, No. 12, Dec. 1984.

Auramaki, E., E. Lehtinen, and L. Lyytinen, "A Speech-Act-Based Office Modeling Approach," *ACM Trans. Office Information Systems*, Vol. 6, No. 2, Apr. 1988.

Austin, L., J. Liker, and P. McLeod, "Determinants and Patterns of Control Over Technology in a Computerized Meeting Room," *Proc. CSCW*, Oct. 1990.

Axelrod, R. *The Evolution of Cooperation*, Basic Books, 1984.

+ Bair, J., "Supporting Cooperative Work With Computers: Addressing Meeting Mania," *Proc. 34th Computer Society Int'l Conf.*, Mar. 1989.

+ Bair, J., and S. Gale, "An Investigation of the Coordinator as an Example of Computer-Supported Cooperative Work," Hewlett Packard internal report, 1988.

+ Bannon, L., N. Bjorn-Andersen, and B. Due-Thomsen, "Computer Support for Cooperative Work: An Appraisal and Critique," in *Eurinfo '88: Information Systems for Organizational Effectiveness*, H. Bullinger, ed., 1988.

* Barber, G., "An Office Study: Its Implications on the Understanding of Organizations," working paper, Massachusetts Institute of Technology, Aug. 1984.

Beard, D., and M. Palaniappan, "A Visual Calendar for Scheduling Group Meetings," *Proc. CSCW*, Oct. 1990.

+ Beaudouin-Lafon, M., "Collaborative Development of Software," *Proc. IFIP WG8.4 Conf. on Multiuser Interfaces and Applications*, 1990.

Begeman, M., et al., "Project Nick: Meeting Augmentation and Analysis," *Proc. CSCW*, Dec. 1986.

Bell, T., "Technical Challenges to a Decentralized Phone System," *IEEE Spectrum*, Vol. 27, No. 9, Sept. 1990.

Bendifallah, S., and W. Scacchi, "Work Structures and Shifts: An Empirical Analysis of Software Specification Teamwork," *Proc. 11th Int'l Conf. on Software Engineering*, May 1989.

+ Benford, S., "Requirements Activity Management," *Proc. First European Conf. on CSCW*, Sept. 1989.

+ Benson, I., C. Ciborra, and S. Proffitt, "Some Social and Economic Consequences of Groupware for Flight Crew," *Proc. CSCW*, Oct. 1990.

+ Berlin, L., and V. O'Day, "Platform and Application Issues in Multiuser Hypertext," *Proc. IFIP WG8.4 Conf. on Multiuser Interfaces and Applications*, 1990.

+ Berman, T., and K. Thorenson, "Can Networks Make an Organization?" *Proc. CSCW*, Sept. 1988.

Bertino, E., Martino, L., "Object-Oriented Database Management Systems: Concepts and Issues," *Computer*, Vol. 24, No. 4, Apr. 1991.

+ Bhandaru, N., and B. Croft, "Architecture for Supporting Goal-Based Cooperative Work," *IFIP WG8.4 Conf. on Multiuser Interfaces and Applications*, 1990.

Bignoli, C., and C. Simone, "AI Techniques for Supporting Human-to-Human Communication in CHAOS," *Proc. First European CSCW*, Sept. 1989.

Bignoli, C., and G. DeMichelis, "Coordination through Multiple Media," University of Milan working paper, 1990.

+ Bikson, T., and J. Eveland, "The Interplay of Work Group Structures," in *Intellectual Teamwork: Social Foundations of Cooperative Work*, R. Galegher, R. Kraut, and C. Egido, eds., Lawrence Erlbaum Assoc., 1990.

Bjerknes, G., and T. Bratteteig, "The Memoirs of Two Survivors: Or the Evaluation of a Computer System for Cooperative Work," *Proc. CSCW*, Sept. 1988.

Bjerknes, G., P. Ehn, and M. Kyng, *Computers and Democracy*, Avebury Publishers, 1987.

Bloomberg, J., "The Variable Impact of Computer Technologies on the Organization of Work Activities," *Proc. CSCW*, Dec. 1986.

+ Bly, S., "A Use of Drawing Surfaces in Different Collaborative Settings," *Proc. CSCW*, Sept. 1988.

+ Bly, S., and S. Minneman, "Commune: A Shared Drawing Surface," *Proc. Office Information Systems*, Apr. 1990.

+ Bodker, S., and K. Gronbaek, "Cooperative Prototyping: Users and Designers in Mutual Activity," *Int'l J. of Man-Machine Studies*, Vol. 34, No. 3, Mar. 1991.

Bodker, S., and K. Gronboek, "Cooperative Prototyping Experiments," *Proc. First European CSCW*, Sept. 1989.

Bodker, S., and P. Ehn, "Computer Support for Cooperative Design," *Proc. Second CSCW*, Sept. 1988.

Bonfiglio, A., G. Malatesta, and F. Tisato, "Conf. Toolkit: A Framework for Real-Time Conferencing," *Proc. First European CSCW*, Sept. 1989.

+ Bornstein, N., and C. Thyberg, "Power, Ease of Use, and Cooperative Work in a Practical Multimedia Message System," *Int'l J. of Man-Machine Studies*, Vol. 34, No. 2, Feb. 1991.

Borenstein, N., "Multimedia Electronic Mail: Will the Dream Become Reality?" *Comm. ACM*, Vol. 34, No. 4, Apr. 1991.

Borenstein, N., and C. Thyberg, "Cooperative Work in the Andrew Message System," *Proc. Second CSCW*, Sept. 1988.

Borning, A., and M. Travers, "Two Approaches to Casual Interaction over Computer and Video Networks," *Proc. Conf. on Human Factors in Computing Systems*, Apr. 1991.

Bowers, J., "Local and Global Structuring of Computer Mediated Communication: Developing Linguistic Perspectives on CSCW in COSMOS," *Proc. Second CSCW*, Sept. 1988.

Bracchi, G., and B. Pernici, "The Design Requirements of Office Systems," *ACM Trans. Information Systems*, Vol. 2 No. 2, Apr. 1984.

Brand, S., *The Media Lab: Inventing the Future at MIT*, Viking Penguin, 1987.

+ Bulick, C., et al., "The US West Advanced Technologies Prototype Multimedia Communication System," *Proc. IEEE Global Telecommunications Conf. (GlobeCom)*, Nov. 1989.

Bullen, C., R. Johansen, "Groupware: A Key to Managing Business Teams?" industrial laison report, Massachusetts Institute of Technology, Aug. 1988.

Bullen, C., and J. Bennett, "Learning from User Experience With Groupware," *Proc. CSCW '90*, Oct. 1990.

Bullen, C., and J. Bennett, "Groupware in Practice: An Interpretation of Work Experience," Research Report CISR WP 205, Sloan WP No. 3146-90, Center for Information Systems Research, MIT, Mar. 1990.

Burke, J., *The Day the Universe Changed*, Little, Brown and Co., 1985.

+ Bush, V., "As We May Think," *Atlantic Monthly*, Vol. 176, No. 1, June 1945.

+ Buxton, B., and T. Moran, "EuroPARC's Integrated Interactive Intermedia Facility (IIIF): Early Experiences." *Proc. IFIP WG8.4 Conf. on Multiuser Interfaces and Applications*, 1990.

+ Caldwell, R., et al., "Conferencing Selection and Implementation: University of Arizona Case History," *The Second Guelph Symp. on Computer Conferencing*, June 1987.

Carasik, R., E. Dykstra, "Requirements for a Semi-Structured Graphics Communication Medium for CSCW," *Proc. First European Conf. on CSCW*, Sept. 1989.

Carasik, R., and C. Grantham, "A Case Study of CSCW in a Dispersed Organization," *Proc. Conf. on Computer and Human Interaction*, May 1988.

Carlson, D., and S. Ram, "Hyperintelligence: The Next Frontier," *Comm. of the ACM*, Vol. 33, No. 3, Mar. 1990.

+ Cashman, P., and D. Stroll, "Achieving Sustainable Complexity through Information Technology: Theory and Practice," *Office: Technology and People*, Vol. 3, 1987.

+ Chalfonte, B., R. Fish, and R. Kraut, "Expressive Richness: A Comparison of Speech and Text as Media for Revision," *Proc. Conf. on Human Factors in Computing Systems*, Apr. 1991.

+ Chang, E., "Participant Systems," *Future Computing Systems*, Vol. 1, No. 3, 1986.

+ Chang, E., "Protocols for Group Coordination in Participant Systems," in *The Structure of Multimodal Dialogue*," M. Taylor, F. Neel, and D. Bouwhuis, eds., 1989.

Clement, A., "Cooperative Support for Computer Work: A Social Perspective on the Empowering of End Users," *Proc. CSCW*, Oct. 1990.

Cockburn, A., and H. Thimbleby, "A Reflexive Perspective of CSCW," *ACM SIGCHI Bulletin*, Vol. 23, No. 3, July 1991.

Conklin, J., "gIBIS: A Hypertext Tool for Exploratory Policy," *Proc. CSCW*, Sept. 1988.

Conklin, J., "gIBIS: A Hypertext Tool for Team Design Deliberation," in *Hypertext '87 Papers*, L. Begeman, ed., Nov. 1987.

Conklin, J., "Hypertext: An Introduction and Survey," *Computer*, Sept. 1987.

Cook, P., et al., "Project Nick: Meetings Augmentation and Analysis," *ACM Trans. Information Systems*, Vol. No. 2, Apr. 1987.

+ Cook, S., and G. Birch, "Modeling Groupware in the Electronic Office," *Int'l J. of Man-Machine Studies*, Vol. 34, No. 3, Mar. 1991.

+ Corey, E., et al., "Multimedia Communication: The US WEST Advanced Technologies Prototype System," *Fifth IEEE Workshop on Telematics*, Sept. 1989.

Cornell, P., et al., "CSCW: Evolution and Status of Computer-Supported Cooperative Work," Technical Report no. 25, University of Michigan Cognitive Science and Machine Intelligence Laboratory, Aug. 1989.

* Croft, W., and L. Lefkowitz, "Task Support in an Office System," working paper, University of Massachusetts, 1984.

+ Crowley, T., et al., " MMConf: An Infrastructure for Building Shared Applications," *Proc. CSCW*, Oct. 1990.

+ Crowley, T., et al., "The Diamond Multimedia Editor," *Proc. Summer Usenix Conf.*, 1987.

Crowley, T., and H. Forsdick, "MMConf: The Diamond Multimedia Conferencing System," *Proc. Groupware Technology Workshop*, Aug. 1989.

Crowston, K., T. Malone, and F. Lin, "Cognitive Science and Organizational Design: A Case Study of Computer Conferencing," *Proc. CSCW*, Dec. 1986.

Crowston, K., and T. Malone, "Information Technology and Work Organization," in *Handbook of Human-Computer Interaction*, M. Helander, ed, North Holland, 1988.

+ Crowston, K., and T. Malone, "Intelligent Software Agents," *Byte Magazine*, Dec. 1988.

+ Culnan, M., and J. Bair, "Human Communications Needs and Organizational Productivity: The Potential Impact of Office Automation," *J. of the American Society for Information Science*, Vol. 34, No. 3, 1983.

Curtis, B., H. Krasner, and N. Iscoe, "A Field Study of the Software Design Process for Large Systems," *Comm. ACM*, Vol. 31, No. 11, Nov. 1988.

Danielsen, T., et al., "The Amigo Project: Advanced Group Communication Model for Computer-Based Communications Environment," *Proc. First CSCW*, Dec. 1986.

DeCindio, F., et al., "CHAOS as Coordination Technology," *Proc. First CSCW*, Dec. 1986.

DeCindio, F., G. DeMichelis, and C. Simone, "The Communication Disciplines of CHAOS," in *Concurrency and Nets*, Springer-Verlag, 1988.

+ DeKoven, C., and T. Radhakrishnan, "An Experiment in Distributed Group Problem Solving," *Proc. IFIP WG8.4 Conf. on Multiuser Interfaces and Applications*, 1990.

DeLisi, P., "Lessons from the Steel Axe: Culture, Technology, and Organizational Change," *Sloan Management Review*, Fall 1990.

Delisle, N., and M. Schwartz, "Contexts — A Partitioning Concept for Hypertext," *Proc. CSCW*, Dec. 1986.

DeMarco, T., and T. Lister, *Peopleware: Productive Projects and Teams*, Dorset House Publishing Co., 1987.

DeMichelis, G., T. DeCindio, and C. Simone, "Groups in a Language/Action Perspective," working paper, University of Milan, 1990.

DeMichelis, G., "Computer Support for Cooperative Work," *Butler Cox Foundation Report*, Oct. 1990.

+ DeSanctis, G., and R. Gallupe, "A Foundation for the Study of Group Decision Support Systems," *Management Science*, Vol. 33, No. 5, May 1987.

Dennis, A.R., et al., "Automated Support for Group Work," *Management Information Systems Quarterly*, College of Business, Dec. 1988.

Dewan, P., and R. Choudhary, "Flexible User Interface Coupling in a Collaborative System," *Proc. Conf. on Human Factors in Computing Systems*, Apr. 1991.

Dollimore, J., and S. Wilbur, "Experiences Building a Configurable CSCW System," *Proc. First European CSCW*, Sept. 1989.

+ Dollimore, J., and G. Coulouris, "Towards a Language for Defining Structure in Message-Based Cooperative Work," *Proc. IFIP WG8.4 Conf. on Multiuser Interfaces and Applications*, 1990.

+ Dongarra, J., and E. Grosse, "Distribution of Mathematical Software Via Electronic Mail," *Comm. ACM*, Vol. 30, No. 5, May 1987.

+ Dykstra, E., and R. Carasik, "Structure and Support in Cooperative Environments: The Amsterdam Conversation Environment," *Int'l J. of Man-Machine Studies*, Vol. 34, No. 3, Mar. 1991.

Dyson, E., "Why Groupware is Gaining Ground," *Datamation*, Mar. 1, 1990.

Eason, K., and S. Harker, "The Supplier's Role in the Design of Products for Organizations," *Computer Journal*, Vol. 31, No. 5, May 1988.

Egido, C., "Videoconferencing as a Technology to Support Group Work: A Review of its Failure," *Proc. Second CSCW*, Sept. 1988.

+ Egido, C., "Teleconferencing as a Technology to Support Cooperative Work: Its Possibilities and Limitations," in *Intellectual Teamwork: Social Foundations of Cooperative Work*, R. Galegher, R. Kraut, and C. Egido, eds., Lawrence Erlbaum Assoc., 1990.

Ehn, P., "The Art and Science of Designing Computer Artifacts," *Scandinavian J. of Information Systems*, Vol. 1, 1989, pp. 21-42.

Ehn, P., "Playing in Reality," working paper, Aarhus University, Oct. 1989.

Ehn, P., *Work-Oriented Design of Computer Artifacts*, Arbetslivscentrum, 1988.

Ehn, P., "Playing the Language-Games of Design and Use," *Proc. Computer Office Information Systems*, 1988.

* Ellis, C., "An Office Information System Based on Intelligent Forms," working paper, Xerox PARC, Aug. 1984.

+ Ellis, C., "CSCW '88 Report," *ACM/SIGOIS Bulletin*, Vol. 10, No. 1, Jan. 1989.

* Ellis, C., "Formal and Informal Models of Office Activity," working paper, Xerox PARC, Aug. 1984.

* Ellis, C., and M. Bernal, "Officetalk-D: An Experimental Office Information System," internal report, Xerox PARC, Aug. 1984.

Ellis, C., "Concurrency Control in Groupware Systems," Technical Report STP-417-88, MCC, Dec. 1988.

Ellis, C., S. Gibbs, and G. Rein, "Design and Use of a Group Editor," Technical Report STP-263-88, MCC, June 1989.

+ Ellis, C., S. Gibbs, and G. Rein, "Groupware: Some Issues and Experiences," *Comm. ACM*, Vol. 34, No. 1, Jan. 1991.

+ Ellis, C., S. Gibbs, and G. Rein, "The Groupware Project: An Overview," Technical Report STP-033088, MCC, Jan. 1988.

+ Ellis, C., and G. Nutt, "Office Information Systems and Computer Science," *ACM Computing Surveys*, Vol. 12, No. 1, 1980.

Engelbart, D., "Knowledge-Domain Interoperability and an Open Hyperdocument System," *Proc. CSCW*, Oct. 1990.

* Engelbart, D., "A Conceptual Framework for the Augmentation of Man's Intellect," in *Vistas in Information Handling*, Vol. 1, P. Howerton, and D. Weeks, eds., 1963 (also in *Computer-Supported Cooperative Work: A Book of Readings*, I. Greif, ed., Morgan Kaufmann Publishers, 1988).

Englebart, D., and W. English, "A Research Center for Augmenting Human Intellect," in *Computer-Supported Cooperative Work: A Book of Readings*," I. Greif, ed., Morgan Kaufmann Publishers, 1988.

Engelbart, D., "Authorship Provisions in Augment," *Proc. IEEE COMPCON*, Mar. 1984.

* Engelbart, D., "Collaboration Support Provisions in Augment," *Proc. Conf. AFIPS Office Automation*, Feb. 1983.

Engelbart, D., "Towards High-Performance Knowledge Workers," *Proc. Conf. AFIPS Office Automation*, Apr. 1982.

+ Engelbart, D., Lehtman, H., "Working Together," *Byte*, Dec. 1988.

+ Engestrom, Y., R. Engestrom, and O. Saarelma, "Computerized Medical Records, Production Pressure and Compartmentalization in the Work Activity of Health Center Physicians," *Proc. CSCW*, Sept. 1988.

+ Ensor, J., "Rapport: A Multimedia Conferencing System," *ACM SIGGRAPH Video Review Supplement to Computer Graphics*, Vol. 45, No. 5, Videotape, 1989.

+ Ensor, J., et al., "The Rapport Multimedia Conferencing System — A Software Overview," *Proc. Second IEEE Conf. on Computer Workstations*, Mar. 1988.

+ Erickson, T., "An Eclectic Look at CSCW '88," *ACM SIGCHI Bulletin*, Vol. 20, No. 5, July 1989.

Eveland, J., and T. Bikson, "Work Group Structures and Computer Support: A Field Experiment," *Proc. Second Conf. on CSCW*, Sept. 1988.

Eveland, J., and T. Bikson, "Evolving Electronic Communication Networks: An Empirical Assessment," *Proc. CSCW*, Dec. 1986.

Fafchamps, D., D. Reynolds, and A. Kuchinsky, "The Dynamics of Small Group Decision Making Over the E-Mail Channel," *Proc. First European CSCW*, Sept. 1989.

+ Fanning, T., and B. Raphael, "Computer Teleconferencing: Experience at Hewlett Packard," *Proc. CSCW*, Dec. 1986.

+ Farallon "Timbuktu User's Guide," user's manual, Farallon Computing Inc., 1988.

Feldman, M., "Constraints on Communication and Electronic Mail," *Proc. CSCW*, Dec. 1986.

Ferwagner, T., et al., "Experiences in Designing the Hohenheim CATeam Room," *Proc. First European CSCW*, Sept. 1989.

564

* Fikes, R., "Automating the Problem Solving in Procedural Office Work," *Proc. Conf. AFIPS Office Automation*, Mar. 1981.

* Fikes, R., "A Commitment-Based Framework for Describing Informal Cooperative Work," *Cognitive Science*, Vol. 6, 1982.

+ Finhold, T., L. Sproull, and S. Kiesler, "Communication and Performance in *Ad Hoc* Task Groups," in *Intellectual Teamwork: Social Foundations of Cooperative Work*, R. Galegher, R. Kraut, and C. Egido, eds., Lawrence Erlbaum Assoc., 1990.

+ Fish, R., R. Kraut, and B. Chalfonte, "The VideoWindow System in Informal Communications," *Proc. CSCW*, Oct. 1990.

Flores, F., and J. Ludlow, "Doing and Speaking in the Office," in *DSS: Issues and Challenges*, G. Fick, and R. Sprague, eds., Pergamon Press, 1981.

Flores, F., et al., "Computer Systems and the Design of Organizational Interaction," *ACM Trans. Office Information Systems*, Apr. 1988.

Foster, G., "Cognoter: Theory and Practice of a Collaborative Tool," *Proc. CSCW*, Dec. 1986.

* Fox, M., "An Organizational View of Distributed Systems," *IEEE Trans. Systems, Man, and Cybernetics*, Vol. SMC-11, No. 1, Jan. 1981.

Fox, M., et al., "Callisto: An Intelligent Project Management System," working paper, Carnegie Mellon University, July 1984.

Freeman, P., *Software Perspectives*, Addison-Wesley Publishing Co., 1987.

Frenkel, K., "The Next Generation of Interactive Systems," *Comm. ACM*, Vol. 32, No. 7, July 1989.

+ Gabarro, J., "The Development of Working Relationships," in *Intellectual Teamwork: Social Foundations of Cooperative Work*, R. Galegher, R. Kraut, and C. Egido, eds., Lawrence Erlbaum Assoc., 1990.

Gaitonde, S., D. Jacobson, and A. Pohm, "Bounding Delay on a Multifarious Token Ring Network," *Comm. ACM*, Vol. 33, No. 1, Jan. 1990.

+ Gale, S., "Adding Audio and Video to an Office Environment," *Proc. First European CSCW*, Sept. 1989.

+ Galegher, J., R. Kraut, and C. Egido, *Intelligent Teamwork: Social & Technical Foundations of Cooperative Work*, Lawrence Erlbaum Assoc., 1990.

Galegher, J., and R. Kraut, "Computer-Mediated Communication for Intellectual Teamwork: A Field Experiment in Group Writing," *Proc. CSCW*, Oct. 1990.

+ Galegher, J., and R. Kraut, "Technology for Intellectual Teamwork: Perspectives on Research and Design," in *Intellectual Teamwork: Social Foundations of Cooperative Work*, R. Galegher, R. Kraut, and C. Egido, eds., Lawrence Erlbaum Assoc., 1990.

+ Garcia-Luna-Aceves, J., E. Craighill, and R. Lang, "An Open-Systems Model for Computer-Supported Collaboration," *Proc. Second IEEE Conf. on Computer Workstations*, Mar. 1988.

+ Garfinkel, D., et al., "The SharedX Multiuser Interface User's Guide, Version 2.0," Research Report STL-TM-89-07, Hewlett-Packard Laboratories, Mar. 1989.

Garrett, L., K. Smith, and N. Meyrowitz, "Intermedia: Issues, Strategies and Tactics in the Design of a Hypermedia Document System," *Proc. CSCW*, Dec. 1986.

Gasparotti, P., and C. Simone, "A User-Defined Environment for Handling Conversations," *Proc. IFIP WG8.4 Conf. on Multiuser Interfaces and Applications*, 1990.

+ Gerrissen, J., and J. Daamen, "Inclusion of a 'Sharing' Feature in Telecommunication Services," *13th Int'l Symp. HFT '90 Human Factors in Telecommunications*, Sept. 1990.

Gibbs, S., "LIZA: An Extensible Groupware Toolkit," *Proc. Conf. on Human Factors in Computing Systems*, Apr. 1989.

Gibbs, S., "Groupware: Issues and Architecture," Technical Report STP-330-88, MCC, Oct. 1988.

Gibbs, S., "Conceptual Modeling and Office Information Systems," in *Office Automation*, D. Tsichritzis, ed., Springer-Verlag, 1985.

Gifford, D., R Needham, and M. Schroeder, "The Cedar File System," *Comm. ACM*, Vol. 31, No. 3, Mar. 1988.

Goel, V., and P. Pirolli, "Motivating the Notion of Generic Design with Information Processing Theory: The Design Problem Space," *AI Magazine*, Vol. 10, No. 1, Spring 1989.

Goldberg, A., *A History of Personal Workstations*, ACM Press, 1988.

+ Goodman, G., M. Abel, "Collaboration Research in SCL," in *Office: Technology and People*, Vol. 3, 1987.

+ Goodman, G., and M. Able, "Communication and Collaboration: Facilitating Cooperative Work Through Communication," *Office: Technology and People*, Vol. 3, No. 2, 1987.

+ Gorry, G., et al., "Computer Support for Biomedical Work Groups," *Proc. CSCW*, Sept. 1988.

+ Gould, J., and S. Boies, "Human Factor Challenges in Creating a Principal Support Office System — the Speech Filing System Approach," *ACM Trans. Office Information Systems*, Vol. 1, No. 4, 1983.

Gould, J., S. Boies, and C. Lewis, "Making Usable, Useful, Productivity-Enhancing Computer Applications," *Comm. ACM*, Vol. 34, No. 1, Jan. 1991.

+ Gould, J., and S. Boies, "Speech Filing — an Office System for Principles," *IBM System Journal*, Vol. 23, No. 1, 1984.

Gould, J., "How to Design Usable Systems," in *Handbook of Human-Computer Interaction*, M. Helander, ed., North Holland, 1988.

Grantham, C., "Can Groupware Get Serious?" *New Science Newsletter*, Feb. 11, 1991.

Gray, J., et al., "Granularity of Locks and Degrees of Consistency in a Shared Database," *Modeling in Data Base Management Systems*, North Holland, 1976.

+ Gray, P., "Group Decision Support Systems," *Decision Support Systems*, 1987.

+ Greenbaum, J., "In Search of Cooperation: An Historical Analysis of Work Organization and Management Strategies," *Proc. CSCW*, Sept. 1988.

Greenbaum, J., and K. Madsen, "Five Easy Pieces: Reframing the Design of Office Systems," *Office: Technology and People*, Vol. 4, No. 2, 1989.

+ Greenberg, S., *Computer-Supported Cooperative Work and Groupware*, Academic Press, 1991.

+ Greenberg, S., "Personalized Groupware: Accommodating Individual Roles and Group Differences," *Proc. Second European CSCW*, 1991.

Greenberg, S., "An Annotated Bibliography of Computer-Supported Cooperative Work," *ACM SIGCHI Bulletin*, Vol. 23, No. 3, July 1991.

Greenberg, S., "Computer-Supported Cooperative Work and Groupware," *Int'l J. of Man-Machine Studies*, Vol. 34, No. 2, Feb. 1991.

+ Greenberg, S., "Sharing Views and Interactions with Single-User Applications," *Proc. Conf. on Office Information Systems*, Apr. 1990.

+ Greenberg, S., and E. Chang, "Computer Support for Real-Time Collaborative Work," *Proc. Conf. on Numerical Mathematics and Computing*, Sept. 1989.

Greif, I., ed., *Computer-Supported Cooperative Work: A Book of Readings*, Morgan Kaufmann Publishers, 1988.

Greif, I., and S. Sarin, "Data Sharing in Group Work," *Proc. CSCW*, Dec. 1986.

* Greif, I., "Software for the 'Roles' People Play," *Proc. Interface Conf.*, Mar. 1983.

Grohowski, R., et al., "Implementing Electronic Meeting Systems At IBM: Lessons Learned and Success Factors," *MIS Quarterly*, Dec. 1990.

Grudin, J., "A Tale of Two Cities: Reflections on CSCW in Europe and the United States," *ACM SIGCHI Bulletin*, Vol. 23, No. 3, July 1991.

Grudin, J., "Interactive Systems: Bridging the Gaps Between Developers and Users," *Computer*, Vol. 24, No. 4, Apr. 1991.

Grudin, J., "Interface," *Proc. CSCW*, Oct. 1990.

Grudin, J., "Obstacles to Participatory Design in Large Product Organizations," working paper, Aarhus University, Jan. 1990.

Grudin, J., "Systematic Sources of Sub-Optimal Interface Design in Large Product Organizations," Report DAIMAPB-321, Aarhus University, July 1990.

Grudin, J., "Why CSCW Applications Fail: Problems in the Design and Evaluation of Organizational Interfaces," *Proc. Second CSCW*, Sept. 1988.

+ Grudin, J., "Perils and Pitfalls," *Byte*, Dec. 1988.

Guindon, R., "The Process of Knowledge Discovery in System Design," in *Designing and Using Human-Computer Interfaces and Knowledge Based Systems*, G. Salvendy and M. Smith, eds., Elsevier Science Publishers, 1989.

+ Gust, P., "Multiuser Interfaces for Extended Group Collaboration," *Proc. Groupware Technology Workshop*, Aug. 1989.

+ Gutek, B., "Work Group Structure and Information Technology: A Structural Contingency Approach," in *Intellectual Teamwork: Social Foundations of Cooperative Work*, R. Galegher, R. Kraut, and C. Egido, eds., Lawrence Erlbaum Assoc., 1990.

Hahn, U., M. Jarke, and T. Rose, "Teamwork Support in a Knowledge-Based Information Systems Environment," *IEEE Trans. Software Engineering*, Vol. 17, No. 5, May 1991.

Hahn, U., eta l., "CoAUTHOR: A Hypermedia Group Authoring Environment," *Proc. First European CSCW*, Sept. 1989.

Halasz, F., "Reflections on NoteCards: Seven Issues for the Next Generation of Hypermedia Systems," *Comm. ACM*, Vol. 31, No. 7, July 1988.

Halonen, D., et al., "Shared Hardware: A Novel Technology for Computer Support of Face-to-Face Meetings," *Proc. Office Information Systems*, Apr. 1990.

Hara, Y., and Y. Kasahara, "A Set-to-Set Linking Strategy for Hypertext Systems," *Proc. Conf. on Office Information Systems*, Apr. 1990.

+ Harper, R., J. Hughes, and D. Shapiro, "Working in Harmony: An Examination of Computer Technology in Air Traffic Control," *Proc. First European CSCW*, Sept. 1989.

+ Hart, P., and D. Estrin, "Computer Integration: A Co-Requirement for Effective Inter-Organization Computer Network Implementation," *Proc. CSCW*, Oct. 1990.

+ Haslett, B., "Structural Pragmatics: Managing Conversations," in *Communication: Strategic Action in Context*, Lawrence Erlbaum Assoc., 1987.

+ Heath, C., and P. Luff, "Disembodied Conduct: Communication Through Video in a Multimedia Environment," *Proc. Conf. on Human Factors in Computing Systems*, Mar. 1991.

Heidegger, M., *Basic Writings*, D. Krell, trans., Harper & Row Publishers, 1977.

Heidegger, M., *Being and Time*, J. Macquarrie and E. Robinson, trans., Harper & Row Publishers, 1962.

Hellman, R., "User Support: Illustrating Computer Use in Collaborative Work Contexts," *Proc. CSCW*, Oct. 1990.

Henderson, D., and S. Card, "Rooms: the Use of Multiple Virtual Workspaces to Reduce Space Contention in a Window-Based Graphical User Interface," *ACM Trans. Graphics*, Vol. 5, No. 3, July 1986.

+ Hennessy, P., "Information Domains in CSCW," *Proc. First European CSCW*, Sept. 1989.

+ Hiltz, S., "Collaborative Learning in a Virtual Classroom: Highlights of Findings," *Proc. CSCW*, Sept. 1988.

Hiltz, R., and M. Turoff, "Structuring Computer-Mediated Communication Systems to Avoid Information Overload," *Comm. ACM*, July 1985.

Hirschheim, R., and H. Klein, "Four Paradigms of Information Systems Development," *Comm. ACM*, Vol. 32, No. 10, Oct. 1989.

Hirschheim, R., "Understanding the Office: A Social-Analytical Perspective," *ACM Trans. Information Systems*, Vol.4, No. 4, Oct. 1986.

Hoffert, E., and G. Gretsch, "The Digital News System at EDUCOM: A Convergence of Interactive Computing, Newspapers, Television and High-Speed Networks," *Comm. ACM*, Vol. 34, No. 4, Apr. 1991.

+ Holland, U., and T. Danielson, "The Psychology of Cooperation — Consequences of Descriptions, the Power of Creative Dialogs," *Proc. First European CSCW*, Sept. 1989.

Holmqvist, B., and K. Madsen, "Initiative in Cooperative Design," working paper, Aarhus University, 1988.

Holt, A., and P. Cashman, "Designing Systems to Support Cooperative Activity," Technical Report CA-8105-0101, Massachusetts Computer Associates, May 1981.

* Holt, A., H. Ramsey, and J. Grimes, "Coordination System Technology as the Basis for a Programming Environment," *Electrical Communication*, Vol. 57, No. 4, 1983.

Holt, A., "Diplans: A New Language for the Study and Implementation of Coordination," *ACM Trans. Office Information Systems*, Apr. 1988.

House, C., and R. Price, "The Return Map: Tracking Product Teams," *Harvard Business Review*, Jan.-Feb. 1991.

Huber, G., "The Nature and Design of Post-Industrial Organizations," *Management Science*, Vol. 30, No. 8, Aug. 1984.

Huff, S., M. Munro, and B. Martin, "Growth Stages of End-User Computing," *Comm. ACM*, Vol. 31, No. 5, May 1988.

+ Hutchins, E., "The Technology of Team Navigation," in *Intellectual Teamwork: Social Foundations of Cooperative Work*," J. Galegher, R. Kraut, and C. Egido, eds., Lawrence Erlbaum Assoc., 1990.

+ Ishii, H., and M. Ohkubo, "Design of TeamWorkStation: A Real-Time Shared Workspace Fusing Desktops and Computer Screen," *Proc. IFIP WG8.4 Conf. on Multiuser Interfaces and Applications*, 1990.

Ishii, H., "TeamWorkStation: Towards a Seamless Shared Workspace," *Proc. CSCW*, Oct. 1990.

Jaques, E., "Development of Intellectual Capability," working paper, Brunel University, 1985.

Jarrell, N., and W. Barrett, "Network-Based Systems for Asynchronous Group Work," *Proc. CSCW*, Dec. 1986.

Johnson, J., et al., "The Xerox Star: A Retrospective," *Computer*, Sept. 1989.

+ Johansen, R., "Groupware: Future Direction and Wild Cards," *Proc. Conf. on Organizational Computing, Coordination, and Collaboration*, Nov. 1989.

Johansen, R., "Groupware: Computer Support for Business Teams," *The Free Press*, 1988.

* Johansen, R., and C. Bullen, "What to Expect from Teleconferencing," *Harvard Business Review*, Mar.-Apr. 1984.

+ Johnson, B., et al., "Using a Computer-Based Tool to Support Collaboration: A Field Experiment," *Proc. CSCW*, Dec. 1986.

+ Johnson-Lenz, P., and T. Johnson-Lenz, "Post-Mechanistic Groupware Primitives: Rhythms, Boundaries, and Containers," *Int'l J. of Man-Machine Studies*, Vol. 34, No. 3, Mar. 1991.

+ Joiner, R., and A. Blaye, "Mechanisms of Cognitive Change in Peer Interaction: Implications for the Design of Computer-Supported Cooperative Learning Environments," *Proc. First European CSCW*, Sept. 1989.

Kaplan, S., et al., "AGENDA: A Personal Information Manager," *Comm. ACM*, Vol. 33, No. 7, July 1990.

+ Karbe, B., and N. Ramsperger, "Influence of Exception Handling on the Support of Cooperative Office Work," *Proc. IFIP WG8.4 Conf. on Multiuser Interfaces and Applications*, 1990.

Kawell, L., et al., "Replicated Document Management in a Group Communication System," *Proc. Second CSCW*, Sept. 1988.

* Kedzierski, B., "Knowledge-Based Project Management and Communication Support in a System Development Environment," *Proc. Fourth Jerusalem Conf. on Information Technology*, May 1984.

* Kedzierski, B., "Communication and Management Support in System Development Environments," *Proc. Conf. on Human Factors in Computer Systems*, Mar. 1982.

+ Keisler, S., J. Siegel, and T. McGuire, "Social Psychological Aspects of Computer-Mediated Communication," *American Psychologist*, Vol. 39, 1984.

Kim, S., "Interdisciplinary Cooperation," in *The Art of Human-Computer Interface Design*, B. Laurel, ed., Addison-Wesley Publishing Co., 1990.

Knister, M., and A. Prakash, "DistEdit: A Distributed Toolkit for Supporting Multiple Group Editors," *Proc. CSCW*, Oct. 1990.

+ Koszarek, J., et al., "A Multiuser Document Review Tool," *Proc. IFIP WG8.4 Conf. on Multiuser Interfaces and Applications*, 1990.

Kraemer, K., and J. King, "Computer-Based Systems for Cooperative Work and Group Decision Making: Status of Use and Problems in Development," *Proc. CSCW*, Dec. 1986.

+ Kraemer, K., and A. Pinsonneault, "Technology and Groups: Assessments of the Empirical Research," in *Intellectual Teamwork: Social Foundations of Cooperative Work*, J. Galegher, R. Kraut, and C. Egido, eds., Lawrence Erlbaum Assoc., 1990.

+ Krauss R., and S. Fussell, "Mutual Knowledge and Communicative Effectiveness," in *Intellectual Teamwork: Social Foundations of Cooperative Work*, J. Galegher, R, Kraut, and C. Egido, eds., Lawrence Erlbaum Assoc., 1990.

Kraut, R., S. Dumais, and S. Koch, "Computerization, Productivity and Quality Work-Life," *Comm. ACM*, Vol. 32, No. 2, Feb. 1989.

+ Kraut, R., C. Egido, and J. Galegher, "Patterns of Contact and Communication in Scientific Collaboration," *Proc. CSCW*, Sept. 1988 (also in *Intellectual Teamwork: Social Foundations of Cooperative Work*," J. Galegher, R. Kraut, and C. Egido, eds., Lawrence Erlbaum Assoc., 1990).

+ Kraut, R., C. Egido, and J. Galegher, "Relationships and Tasks in Scientific Research Collaborations," *Human Computer Interaction*, Vol. 3, No. 1, Jan. 1988.

Kreifelts, T., et al., "A Design Tool for Autonomous Group Agents," *Proc. First European CSCW*, Sept. 1989.

Kuhn, T., *The Structure of Scientific Revolution*, University of Chicago Press, 1970.

Kumar, K., and N. Bjorn-Anderson, "A Cross-Cultural Comparison of IS Designer Values," *Comm. ACM*, Vol. 33, No. 5, May 1990.

+ Kurbel, K., and W. Pietsch, "A Cooperative Work Environment for Evolutionary Development," *Proc. IFIP WG8.4 Conf. on Multiuser Interfaces and Applications*, 1990.

Kyng, M., "Designing for a Dollar a Day," *Proc. Conf. CSCW*, Sept. 1988.

Lafrance, M., "The Quality of Expertise: Implications of Expert-Novice Differences for Knowledge Acquisition," *ACM SIGART Newsletter*, Apr. 1989.

Lai, K., and T. Malone, "Object Lens: A 'Spreadsheet' for Cooperative Work," *Proc. Second CSCW*, Sept. 1988.

+ Lakin, F., "Visual Languages for Cooperation: A Performing Medium Approach to Systems for Cooperative Work," in *Intellectual Teamwork: Social Foundations of Cooperative Work*, J. Galegher, R. Kraut, and C. Egido, eds., Lawrence Erlbaum Assoc., 1990.

+ Lakin, F., "A Performing Medium for Working Group Graphics," in *Computer-Supported Cooperative Work: A Book of Readings*, I. Greif, ed., Morgan Kaufmann Publishers, 1988.

+ Landow, G., "Hypertext and Collaborative Work: The Example of Intermedia," in *Intellectual Teamwork: Social Foundations of Cooperative Work*, J. Galegher, R. Kraut, and C. Egido, eds., Lawrence Erlbaum Assoc., 1990.

Lantz, K., "An Experiment in Integrated Multimedia Conferencing," *Proc. CSCW*, Dec. 1986.

+ Lauwers, J., and K. Lantz, "Collaboration Awareness in Support of Collaboration Transparency: Requirements for the Next Generation of Shared-Window Systems," *Proc. Conf. on Human Factors in Computing Systems*, Apr. 1990.

Lawson, H., "Philosophies for Engineering Computer-Based Systems," *Computer*, Vol. 23, No. 12, Dec. 1990.

+ Lazarov, G., V. Lilov, and M. Nikolova, "The User Illusion Method in Multiuser Interface Design," *Proc. IFIP WG8.4 Conf. on Multiuser Interfaces and Applications*, 1990.

+ Lea, M., and R. Spears, "Computer-Mediated Communication, Deindividualization and Group Decision Making," *Int'l J. of Man-Machine Studies*, Vol 34., No. 2, Feb. 1991.

+ Lee, J., "SIBYL: A Tool for Sharing Knowledge in Group Decision Making," *Proc. CSCW*, Oct. 1990.

Lee, J., and T. Malone, "Partially Shared Views: A Scheme for Communicating among Groups that Use Different Type Hierarchies," *ACM Trans. Information Systems*, Vol. 8, No. 1, Jan. 1990.

Lefkowitz, L., and B. Croft, "Validating Commitments in Cooperative Work," *Proc. Groupware Technology Workshop*, Aug. 1989.

Leibs, S., "The Promise and the Pitfalls: Groupware's Potential," *Information Week*, Feb. 11, 1991.

+ Leland, M., R. Fish, and R. Kraut, "Collaborative Document Production Using Quilt," *Proc. CSCW*, Sept. 1988.

+ Lewe, H., and H. Kremar, "The CATeam Meeting Room Environment as a Human-Computer Interface," *Proc. IFIP WG8.4 Conf. on Multiuser Interfaces and Applications*, 1990.

Liang, L., S. Chanson, and G. Neufeld, "Process Groups and Group Communication," *Computer*, Vol. 23, No. 2, Feb. 1990.

+ Licklider, J., and A. Vezza, "Applications of Information Networks," *Proc. IEEE*, Vol. 66, No. 11, Nov. 1978.

+ Lim, F., and I. Benbasat, "A Communication-Based Framework for Group Interfaces in Computer-Supported Collaboration," *Proc. 24th Hawaii Conf. on System Sciences*, Jan. 1991.

Linton, M., J. Vlissides, and P. Calder, "Composing User Interfaces with Interviews," *Computer*, Vol. 22, No. 2, Feb. 1989.

Liu, K., and W. Saints, "A Multiuser Outline Processor for Technical Documentation," *Proc IEEE Professional Comm. Conf.*, England, 1990.

Losada, M., P. Sanche, and E. Noble, "Collaborative Technology and Group Process Feedback: Their Impact on Interactive Sequences in Meetings," *Proc. CSCW*, Oct. 1990.

+ Lowe, D., "SYNVIEW: The Design of a System for Cooperative Structuring of Information," *Proc. CSCW*, Dec. 1986.

* Lowe, D., "The Representation of Debate as a Basis for Information Storage and Retrieval," working paper, Stanford University, Jan. 1984.

+ Lubich, H., and B. Plattner, "A Proposed Model and Functionality Definition for a Collaborative Editing and Conferencing Facility," *Proc. IFIP WG8.4 Conf. on Multiuser Interfaces and Applications*, 1990.

Ludwig, L., N. Pincever, and M. Cohen, "Extending the Notion of a Window System to Audio," *Computer*, Vol. 23, No. 8, Aug. 1990.

+ Lutz, E., H. Kleist-Retzow, and K. Hoernig, "MAFIA — an Active Mail-Filter Agent for Intelligent Document Processing Support," *Proc. IFIP WG8.4 Conf. on Multiuser Interfaces and Applications*, 1990.

+ Lynch, K., et al., "The Arizona Analyst Information System: Supporting Collaborative Research on Int'l Technological Trends," *Proc. IFIP WG8.4 Conf. on Multiuser Interfaces and Applications*, 1990.

+ Mack, L., "Technology for Computer-Supported Meetings," in *Human Factors Society 33rd Annual Meeting Report*, 1989.

Mackay, W., "Patterns of Sharing Customizable Software," *Proc. CSCW*, Oct. 1990.

Mackay, W., et al., "How Do Experienced Information Lens Users Use Rules?" *Proc. Conf. on Computer and Human Interaction*, May 1989.

Mackay, W., "More Than Just a Communication System: Diversity in the Use of Electronic Mail," *ACM Trans. Office Information Systems*, Vol. 6, No. 7, Oct. 1988.

Madsen, C., "Approaching Group Communication by Means of an Office Building Metaphor," *Proc. First European Conf. on CSCW*, Sept. 1989.

Madsen, K., "Breakthrough By Breakdown: Metaphors and Structured Domains," Report DAIMAPB-243, Aarhus University, Mar. 1988.

Malone, T., and K. Crowston, "What Is Coordination Theory and How Can It Help Design Cooperative Work Systems?" *Proc. CSCW '90*, Oct. 1990.

Malone, T., J. Yates, and R. Benjamin, "Electronic Markets and Electronic Hierarchies," in *Computer-Supported Cooperative Work: A Book of Readings*, I. Greif, ed., Morgan Kaufmann Publishers, 1988.

+ Malone, T., et al., "Intelligent Information Sharing Systems," *Comm. ACM*, Vol. 30, No. 5, 1987.

Malone, T., et al., "Semi-Structured Messages are Surprisingly Useful for Computer-Supported Coordination," *Comm. ACM*, Vol. 30, No. 5, 1987.

+ Malone, T., K. Grant, and F. Turbak, "The Information Lens: An Intelligent System for Information Sharing in Organizations," *Proc. Conf. on Human Factors in Computing Systems*, Apr. 1986.

Malone, T., "Designing Organizational Interfaces," *Proc. Conf. on Human Factors in Computer Systems*, Apr. 1985.

* Malone, T., and S. Smith, "Tradeoffs in Designing Organizations: Implications for New Forms of Human Organization and Computer Systems," Working Paper #1541-84, Massachusetts Institute of Technology Sloan School, Aug. 1984.

+ Mamrak, S., et al., "A Software Architecture for Supporting the Exchange of Electronic Manuscripts," *Comm. ACM*, Vol. 30, No. 5, May 1987.

Manber, U., "Chain Reactions in Networks," *Computer* Vol. 23, No. 10, Oct. 1990.

Mantei, M., et al., "Experiences in the Use of a Media Space," *Proc. Conf. on Human Factors in Computing Systems.*, Mar. 1991.

+ Mantei, M., "Observations of Executives Using a Computer-Supported Meeting Environment," *Decision Support Systems*, Vol. 5, No. 6, June 1989.

Mantei, M., "Capturing the Capture Lab Concepts: A Case Study in the Design of Computer-Supported Meetings," *Proc. Second CSCW*, Sept. 1988.

+ Mantei, M., "Groupware: Interface Design for Meetings," Research Report CMI-88-001, Center for Machine Intelligence, Ann Arbor, Michigan, 1988.

+ Mantyla, R., J. Alasuvanto, and H. Hammainen, "PAGES: A Testbed for Groupware Applications," *Proc. IFIP WG8.4 Conf. on Multiuser Interfaces and Applications*, 1990.

Marca, D., "Specifying Groupware Requirements from Direct Experience," *Proc. Sixth Int'l Workshop on Software Specification and Design*, Oct. 1991.

Marca, D., "Augmenting SADT to Develop Computer-Supported Cooperative Work," *Proc. Int'l Conf. on Software Engineering*, May 1991.

Marca, D., "Experiences in Building Meeting-Support Software," *Proc. First Groupware Technology Workshop*, Aug. 1989.

Marca, D., "Specifying Coordinators: Guidelines for Groupware Developers," *Proc. Fifth Int'l Workshop on Software Specification and Design*, May 1989.

Marca, D., N. McKenna, and S. White, "Computer-Aided Support for Coordination Technology," *Proc. First Int'l Workshop on Computer-Aided Software Engineering*, May 1987.

Marca, D., S. Schwartz, and G. Casaday, "A Specification Method for Coordinated Work," *Proc. Fourth Int'l Workshop on Software Specification and Design*, Apr. 1987.

Marca, D., and P. Cashman, "Towards Specifying Procedural Aspects of Cooperative Work," *Proc. Third Int'l Workshop on Software Specification and Design*, Aug. 1985.

Markus, M., and T. Connolly, "Why CSCW Applications Fail: Problems in the Adoption of Interdependent Work Tools," *Proc. CSCW*, Oct. 1990.

Martial, F., "A Conversation Model for Resolving Conflicts Among Distributed Office Activities," *Proc. Office Information Systems*, Apr. 1990.

Marzullo, K., et al., "Tools for Distributed Application Management," *Computer*, Vol. 24, No. 8, Aug. 1991.

+ McCarthy, J., V. Miles, and A. Monk, "An Experimental Study of Common Ground in Text-Based Communication," *Proc. Conf. on Human Factors in Computing Systems*, Apr. 1991.

+ McCarthy, J., and V. Miles, "Elaborating Communication Channels in Conferencer," *Proc. IFIP WG8.4 Conf. on Multiuser Interfaces and Applications*, 1990.

+ McCarthy, J., et al., "Four Generic Communication Tasks which Must Be Supported in Electronic Conferencing," *ACM SIGCHI Bulletin*, Vol. 23, No. 1, Jan. 1991.

+ McDonald, D., and J. Raymond, "Integration of the Electronic Blackboard and the Electronic Overhead Projector," *Proc. Second Guelph Conf. on Computer Conferencing*, June 1987.

McGoff, C., et al., "IBM's Experiences With GroupSystems," *Interfaces*, Vol. 20, No. 6, Nov.-Dec. 1990.

+ McGrath, J., "Time Matters in Groups," in *Intellectual Teamwork: Social Foundations of Cooperative Work*," J. Galegher, R. Kraut, and C. Egido, eds., Lawrence Erlbaum Assoc., 1990.

+ Minneman, S., and S. Bly, "Experiences in the Development of a Multiuser Drawing Tool," *Proc. Third Guelph Symp.on Computer-Mediated Communication*, May 1990.

+ Minneman, S., and S. Bly, "Managing a Trois: A Study of a Multiuser Drawing Tool," *Proc. Conf. on Human Factors in Computing Systems*, Apr. 1991.

Mirchandani, D., and P. Biswas, "Ethernet Performance of Remote DECwindows Applications," *Digital Technical J.*, Vol. 2, No. 3, Summer 1990.

+ Morgan, T., and R. Anderson, "The Workday World as a Paradigm for CSCW Design," *Proc. CSCW*, Oct. 1990.

Morreale, P., and G. Campbell, "Metropolitan-Area Networks," *IEEE Spectrum*, Vol. 27, No. 5, May 1990.

Mukherjee, B., "Integrated Voice/Data Communication Over High-Speed Fiber Optic Networks," *Computer*, Vol. 24, No 2, Feb. 1991.

Mumford, E., *Designing Human Systems*, Manchester Business School, 1983.

+ Murrel, S., "Computer Communication System Design Affects Group Decision Making," *Proc. Conf. on Human Factors in Computing Systems*, Dec. 1983.

Myers, B., et al., "Garnet: Comprehensive Support for Graphical, Highly Interactive User Interfaces," *Computer*, Vol. 23, No. 11, Nov. 1990.

Nardi, B., and J. Miller, "Twinkling Lights and Nested Loops: Distributed Problem Solving and Spreadsheet Development," *Int'l J. of Man-Machine Studies*, Vol. 34, No. 4, Apr. 1991.

Nardi, B., and J. Miller, "An Enthnographic Study of Distributed Problem Solving in Spreadsheet Development," *Proc. CSCW*, Oct. 1990.

Neches, R., "Tools Help People Cooperate Only to the Extent that They Help Them Share Goals and Terminology," *Proc. CSCW*, Dec. 1986.

Nelson, V., "Fault-Tolerant Computing: Fundamental Concepts," *Computer*, Vol. 23, No. 7, July 1990.

+ Neuwirth, C., et al., "Issues in the Design of Computer Support for Co-Authoring and Commenting," *Proc. CSCW*, Oct. 1990.

Nielsen, J., "Traditional Dialog Design Applied to Modern User Interfaces," *Comm. ACM*, Vol. 33, No. 10, Oct. 1990.

Nielsen, J., "The Art of Navigating Through Hypertext," *Comm. ACM*, Vol. 33, No. 3, Mar. 1990.

Nitzberg, B., and V. Lo, "Distributed Shared Memory: A Survey of Issues and Algorithms," *Computer*, Vol. 24, No. 8, Aug. 1991.

Norman, D., and S. Draper, *User Centered System Design*, Lawrence Erlbaum Assoc. Publishers, 1986.

Notkin, D., et al., "Interconnecting Heterogeneous Computer Systems," *Comm. ACM*, Vol. 31, No. 3, Mar. 1988.

Nunamaker J., Jr., L. Applegate, and B. Konsynski, "Computer-Aided Deliberation," *Operations Research*, Vol. 36, No. 6, Dec. 1988.

Nylund, A., "Aspects of Cooperation in a Distributed Problem-Solving Environment," *Proc. First European CSCW*, Sept. 1989.

Olson, G., and J. Olson, "User-Centered Design of Collaboration Technology," *J. Organizational Computing*, Vol. 1, No. 1, 1991.

+ Olson, G., "The Nature of Group Work," in *Human Factors Society 33rd Annual Meeting Report*, 1989.

+ Olson, G., "Supporting Collaboration with Advanced Multimedia Electronic Mail: The NSF EXPRESS Project," in *Intelligent Teamwork: Social & Technical Foundations of Cooperative Work*, J. Galegher, R. Kraut, and C. Egido, eds., Lawrence Erlbaum Assoc., 1990.

Olson, J., et al., "Concurrent Editing: The Group's Interface," in *Human-Computer Interaction*, D. Diaper, ed., Elsevier Science Publishers, 1990.

+ Olson, M., and S. Bly, "The Portland Experiment — a Report on a Distributed Research Group," *Int'l J. on Man Machine Intelligence*, Vol. 34, No. 2, Feb. 1991.

Olson, M., et al., "Designing Flexible Facilities for the Support of Collaboration," Technical Report 33, University of Michigan Cognitive Science and Machine Intelligence Laboratory, Sept. 1990.

+ Olson, M., *Technological Support for Group Work Collaboration*, Lawrence Erlbaum Assoc., 1989.

Olson, M., "Work-at-Home for Computer Professionals: Current Attitudes and Future Prospects," *ACM Trans. Information Systems*, Vol. 7, No. 4, Oct. 1989.

Olson, M., "Supporting Collaboration with Advanced Multimedia Electronic Mail: The NSF EXPRESS Project," Technical Report 22, University of Michigan Cognitive Science and Machine Intelligence Laboratory, Feb. 1989.

Olson, M., "Encountering Electronic Work Groups: A Transaction Costs Perspective," *Proc. CSCW*, Sept. 1988.

Olson, M., "Remote Office Work Patterns in Space and Time," *Comm. ACM*, Vol. 26, No. 3, Mar. 1983.

+ Opper, S., "A Groupware Toolbox," *Byte*, Dec. 1988.

570

Orr, J., "Narratives At Work: Storytelling as Cooperative Diagnostic Activity," *Proc. CSCW*, Dec. 1986.

Parnas, D., and P. Clements, "A Rational Design Process: How and Why to Fake It," *IEEE Trans. Software Engineering*, Vol. SE-12, No. 2, Feb. 1986.

+ Patterson, J., et al., "Rendezvous: An Architecture for Synchronous Multiuser Applications," *Proc. CSCW*, Oct. 1990.

Patterson, J., "The Implications of Window Sharing for a Virtual Terminal Protocol," *Proc. Groupware Technology Workshop*, Aug. 1989.

+ Pendergast, M., and D. Vogel, "Design and Implementation of a PC/LAN-Based Multiuser Text Editor," *Proc. IFIP WG8.4 Conf. on Multiuser Interfaces and Applications*, 1990.

Pepper, S., *World Hypotheses*, University of California Press, Berkley, 1964.

Pernici, B., "Objects With Roles," *Proc. Office Information Systems*, Apr. 1990.

+ Pettersson, E., "Automatic Information Processes in Document Reading," *Proc. First European CSCW*, Sept. 1989.

Pintado, X., and D. Tsichritzis, "Satellite: A Visualization and Navigation System for Hypermedia," *Proc. Office Information Systems*, Apr. 1990.

+ Piturro, M., "Computer Conferencing: Brainstorming Across Time and Space," *Management Review*, Aug. 1989.

+ Pliskin, N., "Interacting With Electronic Mail Can Be a Dream or a Nightmare: A User's Point of View," *Interacting With Computers*, Vol. 1, No. 3, Dec. 1989.

+ Poole, M., M. Homes, and G. DeSanctis, "Conflict Management and Group Decision Support," *Proc. CSCW*, Sept. 1988.

+ Postel, J., et al., "An Experimental Multimedia Mail System," *ACM Trans. Office Information Systems*, Vol. 6, No. 1, Jan. 1988.

* Pouzin, L., "Team Tools for Teamwork," working paper, Centre National d'Etudes des Telecommunications, Apr. 1984.

+ Powrie, S., and C. Siemieniuch, "IBC and Cooperative Working in the Automotive Industry," *Proc. IFIP WG8.4 Conf. on Multiuser Interfaces and Applications*, 1990.

Prinz, W., and P. Pennelli, "Relevance of the X.500 Directory to CSCW Applications," *Proc. First European Conf. on CSCW*, Sept. 1989.

Rasmussen, J., and L. Goodstein, "Information Technology and Work," in *Handbook of Human-Computer Interaction*, M. Helander, ed., North Holland, 1988.

Reder, S., and R. Schwab, "The Temporal Structure of Cooperative Activity," *Proc. CSCW*, Oct. 1990.

+ Reder, S., and R. Schwab, "The Communicative Economy of the Workgroup: Multichannel Centres of Communication," *Proc. CSCW*, Sept. 1988.

Rein, G., and C. Ellis, "The NICK Experiment Reinterpreted: Implications for Developers and Evaluators of Groupware," Technical Report STP-018-88, MCC, 1988.

+ Rein, G., and C. Ellis, "The NICK Experiment Reinterpreted: Implications for Developers and Evaluators of Groupware," *Office: Technology and People*, Vol. 5, No. 1, Jan. 1989.

+ Rein, G., and C. Ellis, "rIBIS: A Real-Time Group Hypertext System," *Int'l J. of Man-Machine Studies*, Vol. 34, No. 3, Mar. 1991.

+ Rice, R., and D. Shook, "Voice Messaging, Coordination, and Communication," in *Intelligent Teamwork: Social & Technical Foundations of Cooperative Work*, J. Galegher, R. Kraut, and C. Egido, eds., Lawrence Erlbaum Assoc., 1990.

Rivard, S., and S. Huff, "Factors of Success for End-User Computing," *Comm. ACM*, May 1988.

Robinson, M., "Pay Bargaining in a Shared Information Space," internal report, University of Amsterdam, Sept. 1989.

Rodden, T., and I. Sommerville, "Building Conversations Using Mail Trays," *Proc. First European CSCW*, Sept. 1989.

Rooks-Denes, K., "Building a Boardroom," *Presentation Products Magazine*, Feb. 1991.

Root, R., "Design of a Multimedia Vehicle for Social Browsing," *Proc. CSCW*, Sept. 1988.

Rosson, M., S. Maass, and W. Kellogg, "The Designer as User: Building Requirements for Design Tools from Design Practice," *Comm. ACM*, Vol. 31, No. 11, Nov. 1988.

Saffo, P., "Same-Time, Same-Place Groupware," *Personal Computing*, Mar. 20, 1990.

Salisbury, M., et al., "Talk and Draw: Bundling Speech and Graphics," *Computer*, Vol. 23, No. 8, Aug. 1990.

+ Sarin, S., and I. Greif, "Computer-Based Real-Time Conferencing Systems," *Computer*, Vol. 18, No. 10, Nov. 1985.

* Sarin, S., and I. Greif, "Software for Interactive Online Conferences," *Proc. ACM-SIGOA Conf. on Office Information Systems*, June 1984.

Satyanarayanan, M., "Scalable, Secure, and Highly Available Distributed File Access," *Computer*, May 1990.

Schage, M., "The Collaborative Organization," *New York Times*, Nov. 11, 1990.

Schein, E., "Reassessing the 'Divine Rights' of Managers," *Sloan Management Review*, Winter 1989.

Schein, E., "Organization Development: Science, Technology or Philosophy?" Working Paper No. 3065-89-BPS, MIT, Aug. 1989.

Schmandt, C., M. Ackerman, and D. Hindus, "Augmenting a Window System With Speech Input," *Computer*, Vol. 23, No. 8, Aug. 1990.

Schooler, E., and S. Casner, "Multimedia Conferencing in the Internet: The Effect of Long Distances on Groupware Design," *Proc. First Groupware Technology Workshop*, Aug. 1989.

+ Scott, P., "Formal Models of Protocols for Computer-Supported Meetings," Research Report CMI-88-002, Center for Machine Intelligence, Ann Arbor, Michigan, Feb. 1988.

Searle, J., *Speech Acts*, Cambridge University Press, 1969.

Senge, P., "The Leader's New Work: Building Learning Organizations," *Sloan Management Review*, Fall 1990.

Senge, P., *The Fifth Discipline: The Art and Practice of the Learning Organization*, Doubleday Press, 1990.

Shadbolt, N., and A. Burton, "The Empirical Study of Knowledge Elicitation Techniques," *ACM SIGART Newsletter*, Apr. 1989.

+ Sheffield, J., "The Effects of Bargaining Orientation and Communication Medium on Negotiations in the Bilateral Monopoly Task: A Comparison of Decision Room and Computer Conferencing Communication Media," *Proc. Conf. on Human Factors in Computing Systems*, 1983.

Sheperd, A., N. Mayer, and A. Kuchinsky, "Strudel — an Extensible Electronic Conversation Toolkit," *Proc. CSCW*, Oct. 1990.

Sihto, M., "Distributed Hypertext as a Basis for Communication and Collaboration Tools in Distributed Software Environments," internal report, Technical Research Centre of Finland, 1989.

Siewiorek, D., "Fault Tolerance in Commercial Computers," *Computer*, Vol. 23, No. 7, July 1990.

* Sluzier, S., and P. Cashman, "XCP: An Experimental Tool for Managing Cooperative Activity," *Proc. Conf. on Office Automation*, Aug. 1984.

Smith, H., P. Hennessy, and G. Lunt, " The Activity Model Environment: An Object-Oriented Framework for Describing Organizational Communication," *Proc. First European CSCW*, Sept. 1989.

Smith, R., et al., "Preliminary Experiments with a Distributed, Multimedia Problem Solving Environment," *Proc. First European CSCW*, Sept. 1989.

Soares, L., et al., "LAN Based Real-Time Audio-Data Systems," *Proc. Office Information Systems*, Apr. 1990.

+ Sproull, L., and S. Kiesler, "Reducing Social Context Cues: Electronic Mail in Organizational Communication," *Management Science*, Vol 32., No. 11, Nov. 1986.

Sprague, R., K. Singh, and R. Wood, "Concurrent Engineering in Product Development," *IEEE Spectrum*, Vol. 28, No. 3, Mar. 1991.

+ Stanchev, P., and V. Sabev, "CNLS — Computer Network Lecturing System," *Proc. IFIP WG8.4 Conf. on Multiuser Interfaces and Applications*, 1990.

Stankovic, J., "Misconceptions About Real-Time Computing: A Serious Problem for Next-Generation Systems," *Computer*, Vol. 21, No. 10, Oct. 1988.

+ Stasz, C., and R. Bikson, "Computer-Supported Cooperative Work: Examples and Issues in One Federal Agency," *Proc. CSCW*, Dec. 1986.

Stefik, M., et al., "WYSIWIS Revised: Early Experiences with Multiuser Interfaces," *ACM Trans. Office Information Systems*, Apr. 1987.

Stefik, M., et al., "Beyond the Chalkboard: Computer Support for Collaboration and Problem Solving in Meetings," *Comm. ACM*, Jan. 1987.

Stevens, C., "Cotechnology for the Global 1990s," industrial liason report, MIT, Nov. 1989.

+ Stevens, C., "Electronic Organization and Expert Networks: Beyond Electronic Mail and Computer Conferencing," working paper 90s:86-021, MIT, Sloan School of Management, 1986.

+ Storrs, G., "Group Working in the DHSS Large Demonstrator Project," *Proc. First European CSCW*, Sept. 1989.

Straub, D., Wetherbe, J., "Information Technologies for the 1990s: An Organizational Impact Perspective," *Comm. ACM*, Vol. 32, No. 11, Nov. 1989.

Suchman, L., and R. Trigg, "A Framework for Studying Research Collaborations," *Proc. CSCW*, Dec. 1986.

+ Suomi, R., "Inter-Organizational Information Systems as a Tool for Computer-Supported Cooperative Work," *Proc. First European CSCW*, Sept. 1989.

Suzuki, T., S. Shatz, and T. Murata, "A Protocol Modeling and Verification Approach Based on a Specification Language and Petri Nets," *IEEE Trans. Software Engineering*, Vol. 16, No. 5, May 1990.

Swinehart, D., et al., "A Structural View of the Cedar Programming Environment," *ACM Trans. Programming Languages and Systems*, Vol. 8, No. 4, Oct. 1986.

Tang, J., "Findings from Observational Studies of Collaborative Work," *Int'l J. of Man-Machine Studies*, Vol. 34, No. 2, Feb. 1991.

Tang, J., and L. Leifer, "A Framework for Understanding the Workspace Activity of Design Teams," *Proc. CSCW*, Sept. 1988.

+ Tang, J., and S. Minneman, "Videodraw: A Video Interface for Collaborative Drawing," *Proc. Conf. on Human Factors in Computing Systems*, Apr. 1990.

Tang, J., and S. Minneman, "Whiteboard: Video Shadows to Support Remote Collaboration," *Proc. Conf. on Human Factors in Computing Systems*, Apr. 1991.

Tatar, D., G. Foster, and D. Bobrow, "Design for Conversation: Lessons from Cognoter," *Int'l J. of Man-Machine Studies*, Vol. 34, No. 2, Feb. 1991.

Tazelaar, J., "In Depth: Groupware," *Byte,*, Dec. 1988.

+ Thimbleby, H., S. Anderson, and I. Witten, "Reflexive CSCW: Supporting Long-Term Personal Work," *Interacting With Computers*, Vol. 2, No. 3, Mar. 1990.

+ Thomas, R., et al., "Diamond: A Multimedia Message System Built on a Distributed Architecture," *Computer*, Vol. 18, No. 12, Dec. 1985.

Trigg, R., "Guided Tours and Tabletops: Tools for Communicating in a Hypertext Environment," *Proc. CSCW*, Sept. 1988.

Trigg, R., L. Suchman, and F. Halasz, "Supporting Collaboration in Notecards," *Proc. First CSCW*, Dec. 1986.

* Trigg, R., and M. Weiser, "TEXTNET: A Network-Based Approach to Text Handling," working paper, University of Maryland, Aug. 1984.

\+ Tueni, M., and J. Li, "Knowledge-Based Office Automation and CSCW," *Proc. First European CSCW*, Sept. 1989.

* Turoff, M., "Information, Value, and the Internal Marketplace," working paper, New Jersey Institute of Technology, Sept. 1983.

Tushman, M., and R. Katz, "External Communication and Project Performance: An Investigation into the Role of Gatekeepers," *Management Science*, Vol. 26, No. 11, Nov. 1980.

Valacich, J., A. Dennis, and J. Nunamaker, "Electronic Meeting Support: The GroupSystems Concept" *Int'l J. of Man-Machine Studies*, Vol. 34, No. 2, Feb. 1991.

\+ Vertelney, H., "An Environment for Collaboration," in *The Art of Human-Computer Interface Design*, B. Laurel, ed., Addison Wesley, 1990.

Victor, F., and E. Sommer, "Supporting the Design of Office Procedures in the Domino System," *Proc. First European CSCW*, Sept. 1989.

\+ Vogel, D., and J. Nunamaker, "Design and Assessment of a Group Decision Support System," in *Intelligent Teamwork: Social & Technical Foundations of Cooperative Work*, J. Galegher, R. Kraut, and C. Egido, eds., Lawrence Erlbaum Assoc., 1990.

Wagner, G., "Groupware to Augment Face-to-Face Meetings," *Proc. Groupware Technology Workshop*, Aug. 1989.

Wand, Y., and R. Weber, "An Ontological Model of an Information System," *IEEE Trans. Software Engineering*, Vol. 16, No. 11, Nov. 1990.

Watabe, K., et al., "Distributed Multiparty Desktop Conferencing System: MERMAID," *Proc. CSCW*, Oct. 1990.

\+ Watson, R., G. DeSanctis, and M. Poole, "Using a GDSS to Facilitate Group Consensus: Some Intended and Unintended Consequences," *MIS Quarterly*, Vol. 12, No. 3, Sept. 1988.

\+ Weedman, J., "Task and Non-Task Functions of a Computer Conference Used in Professional Education: A Measure of Flexibility," *Int'l J. of Man-Machine Studies*, Vol. 34, No. 2, Feb. 1991.

\+ White, G., "A Formal Method for Specifying Temporal Properties of the Multiuser Interface," *Proc. IFIP WG8.4 Conf. on Multiuser Interfaces and Applications*, 1990.

Whiteside, J., J. Holtzblatt, and J. Bennett, "Usability Engineering: Our Experience and Evolution," in *Handbook of Human-Computer Interaction*, M. Helander, ed., North Holland, 1988.

Whiteside, J., and D. Wixon, "Contextualism as a World View for the Reformation of Meetings," *Proc. Second CSCW*, Sept. 1988.

Whittaker, S., S. Brennan, and H. Clark, "Coordinating Activity: An Analysis of Interaction in Computer-Supported Cooperative Work," *Proc. Conf. on Human Factors in Computing Systems*, Apr. 1991.

Wilson, J., and D. Rosenberg, "Rapid Prototyping for User Interface Design," in *Handbook of Human-Computer Interaction*, M. Helander, ed., North Holland, 1988.

Winograd, T., "Can Office Technology Support Office Dialogues?" in *Information Processing*, G. Ritter, ed., Elsevier Science Publishers, 1989.

Winograd, T., "Where the Action Is," *Byte*, Dec. 1988.

Winograd, T., "A Language/Action Perspective on the Design of Cooperative Work," *Proc. First CSCW*, Dec. 1986.

Winograd, T., and F. Flores, *Understand Computers and Cognition*, Ablex Publishing Company, 1986.

Winograd, T., *Language as a Cognitive Process*, Addison Wesley, 1983.

Winston, P., *Artificial Intelligence*, Addison-Wesley, 1979.

\+ Witten, I., et al., "Livewire: A New Approach to Sharing Data in Social Networks," *Int'l J. of Man-Machine Studies*, Vol. 34, No. 3, Mar. 1991.

Wixon, D., K. Holtzblatt, and S. Knox, "Contextual Design: An Emergent View of System Design," *Proc. Conf. on Human Factors in Computing Systems*, Apr. 1990.

Woo, C., "SACT: A Tool for Automating Semi-Structured Organizational Communication," *Proc. Office Information Systems*, Apr. 1990.

\+ Woitass, M., "Coordination of Intelligent Office Agents Applied to Meeting Scheduling," *Proc. IFIP WG8.4 Conf. on Multiuser Interfaces and Applications*, 1990.

\+ Wright, K., "The Road to the Global Village," *Scientific American*, Mar. 1990.

Wulff, W., S. Evenson, and J. Rheinfrank, "Animating Interfaces," *Proc. CSCW*, Oct. 1990.

Yadav, S., et al., "Comparison of Analysis Techniques for Information Requirement Determination," *Comm. ACM*, Vol. 31, No. 9, Sept. 1988.

Yakemovic, K., and J. Conklin, "The Capture of Design Rationale on an Industry Development Project," Technical Report STP-279-89, MCC, July 1989.

Yoder, E., R. Akscyn, and D. McCracken, "Collaboration in KMS, a Shared Hypermedia System," *Proc. Conf. on Human Factors in Computing Systems*, Apr. 1989.

Ziegler, C., and G. Weiss, "Multimedia Conferencing on Local Area Networks," *Computer*, Vol. 23, No. 9, Sept. 1990.

Zuboff, S., *In the Age of the Smart Machine*, Basic Books, 1988.

573

Author Index

About the Authors

David Marca is a principle software engineer at Digital Equipment Corporation in Nashua, New Hampshire. Currently he consults and trains engineers and managers in the area of socio-technical systems design, and designs groupware systems to support the software engineering practices at Digital.

A trained software engineer, knowledge engineer, and usability engineer, David is dedicated to software industry practices including direct experience during systems analysis, user participation during design, and social responsibility during system development and deployment.

David is a member of the Institute of Electrical and Electronics Engineers (IEEE), the Association for Computing Machinery (ACM), and the Computer Professionals for Social Responsibility (CPSR). He has authored a software engineering textbook, a systems analysis textbook, and several technical papers in the fields of software engineering and computer-supported cooperative work.

Geoffrey Bock is project manager for collaborative systems in the Office Systems Applications Group of Digital Equipment Corporation, and visiting scientist at the Center for Coordination Science, Massachusetts Institute of Technology. Previously a human factors specialist and quality manager, he has contributed to the design of office automation applications and user interface guidelines. He is now designing tools for electronic coworking and is investigating the use of groupware in organizations.

Geoffrey received his bachelors degree from Oberlin College and his doctorate from Harvard University. He is a contributing editor to the Journal of Science Education and Technology and a member of the Association for Computing Machinery (ACM). He is a frequent speaker before user and industry groups.

Other IEEE Computer Society Press Titles

For further information call 1-800-CS-BOOKS or write:

IEEE Computer Society Press, 10662 Los Vaqueros Circle, PO Box 3014,
Los Alamitos, California 90720-1264, USA

IEEE Computer Society, 13, avenue de l'Aquilon,
B-1200 Brussels, BELGIUM

IEEE Computer Society, Ooshima Building, 2-19-1 Minami-Aoyama,
Minato-ku, Tokyo 107, JAPAN

Integrated Services Digital Networks (ISDN)
(Second Edition)
Edited by William Stallings
(ISBN 0-8186-0823-4); 406 pages

Knowledge-Based Systems:
Fundamentals and Tools
Edited by Oscar N. Garcia and Yi-Tzuu Chien
(ISBN 0-8186-1924-4); 512 pages

Local Network Technology (Third Edition)
Edited by William Stallings
(ISBN 0-8186-0825-0); 512 pages

Microprogramming and Firmware Engineering
Edited by V. M. Milutinovic
(ISBN 0-8186-0839-0); 416 pages

Modeling and Control of Automated Manufacturing Systems
Edited by Alan A. Desrochers
(ISBN 0-8186-8916-1); 384 pages

Nearest Neighbor Pattern Classification Techniques
Edited by Belur V. Dasarathy
(ISBN 0-8186-8930-7); 464 pages

New Paradigms for Software Development
Edited by William Agresti
(ISBN 0-8186-0707-6); 304 pages

Object-Oriented Computing, Volume 1: Concepts
Edited by Gerald E. Petersen
(ISBN 0-8186-0821-8); 214 pages

Object-Oriented Computing, Volume 2: Implementations
Edited by Gerald E. Petersen
(ISBN 0-8186-0822-6); 324 pages

Parallel Architectures for Database Systems
Edited by A. R. Hurson, L. L. Miller, and S. H. Pakzad
(ISBN 0-8186-8838-6); 478 pages

Reduced Instruction Set Computers (RISC)
(Second Edition)
Edited by William Stallings
(ISBN 0-8186-8943-9); 448 pages

Software Engineering Project Management
Edited by Richard H. Thayer
(ISBN 0-8186-0751-3); 512 pages

Software Maintenance and Computers
Edited by David H. Longstreet
(ISBN 0-8186-8898-X); 304 pages

Software Quality Assurance:
A Practical Approach
Edited by T.S. Chow
(ISBN 0-8186-0569-3); 506 pages

Software Reuse — Emerging Technology
Edited by Will Tracz
(ISBN 0-8186-0846-3); 400 pages

Software Risk Management
Edited by Barry W. Boehm
(ISBN 0-8186-8906-4); 508 pages

Standards, Guidelines and Examples on System
and Software Requirements Engineering
Edited by Merlin Dorfman and Richard H. Thayer
(ISBN 0-8186-8922-6); 626 pages

System and Software Requirements Engineering
Edited by Richard H. Thayer and Merlin Dorfman
(ISBN 0-8186-8921-8); 740 pages

Test Access Port and Boundary-Scan Architecture
Edited by Colin M. Maunder and Rodham E. Tulloss
(ISBN 0-8186-9070-4); 400 pages

Visual Programming Environments: Paradigms and Systems
Edited by Ephraim Glinert
(ISBN 0-8186-8973-0); 680 pages

Visual Programming Environments: Applications and Issues
Edited by Ephraim Glinert
(ISBN 0-8186-8974-9); 704 pages

Visualization in Scientific Computing
Edited by G. M. Nielson, B. Shriver, and L. Rosenblum
(ISBN 0-8186-8979-X); 304 pages

Volume Visualization
Edited by Arie Kaufman
(ISBN 0-8186-9020-8); 494 pages

REPRINT COLLECTIONS

Distributed Computing Systems:
Concepts and Structures
Edited by A. L. Ananda and B. Srinivasan
(ISBN 0-8186-8975-0); 416 pages

Expert Systems:
A Software Methodology for Modern Applications
Edited by Peter G. Raeth
(ISBN 0-8186-8904-8); 476 pages

Milestones in Software Evolution
Edited by Paul W. Oman and Ted G. Lewis
(ISBN 0-8186-9033-X); 332 pages

Object-Oriented Databases
Edited by Ez Nahouraii and Fred Petry
(ISBN 0-8186-8929-3); 256 pages

Validating and Verifying Knowledge-Based Systems
Edited by Uma G. Gupta
(ISBN 0-8186-8995-1); 400 pages

ARTIFICIAL NEURAL NETWORKS TECHNOLOGY SERIES

Artificial Neural Networks —
Concept Learning
Edited by Joachim Diederich
(ISBN 0-8186-2015-3); 160 pages

Artificial Neural Networks —
Electronic Implementation
Edited by Nelson Morgan
(ISBN 0-8186-2029-3); 144 pages

Artificial Neural Networks —
Theoretical Concepts
Edited by V. Vemuri
(ISBN 0-8186-0855-2); 160 pages

SOFTWARE TECHNOLOGY SERIES

Computer-Aided Software Engineering (CASE)
Edited by E. J. Chikofsky
(ISBN 0-8186-1917-1); 110 pages

Software Reliability Models:
Theoretical Development, Evaluation, and Applications
Edited by Yashwant K. Malaiya and Pradip K. Srimani
(ISBN 0-8186-2110-9); 136 pages

MATHEMATICS TECHNOLOGY SERIES

Computer Algorithms
Edited by Jun-ichi Aoe
(ISBN 0-8186-2123-0); 154 pages

Multiple-Valued Logic in VLSI Design
Edited by Jon T. Butler
(ISBN 0-8186-2127-3); 128 pages

COMMUNICATIONS TECHNOLOGY SERIES

Multicast Communication in Distributed Systems
Edited by Mustaque Ahamad
(ISBN 0-8186-1970-8); 110 pages

ROBOTICS TECHNOLOGY SERIES

Multirobot Systems
Edited by Rajiv Mehrotra and Murali R. Varanasi
(ISBN 0-8186-1977-5); 122 pages